World Premieres *from* Horse Cave Theatre

PLAYS BY KENTUCKY WRITERS

edited by
Liz Bussey Fentress
&
Warren Hammack

WORLD PREMIERES FROM HORSE CAVE
Plays By Kentucky Writers

edited by
Liz Bussey Fentress & Warren Hammack

© 2009
All Rights Reserved.

ISBN 978-1-934894-15-6
ANTHOLOGY

CAUTION: This book contains the literary versions of the scripts it comprises. These are not acting editions. Purchase of this book in no way grants the purchaser the right to perform these plays or read portions of the texts aloud in public. This book may not be used for theatrical productions or for staged readings. For permission to produce one of the plays in this anthology, please contact the playwright directly. Copying these scripts is expressly forbidden by law.

No portion of this book may be copied, transmitted, duplicated, stored or distributed in any form (including but not limited to handwritten, print, mechanical, audio, video, digital or electronic) without prior express written permission from the publisher, with the sole exception of brief excerpts used in reviews or commentaries.

Book design
EK LARKEN & LIZ FENTRESS

Cover painting
(of Horse Cave Theatre on Main Street in Horse Cave, Kentucky)
MARTIN ROLLINS

Photos
WARREN HAMMACK

A percentage of profit from sales of this anthology will be contributed to the MotesBooks Kentucky Voices Fund at The Community Foundation of Louisville. Any Kentucky 501(c)3 organization working on a project involving the development or production of a new play by or about Kentuckians can apply for support. More information about the MotesBooks Kentucky Voices Fund can be found at
www.CFLOUISVILLE.net

LOUISVILLE, KENTUCKY

www.MOTESBOOKS.COM

Praise for
World Premieres from Horse Cave Theatre

"It's thrilling to see a collection of plays from Horse Cave Theatre. I'm a great admirer of Warren Hammack and his fearless team who produced an amazing body of work in true rotating repertory in rural Kentucky, ranging from Shakespeare to Shaw to Pinter to the amazing original works in this collection."
– **Marc Routh**, *Tony Award-winning Producer*

"A small town in rural Kentucky seems an unlikely setting for a professional theatre that produces new plays, but Horse Cave proved fertile ground for Warren Hammack and Pamela White, who fostered playwrights in a unique program at what is now Kentucky Repertory Theatre. These plays by and about Kentuckians capture the dialect and sensibilities of the region while telling stories that would engage audiences anywhere in the world. The playwrights and producers of this remarkable collection deserve our hearty applause."
– **Judith Egerton**, *Theatre Critic (retired)*
Louisville Courier-Journal

"As regional theatres burgeoned across America in the 1960s and 1970s, one of their ideals emerged: professional opportunities for artists of every kind – *even playwrights!* – to ply their craft in the home soil that nurtured their lives and an audience for their work. These Kentucky plays substantiate Warren Hammack's commitment to creating a regional theatre in its purest sense: one that reflects the everlasting truth that art must first be particular before it can become universal."
– **Russell Vandenbroucke**, *Playwright, Director, Dramaturg, Producer*
University of Louisville Theatre Arts Department Chair

"All theatre is local – even if it has an international audience. These works by Kentucky writers are essential reading for those curious to explore who we are in contemporary times."
– **Marc Masterson**, *Artistic Director*
Humana Festival of New American Plays/Actors Theatre of Louisville

"The process of developing a new play and getting it on stage is never easy. That Warren Hammack produced these world premieres at Horse Cave Theatre is an extraordinary testament to his work ethic, his skill at working collaboratively with other theatre artists, his dedication to the art of theatre, and his love for Kentucky. The actors have made their exits, the lights have gone to black, and the applause has faded... but, thankfully, we still have these words. This anthology is a treasure. Bravo!"
– **Liz Engelman**, *Dramaturg*

"Kentucky Educational Television shares with Horse Cave Theatre a commitment to feature and honor talented Kentucky writers. The scripts in *World Premieres from Horse Cave Theatre* offer unforgettable stories, memorable characters, and messages for young and old. Kentucky voices that stir the imagination on the stage and screen – and now on the page – need to be heard."
– **Nancy Carpenter**, *Director of Education, Kentucky Educational Television*

Contents

Preface by WARREN HAMMACK	7
Introduction by PAMELA WHITE	9
East of Nineveh JIM PEYTON	11
Marching to Zion JIM PEYTON	41
Mossie and the Strippers BILLY EDD WHEELER	83
Hopscotch SALLIE BINGHAM	133
Desperate Fortune JOE TERRENCE GRAY	167
His First, Best Country JIM WAYNE MILLER	219
Piggyback SALLIE BINGHAM	271
The Dancers of Canaan RON MIELECH	315
Desert Flower BETTY PETERSON	355
Raven's Gift JOHN HOWELL	399
Just Taking Up Space NANCY GALL-CLAYTON	439
Someday's Gone FRANK SCHAEFER	485
Beating the Varsity LARRY PIKE	539
Liz's Circus Story LIZ BUSSEY FENTRESS	589
Afterword by LIZ BUSSEY FENTRESS	617

Preface

The farm I grew up on in West Kentucky, *the homeplace* we called it, is still there but it's not the same. It's not in the family now. The neighbors who bought the place are good farmers. They bulldozed the fence rows and cut down all the trees in the woods so it would be easier to grow more crops. And then later, the strip miners came in and dug up the whole farm except where the house and barns are. They put the dirt back and the crops are growing again and I guess most people wouldn't notice, but I'd plowed that land, starting when I was nine years old, riding on a cultivator behind two mules, plowing the seventy-five acres of corn three or four times to keep the weeds down while Dad and my brothers put in the soybean crop. To me, what's happened to that farm is a symbol of the changes that have come with time to all of Kentucky.

I've lived in many parts of Kentucky. I attended Georgetown College, surrounded by the horse farms of the Bluegrass. For four summers I was in the East Kentucky mountains performing in *The Book of Job*. I spent eight unforgettable weeks in Basic Training at Fort Knox, and lived more than 25 years in the karst region of Southern Kentucky. Each area of the state has its unique beauty, the people have their unique mind sets, accents and ways of expression, and each area has its own history, stories and even legends.

In 1975, two years before Horse Cave Theatre opened, I wrote in a letter from Los Angeles to Bill and Judy Austin in Horse Cave that, as artistic director of the then-dreamed-of theatre, I wanted to develop and produce original plays about Kentucky. For my senior directing project at Georgetown College I had directed a new play, *The Octogenarian* by Joe Graber and I was thrilled with the process. Later, at the Dallas Theater Center I had directed the world premiere of Charles W. Ferguson's stage adaptation of his best-selling biography of Cardinal Woolsey, *Naked to Mine Enemies*. During the five years I studied and worked at the Dallas Theater Center I was involved with many staged readings and productions of new plays either as an actor or director.

It was 1981, the fifth season of Horse Cave Theatre, before the organization was stable enough for the first new play to be produced. The criteria for choosing the plays had become more narrowly refined: the play must be full-length (no one-acts) and it must be about Kentucky or written by a Kentuckian or both. In most cases as it turned out it was both, but not always. Some of the plays which were chosen were produced as they came to us with only minor changes, some were rewritten over a period of months or even years, and some were developed through the Theatre's playwriting workshop. This process, in all its variety, came to be called Kentucky Voices, and under it the Theatre produced 17 world premieres of Kentucky plays from 1981 through 2001.

Not all of the settings of the 14 plays included in this volume are specific to Kentucky. *Liz's Circus Story* by Liz Bussey Fentress is primarily set in Wisconsin, although there are some scenes in

Kentucky. Billy Edd Wheeler's *Mossie and the Strippers* is really an Appalachian Mountains story. Larry Pike's *Beating the Varsity* portrays a Kentucky high school basketball team but the story is relevant to any high school in America, and Joe Gray's historical play about Aaron Burr, *Desperate Fortune*, is universal in scope and theme. John Howell's *Raven's Gift*, Nancy Gall-Clayton's *Just Taking Up Space*, and Frank Schaefer's *Someday's Gone* could be set in any medium to large American city. The other seven plays, Jim Peyton's *East of Nineveh* and *Marching to Zion*, Sallie Bingham's *Hopscotch* and *Piggyback*, Jim Wayne Miller's *His First, Best Country*, Ron Mielech's *The Dancers of Canaan*, and Betty Peterson's *Desert Flower* all, in my opinion, are tied by language, accents, and characters to Kentucky, which is not to say that they wouldn't play well to audiences anywhere.

The dozen playwrights whose work is printed in this book are talented writers. They have captured and preserved a moment in time from their chosen, changing corner of Kentucky which can be brought to life by theatres now and through the years. It's a valuable gift they have given us. For me, it has been a real privilege and pleasure to know these authors and to work with each of them.

It is expensive, comparatively, to produce new plays and Horse Cave Theatre never had any surplus in the budget to gamble with but I always thought it was worth it. I'm glad to say that all the new plays were well received; they found their audiences. And the audiences at Horse Cave Theatre became some of the most astute and discriminating I know of anywhere. But, to be candid, the only real reason I was willing to take the financial risks I did in order to encourage the writing of plays about Kentucky was simply my love for Kentucky – its landscapes, its history, its traditions, its accents, its people. And, as my playwright friend Preston Jones once told me, in love, risk comes with the territory.

– Warren Hammack

Introduction
about the Kentucky Voices New Play Readings 1990 - 2001

Plays are born on their first reading. Readers give voice to the words, and characters emerge; sounds, rhythms, and patterns of the language take shape; the minds and hearts of the listeners attach meanings to the words; and those meanings assemble and dance over the gathered company. The simultaneous act of speaking and listening that occurs with the lifting of written words to the stage is the moment a play enters the world.

Plays are conceived long before this, of course, and their gestation can take a few days or many years. The writing itself assumes its own guise, colored by obstacles, growth spurts, distressing doubts, or the blissful satisfaction of self-expression. I am not a playwright but I am a writer and I know this to be true in my own writing, and from discussions with other writers. Getting it out, getting it all down, getting it right can be an experience which feels like the rush of a river in spring, or the slow trickle in the dry season.

Horse Cave Theatre began its mainstage series of new Kentucky works in 1981, but it was not until 1989 that the theatre held its first public staged reading, an informal presentation of Joe Gray's *Desperate Fortune*. By 1990, a script development process was initiated, which we called Kentucky Voices. It included an annual spring weekend of staged readings of from three to five original Kentucky plays. Over two densely packed days, these previously unproduced scripts took flight before small but devoted audiences. In the years 1990 to 2001, the theatre staged 43 such readings.

It was, and is, creative work. With occasional trepidation, the playwrights generously handed over their plays to our care. In many cases, these writers had worked with artistic director Warren Hammack in his playwriting workshops. Warren, along with associate producer Liz Bussey Fentress, and I as associate director, gathered readers from the community, people with a passion for theatre and an interest in bringing new plays to life. They were actors, other playwrights, local people who wanted to be a part of something that was not yet quite formed, something that they could help nurture.

We made copies of the scripts for the participants and selected a director – usually Liz, Warren, or myself, but occasionally others (Robert Brock, Joe Gray, Denise Kay Dillard and Karen Terry). Each director scheduled two meetings to read through the play in the week prior to the public readings; the playwrights were encouraged to attend both rehearsals. These read-throughs were held in our newly-purchased building adjacent to the theatre, or in the auditorium itself. If we were planning to do four or five plays in a weekend, often with readers cast in more than one play, it could be a challenge to schedule that many rehearsal slots prior to the public readings.

Depending on our individual styles and the inclinations and talents of each group, we directors might encourage the readers to create characters or to read simply, add movement or remain seated. Lights and sound were kept to the basics. Still, it was the stuff of drama for the attentive community gathered there: lights up on a bank of chairs on the stage, readers giving their best shot, audiences eager to experience the world of a new play. For many, this truly was as good as a Broadway opening.

Following the readings, audiences were given the rare opportunity to meet and speak directly with the playwrights about the work. Over the years, many in our audiences became comfortable and skilled in the process. For those unfamiliar with the delicate nature of the enterprise, we distributed guidelines, lists of questions, things to think about while listening, which we had collected and edited from our own experiences.

These questions included: What were the scenes that gripped you, interested you, and why? Did that interest ever cease as you went on? If so, what was missing from the scene? What were the scenes that you were not interested in? Did they become interesting? When? Is the intent of the characters clear? If so, what are the ingredients that make the intent clear? What is needed when you are confused as to the characters' intent? What causes you to invest in a character? What's missing when there's no bond? Often, the playwrights posed specific questions about an intention, a moment, a theme.

The playwrights could pick and choose what to take from the comments and feedback. After all, the scripts were their babies, not ours. Hearing the words in the air, feeling the language in their ears, and watching the audience conjure images, emotions, and thoughts, the authors gained new and useful insights. They could hear laughter, gasps, sighs, silence. They could sense whether or not something was working.

Plays are rarely perfect the first time around, and readings are just one step in the long march, the noble and courageous process of writing plays. If intended qualities do not register with the audience, if unintended meanings are taken, the maker must revise and revise and revise, until the play is reborn. It can have a second reading and a third, before it emerges as a full production with all the trimmings.

In addition to *Desperate Fortune*, several of the plays presented here first had a staged reading before being mounted as full productions. These included *Desert Flower, The Dancers of Canaan, Piggyback, Liz's Circus Story, Beating the Varsity, Just Taking Up Space, Raven's Gift* and *His First, Best Country*. Many of the playwrights used the process to hear and work on other plays they had written. For me, working with these authors provided some of the most thrilling and creative moments in my 25 seasons. It was an honor to have their trust.

And now, the curtain opens on the words of the playwrights, with their comments about the development process. May these plays go on to new life on new stages.

– Pamela White

EAST OF NINEVEH
A Play in Two Acts
by
Jim Peyton

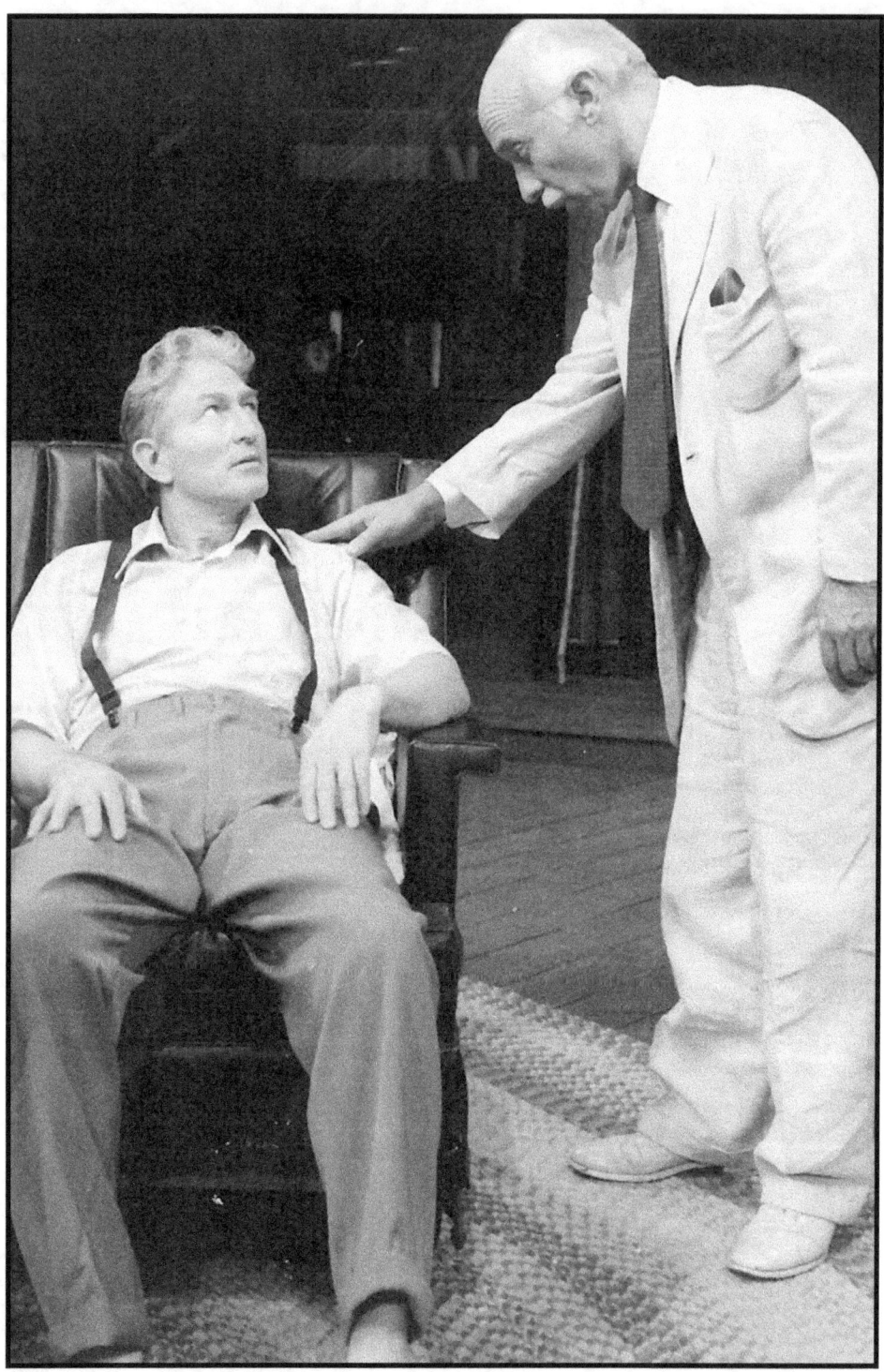
Warren Hammack and Bill Parsons in *East of Nineveh* by Jim Peyton, Horse Cave Theatre, 1985

East of Nineveh opened on July 19, 1985, with the following cast:

JOHN BUMPUS	*Warren Hammack*
B.W. BUMPUS	*William Groth*
FRANCINE BOATWRIGHT	*Breton Frazier*
PRESENCE	*Bill Parsons*

Director: Michael Hankins
Stage Manager: Karen Terry
Set and Lighting Design: John Partyka
Costume Design: Rebecca Shouse
Properties Master: Rob Heberly
Sound Design: Tim Speevack

William Groth, Warren Hammack and Breton Frazier in *East of Nineveh* by Jim Peyton, Horse Cave Theatre, 1985

Characters:

JOHN BUMPUS, a *Bible scholar*

B.W. BUMPUS, *a radio evangelist, John's cousin*

FRANCINE BOATWRIGHT, *B.W.'s admirer*

PRESENCE, *John's friend*

Place: A small community in Western Kentucky. The entire action takes place in John Bumpus' small sitting room. The furnishings are a mixture of antique and the just plain old. The arrangement of the pieces reflects John's preference for comfort and convenience over balance and symmetry. There is a large accumulation of books, some of which are stored neatly in bookcases, others, more frequently used perhaps, stacked handily on a library table. The table is, for John, the central focus of the room... for this is where he has spent many years of his adult life. In addition to the books, the table holds a reading lamp, a water pitcher, a glass with a spoon in it, and a large box of Arm and Hammer baking soda. Beside the table is an easy chair, a platform rocker of a type that swivels as well as rocks, a feature which allows John to swing away from his book on the table, lean back and contemplate some knotty concept he has encountered in his study.

Time: Summer, the year is about 1955.

ACT ONE

It is late afternoon. JOHN is seated at the table, bent over a large, much used Bible. He has reached that time in life when movements tend to be stiff and balance not as sure as it once was. Call it post-middle-age. His dress is casual but neat. He needs glasses to read but he doesn't like to use them and so takes them off whenever he can. He traces the words with his finger and reads slowly, articulating each word carefully, yet with understanding which is evidenced by his appropriate intonation and stress. His speech reflects the slow rhythms and complex vowels of Western Kentucky.

JOHN: "Therefore now, O Lord, take, I beseech thee, my life from me, for it is better for me to die than to live. Then said the Lord, Doest thou well to be angry? So Jonah went out of the city, and sat on the east side of the city, and there made him a" – Wait a minute! "...and sat on the east side ..." I never noticed that before. Now why do you reckon He would go to all the trouble to mention it was the EAST side? B.W., come in here! ...The EAST side, well what do you know? B.W.! ...Well, I expect it would be the east side, now wouldn't it? B.W.!

(While JOHN has been speaking, B.W. BUMPUS has entered and crossed the room and is now standing beside John's chair. He is a young man, in his early twenties. He is in the process of shaving. He is bare to the waist except for a towel draped over his shoulder, has on a pair of sharply-creased mustard colored slacks and is bare-footed. As the dialogue continues, he alternates between the sitting room and an adjoining room finishing his dressing, B.W. and JOHN raising their voices as necessary. B.W.'s complete ensemble includes a white shirt, a red tie, white wingtip shoes with brown caps and heels, and a bright green plaid sport coat. The latter he doesn't put on but drapes across the back of a chair.)

B.W.: What do you want? I'm trying to get ready for my radio broadcast.

JOHN: Looky here. Jonah. Chapter 4, verse 5. "So Jonah went out and sat on the EAST side of the city." Talking about Nineveh, of course. Now why do you reckon he chose the East side?

B.W.: How the hell should I know?

JOHN: Because it was a hill there? Well, of course it was. But it was a hill on the other side, too. Nineveh was in a valley with hills on both sides. Why EAST then? Come on, boy, think. Think.

B.W.: Cud'n John, I'm trying to get ready to go do my radio broadcast.

JOHN: I'll tell you why. So he could smell the smoke! The wind would have been from the west there, just like it is here, and on the east, see, the smoke would drift right over him, the smoke and the wailing and the noise of gnashing teeth. He could hear it and smell it and know for certain they finally got just what was coming to them.

B.W.: Well, if I remember right, they wasn't no smoke for him to smell because God didn't do nothing to them. So I guess he done climbed that hill for nothing.

JOHN: And a damn shame, too, a tragedy, that's what it was! – That bunch of snotty-nosed A-rabs running around hollering We repent! We repent! and him left there in the hot sun ay god with not so much as a whiff of brimstone to make up for all he'd been through. But that ain't the point!

B.W.: Well, what is it, then? I got to finish getting ready.

JOHN: B.W., if you going to preach, you've got to know the Scripture. You got to read.

B.W.: Shoot, I wasn't called to be no Bible scholar. I was called to be a evangelist. Besides, I ain't doing so bad. Just been at it a year and done got me a radio show already.

JOHN: I swear, B.W., you beat anything ever I saw.

B.W.: The Reverend B.W. Bumpus. That's what the announcer calls me when he introduces my show.

JOHN: You do. You beat anything ever I saw.

B.W.: But I been thinking about changing that. Hey, Cud'n John, see what you think about this. I'm going to have him start calling me Brother B. Billy Bumpus, the Radio Preacherboy. How does that strike you? Got a nice ring to it, don't you think?

JOHN: Good Lord!

B.W.: Maybe you right. Might ought to leave off the "boy" part. Ain't really no boy no more anyhow. Maybe just use "preacher" or better still, "evangelist." Yeah ... Brother B. Billy Bumpus, the Radio Evangelist! Hot damn!

JOHN: You ain't got a lick of sense, B.W., you know that? I can't understand why I ever let your mama talk me into this!

B.W.: Pore sainted Mama. I just wish she could be here to see me now.

JOHN: Sainted, my ass. She wasn't no saint. She was a whiner. World class, ay god. That woman could wear the paint right off the walls with her whining. "B.W.'s done had one of them foxhole conversions," she says. "B.W.'s going to make a preacher when he gets back from Korea," she says.

B.W.: Well, that's what I done, ain't it?

JOHN: "Course, I won't live to see it," she says. "No Siree, I don't expect to be here to see it. This old cancer is going to do for me. The doctors say I'm living on borrowed time right now. Could be just any day," she says. "So if I ain't here when B.W. gets out from the army – and you can just write it down that I won't be – well I want you to take him."

B.W.: Pore sweet Mama. I just wish she could be here.

JOHN: Hell fire, Beulah, I says, that boy's over 21. Why can't he look after hisself? "He's going to need help," she says. "He's going to need some help to get started. You take him and teach him and point him in the right direction."

B.W.: Mama always thought highly of you, Cud'n John. "I married into the wrong branch of the Bumpuses," she used to tell me. "Cud'n John's side of the family got all the money and brains and your pore daddy, he didn't get doodledy squat. Cud'n John's the one that never had to hit a lick in his life and could set around all day every day with his nose in the Bible and get to be a authority while your pore daddy worked hisself into a early grave and still never could make ends meet." You know what, Cud'n John? I don't even remember my daddy. He died before I was old enough to remember him.

JOHN: Yeah, I know, B.W. I know, son.

B.W.: Always it was just Mama. Until I went into the Army, it was just me and Mama. And she used to tell me, she'd say, "If anything ever happens to me, why you just go live with your Cud'n John. He'll look after you." She thought highly of you, Mama did.

JOHN: She never thought at all. Never needed to. Got by on whining. Why, if a idea ever struck that woman, it would of split her head wide open just like a ripe watermelon. And you going to wind up just like her if you ain't careful. Here I try to give you a insight into Jonah and I can't even get your attention long enough to listen, much less understand what I'm talking about.

B.W.: Shoot, that ain't nothing new. I don't know what you talking about most of the time.

JOHN: Damn it, I'm talking about Jonah! I'm talking about that pore put-upon son of a bitch that underwent terror and tempest and toss-ment into a raging sea, that endured three stinking days and nights in the belly of a fish with slimy weeds wrapped around his head before he finally had to give in, knowing all the time he was being shoved out onto a limb that was going to be sawed off, but hoping against hope that it wouldn't happen. And when it did, saying, "All right, it's them or me. If you going to let them off scott free, then kill me. Me, who's give up everything in the world for you, who's foregone anything I might have become to learn your ways and will. Me, who's passed up every pleasure I might have had in this world to be at your beck and call and cater to your every whim and fancy. Me, who's time and again stood up for you and counted you a friend and come to expect the same in return, and the one time, the ONE time I wanted a little something for myself, you step in and destroy it. All right! I've had enough! So you choose. Between them, that never give a damn about you, and as soon as your back is turned are going to rip off them sackcloths and get up out of them ash piles and do just like they always done – and you know it as well as I do – now, you just choose between them and me!" And then he marched straight out and climbed that hill on the east. And you know why? Because he was still hoping – pore, desperate son of a bitch that he was – he was still hoping that God would count his life for something –

(*JOHN breaks off abruptly, presses his hand to his chest just beneath his breastbone and grunts. He rocks with the pain and grunts louder.*)

JOHN: Where's my baking sody!

B.W.: Right yonder where you left it. Here, here, sit back down. I'll fix it for you.

(*B.W. pours half a glass of water, stirs in a teaspoon of soda and hands it to JOHN, watching him in some concern as he drinks. JOHN downs the drink in three large gulps, each followed by a long "Ahhhhh." After the last there is a pause and then JOHN emits a loud belch.*)

B.W.: Feel better now?

JOHN: Ahh Lord!

B.W.: I knew it was going to happen. I could tell you was going to get one of your spells.

JOHN: I reckon now you going to claim you a prophet, too. Besides, I keep telling you it ain't no spell, it's heartburn.

B.W.: Well all I know is every time you get yourself all worked up, you get it. Shoot, it don't take no prophet to notice that.

JOHN: Well, I mightn't get all worked up if I could ever get anything through that thick head of yours. Listen to me, boy, if you ever going to be worth your salt, you got to prepare yourself. You got to spend more time with the Scripture and less prissing around showing out for the ladies.

B.W.: I reckon you must be talking about Sister Francine Boatwright, ain't you? You never even met her and you done made up your mind she's just after my body.

JOHN: Her and several others, I expect.

B.W.: Well, let me tell you something. Them "ladies", as you call them, is put me where I am today. Without them "ladies" I'd still be just talking to Sunday School classes and giving my testimony at prayer meetings, instead of having me a pulpit to preach from about every week. And without Sister Francine getting her husband to sponsor me through his furniture business, I wouldn't have no radio show.

JOHN: Well, let me tell YOU something. Them ladies and that Boatwright woman are going to be your ruination! What they don't understand and what I can't seem to get you to understand is you ain't ready yet. You don't know enough to be taking on them preaching engagements and you certainly ain't ready for no radio show. Not everybody that listens to you is going to be a ignorant fool, and the ones who ain't are going to realize you are.

B.W.: Well, let me tell you something back. I ain't near as ignorant as you think I am. All you ever done since I come here to live with you is hammer Scripture at me. Night and day, day and night. And fire questions at me. What kin was Abraham and Lot? Who was Tiglath Pileser? How big was the boil on old Job's ass? Maybe I don't know as much Scripture as you, but I expect I know about as much as I need to.

JOHN: You don't know nothing.

B.W.: Well then, I don't need to. Whatever God wants me to say He puts in my head and I say it. I don't try to add nothing to it nor take nothing away.

JOHN: Just open your mouth and God fills it, does He? Well, He fills it, all right. He fills it with bullshit, that's what He fills it with. I reckon in that radio broadcast of yours last week, when you got to talking about them whited sepulchers, I reckon you going to tell me God put that in your head.

B.W.: Well, yeah, in a manner of speaking. What I done was, see, I just let my Bible flop open and when I looked down, that's what caught my eye.

JOHN: And you had no idea what it was, did you? Couldn't even pronounce it. Called it see-PULL-chers. Must of sounded to you like vultures. So you concluded it must be some kindly of a albino buzzard and went on to talk about how they go to soaring around in the air, pretty to look at but full of rot and corruption and how you better never let one get right over you or it'll puke on you every time.

B.W.: Well, what's wrong with that?

JOHN: Not a thing. Not a god damn thing. Except a sepulcher is a tomb. Where they bury dead people. In this case a old one that's been used and then has been whitewashed so as to look new.

B.W.: Well, shoot, a buzzard is better. People today don't use tombs no more, not very many anyway, so most of them wouldn't know what you was talking about. But everbody understands buzzards.

JOHN: Listen at you! I just wish you could hear what you saying!

B.W.: All I'm saying is buzzards is better.

JOHN: No, that ain't what you saying. You saying being a man of God is easy. It don't cost nothing. Any ignorant, addled-brained son of a bitch that by blind chance becomes so inclined can do it. You don't have to know anything, learn anything, sacrifice anything or suffer anything. All you have to do is say you are and you are. Well, you wrong! You got to learn God. Learn His nature. Learn the way His mind works. And that means you got to spend time, years even, at the Bible. And you got to give up things – friends, family, things you enjoy and that includes women – because He looks upon these things as distractions and He don't put up with no distractions. And then you got to suffer. He'll see to that. After you've done everything He ever asked, busted your tail to please Him and are beginning to think that maybe He's satisfied with you and maybe, just maybe He's beginning to have a little regard for you, when you least expect it, and least deserve it, He's going to do something that's going to hurt you and hurt you bad. Whatever it is you value – and He knows that better than you do yourself – He's going to destroy.

B.W.: Shoot, I suffered. I was in Korea, in the war. I been cold and hungry, stuck in a foxhole with mortar fire landing all around me, shrapnel singing past my ears. That's suffering, ain't it? I seen my buddy raise up to look out and come back down with the whole top of his head blowed off. That's suffering. That's when I clawed the mud in the bottom of that foxhole and cried out to the Lord to just get me out of there and I'd spend the rest of my life preaching the Word. Shoot, I suffered.

JOHN: I've heard that story a hundred times but there's something you always leave out. Tell me this, what was your buddy's name?

B.W.: Damned if I know. He was already in that hole when I jumped in. I never saw him before.

JOHN: Hell, you wasn't suffering, you was just skeered. There's a difference between suffering and being skeered.

B.W.: You know what's wrong with you, Cud'n John? You jealous, that's what. That's right, jealous. You never had no big foxhole conversion like I did. You was converted at some little old piss-ant revival meeting. Shoot, wouldn't nobody cross the road to hear about your conversion. And all you ever done afterwards is set around and study the Bible, maybe go down and argue with that bunch of old farts that hangs out down yonder at Hayes' Farm Store. Never nobody asked you to get up and testify, did they? Never no preachers called on you to come and take their pulpits, did they? Never no women set out there in the congregation clutching their breasts with them white gloves, breathing hard and hanging on your ever word, did they? And you didn't have no Sister Francine Boatwright to talk that rich husband of hers into sponsoring no radio show for you and come and haul you around in a big car wherever you need to go. Naw, didn't none of that ever happen to you and you just jealous because it did to me.

JOHN: You think I give a damn about anything like that?

B.W.: Face it, Cud'n John. God smiled on me and he didn't on you. And I'm going to tell you something else I think He's done. I ain't said nothing about it because Sister Francine just brought me the letter yesterday.

JOHN: What letter? What are you talking about?

B.W.: A letter from a listener. A old lady from down around Mount Tabor. A shut-in. Arthritis so bad she couldn't get around. You remember my show last week when I prayed for all the shut-ins. Well, she claims that she done laid her hand on the radio. Yeah. Laid her hand right on the radio while I was praying. She said pretty soon she felt Power coming through that radio right into her hand. Said it run right up her arm and on into ever part of her body. Said it just spread out all inside her. Claims that when it was over she felt so good she just got up and walked. Been walking around ever since. Feels better than she felt in years. Sent me two dollars. Said she wished it could have been more, but she lives on a pension and it was all she had. Listen, Cud'n John! I think I may got the Gift!

JOHN: Good Lord! That's about all you need. Some silly old woman that you've never seen, don't know nothing about, may be crazy as a coot for all you know, to convince you you got the Gift too!

B.W.: I knew it. I knew you'd say that. You just can't give me credit for anything, can you? You see now why I didn't tell you before? Well, the hell with you. Tonight we'll just settle it once and for all.

JOHN: How you going to do that?

B.W.: You just listen to my radio show, that's all

JOHN: Well, if you promise to stay away from them albino buzzards, I might. I've had about as much of them as I can stand.

B.W.: Shoot —-

 (*B.W. is interrupted by three quick blasts of a car horn.*)

B.W.: Well, here's Sister Francine come to pick me up. She sure as hell believes in me.

JOHN: Yeah, she believes in part of you, I'll grant you that.

B.W.: I keep telling you, she ain't like that at all. You know what I'm going to do? I'm just going to bring her in here and let you meet her and then you can see for yourself.

JOHN: I don't know as I want to meet her.

B.W.: Well, you going to whether you want to or not. I'm tired of hearing your snide remarks.

(*B.W. exits and can be heard offstage.*)

B.W.: (*Off.*) Hey, Sister Francine, get out and come in a minute. I want you to meet my Cud'n John! (*Pause.*) Come on, we got plenty of time.

FRANCINE: (*Off.*) We can't stay too long now. It wouldn't do to miss your broadcast.

B.W.: (*Off.*) Don't worry. We'll make it.

(*B.W. ushers in FRANCINE.*)

B.W.: Sister, Francine, this here's my Cud'n John.

(*FRANCINE is fortyish. Her hair is an unlikely shade of blond and has that rigid just-come-from-the-beauty-parlor look and her makeup has been applied with a heavy hand. She is dressed in a frilly summer outfit complete with white gloves and a wide-brimmed floppy hat worn well off the face.*)

FRANCINE: Oh I'm just so pleased to meet you, Mr. Bumpus. B.W. just talks about you all the time so I feel like I know you already, and I'm just so pleased to meet you at last. I was just saying to B.W., we can't stay too long, now, because it wouldn't do to be late for the radio broadcast, but I just couldn't pass up the chance of meeting you because you've had such an influence on him. I'll bet you're just as proud of him as you can be. Well, of course you are. We all are. Why, the first time I heard him preach I just got goose bumps all over, him, young as he is and been through all that in the war and to see his best friend killed right before his very eyes! Oh, I'll tell you my heart went right out to him and I just wanted to take him and hold him. Oh, it was all I could do, not to. Oh, I've never felt so ... so MOVED in my life. So I said to myself right then, I said, if anybody was ever called to preach, then it was this young man, and if there is any way I can ever help him I'm sure going to do my best. So I went right home and said to Clarence – Clarence Boatwright? He's my husband, you know – so I said, Clarence – He was already in bed asleep and I had to wake him up to tell him – so I said, Clarence, we've got to do something to help him. Then I said, Why don't we put him on the radio? Clarence, my husband, he owns this furniture business – Boatwright Furniture Mart? In Princeton? – and he sponsors a half-hour radio program of gospel music every Friday night to advertise it, you know, so I said, Instead of them just playing old records, why don't we let him preach?

JOHN: Would you care to sit down, Miz ... uh ... Sister ... uh ...

FRANCINE: Well, I'd like to, I really would, but I'd better not. (*FRANCINE sits.*) I can't stay but just a minute. Can't be late for the broadcast. So I said to Clarence, I said, Let's let him preach. People will enjoy it much better than that old gospel stuff. "Well, what if they don't?" he said. "Not ever body likes preaching." Don't you worry your head about that, I said. They'll like this young man. And I'll tell you this, Clarence Boatwright, I told him, I intend to see that he gets his chance. That Clarence, I declare to Goodness, all he ever thinks about is that business of his! So, there we was, last Friday night right there in that radio studio with a desk and a microphone and all, and I said to him, I said, Now B.W., don't be nervous, just speak right out just like you was standing in a pulpit with a church full of people in front of you, there's nothing to be nervous about, I said, and oh, my, he just started in and the words just rolled out of his mouth. He told about his experience in the war and about how the Lord saved him in a foxhole and then he went on to take his text on those white birds – I forget what the Bible called them. What was it the Bible called them, B.W.?

JOHN: See-PULL-chers.

FRANCINE: Why, that's right. That's exactly right. Oh, I should have known you'd know that. B.W. said you was a Bible scholar. B.W. says you know the Bible so well, a person would think you had wrote it yourself. Well, anyway it was a marvelous sermon, Oh just marvelous!

JOHN: I heard it.

FRANCINE: Well what am I thinking about? Of course you did! And wasn't you just as proud of him as you could be! Sitting at that desk, straight as a ramrod and talking into that microphone like it was something he did everyday of his life. Why, I would have been scared absolutely to death! But not B.W. Oh, I could have just hugged him and squeezed him all to pieces. That's what I told Clarence, I said, I was so proud of that boy I could have just squeezed him all to pieces. And I know Mr. Bumpus was proud of you too, B.W., wasn't you, Mr. Bumpus?

JOHN: Proud.

FRANCINE: So there I was in that radio studio, afraid to cough, afraid to move even, afraid they'd hear me on the radio, and B.W. was there at that desk with the microphone and all, and the radio announcer said, "The following program is sponsored by The Boatwright Furniture Mart. And now, live from our studios, we bring you a spiritual message by the Reverend B.W. Bumpus."

B.W.: Hey, Sister Francine, I been thinking about that, and I think maybe we ought to have him change it to Reverend B. Billy Bumpus, Radio Evangelist. See, my middle name is William – that's what the "W" stands for, William – and I think B. Billy sounds better than B.W., don't you?

FRANCINE: Billy! Oh how wonderful! Billy! Oh, it's just perfect! It fits you to a tee! You look like your name ought to be Billy! That's exactly what I'm going to call you from now on!

B.W.: B. Billy. B. Billy Bumpus. It needs that "B" in front to give it the right ring.

FRANCINE: Billy! Oh, I love it. It's perfect, just perfect! So there we was in the radio studio and ... BILLY ... preached this marvelous sermon, and then he prayed for all the shut-ins, you know, sick people and all. And then the most wonderful thing happened! You see, people write in to that radio program all the time. Oh yes, they get several cards and letters every week, requesting songs and all. You'd be surprised how many people listen, you really would. Well, anyway the radio station people go through them and mark down the songs people want to hear and then send them on to Clarence at the store. Well, I just happened to be at the store the other day and I saw this stack of letters on Clarence's desk and I noticed that one of them was addressed to B.W. And guess what! It was from an old lady who had had this disease and B.W. had CURED her! When B.W. prayed for her, it just completely CURED her! Oh, I'll tell you, when I read that I just broke out in goose bumps all over. It was a MIRACLE! An honest-to-God MIRACLE! I wouldn't have believed it if I hadn't seen the letter with my own eyes. It just sent goose bumps all over me. I told Clarence just this morning, I said, See there? And you was afraid people wouldn't like him. And do you know what he said? He said it was just one old crazy woman from Mount Tabor – that's where she was from, you know – just some old crazy woman who wouldn't be buying furniture anyway, living on a pension and all. I'll swear, that Clarence! Well, just you wait, Clarence Boatwright, I told him. One of these fine days you'll be laughing out of the other side of your mouth, because if he can cure one, he can cure a hundred, I said.

B.W.: And I know just what done it. The radio! It was because she done put her hand on that radio. Somehow or other that's what done it. Closed the connection or something and let the Power get through to her body. It was a accident her doing that. Not thinking what she was doing, just laying her hand up there on that radio. It was a accident. But now I know. And tonight, I'm going to tell them all. Just lay your hand on the radio, I'm going to say. Just lay your hand right on up there on that old radio and feel the Power, I'm going to tell them. The Power of God is going to come right through that old radio and it's going to run right up your arm and into that old sick body of yours. Aw, Yes! The Power! The Power of God! And you going to feel it! You going to feel it in your hand. You going to feel it in your arm. You going to feel it all over your insides. Working! Working! Getting shut of all that corruption. All that rot and decay and disease. Aw, Yes! You going to feel it, because God owns the airwaves. He OWNS them old airwaves, and He can send His Power through them if He's a mind to. And He IS a mind to! He's doing it right now. Right this very minute! Aw, don't you feel it? Don't you just feel the Power of God working in you right now?

FRANCINE: So I said to Clarence, I told him I said, Clarence, I said — My! My! would you just look at the time! Mr. Bumpus, do you know what you've just done? You've done made me forget the time and just about made me late. Well, it's been worth it, it certainly has. It's not every day you get to meet interesting people. Now, B.W., we can't waste any more time or we're going to be late, and that wouldn't do now, would it? No, it certainly would not. Well, Mr. Bumpus! It's been SO nice. — No. No. Don't get up. I can see you're not as spry as you once was. Well, none of us are now are we? And B.W. tells me that you have spells. He's right worried about you, B.W. is. Oh, I see you take baking soda for them. Clarence, he takes Alka-Seltzer. I don't see how he can stand that stuff. I told him, I said, Clarence Boatwright, you're going to take so much of that stuff, you're just going to explode. One of these days you're just going to explode, I told him, and then where will I be? Well, these days you just can't be too careful, is what I say. Oh you're such a fine person, Mr. Bumpus, a real gentleman of the old school, as they say, and it's been just a real privilege to meet you. Now, don't you worry about B.W. I'll make sure he behaves hisself and I'll have him back safe and sound real early. I just know you worry about him when he's out and all, now don't you? Come along, B.W., and don't forget your jacket. You want to look nice for your broadcast. Bye-bye, Mr. Bumpus. Come along, B.W. Bye-bye, Mr. Bumpus. Come along, now, B.W.

B.W.: Bye, Cud'n John. Be sure and listen now, you hear?

(*FRANCINE and B.W. exit.*)

FRANCINE: (*Exiting.*) Billy! Oh, it's just perfect! It just suits you, it really does! Billy! Oh, how sweet!

(*JOHN stands listening until all sound of them is gone, then goes over and puts a spoonful of soda in his glass, adds water, stirs and drinks.*)

JOHN: God help Clarence. (*He emits a long and satisfying belch, then sits, swivels his chair around to the table where his Bible still lies open, and begins to read.*) "So Jonah went out of the city, and sat on the east side of the city ..." (*He swings his chair from the table, leans back, gazes at the ceiling for a bit, then speaks softly.*) That pore son of a bitch. That pore put-upon, victimized, double-crossed son of a bitch!

(*As JOHN sits musing, PRESENCE enters. He appears to be a contemporary of John's. He is dressed in white suit, shirt, shoes and large hat. A red tie and pocket handkerchief add a splash of color. His speech reflects the same dialect as John's.*)

PRESENCE: John? ... John? ... John!

JOHN: I hear you!

PRESENCE: Well —-

JOHN: Well, leave me alone.

PRESENCE: Aw, come on John.

JOHN: No! If I told you once, I told you a thousand times, I ain't talking to you!

PRESENCE: Come on, John. It's been years now.

JOHN: I don't care if it's been centuries. I don't care if it's been millenniums.

PRESENCE: You going to have to talk to me sometime.

JOHN: Naw I don't.

PRESENCE: I'm afraid you do, John. We going to have to straighten this thing out between us. We can't just go on forever this way.

JOHN: It's some things that can't never be straightened out.

PRESENCE: I MISS YOU, John.

JOHN: Well you just ought to of thought about that before.

PRESENCE: I'm truly sorry, John.

JOHN: So you said.

PRESENCE: We've had some good times together. I remember when you first come to me. What was it B.W.

called it? A little old piss-ant revival? Well, he just didn't know, did he?

JOHN: That boy don't know his ass from a hole in the ground.

PRESENCE: You wasn't much interested in me that night. Had your mind on other things.

JOHN: Yeah, girls.

PRESENCE: There was one in particular.

JOHN: Nadine Heddin.

PRESENCE: You was planning on taking her home that night.

JOHN: Jr. Pease. You remember Jr. Pease?

PRESENCE: Indeed I do.

JOHN: He was something! A sport. Me and him was running together then.

PRESENCE: I remember.

JOHN: Wore them high-waisted britches, two-toned shoes. We was sports!

PRESENCE: Yeah.

JOHN: Had us a 1928 A Model Ford Roadster. Slickest thing on wheels. Used to go to all them church doings.

PRESENCE: Looking for girls.

JOHN: Yeah, we'd hook up with them there and take them home. Had a lot of church doings in them days – singings, basket dinners, revivals. We took them all in. Hey, you remember Will Theoblod?

PRESENCE: Oh yes.

JOHN: Little man, Will. Ears like a molasses jug. Eyes like a calf. Big and brown and soft-looking, just like a calf's eyes. Buck teeth come down against his bottom lip this away. Remember how rabbity he was? Folks thought he wasn't right bright. I expect up until he was grown, old Miz Theobold was the only one that ever got a good look at him. He was rabbity. Used to hide when company come. Used to crawl up under the house, under of the front porch so he could listen to them talk. Used to peep out through the underpinning, watch them come and go. Told me that hisself, afterwards. Loved to watch people. Couldn't stand for nobody to look at him though. Folks thought he wasn't right bright.

PRESENCE: Will was rabbity, all right.

JOHN: A lot of folks didn't know it but Will used to go to all them church doings, too. Hiding somewhere and watching. Once in a while you'd just catch a glimpse of his face through the bushes or through a window. Had to be quick to do it, though. Me and Jr. Pease, we made us a rule. First one to see Will, the other one had to drive home. You can't do much when you driving, you know.

PRESENCE: I know.

JOHN: Jr. Pease won more than I did. Well, old Junior's dead now. Got caught in a hay baler. Bit his leg clean off, ay god.

PRESENCE: Yeah. That was a shame.

JOHN: The meeting was at old Zions Cause Church. Me and Jr. Pease, we got in and got us a back seat. Singing started and we was looking over the crowd for girls.

PRESENCE: You had your eye out for Nadine Heddin.

JOHN: I'd taken her home once but I had to do the driving. I wanted another crack at her. I was looking all around and Jr. Pease, he nudged me with his elbow this away. Said, "Say, John, I seen him." Seen who? I said. I quit looking for Nadine. "Will," he said. Where? I said. "Why, right through the window yonder. Wait a minute and you'll see him, too." I quit looking for Nadine.

PRESENCE: Not much point, was it?

JOHN: "Say, I got a idea," he said. What's your idea, I asked him. "Listen," he said, "why don't we go out there and catch him and bring him in here." He was a sport. Lead off, I told him, I'm right behind you. I was a sport, too.

PRESENCE: It was before you got sanctified.

JOHN: Well, out the door we slipped and around the church. Come up behind old Will all scrooched down about to pop up and peep through the window again. Both of us grabbed him. He let out a squeal and, ay god, for a while there it was like trying to hold onto a handful of fishing worms. He'd get away from me and Jr. Pease'd grab him, get away from him and I'd grab him. Finally we just throwed him down and laid on him till he quietened down. Then we took him under the arms and in we went.

PRESENCE: Yeah, that was a sight to see, all right.

JOHN: We went right down to the front bench and set down with him. Wedged him between us. Jr. Pease pinned him with one shoulder, I pinned him with another. There we set. Old Will shaking like a dog straining to pass a peach seed. Bottom lip quivering against them buck teeth. Eyes bugged out like a bullfrog. I begun not to feel too good. That Jr. Pease looked like he might bust out in a laugh any minute.

PRESENCE: He was some sport.

JOHN: Bled to death before they could get him to a doctor.

PRESENCE: Yeah. A real shame.

JOHN: You remember how the pulpit was in old Zions Cause Church? Set up on a little platform about two foot off the floor. Little wooden fence around it. Old Brother Uriah was setting up there. Brother Uriah Thompson. There was a man of the Lord, ay god. Make you smell brimstone. Right after we come in, he stood up and give out his text. I never shall forget it. Remember it word for word right today. Found somewhere in Acts. "And there appeared unto them cloven tongues like as of fire, and it sat upon each of them." Word for word!

PRESENCE: That's word for word, all right.

JOHN: Brother Uriah, he begun to preach. Told about all the different kinds of fire. One kind can cook a man's supper. Another can burn up his house. One kind can cleanse a man's heart, another can burn him in hell forever and ever. It was that last kind that he talked most about. Rich man in torment. Lake of fire where the worm dieth not. Set me to sweating, ay god! Will shaking between us. Jr. Pease cool as a cucumber.

PRESENCE: Some sport.

JOHN: Them ole coal-oil lamps around the walls begun to smoke up. Smelled to me like brimstone. I tried to think about Nadine. Will was as white as a flour barrel. Then old Brother Uriah took up the Last Judgment. One shall be taken, another left. Weeping and wailing and gnashing of teeth. Cry to the mountains, Fall on us! Depart from me, saith the Lord, I know ye not. Ay god, that was preaching!

PRESENCE: It was for sure.

JOHN: Brother Uriah went back to that lake of fire. Stood on the edge of the bottomless pit where the smoke arises forever and ever. "What will you do, Sinner," he says, "when the sun refuses to shine? What will you do, Backslider, when the moon turns to blood? Oh ye Unsanctified, when the mountains fly away, what will you do?" My britches was sticking to the seat. Old Will had near about gnawed his bottom lip off.

PRESENCE: Old Jr. Pease's collar was even wilted some.

JOHN: "Aw!" Brother Uriah hollered, "It'll be too late then to call on the name of the Lord. Too late then to beg forgiveness. Too late then to change your ways and get sanctified. Now! Now is the time to do it. Now is the accepted time, saith the Lord. So come on, old Sinner. Come on, old Backslider. And come on, all ye Unsanctified, and let's get right with God! Come on, I say!"

PRESENCE: And Brother Uriah leapt clean across that little fence and landed flatfooted in the middle of the floor!

JOHN: Well, everything busted loose at once. Brother Uriah, he hit the floor and squalled, "Come on!" Old Miz Blackburn setting right behind us jumped up and hollered, "Hallelujah, I'm a-coming through!" Somebody in the back laughed the holy laugh. And Will squealed and jumped and dumped me and Jr. Pease both in the middle of the floor. One minute sitting there not expecting a thing. The next, flat of our backs on the floor. "Get him, John," Jr. Pease hollered. "He's heading for the door!" But he wasn't.

PRESENCE: Brother Uriah had him blocked off.

JOHN: Brother Uriah was standing there squalling, "Come on, Sinner!" And old Will was backing ground. "Grab him, John," Jr. Pease says, "he's backing your way." He was, too. I got all set to spring but about that time old Miz Blackburn cut loose again. She'd done climbed up in the seat. Weighed two hundred pounds if she weighed a ounce. "Hoo, Lordy!" she bellered. "Hoo, hoo, hoo!"

PRESENCE: Might as well of jabbed old Will in the behind with a red-hot poker. He leapt that little wooden fence and tried to climb the wall in back of the pulpit.

JOHN: By now, half of the church was under the Power. Shouting all over. Old Miz Blackburn was making that old bench rock. Brother Uriah was still squalling for the sinners to come on. "I'll drive him out of there," Jr. Pease says. "You head him when he comes down."

PRESENCE: Big sport.

JOHN: Jr. Pease, he run at old Will, flopping his arms this away and hollering "Sooey!" Will, he skinned right up on top of the pulpit. Skinned right up on top of her and hollered, "Let me alone!" "Let me alone," he hollered. Brother Uriah he looked up and seen him there. "Get off that pulpit!" he squalled. "Sooey!" Jr. Pease says. Then it looked like old Will jumped. Or maybe he fell.

PRESENCE: Or maybe he was throwed.

JOHN: Anyway he landed smack-dab in the floor and then begun trying his best to wiggle over and hide under one of them benches. By now, the other half of the church was under the Power. Ever body was shouting. Old Miz Blackburn was trying to climb up on the back of that bench, going "Hoo, Lordy, hoo-Lordy, hoo-Lordy!" Folks was streaming down the aisle to the front. Old Will was laying face down on the floor. Trembling all over. Brother Uriah had him by one leg and was praying him through. Jr. Pease was sitting up on top of the pulpit.

PRESENCE: A natural born sport.

JOHN: "Oh Lord," Brother Uriah prayed, "hear me now. I'm talking to you, Lord. I got a old sin-sick sinner here. Got him down as far as he can go. Can't go no further. I'm calling on you, Lord. Do your stuff now. Lift this old boy up to glory." Well, then it happened to Will. Up he come off the floor. Up he come a-shouting. "Whoop-whoop! Whoop-whoop! Whoop-whoop!" "Praise the Lord!" Brother Uriah squalled. Several laughed the holy laugh. "Hoo-Lordy!" Miz Blackburn hollered. "Sooey!" Jr. Pease went. But he wasn't getting under the Power.

PRESENCE: Sport.

JOHN: Yeah. Well, I couldn't hold back no longer. Old Miz Blackburn, Will, all them folks laughing the holy laugh and that lake of fire – it was too much for me.

PRESENCE: You got sanctified, too.

JOHN: Then and there.

PRESENCE: And I was mighty pleased, John.

JOHN: Me and Will got to be good friends after that. He was a changed man. Wasn't scared of folks no more. Loved to be around them. Used to get under the Power and testify in public. Married.

PRESENCE: Nadine Heddin.

JOHN: Had a youngun ever year for five years and died.

PRESENCE: In the service of his country and happy in the Lord.

JOHN: Me and Jr. Pease, we quit running together. Wasn't much to do after I got sanctified. He never did.

PRESENCE: Too much a sport.

JOHN: He was trying to stomp hay into that baler with his foot, ay god!

PRESENCE: You thought a lot of Jr. Pease.

JOHN: He enjoyed hisself.

PRESENCE: You looked up to him, wanted to be like him.

JOHN: Well, I reckon I did.

PRESENCE: But you couldn't.

JOHN: Not after I got sanctified.

PRESENCE: Why not?

JOHN: Well, it wouldn't of done. It was things I had to give up.

PRESENCE: What things?

JOHN: Well, you know. Things like running around raising hell. And —-

PRESENCE: And?

JOHN: Girls. Women.

PRESENCE: I never asked you to give up nothing, did I?

JOHN: No.

PRESENCE: It was your own decision.

JOHN: Yes, but —-

PRESENCE: Your own free choice. But then after years of just you and me, along come Miss Daisy.

JOHN: I don't want to talk about it.

PRESENCE: You have to, John.

JOHN: Like hell I do! Like hell! You go ahead and do your damnedest. Throw me to the fish like Jonah. I don't care. I ain't talking!

PRESENCE: You growed up with Miss Daisy, didn't you, John? You was both pretty much the same age. How come you never got interested in her back then? She was a right pretty little thing, I remember.

JOHN: It was her that wasn't interested.

PRESENCE: That's right. She used to play the piano at old Zions Cause Church. (*Chuckles to Himself.*)

JOHN: What's so funny?

PRESENCE: I was just remembering something — this was after she was grown woman.

JOHN: I know what it is. You're remembering how when she would get up from the piano stool how her dress would be caught in her crack.

PRESENCE: And there it would remain for the rest of the service.

JOHN: I don't know why ever body thought that was so damn funny. It wasn't her fault. She couldn't help it.

PRESENCE: You're right, of course, John. I meant no disrespect.

JOHN: Used to worry the fire out of ever body, though. Wouldn't nobody tell her because they was all afraid to. But they'd talk about it to one another. I remember hearing some of them after church one day. "You reckon she don't know it's in there," one of them said. "Looks to me like she could feel it." "She can't feel it," another one said. "She backed into me once in a crowd and let me tell you, that thing ain't like you'd imagine. It's as hard as iron. Why, I bet you she could tighten down on them cheeks and crack a hickernut. She ain't about to feel no little old flimsy piece of dress material." I never did think it was funny.

PRESENCE: No, of course not, John. (*Pause.*) She never married.

JOHN: She was particular. Had high standards.

PRESENCE: But you thought since you was both older you might measure up.

JOHN: I tried.

PRESENCE: And broke your word.

JOHN: All right! So I broke my word. What's so damned important about that? Other people break theirs ever day.

PRESENCE: You are not other people, John. Besides, you left me.

JOHN: I never.

PRESENCE: Maybe you never meant to, never realized you had, but all the same, you did. I was just trying to get your attention.

JOHN: Get my attention! Get my attention! Hell fire! It's a thousand ways you could of got my attention. You could of hit me over the head with something. You could of struck me down with a bolt of lightning.

PRESENCE: I couldn't hurt you, John.

JOHN: Couldn't hurt me! Couldn't hurt me! God damn it! If you had studied for a million years, you couldn't have hurt me worse!

PRESENCE: I know that now, John, and I'm sorry.

JOHN: Sorry! You're sorry!

PRESENCE: I want you to know, John, she didn't suffer.

JOHN: Didn't suffer! Why, you —-! Uunnhh! (*JOHN presses his hand to his chest.*) Uunnhh! (*JOHN stumbles to the table, sloshes water into the glass and spoons in soda.*) Uunnhh! (*He gulps the soda water, spilling much of it.*) Uunnhh! (*He stumbles to his chair and sits as gradually the pain lessens.*)

PRESENCE: Bad?

JOHN: Uunnhh.

PRESENCE: It's something I got to tell you, John. Maybe you already suspect it. That baking sody ain't going to do you no good.

JOHN: Why not?

PRESENCE: Cause that ain't heartburn, John.

ACT TWO

A few minutes later. JOHN is seated in his chair, PRESENCE solicitously hovering over him.

PRESENCE: Feeling a little better now, John?

JOHN: Uummhh.

PRESENCE: You know, that old ticker ain't going to hold out much longer. That's why we got to get this thing straightened out between us. You got to forgive me, John.

JOHN: I ain't going to do it. I can't.

PRESENCE: You know I think a lot of you, John. You're my friend.

JOHN: Well, you ain't mine. Not any more.

PRESENCE: I hurt you, I realize that. And I'm sorry. But listen to me, John, she didn't feel a thing. It was like one minute she was sitting in a chair in her living room and next she was in Paradise. She didn't hold no grudge. In fact, she was — is — grateful for it.

JOHN: Still don't make it right.

PRESENCE: I agree. But try to see it from my side, John. It's all in the way you look at time. It's been ten years since I took Miss Daisy. Now to you, that's a long stretch. It represents a big slice out of your life. But time is different to me. When you live in eternity, a thousand years, ten thousand years is like a day, like a minute, even less. In my way of looking at it, I wasn't taking Miss Daisy away from you. Not for more than a split second anyway.

JOHN: Bullshit! You knew what you was doing.

PRESENCE: Honest, John, I never meant to hurt you.

JOHN: Oh yes you did! You done it a-purpose and in cold blood. I ain't the first, and I don't reckon I'll be the last. It's all in here. (*He raps the Bible with his knuckles.*) Ever pore son of a bitch that ever got close to you, you wound up breaking his heart. I guess I got myself to blame. I knew it — Lord knows, you can't miss it, not if you got any sense at all — but I just never thought you would do it to me.

PRESENCE: Now, John —-

JOHN: Just like I reckon Moses never thought you'd do it to him. Forty years he drug that bunch of raggedy-assed, carping, stiff-necked Jews around in the wilderness and when he finally got them to the Promised Land, you wouldn't let him in. HIM! Who'd found favor in your sight, so you said. Talked to you face to face. Been your friend. What did you do? You took him up on Mount Pisgah. Said, "Looky yonder, Moses." Said, "There she is, what you been working for all your life. And flowing with milk and honey, just like I told you. My, my, ain't it pretty! But Moses, old buddy, you can't go in." And why not? Because way back there in the Desert of Zin, when it wasn't no water to be found and that bunch had just about drove Moses crazy with their whining, you told him to speak to a rock and he hauled off instead and hit it with a stick.

PRESENCE: Well now, John, it wasn't because he disobeyed me. I could of overlooked that. No, it was because he doubted my work.

JOHN: So you say. But as I see it, he just lost his temper. And with good reason, I'd say.

PRESENCE: Now you wasn't there, John, and I was. And you got to realize that not ever little detail is recorded in the Bible. As I recall, when I told him to speak to that rock, he said something like, "Shoot, you can't get water out of no rock. I ain't going out there in front of all them thirsty people and say, 'Hey, old Rock, give us some water!' What kindly of a damn fool do you think I am?" No, he definitely doubted my work, John.

JOHN: Well, what if he did? Don't forty years count for nothing?

PRESENCE: Now we're back to the question of time.

JOHN: You know, that's about the flimsiest argument ever I heard. Time ain't got a damn thing to do with it. It's how you treat your friends. It's what you put them through. What about Job? He was one of yours, wasn't he? A perfect and a upright man. Your own words. He never doubted you. Never tried to run away like Jonah. Never broke his word. And what did you do to him? Turned old Satan loose on him, that's what you done. Said, "Don't kill him. But anything else you can think of goes."

PRESENCE: It was kindly of a test

JOHN: A test of who? And at whose expense? First, you take away all his livestock, kill all his servants. Then, you bring the house down and kill all his sons and daughters. Then, you afflict him from head to foot with boils. And even that ain't enough for you, you have to bring in them so-called comforters to gloat over him and say, "Lord, lord. How bad you must have been to bring all this misery down on yourself!"

PRESENCE: Now, I never done none of that.

JOHN: You let it be done. You agreed to it. And then when that pore miserable, put-upon bastard tried to question you about it, asked you why you done it, what did you do?

PRESENCE: I tried to explain it to him. Spoke to him out of a whirlwind as I recall.

JOHN: You mean that part about "Where wast thou when I laid the foundations of the earth?" and so on? Yeah, well that was wind, all right, but it wasn't no explanation. What it amounted to was, "I am strong and you are weak so what business you got questioning me?"

PRESENCE: Well, I tried to put it in terms he would understand. Anyhow, I made it all up to him. Give him more than he had before.

JOHN: What about them ten kids that was killed.

PRESENCE: I give him ten more.

JOHN: And you think that made it up to him? You beat anything ever I saw, you know that? You ain't got no more idea what it means to be human than the man in the moon! You can't go around wiping people off the face of the earth just to suit your every whim and fancy. Because once you done it, you can't undo it. You can't just replace them with other ones. Human beings ain't interchangeable. They're unique! And they feel! They can be hurt!

PRESENCE: You trying to teach me my business, John?

JOHN: Well, somebody needs to. You got a awful lot to learn about being human. You ought to try it sometime.

PRESENCE: I did. I found the experience, as you say, unique.

JOHN: Yeah, well I'm sorry about that. But now that wasn't me.

PRESENCE: Maybe not. But I'll tell you what I found. I found that most of the time the only feelings and hurt human beings care about is their own. That the only side of a argument they are willing to see is their side. That years of friendship don't count for nothing and they ain't about to give you the benefit of the doubt no matter who you are or what you been to them. That they're quick to demand forgiveness when they've transgressed, but unwilling to give it when the shoe's on the other foot. That's what I found. And I can't say as you are much different.

JOHN: You mean I hurt you? Is that what you're telling me? Is that what you're telling me?

PRESENCE: Well, you figure it out. We was friends for years. Close as brothers, closer. We had good times together. Then you got to going to see Miss Daisy. That would have been all right, I wouldn't of begrudged you that. I realize you was awful young when you made that pledge to me, and I wouldn't have held you to it. But you shut me out, didn't have time for me. Then, when I took Miss Daisy, you turn on me completely. Wouldn't listen when I tried to give my side. Wouldn't accept my apology. Just cussed me out and for ten years refused to speak to me. You just figure it out, John.

JOHN: I hurt you? (*He swivels his chair around, leans back and gazes at the ceiling.*) I never thought. The idea never entered my mind.

PRESENCE: That I could be hurt? Don't you think I got feelings, too?

JOHN: And I hurt you.

PRESENCE: If you can love, John, you can be hurt, don't make no difference who you are.

(*There is a pause while they both contemplate this thought.*)

PRESENCE: It's a big risk, to love, and a big responsibility to be loved. (*Another pause.*) And as you pointed out to me, you got to be careful how you treat your friends.

(*JOHN brings his chair down, turns and studies PRESENCE. JOHN smiles, shakes his head slowly, and begins a silent chuckle which soon becomes audible.*)

JOHN: Damned if you ain't done it again! Slickest thing ever I saw! Just let me have rope until I hung myself. Trapped me with my own argument. Lordy, if you ain't something!

PRESENCE: I wasn't just trying to win a argument, John.

JOHN: I know you wasn't. I know that. I understand you. But now you got to admit it was slick. And about the time I thought I had you going, too.

PRESENCE: Well, I confess, you was backing me into a corner.

JOHN: Then WHAMMO! You laid it on me. I swear, you beat all!

PRESENCE: Thank you, John, I appreciate that. (*Pause.*) Well, what about it, John?

JOHN: Well, I reckon I will if you will. You forgive me, I forgive you. We call it even. Fair?

PRESENCE: Fair enough. Friends?

JOHN: Friends.

PRESENCE: I'm mighty pleased, John.

JOHN: Me, too.

PRESENCE: I don't mind telling you, it's a big load off my mind. I was afraid we wouldn't get this settled before that old ticker of yours up and quit on you.

JOHN: You mean otherwise you wouldn't of let me in?

PRESENCE: Now, you know better than that. No, I was afraid, stubborn as you are, you old rascal, you wouldn't of wanted to come in.

JOHN: Hell, I'd of been kicking the door down, hollering for my rights.

PRESENCE: I just bet you would too.

JOHN: You know, it's been many a time this past year I needed to talk to you.

PRESENCE: B.W.

JOHN: What am I ever going to do with that boy?

PRESENCE: Well, he's young yet.

JOHN: He ain't that young. And Lord, is he ever ignorant! You heard about them whited sepulchers.

PRENSENCE: I heard.

JOHN: And when I pointed it out to him, it didn't bother him at all. Hell, he even tried to argue me that buzzards was better.

PRESENCE: Well, that boy's got the bit in his teeth all right.

JOHN: And is headed straight for ruination. He's got all these women mooning over him and egging him on and he's getting all these invitations to preach and now this Boatwright woman whose husband ought to keep her locked up at home – she's done put him on the radio. Say, you didn't give him the Gift, did you?

PRESENCE: Not that I recall.

JOHN: Well, he thinks you did, and now he's hell-bent to become a faith-healer, too. I've tried to tell him he ain't ready yet, but he don't pay no more mind to me than a door-post.

PRESENCE: B.W. thinks a lot like you, John.

JOHN: Sometimes I wonder if he ever thinks at all. I promised his mama I'd see he got started off right, but so far I've failed her. What am I ever going to do with him?

PRESENCE: Not much of anything, I'm afraid. You ain't got that much time, remember?

JOHN: But I can't just leave him like this. I promised his mama.

PRESENCE: You already done more than you know, John. You just leave the rest to me. After all, I did call him.

JOHN: He's a good boy, but that's all he is, just a boy. In some ways a lot younger than his age. Comes maybe from his mama hovering over him too much. Still thinks that ever thing comes easy. You going to have your hands full.

PRESENCE: Well, I like a challenge. Moses stuttered, you know, when I first got ahold of him. But I'll grant you, it'll take a little doing to straighten B.W. out. I'd say he's going to need a mighty strong hand for a while. Well, I expect that's enough talking for now, John. You may not know it but you're beginning to look a little green around the gills. Why don't you just lay back and get a little rest. That's right. Just stretch out and relax. Don't worry about a thing. I'll be right here if you need me. In fact, I'll be here till it's over. Then we'll have all the time in the world.

JOHN: What time is it?

PRESENCE: It ain't quite time yet. You'll last a little longer.

JOHN: Naw, I was thinking about B.W.'s radio show. He wanted me to listen.

PRESENCE: Don't worry about that now. You ain't going to miss nothing. Just lay back and rest. Conserve your strength. Go on, now. Close your eyes. That's right.

JOHN: (*Sitting up again.*) Does Daisy know?

PRESENCE: She knows. Now come on, you old scallywag, lay back down like I told you and get some rest!

(*JOHN leans back again and closes his eyes. PRESENCE withdraws to the back of the room. There is silence for a moment, then offstage can be heard the sound of a car pulling up, its doors slamming, FRANCINE talking.*)

FRANCINE: (*Off.*) Now, wait a minute, B.W. Just wait a minute, can't you. It's no use acting like that.

(*B.W. enters, stomps over to the sofa and sits, dejected, hands between his knees. FRANCINE is still offstage.*)

FRANCINE: (*Off.*) B.W. — B.W. Bumpus!

(*FRANCINE enters.*)

FRANCINE: I declare, B.W., it's not the end of the world, you know.

B.W.: Might as well be.

JOHN: What's the matter? What's wrong?

B.W.: They wouldn't let me on.

JOHN: On what?

B.W.: The radio! They wouldn't let me on the radio!

FRANCINE: No, B.W., I keep telling you, we'll get this all straightened out just as soon as I can get hold of Clarence. Oh, I tell you, Mr. Bumpus, I could just kill that Clarence. I could. I could just kill him. You just wait till I get my hands on him. He's going to wish he was dead!

JOHN: What happened?

B.W.: They wouldn't let me on, that's what.

FRANCINE: Oh, Mr. Bumpus, it was so humiliating. It was absolutely mortifying. I said to that announcer, I told him, I said my husband, Clarence Boatwright, he owns the Boatwright Furniture Mart, and he pays for this program. I said he pays your salary. I said what if he just took his business somewhere else? I said then where would you be? I said I want to talk to the manager.

B.W.: They wouldn't even let me on.

FRANCINE: So he said "The manager's not here." So I said well, where is he? Get him here. I want to talk to him, I said. So he said, "He's done gone home. If you want him, get him yourself." Oh, he was real rude, Mr. Bumpus, real disrespectful. So I said where's the phone.

B.W.: I was fixing to tell them to lay their hand on the radio.

FRANCINE: So I said to the manager, I said what is the meaning of this? I said I'm Mrs. Clarence Boatwright and I want to know just what the meaning of this is. And you know what he said? He said he had already talked to Clarence and Clarence knew all about it! He said Clarence already knew about it and had agreed to it!

B.W.: Just lay your hand right up there on that radio, I was going to say. Just lay your hand right up there.

FRANCINE: I find that very hard to believe, I told him, very hard indeed, I said. "Well, I suggest you talk to Mr. Boatwright about it," he said. Oh he was real snotty. So I told him, I said, I demand to know on what authority you've gone back to playing those old gospel records, on what authority, I said. "Station policy," he said. "The program was not up to our broadcast standards." Well, I said, I'd just like to know who makes those standards. Tell me that, I said. "Now, Mrs. Boatwright," he said, "I really think you ought to talk to your husband about this." I'm talking to you, I said, and I insist on knowing just why you've taken this program off the air. I insist on it, I said.

B.W.: Aw, shoot! Shoot!

FRANCINE: "Popular demand, Mrs. Boatwright, popular demand," he said. And what exactly does that mean? I said. "What it means is," he said, "is after we aired that broadcast last week we've been flooded with letters and phone calls, all of them demanding that we go back to the regular program. Now, I'm a businessman, Mrs. Boatwright. I make my living by the number of people who listen to my station. And if people don't like what I'm airing, they're not going to listen. That program had to come off and I took it off." Businessman! Can you believe that, Mr. Bumpus? Well, you just listen to me, I told him, I said, what about the money my husband Clarence Boatwright pays you to run that program, what about that? So he said to me, he said, "Now, Mrs. Boatwright, your husband's a businessman too, and when I called his attention to all the negative response the program was getting, he said take it off." Can you believe that, Mr. Bumpus? I couldn't. Now I just find that hard to believe, I told him, I really and truly find it hard to believe that my husband would have done such a thing and never said a word to me about it. "Well," he said, "I'd have to suggest you talk to him about that." Well, Mr. Smart-mouth, I told him — that's exactly what I call him, I was so mad — well, Mr. Smart-mouth, I said, I'll do just that and then we'll see. Oh, some people can be so RUDE!

B.W.: Now I'll never get to tell them.

FRANCINE: Yes you will, B.W. Of course you will. I'll straighten all of this out just as soon as I talk to Clarence and you'll be back on next week. You'll see. B.W., he was just crushed, just absolutely crushed. I said to him, I told him, I said, it's not the end of the world. I said it's not like it was the end of the world, but pore B.W., he was absolutely crushed, wasn't you, B.W.?

B.W.: Shoot. Aw shoot!

FRANCINE: So I said, be so kind as to let me use your telephone again and I tried to get Clarence at the store. So then I tried to get him at home. So then I called down at the drugstore, but they said he wasn't there either. If I didn't know better I would think he was hiding from me. Well, it won't do him any good. He's going to have to come home sometime and when he does I'm going to say, Clarence Boatwright — Why, you don't look too good, Mr. Bumpus, are you not feeling well? You don't look too good at all. You look kind of blue. Don't he look blue to you, B.W.?

B.W.: Cud'n John? He don't look blue to me. He looks pale. Cud'n John? Are you all right?

JOHN: (*Weakly.*) Fine. I'm fine.

B.W.: You don't look fine. You look pale.

FRANCINE: I think he looks blue.

JOHN: Is it time?

PRESENCE: Pretty soon, now, John.

FRANCINE: What did he say, B.W.?

B.W.: He wants to know what time it is.

FRANCINE: It's seven o'clock. A few minutes after seven o'clock. What's he want to know that for?

B.W.: It's seven o'clock, Cud'n John. Lord! You're as white as a flour barrel. Are you having one of your spells? Here, I'll fix some sody for you. You want me to fix you some sody, Cud'n John?

JOHN: I don't hurt none. I expected it to hurt.

PRESENCE: No, it's going to be easy, John. You ain't going to feel a thing. I'll see to that.

B.W.: Well, I'm glad you ain't in no pain, Cud'n John, but you look awful white. Don't you want me to help you into the bedroom so you can lay down?

FRANCINE: He's not white, B.W., he's blue. Just look at his fingernails. Blue as can be! You're turning blue, Mr. Bumpus, did you know that? He ought to be laying down, B.W. He's got no business sitting up if he's turning blue. Why don't you help him into the bedroom. Can you walk, Mr. Bumpus? Can you stand up? See if you can stand up, Mr. Bumpus, and we'll help you to bed so you can lay down. B.W., help him get up.

JOHN: I'm all right, I tell you. Just let me be!

PRESENCE: Better do like she says, John. It's the only way you're ever going to shut her up.

JOHN: I reckon you're right.

FRANCINE: Of course I am. I know what I'm talking about. I was a Candy-striper at the hospital once. Listen, when you're all blue like that it's a sign you're not getting enough oxygen or something and you're supposed to lay down. Now, try to get up, Mr. Bumpus. You help him, B.W.

B.W.: Here, Cud'n John. Let me help you.

FRANCINE: Let B.W. help you, Mr. Bumpus. Don't try to do too much yourself. Help him, B.W.

PRESENCE: It's all right, John, I'll be with you. I'll be with you all the way. It won't be long now. Not long at all.

(*B.W. helps JOHN to his feet and he and FRANCINE support him on either side. As they move toward the door, JOHN stops.*)

JOHN: Bible.

B.W.: You don't need your Bible now.

JOHN: Naw, but you do. You read it, you hear me? Study it. Learn it. I promised your mama.

B.W.: Come on, now, Cud'n John.

(*They move a few more steps and JOHN stops again.*)

JOHN: You know I ain't letting you off the hook about Moses and Job, don't you? And Jonah. It's a few things concerning him I ain't satisfied with, neither.

PRESENCE: I ain't surprised. Well, we'll have oodles of time to argue about that later.

JOHN: You sure Daisy knows?

PRESENCE: I'm sure. Now, go on. Get on to bed.

FRANCINE: Who's Daisy? And what's he talking about Moses and Job and Jonah for? I declare, B.W., I believe he's out of his head, hallucinating or whatever they call it. Come along, Mr. Bumpus. We'll get you to bed and then you'll feel better. My goodness, you're blue as a robin's egg, did you know that?

PRESENCE: You're going to like Jonah, John. I can't wait for you to meet him. You know, come to think of it, y'all are a whole lot alike.

(*All exit. FRANCINE and B.W. can be heard off stage getting JOHN to bed and reassuring him. After a moment FRANCINE and B.W. re-enter.*)

B.W.: Sister Francine, you reckon he's going to be all right?

FRANCINE: Well, of course he is. He's going to be just fine. I'll just bet you in a little while he'll be as good as new. Course, his color is bad. No, I don't like his color at all. But don't you worry, he's going to be just fine, you'll see. I'll tell you what. We'll look in on him in a few minutes and if he's not better, I'll go get the doctor to come look at him.

B.W.: I'd sure hate for anything to happen to him. My daddy, he died a long time ago and my mama died when I was in Korea in the war and Cud'n John, he's all I got left.

FRANCINE: Oh, you pore boy. Pore little orphan boy. Let Sister Francine hold you. (*She embraces him.*) There, there, Sister Francine will take care of you. Don't you worry your little head one bit. (*Kisses him on the forehead.*) Sister Francine will be your mama. She'll look after you.

B.W.: I never felt so miserable in my whole life.

FRANCINE: (*Continuing to hold and kiss him.*) Don't you worry, B.W., honey, it'll all turn out right.

B.W.: First, they wouldn't let me on the radio, and now Cud'n John!

FRANCINE: There, there, now, you dear sweet thing, it's not anything serious. In a little while he'll be as good as new, you'll see. And as for that radio program, I'll straighten that out, you can count on that. When I get through with that Clarence Boatwright, he won't know which way is up. You'll be right back on there next week, just see if you're not. Cheer up, now and give Sister Francine a little kiss.

(*B.W. kisses her cheek.*)

FRANCINE: Not there, silly, a real kiss.

(*B.W. kisses her lips. She prolongs it. While this is in progress, PRESENCE enters and observes, shakes his head in disapproval.*)

FRANCINE: There, now wasn't that nice!

B.W.: But that station manager said they got all them bad calls and letters.

FRANCINE: Well, B.W., honey, that smart-mouth just didn't know what he was talking about, that's what. He just didn't have any idea what he was talking about. There was a letter there that he didn't know about. It was addressed directly to you, so he hadn't read it. I saw it laying there at the radio station, so when we was leaving, I just picked it up and put it in my purse. Well, why not? I don't see why not. It didn't belong to them, it belonged to you. Had your name right on the front, didn't it. And I just know it says something good. Maybe it's somebody else that's been cured. Maybe it's another miracle. Now, where on earth did I put that purse? I can never keep up with that thing. I just bet I left it in the car. Now, don't you move a muscle, you hear, not a muscle, dear boy, (*She pats his thigh.*) and I'll just go right out and get it.

B.W.: I'm going to see about Cud'n John.

(*They exit their separate ways. B.W. re-enters first. He wanders about the room as if in a daze and finally sits in John's chair and cradles his head in his arms upon the table. FRANCINE enters with purse in one hand and letter in the other.*)

FRANCINE: Well, that's where it was, pushed back under the seat. I always push it back under the seat when I get in and then as often as not I forget and leave it there. Why, B.W., honey, what's the matter? (*She goes to him, drops the purse and letter on the table, and takes him by the shoulders.*) What is it honey?

B.W.: It's Cud'n John.

FRANCINE: Is he worse?

B.W.: He's dead.

FRANCINE: Oh, now that couldn't be. That just couldn't be. There's just no way that could be. You're mistaken, B.W., that's what. You must be mistaken. (*She exits to the bedroom and shortly re-enters.*) I said I didn't like his color. I remember saying to him, I said Mr. Bumpus, you're turning blue and I don't think that's a good sign at all. That's what I told him. You heard me when I said it.

B.W.: What do I do now, Sister Francine?

FRANCINE: Now, just don't you worry, B.W. Don't you bother your head about that for one single minute. You may have lost Mr. Bumpus, but you won't be alone. I'll be here to take care of you. Just lean on me.

B.W.: But what do I do about him? Ain't I supposed to tell somebody, report it or something? I can't just leave him laying there. I don't know what I'm supposed to do.

FRANCINE: Well, I'm not sure I do either. Maybe we ought to get the doctor.

B.W.: What good is a doctor going to do now?

FRANCINE: Well, he could pronounce him dead and then he'd know what else had to be done. Yes, I think that's exactly what we need to do. Oh, B.W., you pore thing, what an awful thing to happen!

B.W.: I can't believe he's gone. I just can't believe it.

FRANCINE: Shock. That's what it is. You're in shock. Well, don't you worry about a thing. I said I would take care of you and I will. You just leave it all to me. I'll get the doctor and make the arrangements and everything. I'll just go and get the doctor right now. You just sit still, now, and I won't be gone more than a few minutes. I'll be back before you know it. Oh, I hate to leave you in shock and all, but you just sit there and try to keep a grip on yourself and I'll be back before you can turn around. (*Crosses to the door, stops and returns.*) Well, I declare, I won't get very far without my purse and keys, now will I! (*Crosses to the door.*) I'll be right back, now!

(*FRANCINE exits. B.W. sits staring into space for a bit. Idly, he picks up the letter from the table, looks it over front and back and finally opens and reads it.*)

B.W.: Aw shoot! Wouldn't let me on the radio. Cud'n John done left me. And now this! (*He throws the letter on the floor.*) Lord! What do you reckon will be next!

PRESENCE: B.W.!

B.W.: (*Jumping up, looking around.*) Who's that? Who is it?

PRESENCE: Don't ask questions when I talk to you. Just listen!

B.W.: Is that you, Cud'n John?

PRESENCE: No, it ain't your Cud'n John.

B.W.: You mean it's —- ?

PRESENCE: I told you once, don't let me have to tell you again, don't ask questions when I'm talking to you!

B.W.: Yes SIR!

PRESENCE: Now, pick up that letter.

B.W.: Yes SIR!

PRESENCE: Now, read it.

B.W.: You mean out loud?

PRESENCE: I can see your Cud'n John was right about you. Of course I mean out loud. Read it!

B.W.: Dear Reverend B.W. Bumpus.

PRESENCE: Well, go on.

B.W.: I wrote you yesterday about how you cured my arthritis. Well, you did not. Today it is back again. I am now stove up worse than I was before.

PRESENCE: Go on. Read the rest of it.

B.W.: I sent you two dollars. Send it back. I will need it for medicine. Yours truly. Mrs. Stella Yopp.

PRESENCE: Now, what does that tell you about the Gift?

B.W.: I reckon it means I ain't got it.

PRESENCE: That's right. And don't you forget it. From now on, I'll tell you what you got and what you ain't got. You hear me!

B.W.: Yes SIR!

PRESENCE: You see that Bible.

B.W.: Yes SIR!

PRESENCE: From now on, eight hours a day, every day. I'll be asking questions and you better have the right answers.

B.W.: Yes SIR!

PRESENCE: Well, That'll be all for now. (*He moves toward the door.*) But just remember, I got my eye on you ever minute and I better not catch you playing off.

B.W.: Naw SIR!

PRESENCE: (*Stops at the door and turns.*) Oh, and there's one other thing, B.W.

B.W.: Yes SIR!

PRESENCE: GET RID OF THAT DAMNED WOMAN!

(*PRESENCE exits.*)

B.W.: Yes SIR! (*There is silence for a moment. B.W., uncertain whether PRESENCE is still there, looks around.*)

Er ... uh ... Hello. (*Pause.*) Uh ... Hello. (*Pause.*) Uh ... Hello! (*Pause.*) Whew! Gone, I reckon. (*Satisfied he is alone, he wanders over and sits in John's chair, looks around the room again.*) Just like being in the army. Going to make me study the Bible. Going to ask me questions on it. (*He swivels the chair around to the table, looks at the Bible which is still open at the place where John was reading. He places his finger on the page and begins to read.*)

"...So Jonah went out of the city, and sat on the east side ..." The EAST side. Hhhmmm! I just bet you a damn dollar that's one of the questions He's going to ask me. Why did Jonah choose the EAST side? Now, what was it Cud'n John said? Aw, yeah. Now I remember. Because it was a hill there. Yeah, that's it. That's the answer. When He asks me, I'll just tell Him, Shoot, because it was a hill there, that's what I'll say. (*Pause.*) But, Lord! What in the world will I ever say to Sister Francine!

THE END

William Groth and Breton Frazier in *East of Nineveh* by Jim Peyton, Horse Cave Theatre, 1985

Jim Peyton

I was born just in time for the Great Depression. I didn't suffer greatly. On the other hand, it wasn't an easy lot. I reached my teens in time for World War II and volunteered for Air Corps cadet training. They opined that I was just smart enough but far too skinny to fly. They finally took me on as an air traffic controller. Eventually, I was turned loose to begin my pursuit of happiness. Well, not full-time. Eight hours a day I worked, another 10 or so I ate, slept, answered nature's calls, etc. In the time left, I pursued happiness.

Then one day I went through a car windshield. Weeks of pain, doubts of survival and soul-searching followed. It occurred to me that I had been making a bad bargain. The sleep and whatever was necessary. The work wasn't. If I could find something that I enjoyed doing for a living, would do for nothing if I could afford it, I could add those eight hours to my pursuit of happiness.

Although 60 years have passed, I have never worked a day since. I've been a sales manager, a high school teacher, a college professor. I headed the staff of the Education Committee and later directed the research for the entire Kentucky Legislature. I finished my career as a computer consultant and program designer. And to a degree far greater than I deserve, I've found happiness.

Walter Rhodes in *Marching to Zion* by Jim Peyton, Horse Cave Theatre, 1986

MARCHING TO ZION
A Play in Two Acts
by
Jim Peyton

Tony Bush, Pat Sprouse and Warren Hammack in *Marching to Zion* by Jim Peyton, Horse Cave Theatre, 1986

Marching to Zion opened on July 18, 1986, with the following cast:

JIM WELLS	*Walter Rhodes*
SALLY BLACKBURN HOLMES	*Sara Morsey*
ERNESTINE PHELPS	*Joyce Hoke Deskins*
BEECHUM BOATWRIGHT	*Ronald J. Aulgur*
RUBEN (RUBY) CRAWFORD	*Gregory Etter*
HARLEY LEDBETTER	*Kent Logsdon*
RILEY (RILE) BLACKBURN	*Warren Hammack*
BILLY BLACKBURN	*Tony Bush*
MRS. BLACKBURN	*Pat Sprouse*

Director: Warren Hammack
Stage Manager: Karen Terry
Set Design: John Partyka
Lighting Design: Gregory Etter
Costume Design: Rebecca Shouse
Properties Master: Sam Hunt
Sound Design: Tim Speevack

Walter Rhodes, Ronald J. Aulgur, Sara Morsey and Gregory Etter in *Marching to Zion* by Jim Peyton, Horse Cave Theatre, 1986

Marching to Zion

Characters:

MR. WELLS, *Jim Wells, Attorney-at-Law, mid-fifties, a tall, lean man, Lincolnesque in appearance*

SALLY, *Sally Blackburn Holmes, also an attorney, early thirties, attractive, but not strikingly so, junior partner to Jim Wells, daughter to Rile and grand-daughter to Mrs. Blackburn*

ERNESTINE, *Ernestine Phelps, housewife, early thirties but looks older, unattractive, grossly overweight, given to whining*

BEECHUM, *Beechum Boatwright, tinker, toper and teller of tall tales, mid-fifties, a slight, small man who is larger than he appears*

SHERIFF, *Ruben (Ruby) Crawford, county sheriff, mid-forties, a large, powerful man of medium height*

HARLEY, *Harley Ledbetter, mayor of New Zion, mid-forties, bespectacled, lean, medium height, he might have posed for "American Gothic"*

RILE, *Riley Blackburn, farmer, mid-sixties, large, robust, running to fat, son to Mrs. Blackburn, father to Sally and Billy*

BILLY, *Billy Blackburn, eighteen, a young version of his father, Rile*

MRS. BLACKBURN, *Mrs. Blackburn, eighty-two, matriarch of the Blackburn family, a tall, heavy woman accustomed to command*

DUMAS, *Dumas Sims, deputy sheriff (Voice only.)*

Place: New Zion, a small town in Western Kentucky, lying two miles more or less off the western shore of Kentucky Lake. The "New" in the name still has meaning for the older residents, who can remember the original settlement, which was called Zions Cause. Zions Cause had been little more than a wide place in the road, consisting only of a general store, a blacksmith shop and a church. It did, however, boast of a post office, housed in the general store and operated by the storekeeper, which conferred upon the town some measure of legitimacy to the outside world.

Around 1940, when the TVA dam across the Tennessee River was completed and Kentucky Lake was formed, most of Zions Cause was inundated. In anticipation of the deluge, New Zions Cause was established well above the projected water line. The name was very soon shortened to New Zion, and as such the town was incorporated and in due course designated as a city of the sixth class by an Act of the Legislature.

New Zion is centered around a town square and radiates in two directions from it, following the course of a pre-existent road which runs from US 641 on the west to what was once Zions Cause and is now Kentucky Lake on the east. The square contains the business section and the two arms of the two residential sections.

You will find neither New Zion, nor its predecessor, Zions Cause, on the map. The town exists and the residents live and move and have being only in the mind of the author. But if you travel to the Lake area of Western Kentucky, you will find places and people that are remarkably similar.

The entire action takes place in Mr. Wells' law office. The office has three doors: Mr. Wells' private entrance, the door to the reception room and the door to Sally's office. A large window overlooks the street. The furnishings are more suitable to a comfortable sitting room than an office: a couch, easy chairs, occasional tables, one with a modern pushbutton telephone, and a credenza holding a silver coffee service and good china. There is a desk, apparently an afterthought, placed out of the way and rarely used. One has the impression that here business is conducted in an informal, relaxed and friendly fashion.

Time: The year is now 1975. It is the season of mists and mellow fruitfulness, call it late September.

ACT ONE

MR. WELLS *enters from his private entrance, singing. He is dressed in a three-piece, comfortably rumpled suit. Moving to the rhythm of the song, he goes to his desk, picks up a stack of letters and notes, looks through them and tosses them back on the desk, then removes his jacket and pitches it across a chair back, pausing now and then to concentrate on hitting a high note.*

MR. WELLS: "We're marching to Zi-on, / Beau-tee-ful, beau-tee-ful Zion. / We're marching upward to Zi-i-i-on, / That beau-tee-ful city of God." Hey, Boss, I'm here.

(SALLY *has entered from her office and has been observing with mild disapproval. She is wearing a dark business suit and a white blouse. As she speaks, she goes to the credenza and pours two cups of coffee, gives one to him, picks up his jacket from the chair, puts it on a hanger and hangs it on a coat rack. Then she carries the other cup to a chair facing him.*)

SALLY: Well, it's about time. Five minutes more and you would have been an hour late. And stop calling me Boss.

MR. WELLS: Just recognizing the facts.

SALLY: It's a pity you don't recognize office hours, too.

MR WELLS: I took time to smell the roses. I'd recommend it to you.

SALLY: And I'd recommend you take care of business.

MR. WELLS: Oh, have I got business?

SALLY: Mrs. Phelps is waiting to see you.

MR. WELLS: Ernestine?

SALLY: She's been here for nearly an hour.

MR. WELLS: Buford been acting up again?

SALLY: He hasn't come home for the last two nights.

MR. WELLS: Guess we'll have to take him up on the do right law.

SALLY: The what?

MR. WELLS: The law that says everybody has to do right.

SALLY: Now, you're being silly. There's no such law.

MR. WELLS: Well now, that's going to come as quite a shock to Ernestine. Ever time she comes in it's to tell me that Buford's not doing right. "You're a lawyer," she says, "why don't you make him do right?"

SALLY: Shall I bring her in?

MR WELLS: By all means.

SALLY: (*She picks up the phone and punches a button.*) Betty, Mr. Wells is here now. Would you tell Mrs. Phelps to come in.

(ERNESTINE *enters. She is wearing blue jeans that are doing their best to contain her enormous bottom and a quilted vest that accentuates, rather than conceals, her upper heaviness. Her hair is long, parted in the middle, combed flat to her head and hangs straight down her back. Her expression is one of petulance, and she tends to whine when she speaks.* MR. WELLS *rises to greet* ERNESTINE *as she enters, shakes hands, and moves to the credenza to fix her coffee.*)

MR WELLS: Morning, Ernestine. Like some coffee?

ERNESTINE: Not if it's black. I can't drink it black.

MR WELLS: Oh we've got sugar and (*Looking.*) yes, cream too.

ERNESTINE: Two sugars, then, and lots of cream. It gives me heartburn if I drink it black.

SALLY: Won't you sit down, Mrs. Phelps?

MR. WELLS: (*He hands her the coffee.*) Here you go. Well now, Ernestine, what can I do for you?

ERNESTINE: I don't know what I'm going to do, Mr. Wells, I swear to God, I don't.

MR. WELLS: Buford taken off again, has he?

ERNESTINE: Left for work two days ago and not a sign of him since. And not a bite to eat in the house nor a penny to buy nothing with. Now that ain't right, Mr. Wells, and can't nobody tell me it is.

MR. WELLS: No, it's not Ernestine, not right at all.

ERNESTINE: I went down to Heddin's garage. They said he put in a full day but didn't nobody know where he went when he left. Well, he sure didn't come home, I can testify to that.

MR. WELLS: Has he been working pretty regular, then?

ERNESTINE: Oh, regular enough. I ain't got no complaint on that. But that job you got him don't pay nothing. I told him, I said, "Why don't you get out and find you a job that pays something?" But he won't do it. He likes where it is, even if it don't pay nothing.

MR. WELLS: But he hasn't been mistreating you?

ERNESTINE: He ain't hit me lately, if that's what you mean? But he don't hardly come in the house no more except to eat and sleep and sometimes maybe watch a little television.

MR WELLS: Where does he go?

ERNESTINE: He don't go nowheres. He's out in the back yard messing around with them old cars of his. Piles of junk is what I call them.

MR. WELLS: Still crazy about cars, is he?

ERNESTINE: Works on them all day and then comes in and works on them all night. I reckon you might call it crazy. Claims he's fixing them up to sell. Now, who'd buy such as them, I ask you? I'm in one right now. Nothing but a pile of junk!

MR. WELLS: Well, at least it keeps him out of trouble.

ERNESTINE: You call this keeping out of trouble, off and gone Lord knows where and me and the kids left to get by as best we can?

MR. WELLS: Well, I'll have the Sheriff keep an eye out for him. We'll find him.

ERNESTINE: When? That's what I'd like to know. And what am I supposed to do until then?

(*MR. WELLS takes two bills from his billfold and places them on the coffee table in front of her.*)

MR. WELLS: That ought to hold you for a while. Call it a loan. I'll settle with Buford later.

(*ERNESTINE stares at the money for a moment, then sighs, puts down her cup and picks it up. She stuffs it in her purse and rises.*)

ERNESTINE: Well, I reckon I better be getting on. The kids are out in the car if they ain't tore it up yet. Lord knows, they been out there for over an hour.

MR. WELLS: I'm sorry you had to wait, Ernestine. I apologize.

ERNESTINE: Oh, I got to where I just expected it. Seems like all I ever do anymore is wait.

(*MR. WELLS accompanies ERNESTINE to the door, where she stops, turns.*)

ERNESTINE: He just ain't doing right, Mr. Wells, and you know it. Looks to me like you or the Law or somebody would make him do right.

(*She exits.*)

SALLY: You must be overwhelmed.

MR WELLS: By what?

SALLY: By such an outpouring of gratitude.

MR WELLS: Not everybody can afford to be grateful.

SALLY: Humph! (*SALLY moves to the window overlooking the street.*) Well, I agree with her on one thing.

MR. WELLS: What's that?

SALLY: That car. It is a pile of junk. (*Pause.*) I see the kids haven't torn it up yet. Hey, there's somebody in the driver's seat. Now, I wonder who that is?

MR. WELLS: That would be Wesley, I think his name is. Product of her first marriage – no, not marriage – affair. He must be all of fourteen now. Not really eligible for an institution, but definitely retarded.

SALLY: Even so, he probably has enough sense to know that lawyers are not supposed to pay their clients; it's the other way around.

(*MR. WELLS pours himself more coffee, holds the pot out to SALLY. She shakes her head.*)

MR. WELLS: Well, what would you have done?

SALLY: I wouldn't have done anything

MR. WELLS: That's always an alternative, I suppose.

SALLY: But not one open to you, is that it? Did it ever occur to you that you might be doing more harm than good?

MR. WELLS: Often.

SALLY: Then why do you persist? What makes you feel it's up to you to solve everybody's problems? What makes you think you can? Or have the right to even if you could.

MR. WELLS: They're caught in a trap, you know, both of them.

SALLY: If so, they walked into it themselves.

MR. WELLS: Maybe. Or maybe they fell into it because they didn't have enough sense or foresight to know it was there. Or maybe they were born in it. Whatever the cause, they're still trapped. Take Ernestine. What has she got to look forward to but a lifetime of hand-to-mouth existence? Here she is, what, thirty-two or so? Whatever looks she had, and as I recall they were never much, buried under a mountain of fat. Three kids hanging on her, one with a mind stopped forever at eight years old. No education to speak of. No skills. No way to support herself or the kids. Dependent entirely on a husband who's a far cry from being dependable. Her sole strategy for coping is whining.

SALLY: Well, it seems to work.

MR. WELLS: And Buford. His one passion in life is cars, but he's never been able to understand them. No mechanical sense, natural or otherwise. Fit only to bolt or unbolt, provided somebody shows him where. And not even the luxury of whining away his frustrations. About as inarticulate as you can get and not be considered utterly speechless. So he drinks. And sometimes he hits Ernestine. And sometimes he just runs off. Because he knows, whether he is able to express it in words or not, he knows that things are never going to be any better for him.

SALLY: If that's the way it is, then that's the way it is.

MR WELLS: Somehow, I can't accept that. I keep thinking maybe I can make it a little better.

SALLY: Then you're in a trap, too.

MR WELLS: You may be right.

SALLY: It must be in the genes. Your father —.

MR WELLS: Now, you're too young to remember much about him.

SALLY: Well, I've heard enough about him from my father. And my uncles. And my grandmother. And everybody else over forty years old.

MR. WELLS: He was the kind of man you don't forget easy.

SALLY: A meddler.

MR. WELLS: An intervener. But only to even up the odds if they got too one-sided.

SALLY: Well, at least he didn't spend all his time meddling. He must have been a pretty shrewd businessman, too.

MR. WELLS: And since he was, I've never had to be. Anyway, he'd have preferred the term horse trader.

SALLY: Whatever he was, he seems to have been good at it.

MR. WELLS: Well, part of it was luck. Not even he could have foreseen when he was acquiring all that land that one day much of it would end up fronting on the lake.

SALLY: And you've let it just sit there going to weeds and bushes.

MR. WELLS: Not just weeds and bushes. I've let it revert to its natural state. A preserve, so to speak. Besides, I have a lot of memories tied to that area. The lake covered most of it. I'd hate to see the rest go. You think I'm being selfish, don't you?

SALLY: Oh, what does it matter what I think?

MR. WELLS: It matters.

SALLY: Well, I think there's an awful lot of people who would give their eye teeth to live there. People who've worked hard all their lives and are looking for a nice place to retire. And even if they're not all local people, your people, I think they deserve it. I think a docking facility down there would do wonders for the economy of New Zion. And I think it would be good for you to have some neighbors, instead of sitting there in that big house in the middle of a wilderness, alone except for a geriatric cat who's as set in his ways as you are, hanging on to memories of a way of life that passed out of existence thirty years ago and dreaming your life away. That's what I think.

MR WELLS: Developers been at you again, I see.

SALLY: What if they have? There's a group coming in tomorrow morning as a matter of fact. They're looking for a site to build retirement condos. They want to retain us to help find one.

MR. WELLS: Condos! Good Lord!

SALLY: This may come as a surprise to you but not everyone in this world lives in a detached dwelling set in the middle of a forty acre plot, or wants to.

MR. WELLS: But condos!

SALLY: And not everyone knows the genealogy of every person who lives in a twenty mile radius. In fact, that's not true right here and hasn't been for a long time.

(*The phone rings. SALLY picks it up.*)

SALLY: A Beechum Boatwright is out there to see you. And Sheriff Crawford is with him.

MR. WELLS: That saves me from tracking him down. The Sheriff, I mean.

SALLY: Well, I'll leave you to it. I have work to do.

MR. WELLS: What? And miss Beechum!

SALLY: Who's Beechum?

MR. WELLS: Why, he's our famous world traveler, juice harp player and town clock fixer.

SALLY: Oh, <u>he</u> is the one who got the clock running!

MR. WELLS: The same.

SALLY: Where did he come from? And how did he ever find his way to New Zion? He's not local.

MR. WELLS: Oh, yes. Born and raised here. We were boys together. He went off to the war — that's WWII for your information, young lady — and is just now getting back. About thirty years, late, I'd say.

SALLY: Where's he been all that time?

MR. WELLS: That's somewhat of a mystery. It's not that Beechum doesn't say, it's that he says so many different things nobody can decide which if any to believe. There are only two of us that know for sure, Beechum and me. He's been living in a place called Leavenworth, Kansas.

SALLY: Leavenworth, Kansas? Oh, the Federal prison!

MR. WELLS: The reason I know is I found a letter he wrote my father when he was first sent there, and the receipts where my father paid the taxes on that little plot of ground Beechum owns.

SALLY: And you've been keeping them paid up ever since.

MR WELLS: Well, they don't amount to much. Besides, he couldn't very well have done it himself, could he?

SALLY: What did he do to get thirty years?

MR. WELLS: It may not have been that long. He may have been out for some time. As to what he was in for, now, that I don't know for sure. Maybe he got mixed up with the black market while he was in Europe. Or maybe he deserted, got tired and just picked up and walked off. More likely he coldcocked somebody important for insulting him. But it's all just a guess, and I'm not about to ask. In fact, I'm not real sure Beechum realizes that I know where he's been.

SALLY: Well, I certainly wouldn't want to miss meeting anybody as celebrated as that. (*She speaks into the phone.*) Betty, tell Mr. Boatwright and Sheriff Crawford to come right in.

(*BEECHUM and the SHERIFF enter. BEECHUM is wearing a shirt of a Western cut, jeans and high-heel cowboy boots. His clothes look as if he has slept in them, which indeed he has. The SHERIFF is wearing a tan uniform, badge and Smokey-the-Bear hat. MR. WELLS rises to greet and shake hands with his visitors as they enter.*)

MR. WELLS: Morning, Beechum. Morning, Ruby.

BEECHUM: Morning, Jim.

SHERIFF: Morning, Mr. Wells.

BEECHUM: (*He has noticed SALLY and is staring at her.*) Who's that?

MR. WELLS: Oh, this is my law partner, Sally Holmes. Sally, Beechum Boatwright.

SALLY: (*She steps forward to shake hands with BEECHUM.*) How d' you do, Mr. Boatwright. Morning, Sheriff Crawford.

SHERIFF: Miss Sally.

BEECHUM: (*He continues to hold SALLY's hand for a while.*) My! My! Ain't you a pretty thing though.

SALLY: Why, thank you, Mr. Boatwright.

BEECHUM: Beechum. Call me Beechum. (*To MR. WELLS.*) Partner, you say. You mean she's a lawyer, too.

MR. WELLS: That's right.

BEECHUM: Smart, too. Where in the world did you come from?

MR. WELLS: Sally is Rile Blackburn's daughter.

BEECHUM: Old Rile's girl? Thought you said her name was Holmes.

SALLY: Holmes was my husband's name.

BEECHUM: Was? You mean you're a widder?

SALLY: No, just divorced. We're just having some coffee. Will you join us?

(*They find seats and continue to speak while SALLY serves the coffee.*)

MR. WELLS: Ah, Ruby, I'm glad you dropped by. I wanted to ask you if you could help me find Buford Phelps.

SHERIFF: He run off again?

MR. WELLS: Gone two days now, so Ernestine tells me.

SHERIFF: We'll look, but I doubt he'll be in the county. Probably over across the line somewheres. That's where we found him last time.

(*BEECHUM takes a jew's harp out of his shirt pocket and shows it to SALLY.*)

BEECHUM: Bet you don't know what that is? It's a juice harp. Solid silver. Picked it up in Vy-anna, where they make them little sausages, you know. Make juice harps too. Best in the world.

SALLY: I don't think I ever saw one before.

BEECHUM: Couldn't even play the thing when I bought it. Finally learned how from a old Frenchman when I was in France. He taught me how to play "Bonaparte's Retreat." I'll play it for you sometime.

SALLY: Oh, I'd like that.

BEECHUM: Traveled all over the world in the war. Seen everything. Was stationed for a while on a island in the South Pacific. Little bitty place. Full of coconuts and monkeys and bare-breasted women. Had a little hill at one end. Used to climb up there for the view. On a good day, you could see all the way to Spain.

MR. WELLS: Well, Beechum, Ruby, to what do we owe the honor of this visit?

SHERIFF: Don't look at me, I'm just the chauffeur.

BEECHUM: More'n that. He's my witness.

MR. WELLS: Witness to what?

BEECHUM: They've got me in jail, Jim! Me! A war vet'run!

SHERIFF: Now, you ain't in jail, Beechum. He ain't in jail, Mr. Wells. He ain't charged with nothing. He's free to go anywhere he wants to. Fact is, I'm giving him a ride home right now.

BEECHUM: I wasn't free last night.

SHERIFF: Well, this ain't last night. This is this morning.

MR. WELLS: What was the problem, Ruby?

BEECHUM: Harley Ledbetter, that's what.

MR. WELLS: Our illustrious mayor, drycleaner and pillar of the church? What did he have to do with it?

SHERIFF: Him and Beechum got into it. He claimed Beechum was drunk and knocked him into a door and then pulled a knife on him.

BEECHUM: I don't even own a knife. You didn't find no knife, did you?

SHERIFF: Naw, I didn't.

BEECHUM: I wasn't drunk, neither.

SHERIFF: But you was drinking, you got to admit that.

BEECHUM: Well, what if I was? It ain't no capital offense. Didn't give him the right to haul off and coldcock me like he done when I wasn't looking.

MR. WELLS: Now wait a minute. Wait a minute. Back up and tell me how this all came about.

BEECHUM: I was just coming along the sidewalk minding my own business, not even thinking about Harley. It was right after dark and I reckon he was closing up the drycleaners. I didn't even know he was there till I run into him.

SHERIFF: Harley claims he done it a-purpose.

BEECHUM: Well, I never. I didn't even know he was there. Anyway, I must of hit him a pretty good lick because he mashed his head on the door.

SHERIFF: Broke the skin and raised a good-sized pump-knot.

BEECHUM: He never give me a chance to tell him it was a accident, just whipped around and begun mouthing at me. I reach for my juice harp like I do sometimes and damned if he didn't up and coldcock me. The next thing I know, Ruby here was trying to shove me in his car.

SHERIFF: I was over at the office and the mayor called me to come and get Beechum, said he was roaring drunk and attacked him and he'd had to knock him out. Beechum was just coming to hisself when I got there and was madder than fire. It was all I could do to get him in the cruiser and away from there.

BEECHUM: Taken me to jail is what he done!

SHERIFF: I thought it wouldn't hurt none for Beechum to have a little time to cool off. Why, I didn't even lock the cell door.

BEECHUM: It was shut.

SHERIFF: Well, it wasn't locked.

BEECHUM: He didn't tell me that.

SHERIFF: Mad as he was, couldn't nobody of told him anything.

MR. WELLS: Harley didn't sign a complaint?

SHERIFF: No sir.

MR. WELLS: Well now, Beechum, if there's no charge against you, what's the problem?

BEECHUM: Why, I want to sue the hell out of that Harley Ledbetter!

MR. WELLS: On what grounds?

BEECHUM: False arrest.

MR. WELLS: If I understand you right, he didn't arrest you, Ruby did, if you can call it an arrest.

BEECHUM: I ain't got no complaint agin Ruby. It's Harley. Well, if I can't get him on false arrest, how about assault and battery when I wasn't looking?

MR. WELLS: You got a witness?

BEECHUM: Why I done told you. Ruby here.

SHERIFF: Like I said, Mr. Wells, he was on the sidewalk just coming to when I drove up.

MR. WELLS: Where was Harley?

SHERIFF: He was inside with the door locked looking out through the glass.

MR. WELLS: Sally, play Harley's lawyer.

SALLY: Defendant (that's Harley) answers that Plaintiff (that's you Beechum) attacked Defendant first, without provocation or warning. That Plaintiff pushed, shoved, or otherwise propelled Defendant into a door in such a manner as to result in injuries to his person. That Plaintiff exhibited evidence of being under the influence of alcohol, to wit, the odor of alcohol was detectable upon his breath. That when Defendant turned to confront Plaintiff, Plaintiff did behave in a threatening manner, to wit, he drew from his pocket an object of the general size, shape and appearance of a knife. That given the context of the situation and the inadequate light, Defendant did, and justifiably so, believe aforesaid object in fact to be a knife. That then and only then did Defendant, acting in self-defense, strike Plaintiff, knocking him to the ground. That Defendant did then retreat inside his place of business, locking the door to protect himself from further abuse from Plaintiff.

BEECHUM: Lord A' mighty, would you ever listen at that!

SALLY: Seriously, Beechum, you have a pretty weak case.

MR. WELLS: And Harley might be telling the truth, at least, the way he sees it. In any event, without a third party witness, you've practically got no case.

BEECHUM: Well, dammit, it's got to be something I can sue him for!

(BEECHUM *takes the jew's harp from his shirt pocket and plays a chorus of "Bonaparte's Retreat," then speaks to* SALLY.)

BEECHUM: Once I was out in the jungles of Borneo, leading a patrol. Come up on this tribe of savages, buck nekked, ever one of them, could a-been cannibals for all I know. The chief was setting there gnawing on a bone. Didn't have a tooth in his head and was trying to gnaw a bone. I said to one of the boys, I said, "Lend him your uppers." Well, that old chief didn't know nothing about false teeth. Put them in bottom uppards. Et half his head off before we could get to him and stop him.

(BEECHUM *waits until the laughter is over, then speaks to* MR. WELLS.)

BEECHUM: What about the money he owes me for fixing that clock? Can't I sue him for that?

MR. WELLS: That's the city.

BEECHUM: Well, he's head of it, ain't he?

SALLY: How much money is involved, Mr. Boatwright —- Beechum?

BEECHUM: Two thousand dollars, even.

SALLY: That's a lot of money.

BEECHUM: It's a big clock.

MR. WELLS: Even so.

BEECHUM: Well, if you must know, it was what Harley said about me that upped the price.

SHERIFF: That clock hadn't run since Lord knows when until Beechum got aholt of it.

SALLY: I don't even remember it running.

MR. WELLS: The town got it from some outfit up in Cincinnati, and it never did run right. They sent a man down periodically to work on it for a while and then went out of business.

SHERIFF: And for a good twenty-seven years, more'n that, I guess, the official town time was set at exactly twenty-seven minutes after five. People used to have hot arguments over whether that was A.M. or P.M. I remember having to break up a fist-fight over it once.

BEECHUM: Called me a little dried-up piss ant.

MR. WELLS: Now, after all that time, the city council began to agonize over it. Felt it gave New Zion a bad image to have a clock that didn't run. Mentioned it to Harley at ever opportunity.

BEECHUM: About the first thing I heard when I got back was about that clock. That bunch that hangs out in the back of Hayes Farm Store was talking about it. I told them, I said, "I know all about them old clocks." (*To SALLY.*) Learned all about them, see when I was in Germany from the best clock makers in the world. I said, "I could fix that thing if somebody was to pay me to do it." Well, one of them went and told Harley, and you know what he said? He said, "You just go back and tell that little dried-up piss ant if he ain't real careful somebody might just fix his clock so it runs on something besides alcohol," and said, "and tell him they'll do it for free." Well, they come back and told me and I just added it on to the bill.

MR. WELLS: Well now, you've got to understand, Harley is one of these rabid teetotalers that sincerely believes, in spite of all evidence to the contrary, that one drop sullies a man's character forever, not to mention destroys any competence he might have had, and, Beechum, you have been known to bend an elbow now and then.

BEECHUM: Don't give him no call to belittle me the way he done. I just added it to my bill.

SALLY: If Mayor Ledbetter felt that way about it, how did he ever come to hire you to fix the clock.

BEECHUM: He didn't at first. It was that bunch down at Hayes Farm Store. They bet me twenty dollars I couldn't do it. Well, I just skinned up that old rickety ladder to the clock tower and had me a look. Lord, what a mess! Dirty, clogged up with birds' nests, gears with teeth missing, and some parts just plain wore out. I thought, though, I could get it to run for a little while. Didn't need to be much, just a hour or so.

SALLY: It caused quite a stir when you did.

BEECHUM: Didn't it though! I planned it, see. I worked up there all night! Got it going just before daylight. Then I stopped it and waited. At nine o'clock when all the stores was open, I let her rip and started her striking the hour. Whoo-ee! You ought to of seen people running out them stores and into the street. They didn't know what was happening.

SALLY: I know. I was one of them.

BEECHUM: I was up there peeping out through the slats, watching. Ever body was running around looking up and hollering. They had no idea what was happening.

SHERIFF: I ought to of climbed up there and arrested you for disturbing the peace is what I ought to done.

BEECHUM: Hell, that's what a clock's for, ain't it? Anyway, I skinned down out of there and went down to Hayeses and collected my twenty dollars real quick before that blamed thing stopped. Got it just in time, too.

MR. WELLS: Well you certainly stirred the city council up. After they saw it was possible for that clock to run again, they really began to pester Harley.

BEECHUM: Don't I know it! I talked to a lot of them myself. Egged them on. And just like I expected, Harley he sent for me to come by the dry cleaners. Well, I taken two or three with me when I went, so now I got witnesses. Harley looked like he might of just bit down on a green persimmon, mouth all tight and puckered up. Says, "Fix that clock." I says, "That won't be easy. It'll take a complete overhaul." "Don't care what it takes," he says, "just fix it." Now, I got witnesses to that.

(*BEECHUM takes out the jew's harp from his shirt pocket and begins to thump out "Bonaparte's Retreat."*)

MR. WELLS: You planned this thing from the beginning, didn't you?

BEECHUM: (*To SALLY.*) I rescued that old Frenchman from the Germans. They was about to shoot him. Had two daughters. Offered me airy one I wanted. Turned out to be ugly as sin, both of them. I said, "Just teach me how to play "Bonaparte's Retreat" and we'll call it even." (*To MR WELLS.*) Took me more than a month, working day and night. I took me a bedroll up there, slept up there lots of times. Took the whole thing apart. Cleaned ever piece. Even had to make some of the parts from scratch. When I was through, I put it back together <u>right</u>, not the way it come from the factory. Run just like a sewing machine.

MR. WELLS: Until you presented Harley with your bill.

BEECHUM: Yeah.

SALLY: What happened then?

BEECHUM: What he said ain't fitting to be repeated in mixed company.

SALLY: What did he say?

MR. WELLS: Tell her, Beechum.

BEECHUM: Not me

MR. WELLS: I'm afraid Beechum's bill provoked Harley into breaking the Third Commandment, not once but several times. In fact, Harley felt obliged to make a public confession the next Sunday to the congregation down at the church. You can imagine what a problem that posed for him. How in the world to confess his sin without repeating it. It's right interesting how he solved it. He quoted himself as having said, "Blaspheme it, Beechum, that's as much as that blaspheme clock cost in the first place and a whole lot more than it's worth, so you just take your blaspheme bill and stick it up your blaspheme vulgarity."

SALLY: Why is it I don't know any of this and everybody else seems to?

MR. WELLS: Because you're always busy here in the office taking work off me and don't have time to sit around down at Hayes Farm Store or the drugstore or the town square, places where you would learn such things.

SALLY: I'm beginning to see I've been missing out on a lot. So what did you do then?

BEECHUM: Well it didn't suit me to do like Harley said.

SHERIFF: Naw, instead he marched over to the town square and skinned up to the clock tower and took out one of them parts he made. Been carrying it around in his hip pocket ever since.

BEECHUM: I'm still waiting for somebody to ask me if I got the time so I can haul it out and show it to them.

SALLY: Well, what's to stop the Mayor from getting some one else to replace the part?

SHERIFF: Oh, he's done tried that.

MR. WELLS: Harley invested several hours on the telephone and finally tracked down a survivor of that company in Cincinnati that manufactured the clock originally and paid him to come down and give an estimate on what it would take to fix it.

SHERIFF: The old man come in on a Greyhound bus. Didn't spend more'n five minutes up in that clock tower. Told the Mayor, said, "I can tell you two things for sure. One is, that ain't the same clock we made and installed for you. The other is, it ain't no way in hell that clock is going to run again like it is now."

BEECHUM: Like I said, it was put together wrong in the first place. Germans is the only ones that knows anything about clocks.

SALLY: So it's a stalemate.

BEECHUM: Not if I take Harley to court and get my money, it ain't.

MR. WELLS: It would be the city that would be liable, not Harley personally. Beechum, do you really want to do this? I'm sure if you won the judgment it wouldn't break the city, but —-

BEECHUM: It ain't the money. I don't care about the money. It's that Harley! Who in the hell does he think he is! Where was Harley Ledbetter when we went off to fight the war? Nowhere, that's where. And now here he is mayor and so high and mighty ain't nobody good enough for him. Where does he get off belittling me? He's a nothing! And his whole family before him was nothings! And don't let all that mealy-mouthing down at the church fool you. I seen them U-Haul trucks. I seen them.

SHERIFF: Now, Beechum.

MR. WELLS: What U-Haul trucks?

BEECHUM: When I was working on that clock, I seen them pulled up in front of the drycleaners at two and three o'clock in the morning.

MR. WELLS: You got any idea what he's talking about, Ruby?

SHERIFF: Ah, just some of his foolishness.

BEECHUM: Foolishness, hell! I seen them, I tell you. It's something funny going on. It wouldn't surprise me if Harley was running a little bootleg business on the side. Now, wouldn't that be something!

MR. WELLS: Now, Beechum, I can assure you, if it was anything to do with alcohol, Harley wouldn't touch it with a ten foot pole. If there was anything out of the way going on, you'd know about it, wouldn't you, Ruby?

SHERIFF: I sure would, Mr. Wells. I expect Beechum had maybe a little too much and dreamed it.

BEECHUM: Say what you will, I know what I seen, and it wasn't no dream. Anyway one way or another, I want to get that Harley!

MR. WELLS: If I'm understanding you, Beechum, you might be satisfied with something less than the full amount of your bill provided Harley, say, publicly admitted that he was wrong in what he said about you and apologized for saying it.

BEECHUM: What about coldcocking me when I wasn't looking?

MR. WELLS: That, too.

BEECHUM: Then all I would want would be reasonable pay for the work I done, say, a dollar.

MR. WELLS: <u>One dollar?</u>

BEECHUM: Just to make it binding. Ever body knows I was the one who fixed that clock. That's enough for me.

MR. WELLS: I see. Well, why don't we do this? Let me have a little talk with Harley. And for the time being, now you just stay out of it. Let me see if I can handle it. I'll let you know how I come out.

BEECHUM: What about your fee? Lawyers got fees, don't they? What's yours?

MR. WELLS: Standard terms. Twenty-five percent of what you get.

BEECHUM: You ain't going to make much money at a quarter a case.

MR. WELLS: Thank you, Beechum. Now that you've pointed that out, Sally won't have to.

SHERIFF: (*Rising.*) Come on, Beechum, let me get you on home so I can go about my business.

BEECHUM: (*To SALLY as he moves toward the door.*) In Japan they got these bath houses, see. You go in there and geisha gals boil you in hot water and tromp up and down your back with their bare feet, then they feed you raw fish. Prettiest girls in the world. You know what? I never seen one of them as purty as you.

SALLY: (*Laughing.*) Goodbye, Beechum.

MR. WELLS: Nice to see both of you. Ruby, you won't forget to keep an eye out for Buford, will you? And Beechum, I'll let you know how I come out.

(*BEECHUM and SHERIFF exit, ad libbing goodbyes.*)

MR. WELLS: I do believe you've made a conquest.

SALLY: Well, I don't know about that, but he certainly made one.

MR. WELLS: Careful! You're liable to ruin your image.

SALLY: What image?

MR. WELLS: Your no-nonsense, strictly-business, don't-get-involved one.

SALLY: Is that how you see me?

MR. WELLS: Too often. No, that's not true. I really have a great deal of admiration for you.

SALLY: Oh?

MR. WELLS: Your discipline, your orderliness, your self-assurance — I envy you those things.

SALLY: <u>You envy me</u>? Don't make me laugh.

MR. WELLS: I would if I could. I enjoy seeing you laugh.

SALLY: I must make a note to do it more often then. What are you smiling about now?

MR. WELLS: I was just remembering you as a teenager, how skinny and awkward you used to be, all knees and elbows and angles, and so shy you could hardly look anybody in the face.

SALLY: I don't see anything in that to smile about.

MR. WELLS: As I recall, you didn't back then either. I remember you as a mighty serious and determined young lady, determined enough to win yourself a scholarship to the university.

SALLY: Well, I couldn't have gone, otherwise.

MR. WELLS: The next time I saw you, you were a mature young woman, all filled out, with a law degree in one hand and a divorce decree in the other, so to speak, ready to take on the whole world.

SALLY: It took about two months for me to realize the marriage was a mistake.

MR. WELLS: And being you, you ended it on the spot.

SALLY: And why not? It could have only gotten worse. And what do you know about it anyway? You never even got that far.

MR. WELLS: That was not by choice.

SALLY: Don't give me that. You could have had anyone you wanted.

MR. WELLS: Not anyone.

SALLY: You mean someone turned you down?

MR. WELLS: Not exactly.

SALLY: What then?

(MR. WELLS *doesn't answer. He turns away, stares out the window.*)

SALLY: You've told me this much. You're not going to just leave me hanging, are you?

MR. WELLS: She was already married.

SALLY: Well, didn't they have divorce laws back in those days?

MR. WELLS: Not applicable to our situation. She was the preacher's wife.

SALLY: The preacher's wife? Why, who —? That long ago it would have been —. Not Mrs. Thompson! Sarah. Not you and Sister Sarah! I can't believe it!

MR. WELLS: Believe it.

SALLY: Why, she was a saint! Everybody says so! Even my grandmother.

MR. WELLS: No. Just a good woman with a strong belief in God and an infinite capacity to love.

SALLY: But she was so much older than you.

MR. WELLS: Not so much. Ten years. Anyway, it never bothered us. It started when I was eighteen and she was twenty-eight and endured til the day she died.

SALLY: No. It's still going on. That's why you don't want that lake property developed. That's where the town used to be before the lake flooded it and they relocated it here. That's where it happened. You're preserving that land as a memorial to her. God! Who would believe such a thing possible in this day and age?

MR. WELLS: There are environmental considerations, too.

SALLLY: Now you're rationalizing.

MR WELLS: Maybe I am.

SALLY: Oh, you make me so mad! You will never stand up and defend yourself on anything! Sometimes I think you're the most aggravating person in the world!

MR. WELLS: Only sometimes? What do you think the rest of the time?

SALLY: I'm going to my office, something I should have done long ago. I've got work to do.

(*As SALLY turns to leave, the phone rings. She snatches it up.*)

SALLY: Yes, Betty, what is it now? (*She listens a moment, then turns to MR. WELLS.*) Mayor Ledbetter is out there.

MR. WELLS: Sure you won't change your mind and sit in?

SALLY: Betty, ask the Mayor to come in.

(*SALLY bangs down the phone, strides to her office and firmly closes the door.*)

MR. WELLS: Now I wonder what brought that on?

(*MR. WELLS turns as HARLEY enters from the reception room and goes to greet him. HARLEY is dressed in a dark three-piece business suit, white shirt and tie. These are clothes he works in, so the suit is shiny from much cleaning and pressing. There is a small square bandage taped to his forehead.*)

MR. WELLS: Well, Mr. Mayor. Come in, come in.

HARELY: Morning, Mr. Wells.

MR. WELLS: Take your coat off, make yourself comfortable. Let me get you a cup of coffee.

HARLEY: Thank ye, no. I've not got much time. It's a matter of business I want to discuss with you.

MR. WELLS: Well, as it so happens, I need to discuss something with you, too. But you go ahead first.

HARLEY: It's about that lake property you got down there. I want to buy it.

MR. WELLS: All of it?

HARLEY: No, just a piece.

MR. WELLS: You want a place to build you a home down there?

HARLEY: No, a bigger piece than that.

MR. WELLS: Mind telling me what you want to use it for?

HARLEY: I'm not free to say.

MR. WELLS: Well, since I live there, I wouldn't consider even discussing selling unless I had some idea who or what I might end up neighbors with.

HARLEY: I wouldn't want it to get out.

MR. WELLS: I'll respect your confidence, of course.

HARLEY: All right, then. Condominiums, for retired people. And maybe a boat dock.

MR. WELLS: Ah! You know there are some other people around with the same idea, don't you?

HARLEY: Them developers! They ain't already talked to you, have they?

MR. WELLS: No, not directly. But I understand they've got a similar project in mind.

HARLEY: Listen, Mr. Wells, I could pay you cash money for it.

MR. WELLS: Well now, it's been a good few years since I had that land appraised, but using that figure and assuming only, say, a thousand feet of frontage, we'd be talking about a whole lot of money. What in the world would you be doing with that much cash, Harley?

HARLEY: Never you mind. You just deal with me and I'll lay it right on the line.

MR. WELLS: Well, as I said, I'm not inclined to part with any of that land.

HARLEY: Like it is, it ain't doing you or nobody no good. It's just sitting there, going to brush and scrub timber.

MR. WELLS: I kind of like it that way.

HARLEY: You let me have it and at least I'll put it to good use. And having a development down there will be a big boost to the town.

MR. WELLS: I hear what you're saying, Harley, and I concede your point. But let me be very plain, I don't want to sell.

HARLEY: Looks like the least you could do would be think it over and then let's talk about it again. It wouldn't hurt you none to do that, would it?

MR. WELLS: All right, Harley. I'll think it over. But let me warn you, my position is not likely to be very much different.

HARLEY: That's all I ask for the time being, that you give it some serious thought. And when you've done that, us talk about it again. Now, what was it you wanted with me? I need to get back to the store.

MR. WELLS: It concerns Beechum Boatwright.

HARLEY: Yeah, I heard he'd been in to see you this morning, him and the Sheriff. I ought to of pressed charges against him. (*HARLEY touches the bandage on his forehead gingerly and grimaces.*) I may just do it yet.

MR. WELLS: No, as a matter of fact, he wanted me to proceed against you for false arrest.

HARLEY: False arrest? <u>False arrest?</u> Why that stinking little whisky sot! He was falling-down drunk and slipped up behind me and shoved me into a door. False arrest, my eye!

MR. WELLS: You're using some mighty judgmental words, Harley, — "falling-down drunk," "slipped up behind me," "shoved me" — words you might be hard pressed to substantiate in a court of law, if it ever came to that. What were you doing when, as you say, he "slipped up behind you and shoved you"?

HARLEY: Why, I was closing up for the night. I was in the act of locking the front door.

MR. WELLS: Turned all the lights out, had you?

HARLEY: Why of course.

MR WELLS: Pretty dark, was it?

HARLEY: Dark? Well, of course it was dark.

MR. WELLS: Then you probably had a little trouble locating the keyhole. Had to get down close before you could see it.

HARLEY: I was bent over. That's why he was able to shove my head against the door.

MR. WELLS: Beechum claims he was just coming along the sidewalk and didn't see you. Bumped into you accidentally.

HARLEY: Beechum ain't nothing but a liar, lie even when the truth would suit him better. He's apt to say anything.

MR WELLS: But it could have been true? It could have been accidental?

HARLEY: Yeah? Then what about that knife?

MR. WELLS: Was there a knife?

HARLEY: Well, I thought it was. He was drunk out of his head and no telling what he might do. He went for his pocket. I wasn't about to stand there and let him cut me, Christian or not.

MR. WELLS: But as it turned out what you thought was a knife was only a juice harp.

HARLEY: In the dark it looked like a knife to me.

MR. WELLS: And as far as Beechum being drunk —

HARLEY: He was. I could smell it.

MR WELLS: That he'd been drinking. Not that he was drunk.

HARLEY: What's the difference?

MR. WELLS: Legally, a great deal. Ruby didn't think he was drunk and it's his job to know.

HARLEY: He was drunk.

MR. WELLS: Well, again, that's something that would have to be substantiated. That might be hard to do with Ruby disagreeing with you.

HARLEY: I wouldn't be too concerned about Ruby if I was you. He'll say what I tell him to.

MR. WELLS: Oh? Is that a fact, now?

HARLEY: Now wait a minute, Mr. Wells, I didn't mean it that way. What I meant was, when Ruby has time to think about it, I'm satisfied he will see it my way. Anybody would.

MR. WELLS: Well, I wouldn't be too sure. Anyway, as I understand you, you thought he was pulling a knife on you, and so you hit him.

HARLEY: Yes, I hit him. I'd do it again. What are you getting at, anyhow?

MR WELLS: Beechum also wanted me to bring action against you for assaulting him.

HARLEY: Assaulting <u>him!</u> Look what he done to me!

MR. WELLS: It could have been an accident.

HARLEY: Well, it wasn't! He done it a-purpose!

MR. WELLS: Now, why would he deliberately do something like that?

HARLEY: Why, that clock! He's mad over that clock!

MR. WELLS: You mean the bill he submitted for fixing it?

HARLEY: It was clean out of reason! He was trying to beat the city out of two thousand dollars! I told him to just —! Well, anyway, I wouldn't pay it.

MR. WELLS: He didn't tell you it was a big job, that it would require a complete overhaul?

HARLEY: Two thousand dollars for a overhaul? Why, that's the craziest thing I ever heard of in my life!

MR WELLS: You later brought a man down from Cincinnati to look at that clock, didn't you? What did he have to say about it?

HARLEY: He said it was all messed up and wouldn't never run again.

MR. WELLS: But after Beechum reworked it, it was running, until he stopped it.

HARLEY: That's what I tried to tell him. The old fool just kept insisting it was no way it could.

MR. WELLS: How long did that fellow spend with that clock?

HARLEY: Five minutes. I'll bet he wasn't up there more than five minutes.

MR. WELLS: And what did you pay him?

HARLEY: Wait a minute! I don't have to tell you that.

MR. WELLS: It's city business and a matter of public record. I could go look it up.

HARLEY: All right. A hundred dollars, then.

MR WELLS: Plus expenses. Say another seventy-five.

HARLEY: Sixty-eight dollars and some-odd cents.

MR. WELLS? For five minutes work. Well, that's not quite right. You ought to count his travel time, too. Let's call it a full day. And he didn't lay a finger on that clock. Beechum, on the other hand, spent more than a month on it, and fixed it. In comparison, it could be argued that you got a bargain out of Beechum.

HARLEY: You ain't never going to make me believe that, and I ain't going to pay.

MR. WELLS: Harley, Beechum wanted to sue you personally for assault and false arrest. I advised him against it because I believe the whole thing was an accident and a misunderstanding. I did agree, though to represent him in trying to work out this matter of his compensation for fixing that clock. That, of course, is city business, but as mayor, and since you made the contract with him, it involves you.

HARLEY: It wasn't no contract!

MR. WELLS: A contract doesn't have to be in writing, it can be oral as well. And I understand there were witnesses.

HARLEY: I don't care if there was, he ain't getting no two thousand dollars!

MR WELLS: On the contrary, Harley, there's a good chance he will, if he takes the city to court. But there's an alternative.

HARLEY: What do you mean?

MR. WELLS: Beechum might be willing to settle for a token payment under certain conditions.

HARLEY: How much of a token?

MR. WELLS: One dollar.

HARLEY: Just a dollar?

MR. WELLS: Under certain conditions.

HARLEY: Like what?

MR. WELLS: I don't know if you're aware of it, Harley, but Beechum is a proud man.

HARLEY: Well, he ain't got much to be proud of.

MR. WELLS: That may be true. But you insulted him by belittling what little he has.

HARLEY: Well ain't that just too bad.

MR. WELLS: It was bad enough to up the bill for fixing that clock from one dollar to two thousand. And what it will take to bring it back down is for you to make him a public apology for the things you said about him and for hitting him.

HARLEY: Me apologize! Never!

MR. WELLS: Think about it, Harley. It's either that or let the court settle it. And the court won't accept things just on your say-so. You'll have to prove them. And it will all have to come out about your Cincinnati man. All this will take time and that clock is not going to run again until Beechum is satisfied, so the city council's going to be unhappy. You think about it. Better still, talk to another attorney and get his advice.

HARLEY: I'll do that very thing. You can count on it.

MR. WELLS: Fine.

HARLEY: Now if that's all, I'll be getting on back to the store.

MR. WELLS: Oh, there's one other thing, Harley. It has to do with some U-Haul trucks being seen in the town late at night. I wonder if by any chance you would know anything about that?

HARLEY: U-Haul trucks? No! Why?

(*SALLY taps on the door and enters from her office.*)

SALLY: Sorry to interrupt, but Sheriff Crawford is on the phone. I think you had better talk to him. Line two.

MR. WELLS: (*He presses a button and picks up the phone.*) Yes, Ruby.... Where?...In the lake?...Look, I'm coming out. No, no, I'll meet you there....I'll see you in a few minutes....Right. (*He hangs up and speaks to SALLY.*) They've found Buford's car in the lake. There's somebody inside. They think it's him.

SALLY: Dear God!

HARLEY: Buford? Buford Phelps? Well, I ain't a-tall surprised. It was bound to happen. He won't be the first one the bottle has brought to a bad end. Nor the last one neither, I'll warrant.

ACT TWO

SCENE ONE

The next morning. MR WELLS is greeting his visitors who are just entering from the reception room. They are RILE BLACKBURN, his mother, MRS. BLACKBURN, and his son, BILLY. Walking is difficult for MRS. BLACKBURN, and she is being helped by her son and grandson.

MR. WELLS: Well, come in, come in. How are you this morning, Mrs. Blackburn? Rile? Billy?

MRS. BLACKBURN: I'm eighty-two, that's how I am. Get me to that chair yonder, Billy, before I drop. You'd think when you got to be my age they'd leave you in peace, but naw! They got to wag you around all over the place.

RILE: Now, Mama, we tried to get you not to come, you know we did.

MRS. BLACKBURN: Well, it's my land and my grandboy, ain't it? I'll come if I want to. (*She falls heavily into the chair.*) Phew! Feels good to finally set. These old legs ain't lasted like the rest of me.

MR. WELLS: Are you all right now, Mrs. Blackburn? Can I get you something, a cup of coffee?

RILE: Aw, she can't drink coffee no more, Jim. The doctor taken her off it.

MRS. BLACKBURN: Quit talking about me like I ain't here. I'll have coffee if I want it, doctor or no doctor.

RILE: Now, Mama.

MR WELLS: Would you like some coffee, Mrs. Blackburn?

MRS. BLACKBURN: No thank ye, the doctor says it's not good for me.

MR. WELLS: Rile? Billy? Well, sit down, sit down. I'm sorry... Sally's not here. She's out with some clients this morning.

MRS. BLACKBURN: We didn't come to see Sally. We come to talk to you.

MR. WELLS: Well, she'll be sorry she missed you, anyway. So, what can I do for y'all this morning?

RILE: Well, it's Billy, you see, Jim. It's something he seen and it got to worrying us, and we thought you ought to know about it.

MRS. BLACKBURN: It never worried me. I don't think there's a thing to it.

RILE: Why, Mama, you was the one that said we ought to come!

MRS. BLACKBURN: I never done no such thing, Riley Blackburn!

RILE: Well, anyway, we're here. Go ahead, Billy tell Mr. Wells.

BILLY: He couldn't get by, see, cause the truck was blocking the road. Well, they couldn't drive that truck across that muddy field, could they, so they had to leave it in the road, and we had to carry them sacks to it, me and him and that girl.

RILE: That's right, Jim, after that rain you would have stuck that truck for sure.

BILLY: So, when we seen them car lights — see, we was in the back of the field getting another load of sacks — well, when we seen them lights, they said "Uh-oh." They said, "Let's get the hell out of here."

MRS. BLACKBURN: Now Billy!

BILLY: Well, they said it, Grandma, I didn't. I'm just telling you what they said.

MRS. BLACKBURN: Well, you just watch your mouth, young mister!

RILE: Aw, Mama. Go ahead, Billy.

BILLY: Well, when they said — <u>what they said</u>, I says, "Wait a minute. It may not be nobody." So, I slipped down to see who it was. Well, it wasn't nobody. It was him.

MR WELLS: Who?

BILLY: Buford. He was just setting there, behind the truck. I says, "What're you doing way out here?" He said so they wouldn't get him.

MR. WELLS: Who was after him?

BILLY: Nobody. He'd been over to the county line and had a few too many and was taking the back roads so he wouldn't get picked up by the state cops. He's been picked up twice already. They take your license away for good the third time.

MRS. BLACKBURN: It's a sin and a shame is what it is. They ought to shut them places down. They had no business letting them run in the first place.

RILE: Now, Mama.

MRS. BLACKBURN: Don't now-mama me! We don't allow it in this county and they oughtn't to neither!

MR WELLS: What in the world are y'all talking about?

RILE: We trying to tell you. Go ahead, Billy.

BILLY: Well, Buford says, "What's that U-Haul truck for?"

MR. WELLS: It was a U-Haul truck?

BILLY: Yeah. I said we was just hauling off some weeds, and about that time him and the girl come up.

MR. WELLS: Him who and what girl?

BILLY: The people in the truck. I reckon they'd been off there listening. He says, "Who is it?" I told him nobody, just Buford, and told him what Buford was doing there. Him and that girl they backed off and whispered a while. Then he told Buford he was real sorry about this and they'd be out of his way in just a minute.

MR. WELLS: Who were they, the people in the truck?

BILLY: Just a boy and a girl. Well, I guess maybe you'd call him a man; he could have been twenty-three or twenty-four. They seemed real nice. Not from around here, though. She said her home was California. I don't know where he was from. She was kind of pretty.

MR. WELLS: Well, what in the world were they doing there in a truck?

BILLY: Like I told Buford, they'd come to pick up them weeds.

MR. WELLS: What weeds?

BILLY: Aw, you know — them hemp-weeds that grows around the edges of the fields.

RILE: They're a prime nuisance is what they are. Ain't no way you can kill them.

MR. WELLS: Hemp? They were hauling off hemp?

RILE: Aw, you remember, Jim, how during the war they wanted us to grow it, the government did, so America could make its own rope.

MRS. BLACKBURN: Now, how could he remember that? He was away in the war hisself.

RILE: Oh, yeah, I reckon he was. Well, anyway it was the worst mistake we ever made. Didn't nobody know how to break it or whatever you have to do to be able to use it. It just fell over and laid in the fields and finally, we had to plow it under. But you can't get rid of it. It still grows wild in the fence rows and such.

MR. WELLS: Good Lord! That's marijuana!

RILE: Well, that's what they call it now, but it's just that old hemp.

MR WELLS: Let me get this straight. Two strangers were hauling off marijuana — all right, hemp — and Billy was helping and you knew about it?

RILE: Mama, too. It was her land. They'd already taken it off my land.

MRS. BLACKBURN: Course I knew about it. You don't think Billy would of picked it without asking, do you?

MR. WELLS: Billy picked it?

RILE: Well, the boy wanted to get him a car.

MRS. BLACKBURN: He's fixing to get hisself killed. That's what he's fixing to do.

RILE: Now, Mama, Billy's been driving since he was fourteen and never as much as put a dent in a car.

MR. WELLS: I don't believe this!

RILE: See, the way it works is, they'll come in and pick it and pay you so much. But if you pick it and sack it and all they have to do is haul it off, why then they pay you a lot more. Before we've always left it to them, but this year Billy wanted that car, so we let him pick it and keep the extra.

MR. WELLS: Don't you know this is against the law?

MRS. BLACKBURN: Law! That's the same law that lets them sell that whisky and beer just across the county line!

MR. WELLS: You could go to jail for this!

RILE: That's why they pay more if you pick it yourself. It ain't as much a risk to them.

MR. WELLS: What about the risk to you? To Billy?

RILE: Well, Billy was on our land. And it ain't like we was growing it. It grows itself. They ain't no way you can get shut of it.

MR. WELLS: But, my God, it's wrong!

MRS. BLACKBURN: You just watch yourself, Jim Wells! I'll not have no blaspheming! You was brought up better than that, and I'll not have it. Besides, if it's so wrong, why would church folks be doing it?

RILE: Now, Mama, we said we wouldn't talk about that.

MRS. BLACKBURN: I don't care what we said. Some of the finest people I know does it, good Christian people. How could it be so wrong, then?

MR. WELLS: Please listen to me, Mrs. Blackburn. If you get caught, believe me, all of you, even you, Mrs. Blackburn, could wind up in jail. But beyond that, you're dealing with criminals. Since it's outlawed, they're the ones who traffic in it. And I'm not talking about just petty criminals, I'm talking about organized crime, syndicates, maybe even the Mafia.

MRS. BLACKBURN: So much for what you know, Jim Wells. We don't deal with nobody like that. We deal with a fine upstanding Christian gentleman.

RILE: Mama! Now, we said we wouldn't discuss that!

MRS. BLACKBURN: Well, I'll not set here and be accused of consorting with criminals, I'll not! Tell him what we come to tell and take me home! (*Pause.*) I need to go to the toilet.

RILE: Now?

MRS. BLACKBURN: Right now!

RILE: Billy, help your grandma.

BILLY: Here, let me help you, Grandma.

(*BILLY helps MRS. BLACKBURN up and toward the door of the reception room.*)

MR. WELLS: I'm sorry if I upset you, Mrs. Blackburn. I apologize.

MRS. BLACKBURN: And well you should! But I ain't got time to discuss it now. Stir your bones, Billy. I'm in a hurry.

(*MRS. BLACKBURN and BILLY exit.*)

RILE: Don't pay no attention to Mama, Jim, you know how she is.

MR. WELLS: Oh, that's all right.

RILE: It must have been what you said about criminals that got to her. She's had doubts about it all along. That's why she run out of here so quick.

MR WELLS: I thought she needed to use a bathroom.

RILE: Oh I expect she did, but she could of waited. It's a handy excuse she uses to back out of a argument if it ain't going to suit her.

MR WELLS: Rile, I've got to convince you of the seriousness of this.

RILE: I can see you think it is. It just didn't seem so to us. It was just a way to pick up a little extra money.

MR WELLS: Do I understand there are others involved?

RILE: I won't name them, but yes, quite a few. And to some of them, it has made the difference of whether they made it or not. Farming ain't like it once was, you know.

MR. WELLS: How long has this been going on?

RILE: Well, this will make the third year.

MR. WELLS: Three years? How could that happen right under my nose and me not know anything about it?

RILE: Well, we agreed not to talk about it and I reckon nobody did. We wouldn't be here now except for what Billy seen.

MR. WELLS: What did he see?

RILE: Why, he just told you. He seen Buford.

(*BILLY re-enters from the reception room.*)

RILE: But here he is back. I'll let him tell it.

BILLY: Miss Betty is taking care of her. She said when she was through she thought she would just wait out there.

RILE: (*To MR. WELLS.*) See what did I tell you? Billy, you go ahead and tell Mr. Wells what you saw.

BILLY: Well, Buford didn't seem to me to be in too bad a shape, but you know he don't talk much, so it was hard to tell. That man says to me and that girl, he says, "Go get the last of them sacks and I'll stay here and talk to Buford." Well, I was pretty sure he wasn't going to get much talking out of Buford, but anyway, we went on and when we got back, Buford had his head down on the steering wheel. "Taking a little nap," the man says. "He'll be all right in a few minutes." Then he thanked me and said they would take it from there and I might as well go on home.

MR. WELLS: And did you?

BILLY: Yeah. But first I went up to the car window and spoke to Buford.

MR WELLS: Did he respond, answer you in any way?

BILLY: Naw, he was out like a light. Had his hands on the steering wheel, head resting on them, face turned towards me, breathing hard – out like a light.

MR WELLS: You could hear him breathing?

BILLY: And smell him, too. Breath like a brewery!

MR. WELLS: And then you left?

BILLY: Fellow says, "He'll be all right in a minute. We'll look after him. You go on ahead." So I started off across the field. I looked back once and that girl was getting in the driver's seat of that truck. Then a little later I heard that truck start up and looked back again and they was both moving off.

MR. WELLS: Buford's car too?

BILLY: Yeah, tailing along behind that truck. Well, I didn't think anymore about it til we heard what happened to Buford and then I begun to wonder how in the world he could have drove hisself all the way down to the lake and in it.

MR WELLS: You think maybe he might have had a little help? Is that what you're saying?

BILLY: They was both real nice, Mr. Wells, polite and soft-spoken. I don't know.

MR. WELLS: (*To RILE.*) What about you?

RILE: It's worrisome.

MR. WELLS: But what prompted you to come tell me about it?

RILE: Well, I know you been helping Buford out some. Actually, it was Mama said we ought to let you know.

MR. WELLS: And you couldn't tell just that part of it to the Sheriff. You'd have to tell him all of it.

RILE: Maybe you could tell the Sheriff the right part.

MR. WELLS: Damn it, Rile, there's not any right part! It's all wrong! And now you've told me and made me a party to it!

RILE: Aw, you was already a party to it in a way. That's another thing we come to tell you. See, when Billy was picking, he picked some on you.

MR. WELLS: What!

RILE: There where your land butts up to ours, you got a big patch growing. Billy, he got carried away and picked you, too. He'd already done it before he noticed he was over the line.

BILLY: Yeah, and I'm real sorry about it, Mr. Wells. I didn't go to do it.

RILE: I know he didn't mean to, but he done it just the same. And when we get our money, we aim to make it right.

MR. WELLS: Damn it, Rile, I don't want any money! Can't you understand that?

RILE: Now, looky here, Jim! We don't aim to beat you out of it. That was never our intention. You know us better than that. Why, Mama would die if she thought —

MR. WELLS: Wait a minute! You said, "...when we get our money." They don't pay you directly, do they? They operate through a middle-man. Somebody local. Who is it?

RILE: Now, I'm not free to tell you that, Jim.

MR. WELLS: Never mind. I expect I already know. Good Lord, what a mess!

RILE: Now, Jim, I think you're making entirely too big a thing out of this. It ain't like we was hurting anybody.

MR. WELLS: Tell that to Buford! Tell it to Ernestine!

RILE: Now, we don't <u>know</u> them two was responsible.

MR. WELLS: No, but it worried you enough that you had to get it off your mind. You had to pass it on to somebody else to worry about.

RILE: I told Mama you wouldn't like it, that apt as not you'd pitch a fit. I'm sorry we bothered you with it.

MR. WELLS: It's a little late for that now. When you told me, you made me a party to it.

RILE: To what happened to Buford?

MR. WELLS: That and the rest of it. Trafficking in a controlled substance — selling marijuana.

RILE: Well, I don't see how that could be. You didn't know Billy had picked on you.

MR. WELLS: It's not that. It's that you <u>told</u> me. I'm a licensed attorney, which means I'm an Officer of the Court and bound by oath and law, not to mention conscience, to report any crime which comes to my attention. If I don't I'm guilty of malfeasance of office and obstruction of justice. Now, that might not mean much to you, but it means a hell of a lot to me. Not only that, but I'm probably guilty of conspiracy, accessory after the fact and lord knows what else.

RILE: But a lawyer don't have to tell on his client.

MR. WELLS: You're not my client. And even if you were, the only advice I'd be allowed to give you would be to turn yourself in.

RILE: Well, what are you going to do, Jim? Are you going to turn us in?

MR. WELLS: I don't know. I just don't know. But I'll tell you this much. This business is over. I'm going to see to that. If there's anything I can do, and there is, I'm going to put an end to it. Billy, you're just going to have to find some other way to pay for that car. And you, Rile, you and the rest that are involved are going to have to get by some other way.

RILE: Lord, Jim, we didn't know. We never realized —

MR. WELLS: Damn it, Rile! God damn it!....Oh, hell, I know, Rile. I understand. I know you wouldn't deliberately set out to hurt me or anybody else. I know that. But that doesn't change the mess we're in. I don't see how we'll ever straighten it out. I don't even know if we can.

RILE: Jim, I'm truly sorry we got you messed up in it.

MR. WELLS: It's all right. Forget it. Y'all just go on about your business. Give me a little time to think about it, see if I can figure out some way to handle it. A few days one way or the other is not going to make any difference now. And I'll find some way to follow up on that business about Buford.

BILLY: I guess I ought to of stayed with him, made sure he got out of there all right.

MR. WELLS: No, Billy, you couldn't have known, and we're not sure at this point there was anything at all out of the way. You've got no cause to blame yourself.

BILLY: I sure hope not, Mr. Wells.

RILE: Well, come on, Billy, let's get your grandma home. I reckon we've done enough damage for one morning.

MR. WELLS: Forget it, Rile. I'll try to figure something out.

RILE: Oh, I'd appreciate it, Jim, if you didn't say anything to Sally about this. It would upset her something awful. She's a awful lot like her grandma to be so different.

MR. WELLS: I have no intention of telling her, but not for that reason. She's an Officer of the Court, too, you know, and it would make her just as liable as I am. Well, so long. I won't come out. Give your mother my regards.

(RILE and BILLY exit, ad libbing goodbyes. MR. WELLS stares thoughtfully out the window for a moment, then moves purposefully to the telephone and dials.)

MR. WELLS: Ruby, is that you? Jim Wells, here. Ruby, I wonder if you would do something for me? Where is Buford, at the funeral home?...

SCENE TWO

An hour later. MR. WELLS has been staring out the window. The SHERIFF taps on the door and enters from the reception room.

MR. WELLS: Come in, Ruby. Sit down. What did the Coroner say?

SHERIFF: Death was definitely by drowning. And he couldn't find a mark on him. But we already knew that.

MR. WELLS: No, we just assumed it. If somebody has been sitting for two days in eight foot of water, you naturally assumed he drowned, but he might have died some other way. I wanted us to be absolutely sure.

SHERIFF: You know something I don't know, don't you?

MR. WELLS: I know Buford was last seen alive in the company of two people in a U-Haul truck.

SHERIFF: A U-Haul truck? Oh my God!

MR. WELLS: You know about those trucks, don't you, Ruby?

SHERIFF: Yes, Mr. Wells, I do.

MR. WELLS: What in the hell has happened to everybody? Has this whole town gone crazy? Ruby, I've known you all your life. I've never considered you to be stupid. How could you, of all people, get mixed up in something like this?

SHERIFF: I've asked myself that a thousand times.

MR. WELLS: If you needed money, why in God's name didn't you come to me? We could have worked something out.

SHERIFF: Money! Money! Damn you, Jim Wells, I'd never do it for money. There ain't that much money in the world! What makes you so damned high and mighty that you can assume that other people will do anything for money?

MR. WELLS: Nothing, Ruby. Not a thing. I had no right to assume that. I'm truly sorry, Ruby. I apologize.

SHERIFF: I accept it. (*He pauses to cool down.*) By the time I found out about it, it was too many people involved. It was either arrest half my friends and neighbors and kinfolks or look the other way.

MR. WELLS: I can appreciate your dilemma, Ruby, believe me.

SHERIFF: There wasn't nothing I could do.

MR. WELLS: Wasn't there some way you could have stopped it?

SHERIFF: I tried. I went to the man behind it.

MR. WELLS: Harley Ledbetter.

SHERIFF: Yeah. I went to him and told him to put a stop to it, but it wasn't anything he could do either.

MR. WELLS: Why not?

SHERIFF: They wouldn't let him.

MR. WELLS: Who? Not the landowners?

SHERIFF: Naw, the ones that are taking the stuff off.

MR. WELLS: Who are they, Ruby?

SHERIFF: I don't know. And Mr. Ledbetter don't know either. He's got a Chicago number. When he needs to talk to them he calls and asks for Mr. Raymond. Sometimes they talk to him and sometimes they tell him he's got the wrong number.

MR. WELLS: What did they say when he tried to quit?

SHERIFF: They told him they would tip off the state police to ever farm where they'd made pickups. And they warned him to be real careful with his dry-cleaning fluid or it might accidently explode and blow up his store.

MR. WELLS: They could have been bluffing. They would have a lot to lose, too.

SHERIFF: Maybe so. But we wasn't about to find out.

ME. WELLS: There has to be some way to stop them.

SHERIFF: If it is, it's beyond me. If you can come up with something, I'll sure go along with you.

MR. WELLS: Well, there's <u>one</u> thing we can do, Ruby. We can call their bluff.

SHERIFF: But, Lord! What if they ain't bluffing?

MR. WELLS: And they may not be. But think about it, Ruby. If they did tip off the state police, that would mean a thorough investigation, not only by the state but by the Federal boys, too. And no matter how well they've covered their tracks there's always the chance the trail will lead back to them. By stirring up that hornet's nest, they don't have a thing to gain and a hell of a lot to lose.

SHERIFF: I can see that, but what about their threat to Mr. Ledbetter?

MR. WELLS: Now that, they might carry through with. They could be pretty sure that we would play it down, handle it locally, pass it off as an accident if we could. And they would figure on it scaring Harley enough to bring him back in line. I'm afraid we'll have to count on them trying to carry through with that.

SHERIFF: Maybe we could stop them.

MR. WELLS: How?

SHERIFF: Be waiting on them. Put some bullet holes in their car. In them, too, maybe. Scare them off.

MR. WELLS: Just how do you expect to do that? Sit in front of Harley's store and draw down on every strange car that comes by? How many tourists do you reckon you would wing a day?

SHERIFF: Yeah, I see what you mean.

MR. WELLS: Wait a minute! They wouldn't be coming in the daytime. Too much a risk to them and too big a chance of killing somebody and they wouldn't want to do that. And especially, they wouldn't want to kill Harley. He wouldn't be any use to them dead. No, they'd have to do it at night when the store was closed and nobody was on the streets, so probably late at night. Just breeze through, throw a stick of dynamite through the window and keep going. Your idea might work, Ruby. Let's think about it.

SHERIFF: You realize, don't you, that we've made a lot of assumptions here. We might be wrong on every one of them.

MR. WELLS: I know, and it scares the hell out of me, but what other choice do we have?

SHERIFF: Well, we still got to get Mr. Ledbetter to agree, and he's got the most to lose. I'll go talk to him.

MR. WELLS: No, Ruby, let me do it. There are some other things I want to settle with him, too. You go on thinking about how to intercept them. See if you can find some way to separate the sheep from the goats. I'll talk to Harley and get back to you.

SHERIFF: (*Rising to leave.*) Whatever you say. You know, Mr. Wells, this is the first time in a long time I've felt like a half way decent human being.

MR. WELLS: Well, if we do manage to pull this off, Ruby, it still won't absolve us, either one of us.

SHERIFF: I know. But it'll make me feel a hell of a lot better about my sins.

SCENE THREE

Near midnight, a few days later. The lamps are on and the drapes on the window are closed. MR. WELLS is seated, a cup of coffee on the table beside him, his coat and tie draped over the back of one of the chairs. He is turning over a walkie-talkie radio in his hands.

SHERIFF: (*On walkie-talkie.*) Unit One to Unit Two. All quiet on this end, Dumas. What about you?

DUMAS: (*On walkie-talkie.*) Same here, Unit One.

SHERIFF: (*On walkie-talkie.*) Unit One to Unit Three. You still with us? (*Pause.*) Unit three?

MR. WELLS: (*Suddenly realizing that he is being addressed, he fumbles with the walkie-talkie to find and press the transmit switch.*) Yeah, yeah. Still here.

SHERIFF: (*On walkie-talkie.*) Fine Unit Three. Looks like it's going to be another quiet night. Well, check with you later. Unit One, out.

(*During the preceding, SALLY has quietly entered from her office and has been standing arms akimbo, listening. MR. WELLS rises to refill his coffee cup and discovers her.*)

SALLY: Just what do you think you're doing?

MR. WELLS: Good Lord! What are you doing here at this time of night?

SALLY: I might ask you the same thing. This has something to do with that marijuana business, doesn't it?

MR. WELLS: So you know.

SALLY: Grandma Blackburn and Daddy and Billy in here to see you and you never saying a word about it? And then you and the Sheriff with your heads together two or three times a day? Did you think I wouldn't have enough sense to know something was going on? I finally wormed it out of Billy. I just can't believe they could be that stupid! I told them so, too.

MR. WELLS: I'll just bet you did.

SALLY: Grandma Blackburn. Oooh, that woman!

MR. WELLS: She didn't take kindly to being lectured, I imagine.

SALLY: "Just climb right down off that high-horse, Missy! You got no right to talk. You're a divorced woman!" Sometimes I could strangle her!

MR. WELLS: What did you expect?

SALLY: I expected a little common sense.

MR. WELLS: Well, that's what you got. But it's their common sense, not yours. What do they know about marijuana?

SALLY: They read the newspapers. They watch TV.

MR. WELLS: But that's something else. It's not real. No, as far as they're concerned, it's just a weed they can't get rid of. Oh, they know you can get high on it, but that's only theoretical knowledge. It's not ingrained, assimilated, not knowledge they can act upon.

SALLY: So?

MR. WELLS: So, marijuana and the things associated with it are not real to them. Hemp-weed is. And if you can sell some and bring in a little money in hard times, it makes good sense to do it.

SALLY: But they know that's illegal.

MR. WELLS: What does that mean? Why the statute books are filled with laws permitting things that ought to be illegal and others prohibiting things that ought to be lawful. Now if the Bible proscribes it, that's another matter. Unfortunately, the Scripture doesn't directly address marijuana.

SALLY: Try using that argument in a defense and see how far you get.

MR. WELLS: I'll never have the opportunity. If it came to that, I'd be in the dock, too.

SALLY: How so?

MR. WELLS: For concealing a crime, of course.

SALLY: But you didn't conceal it. You told the Sheriff.

MR. WELLS: No. He already knew, had known for some time. I realized he must have and when I asked him, he told me.

SALLY: And he hadn't done anything about it? Why, he's —

MR. WELLS: Caught in the same trap I am, and now, you are. He couldn't bring himself to lock up half of New Zion, so he looked the other way.

SALLY: Couldn't he at least have made them stop?

MR. WELLS: No, Harley —

SALLY: Mayor Ledbetter is in on it, too?

MR. WELLS: He's the go-between.

SALLY: Good Lord! I don't believe this!

MR. WELLS: As I remember, that's exactly what I said.

SALLY: How in the world did this happen? How could it happen?

MR. WELLS: As with so many things, innocently enough. Three years ago, Harley attended a small city mayors conference in Chicago. In a group discussion on drug problems, Harley happened to mention our wild hemp situation. A few weeks later two polite, well-spoken, conservatively dressed business types showed up at his store and proposed a business arrangement. The deal was that Harley would spot the farms where the hemp was growing, square it with the owners and they would send someone in to harvest it and haul it off. Payment would be made in cash to Harley after each pick-up and he could deal with the owners any way he saw fit. Harley did a little selling job on some of his fellow church members and was in business.

SALLY: So he's the one responsible! They ought to lock him up and weld the cell door shut.

MR. WELLS: Now, don't be too hard on Harley. He's a product of New Zion, too. Though, I'll admit, I count him a little more guilty than the rest. He's been justifying it to himself on the basis of helping out his fellow church members, but the fact that he has profited from it personally undermines that argument.

SALLY: Why, that hypocritical bastard!

MR. WELLS: Be careful not to use that language around your grandmother. I expect she's still capable of washing your mouth out with soap and would do it, too. Anyway, the money doesn't seem to have done him any good.

SALLY: Why not?

MR. WELLS: Well, it's all in cash. He couldn't put it in the bank without raising some embarrassing questions. Would you believe he tried to work it off on me in payment for some of that lake property? Anyway I gather it's a right sizeable sum.

SALLY: And growing all the time, I suppose. Isn't there anything to be done about it?

MR. WELLS: It seems that gang Harley's doing business with threatened to turn everybody in to the State Police and as a bonus to blow up his dry-cleaning business if he ever tried to back out of the deal.

SALLY: How could they turn anyone in without implicating themselves?

MR. WELLS: An anonymous tip, I suppose. But I'm convinced it's a bluff. So we've called them on it.

SALLY: What about their threat to Harley?

MR. WELLS: We think maybe we can stop them.

SALLY: With a walkie-talkie?

MR. WELLS: Ruby is parked on the west approach to the town square and Dumas Sims is parked on the east. If they come, they'll have to use one or the other. So Ruby and Dumas are on the lookout for a suspicious car.

SALLY: And then what?

MR. WELLS: They tailgate it til it's past Harley's place. We don't think they'll try anything with a police cruiser on their back bumper.

SALLY: What if you're wrong?

MR. WELLS: Then Harley loses his store and Ruby starts putting bullet holes through their rear window.

SALLY: And they start putting bullet holes through his windshield.

MR. WELLS: And Dumas, who's in touch by radio, comes charging from the other direction to divide their attention.

SALLY: It's the craziest thing I've ever heard of! This time your meddling is going to get somebody killed!

MR. WELLS: That's a possibility we recognized. But what else do you suggest?

SALLY: I don't know. Where is Mayor Ledbetter while all this is going on?

MR. WELLS: Home, if he's following orders. Hiding under the bed, I wouldn't be surprised.

SALLY: I don't like it.

MR. WELLS: None of us do. Harley least of all.

SHERIFF: (*O.S. On walkie-talkie.*) Unit Two, this is Unit One. Heads up, Dumas. I've got a visitor on this end. He just turned off the highway.

DUMAS: (*O.S. On walkie-talkie.*) Right, Unit One.

SHERIFF: (*O.S. On walkie-talkie.*) He's coming pretty slow. I don't recognize the car, course I can't see it much for the lights. (*Pause.*) Here he comes by me. Hey, it ain't no car, it's a pickup camper. Got a motorsickle rack on the back bumper, one of these dirt bikes on it. Got Wisconsin plates.

DUMAS: (*O.S. On walkie-talkie.*) Chicago ain't in Wisconsin, is it?

SHERIFF: (*O.S. On walkie-talkie.*) Naw, it's in Illinois, or was the last I looked.

MR. WELLS: (*He fumbles with the walkie-talkie trying to find the transmitter switch. On walkie-talkie.*) Damn it, Ruby, Wisconsin is right next door!

SHERIFF: (*O.S. On walkie-talkie.*) That you, Unit Three? Maybe I ought to inform you it's against the law to use profanity on the air.

MR. WELLS: (*On walkie-talkie.*) Never mind that. How many in the truck?

SHERIFF: (*O.S. On walkie-talkie.*) Two. Man and woman. She's driving. Now, that ain't just right.

SALLY: What's not right about it? Does he think a woman is incapable of —

SHERIFF: (*O.S. On walkie-talkie.*) I'm right on her bumper. Just about nudging that motorsickle. Got my lights on bright. That'll give them something to think about. All right, Dumas, start easing thisaway, and keep your lights off.

DUMAS: (*O.S. On walkie-talkie.*) On my way.

SHERIFF: (*O.S. On walkie-talkie.*) Here's the square coming up....Here's Harley's place....Naw, she's going on by....Naw nothing....Looks like she's going to circle the square. Yeah, that's what she's doing. Maybe she's going to make another pass at Harley's....Naw, she's turning, going out the way she come in, heading back out to the highway. Guess it was a false alarm. Looking for the campground and turned in here by mistake. Women!

SALLY: What does he mean, women?

SHERIFF: (*O.S. On walkie-talkie.*) Well, that's probably our excitement for the night. Get on back to your position, Dumas and try to stay awake, you hear? This is Unit One, out.

SALLY: Why is it you men assume women can't do anything?

MR. WELLS: Not me. I know better. I wouldn't last a month without you.

SALLY: Yes you would. You'd just have to work harder, that's all.

MR WELLS: It's a little more than that. Who would I talk to?

SALLY: Everybody, just like you do now.

MR WELLS: There's talking and then there's <u>talking</u>.

SALLY: You're upset about all this business.

MR. WELLS: I guess I am.

SALLY: You feel the community has let you down.

MR. WELLS: No, that I have let them down.

SALLY: Because all this happened and you didn't know about it? You're a damn fool, Jim Wells, and an egotistical one at that! Who appointed you their keeper?

MR. WELLS: No one, I guess. Or maybe the same one that appointed you mine.

SALLY: I'm not your keeper. And if I were, it wouldn't be by appointment. It would be by choice.

MR. WELLS: Choice. I wonder if I ever did anything by choice.

SALLY: You chose Sarah.

MR. WELLS: No, that was Divine Providence.

SALLY: Oh come on!

MR. WELLS: No, it's true. At least, she always believed it was. The women of the church took on as a project converting all the young people of the community who were not members of the church. They put our names in the collection plate and each one drew one. Sarah drew mine.

SALLY: And you converted her instead.

MR. WELLS: No, what happened between us just happened. Or maybe she was right after all, maybe it was Divine Providence.

SALLY: What I'll never understand is how you were able to carry it off under the nose of everybody.

MR. WELLS: They thought she was working on me, and in her own way, she was. I was known as a hardened case. Nobody expected her to be successful overnight.

SALLY: But it went on for so long. Didn't they finally get suspicious?

MR. WELLS: Actually, it was only for a summer. Then Brother Uriah was called to another church and she went with him. She saw the separation as Divine Punishment, which she had expected in some form or another, and accepted. I suppose I could have insisted she stay, but I respected her belief too much for that.

SALLY: But you said it lasted until she died.

MR. WELLS: And so it did. We were exiled all those years, but not entirely. We wrote each other regularly. My father and I visited them sometimes and they visited us.

SALLY: He knew about it?

MR. WELLS: The only other one who did until now.

SALLY: And he approved.

MR. WELLS: He had a great reverence for love.

(*There is a loud tapping on the window.*)

SALLY: What on earth?

MR WELLS: Sounds like the window.

(*MR. WELLS rises, goes to the window and opens the drapes. BEECHUM is outside, holding a white plastic bag.*)

MR. WELLS: Well, I declare! Beechum, come around to the side door.

(*MR. WELLS motions the direction, then closes the drapes and moves over and opens his private entrance. BEECHUM enters.*)

BEECHUM: Seen your light. Figured you'd be in here.

MR. WELLS: What in the world are you doing running around at this time of night?

BEECHUM: You'll never guess what I found! Money!

MR. WELLS: What!

BEECHUM: Yeah! A whole sack full! I knew he must be up to something. Why, hi there, Miss Sally.

SALLY: Hi, Beechum.

BEECHUM: I told you, didn't I? I knew it was something going on and here's the proof.

MR. WELLS: Slow down, Beechum. Come over and sit down and tell us what you're talking about.

BEECHUM: Well, I was up there having me a little nap and here come Harley.

MR. WELLS: Up where?

BEECHUM: In the clock tower. I got me a bedroll up there from when I was working on it, see.

MR. WELLS: But why sleep there? Why not at home?

BEECHUM: Well, I got sleepy. Home was too far.

MR. WELLS: I see. Took a little too much sedative, did you?

BEECHUM: Damn it, Jim! What difference does it make? I'm trying to tell you about Harley. Excuse me, Dear Heart.

MR. WELLS: Sorry, Beechum, go ahead.

BEECHUM: Well, I woke up, see, and I was laying there thinking I ought to get up and go home when I heard somebody climbing up that old ladder.

MR. WELLS: When was this?

BEECHUM: Just now. You want to hear this or not?

MR. WELLS: Okay, okay.

BEECHUM: Well, I had no idea who it was. I didn't know what to do, so I hid.

MR. WELLS: It was Harley?

BEECHUM: Yeah. And when he struck that match, I thought sure he would see me, but he had his back to me and his mind on other things, I reckon. Well, he had this sack here and he waved that match around a time or two and then jammed it in behind the clockworks, the sack, I mean, not the match. It went out, the match, and in just a minute I heard him scooting down that ladder again. I give him a minute and then tiptoed over and peeped out them slats and there he was going into his dry cleaners. So I struck me a match and looked in that sack and it was full of money. And here it is!

MR. WELLS: Harley's tithe.

SALLY: Tithe?

BEECHUM: You mean it's church money?

MR. WELLS: Harley took ten percent off the top for his share. He called it his tithe.

BEECHUM: His share of what? Wait a minute, don't tell me. It's that hemp-weed business.

MR. WELLS: You know about that?

BEECHUM: Listen, I wasn't born ever minute. Course, I know about it. But I thought it was Ruby that was heading it up.

SALLY: The Sheriff?

BEECHUM: Well, he knows about it. Even asked me to keep quiet about them U-Haul trucks.

MR. WELLS: No, Harley is the man. Ruby is trying to put a stop to it without having to arrest half the county.

BEECHUM: Why don't he just make Harley quit?

MR. WELLS: It's not that simple.

BEECHUM: I see. It's that bunch Harley is selling it to. They won't let him, I bet you.

MR. WELLS: They've threatened to blow up his dry cleaners.

BEECHUM: Well, let them. It'd be good enough for him. Or better still, when they come in to do it, be waiting on them and blow them up instead. I remember one time when I was in Belgium in that War —

MR. WELLS: That's what we're doing, though we're not being quite that drastic. Right now, Ruby and Dumas Sims are covering both approaches to town and checking out every car that passes.

SALLY: I passed Dumas on my way in. Why didn't he check me out?

MR. WELLS: He recognized you. Wait a minute! How did Harley get past him? Harley was supposed to keep away. Dumas would surely have reported it if he had seen him.

BEECHUM: Maybe he didn't come that way.

MR. WELLS: But if he came the other way, Ruby would have spotted him.

BEECHUM: Well, he could have cut across the fields on foot. That's what I would have done if I didn't want to be seen.

MR. WELLS: Oh good Lord! (*He snatches up the walkie-talkie.*) Ruby! Ruby! Harley is here in town! He's in his store!

SHERIFF: (*O.S. On walkie-talkie.*) That you, Unit Three?

MR. WELLS: (*On walkie-talkie.*) Did you hear me, Ruby? I said Harley was in town!

SHERIFF: (*O.S. On walkie-talkie.*) I heard you, Unit Three. Now what do you reckon he's doing here?

MR. WELLS: (*On walkie-talkie.*) Damn it, Ruby, the point is, how did he get past you and Dumas!

SHERIFF: (*O.S. On walkie-talkie.*) Well, he must have cut through the fields on foot.

MR. WELLS: (*On walkie-talkie.*) Wasn't there a dirt bike on the back of that camper?

SHERIFF: (*O.S. On walkie-talkie.*) Yeah, it was....Oh!....Oh, my God!.... Wait a minute! I hear something!.... I think I hear it!.... Dumas! Get in there! Now! You hear me, Dumas?

(*The ear-splitting roar of an explosion rocks the law office.*)

SCENE FOUR

A month has passed since the explosion. The window drapes are open to the bright sunlight outside. The town clock can be heard very clearly striking the hour of nine. There is a long pause after the last stroke, then MR. WELLS enters from his private entrance, singing. He is dressed in work clothes, a bright quilted vest, high-top shoes and is wearing a bright hunter's cap. He marches around the room in time with the song and on the last line, takes off his cap and tosses it at the coat rack. It misses.

MR. WELLS: "We're marching to Zi-on, / Beau-tee-ful, beau-tee-ful Zi-on. / We're marching upward to Zi-i-i-on, / That beau-tee-ful city of God." Hey, Boss-lady!

(*SALLY enters from her office in time to see the cap fall, retrieves it and hangs it up, goes to the credenza and pours coffee for MR. WELLS and herself.*)

SALLY: Well, aren't we cheerful for a change. Cheerful and late. Been smelling the roses again, I suppose.

MR. WELLS: Wrong. I was up with the sun and I've been taking me a little walk over my lakefront property.

SALLY: A stroll down memory lane, is that it?

MR WELLS: More than that. Those developers still hanging around?

SALLY: No, I couldn't find anything to suit them. They've given up and gone looking for greener pastures.

MR. WELLS: Good! Who needs them?

SALLY: Certainly not you. You made that clear.

MR WELLS: And not anybody. If you want something done to suit you, do it yourself.

SALLY: What's that mean? Are you cooking up another one of those hare-brained schemes of yours?

MR. WELLS: As a matter of fact, it's your hare-brained scheme. We're going to build us a condo, you and I… maybe two of them, and a boat dock!

SALLY: What!

MR. WELLS: Why don't you realize there are an awful lot of people, good, hardworking people, who would give their eyeteeth to live down there? And a docking facility would do wonders for the economy of this community. Besides, I need some neighbors. But most of all, I think New Zion could do with an infusion of fresh ideas. After what's happened, I'd say we're suffering from what in some circles is called cultural lag. It doesn't pay to get too far behind the times.

SALLY: And what about Sarah's memorial?

MR. WELLS: That was just your speculation of what it was. Besides, to everything, there is a season, and it's the nature of seasons to pass.

SALLY: You're not just doing this because of me? I haven't pressured you into it, have I?

MR. WELLS: Of course, you have. Listen, young lady, if you're going to meddle, you're going to have to shoulder the responsibility for the consequences.

SALLY: You won't regret this? You won't be unhappy and blame me?

MR. WELLS: Oh, I expect to regret it. I regret it already. But regret doesn't kill you. It's the lack of hope for something better that does that. Which reminds me, I'm expecting Ernestine. I left word for her to come by. I want to talk to her about investing that money in something that will bring her in a regular income.

SALLY: You're a devious man, Jim Wells — telling her that money was from Buford's insurance policy.

MR. WELLS: Actually, I told her it was from a policy Jack Heddin carried on all his employees.

SALLY: Suppose she says something to Mr. Heddin about it?

MR. WELLS: Oh, I talked to him. Besides, she's not too interested in where the money comes from.

SALLY: I suppose not.

MR. WELLS: Poor old Harley. I told him he wouldn't be able to keep that money, but I guess he just couldn't reconcile himself to giving it up.

SALLY: As disgusted as I was with him, I wouldn't have wished him that.

MR. WELLS: No. If that was an example of Divine Justice, I sure hope it's never meted out to me.

SALLY: And what about that Chicago bunch? Are they just going to get off scot free?

MR. WELLS: Who knows? Maybe Whoever or Whatever it is that orders things, will see to them too. In any case, all we can do is make certain they don't come back.

SALLY: What's to stop them? The hemp is still here. And I guess there will always be idiots around to lead them to it.

MR. WELLS: You may be right about the idiots, but after Beechum and Ruby's Clean-up Brigade get through, there won't be any hemp anymore.

SALLY: Clean-up Brigade?

MR. WELLS: You haven't heard? Beechum's first official action last night after the city council appointed him to finish out Harley's term was to proclaim —

SALLY: What! Beechum? Mayor?

MR. WELLS: Why not? It's largely a ceremonial job. And Beechum will certainly be a hit with the tourists. And as mayor, he'll see to it that the clock keeps running. Anyway, as I was saying, the first thing he did was to establish a joint City-County Clean-up Brigade to eradicate the hemp-weeds from every vacant lot and field and fence row in the area. They're starting this morning, and I intend to do my part, that's why I'm dressed this way. Grub and burn, that's the watch-word!

SALLY: So that will finally end it. Thank God.

MR. WELLS: Oh, no. We've still got the matter of a bunch of unindicted felons running around loose — you and me and Ruby, not to mention half the congregation down at the church.

SALLY: I expect the only one that will ever bother is you.

(*The phone rings. SALLY picks it up.*)

SALLY: Ernestine is here.

MR. WELLS: Well, get her in here. I wouldn't dare keep anybody as rich as she is waiting.

SALLY: Send her right in, Betty.

(*ERNESTINE enters from the reception room. She is sporting a new hairdo and outfit. Her bulk is somewhat disguised by the cut of her new clothes.*)

MR. WELLS: Come in, Ernestine, come in. My, my! Let me look at you!

ERNESTINE: What was it you wanted, Mr. Wells? I ain't got much time.

MR. WELLS: Well, I wanted to know how you're getting along, for one thing, but I don't need to ask that. I can see.

SALLY: It's a very pretty outfit, Mrs. Phelps.

ERNESTINE: It ought to be. It cost enough.

MR. WELLS: The kids all right?

ERNESTINE: They're out in the car. I hope this won't take long. I got business at the bank.

MR. WELLS: Well, that's sort of what I wanted to talk to you about —

ERNESTINE: I'm transferring my account. To Paducah. We're moving there and I'm taking my money with me.

MR. WELLS: You're moving to Paducah?

ERNESTINE: It ain't nothing for me around here. They got a college there. I may go.

MR. WELLS: Why, I think that's great.

ERNESTINE: A beauty college. I might make a beautician. You know, fix people's hair and all.

SALLY: Why, that's wonderful, Mrs. Phelps.

ERNESTINE: Then again, I may not. It all depends. Anyway, I'm getting out of this God forsaken place.

MR. WELLS: You know, I've been thinking, Ernestine. I know that seems like a lot of money, but with the cost of things these days, it can slip away from you real quick. Maybe you ought to invest it in something that would bring you in a little income.

ERNESTINE: I don't think I'd be interested.

MR. WELLS: There are two or three ways you could go. You might want to invest just part of it.

ERNESTINE: I'm not interested.

MR. WELLS: Well, you might just think about it.

ERNESTINE: I don't need to do that, Mr. Wells. I done told you, I ain't interested. (*She rises.*) Now, if that's all you wanted, I'll be getting on to the bank. I expect they'll have a thousand things I can do with my money, too. It sure is funny how when you got money, ever body suddenly becomes interested in you. Goodbye, Mr. Wells, Mrs. Holmes.

MR. WELLS: Goodbye, Ernestine. Good luck in Paducah. I hope the beauty college works out for you.

ERNESTINE: Don't matter if it don't. I ain't real sure I want to be messing around with other people's hair, anyway.

(*ERNESTINE exits.*)

SALLY: Of all the nerve!

MR WELLS: Now, now, don't blow a gasket. It's probably the first time in her life she's had a taste of independence. It's heady stuff!

SALLY: (*At the window.*) Well, she won't be independent long. Come here and see what she's driving.

MR. WELLS: Looks like a new Buick.

SALLY: Cost a fortune, I bet! No wonder she wasn't interested in investments. She's already invested in everything she's laid eyes on!

MR. WELLS: Yeah. Too bad, really.

SALLY: Is that all you've got to say? What will you do in six months when she comes back here whining for help?

MR. WELLS: The best I can for her, I expect.

SALLY: That's the last straw! That does it!

MR. WELLS: Does what?

SALLY: Does *you*, that's what. You're not mentally competent. Your affairs are going to have to be taken out of your hands.

MR. WELLS: Maybe you could get the court to appoint you my guardian.

SALLY: I told you it wouldn't be by appointment, it would be by my own choice.

MR. WELLS: And is it?

SALLY: Yes. Yes, it is.

MR. WELLS: I'm old enough to be your father, you know.

SALLY: So what? You've got a few good years left in you yet.

MR. WELLS: And after they're gone?

SALLY: Will you stop arguing and get over here!

(*As MR. WELLS moves toward SALLY, the phone rings. SALLY answers it.*)

SALLY: Damn! Yes, Betty, what is it now! (*She listens.*) Beechum and Sheriff Crawford are out there.

MR. WELLS: Tell them to wait. No, tell them to go on without me. Tell them to go suck an egg!

SALLY: Now, now. Duty calls. Ask them to come in, Betty.

(*BEECHUM and RUBY enter. RUBY is dressed as usual, but BEECHUM has on a black three-piece suit and is wearing a large golden medallion suspended from a chain around his neck.*)

MR WELLS: Morning, Ruby. Morning, Mr. Mayor.

SHERIFF: Morning, Mr. Wells, Miss Sally.

BEECHUM: Morning, Jim. And how are you this morning, Pretty Lady? Well, Jim, I see you're dressed for the occasion.

MR. WELLS: I can't say the same about you. You're not going to get much work done in that outfit.

BEECHUM: Oh, the only work I'll be doing is to dig up the first weed. After that, I'll just be supervising.

SALLY: What's that around your neck, Mr. Mayor?

BEECHUM: I'll always be Beechum to you, Sweet Thing. Oh, this here's my Badge of Office. Actually, it's just temporary until I can get me one made. It was give to me by the burghomaster of Frankfurt, Germany for capturing them before the Rooshuns got them. They didn't like them Rooshuns a-tall. (*As he speaks, his hand strays to his breast pocket for his jew's harp, but doesn't find it. He frantically searches all his pockets.*) Good Lord, I forgot my juice harp!

SHERIFF: Aw, don't worry about it Beechum. You ain't gong to have time for it today, anyway.

BEECHUM: I don't keer, I ain't going without it. I'd feel nekkid is what I'd feel. Y'all are going to have to run me back to get it. And we better hurry or we'll be late, and that wouldn't do.

MR. WELLS: Why Beechum, they wouldn't start without you. You're the mayor.

BEECHUM: I know that, but I don't want to keep them folks waiting. *Noblesse oblige* and all that. (*To Sally.*) That's French, Darling. Means "Be sure and keep the troops happy." Say, you wouldn't marry me, would you?

SALLY: I'm sorry, Beechum, I'm already spoken for. I wish you had asked me sooner.

BEECHUM: Story of my life. Oh, well. Well, come on, Ruby, come on, Jim. (*He herds them toward the door.*) Time's a-wasting.

MR WELLS: Y'all go ahead. I'll catch up in a minute.

(*BEECHUM and RUBY exit. MR. WELLS looks at SALLY across the room.*)

MR. WELLS: Must I?

SALLY: You must.

MR. WELLS: I could plead pressing business. It would be the truth, you know.

SALLY: You've let your pressing business wait this long. I guess it will keep until tonight.

MR. WELLS: You sure?

SALLY: Besides, I hate to rush. Just make certain you don't wear yourself out today.

MR. WELLS: Yes, Boss.

(MR. WELLS and SALLY exchange blown kisses and he reluctantly exits.)

THE END

Ouida White and Jack Johnson in *Mossie and the Strippers* by Billy Edd Wheeler, Horse Cave Theatre, 1987

MOSSIE AND THE STRIPPERS
by
Billy Edd Wheeler

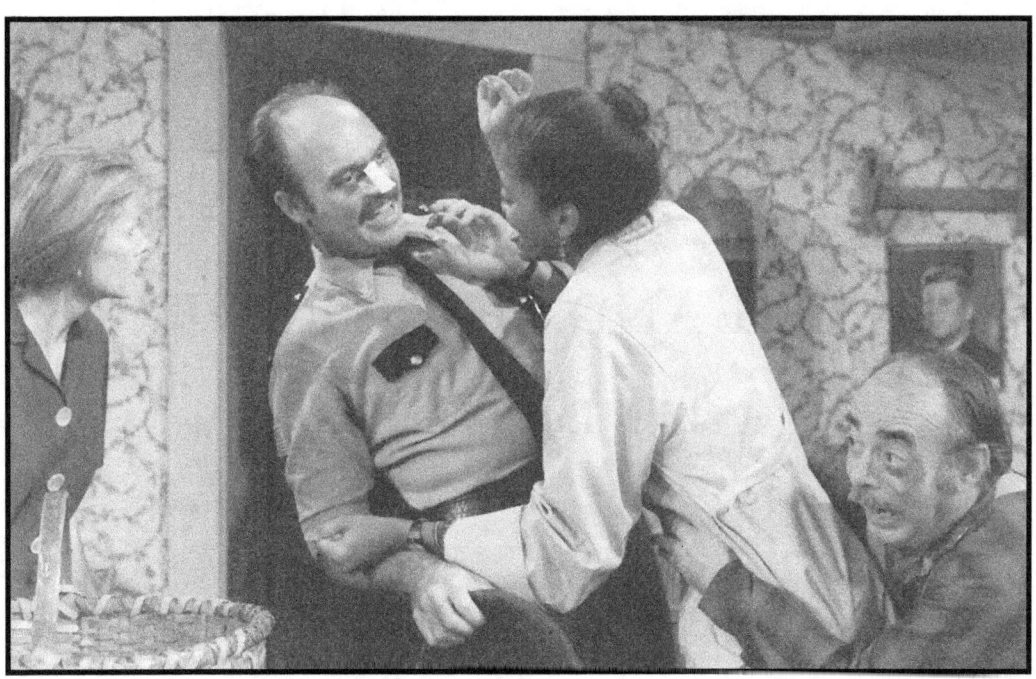

Ouida White, Kent Logdson, Tess Campbell and Jack Johnson in *Mossie and the Strippers* by Billy Edd Wheeler, Horse Cave Theatre, 1987

Mossie and the Strippers opened on July 17, 1987, with the following cast:

MOSSIE	*Ouida White*
GID	*Jack Johnson*
BRUD	*Kent Logsdon*
GINNY	*Tess Campbell*
JUDGE CLAUDE RAMSEY	*Tom Williams*

Director: Warren Hammack
Stage Manager: Karen Terry
Set Design: Sam Hunt
Lighting Design: Gregory Etter
Costume Design: Rebecca Shouse
Properties Design: Sam Hunt
Technical Director: Carl Wolfe

When Warren Hammack approached me about doing a play of mine at Horse Cave Theatre, I was at once pleased and ambivalent. Pleased because several actor friends had told me about the high quality productions being produced at Horse Cave; ambivalent because it meant a lot of hard work loomed ahead.

Mossie and the Strippers was my first and only choice to submit to Warren. It was inspired by a Kentucky lady known as Widow Combs, famous for protesting the strip mining that threatened her home by lying down in front of their big trucks and bulldozers. The picture of her being hauled away by State Troopers – like a sack of potatoes – was forever frozen in my mind. What a brave woman! Yes, *Mossie* was a good fit for Horse Cave. But I knew the play needed a major rewrite, and Warren agreed. That's where the hard work came in.

Warren pointed out that the character who needed the most attention was Mossie's husband Gid. Mossie was rock solid. But Gid, a retired coal miner, was out to pasture, so to speak. He had lost a good bit of his manhood. He was ready to accept any deal offered by the strip mining company and the company-friendly judge. Looking at Gid's character as a director who was also a fine actor, Warren brought a double edged insight to the transformation needed. Likewise, the Jane Fonda reporter character needed more meat on her bones. So, together Warren and I invented more background for her. She ended up having a lot more invested in her job than just a newsworthy byline. Pamela White contributed in this area, too, bringing a woman's insight to problems while also functioning professionally in areas of management, promotion and production. (Not to mention being a gifted actor.) She and Warren were a great team. How lucky can a playwright be!

– Billy Edd Wheeler

Characters:

MOSSIE COCHRAN, *a mountain woman*

GID COCHRAN, *her husband, a retired miner*

GINNY BUCKNER, *a newspaper reporter*

BRUD SHELTON, *sheriff of the county*

JUDGE (*Voice only.*)

Place: A hollow deep in Appalachia.

Time: The year is 1969.

ACT ONE

SCENE ONE

The set is a typical living room in a miner's house. There is a fireplace that is sealed up, a Warm Morning stove in front of it with a coal bucket nearby, a poker and small shovel leaning against the fireplace. Over the mantel in a gun rack is a lever action .30-30 Winchester rifle. There is a couch and a well-worn over-stuffed chair, a large round multi-colored throw rug, the kind that looks plaited by hand. On the rug is a small table covered with a white doily and two framed pictures. On the walls, covered with flower-patterned wall paper, are pictures of John F. Kennedy and Jesus. Upstage is a window, with curtains gathered in the middle with a frilly sash.

People enter the house from outside at stage right and go into the rest of the house at stage left.

Prior to the beginning of the play we hear a medley of recorded music, folky in nature, dealing with coal mining... songs such as "Red Winged Black Bird," "Coal Tattoo," "The Coming of the Roads," "Ain't Goin' Home Soon," "Dark As a Dungeon," "Blue Diamond Mines," etc.

After a period of silence the last music we hear before the lights go down is a banjo tune that begins lyrically, out of tempo, growing into its rhythm slowly. It is not flashy. It is thoughtful, beautiful. It grows into a fairly bright rhythmic piece. This is GID's MUSIC that he has lost. As the house lights go down the music is cross-faded with the noise of big trucks and earth movers, the far-off boom and crash of front end loaders dumping dirt and rock into truck beds. It gets loud during the short time of darkness, fades to silence as the lights come up.

MOSSIE stands at the window looking up the mountain. GID is looking at flies, testing the whip of his fly rod, pulling out line and reeling it back, sticking flies into the big chair arms, transferring them to his hat and the wooly patches on his old fisherman's vest. He is enjoying himself, lost in his thoughts, oblivious of MOSSIE and the concern mounting in her.

MOSSIE: They're getting closer. (*GID doesn't respond.*) They're following the ridge that comes over to Blackberry. Then they'll turn down this way. It won't be just the trucks then. (*MOSSIE sits, tries not to think about it. She looks at GID. He doesn't notice.*) Gid.

GID: Uh-huh?

MOSSIE: They're coming, Gid. They're getting closer.

GID: Uh-huh.

MOSSIE: He don't hear me. Lordy. (*She looks at him, shakes her head.*) Lordy, Lordy.

(*MOSSIE is working up a fit of anxiety but tries to control it. She picks at the couch cover, straightens it, smoothes it, then clasps her hands between her legs.*)

They really are coming, Gid. You said they'd go down Pine Fork and cut some new roads for the trucks, then they'd be gone. Well, they ain't. They're coming. (*She wrings her hands. She springs up and goes back to the window.*)

That rock up yonder worries me, Gid. A good rain and... all them rocks worry me. They didn't have to leave 'em there, with all that dirt. They look like little bitty things from down here, but they're... (*Makes a hoop with her arms.*) That big 'un, he's a granddaddy. If he was to come rolling down the side of the hill... Lordy. Lordy-Lordy. (*She peers at it, backing up to survey it, using her thumb to judge perspective. She marks the spot by the window then backs up to confirm her judgment.*) He'd bust right through the wall. (*She goes to the spot on the other side of the window and touches the wall. Then she goes back to the window, backs up, squats, surveys. GID is still not listening.*) Don't it worry you none, Gid?

GID: Uh-huh.

MOSSIE: Then what we gonna do about it? We gonna just wait til it happens, then let out a squawk?

GID: Uh-huh.

MOSSIE: (*Screaming.*) Gideon!

(*GID almost jumps out of his chair. His rod flies out of his hand.*)

GID: What in the dickens!

MOSSIE: They're coming, Gid. Not just the trucks. The machines. Them strippers are getting closer all the time.

GID: Is that what you're screaming for? I told you they'd head down Pine Fork. Then they'd cut another way out for the trucks and be gone.

MOSSIE: I know you told me that. Come over here.

(*GID follows MOSSIE to the window.*)

MOSSIE: Listen. Hear that?

GID: Well, I don't know. It's something. It ain't...

MOSSIE: It ain't trucks, that's right.

GID: I didn't say that.

MOSSIE: Well, it ain't. Listen. That's drilling. And loading, and haulin'. And look up yonder above Angie's little graveyard.

GID: What?

MOSSIE: That rock.

GID: What about it?

MOSSIE: It's gonna fall.

GID: Oh, Mossie, it ain't done it. It's been there a... it's always been there.

MOSSIE: Last summer. That's when it was. They cut them roads last summer and piled all the rocks up there, and dirt. And that big 'un, Mr. Granddaddy there, he's been there eight months and eleven days.

GID: (*Going back to his chair.*) You got him named, huh?

MOSSIE: They'll bury us. That's all.

GID: For Goodness sake, Mossie. If they do come, and they ain't, but if they do, it ain't nothing to worry about. They'll treat us fair and square.

MOSSIE: Ha!

GID: The company'd see to that.

MOSSIE: Ha-ha!

GID: Mr. Billings'd treat us right.

MOSSIE: Oh, yeah.

GID: And if for some unknown reason he didn't, the Judge would see to it that he did.

MOSSIE: He owns the Judge.

GID: Claude Ramsay? Mr. Billings owns Judge Claude Ramsay?

MOSSIE: And the sheriff. And the company store. And the mine bosses.

GID: (*Incredulous at her stupidity, chiding her.*) Good golly, Mossie.

MOSSIE: I love this place, Gid. This house is the onliest one we ever owned. If they mess it up, they mess me up. You might as well bury me up there beside little Angie.

GID: Quit talking about burying things.

MOSSIE: I can't think about nothing else. You got your fishing.

GID: Big Red. I'm gonna catch that booger this year, you watch. He's a wiley old trout, but I'm fixing him up a fly that'd look like a t-bone steak to me and you. Water's down. But a few rains and…

MOSSIE: The rock comes down. That's all it's gonna take. A few rains.

GID: Mossie… All right. Tomorrow I'll go to the store and buy a new broom.

MOSSIE: What?

GID: My mother used to get all upset when word come up on Coon Creek that the world was coming to an end. Doomsday. The whole town would be scared to death, but Mommy was the worst one of all. She'd set by the window and watch for it to come. Then she'd see Daddy with a new broom walking up the road, and she'd feel all right. She knowed he wouldn't waste money on a new broom if he wasn't gonna need it tomorrow, and the next day.

MOSSIE: I miss my young 'uns.

GID: They've left the nest.

MOSSIE: One day they're here. The next day they're married and having babies of their own.

GID: Jackie's coming up Sunday. And Allewayne, I reckon her old man'll drive her in from Ohio for Easter.

MOSSIE: I don't look for 'em.

GID: They said they'd come.

MOSSIE: Something'll come up. It always does.

GID: Now, don't you fret. Just calm down. Ok?

(*MOSSIE nods. GID finds a fly and starts tying it on the line, dreaming again. The following speeches overlap, but the lines are clear, and they build.*)

GID: Here's a Henryville special. Got Big Red's name wrote all over it.

MOSSIE: The sheriff come by yesterday while you was fishing.

GID: If that don't work, I got a deer hair.

MOSSIE: He said Mr. Billings offered to buy this place.

GID: I've give up on the Adams and the blue dun.

MOSSIE: I told him we'd never sell.

GID: I know in reason I could tip a Montana nymph with a leetle piece o' worm…

MOSSIE: He said something about them cutting off your Silicosis money if we didn't play ball.

GID: ...and drag it across the bottom and snag Big Red with it.

MOSSIE: I said, Buddy, cut 'er all off. Cut off everything.

GID: Ah, but I ain't gonna do that. I'm gonna make him rise to the top.

MOSSIE: But we ain't a-sellin'.

GID: I did hook him once.

MOSSIE: He said, you oughtta be careful talking back to Mr. Billings that way. Ain't you a-feared?

GID: He flipped this way and that and dived straight to the bottom.

MOSSIE: I said, I ain't afraid of nothing, let alone you and that coal company bunch.

GID: My line snapped.

MOSSIE: Sheriff, he said, you watch yourself, Mossie. They's more'n one way of skinning a cat besides choking him on butter.

GID: No wonder. It was just two pound test.

MOSSIE: I said, you'll not outdo me.

GID: I figure I can go to three or four and he still won't see it.

MOSSIE: I'd druther die at a man's feet than to be outdone by him. They wouldn't be up here trying to buy us out if they didn't plan on burying this place.

GID: And I won't jerk so hard.

MOSSIE: If we stay with it, they'll bury us, too. Oh, Gid, you don't hear word I'm saying. (*Shouting.*) Gid!

GID: I'm listening, Mossie. I been thinking. That's what's ailing you, the kids leaving.

MOSSIE: You're crazy.

GID: Well, then it's female trouble.

MOSSIE: Fe...what kind o' female trouble?

GID: It's the mysteries. Something, you know, that happens to the female race.

MOSSIE: (*Amused in spite of herself.*) Oh, Gid, what would you know about the mysteries of anything?

GID: It ain't just me. The doctors can't figure it out, neither.

MOSSIE: Oh...go to hell.

GID: See there! I ain't never heard you talk that way.

MOSSIE: I ain't never been this worried.

GID: I mean cussing that way.

MOSSIE: Are you gonna help me?

GID: Help you what?

MOSSIE: Do something.

GID: Do what?

MOSSIE: I don't know. Fight. Do something. Will you help me fight 'em Gid?

GID: No. I've not gone crazy.

MOSSIE: (*Suddenly tired, resigned.*) Maybe we <u>ought</u> to go ahead and sell the place.

GID: Sell it? Has somebody offered to buy it?

MOSSIE: The sheriff did.

GID: The sheriff?

MOSSIE: Gid, you ain't heard a word I been saying. He come by and said Mr. Billings wanted to buy us out.

GID: You wouldn't sell this place. You couldn't. Could you?

MOSSIE: If the price was right. But they don't have to know that.

GID: But the graveyard.

MOSSIE: You can move graveyards.

GID: But...I don't know. Your flowers, the dogwood trees, I didn't think...

MOSSIE: They want us out of the way so they can bury this place. They'd bury us too and go on their way, if they could get by with it. But I ain't gonna roll over and play dead. Far as they're concerned, Gid, they couldn't prize me loose from this house with a crowbar. But you let 'em mention the right price. I don't mean just any old number that comes into your head, I mean one that's way up here. (*Holds her hand above her head, high as she can reach.*) I can't even count that high.

GID: I still can't believe you'd sell.

MOSSIE: Sssssshhhhh! I wouldn't. Don't you even think it. If you think it, they'll think it. In the between time, now, we've got to fight 'em.

GID: Now it's back to fighting. Mossie...

MOSSIE: You gonna help me?

GID: No. Somebody's got to keep some sense about 'em. You're unsettled in your mind, Mossie. It'll pass.

MOSSIE: All right.

GID: Just calm down.

MOSSIE: All right. All right! (*Thinks. Speaks with resolve.*) I'll do it by myself.

GID: I'm going fishing. (*Quickly gathers his gear, puts on his hat and starts to exit.*)

MOSSIE: (*Yelling after him.*) You're scared, ain't ye?

(*GID waves her off and continues off and out of sight.*)

MOSSIE: That's why you won't stand up and fight! (*To herself.*) No, I don't reckon you are. You ain't got enough sense.

(*MOSSIE takes the rifle from the rack and walks to the window.*) They'll be shutting down pretty soon and parking their big horses all in a row. (*She aims the gun and pretends to fire it, recoiling. She puts the gun back in the rack, goes to a picture and holds it up to look at it.*) Allewayne, if you don't come down here Easter and bring that little dumpling for its grandma to hold, I'm gonna kill you. That goes for you and Shirley Faye too, Jackie. You ain't got no excuse. You don't live that far away.

(*MOSSIE puts the picture down and goes back to the window, looks up the mountain. We hear the sounds of trucks and equipment afar off.*)

MOSSIE: Female trouble. The mysteries. Huh! Men don't know nothing.

(*The noises come up full as the lights go down.*)

SCENE TWO

The lights come up on GID near his fishing hole. He approaches the fishing hole cautiously, sneaking to it, crouching, hiding behind bushes to avoid being seen by the trout. He floats his imaginary line out over the water. GID is dressed in dark pants, the bottoms of the legs stuffed into his socks, tennis shoes, a plain dark work shirt with an old fisherman's vest over it, all kinds of hooks stuck into the vest. He wears a lightweight, soft, cotton, camouflage hat. His creel can be some sort of canvas sack that looks homemade or the dark green expandable pouch with netting at each end that can be purchased at most sporting goods stores. He hums as he presents his line. His eyes glisten with anticipation. He is clearly in heaven.

GID: All right, Mr. Brookie, come and get it. There....you go. Try that. I know you're down there. Are you hungry, old boy? How's that look? Huh? Wanna come up and have a little nibble?

(*As GID fishes, we see that he is a different person from the bland, listless man we saw in the house. As he fishes, his MUSIC creeps in faintly. When he hears it, he cocks his ear listening harder as if wanting it to grow in volume. He stops fishing for a few seconds and starts trying to dance with the MUSIC that has grown somewhat louder, but is still far-off sounding. He is clearly eager, but it begins to fade, so he accepts it and turns back to his fishing.*)

(*As GID continues to fish, humming, talking to the water, GINNY BUCKNER appears, walking very slowly and carefully as if picking her way down a mountainside that is steep and thick with weeds and bushes. From far away she spies GID and calls out to him, but he doesn't hear. GINNY is dressed for the outdoors but still manages to come off as chic. She wears slacks, a shirt or blouse, a light wind breaker, nice leather loafers. She has sun glasses sticking in her hair and carries a writing pad tucked away at this moment in a large, soft leather bag slung over her shoulder.*)

GINNY: Hello down there! Hello! He can't hear me.

(*GINNY picks her way closer, carefully, ducking under bushes, stepping over rocks and brush, until she is ten to fifteen feet away.*)

GID: Hey, Big Red. How you like this, old boy? (*Makes the fly dance on the water by jiggling the rod.*) Looks pretty good, does it? Well, here she goes, flying away. See there, you missed out. (*Casting and recasting.*) Why, there it is again! Better get it while you can, son. You old lazy lunker, I know you're down there.

GINNY: Hello. Hey, there!

GID: Huh? (*Turning, seeing GINNY, surprised almost beyond believing.*) Why, Lordy mercy. What?

GINNY: Hello.

GID: Hello yeself.

GINNY: (*Still shouting a little.*) I'm Ginny Buckner. I write for the Mountain Courier. I've been across the ridge there watching the strip miners. Can I come over there and talk to you?

GID: Me? Why, shore, I reckon. You wanna talk to <u>me</u>?

GINNY: Yes, I'd like that.

GID: You wanna talk to me. Well... (*Looks around.*) Yeah, well I reckon I'm the only one around. You <u>do</u> wanna talk to me, don't ye? Where in the world did you come from, girl?

GINNY: Do you live in the first house down there?

GID: On Blackberry?

GINNY: Right down there.

GID: Me and Mossie lives there. Yep, that's our house, all right.

GINNY: How do I get over there where you are?

GID: You can't get here from there. (*Laughs at his own line.*) Just back up a few steps and start over. Come down that-a-way, there, yeah, right around that ivy patch. That's it. You can step across the creek on them rocks there. (*GINNY is doing this as he directs her.*) Be careful. Looks like them shoes you got on are pretty slicky. (*He backs up to meet her, taking in his line as he does so. She jumps over the creek and he takes her hand to steady her.*) There.

GINNY: Oh! Thank you.

GID: You made it.

GINNY: Oh, wow! Look where I came from. Hi, I'm Ginny Buckner. (*Offers her hand again.*)

GID: Well, I'm Gid Cochran. People call me Gid. My real name's Gideon. That's from the Bible, you see.

GINNY: Having any luck, Mr. Cochran?

GID: Well, I don't know, I.... uh...You can call me Gid.

GINNY: Mr. Cochran, are you a miner?

GID: I was. I'm retired.

GINNY: Do you mind if I take notes?

GID: Why, no.

GINNY: You don't look old enough.

GID: I don't? For what?

GINNY: I mean, to be retired. You look too young to be retired.

GID: I do? (*He turns to the fishing hole, flashing a broad smile.*) Well.

GINNY: Were you a strip miner?

GID: No, I've worked underground all my life.

GINNY: Drift mouth?

GID: Yep. I started out as a trapper, as a boy. Then I was a cutter for years and years. I've drove motors, shuttle buggies, been a 'lectrician, done some blacksmithing.

GINNY: Did you ever think about working at something besides mining?

GID: What for? No, I like coal mining.

GINNY: What did you like about it?

GID: I don't know. They's just something about it. Or they was. I'm retired now. 'Bout all I do is fish.

GINNY: You like fishing?

GID: Do I like it? No, I love it. I been fishing these creeks up here for...They's one fish, right here in this hole, probably, he goes other places, don't ye know, but that fish...if I catch him...I mean, <u>when</u> I catch him... He's gonna get caught. Big Red, I call him. He's a native brookie, got these big red spots, kind of orange-red spots. Most of your natives ain't too big, but this'un, Lordy, I bet he'll go two or three pounds.

GINNY: That's big?

GID: For a native? Ma'am, that's a whale. They ain't never that big up this high. But he's trapped, at least til we get lots more rain. He can't get up that falls yonder, not over the shallows there. He's the boss.

GINNY: He?

GID: Huh?

GINNY: How do you know it's not a she?

GID: Why, I just know. I know in reason he's a he.

GINNY: I don't doubt you, Mr. Cochran, but I'm curious. Why couldn't it be a she?

GID: It just ain't.

GINNY: Can you tell by looking?

GID: No, by feeling.

GINNY: You've felt of her? Him.

GID: It's a feeling. You just know.

GINNY: Oh. He's fast, then. Male trout are faster than females.

GID: Don't reckon, no.

GINNY: Stronger? More aggressive?

(*GID looks at her a second, as if trying to decide where she's coming from, decides to tell her a story.*)

GID: I come here onc't, saw this fish floating belly up. Thought for a minute it was Big Red, but it was too little. But it was a right size of a fish, ten inches or so. I started to move closer and I saw it move. Then something jerked it ever' which way. I snuck up and looked closer and I saw Big Rid had it by the gills. Had a death grip on it. He was killing that fish. You see, they's only room for one bossman in each big hole. And he's defin'ly the boss in this hole.

GINNY: That's why you think Big Red is a male?

GID: He's a fighter. Don't seem right that a woman would be that...that, well, a woman is sort of daintier, or more politer, or something. You know what I mean?

GINNY: No, but if you've got a feeling, I can't argue with that.

GID: I got a feeling, all right.

GINNY: How do you feel about the strip miners above your house?

GID: Don't feel no way at'all.

GINNY: It doesn't bother you?

GID: Not a bit.

GINNY: What if, say, your house was suddenly in danger?

GID: You oughtta talk to Mossie. She's scared to death something is gonna happen. You see, that's a woman for you. Getting all worked up over nothing. I'm the man of the house. I'll fight, if I have to. But do you see me salivating at the gills, getting all worked up?

GINNY: What if they <u>did</u> damage your house?

GID: I'd sue 'em. The Judge would sock it to 'em.

GINNY: (*Writing.*) Uh-huh. Would your wife be at home?

GID: Mossie? Sure.

GINNY: Do you think I could stop and talk to her?

GID: Why shore, shore. You two oughtta see eye to eye.

GINNY: Why do you say that?

GID: It's just a feeling.

GINNY: (*A little whoop of a laugh escaping her.*) You and your feelings. (*She steps past him toward the pool.*) Well, how do I get there?

GID: (*Grabbing her.*) Get back here, sister! Quick.

GINNY: What?

GID: He'll see you. Well, he's seen you for sure. I know in reason he has.

GINNY: How come?

GID: Oh, it's just a...

GINNY: I know, a feeling. Oh, I'm sorry, Mr. Cochran, I've spoiled it for you.

GID: Gid. You can call me Gid.

GINNY: Oh, I couldn't do that.

GID: Why not?

GINNY: Well, I don't know you that well. It would seem disrespectful.

GID: Why's that?

GINNY: You're older than I am.

GID: You told me I looked young. So it's old, is it?

GINNY: No, not at all. You're just about my daddy's age.

GID: You call your daddy mister?

GINNY: No. Oh, wow. I always manage to put my foot in it. I've spoiled your fishing...I've made you think you look old.

GID: I think I look young.

GINNY: You do?

GID: Don't you?

GINNY: Yes.

GID: Then call me Gid.

GINNY: All right, Gid.

GID: (*Smiling that broad smile again.*) Now. Miss Ginny, you go down this creek, and...

GINNY: I don't like "Miss" Ginny. Just Ginny.

GID: Huh?

GINNY: You call me miss, but you won't let me call you mister.

GID: Well, I'm a man. I was trying to show respect. After all, I'm old enough to be your daddy. I'm...I was... (*GINNY looks him straight in the eye, half smiling, half chiding him. He starts over.*) Ok, Ginny. You go down this creek. You can't miss it.

(*Four shots ring out, evenly spaced, from farther up on the mountain.*)

GID: Sounds like rifle shots. Maybe they're shooting rats up there at the strip job.

GINNY: Bye, Mr...er, Gid. (*Shakes his hand.*) Thank you for talking to me.

GID: Why, thank you...uh, Ginny. (*She starts stepping away, carefully.*) You really think I look young?

GINNY: I'd say about thirty-eight.

GID: Aw, go on!

GINNY: Well, maybe forty-eight. Or fifty-two. Certainly not a day over fifty-five.

(*GID smiles a smile that lights up all outdoors and turns back to fishing. Then he looks back at GINNY and watches her disappear. He throws a final word at her.*)

GID: Tell that old woman to heat up the skillet! We'll have fish for supper! (*Concentrates on the pool, humming, joyful.*) Did you get a good look at her, Big Red? She's a looker, now, ain't she? Kinda forward, but I can't say as I disliked it at'all. Hmmm, fifty-five. (*He continues casting, humming, working his way upstream as the lights go down.*)

SCENE THREE

MOSSIE is busy as the lights come up on the living room, as if we have caught her in the middle of some secret actions. She is dragging the table back to its place in the middle of the rug, standing the two pictures back up, looking around to see if everything looks normal. She starts to sit down, notices her muddy shoes, gets up and rushes to the kitchen, comes back in stocking feet and carrying another pair of shoes, sits to put them on, is tying the laces when GINNY comes to the door. GINNY pauses to pick some beggar lice and cockleburs from her pants legs, knocks. MOSSIE jumps up in surprise at the knock. She looks around once more, takes a deep breath to compose herself, and then goes to open the door.

GINNY: Mrs. Cochran?

MOSSIE: Yes.

GINNY: Mrs. Cochran, I'm Ginny Buckner. I'm a reporter for the Mountain Courier.

MOSSIE: You are? Well, my goodness.

GINNY: You know the Courier?

MOSSIE: I've sure heard of it, that's for sure.

GINNY: Can I talk to you for a minute?

MOSSIE: Sure, come in, come in. You come right in and make yourself at home.

GINNY: I won't take but a minute. I was talking to your husband, Gid. Mr. Cochran. He made me call him Gid.

MOSSIE: That's Gid all right. He don't like no misters and stuff like that.

GINNY: I think he's a doll. He told me all about fishing and everything.

MOSSIE: Then you know about Big Red.

GINNY: Oh, yes.

MOSSIE: He vows he'll catch him. But, honey, I hope he never does, to tell you the truth. He'd have nothing left to live for.

GINNY: Mrs. Cochran, can I ask you a few questions?

MOSSIE: Lordy, honey, I'm dumb as a coal bucket. (*Laughs.*) A empty one at that. But you just ask me anything you want to. If I don't know the answer, I'll make something up. Sit down here.

GINNY: I work for the Mountain Living editor. Seems like ever since I started working they've assigned me to strip mining jobs. I covered the one over at Big Balsam.

MOSSIE: That was a mess, wasn't it. Come, sit down.

GINNY: I wasn't the most popular girl in the county after I wrote my story, and this is the same coal company up here.

MOSSIE: It is? Why, yes, I bet it is.

GINNY: Does it worry you?

MOSSIE: Yes. It does worry me.

GINNY: In what way?

MOSSIE: Tell you the truth, it scares me to death. Just having the trucks run that close above us, shaking down all that dust and dirt.

GINNY: I suppose you've lived here all your life.

MOSSIE: Not yet. (*MOSSIE smiles at GINNY who chuckles at the joke.*) No, we've lived here about twelve year.

GINNY: It's so charming, I figured it was the old home place.

MOSSIE: When you marry a miner you've got no home place. You live in this coal camp a while, then move to that one. The last place we worked was right here and when the coal company offered us the chance to buy, buddy, we jumped at it. It's quiet...and peaceful.

GINNY: You love it, don't you?

MOSSIE: I do. I surely do. It's home. The first real home we ever had.

GINNY: What would you do if it looked like you might lose it?

MOSSIE: It's coming. I know it is. Gid says it ain't, but...I said it's quiet and peaceful. Well, it has been...up til now. Honey, I don't know what we'll do. I'm tired of moving. I don't know what in the world we <u>can</u> do, but I hope they's something. (*She pauses a moment, watching GINNY write.*) They was a woman...you might o' heard about her...why, she laid down in front of the bulldozers. (*GINNY recognizes the story, nods her affirmation, but doesn't say anything. She doesn't want to intrude on MOSSIE's train of thought.*) Huh, if I was to do that, why, they'd probably run right over me. Don't reckon it'd do any good, no way. Probably didn't help that woman, neither, but she did it. (*Shakes her head in admiration, chuckles.*) Got her picture in the paper.

GINNY: I saw it. Was her name Combs? Widow Combs?

MOSSIE: Lordy, honey, I don't know. But she looked right funny, all slung down, with a state trooper carrying her by the feet and another by her arms.

GINNY: (*After waiting to be sure MOSSIE has said all she is going to say on the subject.*) Mrs. Cochran, can you tell the difference between a he trout and a she trout just by looking?

MOSSIE: Please, call me Mossie.

GINNY: I'm not going to argue. Mossie.

MOSSIE: Gid says he can tell.

GINNY: Yes, I know. He says the male is more of a fighter.

MOSSIE: He ain't done it! No such a thing. You can't tell by looking. You'd have to cut that trout open to really find out if it was a he or a she.

GINNY: How can you tell?

MOSSIE: Female'll have eggs in her most of the time. Male, he'll have white strips, kinda looks like fat up along his backbone. That's his milk. You know, his whatchamacallit, his...

GINNY: Sperm?

MOSSIE: Yeah. He spews that down on the eggs.

GINNY: Yes, well, I can understand that. But I can't believe the female is any less the fighter than the male.

MOSSIE: I don't think she is.

GINNY: I've noticed, in the mountains, most of the time women walk behind the men. Have you noticed that?

MOSSIE: No. I've never paid it no mind.

GINNY: Do you think men are better than women?

MOSSIE: In some ways. In some ways women's better.

GINNY: Would it bother you to have to walk behind men, or wait on them?

MOSSIE: Somebody's got to look after 'em. (*Chuckles, pauses, turns serious.*) A man ought to wear the pants. A woman ought to cook and take care of the kids. Course, when the kids are gone…

GINNY: Do you have children?

MOSSIE: Got grandchildren. Allewayne's s'posed to come in from Ohio for Easter. Our son Jackie lives right down here at Seneca Falls. We lost Angie when she was thirteen. It was leukemia that finally took her, bless her heart. I miss 'em, I do. I miss 'em a right smart.

GINNY: Now that they're gone, have you ever thought about a career? You know, working at something?

MOSSIE: Lordy, what could I do? I just barely can read.

GINNY: Really?

MOSSIE: I didn't learn til I was sixteen. And, oh honey, learning to read like to broke my heart.

GINNY: Oh?

MOSSIE: I was going with a man. Barlow Burgess. Ohhhhh, he struck me down worse'n Delilah did Samson. He was a handsome thing. Ever' girl in the county drooled over him. They all wanted him. (*Chuckles.*) I think about half of 'em got him. He was stuck on hisself, if you know what I mean. He figured he was the berries above the persimmons. Well, he used to get these letters. All the time. Regular as clockwork. He'd never hide 'em from me 'cause he knew I couldn't read. Then my uncle started learning me my letters, a little at a time, but week after week…til I could, you know, figure it out. One day…I saw one of them letters just laying there. So I read it. Lorrrrrd, honey, I like to a-died. It was a love letter. It was from a girl he was going with hot and heavy. At the same time he was courting me, leading me on!

GINNY: That's a beautiful story.

MOSSIE: It wasn't to me. It broke my heart.

(*Thunder rumbles.*)

GINNY: Uh-oh, I better go, before it starts raining.

(*GINNY gets up, starts for the door with MOSSIE walking behind her.*)

MOSSIE: They're calling for it. Gid's wanting it, to fill up the trout streams, but I hate to see it come. Rocks don't need rain.

(*GINNY doesn't pick up on this ominous note. She extends her hand to MOSSIE.*)

GINNY: Thank you, Mossie. You've been so nice.

MOSSIE: You come back.

GINNY: Can I? Oh, I'd love that. This is one time I hope there's no story, but I would like to come back. Thank you again. Bye-bye.

MOSSIE: Goodbye. Bye, now.

(*GINNY exits. MOSSIE turns back inside, pauses to reflect, speaks to herself.*)

MOSSIE: Mossie, sometimes your jaw comes plumb unhinged. (*Goes to the window, looks up the hill.*) Lord, don't let it rain.

(*As the lights start down we hear it thunder. Then some banjo creeps in and as it plays in darkness we hear it thunder again.*)

SCENE FOUR

A few days later. MOSSIE sits on the couch in the living room, reading the backs of some flower seed packets. GID comes in from the other part of the house. He sits in the big overstuffed chair and takes a letter out of his shirt pocket, unfolds it and reads it. It is raining.

MOSSIE: Gid, you need to read that letter again. She ain't coming.

GID: She don't say for sure they ain't coming. Right here, it says… we "prob'bly won't come for Easter." You see she don't say they <u>ain't</u> coming.

MOSSIE: That's what it means. Allewayne never could just come out and say something.

GID: That's 'cause she took after me.

MOSSIE: Since when have you been at a loss for words?

GID: Since…it don't matter.

MOSSIE: Allewayne's double natured. She's this way one minute and that way the next.

GID: Yeah, wishy-washy.

MOSSIE: Now, Gid. What I mean, she sees both sides of it. She's a deep thinker.

GID: She's got a loose screw, if you ask me. She takes that after you. What would she go and say they're coming for, if she knows they ain't?

MOSSIE: Well, I reckon she wants to come.

GID: She ort to, then.

MOSSIE: I want to see her and that baby much as you do.

GID: She's wishy-washy. Like when she got married. She backed out of it two or three times. Like to wore old Peanuts out. One day he's strutting around like a banty rooster. Next day he's gloomy as a long-nosed undertaker.

MOSSIE: She wanted to be sure.

GID: Don't take up for her 'cause she takes after me. Now, you take Jackie, he's quick to take a side, before he's even thought about it. He takes after you, you see.

MOSSIE: Least he ain't a fence straddler.

GID: Yeah, I know, you think it's better to do something, do it right now, even if it's wrong.

MOSSIE: You don't know it's wrong til you've done it.

GID: And it's too late, then, ain't it, 'cause it's done done. It don't hurt to think about it some.

MOSSIE: Didn't take me long to marry you. I didn't have to think about that.

GID: That's because you'as mad at Barlow Burgess. You'd made up your mind to marry him. Then when you found him out, you wanted to show him, so you went fishing. You hooked the first sucker that swum by. Me. Your folks wanted you throw me back. They didn't think I was a keeper.

MOSSIE: I did. I thought you was a prize catch.

GID: (*With a passive skepticism.*) I was a man. I was alive.

MOSSIE: Alive and kicking. Gid, you struck me down worse'n Barlow Burgess ever could. You know that. Why, when you asked me to dance at that square dance…when you took my hand and twirled me around that dance floor, my heart like to busted wide open, I'as so happy. I knew I had hold of a <u>man</u>. I'd-a-walked through hell barefooted holding on to your hand. It wasn't just your dancing. It was something inside of you, some kind o' power…and music…that come into me when I held your hand. Like touching a lightning rod. I felt like I was a great big tuning fork that you picked up and struck against a star. It set me to quivering with joy.

GID: (*Staring at her a moment, almost unbelieving, then chuckling.*) Must a-quivered something loose in you, like Allewayne. (*GID reads the letter some more, stops, looks up at MOSSIE quizzically.*) I done that to you? (*MOSSIE nods, smiling and sentimental.*) All that lightning rod business, and… (*MOSSIE nods again. He shakes his head.*) Well, Lordy, mercy. (*He reads the letter some more.*) I reckon you're right. She ain't coming. But I bet she'll be here for the Fourth.

MOSSIE: That's a long time off. I wish this rain would stop.

GID: There you go fretting over the rain again.

MOSSIE: It makes mud. And mud slides.

GID: Mossie, for goodness sakes. Them men up there know what they're doing.

MOSSIE: Yeah. I do too. (*GID gets lost in his letter and MOSSIE goes back to flipping through the seed packets.*) I swan, here's a packet o' them forget-me-nots. Remember that feller that was running for the state legislature? He give me these, two or three packs of 'em. I thought I'd throwed 'em away. He said, "Plant these and forget me not." I planted some of 'em and they didn't come up and he didn't get elected and, I swear, I've plumb forgot his name. (*Chuckles.*) Yessir, I'll never forget old what's-his-name.

GID: This rain's getting the creeks up where they ought to be. I like the rain.

(*MOSSIE looks at GID, her face clouding over. She grunts scornfully.*)

(*BRUD SHELTON comes to the door. He is bare-headed but wears a badge and packs a gun on his hip. He walks with a swagger. He is very impressed with himself. And in spite of a certain comic twist to his bearing he is capable of coming off as a very dangerous man. He exudes a physical strength but tries to act casual about the power of his office. He knocks.*)

MOSSIE: Well, now, who could that be?

(*MOSSIE opens the door.*)

BRUD: Mossie, is Gid home?

MOSSIE: Hi-de. It's the sheriff.

GID: Well, tell him to come in. The sheriff. My goodness gracious.

(*MOSSIE nods and BRUD steps past her into the room. GID gets up, folding his letter. BRUD wipes the rain from his face with a handkerchief.*)

Gid: Hello, here, Brud. Come in, come in.

BRUD: Hello, Gid. Little wet outside. You ain't busy, are you?

GID: No, no. I was just reading this letter, here, from Allewayne.

BRUD: How is Allewayne and Peanuts?

GID: She's fine. Fine. They got 'em a fine, healthy baby. Living up there in Ohio.

BRUD: Yeah, where 'bouts?

GID: Why, right down town.

MOSSIE: He means what city, Gid. Ohio is a state.

GID: Cincinnati. That's what I mean. She lives in Cincinnati.

BRUD: (*Looking about, especially over the mantel where the rifle is missing from the rack.*) That's fine. Cincinnati is a nice town. Well, I reckon it is. They got a good ball team.

GID: It is. It's a real fine town.

BRUD: Didn't you used to have a thirty-thirty, Gid?

GID: Still do.

BRUD: Would you let me look at it?

GID: It's right there. Hmmm, I don't remember taking it down. Must be in the closet. I'll get it for ye.

BRUD: I'd appreciate it.

(*GID goes into the next room.*)

BRUD: Been shooting any lately, Mossie?

MOSSIE: Me? I hate guns.

BRUD: Somebody told me you'as a pretty good shot. For a woman.

MOSSIE: Can't believe ever'thing you hear, can ye?

BRUD: (*Studying her, not smiling.*) I reckon not.

GID: (*Coming back.*) Mossie, you seen my gun? (*To BRUD.*) It ain't in there.

MOSSIE: Didn't you loan it to Jackie to go deer hunting with?

GID: I was going to. But I don't think... (*To BRUD.*) Was they something you wanted with it, Brud?

BRUD: They's been some shooting.

GID: Shooting. Somebody get shot?

BRUD: Not some <u>body</u>. Some <u>thing</u>. <u>Things</u>. (*Glances at MOSSIE, speaks to GID.*) Can I talk to you?

GID: Mossie, why don't you make me and Brud some coffee.

MOSSIE: (*Crossing toward the other room.*) I'll put it on.

BRUD: Sit down.

(*MOSSIE exits. GID sits, begins to get apprehensive. The SHERIFF strides around him, letting a little silence and tension build. Then he stands upstage of GID and leans toward him looking serious and stern. GID squirms.*)

BRUD: Have you been shooting that thirty-thirty, say...in the past few days?

GID: No. No, I ain't.

BRUD: You didn't climb up the ridge last Friday and shoot four holes in them Uke tires up there?

GID: Lord, no. Why would I do a thing like that? I ain't fired that rifle in...since...aye gollies, I can't remember when I did shoot it last.

BRUD: Do you know how much them Uke tires costs?

GID: Say...

BRUD: What?

GID: I heard some shots last week when I was fishing.

BRUD: Along about quitting time?

GID: Yeah. I was talking with that girl, that...

BRUD: Ginny Buckner, that reporter?

GID: You know her?

BRUD: Yeah, we know her. (*GID turns sideways to study BRUD's face.*) She's a trouble maker. I think she's prob'bly a lesbian. You know, one of these-here liberated women types.

(*Pause. GID is trying to think things out, trying to determine which side he is on.*)

BRUD: Did you run into her up at the job?

GID: She come down to where I was fishing.

BRUD: What'd she talk about?

GID: Fishing. (*Laughs a forced laugh.*) She don't know nothing a'tall about trout.

BRUD: Where was Mossie all this time?

GID: Here at the house.

BRUD: Can you prove that? Was anybody with her?

GID: That girl. She went down and talked to her for a spell.

(*BRUD eases up, walks around, tries to establish a friendlier atmosphere.*)

BRUD: Is Mossie a pretty good shot?

GID: Shoot, she can shoot good as I can. But, wait a minute. You don't...you ain't accusing Mossie?

BRUD: I ain't accusing nobody. I'm just asking some friendly questions. Trying to be a good neighbor. See, them tires was shot with a thirty-thirty slug. You own a thirty-thirty. You live close to the job.

GID: (*Almost whining.*) It wasn't me, Sheriff.

BRUD: No, I don't think it was. (*Strides around for a minute, thinking, then approaches GID as before, trying to build tension. He speaks in as ugly and menacing tone as he can muster, searching GID's face to see if it betrays any guilt as he talks.*) But if you did do it... (*He lets the threat sink in.*) Four shots. Four Uke tires hit. Do you realize what it's gonna cost the company? One of them Uke tires was on a big cat, a 992-B. That tire sells for forty-one hundred shucks. There was a twenty-seven hundred dollar one, a twenty-nine hundred dollar one, and a thirty-two hundred dollar one.

GID: Lordy, lordy, lordy, what a waste.

BRUD: Them tires may not be wasted. They had spares for all but one of 'em. But they was leaking air.

GID: Oh, that's good. Why, it'd be a shame...

BRUD: (*Getting tougher.*) But do you realize what this son of a buck has done? Do you know how much trouble it is to change one of these-here big Uke tires? (*GID shakes his head, afraid to whisper.*) First, they have to jack up the machine, cribbage it, jack it, cribbage it, til they get it off the ground. That can take a hour. They have to break that front bead, Gid, with a hydraulic boom. (*BRUD is using his big hands to illustrate breaking a stick, his knuckles right next to GID's wide eyes.*) Then they push the tire back so you can get your bar in there and pop this little lock ring off...dig out the O ring, big rubber ring, pull that thing out and get the tire free in the front. They have to do the same thing from behind, til the tire lays loose on the rim. You know, kinda like a man's neck would lay, all limber like, if somebody was to break it.

GID: Whew!

(*GID is almost in a sweat. MOSSIE appears in the doorway, watches.*)

BRUD: Now the tire man takes that shot tire to Akron or Charlotte or somewhere to get it fixed. That can take a week. That down time kills us. It's like the cat peeing on the cash register. It runs into money.

GID: Lordy.

(*MOSSIE comes back in.*)

MOSSIE: Y'all ready for some coffee?

BRUD: I don't drink the stuff myself.

MOSSIE: I didn't make none, noway.

BRUD: I knowed you when you talked more like a woman oughtta talk.

MOSSIE: And I knowed you when you was just a snot-nosed kid.

BRUD: I'm a little bit bigger now, ain't I?

MOSSIE: Yeah, and so's your snot.

(*BRUD stares at her, but she doesn't blink. He breaks away, tries to force a smile.*)

BRUD: When you find that rifle, Gid, you let me know. I wanna look at it.

GID: I sure will. I know in reason it's around here some place, less'n I've loaned it to Jackie. It'll turn up.

BRUD: Let's hope so. (*Starts to exit, stops, speaks to MOSSIE.*) You might wish you'd a-took Mr. Billings' offer before this is all over.

MOSSIE: They're coming down Blackberry, ain't they?

GID: No, now, they ain't. They told me they wasn't. Right, Sheriff? You'as one of 'em that told me.

BRUD: Like Mossie says, Gid, you can't believe ever'thing you hear.

GID: I can't believe it.

BRUD: Fine. What in the hell would you do about it anyhow?

GID: Now, I ain't getting into it with you. We're neighbors. Far as the company goes, I think they're all good decent men. I know they'll treat us fair and square.

BRUD: (*To MOSSIE.*) You think you've seen mud?

MOSSIE: Is that a threat, Sheriff?

BRUD: Just talking about the weather, Ma'am.

GID: (*Lightly, trying to break the tension.*) Like they say, you can talk about the weather, but you can't do nothing about it.

BRUD: You got that right. (*He walks to the door, turns, his face set hard and serious.*) I wanna see that rifle.

(*BRUD exits. MOSSIE starts getting ready for bed. She unbuttons her blouse and walks into the other room. GID talks to her, but he is partly just talking to hear himself talk, as always, and partly to save face. He has lost some of his manhood, we sense, just as MOSSIE knows, but she still loves him for the man he used to be and the man she hopes someday to see again.*)

GID: He's sure got something stuck in his craw. I can't believe he's making all that fuss over a bunch of tires. Still and all they are expensive, I reckon. It's his job to try and find out who done it. As for you, Mossie Cochran, you wasn't none too neighborly. That coal company's done a lot for this country. A lotta people make their living up there. Mr. Billings is a God-fearing, upright Christian man. If anything goes wrong, if they damage one board on this house, you watch, Mr. Billings'll be the first'un to come and set it right.

(*MOSSIE comes back in dressed in a house coat and bedroom slippers. She speaks in a resigned tone, as if she didn't hear him.*)

MOSSIE: Better get ready for bed, Gid.

GID: He joined the First Baptist Church right down here at Ponder. Gave 'em ten thousand dollars to finish that new wing they'as building. He's a Christian. He got baptized.

MOSSIE: Mr. Billings won't worsh feet, testify, or nothing. He claimed he got saved, but I tell ye, he just walked up and shook hands with the preacher. That won't go. Far as I'm concerned he went in a dry sinner and come out a wet one.

GID: (*Taking off his shoes.*) Mossie, why don't ye just get this strip mining business out of your head. It's changing you.

MOSSIE: Will you stand with me, Gid? I need to know you're behind me.

GID: Sure, I'm behind you. But ain't nothing gonna happen.

(*GID walks over and sits by MOSSIE on the couch, takes her hand.*)

MOSSIE: But if it does.

GID: Here, now.

(*They sit a minute. He puts his arm around her shoulder and pulls her close. They sit in silence for a few seconds.*)

MOSSIE: All right, I'll try to put it out of my mind.

GID: That's my girl. (*He gives her a peck on the cheek, then leaves his head next to hers, staring with her into space.*) What ye thinking about?

MOSSIE: The first time we met at that square dance. You'as such a good dancer…made me feel like my feet was made out of cinder blocks.

GID: I thought you said I made you quiver, like a…what was it, a tuning fork?

MOSSIE: You did. But that was my insides. Just holding your hand. Like this.

(*GID takes his hand and lays MOSSIE's head on his shoulder. They look forward, as if staring into a fire. She is starting to feel the warmth of those old memories, finally speaks.*)

MOSSIE: What are you thinking about?

GID: Big Red. This rain's gonna fill up his hole, and he won't be able to see me.

MOSSIE: (*Breaking away, the dream shattered.*) Goodness gracious. I thought you'as getting romantic. I don't wanna hear no fish tales. Let's go to bed.

GID: Well, help me up. My arthur-ritis is coming back on me.

(*MOSSIE gets up and gives GID a hand, then walks into the bedroom. He follows, carrying his shoes in one hand, scratching his head with the other, yawning. Before he walks into the next room, he turns off the lights, leaving the living room in a dim glow. GID delivers the following speech during this business, from the time he gets up until he goes out.*)

GID: I'm going up there tomorrow, even if it's raining. I believe I've caught more fish while it was raining than any other time. Sometimes they'll hit it quicker than you can throw it out. Big Red is no dummy, Mossie. He's as smart as any human being I ever met. Smarter'n me, for sure. (*He sits on the side of the bed, drops his shoes, yawns, scratches, and lies beside MOSSIE.*) Ah, it sure is nice to lay down, ain't it.

MOSSIE: Gid.

GID: Uh-huh?

MOSSIE: I wish you still wanted me the way you do Big Red.

GID: Shut your mouth, woman. You know I do.

MOSSIE: Want me to rub your feet?

GID: No, I don't reckon. I'm too tired to turn around.

MOSSIE: Gid?

GID: Uh-huh?

MOSSIE: Ain't you gonna take your clothes off?

GID: I forgot. I'll take 'em off when I get up to go to the bathroom. Much as I been going lately, with my urinary infection, that won't be long.

MOSSIE: Gid? You really think it's gonna be all right?

GID: I know it is. Now, go to sleep. Ahhhhh, listen to that rain.

(*There is a long silence. GID snores. Then the silence is blasted open by a thunderous, board-splitting, glass-shattering crash. The living room wall and/or window splits open and we see a gigantic rock roll in.*)

MOSSIE: (*Shouting.*) Oh Lord!

GID: (*Also shouting.*) What in the world! What was it!

MOSSIE: Ohhhh, merciful Jesus! What happened? Turn on the light.

GID: I can't find it! Where in tarnation is it? There.

(*GID flicks on the lights. MOSSIE is trying to put on her housecoat. GID rushes to the edge of the living room, stops to stare in horror at the big rock sticking through the wall, glistening wet. The couch has been knocked away and turned over. GID doesn't enter the room, just stands staring.*)

GID: Good God-a-mighty!

MOSSIE: What is it?

GID: (*Approaching the rock cautiously, unbelieving.*) Looks like the south end of a elephant. Heading north. With no tail.

MOSSIE: (*Finally getting her house shoes on and her housecoat wrapped around her, entering.*) Good Lord in heaven! Look at our wall!

GID: Mister, that ain't no regular, ever'day road rock. That's a...that's a, a...

MOSSIE: Granddaddy.

GID: Yessir, you're right. He's a whopper. I bet that thing'd weigh...Lordy, ain't no telling how much it'd weigh.

MOSSIE: And look at the mud. Oh, Gid, our poor house. I got to get a mop bucket.

(*MOSSIE rushes out.*)

GID: Here, here, just calm down. I'll go see about it, soon as it's daylight. That won't be long, now. They'll fix it for us. (*Walking around it, shaking his head, speaking louder so MOSSIE can hear.*) I thought for a minute one of them un-specified flying objects'd hit us. You know, from outer space.

MOSSIE: (*Hurrying back with mop and bucket.*) I gotta get this water mopped up. And this mud. Look at this mud. It's oozing in all over the place. We gotta get this mud cleaned up, Gid. (*She begins mopping and wringing.*)

GID: Now, now, calm down. Can't do it all at onc't. 'Bout knocked me out of bed. Shook the whole house. I'd listen to the rain a while, then drop back off to sleep. Got up and went to the bathroom two times. Well, maybe three times. Hearing that rain makes you want to go. I was asleep, I know I was, when…Boom! I thought I'as dreaming. And when I looked in here and seen it, why, I didn't know what to think.

MOSSIE: (*Working feverishly, growing more angry and confused, frustrated.*) Goodness gracious, what a mess! Look at my curtains. (*The curtains are caught between the rock and the wall. MOSSIE begins pulling at them.*) Give me…give me my curtains. (*She pulls at them to no avail, finally lets them go and picks up the mop and starts to swing at the rock.*) Oh!……

GID: (*Grabbing MOSSIE, pulling her back.*) Here, Mossie, stop that! Ain't gonna do no good to hit it. (*MOSSIE fights to get loose and take a swing.*) Here-now. Stop it! Take a-holt. (*She gives up, drops the mop, goes to turn the couch back upright. GID helps her.*) Here, let me help ye. There. Now sit down. That thing's bigger'n you are. (*She sits and looks utterly dejected. GID sits and starts putting on his shoes.*) Well I never figured it'd happen. But now that it has it ain't nothing to worry about. It's done happened. I'll call the coal company in a little while. Then I'll go see the sheriff. They'll be out here 'fore you know it with a front end loader and pull that thing outta there. You put on the coffee pot. Ain't gonna do no good to sit here and watch it.

MOSSIE: We could be dead, Gid. If that thing'd a-hit our bedroom wall. I wish it had of.

GID: That ain't no way to talk. It ain't the end of the world.

MOSSIE: It is to me.

GID: Here-here. Perk up. Fix us some breakfast and then I'll head on. This old place'll be patched up good as new before you know it.

(*MOSSIE sits up straighter. Something has come to her mind. When she speaks, it is not with the same lifeless tone. There is a resolve in her.*)

MOSSIE: I'll not be here when ye come back.

GID: Huh?

MOSSIE: I'm going up the hill.

GID: What do you think you're gonna do?

MOSSIE: I don't know. But they'll know I'm up there. Comes a time when you got to do something, even if ye don't know what in the world it is. My time has come.

GID: They's no need to go crazy.

MOSSIE: Oh, come on, Gid. First I'll fix you some breakfast.

(*MOSSIE starts out.*)

GID: Then what?

MOSSIE: I don't know. Let's just wait and see.

(*MOSSIE exits, GID following after, shaking his head and muttering.*)

GID: Lordy, lordy, lordy.

(*The lights go down.*)

SCENE FIVE

The lights come up on SHERIFF BRUD SHELTON in his office. He sits at a desk, talking on the phone to the JUDGE. The voice of the JUDGE is heard live over the sound system. Even though the SHERIFF is in his element, feet on the desk, cocky in attitude, etc., he is still kowtowing to the JUDGE.

BRUD: That's right, Judge, he's on his way down here right now. I'll offer him the money and tell him exactly what you said. Only thing...he's all fired up to see you.

JUDGE: Tell him I'm busy. Hell, I am busy.

BRUD: I know you are, Judge.

JUDGE: Was he mad?

BRUD: Aw, you know Gid. I don't think he's capable of getting too mad.

JUDGE: Of course, Mossie may drive him to do something, and...now, there was a time Gid'd make you sit up and take notice.

BRUD: Ha-ha, really? Well, that was before my time. Ever since I've knowed him he's been strictly out to pasture. No backbone a'tall.

JUDGE: I don't think he'll give you any trouble.

BRUD: Naw.

JUDGE: But if he does, call me.

BRUD: Yes, sir, I will.

JUDGE: I'll talk to him, if I have to. I just don't want to see him.

BRUD: All right, sir, I'll handle it.

JUDGE: You're a good man, Sheriff. Thanks. I appreciate it.

BRUD: Uh, thank you.

JUDGE: Goodbye.

(*The JUDGE hangs up abruptly. BRUD looks at the phone, disappointed. But he is pleased overall, lets his chest swell, feeling like he is a very important cog in the machinery of the local power and justice. GID walks in. BRUD treats him like a child. GID is humble and patient, BRUD is impatient.*)

BRUD: Come in, Gid. I've talked to Mr. Billings, I've talked to the Judge, all of 'em. Now, they're real sorry this happened.

GID: I knowed they would be.

BRUD: Just let me tell you the way it is. I think it's fair. Ok. There's gonna be a dozer up there this afternoon. He'll take the rock out. If they's mud in the yard, and such, he'll do his best to push it back. The company's gonna give you a four hundred dollar cash settlement, if you'll take it now and go on your way. Fix it yourself.

GID: Four hundred?

BRUD: That's right.

GID: Uh, that don't seem, exactly...well, it ain't quite...just four hundred...

BRUD: Hey! You could sue 'em. You could go get you a real expensive lawyer. You could end up way in the hole. You want my advice, as a neighbor and a friend? Stick that damn money in your pocket and forget about it.

GID: Well, I'll go talk to the Judge.

BRUD: He's pretty busy today.

GID: Me and him's old friends. We went to grade school together. Course he's went on and got way up there.

BRUD: Yeah, I know y'all go way back. But, like I said, he's pretty busy today.

GID: Ah, he'll see me. I know in reason he will, so I'll just go on around there.

(*GID starts to exit. BRUD is irritated, angry.*)

BRUD: Now, just hold on, Gid! He don't have time to see you today. So I'll get him on the horn. That'll have to do, ok? (*Starts dialing the number.*)

GID: Well, I wanted to…but I reckon if he's that busy…

BRUD: The Judge is a damn busy man. Ok? Now, if you're smart you won't stand here all day, whining and jabbering.

JUDGE: Hello.

BRUD: Hello, Judge. I'm sure sorry to have to bother you, but they's somebody here that insists on talking to you.

JUDGE: Put him on.

BRUD: Yessir. (*Handing the phone to GID.*)

GID: Thank ye, Sheriff. I 'preciate it. Hello, Judge?

JUDGE: Yeah, Gid. Whata-ye-know?

GID: Well, it's about these damages, ye know, and the cash settlement.

JUDGE: Yeah, I'm sorry about that.

GID: I knowed you would be. Yessir, I'as just telling the sheriff…

JUDGE: (*Cutting him off, cooler in tone, very impatient, stern and catering now.*) Now, listen, Gid, like the sheriff said, stick that money in your pocket and be done with it. You can sue, but you may not have a case. Blackwell Consolidated Steel and Coal Company owns the rights to those minerals up there and they have a perfectly legal right to get them out. Rain is an act of God, Gid. Mr. Billings can't control the rain. Now, you get this thing into court, it's no holds barred. You get Silicosis money, right? Can you prove your lungs are damaged? No, you get it because the company doctor put in a good word for you. Mr. Billings told him to. You get things all stirred up, they might just take it away from you. Now, I know you for a reasonable man, so take my advice. Take the money. I've got a heavy docket today, Gid. It was nice talking to you.

(*The Judge hangs up. GID hears it, but speaks into the phone anyway.*)

GID: Thank ye, Judge. I… 'preciate it.

(*GID hands the phone to BRUD who cradles it, watching GID shake his head slowly and sadly and walk out of the office, disappointed and defeated. The lights go down.*)

SCENE SIX

GID walks into the living room and starts measuring the rock with retractable tape. He measures it across, up and down, writing the measurements on a piece of paper as he goes along. He is listless and hollow-eyed. Finally he gives up and sits on the couch staring out into space. GINNY runs to the door, knocks, but GID doesn't get up. Finally GID hears her second knock. He doesn't get up, just calls out.

GID: Come in.

GINNY: (*Extremely excited, talking a mile a minute.*) Gid! They've arrested Mossie!

GID: What? They done what?

GINNY: Took her to jail.

GID: Mossie?

GINNY: I got it on film. It was beautiful. What a story! She was magnificent. You would have been so proud of her, Gid. The sheriff was there, state troopers, coal company officials… everybody.

GID: The sheriff? But I was just with the sheriff two hours ago.

GINNY: It just now happened. I'm hitting the wire services with this one.

GID: They arrested Mossie?

GINNY: Carried her. They had to pick her up and carry her. She wouldn't budge. What a sight, what a beautiful sight…what a story!

GID: How come they carried her? She couldn't walk?

GINNY: (*Noticing the rock, shocked but also thrilled, taking out her camera.*) Oh my goodness! I can't believe this. When did this happen?

GID: Was she hurt?

GINNY: No wonder she went up there.

GID: How come they had to carry her?

GINNY: She laid down. Right in front of those big earth movers. Gid, what a woman you've got there. Listen, I've got to phone this story in. They sabotaged my jeep, took the spark plug wires loose, so I couldn't follow them to the jail house. I'll have to walk to a phone. But I'll be back. Tell Mossie I love her. Tell her I think she's beautiful.

GID: But…she's in jail.

GINNY: They won't keep her, I wouldn't think. I'm sure they'll book her and let her go. Well, I've got to run. Don't you worry.

(*GINNY dashes out the door. GID stares back into space again, unbelieving.*)

GID: Mossie's in jail. Is this the United States of America? (*He gets up.*) Maybe I'll go see about her. Well, no, Ginny says they'll be letting her out. I might miss 'em. (*Sits back down.*) What's a body supposed to do when their wife's in jail? (*Gets up.*) Reckon I'll just go fishing. No, that wouldn't look right, would it, me out there having fun while Mossie's… (*Sits, lets out a deep breath.*) I'll be John Brown if I know what to do. Mossie, I reckon your mind's just pine blank give out on ye. Female trouble. I know in reason it is. They's no understanding it. Makes 'em hop up all of a sudden and do crazy things. (*Stands up, pauses, shakes his head, sits back down, perplexed. He nods, then shakes his head, then nods again, as if carrying on an internal debate.*) Yessir, it's the mysteries. She's crazy. And crazy is as crazy does.

(*Within a few seconds BRUD brings MOSSIE to the door and steps inside with her. He has a harried look, like he's had it. MOSSIE has brown mud stains up and down her back-side. She has a sheepish look as she enters but we know her blood is up.*)

BRUD: Well, here she is. Ain't ye proud of her? Let me tell you something, Gid Cochran, you better start wearing the pants in this dang family. You keep her the hell away from me. Where's that reporter girl?

GID: She left. Went down the road.

BRUD: I got a John Doe warrant in my pocket. I see her and I'm gonna slap it on her. Put her nosey butt in jail. (*To MOSSIE.*) I hope she didn't have nothing to do with you doing what ye done. And you a grown woman. (*Shakes his head in disgust.*) All right, Gid, maybe you can keep her at home where she belongs.

(*BRUD stomps out. MOSSIE stands in place. GID sits, agitated, confused. At first we think he might rise and give her a hug. He seems to have that impulse. Then he stiffens and sulks, thinking of himself. He breaks the silence with a put-out, accusing voice.*)

GID: You went and done it, didn't ye? You've embarrassed the dickens out of me. I been running around all morning trying to fix things up. You been out tearing 'em down.

MOSSIE: I'm sorry, Gid. I had to.

GID: Have you gone plumb crazy?

MOSSIE: Hug me, Gid.

GID: I...

MOSSIE: I need ye to hold me. Tell me you're glad I'm back.

GID: I ain't in the mood for it.

(*MOSSIE sits meekly on the couch. GID gets up and walks around, almost as if he wants to keep a safe distance between him and MOSSIE.*)

GID: They're coming to take out the rock, push the mud away. I got a settlement with 'em. It wasn't much as I wanted, but I had to fight 'em for that. Four hundred dollars.

MOSSIE: That's all right.

GID: I talked to the sheriff. I talked to the Judge. I let 'em know I was pretty doggone mad about the whole business.

MOSSIE: That took nerve, Gid. I'm proud of ye.

GID: (*Sitting, sighing deeply.*) What do we do now?

MOSSIE: On the way up the hill today I passed by Angie's grave. That big rock knocked her headstone down, and gouged out a big rut. The water'd been washing down through it all night, til...oh, Gid, part of the casket was sticking out. I like to died when I saw it. (*The memory of it almost makes her cry.*) They're burying the living and uncovering the dead. They's no peace for nobody. I kneeled down there. I touched Angie's casket. I prayed to God to give me strength to get on up the hill. I didn't think I'd make it. But then, where I was weak, I was strong. Something jumped down in my legs and moved me on up. It was a power like I used to feel come into me when I held your hand dancing. I went fairly bouncing up that hill. I been that way all day...til I come back here and saw you. I was alive. I was strong, and I wasn't afraid.

GID: We'll have to go put the dirt back on Angie.

MOSSIE: Yes. I'll help ye. Then I'm going back up there.

GID: Where?

MOSSIE: To the strip job. They're still running.

GID: (*Getting as mad as he can get, jumping up and pointing a finger at MOSSIE. He has misread her attitude, her meekness, and it gives him extra courage and anger.*) And what do you think you're gonna do up there?

MOSSIE: What I did before. I'm gonna stop 'em.

GID: You ain't gonna do no sich-a-thing! You're gonna stay right here in this house. A woman's place is in the home, and by grabs, that's where you're staying. People ain't laughing at me no more. I've had it. I'm laying down the law.

MOSSIE: (*In utter contempt.*) Oh...hell's fire.

GID: And I don't wanna hear no more cussing. You ain't never cussed before. I don't like it.

MOSSIE: Gid, I'm going back up there and lay down in front o' them trucks.

GID: You ain't neither!

MOSSIE: Are you coming with me?

GID: No, I ain't a-coming, and you ain't a-going!

MOSSIE: How you gonna stop me?

GID: You're my wife, for goodness' sake. I'm your husband. You'll do like I tell ye.

MOSSIE: I been doing that too long.

GID: It's worked, up til now.

MOSSIE: It ain't worked, not for a long time. I ain't had a husband. I ain't got one now. I got a dried up old gourd, with a bunch of dried up seeds for brains, rattling around in a empty shell.

GID: I knowed ye didn't love me. There, that proves it!

MOSSIE: Huh, what I been doing for you takes <u>more'n</u> love. It takes blind devotion. Ever' now and then you toss a scrap my way...a little peck on the cheek. When is the last time you kissed me, really held me close and kissed me?

GID: It ain't always easy for a man.

MOSSIE: You used to have some pride. You used to dance. You heard the music. You said it was your own special music.

GID: I can still dance.

MOSSIE: Let's see. Show me. Get up and dance.

GID: Well, my arthur-ritis.

MOSSIE: You don't do nothing no more.

GID: I go fishing.

MOSSIE: It don't take no backbone to go fishing. You can rant and rave all you want to about catching Big Red, but to me it's give-up talk. When a little old fish is the only thing that gets a man excited, he's really retired. You bring home three or four little old six inch trout and hand 'em to me to clean for ye, like you'as the mighty fisherman coming home from the sea. I do all the work while you sit around and fart.

GID: I got the loose bowels, you know that. I have to fart. The doctor says it's dangerous to hold 'em back.

MOSSIE: You're a good farter, all right. But ain't it something when if somebody was to ask you what you do, the only honest thing you could say is, "I fish and I fart."

GID: Oh that's good, Mossie. You can always talk about somebody's personal habits when you can't think of any other way to get at 'em. I could do that too, if I wanted to. Your breath stinks. Do I complain about it? You eat ramps and onions til you smell like the bottom of a bait bucket. You snore. You grind your teeth.

MOSSIE: I'm going up the hill.

GID: You ain't.

MOSSIE: You coming with me?

GID: I'll not make a fool out of myself.

MOSSIE: Then get out of my way.

GID: (*One last stab at gaining control.*) Mossie! You stay in this house! I don't like you acting like this. I don't like nothing about it. You ain't the woman I married, and, by grabs, you keep acting like this and I may just up and try me a new one on for size. Your place is in this house, right here beside of your husband, and if you can't abide by that, I don't want you. You walk up that hill and far as I'm concerned you can keep on walking. You ain't mine no more. Do you hear that, woman?

MOSSIE: I see your lips moving, but I don't hear a lily-livered thing you say. I've felt good about myself today for the first time in fifteen years. The mountain give it to me, and I'm going back for a second helping. You'll not kick me out of this house. If you won't fight for it <u>you</u> can get out. I've put more sweat in it than you have. I've bore your young'uns and made do for 'em, I've worshed your clothes, I've cleaned and cooked and carried. And let me tell you something, Gideon, I didn't do it to keep walking behind a sorry man like you. I didn't do it to keep calling you Lord and master. I didn't do it so you could tell me to stay in my place because you ain't got the guts to walk up that hill with me. No, sir, your honor, I did it because I am a woman. And I'm proud. And from now on my place is anywhere I want to go. I'm gonna walk tall, or die trying. And I ain't gonna sit back and watch a bunch of strip miners try to bury ever'thing that I hold dear and precious. As long as their mud comes down the hill, I'll be going up. If you're not coming with me, then get out of my way and walk behind me for a change.

(*GID stands looking dumbfounded as MOSSIE exits, walking proud and full of purpose. The lights go down.*)

ACT TWO

SCENE ONE

A week later. GID's MUSIC, the banjo tune, begins just as it did at the beginning of the play. It builds toward a full rhythmic statement, but does not reach the final phase that includes guitars. As the lights come up on stage the music fades and we hear the chirping and calling of birds. The rock is gone, and the wall has been repaired and looks as good as it did before. GID is on the couch sleeping in his clothes, with a bit of a light blanket over him, most of the rest of it on the floor. He is barefoot. He has a rumpled look, a three day beard. He raises up part way, groans, scratches, looks around for his shoes, then decides to try and make it all the way up to a sitting position. The noise of the birds begins to get to him. He looks back over his shoulder without turning, as if he has a stiff neck, yells at the birds.

GID: Shut up! Noisy little die-dappers.

(*GID makes a big issue of reaching for his shoes, putting on his socks, then his shoes, devising ways to make this normally simple task look absolutely near-to-impossible to accomplish. If he weren't groaning and huffing and puffing so much it would pass for a comedy routine. The birds, having died down a bit during all this, now increase in volume. He yells again.*)

GID: Shut up, I tell ye! Oh, my back. I guess the rain put 'em behind in their work. My arthur-ritis is giving me a fit. Shut up! Little prissy, perky devils. They think because they feel good ever' body else ought to. Well, some of us got better things to do than jabber and complain. Ohhhh, my fingers ache, my head hurts, my neck's stiff, my joints feel achy and rusty. Shut up! Join the union!

(*MOSSIE enters, obviously well rested and well groomed. She walks with a spring in her step, as perky as the birds. She sips from a coffee cup and smiles.*)

MOSSIE: Gid, what in the world are you yelling about?

GID: Them gol danged, jabber-beaked, screechy squawky birds out there.

MOSSIE: You never complained about 'em before.

GID: Never heard 'em before. Little sickly feathered devils. They oughtta organize, if they got a complaint, vote 'em in a John L. Lewis, let him squawk for 'em.

MOSSIE: Here's you a cup of coffee. (*Sets it down by him.*)

GID: I ain't speaking to you.

MOSSIE: You want some breakfast?

GID: No, I'll eat down at the boarding house, like I been doing.

MOSSIE: The food's good there, is it?

GID: It's fine. They set it out, I pay for it, I don't have to put up with no sass while I'm eating it.

MOSSIE: What'll ye do when the money gives out?

GID: I ain't talking. Got nothing to say to you, not after the way you struck me down.

MOSSIE: You and Jackie done a bang-up job on this wall, Gid. Why, I can't hardly tell it was hurt.

GID: (*Looking at his fingers, bending them.*) That hammering played hob on my fingers.

MOSSIE: Oh, that'll be good for 'em. They're sore 'cause you ain't used 'em for a long time. My doctor told me, "Mossie, if ye can move it, exercising will help it."

GID: Seems to work better on your jaw than it does my fingers.

MOSSIE: If you won't eat my cooking, is they anything else you want me to do? Want me to lay out some clean clothes for ye?

GID: Just leave me alone. I can get by by myself. You talk like nothing's happened around here. I tell ye, I ain't talking to a wife that's acted like you have. It ain't no kind of a marriage.

MOSSIE: We oughtta started talking a long time ago.

GID: Harsh, mean words? I'd druther not hear 'em.

MOSSIE: They're better'n no words at'all. Marriage ain't some kind of a thing you put up here on a pedestal, Gid. It's fussing and fighting, talking things out.

GID: I don't like fussing and fighting. Marriage ought to be calm and steady as ye go.

MOSSIE: I don't believe a word of it.

GID: Ye know it all, don't ye? Walking up that mountain's made you a regular know it all.

MOSSIE: I know one thing. You Cochrans know how to nurse a grudge.

GID: You going out today?

MOSSIE: You mean, up yonder? I might, if the notion strikes me.

GID: The sheriff warned ye. He said number three would be it. He wouldn't let ye out.

MOSSIE: The third time's a charm, I always heard. (*She walks back by the window.*) I don't know what I'll do. Got to hang my curtains back up; fix up some. Go buy some more salt.

GID: Salt?

MOSSIE: I'm a-hoarding it up. The Judge may not get a garden this year beside his big old fancy house.

GID: Why's that?

MOSSIE: I figure on slinging a little salt on it.

GID: 'Pears to me the Cochrans ain't the only ones that hold grudges.

MOSSIE: They've declared war on us, Gid. I aim to fight back. That Judge. Giving us four hundred dollars to do a thousand dollar job with.

GID: I still say Mr. Billings'll make it right.

MOSSIE: Huh! They's a lot for sale, right next to the Judge's house. I wish we could afford to buy it.

GID: Are you crazy? That's where rich people live.

(*GINNY comes to the door and knocks. She, too, looks fresh and in high spirits. She is dressed in a new outfit and this time she carries a small cassette tape recorder.*)

MOSSIE: I'll get it. Why, hello here!

GINNY: Good morning, Mossie.

MOSSIE: Come in, Ginny. My, don't you look fresh as a daisy.

GINNY: Good morning, Gid.

GID: Morning.

MOSSIE: You're out bright and early.

GINY: I couldn't wait to tell you the news.

MOSSIE: Well?

GINNY: I got arrested too!

MOSSIE: You didn't!

GINNY: Isn't it wonderful? I'm not a virgin anymore. I'm a veteran. All the wire services picked up our story, and they used my pictures.

MOSSIE: I bet that made the sheriff happy.

GINNY: Oh, let me tell you, I thought he'd die. What really got him was when I refused to be served a John Doe warrant. I said, make it a Jane Doe warrant and I'll come along. That's when he picked me up and carried me. He cursed, called me a lesbian, a woman's libber, everything he could think of.

MOSSIE: How long did he keep you in jail?

GINNY: Until my editor came and posted bond. Oh, and look. It's brand new. I can record our interviews now for posterity. Say something, Gid. (*She turns it on.*)

GID: What you want me to say?

GINNY: What are you doing today?

GID: Going fishing.

GINNY: Ok, that's good. Listen to this. (*Rewinds it quickly, plays it.*)

MOSSIE: Welllll, ain't that a dandy.

GINNY: It's got a built-in mike. You can set it anywhere in the room and it'll pick you up.

MOSSIE: Is that right? Well, I never.

GID: Good Lord, it's getting worse in here than all them birds outside.

(*GID leaves to make his gather for fishing.*)

GINNY: Mossie, the networks are really interested in what's happening here. They've got their eye on us. My editor told me the Governor's office called.

MOSSIE: The governor?

GINNY: He's been trying to get a tougher strip mining bill through the legislature, but the strippers have a powerful lobby.

MOSSIE: I don't know nothing about all that.

GINNY: You know what's right. What makes you sick is when the law turns its back. The fines the companies pay are so...inadequate, they just pay them and go on their merry way.

MOSSIE: Laughing, I betche.

GINNY: It's peanuts to them.

MOSSIE: Don't seem right. But what can ye do? What *can* you do?

GINNY: What you're doing, Mossie. If this gets any publicity at all, you'll be a symbol.

(*BRUD appears at the door as GID comes back in with his fishing gear. He also holds his tennis shoes. BRUD knocks, looking to be in a bad mood, impatient.*)

GID: Somebody's at the door.

(*GID expects one of them to open the door, since he has his hands full.*)

MOSSIE: Well, open it up.

GINNY: It might lead to improvements, better laws. You'll be famous.

MOSSIE: I don't care about that. I want to save my house.

(*The SHERIFF knocks again. GID sees that the girls are not going to, so he drops his gear, shakes his head and mutters as he opens the door.*)

GID: Oh! Sheriff.

(*BRUD strides by GID as if he weren't there. GINNY is just placing her tape recorder on the small table and, seeing the SHERIFF, she turns it on "Record" and leaves it lying.*)

BRUD: Well, well, the gang's all here.

(*The ladies don't bother to reply. BRUD stalks around, letting his presence be felt before speaking. GID seems to get a little nervous. The SHERIFF has business with GINNY, but knows it will keep. He zeros in on GID.*)

BRUD: Going fishing?

(*GID nods.*)

BRUD: Wish that's all I had to do. (*Pause.*) Jackie says you didn't loan him the rifle. Where is it?

GID: He said that?

BRUD: That's what I said, wasn't it?

GID: Yeah, well, I...

BRUD: I wanna see that rifle! (*He walks over and picks up the rod and reel.*) Gonna slay 'em, huh? (*Points the tip of the rod toward GID as if measuring him for a fencing thrust.*) Water's kinda muddy, ain't it?

GID: It won't hurt the big ones.

BRUD: Like your famous Big Red? One of them tires was ruined. A four thousand dollar one. The other three come to about a thousand smackers in repair bills. It all adds up about what this house is worth, wouldn't you say? Seven thousand?

GID: We only give thirty-five for it. But we've fixed it up some. And in twelve years it's, what ye call it, growed in....it's...

GINNY: Appreciated.

GID: Yeah, that's right.

BRUD: Mr. Billings is willing to go twelve on this place, if you'll sell and get the hell out of his way. Twelve thousand simoles.

MOSSIE: Most of the sheriffs I know get paid for sheriffing, not running around acting like real estate agents.

BRUD: Mossie, you don't know crap from snappy cheese. Well, what do you say, Gid? It's a hell of a deal. Twelve big ones. Huh?

MOSSIE: No.

GID: Sounds fair to me.

MOSSIE: We won't sell!

GID: Why, you just said the other day, that if they...

MOSSIE: No, Gideon. (*She glares at him for almost betraying their secret.*)

BRUD: What was she saying the other day?

MOSSIE: I said we'd never sell this place. Never.

BRUD: (*Smells a fish, smiles.*) What do you say, Gid?

GID: I'm willing to sell.

MOSSIE: My name is on that deed too.

GID: We could sell it and split her down the middle.

BRUD: (*To MOSSIE.*) Well?

MOSSIE: No, that ain't a fair price. That's highway robbery.

BRUD: Gid, you may never get another offer like this one.

MOSSIE: What kind of a place could we buy for twelve thousand dollars? Just tell me.

GID: Well, Sheriff, you got my answer and you got hers. I'm going fishing.

BRUD: I'll tell Mr. Billings what you said. He'll appreciate it. You know he's all tore up over what's happened here.

(*GID exits with all his gear.*)

MOSSIE: Mr. Billings is all tore up. Brud Shelton, you can go to hell for lying the same as stealing.

BRUD: (*To GINNY.*) They told me you come up this way. I got people watching you, Miss Priss. I got just one word of advice for you. Be careful.

GINNY: Is that a threat, Sheriff?

BRUD: We don't like outsiders nosing around, trespassing, printing lies about us. You're a communist and a damn lesbo.

GINNY: Spoken like a true American.

BRUD: And you oughtta be ashamed for using that poor old woman, just to put a feather in your own hat. Filling her head full of this female liberation crap. Besides that, you just might get her killed.

GINNY: Oh? In the line of duty, I suppose, while you're upholding the law.

BRUD: I ain't gonna do nothing to her.

MOSSIE: If you plan on waiting for me to die of a broken heart, I got news for you.

BRUD: Accidents happen. One of them trucks you're laying down in front of might not see you. Just be a little old greasy spot left of Mossie Cochran.

MOSSIE: That kind o' talk don't scare me, feller, you oughtta know that. And it won't make me give up. Now, we're fixing to sit down and have some coffee. And since you don't touch the stuff, I'll thank ye to leave us alone.

BRUD: That's real hospitality now, ain't it?

MOSSIE: If you got a warrant, serve it. If you ain't, just get out!

BRUD: You're a hard case, Mossie. Maybe you and Miss Priss there deserve each other. She's already butch and looks to me like you're catching up with her pretty quick.

MOSSIE: Get!

BRUD: Be careful. Both of you.

(*BRUD exits. GINNY jumps up and down for joy, clapping her hands, excited and pleased.*)

GINNY: Mossie, we got that on tape. You were great.

MOSSIE: (*Sitting down.*) I don't feel so great. I ain't used to talking to people that-a-way.

GINNY: Men like Brud Shelton deserve it. And it's the only language they understand.

MOSSIE: Makes me nervous. My insides get all quivery-quavery.

GINNY: You're a fighter, Mossie.

MOSSIE: No, I ain't. It don't come natural.

GINNY: But you're doing it.

MOSSIE: I know what I'm fighting for. But what about you?

GINNY: I don't know. I want to be....I don't want to be held back because I'm a woman.

MOSSIE: Don't appear to me like nobody's holding you back.

GINNY: You'd be surprised. It's a man's world out there, Mossie. They get better pay, more promotions, better...But, that's another story.

MOSSIE: How about some more coffee?

GINNY: All right. Please.

(*MOSSIE goes to the next room.*)

GINNY: I'll rewind the tape. (*Imitating the sheriff as she rewinds the tape.*) "Well, how about it, Gid? Mr. Billings is willing to go twelve big ones on this place, if you'll sell and get the hell out!" The sheriff does have a way with words.

(*MOSSIE returns with the coffee.*)

GINNY: Mossie, what if the sheriff had said twenty thousand? Or forty? Could you really sell this place?

MOSSIE: That's for me to know and them to find out.

(*GINNY drops the line of questioning, fiddles with the tape machine. MOSSIE thinks a minute.*)

MOSSIE: Seems to me it takes a little gumption to do what you're doing, Ginny. I think <u>you're</u> the fighter, not me.

GINNY: Oh, not really. I'm just trying to prove I can do a job, I suppose. I don't know, but I don't <u>think</u> I like to fight, either.

MOSSIE: It don't pleasure me none to fight Gid.

GINNY: What are you going to say when the network people put you on TV?

(*The mood brightens. GINNY puts down her coffee cup, makes a square with her fingers and squints through it, pretending to be a movie director looking through the frame at MOSSIE. Then she picks up an imaginary mike and steps in front of the camera, announces.*)

GINNY: Ginny Buckner here, reporting from Blackberry Ridge, where Mossie Cochran rises daily to wage her one-woman fight against the strippers. We're going to hear from the lady herself, to see what words of wisdom she has to pass on to you folks out there in tv land.

(*MOSSIE is a little embarrassed when GINNY kneels in front of her and points the mike at her, shakes her head.*)

GINNY: Go on, Mossie. Say something.

(*MOSSIE starts to speak, blushes, stops, GINNY encourages her, so she does it, self-conscious at first, but game enough to rise to the occasion. She is slowly drawn out of herself and seems to enjoy it as she gets into it.*)

MOSSIE: My fellow Americans. Uh...Abraham Lincoln freed the slaves. John L. Lewis freed the coal miner. And Ginny Buckner, that great... (*Gets tickled at what is coming.*) that great communist lesbo from Kentucky...has freed all of us women. And today, my fellow Americans, I am running for president. I think it's time we had a woman in the White House. (*She jumps up and gestures.*) As your president, I promise you this: all roads will be downhill. Kids will have free ice cream. Women can walk in front of men. Or at least side by side. It won't never rain on Sundays, and...I'm running out of things to say.

GINNY: That was great, Mossie.

MOSSIE: My goodness, what if somebody'd a-walked in!

GINNY: I thought it was fun. (*They sober up a little.*) We're making fun of this whole thing but you know something? You be careful, Mossie. What the sheriff's been saying...he means it. They're liable to hurt you.

MOSSIE: I ain't afraid. Well, I am too, but I ain't running.

GINNY: Let's face it, if we weren't women they might not be so patient. What I didn't tell you about the Big Balsam job. My uncle Jake worked there. Jake Buckner.

MOSSIE: As a miner?

GINNY: Yes.

MOSSIE: A strip miner?

GINNY: No, Uncle Jake worked under ground. He was my favorite uncle. Dad never had much time, but Uncle Jake...well, all he had was time. He had two horses and we'd ride for hours. Uncle Jake loved nature. Woods, hills. Except he never called them just hills. They were always his beloved hills.

MOSSIE: What happened to him?

GINNY: Well...

MOSSIE: You don't have to tell me, if you don't want to.

GINNY: Uncle Jake never spoke out against stripping. It wasn't his way to protest. But one day he had to take a machine part to the strip job, and while he was there some company officials were showing this Japanese coal buyer around...giving him the grand tour, you know. As the Japanese man stood watching the machines at work, he turned to Uncle Jake and spoke to him. He said, "Operations like this would never be allowed in Japan. We have too much love for the beauty of the land." Something snapped. Uncle Jake hit that man. They grabbed him, thought he'd gone crazy. After that Uncle Jake began to speak out against strip mining. One night they beat him up. He went to work with his face all swollen, black and blue, and people pretended not to notice.

MOSSIE: What happened? Did he keep fighting?

GINNY: He wanted to. But the Judge put out a hit on him. I know he did. Pretty soon they were talking out loud about shipping him out of the country in a wooden overcoat...you know, a pine box. He was afraid for his wife and kids. He left.

MOSSIE: Where'd he go?

GINNY: Long Island, New York. He walks by the shore, says he loves it. But, Oh Mossie, he'll never love it there. His heart is in the hills. He loves these mountains. And now he's... (*Almost crying.*) Oh, hell, look at me.

MOSSIE: Here-here. Ain't nothing to be ashamed of.

GINNY: They play hard ball, Mossie. You be careful.

MOSSIE: <u>You</u> be careful. You're the young one. They don't want none of my old elephant hide. But, hey, turn on the sheriff there. Let's see what you got.

(*GINNY rewinds the tape for a second, stops it, pushes the play button and we hear some of the playback as the lights go down.*)

SCENE TWO

The lights come up on GID approaching his fishing hole. He has a quizzical look that turns to a scowl as he walks up the creek. He looks at the water and shakes his head, worried, but not sure why.

GID: I don't like the looks of it. Too many dead fish. The water's muddy, but it ain't that muddy. I never thought I'd live to see it. Strip mining, right down Blackberry. After they told me they wasn't coming, too.

(*He steps forward and goes into his crouch, floats his line out and begins humming.*) All right, Big Red, you old fighter. Come and get it. The world's gone crazy, 'cept for me and you. How 'bout a little lunch. I know they ain't hurt you none. Take a lot more'n muddy water to kill your red speckled butt. The little ones... they're something else. (*He tosses out several times as he talks. Finally he gives up and reels in.*) Ah, heck. You ain't coming up today. I can feel it. (*He tosses his reel aside and just sits and looks absent mindedly into the water, his chin resting on his arms.*) Shucks.

(*He daydreams for a while, looking into the water and seeing nothing. Then his eyes focus on something deep in the pool of water.*) Huh? (*He leans this way and that, looking for a better view to avoid the glare on the water. Then he walks around the pool, staring down. He is heartsick at what he thinks he sees.*) Oh, no. Oh, no. (*He uses his rod to reach down into the water and confirm his suspicions.*) Oh, Lordy, Big Red. You've let 'em get you. (*He breathes hard, getting very worked up and emotional. He gets the fish to the surface and manages to tow it with the tip of his rod to the bushes. He drops the rod and picks up the fish. His breath comes in and out noisily, and he grits his teeth as he holds the fish and looks at it. Then he lowers the fish and looks in anger and outrage up the mountain. He is beside himself. Presently his anger turns to sorrow. He sits down and wipes across his eyes with the back of his hand.*) I'm sorry, buddy. (*He places the fish gently at his feet. He is crying inside.*) I'm just...awful damn sorry.

(*He gathers his gear and starts to walk sadly away, shaking his head. He stops. He turns and looks back at Big Red, a question beginning to form in his face. He drops his gear and reaches into his pocket, pulls out a knife. He walks back, picks up the fish and cuts it open, looks inside.*) Well, I'll be jumped up. You fighting son of a buck. You was a woman! (*He takes Big Red with him, picks up all his gear and exits as the lights go down.*)

SCENE THREE

Soon thereafter. As the lights come up MOSSIE is standing on a chair fixing her curtains. She gets down, pulls at the curtains to straighten and get them to hang to suit her, then moves the chair out of the way. GID enters. He walks to his chair and plops down in a sorrowful daze. MOSSIE notices and starts to say something, decides against it, waits.

GID: I just buried Big Red.

MOSSIE: Aw, Gid.

GID: Yep, I buried her.

MOSSIE: Her?

GID: Big Red was a female. I never would o' believed it.

MOSSIE: The creek was...?

GID: Polluted, I reckon. Must be something draining down from that job up there. I wish they hadn't a-come down Blackberry, Mossie. They told me they wasn't going to.

MOSSIE: Why don't I get ye some coffee.

GID: I need a drink.

MOSSIE: Gid, are you all right? You want a drink...in the middle of the day? The doctor said it was bad for you urinary track. You want a drink?

GID: Yeah, I do.

MOSSIE: Of whiskey?

GID: Please. Straight.

MOSSIE: We ain't got none.

GID: Ah, well. (*Pause.*) They got Big Red. What a fish.

MOSSIE: Why don't I run down to John Henderson's and see if he's got a drink. I know he'd let you have it.

GID: No, wait a minute.

> (*GID walks to the table, moves it, moves the rug, gets a hammer and returns to pry the board loose, in the floor. MOSSIE watches in fascination and anxiety as GID feels around in the space under the floor and produces a bottle of Old Crow, about a third full.*)

GID: Ah, ha!

MOSSIE: Well, I'll be durned.

GID: I'll have me that drink after all.

MOSSIE: I'll fix it.

> (*MOSSIE takes the bottle and heads for the kitchen, glancing curiously back over her shoulder.*)

GID: Huh, what's this?

> (*GID takes out the rifle and carefully unwraps it, gets a knowing look on his face as MOSSIE returns. He smiles at her.*)

GID: So it was you? (*MOSSIE nods sheepishly.*) Good. I told 'em you could shoot better'n me.

MOSSIE: (*Handing him the drink.*) I didn't know you knew about that board.

GID: I didn't know you did. Well, here's to Big Red. (*Tosses a drink down, sets down the glass and rewraps the rifle, lays it back to rest under the floor. Then he replaces the board, the rug and the lamp, and finishes off the glass.*) Can I have another?

MOSSIE: What about your urinary track?

GID: Piss on it.

MOSSIE: Doctor said it was bad for your tubes.

GID: I'll get me another doctor. (*MOSSIE takes the glass.*) Put a ice cube in it. And some water this time. Please. Wanna have one with me? (*She just grimaces at him.*) I don't know as I've ever seen you take a drink, Mossie.

MOSSIE: You ain't going to neither. But I'll get you one.

> (*MOSSIE exits. We hear some of the BANJO MUSIC, just a touch, but enough to make GID stop and listen. He acts like he wants to start dancing with it but it is over too soon. MOSSIE comes back.*)

GID: Big Red. She was a hell of a fighter. Just like you, Mossie. (*Swallows some of the drink.*) You're a hell of a fighter too.

MOSSIE: Awww.

GID: And me? I'm a regular milk sop, if they ever was one. I lied about fighting the sheriff and the Judge for that four hundred. They tossed it to me like a bone to a dog, and I jumped all over it.

MOSSIE: You went to see 'em.

GID: They backed me down.

MOSSIE: You believed in 'em, Gid.

GID: You don't have to take up for me.

MOSSIE: You're being too hard on yourself.

GID: Not as hard as I was on you.

MOSSIE: Gid.

GID: I ain't even got the guts to tell you I'm sorry.

MOSSIE: You don't have to.

GID: Or you'as right about that marriage business.

MOSSIE: Hush, now.

GID: Am I getting drunk? I must be. Maybe if I have a couple more I'll get up the nerve to go bust Brud Shelton one in the snot box. Huh. That'll be the day. If I done that, he'd hit me back, and the trouble with getting hit back is, it hurts.

MOSSIE: Ever'body can't be brave.

GID: (*Snapping.*) Why can't they?

MOSSIE: I mean...

GID: You said exactly what you mean. You're right. I am a coward. I been one all my life. Get me a drink.

MOSSIE: Sure

(*He downs the rest of the glass.*)

GID: Bring me the bottle.

(*MOSSIE goes for it quickly. He continues to talk, and she comes back during the speech.*)

GID: There's a old folk song...daddy used to sing it. Sam Hall, it's called, and I've always loved that old song, but I didn't have the guts to even sing it, let alone be like Sam Hall. Here they was getting ready to hang him, and he's telling 'em where to go.

(*GID takes the bottle from MOSSIE, pours and has another drink. He is getting a little buzz on, just enough to loosen him up.*)

MOSSIE: Sing it, Gid.

GID: Nah.

MOSSIE: Come on, sing it.

GID: (*Singing.*) Oh my name is Sam Hall, it is Sam Hall
Oh my name is Sam Hall, it is Sam Hall
My name is Sam Hall and I hate you one and all
I hate you one and all...........Damn your eyes

(*Speaking.*) I love that song. That's the way I feel sometimes, but I can't never say it. That's the way I feel about them up there, for killing Big Red. I felt that way about you last week, too.

MOSSIE: You should a-said it. I told ye what I thought.

GID: I say ye did. My ears are still burning.

MOSSIE: But that was last week. This week I love you.

GID: Ye do? Milksop, coward and all?

MOSSIE: (*Sitting by him, putting her arms around him.*) Coward, hero, good, bad. Ain't much difference in 'em. You don't have to prove nothing to me. I love you just the way you are.

(*GID squirms, finally lets out a big howl. He pushes her away.*)

GID: No! Get offa me. Get away. I don't want your pity.

MOSSIE: It ain't...it's...

GID: One day you're telling me you can't stand me. The next day you're falling all over me with your....pity, and calling it love. It ain't. I <u>am</u> a coward. But I'm gonna change. Leastways, I'm gonna try. You might have to help me.

MOSSIE: All right, Gid.

GID: I'm going up that mountain. Lordy, I don't know how I'll do it. But I'd like to give her a try.

MOSSIE: You can, Gid.

GID: I need a drink.

MOSSIE: I do too. You're ahead of me.

(*MOSSIE pours herself a drink. GID declines.*)

GID: No, no, I think I need some coffee.

MOSSIE: (*Drinking.*) Oooooo, that's hot as fire. I'll put the pot on for you.

GID: Put the washtub on. I need a lot of it, 'cause I'm going up the mountain. Today.

MOSSIE: Oh, Gid, you can do it. I'll drink to it, cause I know you can do it. (*Drinks, shivers, smiles.*)

GID: You better hurry and make that coffee. I'm liable to back out any minute.

MOSSIE: You want honey or sugar in it?

GID: Put black strap molasses in it. Sticks to your ribs.

MOSSIE: (*Starting to exit, stopping, getting a flash of inspiration.*) Wait, Gid, I've got it! Oh, Lordy, this is good. Guns make noise, right? But molasses don't make no noise.

GID: Don't make sense, neither.

MOSSIE: We pour it in their gas tanks. Shut down ever' durn machine up there. Maybe for good. Gid, they won't know it's in there til the engines start gumming up. That stuff'll be all through 'em, the carburetors, the blocks....froze stiff.

GID: We could use honey and sugar, too.

MOSSIE: Gid, bless your sweet old hillbilly heart. You've come up with a good one this time.

GID: You thought of it.

MOSSIE: The bottle give it to me. Maybe there's something to this daytime drinking, after all.

GID: Coffee, Mossie! My knees are turning to jelly. If we're going up the mountain, we better get to it.

MOSSIE: I'll get the coffee. You get the molasses.

(*GID's MUSIC begins to play as they scurry about. The lights go down.*)

SCENE FOUR

The MUSIC continues to play as the lights come up on BRUD in the Sheriff's office. It is early next morning. BRUD stands looking into a small imaginary mirror to one side of his telephone, so that he is looking straight out at the audience. He is trying to put a patch on his black and blue nose, measures it for size, then lowers it to cut it with scissors. Then he cuts strips of adhesive tape, attaches them to the gauze and tries to make them stick to his nose. When he presses the tape to his nose it is painful. He grimaces. SHERIFF BRUD SHELTON is definitely in a fowl mood. After all this gauze and tape business, the MUSIC is faded back to nothing.

BRUD: What a schnowzer. Looks like a damn red-black-and-blue pickle. (*Looks toward the jail.*) Little dried up fart. One lucky damn punch. (*Holds the gauze in place, seeing how it looks.*) That looks worse than the pickle! (*Yells at GID back in the jail.*) You son of a weasly-eyed coward! (*Muttering to himself.*) Them back there sleeping like babies. I oughtta go wake 'em up. Almost daylight anyway.

(*He studies the nose without the gauze.*) Ah, I can't go 'round like that. Cover that ugly thing up. (*He begins taping it into place.*) You're a fine sight, Brud Shelton. And one dumb booger. You had the light; he had the can of molasses. Ouch! (*Replying to what he has just said, as if he were two people carrying on a conversation.*) Well, how was I to know he was gonna toss me the can? How did I know his little tinker toy fist was heading for my nose at the same time? Ooooooooo. (*Makes a face full of pain.*) You didn't have to catch the can, like it was a egg you didn't want to see get broke. You coulda punched him in the kisser, 'stead of letting the deputies pull him off of you and do it for you. He's gonna be strutting around like a banty rooster, while you…wear this…first aid kit on your nose, like a little white flag of stupidity.

How's that look? (*Steps back, looking from different angles.*) Fine. Beautiful. Best looking sheriff in the U.S. of A.

Hell, I am gonna wake 'em up. What they think this is, some kinda resort hotel? (*He picks up a metal waste basket, walks back to the jail banging it with his night stick.*) Ok, ok, time to wake up. Off your cans and on your feet. Rise and shine.

(*MOSSIE and GID raise up slowly behind the bars of their tiny cell. They respond very sleepily. GID looks bad, banged up with cuts and bruises, and he can hardly move.*)

MOSSIE: What in the world?

GID: Ohhhhh, Lord, I'm dead. What is it?

BRUD: Wake up in there, you two. Almost time for breakfast.

GID: What time is it?

MOSSIE: I don't know. When is breakfast, Sheriff?

BRUD: Eight-thirty sharp.

GID: Ohhhhh, Lord.

(*GID lies back down. BRUD beats on the wastebasket again to torment him.*)

BRUD: Here-here! Sit back up there!

GID: Ohhhhhh, my head. Stop making all that noise.

BRUD: Got a little headache this morning?

MOSSIE: No, his head feels fine. Don't it, Gid?

GID: Huh? My Lord, no, it's about to come off.

MOSSIE: He feels good, Sheriff. How's your nose?

BRUD: Not a scratch on it. Feels great.

MOSSIE: How come you got it gift wrapped, then? You know what hurts about Gid? His fist.

GID: By golly, you're right, Mossie. I think I got a busted knuckle.

BRUD: No harder'n you hit! Hell. Well, you two love birds have fun. We'll get you a good luke-warm breakfast in here in about three hours.

(*BRUD walks back to his chair, sits and unfolds the paper. Lights stay up on both areas.*)

MOSSIE: That low-life scab.

GID: I need to go back to sleep, Mossie.

MOSSIE: No, you ain't. You sit up here. We'll not be outdone.

GID: I need some coffee.

MOSSIE: Hey, Sheriff, bring us some coffee!

(*BRUD hears, smiles, goes on reading.*)

MOSSIE: Come on, Gid. Let's let him know we're back here. Coffee, coffee, we want coffee! Coffee, coffee, we want coffee!

GID and MOSSIE: Coffee, coffee, we want coffee. Coffee, coffee, we want coffee.

GID: I ain't got the energy for this. I'm going back to sleep.

MOSSIE: Let's sing a song.

GID: At six in the morning?

MOSSIE: For the sheriff. Let's sing one for him.
(*Singing.*) Write me a letter, sent it my mail
Send it in care of the Birmingham jail

(*Speaking.*) No, the Blackberry jail. Come on, Gid.

GID and MOSSIE: (*Singing.*)
Blackberry jail, love, Blackberry jail
Send it in care of the Blackberry jail

(*Lights go down on the jail and their song tapers off. GINNY enters. BRUD folds his paper, an evil grin appearing.*)

BRUD: Well, hello there.

GINNY: Can I see the prisoners?

BRUD: I thought I ran you off last night.

GINNY: You did, while your brave deputies were beating up Gid. Can I see them?

BRUD: No, I'm busy. Come back after breakfast.

GINNY: Are they all right?

BRUD: Just go on and mind your own business.

GINNY: You ought to treat me a little nicer, you know.

BRUD: How's that?

GINNY: I might put you on television. (*GID stares at her, eyebrows raised.*) That's right. I called the story in last night. All three networks are coming. Today.

BRUD: Oh, yeah. So is President Nixon.

GINNY: You don't believe me. (*GID squints at her.*) Can I ask you a question? (*He shrugs.*) How did you know they were going up there last night?

BRUD: I got a nose for trouble.

(*BRUD is instantly sorry he said it, and GINNY has to repress a giggle.*)

GINNY: Can I see the prisoners now?

BRUD: I'll have to search you.

GINNY: Your female deputy can.

BRUD: Fine. Let's just wait on her. Since I ain't got one, that might take a while.

GINNY: Ok. Search me.

(*BRUD looks like a hungry tomcat about to get fed. He walks around GINNY, looking her over.*)

BRUD: Raise your arms.

(*GINNY does so. BRUD feels of her arms, under her arms, under her breasts, the sides of her breasts.*)

GINNY: That's all me, Sheriff. No guns or files.

BRUD: Just checking.

GINNY: I noticed.

(*BRUD runs his hands down around GINNY's buttocks, squats, puts his hands around one of her legs, works his hands up toward her thigh.*)

GINNY: Hey, wait a minute!

BRUD: How do I know you ain't got a knife taped to your leg?

GINNY: Take my word for it.

BRUD: I'll have to check. (*Indicates GINNY should raise her skirt in lieu of letting him feel. She raises her skirt. BRUD gestures for her to go higher.*) You don't look all that bad for a lesbian. What a waste.

GINNY: Can we go now?

BRUD: Go on back.

(*GINNY goes back as the phone rings.*)

BRUD: Sheriff's office. Oh, good morning, Judge. Yep, locked up tighter'n Dick's hat band. Let 'em back out? But, but...huh? They are? All three of 'em? Great turkey gobbler! The governor too! No sir. Yessir. (*Feels his nose.*) No, sir, it's just bruised. Naw, it ain't broke. Well, no, I wouldn't say it'd look too good on TV. I guess I could. Well, there's this sheriffs' convention out in Denver. I could go to that. Right, Judge. Ok, put him on.

(*Breathes deeply and changes positions.*) Morning, Mr. Billings. Sure, I guess I can. Yessir, I <u>know</u> I can, but... ok. How much? Holy simole! Why, they'd be crazy not to. Yessir. Got you. All right, I'll drive 'em home and see if I can work on 'em. Yessir, I'll call you. You're welcome. (*He hangs up, looks glum. Then gets mad.*) Don't that frost your eyeballs. (*Slams his fist into his palm.*) Son of a buck.

(*BRUD gathers himself together, tucks in his shirt, combs his hair in the mirror, tries a big false smile, rejects it, tries a smaller one. Looks toward the jail, then back to the mirror, shakes his head and smiles ruefully.*) Shelton, ole son, it's time to open up a can of kiss-ass. (*He plasters on the big false smile and walks toward the jail area as the lights go down.*)

SCENE FIVE

Later that morning. BRUD ushers MOSSIE, GID and GINNY into the house as the lights come up. He still wears the big smile, the epitome of sweetness and light.

BRUD: Watch your step there, ladies. There ye go.

(*MOSSIE and GINNY look sideways at BRUD, skeptical about his new attitude, and amused.*)

GID: We sure thank you for the ride, Sheriff.

BRUD: Call me Brud, Gid. You always did. Say, you know something? You pack some power in that right of yours.

GID: Why, thank ye, Sheriff...uh, Brud. How's your nose?

BRUD: Hurts like hell. How's your fist?

GID: It hurts too.

(*MOSSIE comes up with a long strip of bandage and goes to work on GID.*)

MOSSIE: Here, Gid, sit down here and let me work on you a little bit. That one place there is still oozing a little blood. Sit down, Sheriff.

BRUD: Thank ye, thank ye.

MOSSIE: Sheriff, what's going on? You've went from beating on us to bragging on us. How come you let us out so quick?

BRUD: Judge told me to. Said you had a right to protect your property, same as the coal company.

MOSSIE: That a fact.

BRUD: (*Sitting, but leaning forward to talk. He is really trying to do a selling job.*) Now, Gid, Mossie, Mr. Billings called me this morning. He's gonna come by and talk to you in person, as soon as he gets back. This Pittsburgh seam he's been following down Blackberry comes awful close to your house, so there ain't no way he's gonna keep mining it.

GID: Really?

MOSSIE: What's the catch?

BRUD: He'll shut 'er down, if that's the way you want it. Go somewhere else. Or, he'll offer to buy you out, at a good price. I didn't say a fair price. I said a good price.

MOSSIE: How good?

BRUD: Four times what he offered before.

GID: Lordy, mercy! That comes to...

BRUD: Forty-eight thousand dollars.

MOSSIE: That's what I was going to say.

GID: I was afraid to say it.

MOSSIE: That's something to think about. But poor little Angie. The graveyard.

BRUD: We'll move the graveyard. Wherever you buy your next place, we'll put it there for you. You just tell us where you want it.

MOSSIE: I don't know.

GINNY: Think about it, Mossie. You don't have to be in a hurry. Right, Sheriff?

BRUD: Why, no. But if they's gonna be a deal, it might as well be made, you know, pretty soon. They don't like to keep them machines idle. They lose money.

MOSSIE: If he was to throw in one more little something, I think we might do it. I ain't talked it over with Gid, but...

BRUD: What?

MOSSIE: They's a piece of property over next to Judge Ramsay's place...just three or four acres. If he'd throw that in with the deal, we'd prob'ly do it. If Gid says so.

GID: I'd say so. I sure would.

BRUD: You got a deal.

GINNY: Wait, Mossie. What's the rush?

MOSSIE: They've offered us what we want.

GINNY: But you love this place.

BRUD: She's thought it out, little lady. She said we had a deal.

GINNY: Why can't we wait until she's been on television? You're trying to de-fuse the story. Mossie, think about it.

BRUD: Now, by grabs, this ain't none of your business. I mean, with all due respect to the press. You think Mossie don't know what she wants?

GINNY: Not with you pressuring her.

BRUD: Me? What about you?

GID: Would you two just shut up!

BRUD: Sorry, Gid.

GID: Just let Mossie decide.

MOSSIE: (*Thinking a minute while they wait.*) Ginny, I know what's in your mind. It's your Uncle Jake.

BRUD: Jake? Jake Buckner, he was your uncle? Why, sure, it all makes sense. Son, talk about a damned communist.

GINNY: Watch your mouth, Sheriff!

BRUD: (*Loves seeing her lose her temper.*) They tell me Jake was double gaited. You know light on his feet.

GINNY: What's that supposed to mean?

BRUD: He was queer as a three dollar bill.

GINNY: (*Losing control completely, flying at him, fists swinging, kicking at him.*) You son of a...!

GID: (*Grabbing her around the waist from behind, pulling her back while she thrashes.*) Here, now! Here, now. Back off, Brud. You got no call to talk about her uncle that way.

MOSSIE: She loved that man. Did you ever meet him, Sheriff? Tell the truth.

BRUD: No, but I heard 'em talk.

MOSSIE: There. Gid, you gonna hold her all day?

(*GID lets GINNY go. She composes herself.*)

GID: Brud, I figure you owe her a kind word or two.

BRUD: You gonna sell this place or not?

MOSSIE: We might and we might not.

BRUD: I'll apologize, Miss Ginny, if...

GINNY: I don't like "Miss" Ginny.

BRUD: Ginny, dang nab it.

GID: Is that all you got to say?

BRUD: That's far as I'm going.

GINNY: He doesn't have to apologize. Forget it.

BRUD: What's your answer, Mossie?

(*MOSSIE thinks.*)

GINNY: Mossie, don't sell out.

(*BRUD is exasperated by this remark, but manages to keep quiet, watching MOSSIE.*)

MOSSIE: Ginny, I don't know what you mean. Selling, to me, means mule trading. I think we've come out pretty good on this one.

BRUD: It's a deal, then?

MOSSIE: If Gid says so.

GID: Why, shore, I do. You know I do.

BRUD: Son of a buck! All right! Put 'er there, Gid. Well, as they say, it's been loverly, but I've got to Pull a Hank Snow and be moving on. There's this sheriffs' convention out in Denver. (*Starts to exit.*)

GINNY: Why don't you stick around? I'd love to put your nose on TV.

(*BRUD pauses, reacts without turning around, goes on off quickly.*)

MOSSIE: Ginny, I'm sorry about your Uncle Jake, but...

GINNY: No, you did what you thought was best.

MOSSIE: Why, if it wasn't for you bringing them TV people in, and then the governor and all...I know we'd a-never got nothing outta this place.

GID: They'd a-buried us.

MOSSIE: That's the truth, 'cause I wouldn't a-budged.

GID: Me neither.

MOSSIE: Thank you. I know you're disappointed.

GINNY: (*Hugging her.*) You're happy, that's all that matters. I...I guess I <u>was</u> thinking a little of myself, like the sheriff said. But I've still got one fine story. Which reminds me, I've got to run, too. I don't want to be late.

GID: Ginny, I forgot to tell you. They got Big Red.

GINNY: Oh, Gid.

GID: That's all right. I just wanted to tell you...Big Red was a woman.

(*GINNY hugs GID.*)

GINNY: I've got to run. Bye. I love you both. Bye-bye.

(*GINNY exits quickly, waving.*)

MOSSIE: Bye. You come back, now.

GID: I was scared to death, Mossie.

MOSSIE: I was too.

GID: When the sheriff stepped up behind me up there in the dark, and said, "Hold on, Gid!" I almost went right in my britches. (*He looks at his fist and smiles.*)

MOSSIE: Does your head still hurt?

GID: No, I feel fine.

MOSSIE: I do too.

GID: Big Red didn't mean that much to me, Mossie. I thought she did. But I was just taking up slack. What really scared me was the thought of losing you.

MOSSIE: I was scared too, Gid. But I ain't no more. (*The air begins to warm between them.*) Looky here. (*Takes a piece of magazine paper out of her pocket and unfolds it.*) I tore it out of Better Homes and Gardens.

GID: What is it?

MOSSIE: House plans. Look at the picture. It's about wore out, but...ain't it pretty?

GID: Not as pretty as you are.

(*MOSSIE's eyes meet GID's. Emotion swells between them. They reach out and hold hands. He smiles, then cocks his ear, hearing his MUSIC start to play. He looks up.*)

GID: My music. (*Listens a minute.*) It's come back to me.

(*GID starts to move his body to the music. Then slowly, slowly he begins to dance, in spite of his stiff joints. He starts to fill with pride. His steps come tentatively and small at first. Then as the music gets going, so does he. It is an individual sort of clog step, but not frantic and all-out. It is contained, strong, joyous.*)

(*MOSSIE watches with great pride and appreciation, touched deeply. At the height of his expression, he turns to her and holds out his hand. She rises to take his hand and they finish the dance in a vigorous, rhythmic celebration of life and love.*)

(*When the dance builds to its final chord, they are at center stage with their hands joined and held high. Then GID pulls MOSSIE close and kisses her during the applause. It is a long passionate kiss. They part, hold hands and bow.*)

(*Before the applause ends, ENCORE MUSIC starts to play and GID and MOSSIE motion for BRUD and GINNY to come on for a bow. All four bow and begin to dance in a line, left, right, perhaps circling and swinging partners, then joining in a straight line to end the dance with their hands held high. Stage lights go down.*)

THE END

Ouida White, Jack Johnson, Tess Campbell and Kent Logdson in *Mossie and the Strippers* by Billy Edd Wheeler, Horse Cave Theatre, 1987

Billy Edd Wheeler

Born and raised in Boone County, West Virginia, Billy Edd Wheeler graduated from Warren Wilson Junior College, Swannanoa, North Carolina, and Berea College at Berea, Kentucky. After service in the Navy's Air Force, he did graduate studies at Yale's School of Drama, majoring in playwriting.

Wheeler has received 13 awards from ASCAP for songs recorded by Judy Collins, Bobby Darin, The Kingston Trio, Neil Young, Kenny Rogers, Elvis and 150-some other artists, selling over 57 million units. The songs include "Coward of the County" which was made into a movie, and the classic "Jackson," recorded by Johnny Cash and June Carter.

Wheeler is author of a dozen plays and outdoor dramas that include the long-running *Hatfields & McCoys* and *Young Abe Lincoln*. His newest one, *Johnny Appleseed*, premiered in 2004. He has authored or co-authored several books of humor. His most recent one, *Real Country Humor – Jokes from Country Music Personalities*, was published in the spring of 2002 by August House.

Recently inducted into the West Virginia Music Hall of Fame, he is the recipient of Distinguished Alumnus awards from Warren Wilson College and Berea College. In 2004, Berea College conferred on Billy Edd the honorary degree of Doctor of Humane Letters.

Married to the former Mary Mitchell Bannerman, the Wheelers have two adult children, Lucy and Travis, and continue to live in Swannanoa. Billy Edd Wheeler's website is www.billyeddwheeler.com.

Tess Campbell in *Hopscotch* by Sallie Bingham, Kentucky tour, 1988

HOPSCOTCH
by
Sallie Bingham

Tess Campbell, Andrea Gallo and Sylvia Cardwell in *Hopscotch* by Sallie Bingham, Kentucky tour, 1988

Hopscotch opened on March 8, 1988, with the following cast:

ACTOR I — *Sylvia Cardwell*
  MARY TODD LINCOLN
  MRS. ULYSSES S. GRANT
  SCHOOL TEACHER
  ENID'S FRIEND
  SECOND CHANTER
  ELIZABETH MADOX ROBERTS
  SECOND PIONEER WOMAN
  CARRY'S MOTHER
  MOTHER GLOYN
  BAR KEEPER
  JUDGE
  JOINTIST
  SECOND YOUNG GIRL

ACTOR II — *Tess Campbell*
  ENID YANDELL
  EVANGELIST
  CARRY'S BROTHER
  FIRST CHANTER
  VILLAGE GOSSIP
  BLACK SLAVE
  MANDY
  FARM WIFE
  REPORTER
  FIRST YOUNG GIRL
  JANET LEWIS

ACTOR III — *Andrea Gallo*
  CARRY NATION
  GEORGINE
  FIRST PIONEER WOMAN
  LAURA CLAY

Director: Warren Hammack
Tour Manager: Breton Frasier
Stage Manager: Beverly Nachimson
Set & Properties Design: Sam Hunt
Costume Design: Rebecca Shouse
Lighting Design: Greg Etter
Technical Director: Greg Etter
Assistant Technical Director: Paul Kaufman
Wardrobe & Properties: Kelly Ferguson

From childhood I've known the long road from Louisville to cave country – we often visited Mammoth Cave – and although the road is now a throughway, not much else has changed. After Elizabethtown, the throughway seems to slope for many miles, through half-abandoned fields, barns, and small towns hidden behind their trees. The turn-off for Horse Cave leads across railroad tracks. The appearance of Horse Cave Theatre seems almost a miracle: a beautiful, modern, fully-equipped regional theatre.

I remember feeling that the productions of my four plays there – *Paducah, Hopscotch, Piggyback,* and a stage version of Kate Chopin's *The Awakening* – were also miracles. Readings and rehearsals, at least in hindsight, seemed to roll smoothly along, under Warren's sometimes invisible directing, graced with Pamela White's acting. I remember her especially as Edna in *The Awakening,* an almost entirely internal story, which she brought luminously to light. The casts of my plays were always theatre professionals, somehow drawn down to this tiny Kentucky town, and the audiences were, very often, rapt, giving my plays the unquestioning attention and response that is perhaps only possible when theatre is, literally, life-giving.

And when I went with Warren and Pamela to the "coffees" that were both fundraisers and gatherings of friends, I saw, too, that the plays the theatre was offering were life-giving. How amazing that was, even when the praise was sometimes a little off, as when a woman exclaimed after one of my plays, "It's just like 'Gone With the Wind!'"

– Sallie Bingham

Characters:

MARY TODD LINCOLN
ENID YANDELL
CARRY NATION
MRS. ULYSSES S. GRANT
EVANGELIST
CARRY'S BROTHER
SCHOOL TEACHER
LOUISVILLE LADY
FIRST CHANTER
SECOND CHANTER
ELIZABETH MADOX ROBERTS
GEORGINE
FIRST PIONEER WOMAN
SECOND PIONEER WOMAN
VILLAGE GOSSIP
BLACK SLAVE
MANDY
CARRY'S MOTHER
FARM WIFE
MOTHER GLOYD
BAR KEEPER
JUDGE
JOINTIST
REPORTER
LAURA CLAY
FIRST YOUNG GIRL
SECOND YOUNG GIRL
PROFESSOR JONES
TRAVELING COMPANION
MALE VOICE

(*All characters played by three women.*)

ACT ONE

SCENE ONE

On stage there are three trunks, one large and two medium sized, and two stools, both built to look like old fashioned hat boxes. These are moved about the stage by the actors to define space and to become different objects: a train, a coach, etc. The stage may be chalked for a hopscotch game. Three women are seen, posing behind ornate picture frames. They are MARY TODD LINCOLN, CARRY NATION and ENID YANDELL. Each may hold or wear an item which will identify her during the play: MARY TODD a fan, CARRY NATION a small hatchet, ENID YANDELL a sculptor's tool. They pose for a beat, then step around the frames and turn towards them to adjust hair and costume, using the frames, now, as mirrors.

MARY TODD: Why, Enid Yandell... I didn't know you were in Washington!

ENID: I come as often as I can, to study the great public statues. A sculptor must keep up to date...

MARY TODD: And... Mrs. Carry Nation, isn't it?

CARRY: I've been wanting to meet you, Mrs. Lincoln. You've had grief of your own from demon rum...

MARY TODD: You mean Abraham's law partner and that evil book he wrote? Liquor inspired it, everyone says.

CARRY: I know how hard it can be to face the truth, Mrs. Lincoln. It took me years to understand it was demon rum that wrecked my first marriage.

ENID: (*Looking at the hopscotch design.*) I watched some little girls playing here a while ago. I was tempted to sketch them, but then I remembered: I'm here to draw the public monuments...Lincoln, and Jefferson, the great men... (*Tentatively, she hops on the board.*)

MARY TODD: Hopscotch... that was always my favorite.

CARRY: We used to scratch out the design in the dirt...

(*They run to the hopscotch court. The THREE WOMEN begin playing hopscotch, their skirts gathered up, laughing together. They are impeded by their costumes, which involve articles from the late nineteenth-century: a bonnet, a shawl, a fan. Their laughter derives from these impediments, as should be clear to the audience. Other props are available on the stage, and the three actors use them to indicate changes from one character to another.*)

MARY TODD: (*Stopping, rather breathless.*) I insist on very long strings to my bonnets—that's where the true elegance of a bonnet lies—but how they do fly when I move fast!

CARRY: I've been trying for years to find shoes I can run in—a considerable amount of my time is spent running away from angry men—but they haven't invented running shoes for ladies.

ENID: Ladies' shoes are supposed to be picturesque... When I went to Chicago to design the caryatids for the Women's Pavilion they told me to wear something "picturesque" for the visitors to my studio. I put on my apron, the one I always wear for sculpting, and topped it off with a beret—to keep the marble dust out of my hair...

MARY TODD: Now Enid, you never did use marble for those statues...

ENID: Just plain old plaster for the caryatids, the committee said marble was too expensive. Besides they doubted I'd have the arm strength to carve marble, though I'd been carving it for years... Mrs. Grant was there, you know.

MARY TODD: That woman! That woman was given a pension when the senators wouldn't allow me a cent! And MY husband was a martyr to his country. You could hardly call Ulysses S. Grant a martyr to anything but a liquor bottle.

CARRY: I wish I'd had a chance to tell him what I thought about that.

MARY TODD: I always thought Mrs. Grant was common. But people never criticized her the way they criticized me.

(*ACTOR I puts on a little ruffled widow's cap, and speaks to ENID as MRS. GRANT.*)

MRS. GRANT: I don't approve of women sculptors. There was one of them buzzing around the General, I made short shrift of her. A fifteen year old girl, would you believe it, came all the way to Washington to do a bust of Mr. Lincoln, but then of course the tragedy intervened and she ended up trying to make a PORTRAIT of the General.

ENID: So you do not approve of me, Mrs. Grant?

MRS. GRANT: I don't disapprove of YOU, Miss Yandell, but I think every woman is better off at home taking care of husband and children. The battle with the world hardens a woman and makes her unwomanly.

ENID: And if one has no husband?

MRS. GRANT: Get one.

ENID: But if every woman were to choose a husband, the men would not go round; there are more women than men in the world.

MRS. GRANT: Then let them take care of brothers and fathers. I don't approve of these women who play on the piano and let the children roll about on the floor, or who paint and write and embroider in a soiled gown and are all cross and tired when the men come home and don't attend to the house or table. Can you make a better housewife for your cutting marble?

ENID: Yes. I am developing muscle to beat biscuit when I keep house.

CARRY: (*To ENID.*) Bravo! She'll find nothing to say to that.

ENID: But Mrs. Grant, are there no circumstances under which a woman may go to work?

MRS. GRANT: I may be old-fashioned. I don't like this modern movement. But I don't think so. Although there are certain sorts of work a woman may do: teaching, being a nurse, or taking care of children.

CARRY: Those jobs don't pay enough to keep a woman in potatoes and onions.

MARY TODD: (*No longer as MRS. GRANT.*) You carry the day! (*She takes off cap, pins flower in her hair.*) I've worn widow's weeds long enough… I always was partial to a posy in my hair. That was one of the things people never could understand—and yet flowers in the hair were all the style.

(*During this speech, CARRY begins to listen intently to a sound offstage, a creaking as of a cart being driven slowly along. The trunks have become a cart in which CARRY is riding. The lights change.*)

CARRY: Father, don't drive us that way—the battle's hardly over.

ENID: Come along, Mary—tuck up those long skirts. I'll beat you to the other end.

(*MARY TODD and ENID proceed with the game of hopscotch while CARRY, alone, speaks to the invisible presence of her father.*)

CARRY: Pea Ridge Battle ground, the boys lying tossed around on the bare earth, they seemed to be sleeping until you got close enough to see the wounds. Stop, Father! Here's one that's still alive—he's calling for water! Somebody run up to the spring and see if there's a cup—everybody's gone, I forgot, there's nobody anymore to run for anything. Our slaves all left as soon as they heard they were free—even Nancetta who used to rock me to sleep in her arms. What will I do now when I can't sleep, after they've been talking about the sights in the old graveyards, the spirits of all those old masters walking at night with their chains clanking, and the sights of hell, where some of the white men would be on gridirons, some hung up to baste, and the devil with his pitchfork tossing the poor creatures hither and thither, just the way the boys were tossed around on the ground after the battle at Pea Ridge… My nurse used to hold me in her arms until both of us were asleep, but now she's gone… Father! Wait for me, I'm coming… Mother has to ride in that old coach with the worn-out velvet on the inside, she thinks she's Queen Victoria. She despises the rest of us because we're lower class, no dukes or duchesses among all her children… I'm coming! I only want to get back to Garrard County, to Preacherville where I was born, where I filed my teeth down with a metal rasp so I'd look like Father.

(*The lights change.*)

MARY TODD: You're cheating, Enid. I won't play with a cheat. (*She steps out of the game.*)

ENID: I just took natural advantage of the lay of the land —-

MARY TODD: Come along, Carry, you've been yammering long enough. See if you can get to the end ahead of Miss Enid. (*As CARRY tucks up her skirts and enters the game.*) Now, laugh, you two—laugh louder! I've started to hear them again. Mr. Lincoln said he heard them nearly every night... Down in the old slave pens, behind Grandmother's house in Lexington—Mr. Lincoln had never seen human beings in pens before! They keep the runaways there, and the ones they're getting ready to sell, and some of them, why, they cry and moan, you can hear them all through the night, even through Grandmother's lace curtains and the eiderdown I pull over my head... Hush now, down there! We don't want to hear that caterwauling. Slaves HAVE to be sold sometimes, you all know that, and if the overseer has to beat you, why, it's because you've been stealing again... I saw one once in the field—I don't know her name—she had a little baby laid under a honeysuckle bush, and every time she got to the end of a row of tobacco, she'd run over to check on him... Where are my babies, where are Eddy and Willy and Tad? Why did they all have to die? Down at the end of the row, under a honeysuckle bush—hardly any shade in the month of May! The overseer saw her and he came running with his whip. (*She speaks directly to the audience.*) Now I'm a believer in dreams. Mr. Lincoln is, too. Why, he saw just about every tragedy that was coming to us, saw it in detail, too—even saw the coffin in the White House and the people on their knees weeping and praying beside the train track all the way back to Illinois...

(*Train whistle.*)

MARY TODD: I saw it coming but I couldn't do anything to stop it, anymore than I could do anything to save Eddie and Willy and Tad, my three precious sons, my babies—I saw them die. People blamed me for Willy's death, said I was an unfeeling mother because I had a big banquet in the White House the night he was taken ill, dancing, and candles, and food, and my baby lying sick upstairs.

Later on those same people said I cared too much about bonnets and china and flowers but what they never could understand is just for a minute when I put a new bonnet on my head – just for a minute I don't hear Willy crying.

(*The lights change.*)

CARRY: (*As the YOUNG CARRY MOORE. Stopping suddenly.*) I was greatly shocked to find myself a thief.

(*ACTOR II takes up a staff, assuming the role of an EVANGELIST.*)

EVANGELIST: Petty thieves are just the same as bank robbers—equally pernicious in the eyes of the Lord!

CARRY: I borrowed Mama's brooch to wear to the Great Revival, and it fell out somehow when I got the jerks—

EVANGELIST: Little thief! God is watching you—

CARRY: I WANT to be saved—

EVANGELIST: Won't you come to Jesus? (*CARRY kneels in front of her. The EVANGELIST speaks directly to the audience.*) Folks, I know there's them amongst you that's had a mighty tussle with old John Barleycorn, starved for him, stole for him, wallered in the muck and the mire, too hang-dog to hold up your heads, friends looking the other way when you pass, see your wife and babies shoved from pillar to post, clothed in rags to the shame of blessed Jesus—won't you stand up and swear to throw down that bottle? Yes, throw it down for good and all, bury old John Barleycorn and come to the Lord with clean hands on judgment day.

(*CARRY begins to shake uncontrollably. The EVANGELIST holds her in her arms. MARY TODD sings an old hymn: "Are you washed in the Blood".*)

CARRY: When I heard the preacher's words, I began to weep bitterly—I was just a little thing—I could not have told anyone what I wept for, except it was a longing to do better... Then they carried me down to a stream—it was winter time, and the stream was fringed with ice. And they pushed me under the ice-cold water... The little Carry who walked into the water was quite different from the one who walked out. I said no word. I felt I could not speak, for fear of disturbing the peace that passeth understanding. Kind hands wrapped me up and I felt no chill.

(*The lights change. ACTOR II puts on a vest, playing the role of CARRY'S BROTHER.*)

CARRY'S BROTHER: Carry, little sister, I believe you know what you are doing.

CARRY: NO, I DON'T! I want someone to explain it to me!

CARRY'S BROTHER: So those damned Campellites took you to the creek and soused you, did they, Cal? And you never understood a thing about it?

MARY TODD: Don't you talk that way! She's born again in Jesus.

CARRY'S BROTHER: She's still going to need to learn how to use her mind. Going on seventeen and not a day in school yet—

(*The lights change. ACTOR I assumes the role of SCHOOL TEACHER, picking up a long pointer.*)

SCHOOL TEACHER: The problem for our discussion is, "Do animals have reasoning faculties?" Carry Moore: you'll be first to answer. Don't look so stricken, Miss Carry. If you hadn't of been looking out the classroom window all morning, you'd know what we're talking about.

CARRY'S BROTHER: Go on, Carry, you can answer the question.

(*CARRY struggles for words.*)

CARRY'S BROTHER: Just go ahead and tell her.

SCHOOL TEACHER: Speak up, Carry. I can't hear you...

CARRY: Miss President...

SCHOOL TEACHER: You've said that already, Carry Moore. You're going to have to stand there in the front of the room until you find your voice. You use it enough when it's time to play.

(*CARRY stands for another agonizing moment, trying to arrange her thoughts, then bursts into tears and runs offstage.*)

CARRY'S BROTHER: Poor Baby Sister, always trying to do more than she could. Lay in bed for five years after that baptism in the freezing cold water. Many are called but few are chosen, as I have reason to know.

(*ACTOR II lays aside the vest and becomes ENID again. The lights change.*)

ENID: (*Takes out a letter.*) I submitted my design for the Confederate memorial in Louisville—a very fine drawing indeed! Marse Henry Watterson wrote to recommend me: (*She reads.*) "I have always been much interested in Miss Enid Yandell personally and was very anxious for her to be the favored competitor." But the ladies in Louisville saw to it that I lost the competition.

I worked on bigger statues in Chicago. There were five of us. Five women sculptors. We were all together then. The men had said, "Hire anything—white rabbits—if they'll do the work..." So we were called the white rabbits...

We worked in a vast hall of iron girders and glass walls and roof. It was like some giant's studio. It was surely crowded with giants. We gradually filled it with those huge figures, and they were then hauled away and put in position on the fairground.

In the winter we were kept from freezing by large braziers filled with glowing fires; in the summer we were saved from heat prostration by awnings stretched across the roof... Scaffolding, iron armature, huge mounds of plaster, designs hanging from the walls and everyone rushing around in mad haste: it was a fantastic sight!

My energy then was inexhaustible. No scaffold was too high for me to mount, carrying a pail of plaster in one hand and tools in the other!

LOUISVILLE LADY: It's a wonder you didn't fall and break your foolish neck!

ENID: Once, when I had climbed up twenty feet or more and was covering an iron bar with plaster, I lost my balance, slipped and fell down between the statue and the scaffold!

LOUISVILLE LADY: Gracious!

ENID: It was rather thrilling! As I went dropping, dropping, dropping, very slowly, I had heaps of time to think. I was filled with regret that my career should be cut off at such an interesting moment... When I finally hit the ground with both feet, I shook myself as a cat does who has jumped from a fourth story window, looked around, and smiled at my friends who had come to pick up my fragments...

LOUISVILLE LADY: And didn't even break a bone?

ENID: I was bruised from head to foot—a sort of study in blues and greens and blacks! But it didn't occur to me to take even a day off from work... But now this Confederate Memorial. Why wasn't I chosen?

LOUISVILLE LADY: I happened to notice that the judges had left your name on your entry—and that, you know, was entirely against the rules. You had to be disqualified, Enid, and that nice Mr. Muldoon designed the monument instead.

ENID: You called yourself my best friend, yet you took it upon yourself to prevent me from being chosen.

LOUISVILLE LADY: Enid, women artists must have standards just like the men. They can be difficult to adhere to, especially in the face of your kind of ambition—

ENID: What about support, encouragement?

LOUISVILLE LADY: Now you're asking for special treatment. That's just the sort of demand that gets us in trouble, Enid. The men say we're not professional about our work.

ENID: But I'm qualified to make that statue—my father was a Confederate officer!

(*The lights change. CARRY enters. She is calm. She walks to ACTOR I, who picks up the pointer and resumes her SCHOOL TEACHER's role.*)

SCHOOL TEACHER: I see you've gotten control of yourself, Miss Carry.

CARRY: Miss President, I am ready now to state my case. I know animals have reasoning power because my brothers cured a dog of sucking eggs by having him take a hot one in his mouth and it was the last egg we ever knew him to pick up.

That was the last time I was afraid to address an audience.

(*The lights change. ACTORS I and II sit down and become members of her audience, CHANTERS, as CARRY begins to speak.*)

FIRST and SECOND CHANTERS: (*As followers, chanting.*) Devil's broth and devil's brew will be the end of all of you... (*Chanting continues under Carry's speech.*)

CARRY: One time when I was speaking at Elizabethtown, I happened to walk down the street past a tavern, and the owner was sitting in a chair tilted back against the wall outside the door. I said, "Aren't you ashamed to sell devil's broth inside there? Those are innocent souls you are sending to perdition." He stared at me, went on chewing his cud of tobacco, never said a word... On my way back, after the speech, I saw him sitting there still, tilted back against the wall, chewing his cud. I was fired up, the speech had roused enormous support... "Aren't you ashamed?" I began again, just like the first time, but he stood up before I could finish, raised his chair, and struck me in the head. My bonnet saved me from serious injury, but I fell to the ground, senseless, and spent the next three days, recovering, in bed.

FIRST and SECOND CHANTERS: (*As followers, chanting.*) Devil's broth and devil's brew will be the end of all of you...

CARRY: Kentucky was the worst place of all the many I preached—and my own birthplace, to boot! The distillers have this state by the throat. They hired men with pistols to go to all my meetings, stand in the back of the room, note down the names of anyone in the gathering who spoke up to agree with me... God knows what they did to those good people who saw the wickedness of their ways.

FIRST and SECOND CHANTERS and CARRY: (*Chanting, pointing at the audience.*) Devil's broth and devil's brew will be the end of all of you. Devil's broth and devil's brew will be the end of all of you...

(*The lights change.*)

MARY TODD: Mr. Lincoln rarely took a drop. But his law partner—he had trouble with the bottle all his life. I always say it was drink drove him to write that scandalous book about me. He said I screamed so at Mr. Lincoln the neighbors used to hear it through the walls. I never raised my voice at Mr. Lincoln—and he could be provoking! Lying on the floor with his back against an upturned chair, or sliding around the house in those terrible old carpet slippers... I threw them away when we went to the White House.

(*The lights change.*)

ENID: (*In her studio, at her easel, sketching MARY TODD.*) Neither of you ever lived abroad—I've always said that's a terrible limitation for a woman, especially a woman born and bred in Kentucky.

MARY TODD: Why, I spent years abroad after Mr. Lincoln's death. Of course I had no choice. The hatred that was spewed out on me after he died... My own son had me committed, then tried to jail me with my sister. We didn't get along. I could live cheaply, and with dignity, in a French *pensione* when I would have been out on the streets of Washington... The French understood my problems, they always called me "Madame President."

ENID: But by then it was too late for you to learn anything.

MARY TODD: My life ended when Mr. Lincoln died.

CARRY: I spent three months lecturing in England. Raised barely enough money to pay for my return ticket. The only positive thing I can say about England is that the people do not chew gum. In that America could well imitate them.

ENID: When I went for my first class at the academy in Paris, and saw the naked male models we were allowed to draw from—when I saw that, I thought, this is the way the world is, not the way it was back home in Kentucky.

CARRY: Weren't you lonely?

MARY TODD: Didn't you miss your people?

ENID: I never knew I had any people until I went to live in France. I always thought I was just a queer little thing, carving bits of wood and molding mud into figurines, the way I felt when I was five years old in the old backyard in Louisville.

MARY TODD: But they say nearly all your grand statues have disappeared now, torn down when the cities were fixed up.

ENID: Yes, even my Athena in Nashville. She was my masterpiece. At the time the biggest statue ever carved by a woman—forty feet tall! I had to make her in three pieces, in my Paris studio, and when it was time for her to start the journey home, I held a farewell party.

CARRY: They say the French people drink like fishes.

MARY TODD: I was often reproached for the amount of money I spent on those beautiful evening parties at the White House—

ENID: Everyone was there, eating cold poached salmon off tables I'd had set up in the stomach—the widest part—of my statue of Athena.

CARRY: Who was there?

MARY TODD: Did you have any dukes and duchesses?

ENID: I had the world. Artists are the world, my dear. That's something neither one of you has ever understood.

CARRY: Artists drink like the rest of the world—even more so.

MARY TODD: They never did a thing for Mr. Lincoln. All those terrible portraits, showing every wrinkle and wen—

ENID: But artists SEE, my dears.

MARY TODD: The little man who made my bonnets called himself an artist and as far as I'm concerned, he was one!

ENID: Come along, the party's starting—they've lit the candles inside Athena. You can see the glow from here.

CARRY: I'm not dressed for anything fancy.

MARY TODD: I would have put on my new spring bonnet, had I known—

ENID: You are my guests.

(*The lights dim. Transition music. ENID and CARRY arrange the trunks and stools into chairs and a table on which they lay out a tea serving set, creating Enid's Paris studio.*)

SCENE TWO

The trunks and stools have become Enid's Paris studio. ELIZABETH ROBERTS, wearing a turban and carrying a parasol, appears in the center picture frame. She holds a pose for a moment then steps through the frame. CARRY NATION and ENID YANDELL enter.

ENID: You're early, Elizabeth! I said seven o'clock.

ELIZABETH: I left home at four—it's an old habit of mine. When I take the train to Florida, I leave for the station at daybreak and sit on my suitcase all day . . . I wonder if other writers have this problem with time? It lengthens out in front of me in the most extraordinary way and then it snaps up short like a rubber band.

ENID: Let me introduce you. Carry, this is our famous novelist, Elizabeth Madox Roberts, from Springfield, Kentucky.

CARRY: I'm honored to make your acquaintance.

ELIZABETH: Why, thank you. (*They shake hands.*) What a strong hand you have, Mrs. Nation!

CARRY: Call me Carry—everybody else does, even the drunks who throw bottles at me in the bars.

ELIZABETH: Very well... Carry. We've heard of you in Springfield; we know of your battles to close the saloons.

CARRY: There's been a lot of changes since I sat in my room over the hardware store and watched the men going in and out of the bar across the street. I always believed my marriage failed because of demon rum.

ELIZABETH: Some say you drove him to it.

CARRY: Some say anything.

ENID: Let us sit down before there's an argument. Elizabeth, you should hesitate to cross swords with the likes of Carry Nation! I've felt her hand, too—she has the strength of a woman who carves in marble... Sit here. (*She indicates a place next to ELIZABETH.*) Where is Mary Todd?

CARRY: She slipped out as we were walking over. Said she wanted to catch the next steamer home.

ELIZABETH: I wonder what she will use for cash.

ENID: The Senate finally voted her a pension...

CARRY: After her son took all her money and had her closed up in a madhouse! But I know about children—the grief...

ELIZABETH: I never had any... children, I mean. Of grief there was always plenty. And I have a sort of child now, you know—my poor old father. He can't leave his bed unless I carry him, and he's so heavy. Yesterday when I did manage to drag him out on the porch—the first time in weeks—he said, "It's so pretty out here!"

ENID: I have neither children nor parents—sprung whole, I sometimes think, like Minerva, from the head of Zeus. For an artist it's important to be unencumbered...

CARRY: I love my little girl but she has been sick all her life—first with that terrible problem with her mouth. She couldn't open it wide enough to take a good bite. Had to live off liquids for years. Finally I sent her to a surgeon who pried it open—but she suffered so, and of course she blamed her suffering on me.

ENID: Is she alright now?

CARRY: Well, she can eat—but she still can't talk. I guess I talk enough for the two of us.

ELIZABETH: I never did feel what they say all women feel: the love of children. When my nieces and nephews come to call, I like to see them, of course—but I would hardly call that love. I feel more genuine affection for the birds and the flowers in my garden than I do for human beings.

ENID: Now, that's shocking. I wouldn't dare to say as much.

CARRY: But honest—

ENID: You can go too far in that direction, Elizabeth. It loses you sympathy with the general public.

ELIZABETH: I never had much faith in the general public.

ENID: You wrote all those books for them.

ELIZABETH: For some of them—I invite them in, the way I invite old friends into my garden.

CARRY: Tell us about your garden.

ENID: I'll pour the tea... (*She does so.*) In Paris I always served *petit beurres*. But here—well, cucumber sandwiches. I suppose they'll do.

ELIZABETH: Right now the redbud tree, out my window, is blooming, and I have trillium and bloodroot and wild flowers in my wild flower bed. Sometimes when I'm writing a letter, I forget what I had planned to say—just carried away by the birds. I wish you could hear my mockingbird—he sings all night out in the garden near the blooming pear tree—and then there's the brown thrasher and the bluebird and the catbird and the yellow warbler and the cardinal.

ENID: I can tell you're a poet as well as a novelist, Elizabeth.

ELIZABETH: I started out as a poet but lately the words come in a different way. I still like to say my old poems, though. Here is one I love especially:
"I never could have thought of it—
To have a little bug all lit—
And made to go on wings!"

CARRY: Why, that's a firefly.

ENID: Did you write that, Elizabeth?

ELIZABETH: Yes, and it's one I'm proud to claim. It's poetic, descriptive, musical, and at the same time, profound.

CARRY: I can't say as I see the profound.

ELIZABETH: Why, to think that a mind existed which could conceive of such a thing—that's profound!

CARRY: I always thought a firefly was a kind of toy, the sort of thing a child might make with a pin and a bit of thread and candle wax.

ENID: I never thought about fireflies at all. I don't believe they exist in France... Did you say that mind "existed," Elizabeth? Don't you believe in God anymore?

ELIZABETH: Why, that's the problem, isn't it? I feel the need to believe, but I can't find anything to believe in.

CARRY: It's God that has carried me this far, I know that!

ENID: My strength and my redeemer. I haven't been to church since I was a little child in Louisville. Then I liked Sundays because after lunch everybody took a nap, and I could go out in the back yard and make my "mud pies." Mama always called them my mud pies because they were made of mud—I did not know there was such a thing as clay. But they were not pies. They were men... Do you know, the great sculptor, Rodin, made men, too, when he was a child? He made his men out of dough, and his mother fried them up for him.

CARRY: Did you never make a woman?

ENID: Why, later, of course—when rich and fashionable ladies came to me for their portraits, in marble. One I was especially proud of, made in three differently colored marbles, brought me nothing but criticism; Saint-Gaudens said it was against nature to work in different colored marbles! As though the white marble he used wasn't against nature, as well. The men in Paris—the Great Men—never liked my work. I don't know why. They seemed to think me proud.

ELIZABETH: People here at home were proud of you. I've heard them talk about your statue of Daniel Boone—

ENID: But those same people—the ladies among them, at least—refused to allow me to make the confederate monument in Louisville—even when a majority had voted for my design! "Our intention," they said, "was not to perpetuate Miss Enid Yandell, but the memory of the Confederacy!"

ELIZABETH: I heard you wanted to put a woman on top of that column, and they wanted a man.

ENID: She was to have been an allegory—all my women are allegories!

(*CARRY laughs.*)

ENID: Does that amuse you?

CARRY: To tell you the truth, Miss Enid, I don't know what it means!

ENID: Why, it means my women are bigger than life. They represent the eternal verities: Truth, Honor, Love—and so forth. Saint-Gaudens made fun of the fountain I designed for Providence, Rhode Island—he said I made a fool of myself in bronze in the public streets! But other critics found my design very powerful. I showed life as an enormous woman, struggling with three small men who represented Avarice, Duty and Passion.

CARRY: Who won?

ENID: Why, nobody won, of course, it was the struggle which created a dramatic moment. I wanted the sculpture to be so fine people would miss their trains to look at it—and I succeeded, at least for a while...

ELIZABETH: The struggle... always the struggle, at the heart of it...

(*The lights change. Dressed as Elizabeth's little niece, GEORGINE, ACTOR III, enters and goes directly to ELIZABETH, puts out her arms and kisses her.*)

GEORGINE: Aunt Elizabeth!

ELIZABETH: Why, Georgine—my darling little niece! I had no idea you were here—

GEORGINE: Mama sent me to you, Aunt Elizabeth. She told me to say this to you: "Take care of my little darling for today and I will come and claim her tomorrow."

ELIZABETH: But today I'd planned to work on the seventh chapter of "The Time of Man"—I have my notes all laid out, and I've sharpened seven pencils—-

GEORGINE: Can we make taffy, Aunt Elizabeth? You told me the next time I came to visit we could make taffy and pull it all afternoon.

ELIZABETH: Why, of course, darling... (*ELIZABETH turns to address the audience.*) "It's so pretty out here," Father said when I carried him out onto the porch—but I lost a day's work, tending to him. How can you stack a page of writing, or ten pages of writing, or a hundred, against the look on his face? "It's so pretty out here..." And now my darling little niece... Georgine is a wonder child, an exquisite baby and a personage. She is four and a quarter years old and it amazes me to see her mind imagining just as mine used to do at her age. She has friends about her—"pretend people"—

GEORGINE: Pretend people. Lefus and Beman. They live upstairs. Lefus is seven and Beman is five.

ELIZABETH: She has converted my room into some other place...

GEORGINE: Lefus works downtown in an office. This bench is a bed, and let's pretend the bed is a grand piano. The chair could be a table and the fireplace is downtown. What could the cushion be besides what it is? Pretend something for it...

ELIZABETH: Mind trying to strip itself clean of matter, trying to assert itself over things, to fly free—-

GEORGINE: Lefus has come home from downtown and he wants some taffy candy.

(*GEORGINE starts to lead ELIZABETH offstage. ELIZABETH stops and GEORGINE exits singing a nursery rhyme.*)

ELIZABETH: Beautiful child. Yellow curls that will not stay bobbed and combed as her mother designs. Her plump little body shapely and tall and lithe, her pink skin and her quick and ardent little mouth. She is full of singing and dance. Every song sets her a-stepping and a-bowing... At night she carries the candle up to bed, just as her mother used to do... lying in her bed with her eyes closed, she says the Lord's Prayer with a little tired voice.

GEORGINE: (*Entering, with her thumb in her mouth.*) Our Father who art in heaven, Hollywood be thy name...

ELIZABETH: She knows all of it without a moment's hesitation. In her sweetness and purity, man is made over again—as good as new. I am a form against which she leans... (*As the little girl, GEORGINE. leans against her.*) Ah, there. A woman talks of her niece, the offspring marvelous, the child of the house... Goodnight, precious.

(*GEORGINE exits. The lights change.*)

ELIZABETH: I must get back to my garden. Tonight will be very cold, and the scarlet flowers will probably crumple down into black masses... I have planted iris roots and peonies and lilies-of-the-valley and hollyhocks for next year. The garden and the prose run high and remote, wing touching wing, in the thin air. I have overcome enormous difficulties in the garden, and I have accomplished what I have accomplished there with infinite hardship. The soil was heavy and dry, beaten down and sodden. I was a pioneer. I have eradicated the poison ivy. The prose, too... I am a pioneer there. I speak of the masses of confusion through which I have hacked and chopped. The kind of living I have experienced ought to make my words cut like axes and beat like mauls... I write of the early days, the times before—the pioneer Kentucky, dark and bloody... Indians!

(*Drums are heard. Some of the trunks have been turned on end to suggest trees. The lights change.*)

FIRST PIONEER WOMAN: Listen! They have noticed my absence. Now, quick, quick, quick—old limbs, old feet, bear me away through this dark wood! (*She gazes around in panic.*) Which way? I do not know the trees—which side does the moss grow on? Arthur, you knew the ways of the woods, but you failed to instruct me... Listen!

(*Drums continue to be heard.*)

FIRST PIONEER WOMAN: Nearer! They have picked up my trail at the edge of the settlement, they have seen the bucket I left at the spring... Fly! Fly! But which way?

MARY TODD: Indians. When the Shawnees passed through Lexington, Pa said they were friendly, but I prayed to God to hide me from them.

ENID: It was the same when the Germans marched toward Paris in 1917. Fly! But where? And then we had the children to care for—

FIRST PIONEER WOMAN: Something holds me back, stays my feet, holds my heels like the mud in the buffalo wallows we passed through in the Kentucky canebrakes! Oh we were flying, then—before the storm, before the creditors who had taken everything we had in Virginia, before the wrath of my Father-in-law who said Arthur had married beneath him... If I cannot escape them now, they will seize me and treat me with the devilish cruelty I watched them inflict on Arthur and our infant... when we first came to Kentucky. Long ago when we were so young... How they tore his back with their thongs, how they bound him, lifeless nearly, to the back legs of the horse—Oh God! I had to see it, I could not bring myself to close my eyes. And then the babe—she cried on the journey west, I could not quiet her, my milk was gone, quite gone... They made signs to me to quiet her, with threatening looks, terrible frowns—I knew what they meant! I hid the poor thing in my bosom, wrapped my cloak around her to stifle her screams—but they snatched her from me and beat her brains out against a tree...

ELIZABETH: She will not flee.

ENID: We must leave Paris before the Germans come—before it is too late! But how can we leave the children—the orphans we took in when their fathers left for the front? I have a train ticket—two—but how can I leave her behind—six years old—such a face!

FIRST PIONEER WOMAN: I saw something in the Indian's eyes as he beat out my babe's brains, I saw something that ran down my spine like lightning down the carcass of an old tree...

ENID: Still she stands! And I must wait, as well!

(*ACTOR I puts on a cloak, becoming a SECOND PIONEER WOMAN.*)

SECOND PIONEER WOMAN: I'll wait no longer... The babe I must leave behind, his wailing would give me away... (*As though kissing a baby.*) Goodbye, Sweet Dove. Pray God you will outlive me and never know your mother went on without you... (*She lays the baby down.*) Stay there... (*She turns to FIRST PIONEER WOMAN.*) Come along, Mother. We're going down the south bank of the Ohio, through creeks, swamps, and the terrible canebrakes... where a man can lose his mind trying to tell north from south, or sink down in the mud and lose his life to the poisonous snakes. (*She takes FIRST PIONEER WOMAN's hand.*) They've left us without a guard—now is our chance!

FIRST PIONEER WOMAN: (*As they move across the stage.*) It's too quiet in these high woods—I think I hear them breathing...

SECOND PIONEER WOMAN: They haven't missed us yet.

FIRST PIONEER WOMAN: Ah, I hear them, I hear them—they'll kill and eat us—

SECOND PIONEER WOMAN: Come along!

FIRST PIONEER WOMAN: You've brought me here to my death, but I'll not have it! I'll kill and eat you before you do the same to me!

SECOND PIONEER WOMAN: The woods have turned your mind. We'll draw straws to see who will eat who. I have a good appetite myself, and there's some succulent flesh yet hanging on your old bones. (*She takes out two straws.*) Now whichever one of us draws the shorter straw will have the privilege of being eaten...

(*The FIRST PIONEER WOMAN, demented, throws herself on the SECOND PIONEER WOMAN and they struggle fiercely. Finally the FIRST PIONEER WOMAN rushes offstage.*)

SECOND PIONEER WOMAN: (*Panting.*) There—she's done for now—poor old woman! The woods will eat her for sure if the Indians don't... (*She continues her journey.*) Forty days in the wilderness, and I reached a cabin fifteen miles from home.

ENID: And the old woman?

SECOND PIONEER WOMAN: She found a hunter's camp where there was some food, and she caught a stray horse, and rode on into town. With food and rest, her mind cleared, and she was delighted to see me again. Later she joined a party headed through the Shenandoah to her home in Pennsylvania. I never heard from her again.

ENID: Your child—

SECOND PIONEER WOMAN: With the help of God, he, too, was found—but only after eighteen years with the Indians. The ways of the Lord are wondrous. He was a Shawnee—in language, habits, attitudes. He did not want to return to me—to the white man's world. Finally he returned, but not in spirit. He kept the wilderness in his soul...

(*FIRST PIONEER WOMAN enters with a stool. She sits with SECOND PIONEER WOMAN as though brooding over a fire.*)

FIRST PIONEER WOMAN: We lived in the very inside of the war...

FIRST and SECOND PIONEER WOMEN: In the middle and midst of hate and kill. There's blood on every side of us.

SECOND PIONEER WOMAN: Every man I could name in the fort has had someone killed,

FIRST PIONEER WOMAN: A brother or a father or a child.

FIRST and SECOND PIONEER WOMEN: A sister or a wife carried away.

FIRST PIONEER WOMAN: Martin Wilson's wife...

FIRST and SECOND PIONEER WOMEN: ...up on the Kanawha

SECOND PIONEER WOMAN: ...found her way back home after two years gone...

FIRST PIONEER WOMAN: ...came back with the Indian baby she had two months later...

FIRST and SECOND PIONEER WOMEN: ...and Martin Wilson can't go back to his home because he can't mend his hate for the little Indian child his wife, Lettie, has got in her cradle...

FIRST PIONEER WOMAN: ...her own baby that she pities and holds in her arms.

SECOND PIONEER WOMAN: He can't find his way in so much trouble...

FIRST and SECOND PIONEER WOMEN: ...his hate torn in two...

VILLAGE GOSSIP: The Tolliver woman was thin and broken and covered over with sadness... it was forever present in her abstracted and dull face...

FIRST PIONEER WOMAN: Who speaks back to Sallie Tolliver when she mutters on the stairs?

SECOND PIONEER WOMAN: It's because she's been far into the wilderness...

FIRST PIONEER WOMAN: She talks to Indians.

SECOND PIONEER WOMAN: She talks to scalps, maybe. Old scalps, dry and withered.

FIRST PIONEER WOMAN: To far-off places she remembers.

VILLAGE GOSSIP: She talks to the dead.

(*Pause. The lights change.*)

MARY TODD: As I talked to my Willy... In the south of France, where I went to take the waters—a medium there came to see me every afternoon at five o'clock, she said it was Willy's hour, and she was right: my son always liked the end of the day better than any other time. "What's prettier than the light just before the sun sets?" he whispered to me, the day he died—and it was nearly four then, and he did not last beyond sundown... Oh, it's a great consolation, to talk to the dead.

CARRY: I have no fear of the dead. I've sent too many of the men I loved that way—or so some have claimed: deprived them, both my husbands, of the will to live, because my will to live was so large... (*Taking out a hatchet.*) Will you buy a memento, ladies? It's only fifty cents—an authentic replica of the hatchet I used in Kansas on my first smashathon.

(*CARRY holds out the hatchet. ENID shrinks back in horror, but ELIZABETH takes it and looks at it with interest.*)

ENID: When the war came, there were orphans in the street, and I took up the work of caring for them. After the war, there was no art—only suffering. One morning I walked around the studio and took the cloths off all my work—the heads of beautiful ladies from before the war, the sketches and models for triumphant city statuary—and they looked childish to me, ridiculous. What streets would they grace, now? The streets were gone, the entire scale was changed. I should have spent my time on the children.

ELIZABETH: (*As she examines the hatchet.*) They made her walk every step of the way, and made her carry around her neck the bloody scalps of her own children, tied around her own throat.

CARRY: (*Holding out her hand.*) Fifty cents. A genuine replica...

ELIZABETH: Here.

(*ELIZABETH pays CARRY the money. CARRY pockets it with a mocking curtsey.*)

CARRY: Thank you, Ma'am.

(*ACTOR II appears as the figure of a black slave woman. (May be a slide.) The lights change.*)

BLACK SLAVE: My mother's name was Elizabeth... She had seven children... No two of us were children of the same father. My father's name, as I learned from my mother, was George Higgins. He was a white man, a relative of my master, and connected with some of the first families in Kentucky.

CARRY: The slave woman Eliza was handcuffed and got away at Ruddles Mills on her way down the river; it is the fifth time she escaped when about to be sent out of the country.

MARY TODD: Everyone in Lexington knows the black Todds. There are many of them. Sometimes their master would say, "You all belong to me and if you don't like it, I'll put you in my pocket" – meaning, of course, that he would sell the slave and put the money in his pocket. The day he was to sell the children from their mother he would tell that mother to go to some other place to do some work.

CARRY: Sarah is the biggest devil that ever lived, having poisoned a stud horse and set a stable on fire, also burnt General R. Williams' stable with seven horses...

BLACK SLAVE: The white folks weren't good to me. My master was a good man but my mistress wasn't a good woman. She used to box my ears, stick pins in me and tie me to the cedar chest and whip me as long as she wanted. Oh, how I did hate that woman. My master wasn't as mean as most masters. Hugh White was so mean to his slaves that I know of two girls that killed themselves. One nigger girl Sudie was found across the bed with a pen knife in her hand. He whipped the other nigger girl almost to death, for forgetting to put onions in the stew. The next day she went down to the river and for nine days they searched for her and her body finally washed up on the shore.

(*The BLACK SLAVE turns. The other TWO WOMEN take her hands and they exit as...The lights fade.*)

ACT TWO

SCENE ONE

ELIZABETH is alone on the stage. She wears an apron, and is chopping something on a small chopping board. (This may be mimed.)

ELIZABETH: She chops the meat with a golden knife
And cooks it in a golden skillet.
For coal she has a golden hod;
There is always a plenty to fill it.
She has some tongs made out of pearl
To poke the fire and make it burn.
She pours the milk in diamond crocks
And churns the cream in a silver churn.
And when she's tired she has a stool.
It's made of jade with pearls set in it.
She sits down here and wipes her face
And gets her breath a minute.
On Saturday she stirs a cake
With gold, and when the water is hot,
She kills a hen with a golden ax
And scalds her in a golden pot.

(*MANDY, a black woman, enters silently. She takes the knife and the board from ELIZABETH and continues chopping. The lights change.*)

ELIZABETH: Mandy raised me from the time I was two days old—they didn't expect Mama to pull through. Just appeared out of nowhere and took over—"Hand me that pore chile." Stayed with us till I was seventeen—

MANDY: And wouldn't listen to ole Mandy no more.

ELIZABETH: You didn't have anything to say...

MANDY: Growed up and going to dinner parties. I talked to you when you was still making mud pies. You listened, then.

(*CARRY enters. She is wearing a cloak, dressed for travel, and is now a young girl. The lights change.*)

CARRY: Mandy! Papa says he's selling you, we can't afford to take you out to Kansas... Oh I cried and cried, I got down on my knees—

MANDY: No use, Miss Carry.

CARRY: But you're family, Mandy—been family since I was two days old and...

(*ELIZABETH joins the rest of this speech.*)

CARRY and ELIZABETH: ...they didn't expect Mama to pull through... Came out of nowhere... "Give me that pore chile." Stayed till I was seventeen years old—

MANDY: And wouldn't listen to ole Mandy no more.

ELIZABETH and CARRY: You didn't have anything to say...

(*The lights change.*)

CARRY: I was seven or eight before I ate at the white folks' table. When I was sick—and I was sick most of the time I was growing up—our slave women comforted me. One of them brought me a hot toddy after I was baptized through the ice in the pond—I wasn't cold then, but later the cold came into my bones. She wrapped me in a blanket and held me in her arms in front of the fire...

MANDY: Sold down the river to New Orleans when you all went out west.

CARRY: But I got down on my knees, Mandy! I cried and cried!

MANDY: Sold down the river, Honey. You can cry all you wants.

(*The lights change.*)

CARRY: Mama went crazy again on the flatboat heading west...

(*As CARRY speaks, MANDY slowly exits. ACTOR I takes off Elizabeth's cloak and puts on a crown, becoming CARRY'S MOTHER.*)

CARRY: She'd been bad before, in Kentucky, but after Papa ordered her royal coach she seemed satisfied, for a while. She would drive out into the countryside with old Pete on the driver's seat, dressed up in livery and a top hat. Mama would stop the coach when she saw a farmer hoeing his field; she'd call out the window,

(*CARRY'S MOTHER sits on an upturned trunk, which now is the coach.*)

CARRY'S MOTHER: Your Honor! Duke of Northumberland! How can you disgrace your high degree by digging in the dirt?

CARRY: Then call to Peter—

CARRY'S MOTHER: DRIVE ON!

CARRY: And leave the poor farmer staring.

CARRY'S MOTHER: They never listened. Dishonored themselves in the eyes of their own peasantry! Why, a country's ruined when its aristocracy doesn't know how to behave.

CARRY: When Father decided to head west—he had the wandering foot, was never satisfied more than three years in one place—Mama had one of her fits:

CARRY'S MOTHER: If you insist on dragging me out of my castle, young man, you must at least permit me to ride in appropriate state, in my coach...

CARRY: So the coach, which was fairly worn out by now, was loaded on the flatboat heading west... A long trip, the wrong time of year—cold, and ice floes, and the fear of bandits in the caves along the Ohio...

CARRY'S MOTHER: (*She has left the coach.*) Cold, cold—so terribly cold! My feet are turned to stone... They have brought me here to see me die—regicides, loose in this wild land...

CARRY: Cold and homesick and very lonesome, I crept into the royal coach on one of those long days when the mist never rose off the river. (*CARRY crawls into the coach.*)

CARRY'S MOTHER: Beggar girl! Misbegotten creature! Quit my coach of state before I scratch your eyes out... (*CARRY'S MOTHER throws CARRY from the coach.*)

CARRY: I married early.

(*The lights change.*)

FARM WIFE: Miss Carry, people around here say you know how to bring on rain.

CARRY: It was the Lord's doing, although I was his instrument... After the meeting, we were standing on the platform in front of the church, and I prayed and prayed—west Texas had been dry all spring—and then a sprinkle of rain fell out of a cloudless sky—

FARM WIFE: (*Holding out her hands.*) Praise the Lord! Rain!

CARRY: The next day clouds began to gather in the sky and the moisture started to come down in the gentlest manner and continued in this way for three days...

FARM WIFE: Rain! Rain! Praise be—

CARRY: To the Lord, who made heaven and earth. I am only his instrument... (*As the FARM WIFE sinks to her knees, rejoicing and thanking her.*) It takes so little to make people happy.

(*CARRY raises the FARM WIFE and leads her to sit on one of the trunks. The FARM WIFE is now an OLD WOMAN.*)

CARRY: I first felt the sweet presence of God after I got up in the night to take care of one of my roomers. I was running a boarding house to make ends meet after my first husband died of drink. Standing there by her bed, I felt for the first time in my life the sweet presence of God, like a pulsating golden glow that followed me out the door. I knew then my life was designated for a particular purpose, although it was some time before I divined what that purpose was...

(*CARRY goes to MOTHER GLOYD, the mother of her first husband. The lights change.*)

CARRY: Mother Gloyd, you know I love you better than my own mother, locked up these fifteen years in that hospital in Missouri... But David says we must move so that he can take up his ministry at a new church in Kansas, and he says we have to leave you behind...

MOTHER GLOYD: Don't leave me, Carry, Daughter—I won't live without you. I'm an old woman, give me house room a few more years...

CARRY: David says he can't afford to carry you all the way to Kansas... Goodbye, Mother Gloyd! Goodbye... (*CARRY sits on one of the trunks, which is now the seat of a railroad car.*)

CARRY: Oh, she's come to the train station, she's standing by the train, David, she's got her little suitcase in her hand... (*Weeping.*) One mother closed up in a madhouse and the other left behind by the railroad track...

(*MOTHER GLOYD exits. The lights change.*)

CARRY: I prayed that first night, advancing on my knees, the way I'd learned to do, prayed for the vision—and it came to me when I remembered the way my first husband died, stinking of whiskey so the preacher had to hold his handkerchief to his face. Rum! Demon Rum! That's what has been the ruin of this country... Liquor is illegal in all but four states, but bars and drugstores get around the law, bribing policemen and politicians, and the liquor industry makes more money than any legal business in the country.

(*CARRY crosses to the BAR KEEPER. The lights change.*)

CARRY: Hello, you rum-soaked Republican Rummy!

BAR KEEPER: I'll drink what I please, where I please, it's a free country, and no hatchet wielding daughter of Satan...

CARRY: (*Singing.*) Touch not, taste not, handle not
Drink will make the dark, dark blot,
Like an adder it will sting,
And at last to ruin bring
They who tarry at the drink.

(*To her followers - the audience.*) Roll out that barrel of rum they claim is for medicinal purposes! Roll it into the street and I'll crack it open with one blow! Let the liquor flow in the gutters—roll out the broth of hell!

BAR KEEPER: If you destroy my bar, you hell cat, I'll burn your house to the ground!

CARRY: Should my home be burned, it would be a lecture in favor of my cause that would be worth more than my home.

(*She sings.*) Touch not, taste not, handle not—

(*She stops, suddenly.*) What's that? (*She strains to hear.*) My voice, again! Calling me to a higher purpose—Go to Kiowa! Is that what you say? Who am I to carp at the Lord's calling...

(She *takes a few steps. ACTOR I as a DEVIL bars her way.*)

CARRY: There are devils dancing on the bridge that leads to Kiowa! I cannot pass— (*She makes the sign of the cross. The DEVIL cowers.*) I am called to Kiowa as Joan was called from the fields at Doremy. The liquor interest formed the Mystic Order of Brotherhood to combat me, but the women and the children were always on my side—they had seen the destruction wrought by demon rum! I met tramps who had been their mother's greatest treasure—ruined by demon rum! It was for their sake I smashed the bars in Kansas, and I always left them with a blessing: God be with you! I smashed in the name of love!

(*ENID enters and stands watching. The lights change.*)

JUDGE: You are sentenced to ninety days in the county jail for willful destruction of private property, vis., a bar decorated with carved blocks from the 1893 world's fair in Chicago—

ENID: My world's fair! Why, you might as well smash the caryatids I modeled for the Woman's Pavilion!

JUDGE: SILENCE IN THE COURT!

CARRY: The monkey wants to speak. Yes, Your Dishonor, I'll spend my time in jail—I've made up my mind to it... (*She moves to the jail.*)

(*The lights change.*)

CARRY: When it was time for me to leave, the inmates wrote a song for me, and gave it to me the day my sentence was up:
(*She sings.*) Some who'd never known a mother,
Ne'er had known to kneel and pray,
Raised their hands their face to cover
Til her words had died away...

(*Speaking.*) I was supported by decent women, and by all the children—but I was attacked by whores and jointists' wives for interfering with their trade.

(*She stands as though addressing a crowd.*) There is a spirit of anarchy abroad in this town! (*Raising a hatchet.*) For your sake, Jesus!

(*Bringing hatchet down, beginning to sing.*) Praise God from whom all blessings flow...

ENID: Anarchy is the enemy of art, it is the destroyer of everything fine and beautiful—

CARRY: After I got out of jail my husband, David, bought a new suit and came to join me; he wanted to lead the next crusade with me but I told him frankly he was far too old. He told the newspapermen stories about me, then—said he never wanted to live with me again. (*Raising hatchet.*) For your sake, Jesus!

(*Bringing hatchet down, singing.*) Praise God from whom all blessings flow...

ENID: It was the anarchy and the destruction of the war that ended my life as an artist, in Paris. After the war, there was only suffering. Sometimes I think there must be an art which can survive in the face of such suffering, an art made of the faces of women and children—but that was not the kind of art I made. Mine was always beautiful—

CARRY: One jointist suspended a cage of starving rats and mice over his door—said he'd turn them loose on me, but the poor critters ate each other before I arrived... DOG EAT DOG, AND RAT EAT RAT.

JOINTIST: You have strength in your tongue and venom in your nails. I expect you to be dead soon... I will break a Colt's forty-five over your head and let my dogs gnash your skull bones.

CARRY: Hell letters, and letters from hell... (*Cowering, as though struck.*) Oh—don't raise that chair again at me, you villain! You've knocked me slabsided already—only my bonnet saved me from serious harm...

(*The JOINTIST and ENID laugh at her.*)

CARRY: I lay there in the street while they laughed at me—knocked down flat by a jointist's chair.

ENID: Insanity!

(*The lights change.*)

CARRY: Yes, I did plead insanity at the next trial—to shorten the time I would have to spend in jail—my time was too valuable to waste! David filed for divorce shortly thereafter. (*As though speaking to a REPORTER.*) All this time he has been an encumbrance on me...

REPORTER: Is it true you call McKinley the Brewer's President?

CARRY: It certainly is. Why, he's done everything the liquor lobby wants—and you know they gave thousands of dollars to his campaign.

(*Pistol shoots off. CARRY is horrified.*)

CARRY: Shot by an anarchist in Buffalo—poor suffering human! What will become of our country, now?

REPORTER: The New York Times says you prayed for President McKinley's death—

CARRY: I never prayed for anyone's death; the newspaper misquoted me.

(*Enter MARY TODD.*)

MARY TODD: You reporters always turn around the things I say, twist them to another meaning! You claim I have fourteen first cousins fighting for the Confederacy—but you don't bother to explain they are cousins I'd never seen in my life. You claim I used my southern connections to smuggle military secrets out of the White House... But I love my husband, I love my country, I would die before I would do either one a disservice... There's one thing I never have understood: Why do you gentlemen of the press hate us so?

CARRY: We are only trying to fulfill our destinies as they are handed down to us by the Lord.

REPORTER: I only report the news, ladies. Facts is facts.

MARY TODD: But they are not facts. Only you have the power to make them appear to be.

CARRY: The way you turned the whole country against me, claiming I'd wished the president's death. My speeches in the Northeast were cancelled because of the hostile reaction to your lies. My career nearly sidetracked. I had to resort to speaking on college campuses—and those young men at Yale and Harvard were the toughest proposition I ever met!

MARY TODD: After Mr. Lincoln died, your attacks increased; you knew I was without protection. When my poor misguided son had me judged insane—

CARRY: When my poor misguided ex-husband had our daughter Charlein judged insane—

MARY TODD: When they locked me away in that mental asylum—I who had been first lady of the land—

CARRY: They said I wished the president's death, but never mentioned the fact that he'd killed 500,000 Filipinos to get the Philippines. And then my voice told me, "Go to Washington," but I was sentenced to the workhouse for drawing a crowd... The hells of capitalism create the desperate—and the desperate act—desperately... (*She gets down on her hands and knees, mimes scrubbing the floor.*)

MARY TODD: When they told me I had to do what they called occupational therapy, which meant scrubbing the floor of my miserable cell... (*She gets down on her hands and knees, mimes scrubbing the floor.*)

CARRY: I never allowed myself to murmur and complain about anything, for my fellow prisoners were in a worse position than I. After all, I was praying... Advancing on my knees.

MARY TODD: Take this filthy water away—and these rags! I am the widow of the president of the United States, martyred for his country!

REPORTER: Ladies, ladies, ladies, ladies, ladies... (*She moves away.*)

MARY TODD: They let me go, at last. A few friends were left, and they intervened. I went to France, Germany, Switzerland—it's cheaper living abroad—trailing my days through those foreign countries, invisible as a ghost...

CARRY: When I die, daughter, see they put this on my marker: She has done what she could.

CARRY'S DAUGHTER: I tried, Mother—but I was sick again, I had to go to the rest home again, and there was so little money left over after what we needed for my doctor and for the babies... I tried, but it was quite a while, many years in fact—

CARRY: You mean I have no marker?

MARY TODD: They promised to bury me at the President's side. The widow of a president has some rights, after all—at least after she's dead.

CARRY: Nothing at all?

CARRY'S DAUGHTER: Times were so very hard, and I was sick, and the babies needed so much—

(*CARRY drops to her knees and resumes the floor scrubbing. As she progresses across the floor towards the exit, she begins to sing.*)

CARRY: (*Singing.*) Onward Christian Soldiers, Marching as to war...

(*She exits, still singing and scrubbing. The lights change.*)

MARY TODD: Yes, Your Honor, I bought six sets of the finest lace curtains when I had not a single window to hang them in, or a house, or even a room I could call my own. Yes, indeed, Your Honor, I am "that kind of woman." I am used to the best. (*Turning to the audience.*) My son was quite correct when he brought up the lace curtains in court, at my competency hearing. Exhibit number one in the case against Mary Todd Lincoln's sanity! For indeed I HAD dressed myself in my deepest mourning and gone down to Main Street and ordered six pairs of the finest lace curtains at the Dry Goods Store, where Mr. Homer was always so kind to me. He took out everything they had, spread each lace curtain on the counter for me to consider—and never even mentioned my long-overdue bill. Oh they knew how to treat ladies, once—and in Mr. Homer's Dry Goods Store, they know how to treat ladies even today! It's not a question of money, or bills, paid or unpaid. Mr. Homer KNOWS me. He is my friend! Buying the finest at Mr. Homer's emporium where no questions were ever asked kept me alive, kept my battered spirit alive, during the long years of my widowhood... "O! reason not the need; our basest beggars are in the poorest thing superfluous: Allow not nature more than nature needs, Man's life's as cheap as Beast's..." Not to mention lady's.

Of course my son could never understand Shakespeare—such sentiments are beyond him! The only son left to me of my four fine boys—and the least sympathetic! He thinks only of dollars and cents, bills paid and unpaid. He cannot see the joy for a woman neglected in old age, deserted by all her friends, her husband and children gone—the joy in putting on a shawl (not new, but nicely darned, a fine black lace left from the good days) and a pair of handsome kidskin gloves, and my best black bombazine, and underneath, my white *poie de soie* underthings. Oh yes! Even in all my years of fullest, blackest, deepest mourning, I wore the finest white silk underthings, next to my skin. We are owed something, after all, for our suffering.

It was MY money! They could not understand that—they can never understand that! A woman in Kentucky does not own the clothes on her back, she cannot make a will, or sell her property!

For the price of six sets of lace curtains, never hung, I was shut in that asylum—the president's widow, closed up with shrieking idiots!

(*Lights dim. Music.*)

SCENE TWO

LAURA CLAY, as a young girl, is posing in the empty picture frame. She holds her diary. She steps through the frame. MANDY enters and tries to take the diary away from her.

MANDY: Laura Clay—give that here to me! Fourteen years old, and still scribbling...

LAURA: I have something serious to write, Mandy! I am trying to save my immortal soul.

MANDY: Immortal foolishness!

LAURA: Please, Mandy! Writing's like praying, you know—it's talking to God...

MANDY: Well, maybe... I see you're set on it. Don't be late to dinner!

LAURA: (*She begins to write in the diary.*) I have this night resolved to lay down my own will, and follow God's, as he will most mercifully help me. I pray him to grant me his grace, that I may carry out my resolve for the love of his only son, Jesus Christ our Saviour. (*Closing diary.*) Mr. Shipman's text for tonight's service was taken from the 23rd chapter of St. Luke, the 42nd verse: "Lord, remember me when thou comest into thy kingdom." (*She goes to an imaginary mirror and adjusts her hair and dress.*) I always used to wonder whether the streets in that kingdom are really paved with gold. When I was little, I wondered before I put away such childish things. Mandy used to tell me the streets were paved with gold and the sidewalks were paved with rubies, but that sounded gaudy to me. I don't believe I would like to walk on rubies.

Mr. Shipman said in his sermon tonight that the moment of conversion is when one resolves to lay down his own will to that of God. Perhaps that is easier for men than for women? The scripture always refers to men, although there are a great many more women in every congregation, it seems to me. As Mr. Shipman preached, I resolved to lay down my will to God's and I intend soon to be baptized and confirmed. But my sorrow and repentance for my sin is not deep, nor is my wish to become a Christian very steadfast—I have many wrong thoughts, and grievances, particularly now when I am away from home, and the people here in Aunt's house, although they try to be kind, do not always succeed—especially the boys, my cousins, Richard and Elijah.

Yesterday evening at dinner Elijah walked in front of me into the dining room, and made it impossible for me to pass. I know this is simply foolish boyish behavior, but it made me angry, and afterwards I prayed for forgiveness...

I am a woman, but I think I have a mind superior to that of many boys my own age, and equal to that of many more, yet the world is so fixed that I am not able to continue my studies, while my brothers have tutors and are soon to go to college. Even Elijah, who takes such spiteful pleasure in angering me, will soon go to the University of Michigan at Ann Arbor.

Surely when we get to heaven we will be equal.

I am not perfectly submissive—I will pray to God to make me so. (*She kneels.*)

Mama says there is no money for me to go to Italy, as I had planned to do, next summer. Aunt Mary advises me to teach Mrs. White's children instead; she thought it was my duty, as I might thereby save a soul.

Lord, grant me patience and a humble spirit—apparently I was born with neither. (*She rises.*)

Pa is still in Russia; this will mark the fourth year of his ambassadorship there. Of course we are all very proud of him, but it has been hard work, for Mama, keeping the farm going and taking care of all the family, especially now, with the Rebel army foraging around Lexington...

Mama says I must have Pa's permission to be baptized, and that he is unlikely to give it, since he does not wish for any of his children to join the church...

I have a great deal of work to do to forge a forgiving spirit, for I must admit that I do hold grievances and grudges for a very long time, which is hardly Christian.

I still have not been able to forgive Pa for selling Mandy South to work as a field hand. Mandy raised us, and the jury in Madison County acquitted her of that vile suggestion that she poisoned little Cassius. Mama says I must understand that Pa gets these wild notions, and can't rid himself of them—but Mandy is gone South, to work in the cotton fields, and she never worked in the fields here a day in her life.

I will be so glad when I am a member of the church. I have so long wished it. I have had an idea that those who were converted loved God with a very great love, and had a horror of sin, and felt very sorrowful and repentant. I do not feel much at all...

I have made a list of the things it is my duty to do. (*Takes out the list, reads.*) I must always get up in time for breakfast, must study my lessons diligently, must give up many day dreams in which I waste so much time, must be more kind and forbearing to the servants, must be polite to Richard and Elijah, who are often not at all polite to me, must keep down many evil thoughts and feelings and do all things for the glory and love of God.

I must forgive Pa.

My! I feel exhausted...

(*The lights change. ENID and ELIZABETH enter, in the character of YOUNG LEXINGTON GIRLS, and begin to play hopscotch, laughing and teasing. LAURA watches, unobserved for a moment.*)

LAURA: Really I have only one wish: to be loved in this world by all who know me.

FIRST YOUNG GIRL: Laura! We are going to the circus—

SECOND YOUNG GIRL: Come with us, Laura! There will be clowns—

LAURA: But this is the day I have appointed as a fast day... Ah, I can hear the band playing... Is it a sin that keeps my spirits so low? Sometimes I think if I could paint, I would not feel so...

SECOND YOUNG GIRL: Come along, my dear! This is no time for low spirits...

LAURA: I do so long to be roused... I have strong feelings, and a great capacity to love—I wish I were good!

SECOND YOUNG GIRL: Why, you are good, Laura—the best of any of us! Come along! I'll put on my new dress—

(*Band music.*)

LAURA: I can hear the music plainly! It is a very good band—how delightful! I wish to go very much—I was expecting to go—if we heard that many respectable people went... But I fear that it would be drawing my mind from serious things, and so I will stay home, and put the fifty cents it would have cost me in the contribution box next Sunday. (*She sighs.*)

FIRST YOUNG GIRL: Very well, if you've made up your mind—

SECOND YOUNG GIRL: She seems so indifferent about everything!

FIRST YOUNG GIRL: Come along or we'll miss the clowns.

(*FIRST YOUNG GIRL and SECOND YOUNG GIRL exit.*)

LAURA: Not indifferent—never indifferent! I have strong feelings—but they wait to be roused... (*Taking out coins.*) I wish I could do this in a perfectly right spirit, and without any self-righteousness, but I do not, and scarcely hope that my self-denial can be pleasing to God.

(*The lights change. ELIZABETH enters. She seizes LAURA's hand.*)

ELIZABETH: I could see the band was laughing some!
   And then the big black man that was wild
   Looked hard at us and blinked his eyes,
   And even the golden ladies smiled...

(*ELIZABETH hustles LAURA offstage.*)

ELIZABETH: The morning is late and her duties are over.
She's pressed her ribbons and curled her hair.
She's watched the road for a friend to be passing,
For Laura is waiting to go to the fair...

(*Blackout. Calliope music. Lights up. LAURA is again seen in the picture frame.*)

LAURA: I have been to the circus. I could not refuse. Elizabeth supposed that I wished to go... I enjoyed it very much indeed. The riding was perfectly beautiful, and the clown said nothing at all disagreeable. The gymnastics were wonderful and sometimes painful on account of their seeming danger... Now I cannot put anything in the box next Sunday, since I spent the fifty cents.

(*LAURA steps out of the frame, turns toward it, and puts a grownup woman's bonnet on her head. As she adjusts it, she speaks. ELIZABETH, now as LAURA'S TRAVELING COMPANION, enters with a small suitcase for LAURA. The lights change.*)

LAURA: I never gave up my desire for an education, but I no longer took lessons under a tutor, as I could not find a French tutor who suited me. So I had about given up studying. (*She takes the suitcase from her COMPANION.*) But one day I received a letter from Mr. John Tree, saying that he had heard from my brother Brutus that I hoped to come here, to Ann Arbor, to study, and Mr. Tree felt moved to write to urge me on... This was what turned the balance, although Pa opposed it with all his might—and I determined to come the next semester. If I could not enter college, I would enter High School, and spend the year in preparing for college.

COMPANION: Your mother was very generous, in offering to pay for your year of studying.

LAURA: Fortunately, that was not necessary. I have a little money of my own, a bequest from Aunt Anne, who died last year. So I told Ma that if I found I could possibly afford it, I would come to Ann Arbor; and I began to study again to prepare myself. The bliss of setting up my work table again, spreading out my books, sharpening my pencils, buying paper and ink—

COMPANION: And your distinguished Pa?

LAURA: Ranted and raved, as usual—said learning did nothing but ruin girls; he has no notion that I am hardly a girl any longer. But you know we live in separate establishments now.

COMPANION: I did not like to inquire...

LAURA: It's public knowledge. When Pa came back from Russia, he brought a four-year-old Russian boy.

COMPANION: Gracious!

LAURA: Ma had tried to reconcile herself to his nature—the terrible fighting and railing—but the sight of that child at her own table—-

(*A VOICE is heard.*)

VOICE: Good morning, ladies. You may come in. I have been expecting you, Miss Clay.

LAURA: It is Professor Jones.

VOICE: It is fortunate that you have come early, so that you can see what will be required of you here. I am not at all certain that you are qualified...

LAURA: But I understood that, since I am over twenty-one, I may enter as a student of select studies.

VOICE: That remains to be seen. Come in...

COMPANION: I will wait for you here.

LAURA: I intend to come out of Professor Jones' office with a course of study which will please me.

(*LAURA exits. The lights change.*)

ENID: After the war there was no art—too many men had died. But there were many ladies left, and ladies love gardens, and statues for their gardens: I made those, in plenty, and earned good money. Cupids, with little bows and arrows... Frogs, on lily pads... And marble portraits of ladies, too, but not for gardens: for sitting rooms and parlors... Decoration. Not art. I made one statue of a real woman—no lady: Emma Willard, who started the first woman's college in this country. And... I have two things left, even now: I can support myself. And I have the clay...

When I began, in Chicago, in the first arts sweat shop, I made five dollars for each weekday I worked, and seven-fifty on Sundays: fat wages! When our first month's work was finished and we took our place in line with hundreds of workmen to receive our pay envelopes, we were about the happiest white rabbits that ever existed. We rushed back to our rooms at the hotel and poured out the five-dollar bills and carpeted the floor with them. We wanted to see what it felt like to walk on money! I still love money. And I still love clay.

The beautiful clay! Every day, I carry a bit of clay in my hand—just to feel it, to mould it... I roll it between my fingers, and suddenly an almost overwhelming delight comes through me. The feel of that clay in my hand—just the mere sensual part of it, the touch, seems to fire me with something tremendously stimulating!

Mine was a wholesome, happy, stimulating life...

And so that must be added to the sum: the feel of the clay, and of my independence—and the friendship of women...

"Better to marry than to burn," my sister told me when she was engaged. But I have burned—I have burned with a lovely light!

I sent her, for a wedding gift, my "Kiss tankard" made of silver, with a little faun who kisses a nymph when the tankard lid is lifted...

But it was cast wrong. When the lid is lifted, the faun's nose strikes the poor nymph's collar bone, and she is left staring at his adam's apple! (*She laughs.*) I don't believe my sister ever noticed...

Better... to... burn...

(*The lights change.*)

ELIZABETH: Pardon me. Is this the Poetry Club of the University of Chicago?

ENID: It is.

ELIZABETH: Why are we required to take off our wraps and leave them here in the vestibule? (*Lays coat down.*) I am always cold, I prefer to keep my coat.

ENID: The smoke from the Illinois Central Railway makes everything sooty here in Chicago, and so our wraps must come off so that they will not sully the upholstery...

ELIZABETH: I am Elizabeth Madox Roberts, from Kentucky. Excuse me, I must sit down.

ENID: Was your trip tiring?

ELIZABETH: No, but I have been ill for a very long time—I had to give up my teaching, my nerves simply wouldn't allow—-

ENID: Were you teaching in Kentucky?

ELIZABETH: Backwoods boys. They did everything in their power to wear me out. One day I came into class and found my blackboard had been scrawled with common four-letter words of bodily excretions. Before I cleared the board, I added one more word: tear. Also a four-letter word, also an excretion of the body—a true juice of the human frame. And I told my pupils, "Let the boy, whoever he was, who wrote for the whole people of the community, let him write the last word: tear. He will write it in time, this supreme juice from the body of man, the point where he stands above himself, where he outdoes the cattle."

ENID: It does not sound as though they succeeded in wearing you out.

ELIZABETH: Ah, but they did. I had to return to my parent's house, in Springfield—in the Little Country.

ENID: The Little Country?

ELIZABETH: Kentucky. I have the phrase from Willa Cather, and I also adopted from her the line of Horace which is my motto: *Primus ego in patriam mecum... deducam Musas.* I WILL BE THE FIRST TO BRING THE MUSE INTO MY OWN COUNTRY. Cather had to leave the west in order to write about it, and I needed to leave my Little Country, for a while, in order to be able to return and write about it, without feeling imprisoned...

VOICE: The annual meeting of the Poetry Club of the University of Chicago will come to order...

ELIZABETH: I must go in—I am fairly in the town of my hopes.

(*The lights change. LAURA reenters.*)

LAURA: I am fairly in the town of my hopes!

ENID: So you are admitted?

LAURA: To one year's course of study—without any trouble at all! French and Algebra—no difficulty there! History and drawing—I will have to study harder than I have ever studied before, to keep up with my classes; they are all men who have had the benefit of formal training. I will take private lessons in geometry. I will be very happy.

ENID: But, Laura—you've only begun. How do you know?

LAURA: I have waited fifteen years! I have seen all my brothers educated, leaving home. I have seen in front of me the life of my Aunt Ann—the life of service. Now I have nothing against the life of service, but I must see my way clear to choosing what or whom I am to serve. Now, however, I must return to our boarding house and continue to make the list of the contents of my trunk. Mother has asked for an inventory.

(*As LAURA and ENID cross the stage toward the exit, the lights change. LAURA recites in a singsong which communicates her delight.*)

LAURA: CHEMISES, TEN.

ELIZABETH: DRAWERS, NEW, SIX.

ENID: DRAWERS, OLD, FOUR.

LAURA: DRAWERS, FLANNEL, SIX.

ELIZABETH: PETTICOATS, OLD COTTON, FIVE...

ENID: PETTICOATS, PERCALE, THREE...

LAURA: PETTICOATS, NEW COTTON, THREE...

ELIZABETH: PETTICOATS, FLANNEL, FIVE...

(*They join hands and they are children again, hopping together along the hopscotch.*)

ENID: (*Hopping and singing.*) TOWELS, HAND, NINE! TOWELS, FOOT, SIX!

LAURA, ENID and ELIZABETH: UNDER SLEEVES, ONE! UNDER BODIES, THREE! CORSETS, TWO! —

(*Laughing, they run off the stage. ELIZABETH stops just before she exits. She looks after LAURA and ENID incredulously, shaking her head.*)

ELIZABETH: What IS the new generation of girls coming to?

(*Transition music.*)

SCENE THREE

EPILOGUE

Many years later. All are present except CARRY and MARY TODD who have died. They have gathered to view the marker, which has finally been erected on CARRY's grave. They carry a wreath.

LAURA: Well, it's a fine sight, and Carry would approve of it—simple, dignified, made of granite.

ENID: Yellow Cararra marble, Italy's finest—that's what I wanted.

ELIZABETH: But I knew Carry would want plain Kentucky granite. Hard as she was—

ENID: She was not hard.

LAURA: You have to be hard, to survive in this world. Look what happened to poor Mary Todd—

ELIZABETH: She had to wait till she died to be treated the way she wanted. At least they buried her with Abraham.

ENID: But you don't see her name on Abraham's big monument in Washington. I'm glad we put a wreath there, with her name on it—people will see that and think of her, for a while.

LAURA: My work is my monument... I spent twenty-four years slaving for the Kentucky Equal Rights association—twenty-four years of writing letters, speeches, signing petitions—-

ELIZABETH: Black men were given the vote in 1870.

LAURA: We had to wait till 1920—and then it was the federal government, butting in. Kentucky should have given the vote to women.

ENID: By 1920 I was home again, teaching young women, telling them to marry rather than to burn— and when I went to vote that first time, I thought: So this is what Laura was carrying on about, all those years—

ELIZABETH: All that never mattered much to me... I was writing.

ENID: You must have felt it, Elizabeth.

ELIZABETH: Well, yes, I felt it: It's in the air we breathe... But I had faith in men. That someday it would all be made right...

LAURA: Alice Paul took over the women's movement... She wrote the equal rights amendment, finally, in 1923— "Equality of rights under the law shall not be denied or abridged by the United States or any State on account of sex." But Congress wasn't ready—the men weren't ready, Elizabeth, to tell us we could be their equals! Twenty-nine years later, Congress passed the amendment! Twenty-nine years—nearly a lifetime.

ENID: And Kentucky didn't ratify the amendment for a long time after that—

LAURA: We were the 19th State in 1972.

ELIZABETH: But didn't they try to rescind the amendment?

LAURA: The legislators did, one time when the governor was away— but we had a woman, the lieutenant governor, Thelma Stovall, who wouldn't let that pass—-

ENID: It's not the law even now, and still some people wonder what it's all about.

LAURA: They're going to be feuding and fussing about the amendment for years, long after all of us are gone! They'll be telling lies, saying equal rights means men and women will have to use the same bathrooms, or women will have to join the army—lies! All lies! But foolish people will believe them.

ELIZABETH: You may say I never did a thing to help—but my girls—the young women in my books—they show our fighting spirit! Look at my Ellen—playing with a colt in the field, forgetting her fear of fences... Ellen's just as much a fighter as Carry Nation! I had the women in my books—and Carry had her axes.

ENID: And I had my marble ladies, all lost now, who never needed to worry about equality.

LAURA: But privilege is no protection. It comes from men, husbands and fathers, and husbands and fathers can take it away.

ELIZABETH: I brought something I'd like to read—it's by Edna St. Vincent Millay. It wasn't written about Carry, but it made me think of her.

LAURA: Go ahead, Elizabeth.

ELIZABETH: (*Reading.*) Upon this marble bust which is not I
Lay the round, formal wreath, which is not fame;
But in the forum of my silenced cry
Root ye the living tree whose sap is flame.
I, that was proud and valiant, am no more;
Save as a dream that wanders wide and late,
Save as a wind that rattles the stout door,
Troubling ashes in the sheltered grate.
The stone will perish; I shall be twice dust.
Only my standard on a taken hill
Can cheat the mildew and the red-brown rust
And make immortal my adventurous will.
Even now the silk is tugging at the staff:
Take up the song; forget the epitaph.

(*THE WOMEN lay their wreath. Then they embrace. They may repeat sentences from the poem to each other. ALL THREE then approach the marker, as though to tell CARRY goodbye.*)

ENID: I wish we could have given her that poem.

ELIZABETH: Oh no—she told us what she wanted.

LAURA: (*Reading the inscription.*) She has done what she could.

(*THE WOMEN walk back to the picture frames and step behind them. Slowly, gravely, they take up their poses again as the lights fade.*)

THE END

Sylvia Cardwell in *Hopscotch* by Sallie Bingham, Kentucky tour, 1988

SALLIE BINGHAM

Born in the shadow of World War Two, I was raised and schooled in Kentucky until going to Radcliffe College where I graduated with an English degree in 1958. My first novel was published shortly after that, and I continued to live on the East Coast.

Two collections of short stories were followed by a long hiatus while I was raising my three sons. I began writing for the theater in 1980 with the founding of The Women's Project and Productions in New York, which produced my first three plays. My other plays have been seen at various regional theatres as well as the Perry Street Theatre in New York.

After moving back to Kentucky in 1977, I wrote a memoir and published three novels, followed by two more collections of short stories, including *Red Car*, published in the spring of 2008.

As a feminist and a philanthropist, I have had the pleasure of founding the Kentucky Foundation for Women and The Sallie Bingham Archive at Duke University.

I live in Santa Fe, New Mexico.

Ronald J. Aulgur and Warren Hammack in *Desperate Fortune* by Joe Terrence Gray, Horse Cave Theatre, 1990

DESPERATE FORTUNE
by
Joe Terrence Gray

Kevin Haggard and Jack Johnson in *Desperate Fortune* by Joe Terrence Gray, Horse Cave Theatre, 1990

Desperate Fortune opened on July 13, 1990, with the following cast:

JOSEPH STREET	*Kevin Haggard*
JOHN WOOD	*Jack Johnson*
THOMAS JEFFERSON	*Ronald J. Aulgur*
DOLLY MADISON	*Phoebe Hall*
THEODOSIA BURR ALSTON	*Amy Stewart*
JAMES MADISON	*Chris Burmester*
AARON BURR	*Warren Hammack*
ANTHONY MERRY	*Scott Edmonds*
HENRY DEARBORN	*Randall Ervin*
HUMPHREY MARSHALL	*Gregory Etter*
GEORGE ADAMS	*Robert Poe*
JOSEPH HAMILTON DAVEISS	*Steve Wise*
JOHN BROWN	*Chris Burmester*
MARGARETTA BROWN	*Pamela White*
JOHN ADAIR	*Ronald J. Aulgur*
HENRY CLAY	*Tim Van Metter*
HARRY INNES	*Scott Edmonds*
EZRA BROOKS	*Randall Ervin*
JOHN BRADFORD	*Thomas Harner*
JOHN POPE	*Amahl Lovato*
ABRAHAM HITE	*Joseph Gray*
PETER TAYLOR	*John Conlee*
SHERIFF	*Matthew Stone*
CITIZEN of FRANKFORT	*Thomas Harner*
SPEAKER of the KENTUCKY GENERAL ASSEMBLY	*Robert Singleton*
SERVANT	*Christi Spontak*
SPECTATORS	*Jane McNeill, Thomas Harner*
	Eric Blanton, Robert Singleton

Director: Walter Rhodes
Stage Manager: Karen Terry
Set Design: Sam Hunt
Lighting Design: Gregory Etter
Costume Design: Becca Shouse
Properties Master: Julie Whichard
Technical Director: Eric Wegener
Original Music Composed by: Gabrielle Mattingly Gray
Violin: Mason Newman
Percussion: Steve Tucker
Choreographer: Melanie Asriel
Assistant Choreographer: Christie Spontak

Kentucky history provides many fascinating stories, but few as intriguing as the mystery surrounding Aaron Burr's trials for treason in Frankfort in the winter of 1806. The former vice-president, war hero, and duelist flat-boated down the Ohio collecting men and supplies for a colony along the Ouachita River. Or so he said. But was it a settlement or an invasion force that the little colonel was enlisting? Was his objective the conquest of Spanish Mexico or secession of the new Louisiana Territory? To this day, nobody knows.

With Warren Hammack's encouragement, the guidance of state historian Jim Klotter, pointers from Jim Peyton, and aid from the Kentucky Humanities Council, I began to knit together a narrative that hued as close as possible to the events of history.

I had fallen into a cauldron of political ambition and physical jealousies. Could I balance these contradictory affections and overlapping allegiances? I spun the conclusion as I would a documentary film; I set down what facts I uncovered and left interpretation of motives and consequences to the public.

My biggest thrill personally was being a member of the acting company and watching from the wings as Warren leaned into Burr's closing monologue, the haunting benediction of an old soldier fading away.

– Joe Terrence Gray

Desperate Fortune

Characters:

JOSEPH STREET, *23 years old, a good-looking arrogant son of a land-poor Virginia farmer*

JOHN WOOD, *a Scotch immigrant, elderly looking, of middle size, and ordinary dress*

THOMAS JEFFERSON, *at 63 years, the tall President is casually elegant in a black suit and stockings; slow to anger but unrelenting in defeating opposition*

DOLLY MADISON, *38 years old, a buxom, social climber*

THEODOSIA BURR ALSTON, *23 years old, the only child of Aaron Burr; a paragon of brains, beauty and wit*

JAMES MADISON, *56 years old and physically unimpressive*

AARON BURR, *50 years old, five foot six inches tall, with deep-set hazel eyes; a high forehead accentuated by long thick hair, generously powdered and anchored by a small shell comb; often clad in a single-breasted jacket, usually blue, a standing collar, a buff vest, and dark trousers; displaying an urbanity which... while it precludes familiarity... banishes restraint*

ANTHONY MERRY, *a middle-aged English bourgeois, plain, unassuming, and sensible*

HENRY DEARBORN, *middle-aged, very much a farmer*

HUMPHREY MARSHALL, *46 years old, six feet two inches, lithe and muscular; a luxuriant growth of black hair atop a handsome face, coal-black eyes; wears scrupulously clean, white linen and a suit of plain homespun cloth cut to show off his fine form to advantage; carries a large cudgel, "Uncle Ratha"*

GEORGE ADAMS, *a young firebrand*

JOSEPH HAMILTON DAVEISS, *32 years-old, six feet tall, fine personal appearance and impressive bearing*

JOHN BROWN, *49 years old, a portly frame of medium height, pleasant features and rosy cheeks*

MARGARETTA BROWN, *34 years old, mother of two, red hair, hazel eyes, daughter of a New York City clergyman; starved for good society in her new frontier*

JOHN ADAIR, *49 years old, an ex-Indian War officer, Revolutionary Army officer, and prisoner of war*

HENRY CLAY, *29 years old, six feet, one inch with premature white hair, a tall forehead, large mouth, small grey eyes, a pallid face*

HARRY INNES, *54 years old, a bald man of medium height, long pointed nose; an asthma sufferer, stutters when under pressure*

EZRA BROOKS, *a middle-aged farmer and war veteran*

JOHN BRADFORD, *a partisan Republican newspaper editor*

JOHN POPE, *a 40 year-old legislator, a zealous speaker, a missing right arm*

ABRAHAM HITE, *a tradesman, simple and sincere*

PETER TAYLOR, *a young gardener*

SHEFIFF; BAILIFF; DOCK WORKERS; CITIZENS OF FRANKFORT; SPEAKER AND MEMBERS OF THE KENTUCKY GENERAL ASSEMBLY; GUESTS AT A GALA; A KENTUCKY GOVERNOR

Place: Kentucky, Washington, Philadelphia

Time: First decade of the 19th century

The stage setting is minimal, the better to emphasize the revolutionary ideal that individual will is the primary force shaping the human environment; thus a table or a bush, a chair or a hitching post serve to distinguish interiors from exteriors. The costumes should be as authentic to the era as is practical.

This first decade of the 19th Century was an unstable period, following years of tremendous social upheaval. A man's mode of dress was a badge of his politics. The new American republic, followed swiftly by the more radical revolution in France with its doctrine of liberty and equality chillingly enforced by mass executions, had hardened partisan loyalties on this side of the Atlantic. Once he was inaugurated President in 1801, Thomas Jefferson, the leader of the "Jacobin" party in America, implemented his egalitarianism by doing away with fancy dress at state functions. Long pants and broadcloth replaced lace cuffs and periwigs among Jefferson's Republican followers. If you were a "federal man" —- that is, an opponent of Jefferson's style of democracy —- dressing in the older fashion of your party's exemplar, George Washington, with knee britches and powdered wigs, was an indication of your conservatism. On the frontier, however, which was Kentucky, these distinctions tended to blur. Garments made of homespun cloth and suits of buckskin were preferred by the pioneers who were devoted to making Kentucky commercially, if not politically, independent of the dominant Atlantic states. In Lexington and Frankfort, a suit of richly colored imported English broadcloth marked you as an Easterner, whatever your political party.

The contrast in clothing among the characters is important, not only to demonstrate their nominal allegiances, but as a dramatic device to reveal personality and political acumen, as characters mix their styles of dress to be accepted by one segment of society or another.

ACT ONE

SCENE ONE

Morning sunlight sparkles through a frosty mist. A heron calls. A flatboat floating down the Ohio. Two men unwrap themselves from a common bedroll. A young man, JOSEPH STREET, stands up shivering. He slaps his arms around his shoulders to warm himself. He wears what was once a fine brown suit, but is now soiled and tattered. The second man, JOHN WOOD, gets to his feet slowly. He pulls the blankets around his shoulders and sits atop the stacks of crates on which they have been sleeping.

STREET: How long are we to float down this endless river? I've not seen a civilized soul in days.

WOOD: Ah, but laddie, we have each other.

STREET: Yes, and the elements <u>have</u> us both.

WOOD: You're too captious, lad. We'll soon reach our destination: quiet little Frankfort, the new capitol in the new state of Kentucky.

STREET: If I'd a-known what a wilderness we'd encounter, I'd a-stayed in Richmond.

WOOD: Ah, but out here we'll embrace a new sort of man, loyal to nothing but his own toil and ambition— devoid of the false flattery of your slave-flogging Virginia gentry.

STREET: You have a short memory, John. It was the price of my manservant, William, that has provided us this raft and the food we finished, yesterday.

WOOD: Aye, but now you're free. Free to ply your own talents instead of relyin' on the labor of the black man. Rejoice, me boy. For the first time in your life, you are truly free.

STREET: Even if William is not.

(*WOOD smiles, then looks into STREET's eyes. He chortles.*)

WOOD: Laddie, you must learn to live off the land as you find it, whether a state of nature or a state of man. When I came ashore six year ago, a penniless Scotsman on the quays of New York, I had only my instincts to guide me. Today me' name is known by all the reflectin' men of this country as the brave journalist who exposed the tyranny of one President and clipped the wings of another who came within a talon's grasp of that high office.

STREET: Yes, but are you certain your famous Colonel Burr will return to the West?

(*WOOD picks up a length of string, and proceeds to tie small hooks into the cord at various points along the line.*)

WOOD: "He needs must go that the devil drives." Ol' Cootie will be back. Never fear. There be too many souls ripe for the temptin' and too many fat purses for clippin' for me Colonel to resist such fabulous lure.

STREET: (*Slapping his shoulders.*) 'Tis a pity you're so fond of your own words. Those old newspapers you're carrying would make good wadding inside my coat. I'm freezing.

WOOD: Patience, laddie. (*Offering him a sip from a flask.*) Let your spirit keep you warm. Soon we shall ignite me old rags. But ne'er so 'umble a fire as to fizzle in a morning's dew. Nay. (*Patting his knapsack.*) Me thinks these scribblings will spark a noble's pyre that will smelter both our ambition's due. (*WOOD smiles as he drops the hooks into the water.*)

(*Lights cross fade.*)

SCENE TWO

The President's House. A long dinner table sits atop an elevated platform. The table forces our perspective to narrow toward the head, upstage; thus the GUESTS downstage appear farther apart than those near the head. At the head of the table sits a tall sandy-grey-haired man in his sixties – THOMAS JEFFERSON. On his right, a plump, cheerful woman, DOLLY MADISON. On JEFFERSON's left, a red-faced, middle-aged man, the British Ambassador, ANTHONY MERRY. Beside MRS. MADISON sits her husband, the Secretary of State, JAMES MADISON. Opposite MADISON, a petite and attractive young woman, THEODOSIA BURR ALSTON, drains her wine glass. On MADISON's right, the Secretary of War, HENRY DEARBORN, slowly finishes his meal. Opposite DEARBORN, sits an immaculate figure, erect and alert, AARON BURR. JEFFERSON pours wine in DOLLY's glass, hands the bottle to MADISON, who pours his own and sends the decanter down the table.

THEODOSIA: Mr. President, I must compliment you on one policy you announced during your first inaugural address. How did you phrase it? (*Feigning forgetfulness.*) Oh, yes. "The energies of our men ought to be principally employed in the multiplication of the human race."

JEFFERSON: (*Seriously.*) And so they must, if we are to populate our new Louisiana Territory.

DOLLY: Perhaps, Mr. President, the women folk would be more dutiful, if the men were more forth-coming.

(*The GROUP laughs.*)

MADISON: Tell us, Colonel Burr, how stand you now with the courts?

BURR: In New York, I'm disenfranchised, and in New Jersey, I'm to be hanged. Having substantial objections to both, I shall hazard neither, but shall seek my fortune in our West.

JEFFERSON: We must see if our friends in New York can't be more helpful, mustn't we, Jemmy? After all, your duel with Hamilton was in New Jersey. Was it not?

BURR: Yes, and the Federalists there don't plan to allow anything as petty as the law to obstruct their vengeance. Old Judge Boudinot charged the grand jury, "Indict Burr, or God will desolate your family and lay waste to your crops."

(*Part of the GROUP laughs.*)

JEFFERSON: These High Federalists make a mockery of justice. God would we were rid of 'em all.

MERRY: Your expedition through your western country caused quite a stir here in Washington, Colonel.

MADISON: The <u>Philadelphia Gazette</u> suggests that you are plotting some sort of revolution out there.

BURR: (*Laughing.*) Ha. Ha. I'm surprised at you, James; surely you know me better than that? The only active conspiracy I know is the one perpetrated by the newspapers to entice more subscribers.

(*All the GROUP laughs.*)

THEODOSIA: If Your Excellency will allow us, Mrs. Madison and I will withdraw. Now that the Madeira is served, I fear the appearance of those terrible cigars. Besides, Dolly and I have a plot of our own to construct: how to find our Chief Executive a first lady.

DOLLY: Come, Theodosia, let's see to our patriotic duty. The companionship of an attractive lady might make our President's habitation in this drafty barn more hospitable.

(*The MEN stand as the two WOMEN exit. JEFFERSON passes around a box of cigars. The MEN move down a staircase in groups of one and two, passing a taper with which to light their cigars.*)

JEFFERSON: Gentlemen, in a few days I shall deliver my annual message to Congress. I should like to have your opinions, particularly yours, Mr. Merry, as what I have to say deals directly with the actions of your British Admiralty.

(*JEFFERSON takes up a manuscript and reads.*) At a moment when the nations of Europe are arming against each other, a meeting of both Houses of Congress has become more than usually desirable. Our coasts have been infested by private armed vessels. They have captured not only the vessels of our friends, but our own also. (*JEFFERSON's delivery falters, and his voice lowers to a whisper.*) New principles have been interpolated into the law of nations, which if pursued in practice, prostrate our neutral navigation and make us merely subservient to the purpose of a belligerent — Strike that last phrase. "Merely subservient" may be at once too inflammatory for our Congressmen and too gratifying to the British Navy.

MERRY: I protest. This is crass indignity, sir, reading such insults to my face. (*MERRY stands drawing all his authority into himself.*) As the minister of His Majesty King George of Great Britain, I must object to these accusations. (*MERRY starts to exit.*)

JEFFERSON: A moment, sir. You will want to make a full report to London. (*JEFFERSON continues reading.*) Your England takes to itself commerce with its own enemy, which it denies to us, a neutral nation. Reason revolts at such inconsistency. The duty of maintaining the authority of reason, the only umpire between just nations, imposes on us the obligation of providing a determined opposition to such a doctrine.

DEARBORN: Good stuff.

MADISON: The passage as it stands has a good countenance. But if I may make a suggestion…

MERRY: (*Sarcasm concealing his shock.*) If my presence is no longer required, I will withdraw and allow you, gentlemen, to refine your effrontery. Good night.

(*MERRY exits.*)

BURR: Determined words, Mr. President. But the message would be more effective were it writ with gunpowder and lead rather than pen and ink.

JEFFERSON: Our Constitution is a peace establishment, Mr. Burr. War would endanger its very existence.

BURR: If it be so insubstantial, perhaps it is better replaced with a more energetic government. (*A beat. BURR surveys the reaction of each man in the group, then smiles.*) Gentlemen, I will say good night. Since I am no longer an officer of the federal government, I think I will join the more subtle sovereignty the ladies are plotting in the parlor.

(*GROUP laughs.*)

JEFFERSON: I'm afraid your conspiracy will be foiled, Colonel. Two terms as President and one marriage is plenty enough for any man.

BURR: Or too much? Am I right, sir?

JEFFERSON: (*Laughing.*) Yes, I'm sure at my age, either one would be too much. Good night, Colonel.

(*BURR exits.*)

MADISON: Sir, I think Colonel Burr warrants watching. He loves intrigue more than life itself.

JEFFERSON: Let him stand undisturbed as a monument to the safety with which error can be tolerated where reason is free to combat it.

DEARBORN: I never knew reason to fire a musket, sir.

JEFFERSON: Gentlemen, this is 1805, not 1800. The two political factions have melted into one.

DEARBORN: Our domestic policies are popular, true. But as Secretary of War, what I see is a nation, with no army to speak of, surrounded by foreign armies and navies, with rebels North and South plotting openly to make of us several separate nations.

MADISON: However, having a man with the Colonel's military reputation openly operating on the western frontier might give the Spanish Commandants second thoughts about moving further into Louisiana.

DEARBORN: On the other hand, Burr might already be plotting with the Spanish.

MADISON: Or the English.

DEARBORN: Or both, for that matter.

MADISON: We must be very careful. Burr is extremely popular on the frontier. Killing Hamilton endeared him to every whiskey rebel in Christendom.

JEFFERSON: I grant you, the little Colonel is a crooked gun. But we've sighted him before and hit our mark. I think we can aim him safely.

(*Lights cross fade.*)

SCENE THREE

DOLLY and THEODOSIA talking.

DOLLY: My heart sinks when I think of that lonely, disconsolate man.

THEODOSIA: I understand the President's sons-in-law are perpetually at each other's throats.

DOLLY: Oh my, Dear, I don't mean Mr. Jefferson. I'm talking about your father.

(*BURR enters.*)

BURR: Any progress in your match-making, ladies?

DOLLY: You and Mr. Jefferson are too single-minded, I fear. I want you to know, Aaron, that Jemmy and I don't believe a word of what the newspapers are saying about you.

BURR: I could tell you of many a tale at which you would laugh, at my expense.

DOLLY: (*Laughing.*) Oh, Aaron, no matter how sad your prospects, you never lose your sense of humor. (*Assuming a matriarchal tone.*) You must console yourselves as I do with the old saying, "Vain his attempt who strives to please them all."

BURR: My dear Dolly, if memory serves, you would know the proof of that adage better than I.

DOLLY: Theo, your father is too naughty for words. See if you can rein in his galloping wit, before it runs away with him.

(*DOLLY exits.*)

BURR: I'm pleased to see Dolly still so attractive.

THEODOSIA: But oh, that unfortunate propensity to snuff-taking.

BURR: You hardly touched your dinner. In China, ginseng is the panacea for a poor appetite. Shall I have my chemist send some 'round?

THEODOSIA: I was too agitated to eat. How that beast, Jefferson, can feign concern for your welfare after depriving you of the vice presidency...

BURR: When my stomach wants tone, nothing serves so effectually as a cup of chamomile tea, without sugar or milk.

THEODOSIA: More needs repairing than my appetite, father. My spirits rise and fall with your fortune.

BURR: So little fortune have I to speak of. I've sold my house and furniture for about twenty-five thousand. But I still owe seven or eight thousand. The library and the wine remain. They are yours, for I see no way to repay your husband his generosity.

THEODOSIA: Do not concern yourself about Mr. Alston. His Carolina plantation produces more rice every year.

BURR: And more black babies, too, I warrant.

THEODOSIA: (*Looking downcast.*) Yes, and those too. (*She looks up toward her sire.*) But tell me, Papa, how are you bearing up?

BURR: If you have a friend who is dying of ennui, recommend to him to engage in a duel and a courtship at the same time.

THEODOSIA: *La pauvre Celeste?*

BURR: *Oui.* At five in the morning, I start for Philadelphia.

THEODOSIA: Must you, father? We see so little of each other. You have furnished this Celeste ample arguments against matrimony. Yet she has called you back. I would have seen you to Japan before I should have done so much.

BURR: If the President will oblige me, I should prefer a posting to London.

THEDOSIA: (*Adjusting his tie.*) Dress warmly for your trip tomorrow. It will be bitterly cold at that hour of the morning.

BURR: How little the truth is suspected by the hundreds who ascribe to my every move a profound political importance.

THEODOSIA: Go, then. Go to your mistress! I shall postpone my departure for Charleston until you return. Husbands can be kept waiting more easily than lovers. *Bon jour, mon cher petit pere.*

BURR: *Adieu.*

(*BOTH exit. Lights fade to dark.*)

SCENE FOUR

The residence of the British plenipotentiary in Philadelphia. MERRY walks ahead of an unseen guest wearing a cloak.

MERRY: Welcome to my home. I hope your journey was not arduous. I am afraid my wife refuses to leave Philadelphia for that swampy bog you've chosen for your capitol.

(*BURR steps from the shadows.*)

BURR: Philadelphia has much to recommend it, I agree.

MERRY: Your President would do well to study its etiquette, I can tell you that. I am becoming intolerant of his discourtesies.

BURR: He's quite tame, I assure you. Mr. Jefferson savors strong rhetoric at table. But he has no stomach for real warfare.

MERRY: Yes, so I'm informed.

BURR: Any word from Lord Mulgrave?

MERRY: I am sorry to report that my dispatch containing your request was lost at sea.

BURR: Lost? You can't be serious? This is a severe setback. Everything is prepared in every other quarter. New Orleans is so completely prepared that a revolution can be accomplished there without a drop of blood being shed.

MERRY: That's encouraging.

BURR: Once Louisiana declares itself independent, the Eastern states will separate from the southern and these United States will be united no longer.

MERRY: That seems likely, if your plan succeeds.

BURR: To assure success, send me two or three ships of the line and an equal number of frigates to guard the Gulf of Mexico. I must impress upon you the importance of prompt action. If we delay even for a season, all opportunity will be lost. France will intervene, regain Louisiana and annex Florida.

MERRY: (*Becoming nervous at the prospect.*) We must certainly prevent that. If the Austrians fail to stop Napoleon in Italy, Europe is lost. God knows who or what could stop that little tyrant then?

BURR: For a fraction of what it will cost England to regain Europe, you can have ten times the continent here. Loan me one hundred thousand pounds to outfit my army of volunteers, and I will make you masters of North America forever.

MERRY: Getting money from England with war threatening may be difficult.

BURR: I have a plan to avoid the necessity of exporting specie: get your government to purchase stock in an American company, say my Indiana Canal Company.

MERRY: That could be arranged, I suppose.

BURR: Then arrange it, and quickly.

MERRY: Your plan has much to recommend it. I will detail your requests to the Admiralty and relay their decision to you, when, and if, my government chooses to act. You will, of course, make no mention of my role in this business.

BURR: Sir, I never take the least liberty with any man's secrets but my own.

(*Lights fade to dark.*)

SCENE FIVE

A tavern in Frankfort. Three MEN stand drinking ale. Behind them WOOD and STREET sit at a table.

FIRST PATRON: They say Miranda has sailed from New York bound for the Caribbean.

SECOND PATRON: If his armada liberates Caracas, all South America will revolt against Spain.

THIRD PATRON: And the Floridas will be ours for the taking.

FIRST PATRON: Get your muskets ready, boys.

THIRD PATRON: (*Lifting his mug and shouting.*) On to Mobile!

STREET: What gentleman would keep us waiting half a day to make his acquaintance?

WOOD: One who requires proof that our confidence in him is greater than our concern for ceremony. If there be 'er a man who knows where the political skeletons are buried in this state, it's Humphrey Marshall.

STREET: You said we were to stay clear of political factions?

WOOD: Factions, yes. But money and power? Not and succeed in this business, laddie. Humphrey Marshall is the one man with the motive, the fortitude, and the fortune, to support our newspaper. (*He leans toward STREET and lowers his tone of voice.*) People say ol' Humphrey is the richest man in Kentucky, that he owns more than a hundred thousand acres of this overgrown Paradise.

STREET: Is money your sole moral philosophy?

WOOD: I speak only that ye may profit by my example. While I was in the employ of Colonel Burr, as private tutor to his smart aleck daughter, I kept my mouth closed and me' ears open. At table I listened as Colonel Burr described the idiocy of incumbent President Adams. When I published these observations, Burr was outraged and suppressed my wee' book. But nothing is done, the saying goes, that is done in secret. Colonel Burr's enemies in his own party seized on this as proof of his connivance with the Federalists.

STREET: What man doubts he is not secretly a Federalist? Every Federalist member of Congress voted for Burr over Jefferson when the two tied for the Presidency in 1800.

WOOD: Party politics is a dull sword that will sooner tire the man who wields it than bloody his opponent. The good journalist, however, keeps himself above party strife; only, ne'r so far out of the fray as to be beyond belief in all that he writes.

(*A tall, dark-haired man, HUMPHREY MARSHALL, dressed in a homespun suit and carrying a large cudgel, approaches.*)

MARSHALL: Mr. Wood?

(*WOOD and STREET stand.*)

WOOD: Aye, sir. (*He extends his hand. MARSHALL shakes his hand reluctantly.*) This is my associate, Joseph Street of Richmond.

MARSHALL: Mr. Street. (*MARSHALL shakes his hand vigorously.*) Always pleased to meet a fellow Virginian.

WOOD: That's quite a shillelagh you're carrying.

MARSHALL: (*Pounding his cudgel on the floor.*) Meet Uncle Ratha. His namesake attempted to cane me with him. But I disarmed the culprit and thrashed him with his own cudgel. I carry it now to remind my political enemies how easily I may turn their own weapons against them.

WOOD: Mr. Street and I are journalists. We are thinking of inaugurating another newspaper in Frankfort. What do you think of our prospects for success?

STREET: We are concerned that Mr. Hunter's <u>Palladium</u> and Mr. Bradford's <u>Kentucky Gazette</u> may prove stiff competitors.

MARSHALL: Nuisances, the both of them. No man of quality puts stock in what they say. They rhapsodize over every word Thomas Jefferson utters.

WOOD: That is why we were thinking an independent newspaper, rigidly pursuing the path of truth...

STREET: .....regardless of the anathemas of political maniacs...

WOOD: .....would be a welcome addition to local political discourse.

MARSHALL: You want my opinion? This state needs a journal whose editors believe in the Constitution of the United States.

WOOD: We will ever support those characters whose conduct proclaims their attachment to that document.

STREET: And whose acts evidence purity of motives.

WOOD: Purity of motives is well and good. But will we have enough subscribers to make our enterprise pay its way, and ours?

MARSHALL: Subscribers are like cattle. They gather around the trough with the sweetest grain. And, I do believe there is fodder enough in Kentucky to feed a sizable beast of controversy.

STREET: Then will you open your granary to us?

MARSHALL: That depends on whose ox you intend to gore.

WOOD: Why, the fattest, of course.

(*WOOD and MARSHALL laugh. STREET looks troubled. Lights fade to dark.*)

SCENE SIX

The President's Office. On an elevated stage JEFFERSON stands with his back to the audience. A violin under his chin, he draws a bow over the instrument, but fails in his attempt to push it harmoniously back across the strings. BURR enters and watches silently as JEFFERSON repeats the gesture with the same results, then lays the instrument aside.

JEFFERSON: (*Massaging his right wrist.*) My apologies for so discordant a fanfare. As a young man, I was quite a fiddler. But no more. Now I must content myself with other instruments. I broke my wrist some years ago, and I'm no longer able to play with any felicity.

BURR: A fall from a horse?

JEFFERSON: A missed jump, you might say. (*JEFFERSON sits in his swivel chair, lifts a large fossil on his desk and takes some papers from beneath it.*)

BURR: An affair of the heart?

JEFFERSON: (*Looks up.*) Your astuteness rarely fails you, does, it, Colonel Burr?

BURR: I believe you will agree it played no small role in placing you initially in this office.

JEFFERSON: Your management of our party's victory in New York in 1800 was superior. I will be the first to admit that. (*JEFFERSON turns his seat then stands.*) Now, tell me, what new challenge have you found equal to your talents?

BURR: (*Walking away.*) I am presently disengaged from all particular business. While I have never asked for any position, I believe I possess certain qualities that may be of service, particularly in our delicate relations abroad.

JEFFERSON: If you're referring to the vacant post in London, I have in mind to name Governor Monroe.

BURR: Your preference for appointing Virginians to all the important positions will no doubt be noted by your enemies.

JEFFERSON: Monroe proved his diplomatic skill in concluding our Louisiana Purchase. I foresee no objections from any person of influence to his continuing service.

BURR: I see. Then allow me to inquire of another matter. Among the private ventures I am considering is a large grant belonging to Lord Bastrop along the Washita River near our disputed boundary with Spanish Mexico. I would like to reassure the settlers that I lead there as to their nation's intentions in that quarter.

JEFFERSON: As you are probably aware, Colonel, we are ill prepared for war, even with the decrepit Spanish garrisons in Florida and Mexico.

BURR: The Spanish obviously think so. Thirteen hundred Spanish soldiers now occupy territory claimed by your government. Opinion is that we shall be at war with Spain before the year is out.

JEFFERSON: Peace is our policy, now and always. It is my firm belief that a just and friendly conduct on our part will produce justice and friendship from others.

BURR: Pardon me, sir, if I beg to differ in my view of what motivates men and their nations.

JEFFERSON: If I were you, I would not gamble too heavily on the eventuality of war. The Congress in secret session has appropriated two million dollars to purchase the Floridas from Spain. And the French minister, Talleyrand, has sent us terms by which the Spanish will part with these territories.

BURR: I can't believe you'd trust anyone as duplicitous as Talleyrand. He is like excrement forever floating to the surface of whatever tide sweeps France.

JEFFERSON: Perhaps your character is better suited to our negotiations with Monsieur Talleyrand?

BURR: He sold his nation's title to half a continent in ceding us Louisiana. He will not allow his pocket to be picked so easily again.

JEFFERSON: As much as I might personally enjoy seeing you off to Paris, Colonel, a government like ours must embrace a great mass of public confidence. As a consequence, I must employ, not merely those whose talents I may appreciate, but men who have the public's confidence in their own right.

BURR: You of all people, whose reputation has been sullied in every newspaper from here to Newfoundland—where daily one reads ribald ballads about your romance with your black chambermaid—surely, you cannot put faith in what the newspapers are writing about me.

JEFFERSON: The judgment of a few newspapers does not concern me. However, during the past Presidential election, although you were in possession of the office of Vice President, there was not a single voice heard in the Republican caucus for your retaining that office.

BURR: You're well aware that a small faction in Congress was untiring in spreading rumors that I sanctioned the Federalist cabal that would have put me in this office ahead of you.

JEFFERSON: Rumor frequently is born of truth.

BURR: Truth? What do either of us know of truth? We move in a world where action carries the sword while truth labors in chains. Lately, I've instigated legal action to obtain sworn affidavits to reveal what actually took place during the deadlock of 1801. Testimony which I fully expect will show you, sir, not I, to have been the trimmer.

JEFFERSON: (*Self-righteous anger.*) Do not imagine for an instant that the threat of some ancient disclosure will move me to any action. I have never done a single act which I fear to have laid fully open. Never have I done anything with any other motive in view than the greatest public good.

BURR: I am sure it gratifies your spleen to think so. We all want to believe we hold the key to our own conscience.

JEFFERSON: (*Resuming his composure.*) I have a profound pity for your predicament, sir. What might you be, save for an errant bullet lodged in the abdomen of an inveterate foe? Perhaps a power in New York still, or even the nation. Now, you are hardly more than a ghost of your former self.

BURR: This Lazarus you see before you can still walk on his own two legs.

JEFFERSON: Yes. And we shall see where they carry you. Now, as to your new expedition, let me say this. It has long been the policy of this government not to intervene in commercial ventures of a strictly private nature.

BURR: Then I shall arm the settlers I lead to the Washita River for their own protection. And come war, you can be certain that I shall be at the head of the first volunteer regiment to engage the enemy.

JEFFERSON: (*Looking distractedly out the window.*) Have you been following the progress of the mechanics along our inland waters? I observed an experiment recently by a man who wanted the Navy to purchase a boat which he said would sail against the current. He powered it with some sort of steam jenny. As we watched from the shore he proceeded promptly to run his craft aground. I think some men's lives are like that steamboat. While their ideas may be perfectly correct, when they put them in motion it is impossible for them to guide them or even say where they will end up. (*JEFFERSON walks across the room.*) You will excuse me, but I have an appointment with the nurseryman. He has a new variety of thorn bush he says will make a fine hedge for my farm.

BURR: Tell me, sir, when determining how many thorns you require, do you calculate by the quantity of land you own, or by the number of slaves you must confine?

JEFFERSON: (*He halts, turns slowly and gazes down at his diminutive caller.*) Perhaps, Mr. Burr, in your travels around our country in your capacity as a private citizen, you will observe whether it is preferable to be hemmed in, or hemmed out. Good day to you, sir.

(*Lights fade to dark.*)

SCENE SEVEN

The office of The Western World. *WOOD is holding up a copy of a newspaper. STREET is writing at a desk.*

WOOD: (*Admiringly.*) Ahh, the sweet aroma of "guid black prent."

STREET: Will you stop admiring this week's edition and start writing copy for next week's issue.

WOOD: Josey, me lad, you must learn to let y'r organ do y'r work. There'll be no lackin' copy now that our Western World has published the names of Spain's agents in Kentucky. We have thrown down the gauntlet. Which culprit will stoop to fetch it up?

STREET: Don't patronize me, John. Our reputation demands we follow through our investigation, whatever the consequences.

(*A man – GEORGE ADAMS – enters stage right with a newspaper crumbled in his fist.*)

WOOD: Right you are, laddie. And I do believe I see the first'n a'comin'.

ADAMS: (*To WOOD.*) Are you the man responsible for this calumny against Senator Brown?

WOOD: Mr. Street and I are the editors of The Western World, aye.

ADAMS: George Adams is my name. The Senator is as worthy a patriot as any man in this state. I demand you print a retraction of your slanders.

WOOD: We would be pleased to print your letter to the editor refuting our observations.

ADAMS: Sir, you must provide proof of your allegations. If you cannot, then you must retract your libels, or I shall be forced to call you out.

WOOD: I only do the writing, sir. My associate, Mr. Street, does the fighting.

ADAMS: (*Turning to STREET.*) Will you disavow these lies?

STREET: If they were lies, I should not have printed them.

ADAMS: I say they are lies, sir. Worse. They are mere innuendo, impossible to disavow without raising more suspicions. I insist you print a full account of Senator Brown's public career.

STREET: We cannot print an encyclopedia on every subject.

ADAMS: You will, sir, on this subject, or have your nose broken.

STREET: (*Standing.*) No common bully stepping out of the back alley will dictate to me the contents of my newspaper.

ADAMS: Then I shall have my Negro take a lash to you.

STREET: I should think the black man will have the more honorable duty than the coward who sent him.

ADAMS: You will receive my seconds.

STREET: If you have the courage, send them. But make no mistake, sir, you cannot disguise this as a private quarrel. I shall publish your challenge for the information of the public.

(*ADAMS exits. STREET shouts after him.*)

STREET: You are attacking the freedom of the press and the right of the people to know the secret actions of their public officials.

WOOD: (*Stepping from the shadows.*) Well spoken, m'lad, well spoken, indeed. There is nothing like a duel to promote circulation.

STREET: I will show these heathens they can't intimidate Joseph Street.

WOOD: Go to it. Go to it.

STREET: You sidestepped the matter quick enough.

WOOD: One of us must stay healthy enough to report the outcome of the contest.

STREET: Duty before honor, eh?

WOOD: How does the Bard put it?
"Sir Wisdom's a fool when he's fou (*Full.*)
Sir Knave is a fool in a session;
Here's a we' apprentice I know
That be a fool by profession."
(*Laughs.*) Ha. Ha. Ha.

(*Lights fade to dark.*)

SCENE EIGHT

BURR and THEODOSIA walking up a gang plank.

BURR: Ohio is such a verdant paradise. I shall be sorry to leave it.

THEODOSIA: I doubt Mexico holds any greater promise.

BURR: Mexico, my dear?

THEODOSIA: You can stop pretending with me, father. Mrs. Blennerhasset bragged about the empire you and her husband will build. What is it you are planning, father? I thought we were starting a new colony on the Washita?

BURR: Do not bother yourself. The Blennerhassets live in a world of their own making.

THEODOSIA: But they are about to abandon their world for yours. Why do you not reveal these plans of yours to me, father? Am I not more trustworthy than strangers?

BURR: Why would I deceive my little Theodosia?

THEODOSIA: Like most men, you have no confidence in a woman's judgment. You must not forget what you've taught me, father. Everything in our world is ruled by Newton's two laws of mechanics. Am I not right? Then that must include a woman's affections. Once we repose our attachment on one person, it requires a great exertion to move us from that regard. But beware, lest you set us in motion. Push us away, and our love moves away continuously.

BURR: You must know that man alone of all the species is forever discontent, ever sacrificing the present for the future. Never enjoying, always hoping.

(*This is not the reply THEODOSIA was seeking. She turns away. BURR goes and takes her in his arms.*)

BURR: Oh my sweet little girl, if I had a kingdom, I would gladly give it to you and content myself to brave the world's storms a washed-out old monarch in search of a crown.

THEODOSIA: I'm sorry, father. But you know that you and your concerns are the highest, the dearest interest I have in this world. In you, are centered all my wishes, all my desires, all my fears.

BURR: Calm yourself and come aboard. "Nothing will come of nothing."

(*They exit the plank.*)

SCENE NINE

A Frankfort street corner. WOOD and STREET arguing.

STREET: How long do you suppose our readers will be satisfied with this stale diet of ancient accusations? We have nothing to link the old Spanish conspiracy with any new treason.

WOOD: We must play the proper overture, laddie. Our audience has to be prepared for the entrance of the prima ballerina.

STREET: You gamble heavily on Burr fulfilling your fantasies.

WOOD: The political journalist, my dear Joseph, is a barnacle clinging to the hull of the ship of state—-feeding off the flotsam in its wake.

STREET: Your prose style is like your personality, John—colorful but frail. I can see I myself must do more of the writing for this enterprise. Our benefactors will soon enough realize which of the two of us is the more steadfast patriot. (*STREET walks away.*)

ADAMS: (*Off.*) A moment, sir.

(*ADAMS enters angrily. He strides up to STREET, and jabs his finger at STREET's face.*)

ADAMS: (*To STREET.*) I've heard that you have spoken very insultingly of me to several persons.

STREET: Some might consider the phrase 'whining cur,' an insult—to the canine population.

ADAMS: For that remark, sir, I shall have to give you the caning you deserve.

(*ADAMS lifts his cane to strike STREET. STREET lunges at ADAMS with the knife.*)

ADAMS: You are quick, sir. But perhaps not quick enough.

(*ADAMS draws a pistol and fires. STREET absorbs the shot, then stabs ADAMS. ADAMS drops the pistol and runs off.*)

WOOD: (*Supporting the staggering STREET.*) God's body, they've killed you.

STREET: If these traitors wish me dead, they'll have to send a better marksman.

(*STREET collapses. Two men, the SHERIFF and a DEPUTY, walk up to STREET and WOOD.*)

SHERIFF: As sheriff of Frankfort, I'm arresting you for assault with a deadly weapon.

WOOD: What? My friend is wounded.

(*The SHERIFF reaches down and picks up STREET by his unwounded arm.*)

SHERIFF: I'll fetch a doctor to his cell.

STREET: You can incarcerate my body, sir, but you cannot so easily imprison the truth.

(*The SHERIFF starts to lead STREET away.*)

STREET: (*To WOOD.*) Help me, John. I have no money for bail. And I'll starve on their jailhouse gruel.

(*SHERIFF and his prisoner exit right. WOOD stands bewildered a beat, then exits quickly left.*)

SCENE TEN

HUMPHREY MARSHALL's office. MARSHALL sits reading The Western World. *JOSEPH DAVEISS paces the floor in front of him.*

MARSHALL: (*Laying the paper aside.*) Our friend, Mr. Wood, has outdone himself. Every Republican in Kentucky seems now to be a conspirator. (*He laughs.*)

DAVEISS: While I was in St. Louis, I interviewed Burr's collaborator, General Wilkinson, the commander of our entire U.S. Army. The General showed me a map of New Mexico. He tapped his finger on it and told me in a low and significant tone, "Had Colonel Burr been President, we would have all this before now." Then he pushed out his breast like a peacock and said, "Colonel Burr will prove to be the savior of our western country."

MARSHALL: I should like to know more about the doings of this savior of ours.

DAVEISS: I have made a particular examination of the law and there is no statute which forbids an attempt to disunite the union.

MARSHALL: My dear brother, the very act of bringing an indictment against the cabal will alert the nation to its peril.

DAVEISS: I shall not bring a frivolous court action.

MARSHALL: Burr is no ordinary criminal. And ordinary means will not stop him. He has escaped two murder indictments already. He does not dare run from a court challenge, here. He knows politics only too well. He's well aware that turning tail on a fight in this country is a far greater sin than sending a man's soul to hell with a well-aimed pistol shot. He must save face, if ought else.

DAVEISS: I didn't know you believed in a soul, Humphrey. You've so often said you were an atheist.

MARSHALL: Even an atheist can recognize Beelzebub in his own garden.

(*A knock at the door.*)

MARSHALL: Come in.

(*WOOD enters.*)

MARSHALL: Mr. Wood. Welcome. I believe you know my brother-in-law, the U.S. Attorney, Joe Daveiss.

WOOD: (*Agitated.*) How do you do? Your pardon, sirs, but the most horrendous thing has just happened. Joseph Street has been shot and wounded in the public highway. And then, insult upon injury, arrested as he lay bleeding in the gutter.

DAVEISS: Is he mortally wounded?

WOOD: No, thank heaven. But we have no means of securing his release.

MARSHALL: A man of such exceptional courage should not languish in jail.

WOOD: Aye, Josey is fearless, right enough. He would have cut the blackguard's heart out, if the fellow had been a mite slower on the trigger.

DAVEISS: His assailant fired in self-defense?

WOOD: Ah? No, sir. About that I cannot say, exactly. You see, this man Adams began to employ his cane about Josey's head and shoulders, when all of a sudden this dirk appears, so quick it did, that the flashing of the blade verily blinded me.

MARSHALL: First we must attend to Mr. Street's release. The court will sort out the details. (*Writing a note.*) Take this surety to Judge Mutter, and your friend will be released. We cannot allow a man of such sterling mettle to be treated like a common criminal.

WOOD: Aye, sir, that we cannot. Our profession is too ill thought of as it is. I shall not trouble you gentlemen further. Thank you. I was sure we could count on your.... compassion. I will attend to Mr. Street's freedom. (*WOOD accepts the note.*)

MARSHALL: See that you do.

(*WOOD exits.*)

DAVEISS: You have picked a dappled pair to haul this load of suspicion before the public.

MARSHALL: The surgeon cannot always choose his instruments.

(*Lights fade to dark.*)

SCENE ELEVEN

Liberty Hall, John Brown's home in Frankfort. JOHN BROWN, his wife, MARGARETTA, THEODOSIA, and BURR are playing whist.

MARGARETTA: (*Laying down a card to catch a trick.*) The Queens are much in favor this evening.

BURR: Are they not always?

THEODOSIA: I did not play cleverly on that trick, Father. Forgive me.

BURR: The game has only begun, my dear.

(*During the following, the FOURSOME play out their hands of cards.*)

BROWN: You've plopped yourself into quite a ruckus this trip, Aaron. My old nemesis, Humphrey Marshall, is pouring considerable coin into a new journal here in Frankfort, The Western World. I believe you may know one of his editors, John Wood?

THEODOSIA: Wood? My old tutor? Is he here? That retched little man trails father like vermin.

BURR: My dear, your language.

BROWN: Disappointed ambition can be quite a motive force.

MARGARETTA: Whist, Whist, gentlemen. Silence, please. I can't concentrate on the cards if you insist upon talking.

BROWN: You remember Humphrey Marshall, Aaron. He was with us in the Senate during Washington's Presidency.

MARGARETTA: My dear Theodosia, you haven't said a word about my house. Don't you simply love it? John had it built precisely to the design President Jefferson drew for us.

THEODOSIA: Yes. Yes. It has a certain... airiness.

BURR: Our President is a master of many talents.

BROWN: Indeed, he is. He has saved us from war with England, when few men could, or would.

BURR: Yes, but will he save us from war with Spain?

MARGARETTA: Theodosia, I am so pleased you're here. Your father has been perfectly ebullient about your musical talents. Will you favor us with a tune?

THEODOSIA: My pleasure.

BURR: Bach, perhaps?

THEODOSIA: Father, you are so traditional. I have this wonderful violin sonata which Nathalie has sent me from Paris. The young composer is the rage of Europe.

BURR: And who is this young genius?

THEODOSIA: Von Beethoven. His music is so... so radical. (*Laying down her last card.*) I believe we may have won, Father.

BURR: So we have, my dear. So we have.

MARGARETTA: John, you weren't paying attention.

BROWN: All your talk about music and architecture distracted me.

MARGARETTA: Please excuse me, I'll see to your rooms.

(*MARGARETTA exits.*)

BROWN: Aaron, how about a dram? I believe I have an eight-year-old keg that needs tapping.

BURR: Nothing would please me more, John.

BROWN: (*Standing.*) You shall have it.

(*BROWN exits.*)

BURR: My dear, you must be more civil. Your conduct is unworthy of my daughter. Reflect a moment and you will see that your manner could be construed as arrogant.

THEODOSIA: I was only playing the game as you taught me.

BURR: The real game is not always the one at hand.

THEODOSIA: Forgive me, Father. I am overwrought. I cannot believe that nasty John Wood has followed you all this way.

BURR: Mr. Wood menaces only himself.

THEODOSIA: Can you be sure? You tell me so little of your plans. Meanwhile the newspapers all but accuse you of treason.

BURR: The best retort to slander is silent contempt.

THEODOSIA: You were silent in New York too long, and the newspapers destroyed your reputation. Why entangle yourself in these petty provincial quarrels? Let us go on to the new settlement you're making on the Washita. Be done with politics.

(*BROWN enters with a decanter of whiskey.*)

THEODOSIA: Please excuse me. I believe our hostess is anticipating a recital.

(*THEODOSIA exits. Violin music rises off stage.*)

BROWN: I find music always goes better with the right spirit. (*BROWN pours a glass for each of them.*) That was an interesting variation of whist you showed us this evening. What's it called?

BURR: It's Russian. They call it "Biritch." I think it means "surrender." I suppose it refers to the exposed hand.

BROWN: I don't know how you managed to beat us when your cards were all on the table in plain sight.

BURR: It's an old rule that works equally well in politics: When you are not strong enough to lead trumps, you are weak enough to force them. (*A beat.*) The Republican Party will miss your leadership in the Senate next session.

BROWN: I have given twenty years of my life to public service, and what has it gotten me? It's made a poor man of me, that's what it's done. I helped secure Kentucky's statehood, and now ol' Humphrey and his hired character assassins accuse me of being a Spanish agent. There are men in this state who have pledged their allegiance to Spain, but I am not one of them.

(*A knock at the door.*)

BROWN: Who's there? John, is that you? Come in.

(*A tall man of middle age – JOHN ADAIR – enters. He is dressed in a suit but wears Indian leggings.*)

BROWN: Come in. I want you to meet a friend. This is our former Vice President, Aaron Burr. Mr. Burr, our junior United States Senator, and the adjutant general of our state militia, John Adair.

BURR: (*Steps forward. The two men shake hands.*) Senator, how do you do?

ADAIR: Colonel Burr. My congratulations.

BURR: Congratulations? I am sorry, sir. You have the advantage of me.

ADAIR: Alexander Hamilton was a scoundrel that needed killin' and you were the man with the gumption to do it.

BURR: Sir, General Hamilton was a gentleman or I should not have met him.

ADAIR: If you say so. But here he was roundly hated. His National Bank skinned more of our farmers than the red savages could ever hope to.

BROWN: Tight money is the ruination of any frontier. We had to charter an insurance company and issue notes to have any currency out here whatsoever. Oh, you'll be pleased to hear that our Indiana Canal stock is looking up. A large subscription has been taken up in London, I'm told.

BURR: Excellent. The British are a keen lot when it comes to good investments. Then it is not indelicate to ask for my retainer for serving as the company's legal counsel this year. I am stocking provisions in Louisville for the Washita expedition and must pay my purchasing agent. You know, John, I am keeping back a tenth of the Washita stock for you, should you choose to subscribe.

BROWN: I may. Will you accept notes on the Kentucky Insurance Company?

BURR: They will be honored locally with little discount, I suspect?

BROWN: They're easier to borrow against than a land grant in Louisiana at the moment. (*The MEN laugh.*)

BURR: They'd better be. (*Holding up his glass.*) Your fortune, sir.

BROWN: (*Touching BURR's glass with his.*) And yours.

ADAIR: Salud.

(*The three MEN drink.*)

BROWN: Our little insurance and banking enterprise didn't please the squatters downstate. The legislature would have revoked our charter, but Henry Clay maneuvered the vote off the floor.

BURR: Young Clay seems quite the man of the hour.

BROWN: There's talk of sending him to Washington.

BURR: So, he's ambitious?

ADAIR: Exceedingly.

BROWN: Fortunately, his shrewdness matches his appetite. (*BROWN is filling his guests' glasses from the open decanter.*)

(*Lights dim on the main scene, rise at the opposite side of the stage. MARGARETTA listens as THEODOSIA plays the violin.*)

THEODOSIA: Forgive me, a string slipped. (*She tunes the violin.*)

MARGARETTA: You play marvelously, my dear.

THEODOSIA: I dare say, I'm a better pistol shot than a musician.

MARGARETTA: Oh, indeed?!

THEODOSIA: Father insisted that I master several of the manly arts to compliment the female graces.

MARGARETTA: Your father is always so avant-garde.

THEODOSIA: It was little enough to do to please him. His life has been filled with such sorrow, such broken dreams. Since mother's death, I have been both wife and daughter to him since I was ten years old, leaving my dolls to play the hostess to his dinner guests. I only wish I could do more.

MARGARETTA: If it would ease your burden to have me...

THEODOSIA: (*Continuing her thought.*) Father gets quite lost without me, emotionally, I mean.

MARGARETTA: I would never have suspected he was so... so vulnerable.

THEODOSIA: Wherever he goes, women throw themselves upon his affections. You would never guess that so resolute a man in the company of other men would become so helpless before a woman's charms. Fortunately, he has me to protect him from his one silly weakness.

MARGARETTA: You must forgive the shortcomings of your sisters. With men as their chief examples, how can women ever learn to master their passions? When one love ebbs, we wait patiently for the tide of another to rise and carry our hearts away. Oh, Theodosia, you have no idea how I miss New York: the teas and socials that kept us in a flurry; the balls that gave energy to our thoughts—dancing first with Mr. Hope, next with Mr. Fear.

(*THEODOSIA resumes her music as MARGARETTA dances around her. Light dims to dark on the two WOMEN and rises on the MEN in the first part of the scene.*)

BURR: This Bourbon whiskey, John, is strong enough to resurrect its dead namesake.

BROWN: (*Holding his glass and admiring the color of the liquor.*) Yes, I think it is more potent than its Scotch cousin.

BURR: As it should be. A new liquor for a new world, strong and dark.

(*A SERVANT enters.*)

SERVANT: Mr. Clay has arrived, sir.

BROWN: I invited Henry to join us as you suggested, Aaron. (*To the servant.*) Show Mr. Clay in.

(*SERVANT exits.*)

BURR: Wonderful! I am anxious to meet this new star in the western firmament.

(*CLAY enters.*)

BROWN: Are you gentlemen acquainted? Colonel Aaron Burr, Mr. Henry Clay.

BURR: (*Extending his hand.*) A pleasure to meet you.

CLAY: (*Crosses the room to the stationary BURR...shaking hands.*) The honor is mine, sir. (*Turning to the tall man in leggings.*) Senator.

ADAIR: Mr. Clay. (*ADAIR turns to fill his glass just as CLAY starts forward to shake his hand.*)

BROWN: Henry is the master of the courtroom. When he goes to trial, the gallery is always packed with spectators. Many of them attractive young ladies.

ADAIR: Young Clay rarely fails to entertain. Tell the Colonel how you got that murderer, Willis, acquitted.

CLAY: Ah, Willis —- I fear I have saved too many like him who ought to have hanged.

BURR: Let's just hope they don't start hanging lawyers along with their clients, or we will all be short-winded.

(*MEN laugh.*)

BROWN: Henry, what's your opinion of Charles Lynch's title to Baron Bastrop's land grant along the Washita? Is Lynch within his rights deeding it to Colonel Burr and his partners?

CLAY: In my opinion, perfectly within his rights.

BROWN: That's good enough for me. Henry's the best land lawyer west of Philadelphia. Hell, even old Judge

Innes reversed himself after listening to Henry's argument.

CLAY: For eight hours.

(*MEN laugh.*)

BURR: I am prepared to give Mr. Lynch four thousand dollars as surety for a mortgage on the whole 350,000 acres.

CLAY: Mr. Lynch has empowered me to accept any reasonable offer. Will you assume Lynch's debt to Mr. Livingston and agree to a second note of 30,000 payable in yearly installments?

BURR: Done.

(*BURR holds out his hand to CLAY. They shake.*)

BURR: In fact, we will give you our binder tonight. (*BURR turns to BROWN.*) John, have you those notes you mentioned?

BROWN: (*A moment's hesitation.*) Ah, why, of course.

(*BROWN exits.*)

ADAIR: You have made a good bargain, gentlemen.

CLAY: If you can keep the Spanish from dispossessing you.

BURR: I believe a brigade could be raised in this western country which could drive double their number of Spaniards or Frenchmen off the earth.

CLAY: Surely, this is a fortunate moment to show the world when American rights are violated, we are not afraid to engage in war with alacrity and effect.

ADAIR: A brave speech for a man who has never felt the hot breath of battle.

CLAY: A nation must maintain a certain military ardor. Your generation had your war. Now it's time for a new race of heroes.

BURR: (*To ADAIR.*) Our friend James Wilkinson tells me you were in a British prison during our Revolution, Senator?

ADAIR: For nine torturous months. Every day we were threatened with execution. There were a couple of times they even marched us out in front of a firing squad. Then we were exchanged and I fought at King's Mountain with Shelby.

BURR: Hard fought, I've heard. Turned the War.

ADAIR: Some say Monmouth Courthouse was the battle that got things going our way.

BURR: Monmouth, ha. Another of Washington's so-called, "victories." Believe me, sir; any man who was there knows the truth. I was at the head of my regiment on the left flank of our Army at Monmouth, on the 28th of June in '78. A hot, airless, interminable day, it was too. We had a detachment of Redcoats cut off from the main body of the British Army. We were preparing to charge into them when I was overtaken by an officer from Washington's staff with orders to hold my position. I was maneuvering in a muddy ravine in full view of the British artillery. I sent Washington word of my exposed position. But no, I had to hold where I was. Presently, we came under heavy fire. But every request I sent to Washington asking that I be allowed to reposition, was curtly denied. Volley after volley of British cannon fire cut down my lines. My second in command was crushed by a cannon ball as he stood beside me. If I had been allowed to attack, I could have rolled up the British flank, and we could have ended the war then and there. Those Federalist fanatics who boast of General Washington's military genius have never had a horse shot out from under them following his timid tactics.

ADAIR: Which of us has not been the victim of bad commanders? They rise through the ranks during peacetime, then in war send many a poor soldier to his grave—-until better men can be promoted over them.

BURR: Or defeat them. (*A beat.*)

(*Lights fade to dark.*)

SCENE TWELVE

The steps of the Frankfort courthouse. Two CITIZENS exit, followed by others, including STREET, MARSHALL, and WOOD.

FIRST CITIZEN: That was a curious trial.

SECOND CITIZEN: How can a man be found guilty, and then discharged?

FIRST CITIZEN: It's that young Clay. He's sharp as a briar.

(*The CITIZENS exit. STREET, MARSHALL, and WOOD descend the steps.*)

STREET: Is there no justice in this state?

WOOD: Be calm. You are acquitted.

STREET: But my assassin goes free.

(*DAVEISS approaches.*)

DAVEISS: What was the verdict?

(*At the top of the stairs, ADAMS appears, grasping the hand of a dapper young man, HENRY CLAY.*)

WOOD: The jury found Adams guilty. But his lawyer, Henry Clay, objected, saying that the Attorney General had not alleged in his indictment that the shooting was with intent to kill. So the judge turned him loose.

DAVEISS: Such are the morals of our public functionaries, ever befriending crime.

STREET: Confound them all. The whole judiciary is compromised. They are all conspirators.

(*Escorted by MARSHALL and DAVEISS, STREET exits.*)

STREET: (*Shouting.*) The Western World will mete out justice of its own.

(*ADAMS and CLAY walk to the foot of the stairs. ADAMS exits opposite of STREET and friends. WOOD approaches CLAY.*)

WOOD: Mr. Clay, may I speak with you, sir?

CLAY: Your servant, sir. I hope you and your partner bear no ill will. The law is quite clear regarding correct procedure.

WOOD: I have no quarrel with you, sir. You're an outstandin' barrister. It's for that reason that I would talk with you. Would you be representin' me in these libel actions against The Western World?

CLAY: Now that this little shooting spree has been fairly settled, I see no conflict of interest in representing you in a civil action. Your newspaper is prospering, is it not?

WOOD: More than we dreamt. We have some 1,200 subscribers, half again the entire population of Frankfort.

CLAY: Do you speak for your partner in this?

WOOD: No, sir. That's just it. I would like you to be my private counsel. Humphrey Marshall is Mr. Street's advocate. And frankly, I'm not sure how he'll respond to my employin' a separate lawyer.

CLAY: Most libel suits arise from a flash of anger. Once the delays of a trial begin, tempers subside, and out-of-court settlement becomes the easiest solution. I should think in your case you could undo any injury by recourse to the same means by which offense was given, namely, your newspaper.

WOOD: Mr. Street will never print a retraction.

CLAY: A few soft words may be preferable to forfeiting your whole enterprise.

WOOD: True enough. I suppose I could inject a temporizin' word or two into each issue without rousin' my partner's suspicions. I tell you, sir, my principal desire is to confine the lead in this business to the printin' presses, and leave off its fiery flyin' so near me 'ead.

CLAY: A capital ambition. But on the frontier, Mr. Wood, peace and justice can be scarce commodities. And like other luxuries, they tend to be rather expensive.

(*Lights fade to dark.*)

SCENE THIRTEEN

Liberty Hall. MARGARETTA and BURR are finishing a game of chess. MARGARETTA captures BURR's Queen with a Bishop.

MARGARETTA: Your move, Colonel.

(*BURR checks with a Rook to the King row.*)

BURR: Mate, Madame.

MARGARETTA: *Vous jouez bien, mon Colonel.*

BURR: *Aussi bien que la situation le permet.*

MARGARETTA: How I miss Theodosia's sweet music.

BURR: She wanted to visit friends in Louisville before we set off for Louisiana. Tell me, Margaretta, do you think she chafes under my strict hand? I fear I injure her soul with my constant reproofs. But how is a father to stop worrying about his only child?

MARGARETTA: Do not worry. It's quite obvious that she loves you dearly.

BURR: I have taught her to rely on herself. Now I must be content to rely on her pride.

MARGARETTA: I know I'm wicked in asking. And you must not tell me, if you think I'm not to be trusted with your secrets. But, is it true you are going to revolutionize the whole Mississippi Valley?

BURR: If I could accomplish the half of what I am credited with, I would be more of a man than I am.

MARGARETTA: (*Smiling.*) There are far easier conquests much closer at hand, my dear Colonel.

(*BROWN enters.*)

BURR: Yes, and fraught with just as many dangers.

BROWN: My apologies for being detained. I trust Margaretta has entertained you.

BURR: Oh, yes. You are fortunate to have such a cultivated companion.

MARGARETTA: I think our Colonel should settle in Kentucky and campaign for Congress. Don't you, John?

BROWN: Why not? (*BROWN pours whiskey into a glass.*) If ever I'd hopes of holding public office again, Humphrey Marshall has scotched them. Damn him. And damn his passel of scribbling devils. Even libel suits don't tame their wild slanders. Only in newspapers can guilt be proven by association. Ben Sebastian may have sold out to Spain and our friend Wilkinson may have too, for that matter. Our genial General has certainly done little enough to stop their raids into Louisiana. (*He gulps his drink.*) If we go to war with Spain over this border issue, I'm of a mind to march to Louisiana, as a simple private.

MARGARETTA: (*Amused.*) John, you're no soldier.

BURR: (*Moving between the BROWNS, and embracing each.*) Margaretta is right, my old friend. To be a good soldier, you must hate—and hate hard—hard enough to do anything to defeat your enemy. You have many qualities, but hatred is not among them.

MARGARETTA: Our Colonel is right, John. You're too kind to be a warrior.

BURR: You'll do the cause more good by staying here and enlisting volunteers to send on to us, than sloughing through Texas. Margaretta, if you will excuse me, I'll say good night.

MARGARETTA: Sleep well. Our prayers are with you.

BURR: Thank you, Madame.

(*BURR exits.*)

BROWN: An extraordinary individual. I doubt I could withstand the misfortune he has suffered and retain such poise.

MARGARETTA: He is grappling with powerful forces, the fiercest of which are within him.

(*Lights fade to dark.*)

SCENE FOURTEEN

A Frankfort courtroom. DAVEISS stands before the bench. HARRY INNES presides.

DAVEISS: (*Reading from a document.*) If it please the court, Your Honor, I, Joseph Hamilton Daveiss, Attorney for the United States in and for the Kentucky District, upon my corporal oath, doth depose and say that a certain Aaron Burr, Esq., late vice-president of the said United States, for several months past hath been and is now engaged in preparing and setting on foot a military expedition within this district for the purpose of descending the Ohio & Mississippi therewith and making war upon the subjects of the King of Spain, who are in a state of peace with the people of these United States. Wherefore, I pray that this court compel the personal appearance of the said Aaron Burr, to answer such charges as may be preferred against him; and in the meantime, that he desist from all further preparations in the said armament within the said United States, or the territories thereof. (*DAVEISS places his document on the bench before INNES.*)

INNES: (*Looking at the affidavit, then at DAVEISS.*) Attorney Daveiss, this is a serious charge you have brought against an individual with a long and distinguished record of service to his country. The magnitude of this case requires that the proceedings be pursued with regularity, caution, and circumspection. I have no doubt of the truth of your affidavit—that is, that you have been informed of the fact stated—and it is possible that the fact stated is true—yet, it is not legal evidence, because you have been informed by one not under oath. Not being legal evidence, the court cannot act upon it. The motion is denied.

DAVEISS: (*Vehemently.*) Your Honor, I have further information that all the western territories are the next object of this scheme—and finally, all the region of the Ohio is to be drawn into the vortex of the proposed revolution.

INNES: To award process would be improper, Attorney Daveiss. There are two well-understood modes of proceeding, either by obtaining a warrant upon legal evidence, or by the Court ordering a Grand Jury to be summoned and preferring an indictment.

DAVEISS: Your Honor, I pray you to issue a warrant to the Marshall to summon a Grand Jury…

(*At the rear of the auditorium behind the audience, BURR speaks.*)

BURR: Your Honor, if it please the court, may I approach the bench?

INNES: Colonel Burr?

(BURR *comes forward.*)

INNES: This court was informed that you had left the state. (*INNES looks hard at DAVEISS.*)

DAVEISS: I object, Your Honor. Mr. Burr has no standing in this Court. No charge has been formally brought against him by this court.

INNES: Mr. Attorney, a moment ago you wanted me to issue a process to compel his attendance.

DAVEISS: Your Honor...

INNES: Mr. Burr, you may proceed.

BURR: Your Honor, regarding the motion before the Court for empaneling a Grand Jury, my fervent hope is that this court... will summon the Grand Jury to investigate these allegations of the Federal Attorney impugning my character. As an officer of the court, as a veteran of our Revolution, and as a citizen of this free nation, I demand... Justice.

(*All lights fade to dark.*)

ACT TWO

SCENE ONE

Jordon's Tavern in Lexington. ADAIR and BURR are drinking wine.

ADAIR: Another cup, Colonel? It'll thin the blood and let you rest for tomorrow.

BURR: Tomorrow is of little concern. It's difficult to obtain an indictment without evidence. I am counting on this little courtroom skirmish to publicize our objective throughout the state. Far from stalling our expedition, the U.S. Attorney may help us in enlisting more volunteers.

(*A knock at the door. CLAY enters.*)

CLAY: Excuse me, gentlemen, but I need to speak with you, John, in private. It concerns what happened in the state assembly today.

ADAIR: No need to be circumspect, Henry. The Colonel here is no stranger to politics.

CLAY: My news is not good. John Pope has beat you out of your seat in the U.S. Senate.

ADAIR: Was I not considered?

CLAY: Your name was among the five nominated. Some of the legislators questioned your loyalty—to the President. Your vote against Jefferson's request for two million dollars to purchase Florida was mentioned.

ADAIR: And why should we pay <u>twice</u> for the same property? West Florida was part of the Louisiana Purchase. What we should do is march in and take it.

BURR: We had better. If the French capture New Orleans—as they could at any moment—there will be a lot more blood shed trying to recover it than marching on Mobile now. (*BURR offers to pour CLAY a glass of wine, but CLAY declines.*)

ADAIR: That's the truth, even if Jefferson is blind to it. Come, Henry, share our bottle. (*CLAY accepts the glass.*)

BURR: We are free men everywhere but in our legislatures. There, loyalty to party and obedience to a senile chief executive are the only measure of a man's virtue.

ADAIR: It's men like you, me, and Andy Jackson, men who aren't afraid to fight, that made this country free, not the politicians. And it will be the likes of us that keeps her free.

CLAY: (*Lifting his glass.*) Millions for defense....

ADAIR: .... but not one penny for tribute.

BURR: Salud.

(*The three MEN drink.*)

CLAY: Had I known the discontent of my colleagues, I might have worked harder in your behalf. But as a member of the conference committee comparing the ballots of the two chambers, I felt my status required me to be neutral. You understand?

ADAIR: I'm sure you did what you could.

CLAY: It's a tough problem you have now, John, going back to Washington to finish your term. I cannot imagine how I would be able to have two minds on every subject —- what I believed and what I thought the Assembly would prefer.

ADAIR: I am my own man – first, last, and always. Colonel, have you a coin in your purse?

(*BURR fetches a silver coin from his vest pocket, and hands it to ADAIR.*)

ADAIR: (*Taking the coin.*) Ah, good British sterling. (*Bites the metal.*)

BURR: A souvenir of a skirmish in Paramus in '79.

ADAIR: Heads: I do the bidding of the Assembly; Tails: I do my own. (*He flips it in the air. The coin clinks on the table. ADAIR examines it without picking it up.*) Henry, inform your colleagues that I resign my seat as Kentucky's United States Senator.

CLAY: John, don't be rash. It's not necessary to step down.

(*ADAIR writes hurriedly.*)

ADAIR: I'm tired of other men's necessaries. I can resign and consider no man's opinion but my own.

BURR: Your decisiveness is commendable, Senator. I tried to hold on in New York too long. It was an expensive mistake. It cost me my fortune and another man his life.

ADAIR: (*Handing CLAY his note.*) Chuck that on the Speaker's table and I'll be done with politics.

CLAY: I shall hold your resignation at my room at Bush's Tavern tonight. If you change your mind, send me word before noon.

ADAIR: A needless precaution. My mind is fixed.

BURR: Mr. Clay, I may have need of your legal services in this little annoyance in Frankfort. Will you serve as my counsel?

CLAY: You honor me, Mr. Vice President. The whole world knows you are the best lawyer in America.

BURR: It is a vain attempt to criminate me, we all know that. Be that as it may, it is an error of court etiquette for one accused of so great an offense to represent himself. Don't you think?

CLAY I am a firm believer that the law protects the innocent.

BURR: The law, Mr. Clay, is what we lawyers boldly assert and plausibly maintain. (*A beat.*)

CLAY: (*Masking surprise.*) It would be my privilege to defend you, sir, in esteem for your years of distinguished service to our nation.

BURR: Thank you, sir. It should prove an amusing diversion for a man of your skills.

CLAY: If you will permit me, gentlemen, I will withdraw. We have a heavy session tomorrow, particularly now that, John, you have added this unforeseen item to our agenda.

(*CLAY shakes hands with BURR, nods to ADAIR.*)

ADAIR: Good night, Henry.

CLAY: Colonel Burr. I'll speak to Judge Innes. He's a good friend of John Brown's; I doubt we will have any problem in his court. Good night.

(*CLAY exits.*)

ADAIR: Oh, he's a sly fox. He hates me with a passion. And I happily return the favor.

BURR: (*Picking up the coin on the table.*) In politics friendship can be a counterfeit currency. It's best to bite hard on every pledge, testing it like you would a strange coin. (*BURR rolls the coin across his knuckles before returning it to his pocket.*)

ADAIR: Clay secured my defeat simply by withholding his support. That man is tempted by nothing but his own advancement.

BURR: Good. Then he can ill afford to fail me in the courtroom.

(*Lights fade to dark.*)

SCENE TWO

Courtroom in Frankfort. MEN enter and sit in gallery of rough-hewn benches in front of the first row of audience. DAVEISS sits at one of two tables in front of the judge's bench. CLAY and BURR enter. BURR wears the uniform of a field officer in the Continental Army. The gallery applauds. A middle-aged man, EZRA BROOKS, approaches BURR.

BROOKS: Colonel, I was with you and Montgomery in our march on Quebec in '75. I want you to know that you've got many friends in these parts who fought beside you, and would again.

BURR: Thank you. What's your name, friend?

BROOKS: Ezra Brooks, sir. I heard your rallying cry that cold December morn, but my captain wouldn't permit us to advance. If we'd followed your lead, Canada would be in the Union now and the British off our continent.

BURR: Quite possibly. But today, I think we shall make short work of these local Tories, huh?

BROOKS: Well said, Colonel. We're with you. Ain't we boys?

(*Hoots and hollers from the CROWD. BURR shakes BROOKS' hand then joins CLAY at the second table. STREET enters. Boos and hisses from the crowd.*)

SPECTATOR: Hey, Street, you gonna pull a knife on Aaron Burr?

SECOND SPECTATOR: (*Laughing.*) Watch out he don't shoot you.

BROOKS: He's killed better men than you'll ever be.

(*STREET ignores the gallery. He finds his seat next to another man, JOHN BRADFORD, with writing materials.*)

STREET: Mr. Bradford, good to see you're taking your own notes today. I notice your <u>Gazette</u> is not publishing excerpts from our <u>Western World</u> as regularly as in August.

BRADFORD: I'd sooner the <u>Gazette</u> not reek of the stench you have sprayed over Frankfort, thank you.

STREET: Holding our noses mighty high today, aren't we?

(*BALIFF enters.*)

BAILIFF: Hear, ye... hear, ye. The Court of the United States in and for the District of Kentucky is now in session, the Honorable Henry Innes presiding. All those having business before this court draw near and be heard.

(*INNES enters and sits behind a bench elevated above the others.*)

INNES: Mr. Daveiss, the Grand Jury is sitting. Have you charges to proffer?

DAVEISS: Your Honor, if it please the court, of the thirteen witnesses summoned to testify in this case, all but one are in court today. But the testimony of the absent individual is indispensable. This man, Davis Floyd of Jeffersonville, is currently attending the session of the Indiana Territorial Legislature in Vincennes. I beg your indulgence, Your Honor, and move a postponement of these proceedings.

(*Whispers in the gallery.*)

INNES: (*Banging his gavel.*) Hearing no objection, I so order. Bailiff, dismiss the Grand Jurors.

BURR: (*Standing.*) Your Honor, I would like to move that the reason for this action be recorded, for I am certain that the U.S. Attorney's suspicions are as groundless as my appearance in this court today has been fruitless.

(*Applause from gallery.*)

INNES: Mr. Burr, the Attorney's motion will be duly entered into the order book. This court stands adjourned. (*INNES pounds his gavel, exits.*)

FIRST SPECTATOR: (*Singing to the tune of "Froggy Went a Courtin".*)
Joe Ham Daveiss went t' court, uh-huh, uh-huh.
To try Aaron Burr and have some sport, uh-huh, uh-huh.
There he found he had no luck, uh-huh, uh-huh.
Without his witness he was ******, uh-huh, uh-huh.

(*More laughter, as the spectators file out of the courtroom behind BURR. CLAY walks over to DAVEISS.*)

CLAY: If I knew you were going to argue both sides of the case, Joe, I would have stayed in Lexington today.

(*CLAY extends his hand. DAVEISS turns his back. CLAY exits smiling. STREET and MARSHALL converge on DAVEISS from opposite corners of the now empty room.*)

DAVEISS: What is a righteous man to do? Burr is having boats built, beef cattle bought and more demanded. Volunteers are being engaged with the promise of a hundred acres in New Mexico in which to grow their dreams. And the only weapon I have to arrest this diabolic scheme is this ponderous court of law and its one, old, partisan judge.

MARSHALL: Perhaps now is the time to turn our attention to Benjamin Sebastian. Of his treachery we have hard evidence.

STREET: Evidence?

DAVEISS: In my next letter to the President, I will add the names of Adair and Clay to the list of conspirators.

STREET: You've written President Jefferson of this plot?

DAVEISS: Numerous times. But to no avail.

MARSHALL: We are trying to awaken a snoring Administration.

DAVEISS: How wonderfully numerous are the friends and neutrals of this infernal scheme.

STREET: Do you have copies of your letters to the President?

DAVEISS: Of course.

STREET: May I see them?

DAVEISS: They are confidential correspondence between a subordinate official to his superior – not meant for publication.

STREET: But with these, <u>The Western World</u> could really assist you. Allow me to print your letters to the

President. Expose the full extent of this conspiracy.

DAVEISS: I cannot. My duty comes before my pride.

(*WOOD enters.*)

MARSHALL: If it were a giant fossil you had uncovered, instead of a plot to overturn the government, Tall Tom would have dispatched a regiment of cavalry to retrieve it.

(*DAVEISS and MARSHALL exit.*)

WOOD: (*Steps out of the shadows.*) Careful, laddie. Daveiss is a zealot. He thinks he's saving his soul by hanging Aaron Burr.

STREET: You're a brave one behind a goose quill, John Wood, but measured beside a true patriot like Joe Daveiss, you are weak tea.

WOOD: You best be rememberin' who your true friends are, laddie. These public men will smile at you one minute and be puttin' you in prison the next. We'd best be attendin' to the plethora of libel suits your pernicious name-calling has brought against us.

STREET: Let them sue. They but provide more proof of our independence.

WOOD: And what if they win?

STREET: So? What have we worth the taking?

WOOD: We have each other, laddie. If they take our <u>Western World</u>, I'm afraid they will drive a wedge between us. Ours is more than a mere business arrangement, me lad. You know that. Surely, you know that? Can't you see how fond I am of you? How sorely attached to you I am? If you're not sharing my ale, I durst not drink. Unless you are in the room with me, I cannot sleep.

STREET: Do you think I'm some mongrel pup you've taken in to feed and pet so it can scare off rats and bark at intruders? Is that how it is? Well, beware. This dog can bite.

WOOD: Oh, Josey, Josey. Don't abandon me for some zealous stranger. He will never have the regard for you that I do…

(*STREET exits. WOOD stands alone. Lights cross fade.*)

SCENE THREE

Liberty Hall. BURR and THEODOSIA enter wearing riding apparel and carrying small whips.

THEODOSIA: That was wonderful, Father! There is nothing like a gallop through the morning mist to awaken the body humors.

BURR: My dear Theodosia, how audacious you are.

THEODOSIA: So I am. Just as you made me.

BURR: Yes, my dear. Yes. In you I see accomplished my fondest ambition: to convince the world what neither sex appears to believe—that women have souls.

THEODOSIA: How skillfully you weave your words, father, insulting as you appear to flatter. You honor women with possession of a soul while denying us the faculty of good sense.

BURR: I beg your pardon?

THEODOSIA: I discovered your maps.

BURR: Naturally, I had maps prepared for our new settlement.

THEODOSIA: Please, father. I know a nautical map when I see it. One chart had sea depths marked in the Gulf all the way to Vera Cruz.

BURR: Your anxieties evince a sort of sickly sensibility. I fear that you are suffering a debility affecting both your mind and body.

THEODOSIA: I'm torn apart, you're correct in that. Love and malice war in my soul over you, father. Each so well maintains its ground that my heart has become a refugee within my breast; my emotions spinning like a dervish.

BURR: When you are in health, you have no sort of apprehension about me. Resume, I pray you, that confidence, so flattering to me, so consoling to yourself, and may I add, so justly founded.

THEODOSIA: One day you must write me a history of your life, complete with all your remedies. I'll bind it in red morocco and keep it for advantage and instruction. Perhaps after sufficient study, I'll divine its meaning and know my true place in your heart. I must dress now, father—excuse me.

(*THEODOSIA exits. Lights fade to dark.*)

SCENE FOUR

The Kentucky General Assembly. As the SPEAKER OF THE HOUSE reads from a platform high above the rear of the stage, men gather in knots in the isles.

SPEAKER: Gentlemen, the results of the balloting to elect a Senator to complete the unexpired term of John Adair are as follows: the Honorable George Bibb, Circuit Judge of Fayette County, ten votes; the Honorable Henry Clay, Representative to this body from Fayette County, sixty-eight votes.

(*Cheers from the ASSEMBLY.*)

SPEAKER: Mr. Clay, pack your bags. You're going to Washington City.

(*A representative, JOHN POPE, approaches from the back of the auditorium.*)

POPE: Mr. Speaker?

SPEAKER: Mr. Pope, you have the floor.

POPE: I wish to address this assembly on a serious matter which has only lately come to my attention. A broadside has been circulated among our members, charging one of our supreme judges with a crime most depraved. To wit, Judge Benjamin Sebastian has, for many years, received a pension of two thousand dollars per annum from the King of Spain.

(*CROWD mumbles.*)

POPE: I move a special committee be formed to investigate this matter, forthwith.

VOICES: Second. Second. Second.

(*Lights fade to dark.*)

SCENE FIVE

The Falls of the Ohio. BURR is aboard a flatboat supervising its loading. Two MEN roll a barrel into place beside BURR. A third MAN approaches and hands him a letter. BURR scans it.

BURR: Tell Mr. Clay to come aboard.

(*The COURIER exits and CLAY boards.*)

CLAY: You're a busy man, sir. The <u>Palladium</u> reported you had left for Cincinnati.

BURR: Provisioning this expedition seems to require that I be everywhere at once.

CLAY: I assume you know that the U.S. Attorney is resuming his prosecution.

BURR: This private vendetta of his frustrates my whole enterprise.

CLAY: Notwithstanding the U.S. Attorney's aberrant species of vengeance, I fear I must...

BURR: (*Interrupting.*) Withdraw from the case?

CLAY: Yes. It is a difficult decision and one I do not make lightly. But given my new status...

BURR: (*Interrupting.*) I hope further consideration will induce you, even at some personal inconvenience, to continue as my counsel. It would be disagreeable to me to form a new connection at such a critical moment. Of course, I shall insist on paying you a liberal compensation.

CLAY: Money is not a factor in my decision. But owing to my new position as a United States Senator...

BURR: By no means would I urge a measure inconsistent with your interest, but a delay in starting your journey to Washington cannot be very material. No business is done in Congress till after New Year's.

CLAY: I must in no way neglect my new duties.

BURR: I, too, found it difficult to continue my law practice when I became a Senator. However, I felt morally bound to stand by my clients whose cases were in the midst of trial. The public's trust begins with honoring one's personal commitments.

(*Another barrel is rolled into place. BURR marks his list.*)

CLAY: I agree. Nevertheless, I believe it would be unseemly for a United States Senator to argue in open court against a United States Attorney.

BURR: As unseemly as seeing an innocent man hanged? (*A beat.*)

CLAY: It is by no means certain that you will be indicted.

BURR: Given the calumny surrounding this case, I am sure you can see what an adverse impression it will make on a weak-minded jury, were my chief counsel to abandon me midstream.

CLAY: Yes, there is that. But, I have been placed in a high station by the General Assembly. It would be improper for me to endanger my effectiveness in Congress by seeming to be at odds with the President.

BURR: Of course. At the onset of your national political career, you cannot risk having your tender reputation tainted by a traitor's kiss.

CLAY: My friends all advised me that my association with you could be dangerous—politically, that is.

BURR: "Ye are the salt of the earth; but if salt have lost his savior, wherewith shall it be salted?" This Marshall clan and the whole Tory Federalist faction would like nothing better than to promote more dissention among leading Republicans. If the Federalists succeed in prosecuting me, whatever the verdict, Republicans will have been dealt a severe blow in this Western region. Every candidate we offer for public office will have to labor under the stigma of being a traitor, whatever the truth of the matter.

CLAY: True. It will make it bad for all of us.

BURR: I assure you I have not taken any measure to promote a dissolution of the Union. I have neither issued, nor signed, a commission to any person for any purpose. I do not own a musket, nor a bayonet, nor any single article of military stores.

CLAY: Are you willing to put as much in writing?

BURR: Without hesitation.

CLAY: Such a concrete denial would increase my confidence in presenting your case.

BURR: And make a handy letter of introduction to the President. But no matter. We must not allow inflammatory newspaper articles and half-baked judicial maneuvers to separate the two best legal minds in the country. Together we can defeat these old Federalists and their ploy of using the courts to destroy their political opponents. Can we not?

(*BURR offers his hand. CLAY hesitates, then shakes. Lights fade to dark.*)

SCENE SIX

Courtroom. SPECTATORS are gathered around the gallery. DAVEISS enters to boos and hisses. BURR and CLAY enter to applause. INNES enters to whispers.

INNES: Attorney Daveiss, the Grand Jury has been sworn and sequestered. Have you charges to proffer at this time?

DAVEISS: Your Honor, I would like to request a postponement. Two of the witnesses necessary for me to proceed are not present.

(SPECTATORS boo. INNES pounds his gavel. CLAY jumps to his feet.)

CLAY: Your Honor, how much longer must my client dance attendance on the attorney's mock prosecutions? The U.S. Attorney should be compelled to proceed, or abandon his allegations.

DAVEISS: *(Angrily.)* Mr. Clay and his client are attempting to force matters to an abrupt conclusion, Your Honor. No one has summoned Aaron Burr to appear in this court. He has not been indicted and therefore it is not for him or his counsel to interfere with these proceedings.

CLAY: I trust that freedom of speech is still sacred in this country. Is a man to sit idly and see a net spread for his liberties? The accused has duties as high and as honorable as the prosecutor. Colonel Burr should not be forced to remain under the shadow of a grand jury which has made no indictment, and which may never make one. Is this not the land of liberty? Can no stranger pass through Kentucky without the most atrocious charges being advanced against him? No, Your Honor, we are not so barbarous.

DAVEISS: Yes, this is the land of liberty. Men are free to say what they please and act as they please. But liberty does not give license to treason. Some men have used their freedom to make a commissary out of Kentucky to stock up provisions to carry out their evil designs. Are the guilty to go unpunished because the time necessary to establish their guilt might not be had? A little delay is all that the culprit requires. For soon he expects to be beyond our law and become a law unto himself. This Burrrh—he has no business in this courtroom. He is not a defendant and cannot therefore claim the rights of a defendant.

CLAY: Can the U.S. Attorney expect Colonel Burr to be indifferent to such enormous accusations? Is this man to be made the butt of slander because there is no court order out against him, because no deputy marshal has laid his hand on his shoulder? Is he to be treated with scorn and contempt because he has not run off, as the U.S. Attorney continually expects, and endeavored to escape an investigation?

SPECTATORS: Here. Here. Well said. Tell 'em, Henry.

(INNES pounds his gavel.)

CLAY: I object. I strongly object to the Federal Attorney's singular action to force upon the court principles which were never heard of before—to call and adjourn the grand jury at his pleasure; to make a weathercock of this court to twist with his whim. If the U.S. Attorney is allowed such license, there is no saying where his quest for power will lead. He might, for all I know, take into his head to make presentments as well as to draw conclusions—in short, sir, he might proceed to assume and exercise all rights of a grand jury...

DAVEISS: *(Interrupting.)* Your Honor...

CLAY: *(Interrupting.)* In fact, to become a grand jury himself.

DAVEISS: Your Honor?

INNES; I am going to grant Mr. Daveiss' motion for a postponement, not for the reasons the Federal Attorney offers, but because of the lateness of the hour. I regret that I was persuaded to release the first grand jury. Mr. Daveiss, this court feels you have had ample time to prepare. You will be prepared to call witnesses before the grand jury tomorrow, or I will dismiss this case. *(INNES pounds his gavel.)*

(Lights fade to dark.)

SCENE SEVEN

An attic room. BURR is writing at a table. A knock on the door, MARGARETTA enters. She carries a basket covered with a cloth.

MARGARETTA: Theodosia charged me with seeing you well fed. So I have brought you a late supper.

BURR: Thank you. But you needn't have troubled yourself. Years ago while I was at Princeton, I discovered my powers of concentration could be increased by fasting.

MARGARETTA: If you'll not take these vitals perhaps you'll accept spiritual nourishment. (*She pulls a small Bible from the hand basket.*) The church lost a wonderful steward when you chose the law over God's service.

BURR: There were so many divines in my family, so much rigorous godliness, that I was inured to its spell.

MARGARETTA: But you are still winning converts?

BURR: Arousing passions is easier than employing them.

MARGARETTA: Having fanned affections so near, will you not inspire them more by returning them?

BURR: Reason teaches passion to yield to duty.

MARGARETTA: Please? If I prayed for you, perhaps... (*She grasps his arm.*)

BURR: (*Removing her hand from his.*) As a child, prayer was my sole companion. What I wanted; what I needed was a living father, not a holy ghost. Prayer for me is a bell without a clapper. God turned deaf when He took my parents from me before I could even know them.

MARGARETTA: You should rejoice, for their faith saved them.

BURR: My parents' faith brought them nothing but an early grave. They worked themselves into it cultivating God's vineyard.

MARGARETTA: Perhaps their early demise was their salvation. Not to confront the injustice and treachery of this world—surely that's a blessing. How wonderful it must be to go to our Maker with our hopes intact.

BURR: If I had to live without the smallpox which killed my mother or live without hope, I would do without hope, thank you.

MARGARETTA: God may reward you yet.

BURR: (*Reflecting.*) I could hear her moans through the heavy oak door. But none of them would let me see her. My mother was dying on the other side of that door and I couldn't get to her. Two years old, and I knew I would never see my mother again. I hated them. I hated them all for taking her away and giving me instead their divine recollections of her to love. My poor aunt—she grieved long after I was only bitter. And my uncle was too concerned with the size of his purse to worry about the chilling heart of his tiny nephew. They were a stern couple. They may have loved God, but no one else.

MARGARETTA: I have admired you for so long. As a little girl, growing up in New York, I used to pray each day would bring you to our house. Your clothes were elegant, your movements graceful. I can remember how happy my father was when you were his dinner guest. And I remember my brother saying you were the most brilliant man in America. How I trembled when you entered the room. I still do.

BURR: Your brother's investment in land in western New York doubtless encouraged your husband to invest with me on the Washita.

MARGARETTA: The Senator needs no encouragement to speculate with my money.

BURR: Yours, you say? (*Standing.*) The Washita, the West—it's more than mere speculation. It's the future. America's destiny is its frontier.

MARGARETTA: Oh, how I admire your courage, to risk your life to create a new world out of nothing.

BURR: Few men have less with which to gamble.

MARGARETTA: (*Kneeling.*) In the name of the Lamb whose blood cleanses all sin… Won't you join me? We must be washed or all our hopes will be for naught. (*She rises and approaches the rigid BURR.*) Salvation is only one step beyond repentance.

BURR: (*Making the sign of the cross.*) Remembrance, regret, and repentance, the cross of religious obedience. No thank you. I am satisfied to keep a firm grip on my own soul.

MARGARETTA: Loosen thy grip on thy self and embrace the world.

BURR: Ah, but it is the world that has me too much in her embrace.

MARGARETTA: (*Closing her eyes in prayer.*) "I come a light into the world that whosoever believeth should not abide in darkness."

BURR: It is your tender heart which enlightens my life.

MARGARETTA: These are not my words which comfort you, but the voice of one who speaks through me.

BURR: At this moment it is only your beautiful countenance which shines through my gloom. (*He takes her hands in his.*) "He that believeth on me, as the Scripture hath said, out of his belly shall flow rivers of living water."

MARGARETTA: (*Moving closer.*) Is it God's voice I hear, or…?

BURR: The god who says: … I am love.

MARGARETTA: Oh, I want to believe. God help my unbelief.

BURR: God will. (*He embraces her.*)

(*Lights fade quickly.*)

SCENE EIGHT

The offices of The Western World, *the darkened mass of a huge, idle press looms in the background. WOOD and STREET are setting type furiously.*

STREET: You got an extra "e"?

WOOD: English has too many "e's"; leave one out.

STREET: Are you going to tell me how to spell, now?

WOOD: You finished with the first page?

STREET: Give me your type stick if you're finished. (*STREET crooks his neck to read what WOOD has composed.*)

WOOD: Buyin' our own press, Josey, was a master stroke.

STREET: With our circulation rising it's kept the cash in our pockets and out of the hands of our competitors.

WOOD: Did I not tell you Colonel Burr would make our fortune? Was I right or not?

STREET: (*Rubs a pestle with ink over the lead, puts a piece of proof paper over it and rolls a heavy cylinder across the type. Holding the wet paper.*) What's this? (*Reading aloud.*) "Colonel Burr was manly and dignified, as usual. True, his constitution appears to have suffered considerably with the passing years, and his many misfortunes have left the traces of care and anxiety deeply impressed upon his features. His eye, however, retains all its natural penetration." Are we publishing novels, Mr. Wood, or is this a newspaper? What has any of this to do with the fact of treason?

WOOD: The whole town knows Daveiss is mad. He marches around Frankfort babbling to himself and fencing the wind.

STREET: Who wouldn't be seized with anger, tilting against these treacherous Republicans?

WOOD: Everyone knows he is prosecuting Burr for Hamilton's murder. Invade Mexico? Every other man out in that thicket yonder would march there tomorrow if Burr, or Wilkinson, would lead them.

STREET: You are infatuated, old man.

WOOD: Not I, lad. 'Tis you who have let your affection distort your reason. But you'll never have Joe Daveiss, if that's what you're hopin', not the way he has you, now.

STREET: You are evil, John Wood. As evil as the very one you worship. You want this would-be Bonaparte to drift down the Ohio to gold and glory, don't you? You'll trail after him like the faithful dog you are. Whatever your scheme, old man, I'll not let your new centurions nail my nation to a cross and cast lots for its raiment.

WOOD: Laddie, the story is what makes the newspaper, not the paper the story.

(*STREET overturns WOOD's type carriage. The type scatters across the floor.*)

STREET: Fatuous adulation! Your craven cowardice sickens me. Out! Get out of my sight. Get!

(*STREET picks up the type and throws it at WOOD. Suddenly remembering the dirk in his boot, he hurls that at WOOD. Lights fade to dark.*)

SCENE NINE

The Courtroom. DAVEISS is near the Judge's bench when CLAY and BURR enter. BURR wears only the coat of his old uniform now, having replaced the short pants with riding britches and fine Spanish riding boots. DAVEISS is dressed in a buckskin shirt, a hunting knife strapped to his belt. INNES appears sunken in his seat of power. His face is white. The whole scene has the feeling of being antique. CLAY whispers to BURR as they approach their seats.

CLAY: (*Anxious.*) I hear Innes had such a severe attack of vertigo after testifying before Pope's committee investigating Sebastian that he had to be bled twice.

BURR: Politics makes us all either victims or assassins—and sometimes both at once.

DAVEISS: Your Honor, I move the indictment of Aaron Burr for conspiring to make war on Mexico, the colony of the King of Spain, a foreign power at peace with the United States.

INNES: Bailiff, if the United States Attorney has qq-qq-questions to be submitted to the Grand Jury to guide tt-tt-their i-i-inquiry, convey them to tt-tt-the jury room.

DAVEISS: Your Honor, I must interrogate the witnesses personally before the Grand Jury.

CLAY: Your Honor, I object to this novelty in the code of criminal jurisprudence.

DAVEISS: The only novelty which I see in this court is Mr. Clay. With all due respect to the gentlemen of the Grand Jury, no person who is a stranger to the machinations of this conspiracy can hope to link together the chain of circumstances that constitute legal proof.

CLAY: Your Honor, I cannot idly stand by as the institution of the Grand Jury, that great palladium of the people's rights, is turned into an inquisitorial tribunal. Does the Attorney for the United States believe himself to be a modern Torquemada? Would he fashion himself the Grand Inquisitor of Kentucky, examining virtuous citizens behind sealed doors to obtain such confessions as will best suit his purpose?

DAVEISS: The evil which this indictment seeks to arrest is far more threatening to the liberty of our countrymen than any fanciful dangers Mr. Clay can impute to my motives. What I ask is no novelty. It is the practice and has been the practice in every court with which I am acquainted. Were Mr. Clay not in the employ of this … this wanted murderer, Mr. Clay would in no wise challenge this innocent procedure, the sole aim of which is to expose the seditious crimes of this patriot-turned-lunatic.

BURR: Hold, sir. (*A beat.*) I defy you to name a single instance, a single court in this nation, where such a practice was ever tolerated. (*A beat.*) Silence, Your Honor, for you and I know he cannot. For many years before becoming Vice President of the United States, I served as the public attorney in New York. And never in my tenure in that office did I ever examine, or ever propose to examine, witnesses before a Grand Jury. You may even appeal to the courts of Great Britain, where law is tyranny and its ministers tyrants, and such a proposal as the one just made would be rejected with the contempt it deserves.

INNES: (*Pounds his gavel.*) Gentlemen, on no occasion but extreme nn-nn-necessity ought a judge be ii-induced to exercise a power which results from his own dd-dd-discretion. The strong arm of the law ought to be cc-cc-confined within its pp-pp-proper limits—the known rules of pp-procedure. Attorney Daveiss, I find your request improper, unsupported by legal pp-precedent. Motion overruled.

DAVEISS: Your Honor must then be of two opinions, one private and confidential, the other public and official.

(*INNES pounds his gavel. BAILIFF enters and whispers to INNES.*)

BURR: "O, that a man might know the end of this day's business ere it come."

CLAY: Let us hope I have not played Strato to your Brutus and held the sword which caught your fall.

BURR: Fear not, friend. "For Brutus only overcame himself."

INNES: Attorney Daveiss, the Grand Jury wants to question two witnesses not on your list. Do you have any objection?

DAVEISS: You have removed all grounds for objection, Your Honor. Therefore, I have none.

CLAY: May we know whom, Your Honor?

(*INNES nods to the BAILIFF.*)

BAILIFF: The Court summons Joseph Street and John Wood, editors of <u>The Western World</u>, to appear in this court before noon tomorrow.

(*CROWD murmurs. INNES pounds his gavel. Lights fade to dark.*)

SCENE TEN

The darkened office of <u>The Western World</u>. STREET hunches over a barrel, a sole candle burning in front of him, a bottle open beside the candle.

STREET: It's as if Burr had wrought a spell of enchantment on the whole people and their magistracy.

DAVEISS: (*Steps from the background.*) Throughout history, there are times in which whole nations are blind.

MARSHALL: (*Appears out of the dark.*) Gentlemen, your chins will be full of splinters if you continue to drag them on the floor. Our cause is not lost. We have drawn first blood. Today Judge Benjamin Sebastian resigned from the Appeals Court. Rejoice, for we have pulled down a mighty pillar of injustice.

STREET: While the arch fiend makes ready his escape.

MARSHALL: These intriguing Republicans have made Kentucky government their exclusive prize since their plotting began in '88. This is a war of attrition we are fighting. We must wound them, one at a time, in engagement after engagement, until they bleed their last at the polls on election day.

DAVEISS: Are you preparing to stand for election?

MARSHALL: If there was ever a man who voted on any public question from pure motive, from the full conviction of his best judgment and responsibility, I am bold to say that on that question, I was that man.

DAVEISS: That the courts should be so ill used. Not to be able to stop treason. Innes told me privately he would allow me to question my witnesses before the Grand Jurors.

MARSHALL: It is a matter of doubt whether the head or the heart of Harry Innes is most to be pitied, censured, or despised. He recklessly dismissed a suit in which I was seeking damages after an advisory jury inferred I had mutilated the land office records to conceal a transaction.

STREET: You had a case before Innes' court?

MARSHALL: I did, until a few days ago.

STREET: Have you suits pending in Sebastian's court?

MARSHALL: A man of my extensive holdings has lawsuits constantly. This country grows ambitious lawyers like hemp, strong and plentiful.

STREET: I should have known this before we published your attacks on Judge Sebastian.

MARSHALL: Benjamin Sebastian is a vile traitor. He has now been exposed, and pulled down from the bench; as we shall soon expose his collaborators: Innes, Brown, Adair—the whole rotten lot.

STREET: I feel <u>The Western World</u> has been ill-used by your failure to confide your overlapping of interests.

MARSHALL: You know, Mr. Street, it is not necessary to tell the whole truth under all circumstances.

(*Lights fade to dark.*)

SCENE ELEVEN

The Golden Eagle Tavern. A large banquet is set. Guests enter including BURR, THEODOSIA, CLAY, ADAIR, ADAMS, BROWN, MARGARETTA, and JUDGE INNES. All take seats around the table.

ADAMS: Superstition and Christianity are inseparable. To give up belief in witchcraft is to give up faith in the Bible.

CLAY: Even a reformer as great as John Wesley believed in miracles and visions.

BROWN: Tell us, Colonel Burr, what is your opinion of the Christian religion?

BURR: I hold with Voltaire, if God did not exist it would be necessary to invent him.

MARGARETTA: *Mais toute la nature nous crie qu'il existe.*

THEODOSIA: But all of nature cries out He exists.

BURR: *Touche.*

ADAIR: I trust I do not give offense when I say: this company admires the way in which you have maintained your bearing through this ordeal, Colonel.

BURR: Composure under fire is the first quality of any soldier, private or general. I remember during the revolution there was but one entry by which the British could approach us in our winter quarters at Valley Forge. We called this the Gulch. The militia holding this outpost was an unruly lot. And they had gotten into the habit of raising the alarm whenever their fancy suited, causing the whole camp to be called to arms.

(*A WAITER hands a note to CLAY.*)

BURR: Admiring the discipline of my unit, Washington put me in command at the Gulch. I proceeded to take them in hand, drill them regularly and inspect their posts at all hours. A few malcontents resented discipline and plotted to kill me. I learned of their plan, and on the night they had set for their mutiny, I called out the entire detachment for inspection.

(*CLAY leaves the table.*)

BURR: As I passed in front of the first rank, a soldier stepped forward, aimed his musket at my chest, shouted, "Now's the time," and pulled the trigger. The hammer fell, the powder flashed—but I had seen to it that the balls had all been removed from their muskets.

(*The GROUP laughs. Lights fade to dim and rise at stage right.*)

SCENE TWELVE

In an alley behind the tavern. CLAY approaches a man in a hooded cloak, JOHN WOOD.

CLAY: Didn't we agree to keep our communications confined to an exchange of letters?

WOOD: I'm caught in the most distressing circumstances.

CLAY: Your columns of late have been quite conciliatory. The chance of settling your libel suits out of court has improved.

WOOD: You know the reciprocal attachment that has existed between Mr. Street and myself?

CLAY: Sir, I make it a rule never to pry into a man's private life.

WOOD: Perhaps such an ardent friendship is unfortunate, as it commonly entails misery for those who are slaves of such a passion. But this solitary regard constitutes my only happiness.

CLAY: Why confide this affair to me?

WOOD: My principal inducement in commencing the investigation of the so-called Spanish conspiracy was a hope that the enmities we would incur in the undertaking would be the means of binding Street and me closer together. But Mr. Marshall and Mr. Daveiss have employed every art of which they are master to produce distrust between Mr. Street and myself. It is now my sincere wish that a total stop be put to the conspiracy investigation, if not the paper itself.

CLAY: No doubt both would be a good thing for the tranquility of the community. But I confess, sir, I don't see how in either instance I can be helpful.

WOOD: I can see the deplorable situation into which Street and myself have fallen, but he does not. Those in whom he confides, far from assisting him, only urge him nearer sedition.

CLAY: As you know, the gentlemen you mention have considerable resources at their command, either to persuade, or purchase, what they desire.

WOOD: How well I know. My only object is to procure a settlement which will afford the means of carrying me to Richmond, Virginia, where I know I can find employment as a tutor. If it is in your power to advance me a sum sufficient to carry me to that destination, I should esteem it a most singular favor.

CLAY: How much do you require?

WOOD: I should say a hundred dollars will cover my expenses in leaving this factious country.

CLAY: And how soon will you depart?

WOOD: As soon as I can settle with Mr. Street. If he will give me a note for my share of the enterprise, I could then place that with you as surety for your loan.

CLAY: Yes, that would probably be the best. (*CLAY pulls out his pocket book.*) I expect you now view this whole matter in rather a new light?

WOOD: That I do, sir. I most certainly do.

(*WOOD accepts the money CLAY holds out to him. Lights fade to dark on scene in the alley and rise on the banquet.*)

ADAMS: What if the rebellion of the blacks on Santa Domingo should succeed? Every slave in the western hemisphere will be inspired to rise up against his master.

BURR: Not necessarily. Santa Domingo is but a tiny island, whereas we stand on the threshold of a great unsettled continent. So long as there is ample land to offer the hope of escape, the spirited black will seek freedom first in flight before he stands and fights.

THEODOSIA: Father is a true democrat. He introduced the first manumission bill in the New York Assembly.

BURR: Yes, only to see it fail, my dear.

MARGARETTA: Slavery is a sin that must be abolished.

BROWN: My dear, that's not the issue.

ADAIR: Virginia is none the worse for having suffered through slave rebellions. Witness how swiftly James Monroe, when he was governor, handled Gabriel's revolt in 1800. Hang those involved, then a few more, and all is quiet.

(*CLAY enters and stands at the rear.*)

BURR: Monroe's knotty justice will come as near making him President as any deed in his public career. What do you say, Henry?

CLAY: I'll say this, it's a sure bet that Virginia will give birth to more than one President.

BURR: Indeed. Young Mr. Clay must know, for he was born in Virginia, I believe.

(*GROUP laughs.*)

BURR: Gentlemen, if you will excuse me, I have a trying day ahead of me tomorrow.

(*GROUP laughs again.*)

THEODOSIA: Father, will you see me to my room.

BURR: With pleasure, my dear. (*BURR offers her his arm, they start to exit.*)

CLAY: A toast. To the last nail in the coffin of the last Federalist, and may his name be Joseph Hamilton Daveiss.

(*GROUP cheers, drinks.*)

BURR: We must be merciful in victory, Henry, just as we have been merciless in its pursuit. (*BURR stands and puts his hand on the sitting CLAY's shoulder.*)

MARGARETTA: That's not the sort of sentiment I'd expect from a military man, Colonel.

BURR: Perhaps, not. But the quality of his mercy *is* the measure of a good emperor.

(*The GROUP laughs—all but the stunned CLAY. BURR and THEODOSIA exit.*)

BROWN: Our Colonel is an enigma I cannot cipher.

MARGARETTA: A pity you weren't born a woman.

(*Lights fade to dark.*)

ACT TWO

SCENE THIRTEEN

BURR and THEODOSIA on a stairway.

THEODOSIA: You put on a brave show, Father.

BURR: Is my trepidation so clearly visible?

THEODOSIA: Only to experienced Burr-watchers.

BURR: I do nothing that I intend, and... what is worse, many things not intended and better left alone.

THEODOSIA: Confide your plans to me, father. I can help you, if you'll let me.

BURR: Hamilton's ghost haunts me at every turn. His slanders against me were tame so long as he alone uttered them. By dying at my hand he has given life everlasting to his lies. My aim was too unerring. I slew the man but not the slander.

THEODOSIA: Whatever you do, you must not lose faith in yourself.

BURR: This federal attorney thinks he's St. George and can advance his political career by slaying the democrat dragon. I am caught in this courtroom farce like an animal in a snare. I shall be forced to chew off a limb to escape this trap.

THEODOSIA: Voltaire is right. History is little more than a long succession of useless cruelties. What can I do to help you, father?

BURR: Nothing, my dear. Making war is a man's business.

THEODOSIA: (*Sighing.*) Good night, then. I will not wish you good luck for the trial tomorrow, because I know you do not trust Lady Luck either.

(*THEODOSIA exits.*)

BURR: "You do me wrong to take me out o' th' grave. Thou art a soul in bliss; but I am bound upon a wheel of fire, that my own tears do scald like molten lead."

(*Lights fade to dark.*)

SCENE FOURTEEN

The Jury Room. ABRAHAM HITE stands before a seated JOSEPH STREET. The BAILIFF stands in front of a door leading to the larger courtroom, which is unseen.

HITE: Mr. Street, you are the publisher of the newspaper, The Western World, are you not?

STREET: I am.

HITE: I will read to the Grand Jury a passage from your edition of Friday, November 28, this year. Quote: "Unapprised as we are of any evidence which it may be in the power of Mr. Daveiss to produce upon the trial of Colonel Burr, the purpose of prevention would have been answered by the wide diffusion of the evidence and corroborative facts which are in our possession." Unquote. Sir, this Grand Jury asks you to produce this "evidence" to which you refer.

STREET: Gentlemen, please understand that I relied on Mr. Wood, my associate editor, almost exclusively in this matter. It was he who gathered the information and who wrote most of the columns on this subject. I confined myself to what you might term, "commentary on their importance;" and to upholding the reputation of our journal among the public.

HITE: Yes, Mr. Street, I think most of Frankfort is familiar with your militant efforts in that regard. Sheriff, bring in Mr. Wood.

(*The BAILIFF opens the door at the side of the stage and beckons. JOHN WOOD enters, his eyes fixed on STREET. STREET avoids WOOD's glance.*)

HITE: Thank you, Mr. Street. You may go.

(*STREET exits quickly.*)

HITE: Take a seat, Mr. Wood.

(*WOOD, proud to be the center of attention, sits with distinction.*)

HITE: (*Continues.*) Mr. Wood, this Jury is given to understand that you may have certain evidence to offer us in regard to the alleged conspiracy purportedly masterminded by Aaron Burr.

WOOD: Your Honor, I have heard a good deal reported about Mr. Burr's plans, but I have no direct, personal knowledge of his intentions. The Colonel and I have not spoken in several years.

HITE: In July of this year, you, I suppose it was you, wrote in *The Western World*, quote: "We know the proceedings of Burr's agents in this state, at Orleans, and at St. Louis; we are perfectly informed of the nature of his contract with General Wilkinson, as likewise the articles agreed to at Frankfort between him and Mr. John Brown," unquote. All this in an article about a plot to disjoin Kentucky, Ohio, and Tennessee from the union.

WOOD: I'm sorry to say I was misguided in that instance. Further investigation satisfied me that the "articles" agreed to with Mr. Brown concerned the Indiana Canal Company, and the "contract" with General Wilkinson pertained to Colonel Burr's settlement along the Washita River. At the time I was writing about various conspiracies which have grown up in this country… some involving Spain and prominent men in Kentucky; others by France through Citizen Genet to invade Spanish territory with American volunteers; and a separate compact between Tennessee's Senator Blount and the British to invade the same territory.

HITE: Your command of history is impressive, Mr. Wood. But what can you say to this Jury to substantiate the current charges?

WOOD: That's a difficult question to answer, Your Honors. As I see it now, all these facts I was relating about these schemes from the past, led to speculation about the present, and speculation to suspicion, and suspicion to fantasy, n'r as not. Sort of the way Mr. Burns describes, "Backward cast my e'e on prospects drear, an' forward, tho' e canna see, I guess an' fear."

HITE: Is a poetical recitation all you have to offer this Jury, Mr. Wood, after months of printing accusations against Colonel Burr and his associates?

WOOD: Aye. The newspaper trade is a cut-throat business, Your Honors. A man cannot be about printing his wife's recipes and hope to survive. In fairness, after studyin' the matter, I am persuaded to believe that the present designs of Colonel Burr are neither against the government nor the laws of the United States.

(*Lights fade to dark.*)

SCENE FIFTEEN

Jordon's Inn in Lexington. BURR leans over a table studying a large map. ADAIR enters.

BURR: Senator Adair, come in.

ADAIR: Colonel, I bring you the information you've been waiting for. I just received this letter from our friend Wilkinson at the head of the Army facing the Spanish across the Sabine River. The time looked for by many, and wished for by more, has now arrived for subverting the Spanish government in Mexico. (*Reading.*) "Be ready and join me; we will want little more than light troops. More will be done by marching than by fighting."

BURR: We must lose no time. If I know Wilkinson, he will do far more marching than fighting, whatever the situation. Unless I take command, he will allow the Spanish garrison in Texas to fall back into southern Mexico.

ADAIR: I was Wilkinson's aide in the Indian campaign of '92. He is not a man to take orders.

BURR: He will, sir, from me. (*BURR stares coldly at ADAIR. Then resumes his affable manner.*) You and I will go immediately to Nashville. There we will spur our friend, Andy Jackson, to mobilize his Tennessee militia. (*BURR reaches in the desk and pulls out large bank notes.*) I'll give him three thousand dollars worth of these Kentucky Insurance Company notes and have him buy boats and provisions. Look here. (*BURR points to the map.*) You're a military man, Senator. Or should I say, General? What do you think? Should we halt at Natchez or descend the river and seize Baton Rouge with its arms cache?

ADAIR: If we capture Baton Rouge, we are masters of Spanish West Florida, and can bargain with whatever government we please.

BURR: My thought, precisely. (*BURR goes to a trunk behind the table and retrieves a document.*) You see this document? This is a declaration of independence for the republic of Louisiana. I have it completely drawn up. If the Creoles of New Orleans are prepared to act, I am ready to assist them.

ADAIR: New Orleans is United States territory, Colonel. I'll not fight my own countrymen.

BURR: Oh, no. No. That must be avoided. We're revolutionaries, not traitors.

(*Lights fade to dark.*)

SCENE SIXTEEN

A ballroom. A file of dancers in elegant attire step to the music of a string trio playing a minuet. VARIOUS CHARACTERS circulate around the dancers.

A WELL-DRESSED LADY: Colonel Burr was the most perfect gentleman throughout this dreadful affair.

ADAMS: Without question, Aaron Burr is the most erudite man I've ever met.

BROWN: (*To his wife as they dance.*) Our young Henry was magnificent. He demolished Daveiss' arguments with the most flowing language ever uttered in a courtroom. This trial will make him famous even before he reaches Washington City.

MARGARETTA: The whole episode makes me sad.

BROWN: Aren't you pleased our little Colonel was vindicated?

MARGARETTA: Yes, of course. But how much more gratifying it would have been to have given refuge to the liberator of Mexico. Now, I fear our dear Colonel will take all this excitement with him.

FOOTMAN: (*Announces a new guest.*) Ladies and gentlemen, the Governor of the Commonwealth, the Honorable Christopher Greenup and Mrs. Greenup.

(*A white-haired MAN and a finely dressed WOMAN enter. Polite applause. The young ADAMS steps beside the FOOTMAN.*)

ADAMS: Ladies and gentlemen, the inimitable, the incomparable, Aaron Burr.

(*BURR enters to wild applause. He is dressed in a suit of velvet, a deep blue waistcoat and gold knee britches. On his head a powdered wig tied in the back by a golden ribbon; on his feet, dancing pumps with immense rosettes. The LADIES crowd around him. MARSHALL and DAVEISS stand apart. MARSHALL carries his cudgel adorned by a blue ribbon.*)

MARSHALL: His Majesty, Aaron the First.

(*MUSICIANS begin a contra dance and BURR is in the center of it with a lady on either arm. POPE walks over to MARSHALL and DAVEISS.*)

POPE: Mr. Daveiss, my congratulations on a valiant effort.

DAVEISS: See how the people vie with each other to caress their little traitor.

MARSHALL: You're to be congratulated, Senator, on your role in revealing Sebastian's treachery.

POPE: And when I arrive in Washington City I shall move an examination of his co-conspirator, Harry Innes.

MARSHALL: Excellent.

DAVEISS: You'll find little encouragement in that effort. Jefferson did nothing to aid my prosecution of Burr.

MARSHALL: Careful, brother, you don't want our new Senator to think you were motivated solely by politics.

DAVEISS: Whether my motives be set down to malice, federalism, or candor, I care not. But were I in Congress, I would move an impeachment against Thomas Jefferson for his negligent and flagitious conduct relative to this conspiracy.

POPE: If you gentlemen will pardon me, I must speak to the Governor. (*He moves off.*)

MARSHALL: That was an untoward statement. As a first-term senator, Pope will want to ingratiate himself with the President. You may have just handed him his tribute, the head of a Federalist U.S. Attorney—your own.

DAVEISS: So be it. I shall never imitate Thomas Jefferson and make my judgment play the whore to my ambition.

(*BURR, THEODOSIA and MARGARETTA on each arm, walks up to MARSHALL and DAVEISS.*)

BURR: Senator Marshall, we meet again. That's a weighty scepter you're carrying. Is there a significance in the blue ribbon?

MARSHALL: A symbol of a recent victory. Although, I would prefer it were Sebastian's scalp dangling here.

BURR: A pity you have no gold ribbon to match it.

MARSHALL: Ah, Colonel. It would not be sporting to kill all the game in the forest.

BURR: No fox, no hunt, eh, Senator?

(*BURR sees ADAIR and a commonly dressed man, TAYLOR, approaching.*)

BURR: You will excuse us; I have a great many friends to greet tonight.

(*BURR and the LADIES move off. The MUSICIANS begin another reel and BURR leaves the LADIES to talk with ADAIR and his companion.*)

DAVEISS: (*To MARSHALL.*) I wonder if he intends to dance his way into Mexico?

(*BURR moves with ADAIR and TAYLOR to a corner of the room.*)

ADAIR: This man has distressing news. (*To Taylor.*) Tell the Colonel, here, what you told me.

TAYLOR: All Ohio is in an uproar. Virginia too. The militias are mustering along both sides of the river.

BURR: I beg your pardon?

TAYLOR: No good in begging me, sir, for I'm a poor man. People in Ohio say Aaron Burr is a traitor and using Blennerhasset's island to store weapons for a rebellion. Some say he's going to make himself king of St. Louis, and Mrs. Blennerhasset his queen.

BURR: (*Stunned.*) Has the whole country gone insane?

TAYLOR: No more than you, sir, if you're the gentleman I take you for.

ADAIR: Enough. Go back to Blennerhasset and tell him you've delivered the message.

TAYLOR: I can't do that, sir. He's left the island in the dead of night. Boarded three flatboats with the men that had gathered there, and set off down the Ohio. Only Mrs. Blennerhasset and the house servants are left.

BURR: Embarked, you say? When?

TAYLOR: Two, three nights ago.

BURR: Thank you. Get yourself a glass of the grog. You've accomplished your mission.

(*TAYLOR pushes into the background.*)

ADAIR: Sounds like you've been outflanked, Colonel.

BURR: One can't be sure until the battle's joined. (*A beat.*) Did I tell you how I foiled a mutiny in the ranks at Valley Forge?

ADAIR: Yes, last evening.

BURR: Yes, but not all the story. I can see as though it were yesterday the mutineer's face as he held the harmless musket pointed at my chest and I drew my sword and sliced off his wrist.

ADAIR: A brave tale. But on this occasion, Colonel, the militia's muskets may not only be primed, but loaded.

BURR: (*Relishing the idea.*) Ah, yes, General. But in war, there is no gain without risk. Ride with me to Nashville. With two old Indian fighters like you and Andy Jackson by my side, Mexico will fall like a ripe fruit into my palm.

(*ADAIR notices THEODOSIA approaching behind BURR. BURR notices ADAIR's expression change and turns to his rear.*)

BURR: How lovely you are tonight, Theodosia.

(*ADAIR moves off.*)

THEODOSIA: Am I worthy to be the daughter of an Emperor?

BURR: Simple ambitions, my dear, like simple food, preserve the appetite.

THEODOSIA: Tell me, father, will you have slavery in your new nation? Will women have the vote?

BURR: You mustn't allow your fantasies to run away with your reason.

THEODOSIA: Oh, father, how I've come to loathe your endless games: your word games, your financial games, your political games. You play at land speculation as if it were tether ball. When that becomes tiresome you launch into politics. If you fail to master your opponent there, you load your pistol and turn the contest into a deadlier sport.

BURR: You should retire, my love, the wine has gone to your head.

MARGARETTA: Better I, too heady, than you so very head strong.

(*BURR watches MARGARETTA across the dance floor.*)

BURR: We often persuade ourselves that certain things are our choice, when in truth we have been unavoidably impelled to them.

THEODOSIA: As you have been impelled to make love to our hostess?

BURR: A moment of irritation is not the time for explanation.

THEODOSIA: Are you so sure? For years, I have observed how you soothe your irritations by explaining away other people's virtues. So far as I can tell, your sense of morality consists of limiting yourself to one mistress at a time.

BURR: *Ma maitresse est le pouvoir.*

THEODOSIA: Power is a frigid companion who will never return the love you bestow her.

BURR: If it will ease your troubled mind to know what my plans are, then, I will confide them to you. Tomorrow at daybreak, I go...

THEODOSIA: (*Interrupting.*) No, no. Don't tell me. You mustn't spoil me with your confidences. My soul could not stand the torment of trying to decide whether you had told me the truth or not. Better the doubt that keeps me loving you than the truth which would make me hate you forever. I am not well enough to carry such a burden. A horrible sensation like a spike running through me tortured me all yesterday.

BURR: Perhaps it's better if you do not hazard this expedition further.

THEODOSIA: Yes. Yes, that would be best. If I return to Charleston, I can still serve you. Here I am nuisance but there I can imprison myself in their slave-grinding elegance—forever the hostage—a living pledge for all the guarantees my husband has provided your creditors. (*She whirls around the ballroom.*) Dear delightful confusion. It gives a pulse to the blood, an activity to the mind, and a bounce to every step.

(*BURR grabs his daughter's arm and pulls her away from the crowd.*)

BURR: Get to bed, you hussy.

THEODOSIA: (*Slaps BURR.*) Confine your tyranny to yourself, father.

(*THEODOSIA runs off crying. BROWN and MARGARETTA walk over to BURR.*)

BROWN: Colonel, what a victory. Daveiss must be deranged like they say. Only a madman could believe you would attempt to sever the Union.

BURR: Sometimes it is more convenient to be mad among madmen than to be wise all alone.

(*BROWN and MARGARETTA laugh.*)

MARGARETTA: John, shall we share our good fortune with our friend?

BROWN: Of course, my dear.

MARGARETTA: I'm expecting another child in spring.

BURR: Congratulations, Madame. (*He kisses her hand.*)

BROWN: What a triumphant day. My friend escapes the scaffold and my wife multiplies my joys.

(*BROWN picks up glasses of champagne, hands them to his three companions. Among the DANCERS, a WOMAN screams. ADAMS and BRADFORD have grabbed an INTRUDER and are trying to eject him from the room. The INTRUDER breaks free and turns on the audience. It is STREET.*)

STREET: Fools, be warned! The robber is in your midst.

BROWN: Sir, your presence is not desired here.

STREET: You may fight and you may conquer, but many must fall your victim.

(*The SHERIFF has moved behind STREET and grabs his arms. ADAMS and BRADFORD move forward to help. STREET breaks an arm free, reaches in his cloak, pulls out his dirk and lashes at his assailants.*)

STREET: Even I may fall on the field of battle.

(*STREET's dagger misses its target and sticks in the woodwork. STREET tries to pull it free, but cannot. A GROUP OF MEN grab him and throw him through an open window.*)

MARSHALL: (*Steps to the podium and lifts his glass in a toast.*) Ladies and gentlemen, a toast. To the United States of America. May the seventeen glorious states of our Union be welded into one united empire by the hammer of peace on the anvil of reconciliation.

(*The CROWD cheers.*)

BURR: (*Lifting the glass.*) And may the man that pumps the bellows of discord be burnt up by the flying sparks.

ADAIR: The Eagle and the seventeen stars!

(*The CROWD cheers. The MUSICIANS play "The Liberty Song," and the CROWD sings.*)

CROWD: Come join hand in hand brave Americans all
By uniting we stand, by dividing we fall;
No tyrannous acts shall suppress your just claim
Nor stain with dishonor American's name
In freedom we're born and in freedom we'll live
Our purses are ready; Steady friends, steady,
Not as slaves but as free men our money we'll give.

(*CROWD exits singing. Lights fade to dark.*)

SCENE SEVENTEEN

The offices of The Western World. *WOOD and STREET examine the type they have set.*

WOOD: (*Reading.*) "The jury has whitewashed Aaron Burr." That's fine language but a wee bit strong for the opening paragraph.

STREET: That's the fact of the matter. The Grand Jury has made a lie of every suspicion.

WOOD: Perhaps it would be of interest to our readers to know the important role we played in the proceedings.

STREET: The perfidious Judge Innes is now the subject of scrutiny. But no matter. Your views no longer guide the content of this newspaper.

WOOD: I write not less than the truth allows.

STREET: Yes, and no more than libel will permit.

WOOD: Give up this quarrel, Josey. Go with me to St. Louis. There we can use our winnings in this little game to start another newspaper, bigger and better, and be free of these libel-batting lawyers and infernal speculators.

STREET: Leave all this, when it's finally paying off? You are daft. Have you forgotten, old man, that it was you who taught me this alchemy? You who gave me this Philosopher's stone and showed me how to turn lead into gold. Now I intend to profit by the secret. (*STREET picks up the letters from a tray and lets them spill through his hands like coins.*) I aim to mine this vein for all it's worth. (*He reaches beneath a stack of manuscripts and pulls out two legal-looking documents.*) Sign this quit claim, and I shall give you my note for what you have invested in* The Western World.

WOOD: "Rapture sweet that hour we meet
wi' mutual love an' a that;
But for how long the fly may sting
Let inclination know that."

(*WOOD signs one document. STREET hands him the second document.*)

STREET: Now, take your whore's fee and be gone. You have no claim on anything around here anymore.

WOOD: (*Examining the note.*) Only sixty dollars. Little enough recompense for a year's love and labor lost. It's a cold heart you have, Joseph Street.

STREET: I had a good tutor.

(*Lights fade to dark.*)

SCENE EIGHTEEN

A flatboat adrift on the Cumberland River. BURR is seated on a small keg surrounded by larger casks. Another keg in front of him he uses for a writing desk. ADAIR stands beside him holding a newspaper.

BURR: You remember last summer?—that day when the skies darkened at midday and the moon passed in front of the sun? I took that as an omen for our success—that the orbit of our adventure would soon eclipse the brilliance of Thomas Jefferson. But all it meant was a harsh winter and cold earth in which to germinate our uprising.

ADAIR: Our seed is well planted. Water it with a little American blood on the Spanish frontier and it will erupt into a tree of liberty in the center of Mexico City.

BURR: Read the President's proclamation to our volunteers. Let them vote among themselves what course we're to follow.

(*ADAIR exits.*)

BURR: (*Writing.*) My dearest Theodosia, We left without Jackson and with but few recruits. Today we spend Christmas at the confluence of the Cumberland and Ohio Rivers. As I watch the two waters converge, I reflect how our individual fates co-mingle with larger currents...

(*BURR continues writing as ADAIR appears on the deck over BURR's cabin.*)

ADAIR: (*Reading.*) "I have thought fit to issue this proclamation enjoining all citizens who have been led to participate in conspiring to set afoot a military expedition against the dominions of Spain to withdraw from the same without delay or incur prosecution with all the rigors of the law. Given at the City of Washington on the 27th day of November, 1806, in the year of the sovereignty and independence of the United States the thirty-first. Signed, Thomas Jefferson."

BURR: In childhood I was taught to believe that I was among the elect of God—the next in an honorable line of divines—grandfather Edwards, father, myself: God's chosen instruments. I was nineteen when our war of independence began. And all my life has been a battle against the sinful men in control of government—first a spiteful king, then a landed aristocracy. But the assumption of power is its own corruption. Honor soon perishes amid the many conflicts needed to sustain it.

(*A ROAR of voices above.*

BURR: (*Continues.*) As I write, my corps of volunteers determines my future: whether on to Mexico and its shining promise, or backward to Jefferson's America, poverty and a hangman's knot. My dear, if words could contain the full measure of my love for you, the extent of my sorrow at our parting, then I ....

(*ADAIR enters.*)

ADAIR: The men have voted, sir.

BURR: And what is their will?

ADAIR: On to Mexico. Fame and fortune.

(*BURR picks up a wicker of wine and pours two gourd cups full.*)

BURR: Then onward it must be. (*He hands a cup to ADAIR then lifts his own gourd in a toast.*) To our one undeniable fortune: — fame. (*They touch cups.*)

THE END

Joseph Gray, Jack Johnson, John Conlee and Kevin Haggard in *Desperate Fortune* by Joe Terrence Gray, Horse Cave Theatre, 1990

Joe Terrence Gray

Joe Terrence Gray was raised on a farm in Southern Kentucky. He is a graduate of combat in Vietnam (CMB, '69) and Yale University (BA '72).

For 40 years, he has been a writer, producer, and director of documentary films and videos set in his native state.

His "intimate" film on share-cropping tobacco, *Lord and Father* is available on DVD at www.appalshop.org. The sequel in this family saga, *Green Blood Red Tears,* reveals the danger to farmers of mixing stress, pesticides, and antidepressants. His new film, *Big Nam*, is a drama/documentary about "war stories," who tells them and why.

Scott Morgan and Dave Ducey in *His First, Best Country* by Jim Wayne Miller, Horse Cave Theatre, 1992

HIS FIRST, BEST COUNTRY
by
Jim Wayne Miller

Scott Morgan and Scott Hubbard (foreground) and Charles K. Brown, Bob Carner and Jack Johnson (background) in *His First, Best Country* by Jim Wayne Miller, Horse Cave Theatre, 1992

His First, Best Country opened on July 17, 1992, with the following cast:

JENNINGS WELLS	*Michael Hankins*
ROMA JEAN LIVESAY	*Trigger Manning*
BUDDY SHELTON	*Scott Morgan*
EDNA RAE	*Peggy Howell*
LLOYD SUTHERLAND	*Dave Ducey*
HILLARD SHELTON	*Gregory Etter*
CECIL PEDIGO	*Scott Hubbard*
DELANO CRUM	*Jack Johnson*
WILEY WOOLFORD	*Bob Carner*
DEE RHODOMMER	*Charles K Brown*
TOWNSPEOPLE	*Roger Bell*
	Jeffrey Bracco
	Kip London
	Bruce Racond
	Kari Todd

Director: Warren Hammack
Stage Manager: Rebecca Monroe
Set Design: Sam Hunt
Lighting Design: Gregory Etter
Costume Design: Jennifer Noe
Sound Design: Wesley Jay Akers
Properties Master: David Phillips
Technical Director: Steve McCormick

I saw more of my father's writing process in the development of *His First, Best Country* at Horse Cave Theatre than in anything else he wrote. I'm grateful to Warren Hammack, as a director, producer, and actor – for his artistry and vision – and to Horse Cave Theatre and everyone involved in the new play program, and for plays I saw there back to my childhood.

His First, Best Country began as a story, published by Gnomon, in 1987; it then went through successive drafts as a play, with staged readings and workshop discussions. The production was in 1993, sponsored by WKYU-FM, and produced and directed by Hammack. I wrote comments on the drafts, went to the staged readings and workshop discussions, wrote letters to Dad, and made suggestions he didn't wind up using. But I think he appreciated the exchange. He said it sometimes got him going again after he'd set the play aside.

I remember that scenes in drafts I'd read often surprised me when I saw them read, or acted, and that things worked in ways I hadn't expected. The loafers, guys on a bench at a local store, were so brilliantly acted – the loafer scenes may also stand out in my memory because they are, for me, about as good an earthly vision of paradise as ever represented by art.

I don't know if many people enjoy watching a story go through editing, and changes, and readings, and performance, but I think it's an amazing thing to see. I remember watching my father's play develop in a process that involved the collective contributions of many people, and I think this book celebrates that, and is something itself to be celebrated.

– Frederic Smith Miller

Characters:

JENNINGS WELLS, *a professor/writer, mid-to-late forties*

ROMA JEAN LIVESAY, *a divorcee, twelve years younger than Jennings*

BUDDY SHELTON, *a sixteen-year-old, son of Jennings Wells' one-time fiancé*

EDNA RAE, *Jennings Wells' cousin, mid-fifties*

HILLIARD SHELTON, *older brother of Jennings Wells' former fiancé, and uncle of her son Buddy*

CECIL PEDIGO, *Hilliard's enforcer*

LLOYD SUTHERLAND, *farmer, sixty-five years old*

DELANO CRUM, *occupant of loafers' bench at a local store*

WILEY WOOLFORD, *occupant of loafers' bench at a local store*

DEE RHODOMMER, *occupant of loafers' bench at a local store*

OTHER RESIDENTS OF THE KINGDOM COMMUNITY, and MEMBERS OF SCHOOL BOARD, *present at the school board meeting*

Place: Eastern Kentucky

ACT ONE

SCENE ONE

As lights come up on an area that represents Jennings Wells' house, the song "The Coming of the Roads," words and music by Billy Edd Wheeler, is heard. Strumming a guitar, JENNINGS WELLS sits turned away from a desk. As the music fades, he puts the guitar aside and turns to a typewriter which sits on the desk that is cluttered with magazines, books, and papers. He pulls a sheet of paper out of the typewriter and rolls another one in. He looks back at the last line on the finished page.

JENNINGS: Gerald, do you remember that time back on Doggett Mountain, when you drove a log truck up to our camp at Double Springs...?

(*BUDDY SHELTON enters, leans a bush ax against Jennings' table.*)

JENNINGS: (*Without looking up.*) What say, Henry?

BUDDY: My name's not Henry. I finished mowin that branchbank.

JENNINGS: Good. (*Continues to type.*)

BUDDY: (*Watches him type.*) You gonna pay me?

JENNINGS: I thought I paid you with the driving lessons.

BUDDY: Drivin lessons was for cleanin up around the barn. You said you'd pay me for mowin the branchbanks.

(*JENNINGS reaches into his pocket, peels a bill off the folded money, and lays it on the table.*)

BUDDY: (*Steps over and pockets the bill.*) When can we go and get my license?

JENNINGS: I think you need to practice some more.

BUDDY: (*Sits in a ladder-back chair.*) Let's do it, then! Let's go ride around.

JENNINGS: Not today. I'm busy, Henry.

BUDDY: I'm Buddy! Not Henry. (*Sits watching JENNINGS type.*) You get paid to write stuff?

JENNINGS: Sometimes.

BUDDY: Pay me, I'll write you somethin. (*When JENNINGS doesn't respond.*) What are you writin this time?

JENNINGS: I'm writin a letter.

BUDDY: Who to?

JENNINGS: My cousin, Gerald.

BUDDY: You write to him a lot?

JENNINGS: No. (*Turns from the typewriter.*) This is the first time I've ever written to him. The last time I saw him, Henry, was twenty-four, twenty-five years ago, when he left out of here. I promised him then I'd write. So I'm writing.

BUDDY: You tellin him about comin back to Newfound to live?

JENNINGS: Yeah.

BUDDY: What you tellin him?

JENNINGS: I'm telling him about how Cordell County's changed. (*Picks up one of the finished pages and refers to it as he talks.*) How one end of the county's filled up with Hare Krishnas, and back-to-the-landers... raising Nubian goats and living in renovated barns and geodesic domes. How the other end of the county, where the coal seams run, 's been pretty well trashed by strip-mining. And I've come home and I'm trying to write a book—but this feller who wants to quit school and live in the woods like Henry Thoreau keeps coming around pestering me to teach him to drive.

BUDDY: (*Half-believing, gets up from the chair and comes over to look over at the page in the typewriter.*) That's not what it says, either! Says: (*Puzzling this out, slowly.*) The woods are full of solar carpenters, potters, spiritualists, dulcimer makers—-

JENNINGS: Go home Henry.

BUDDY: We could go down to the lake and ride on your tract, or if you don't want to ride around, at least let me practice driving some more.

JENNINGS: Not today, Henry.

BUDDY: Not out on the big road, just up and down the driveway here—between the barn and mailbox.

JENNINGS: Be sure you don't get out on the road.

BUDDY: (*Heading off.*) Is the key—?

JENNINGS: In the ashtray. And don't jerk that truck around, Henry.

(*BUDDY exits. He can be heard starting the truck. As JENNINGS resumes typing, the sound of the motor can be heard approaching and receding, as BUDDY drives it up and down the drive between the barn and the mailbox.*)

JENNINGS: (*Types, reads aloud as he types.*) What I want to know, Gerald, is... did you have some early warning system... and foresee all this? Is that why you got out so fast and never came back? —This is the letter I said I'd write you—all those years ago. If I knew where you were, I'd mail it to you.

(*As he rolls the sheet of paper out of the typewriter, a car horn sounds offstage, another horn answers, and there is the sound of a car coming to a stop just offstage. Music, the Judds' "Mama, He's Crazy," is heard.*)

(*ROMA LIVESAY enters in blue jeans and an "Outlaws" tee shirt. She has left the radio—or tape player—playing in her car.*)

JENNINGS: (*Gets up from desk, goes to door.*) Hello?

ROMA: Hi! Heard you were home!

(*JENNINGS welcomes ROMA with a gesture. She sits down on the bench where Buddy sat earlier. Looks up at him and slaps both knees with her hands, rocks back and forth expectantly.*)

JENNINGS: (*Sits on edge of desk. Speaking awkwardly.*) Well, yes, I—I've been home a week now, and it's been pretty much—open house. I'm Jennings Wells.

ROMA: (*Smiles.*) I know who you are, Jennings Wells. —I'm Roma!

JENNINGS: Hello... Roma.

ROMA: (*Suppresses laughter.*) Come on, now. Try to remember!

JENNINGS: Roma? Roma?

ROMA: You went to school with my sister, Barbara.

JENNINGS: Barbara... yes.

ROMA: You used to come by the house to go squirrel hunting with my brother Clyde, and you'd be there in the yard waiting and I'd dance for you. (*Stands, reenacts the dance.*)

JENNINGS: Clyde. Clyde Livesay? (*Finally remembering.*) Little Roma? Roma Livesay! But you were just a....little Roma—then!

ROMA: (*Sits again.*) Who is that drivin your old truck? Almost ran me in the ditch. Was that Buddy Shelton?

JENNINGS: Buddy, yes. —You're little Roma?—I mean, of course, you are. But—I remember you with your hair in dog ears!—Sit down, Roma!

(*ROMA looks up at him, amused by his awkwardness.*)

JENNINGS: Oh, you are sitting down. (*He turns in the direction of the door, then back to her.*) Yes, Buddy Shelton. That boy came by the other day wanting to work for me. I'll speak to him about his driving.—Roma! (*Turns toward the door again, then toward the typewriter.*) Look, I was just about ready to knock off this (*Gestures toward the typewriter.*) — and have a...have a drink. Do you —would you?

ROMA: Got any Jim Beam? I like that boy!

(*JENNINGS steps offstage into kitchen. From offstage we hear sound of glasses, cabinet doors opening.*)

JENNINGS: (*Off.*) Don't think I have any Jim Beam.

(*ROMA, alone, begins to sway to the music on the car radio. Dances across to the worktable, picks up JENNINGS' guitar which has been leaning against the table.*)

ROMA: See you still play the guitar.

JENNINGS (*Off.*) Oh a little.

ROMA: Like you used to at the Rocky Top Festival.

JENNINGS: (*Off.*) Not as well as I did then.—I don't have any Jim Beam. How about Elija Craig?

ROMA: Whatever! —You and Roseanne Shelton played and sang together at the Rockytop Festival. I remember. I used to wish it was me up there singing with you. — You keep up with Roseanne?

(*JENNINGS comes back with drinks. ROMA puts down the guitar and takes one of the drinks.*)

JENNINGS: No, I've not seen her or heard from her in years.

ROMA: Surely you knew about Buddy.

JENNINGS: I heard she'd brought her boy back here and left him with her Mama and Papa. Didn't know he was still here. I think he's adopted me.

ROMA: (*After an awkward pause.*) I can't drink anywhere but in a car! Come on, let's sit!

(*Exits with JENNINGS in tow in the direction of the offstage car, as the music comes up, still playing "Mama, He's Crazy."*)

SCENE TWO

Hilliard Shelton's office. JENNINGS knocks. HILLIARD, a man in his fifties, is wearing a short sleeved shirt with a pocket full of pens, a loosened tie. HILLIARD speaks loudly, forcefully, smiles a lot, plays his cards close to his chest, seems less informed than he is, gives the impression that no obstacle is too great to overcome.

HILLIARD: Come in!

JENNINGS: (*Enters.*) Hilliard.

HILLIARD: Well, well, well! The seldom seen and often heard about Mr. Jennings Wells! Professor Wells, I guess it is, eh? You still stompin out ignorance at that college over in Virginia?

JENNINGS: Well, no, Hilliard, I'm taking a little time off.

HILLIARD: Now, seems to me I <u>did</u> hear somebody say you's back up on Newfound.

JENNINGS: I guess you know— I bought your Mama and Daddy's house, down there by the lake.

HILLIARD: Heard that, too—and wondered about it.

JENNINGS: There's no rush—no rush at all. But I thought you might know when your Mama and Daddy would be out of that house.

HILLIARD: It's a sticky situation. Nothin' I can't handle, though. I've been trying to get Mama and Papa out of that old house for a long time, get 'em over to my place. Not been able to budge them till this new lake come in. I reckon Papa's gonna have to have the papers read, though, before he'll leave. I'll have 'em out before long.

JENNINGS: There's the boy, too. Buddy. Roseanne's boy. I've run into him.

HILLIARD: He's welcome to come, too— finish his school. As long as he understands he'll be livin in my house. Headstrong, that boy— Roseanne's boy.

(*The door opens, and CECIL PEDIGO enters, wearing khaki pants, khaki shirt and Cordell County Sheriff's Department hat, a beeper on his belt. CECIL PEDIGO has a furtive look.*)

HILLIARD: (*To JENNINGS.*) You know Cecil, here, I guess, don't you?

JENNINGS: (*Turns to CECIL.*) Cecil Pedigo. —Yeah. We go way back.

HILLIARD: You fellers probably went to school together.

CECIL: (*Crooked grin.*) What little I went.

JENNINGS: (*Notices the lettering on Cecil's cap: Cordell County Sheriff's Department.*) Thought you were off the Sheriff's Department, Cecil, after that last election.

CECIL: (*Looks knowingly at HILLIARD.*) I'll be back on, come another election.

HILLIARD: (*Grinning.*) Maybe before that. Cecil's on my payroll—for now. (*HILLIARD turns in his swivel chair and twirls a yellow pencil between his fingers.*)

JENNINGS: You think our new sheriff—who is it? Ratliff?—You think he's gonna be indicted for dealing drugs?

CECIL: Prob'ly

HILLIARD: I want Ratliff on the job at least till he can read the papers to Papa, get him and Mama out of that old house. (*HILLIARD picks up some papers on his desk, looks up at CECIL.*) Cecil, go out to the trailer park, see if you can fix the leak in number 12. (*Hands CECIL a piece of paper, picks up another one.*) Go by 21, tell that no-'count sonofabitch Jack Price if I don't have my rent by the fifth of the month, I'm sending the sheriff to put him out.

CECIL: (*Looking around slyly, proud of his inside knowledge.*) He'll pay after he sells his marijuana crop.

HILLIARD: (*Hands CECIL another piece of paper.*) You tell him what I said.—And go by Troy's and see if he's got them air conditioners ready.

CECIL: (*Summoning up his wit.*) See you in the funny papers.

(*CECIL exits.*)

HILLIARD: (*Resuming conversation with JENNINGS.*) Yeah, it may take a week or two, but I'll have Mama and Papa out of there.—What I was wonderin, what did you want with that old house, anyway? You can't hardly get your money out of it, can you?

JENNINGS: I'm not interested in getting my money out of it. It's just that— that old house seems to stand for everything Cordell County used to be, before the roads came.

HILLIARD: (*Looks at JENNINGS with disbelief, then, as if he understands.*) Perfessor Wells must be into this "heritage" business.—I saw your little article in the paper.

JENNINGS: Yeah, it has to do with that. Heritage.

HILLIARD: (*Makes circles on a note pad with his pencil.*) Any money in "heritage"?

JENNINGS: I guess not.

HILLIARD: I've never been interested in gettin into anything that wouldn't pay somehow.

JENNINGS: I guess not.

HILLIARD: You always did have ideas, Perfessor Wells. And that's been your trouble.

JENNINGS: Yeah. Ideas'll get a feller into trouble. Is that how you've stayed out of trouble, Hilliard?

HILLIARD: (*Misses or ignores the dig.*) Why, I was raised up in that old house.

JENNINGS: That's why I thought maybe you'd want it.

HILLIARD: Hell, no! I wouldn't give a nickel for that old house. I've always wanted to go forwards. What's the sense in going backwards? —We've sucked the hind tit too long here in Cordell County. Didn't even get decent roads till 1969. You know how it was.

JENNINGS: Coal roads. That's all they are. You know that better than anybody, Hilliard.

HILLIARD: What difference does it make? We got 'em. Couldn't get the coal without the roads!

JENNINGS: (*Grins.*) You know, Hilliard, you put me in mind of a state legislator I was readin about the other day. He owned a bunch of liquor stores, and when some liquor legislation came up, he was asked not to vote on it— because of the conflict of interest. He said, "How does that conflict with my interest?"

HILLIARD: (*Missing or ignoring the point.*) If a man don't look after his interests, who's going to?

JENNINGS: We got the roads—and now half the county's torn up.

HILLIARD: We're still better off than before—a lot better off!

JENNINGS: A few people are. You sure are.

HILLIARD: Damn right. I was born poor, and I'm not ashamed of it. But I didn't stay poor. And I would've turned over ever foot of land in Cordell County if that's what it'd took. Besides, it don't hurt land to strip-mine it. Not in the long run. I've said it before and still believe it.

JENNINGS: What's scary, Hilliard, is you probably <u>do</u> believe it.

HILLIARD: Once you get the coal out, see, you can put the land back with a better contour. Make it good for something. You can raise cattle on land that's been stripped and then contoured right—where before, that land would've been so steep a goat'd fall off of it!

JENNINGS: What about water, Hilliard?

HILLIARD: We've got plenty of water.

JENNINGS: (*Shakes his head.*) Acid water. And polluted water. Cordell County's water's in bad shape, Hilliard, and you know it. It's making people sick. We don't have the sewage system for this much development.

HILLIARD: We got good water… and plenty of it.— If I had my way, ever foot of land in Cordell County'd be as flat as a pool table.— Airports. Once the land has been leveled, you can put a airport on a strip-mine site. I think we may be able to get one.

JENNINGS: If one can be got, you'll get it for us, Hilliard.—And how about another landfill? They're pretty popular nowadays. Maybe you can do deals and get us two or three landfills.

HILLIARD: (*Leans forward.*) Me and you differs on lots of things, Perfesser Wells, but one thing we agree on: (*Almost choking with emotion.*) We both <u>love</u> this place.

JENNINGS: (*Nods.*) Yes, Hilliard, you've been talking that line for over twenty years. You love your country, love your state, love Cordell County. (*Gestures toward flag displayed on the wall.*)

HILLIARD: Hell, yes!

JENNINGS: How can you love this place and still want to see it cut up and abused. If you love your dog, you don't kick it, do you? If you love a woman, you don't mistreat her, do you?

HILLIARD: (*Derisively.*) What's a woman got to do with it?— Listen, I knowed you's back home. I've been meanin to get up there on Newfound and talk to you. Here's the deal? We differ. Always have. But I can differ with a man and still do business with him.

JENNINGS: Business?

HILLIARD: This lake comin' in and all, I need a man like you—educated—to help me out here in the county. Man that can handle paperwork, talk to people, do deals.—You take Cecil, there's just certain things Cecil can do.

JENNINGS: (*Incredulous.*) I'm not looking for work, Hilliard!

HILLIARD: Thought you might be.—Anyway, you think about it. Feller like you—you know this county, know the people, how they think. You could put together parcels of land. (*He picks up a sheaf of papers.*) Land. (*He leans forward toward JENNINGS, his eyes brightening.*) Heritage Acres! How's that sound?

JENNINGS: Hilliard, I want to come home—but not to work for you. Or start speculating in land. (*Shakes his head.*) Here we are, doing it again. The same argument we had twenty years ago and more.

HILLIARD: Thought maybe you'd smartened up since then.

JENNINGS: Ever hear from you sister?

HILLIARD: Roseanne. No, I don't hear from her. Hell, even Roseanne knowed back then I was right about the roads. She sided with me, remember?

JENNINGS: Yeah, I remember.— (*Stands.*) Well, like I said, no rush about the house.

HILLIARD: Me and you can do business.

JENNINGS: (*Moving toward the door.*) Hilliard, I won't be working for you—or with you. I'm probably just going to make trouble for you.

HILLIARD: Trouble? You won't make trouble for <u>me</u>! You mean them books you wrote? These little articles

His First, Best Country

(*Picks up newspaper.*) you're always puttin in the paper? They don't bother me! That stuff—it may be right, somewheres else. It may be right in your house. But not in my house.

JENNINGS: (*Grins.*) Now that's curious, what you just said, Hilliard. I thought if somethin was true, it was true everywhere.

HILLIARD: (*Repeats.*) Not in my house.

(*JENNINGS turns to go.*)

HILLIARD: You <u>say</u> anything you want to—

JENNINGS: Thanks, Hilliard. But I didn't know I had to have your permission.

HILLIARD: (*Comes from his desk. Confidently.*) No sir, you won't make trouble for me, Mr. Perfesser Wells. Least, nothin I won't know how to handle.

JENNINGS: Take care, Hilliard.

HILLIARD: (*With rising anger.*) No, you take care.— Somethin I'd like to know: Perfesser Wells is coming home!— How in the hell can you even call a place home if you've not lived here for twenty years and more? What right do you have to call Cordell County home? It's people who've lived here, and built it up— I've <u>lived</u> here, Mr. Perfesser! You've not.

JENNINGS: (*As he exits.*) It's been about the same talkin to you, Hilliard.

HILLIARD: (*Repeats.*) Go on, say anything you want to. Just watch what you do.

SCENE THREE

Local LOAFERS at crossroads store, The Trading Post.

WILEY WOOLFORD: (*To DELANO CRUM, who is reading a newspaper.*) Anything in the Cordell County Curious Journal I ought to know?

DELANO CRUM: (*Turning a page.*) I see Jennings Wells's got a letter to the editor here—about progress in Cordell County.

WILEY: He for it or agin it?

DELANO: (*Cocks his head as if making a difficult judgment.*) He's not agin it, exactly. Appears to be for it—as long as it's goin somewhere.

DEE RHODOMMER: I'm agin it. My opinion, we've enjoyed about all the progress in Cordell County we can stand.

(*DELANO hands newspaper to WILEY WOOLFORD as SUTHERLAND, a farmer in his late sixties, enters.*)

DELANO: Howdy, Lloyd. How's things over in the Kingdom?

LLOYD SUTHERLAND: We've seen better days over home. The strip-minin on Lost Creek's hurtin us still. Made our water run black, killed the little minners and crawdads in the creek! Now they're talking about closin our school.—How're you fellers?

WILEY: (*Taps his knee with rolled-up newspaper.*) Keepin up with Cordell County doings keeps us pretty well occupied—full time.

LLOYD: (*Points to the newspaper WILEY is holding.*) Saw that piece Jennings Wells's got in the paper. Understand he's back home. Jennings Wells—he's the kind of feller that stirs things up. I'm thinking he might be able to help us.

WILEY: Messin' in school business—that's what got Jennings Wells in trouble here years ago, wasn't it?

DELANO: Why do you reckon he has come home? I'd be curious to know.

WILEY: One thing's for sure— it's not the place he left, is it, boys?

DEE: Cordell County's changed, all right. Used to be, folks eat supper in the house and done their business out of doors. Now, it's the other way around. What you call <u>progress.</u>

WILEY: I'm <u>for</u> progress on a cold morning, I tell you!

LLOYD: I'm for anything that helps. But closin down our school and haulin our younguns clear across Cordell County—they're sayin that'd be progress— I'm not so sure it is, and I'm agin it. All of us over in the Kingdom's agin it.

DEE: I tell you who's for it—Hilliard Shelton.

LLOYD: I know he is. And he runs the school board. And I'm still agin it. (*Turns to leave.*) You fellers take care.

(*LLOYD exits.*)

DELANO: You too, Lloyd.

WILEY: See you Lloyd.

DEE: Lloyd. (*Reflecting.*) Old Lloyd Sutherland. Old-timey as can be, but you wouldn't find a better neighbor. Or farmer.— Not many Lloyds left around here, though.

DELANO: I still farm a little. But I never have farmed as well as I know how to! — If Jennings Wells has come back in here to tell people how to run their business, he's got his work cut out for him, my opinion.

DEE: Maybe he's turned out like that teacher they had over at Jewell Hill one time. Said this teacher had two cats, big cat, and little cat, — cut two holes in his back door so them cats could come and go—big hole for the big cat, little hole for the little cat!

(*JENNINGS WELLS enters.*)

DELANO: Well, looky here what the cat drug in! Jennings Wells! I bet your ears has been a-burnin cause we been talkin about you.

JENNINGS: Delano. Wiley… Dee. How're you fellers gettin along?

DELANO: 'Bout as well as common. How long you home for this time, Jennings? Give us the straight of it. You've been runnin in and out of Newfound for twenty years. We heard you's settlin back in this time.

JENNINGS: Yeah. I've been gone too long, Delano.

DELANO: Your mama passed—what?—two year ago, was it?

JENNINGS: Three.

WILEY: I recollect your daddy, too.

DEE: Thought the world of old man Chris Wells.

WILEY: I recollect somebody asked your daddy once, "Have you read Jennings's last book?" He said, "I hope so."

JENNINGS: Turned out, he hadn't.

DELANO: Did I hear right? You bought the old Shelton house down by the lake?

JENNINGS: That's what I wanted to talk to you fellers about—that old house. Thought maybe I could get you to dismantle it for me—take it down, haul it up home. I aim to put it back together there at my place.

DELANO: (*Looks around at WILEY and DEE.*) We might be able to work that into our schedules. What you aim to do with that old house, Jennings?

JENNINGS: Just want to keep the old house in the county. So many of the old houses have been bought up and hauled off to other places.—I want the logs marked before the house is taken down—so it can be put back right.

DELANO: (*To DEE and WILEY.*) We've done that a time or two, ain't we, boys?

WILEY: Yeah. Old houses.

DEE: But Miz McCreary's smokehouse, that did beat all.

JENNINGS: Who bought her smokehouse?

DELANO: I did, was how it started. I was up there at her place one day, in my truck, Miz McCreary said how much would I give her for them logs in her smokehouse. Well, I didn't need the logs, but I knowed she wouldn't have offered to sell 'em if she didn't need money. I give her ten dollars for 'em.

WILEY: It wasn't no job to knock down. Old smokehouse was mostly already fell in on itself.

DELANO: I sold them logs to a feller named Tweed. For $35.00. (*Winks at JENNINGS.*) Tweed never got around to haulin 'em off, so they stayed stacked for about a year. Saw Tweed over in Jewell Hill, he asked me would I buy them logs back. I did—for $25.00. (*Winks again.*)

DEE: Don't trade pocket knives with this feller (*Jerks his head toward DELANO.*) if you don't want to get slicked.

DELANO: (*Continuing.*) —Then the TVA got interested in my logs! They aimed to build log cabins, put 'em on truck beds, make what they call a mobile museum, haul 'em around to show folks how it was back in the old days. Spent close to a million dollars doin it—what I heard.—But I'm gettin' ahead of myself.

WILEY: Remember, though, Delano—at first they wasn't interested in <u>old</u> logs.

DELANO: Right. They'd hired a company out of Chicago to build a "pilot" log cabin.

JENNINGS: Now, come on, Delano!

(*DELANO holds up his hand as if swearing an oath.*)

WILEY: (*Nods.*) Hit's the tom-truth!

DELANO: So they flew somebody in over at Bristol, made field trips, looked at some old log houses, took pictures, called around. Flew back to Chicago, back to Bristol, wound up drivin around up here in a rented car. That's when they heard I had them logs from Miz McCreary's smokehouse. Would I sell 'em?— Well, I might.

JENNINGS: How much, Delano?

DELANO: $800.00.

JENNINGS: Delano—

DELANO: I've got the paper on it. Sale slip.—Why, they sent two trucks in here, wrapped them logs ever one in a separate shippin quilt, hauled 'em to Chicago. Then they hired me on as "project consultant."

JENNINGS: Pay you well for that, Delano?

DELANO: Right well! Then—I reckon it was three or four year after I sold them the logs, they had that cabin they made out of 'em on a flatbed truck out there on the school ground, showin it to younguns—in full view of Miz McCreary's house—and the very spot where that old smokehouse had stood for maybe a hundred year. —I tell you!

JENNINGS: You're not gonna slick me the way you did the fellers from Chicago, are you, Delano?

DELANO: (*Tips back his hat, scratches his head.*) I'll treat you right.

JENNINGS: I was hopin I could get the Shelton house dismantled, hauled over home, and stacked up, for—I thought maybe—two, three hundred dollars.

(*JENNINGS gauges DELANO's reaction. DELANO squints with his right eye, his chin juts out.*)

JENNINGS: I'm not the TVA, Delano!

DELANO: What do you think, boys?

(*DELANO looks at DEE and WILEY, who don't commit themselves.*)

DELANO: Bein' it's Jennings. (*After DEE and WILEY nod approval.*) I believe we can do it.

JENNINGS: All right.

DELANO: So you've come home!

JENNINGS: And it's good to be back. I couldn't tell you how good it is.

DELANO: I'm glad to hear it. You can pick and sing for us like you used to. We need you back in here. It's all we can do, and more—just me and Dee and Wiley here—to run Cordell County.

JENNINGS: I'll help out all I can, Delano!

SCENE FOUR

Lights come up on the Shelton house, an old-fashioned log structure. BUDDY SHELTON comes out the front door, carrying two large oval picture frames. At the sound of a car door slamming offstage, BUDDY steps back inside the house. JENNINGS WELLS enters. Behind him DELANO CRUM, WILEY WOOLFORD, and DEE RHODOMMER enter, carrying sledge hammers, and a crowbar. JENNINGS WELLS stands in front of the house snapping photographs from several angles as the other three comment on the house.

DELANO: Nice old house, all right.

WILEY: Good shape.

(*DEE takes a marker out of his pocket and begins chalking numbers on logs—1F, 2F, etc.*)

DEE: Look at that end-notchin.

(*DELANO, WILEY, and DEE go to the back side of the house. From time to time they can be heard pounding on the house from the back. BUDDY comes out of the house just as JENNINGS snaps a photo, and, seeing BUDDY through the viewfinder, looks up at BUDDY.*)

BUDDY: What are you all doing?

JENNINGS: What say, Henry? Thought you'd be gone with your Grandpa and Grandma.

BUDDY: (*Turning in reaction to a pounding noise from the back of the house.*) My name's Buddy.—What are you all doing?

JENNINGS: We're taking pictures and marking the logs—so we don't get them mixed up after we take them apart, Henry.

BUDDY: Apart? You can't take this house apart!

JENNINGS: Well, yes, Henry, I reckon we can. And we are.

BUDDY: (*Comes out into the yard.*) You're not taking this house apart!

JENNINGS: Henry, all these buildings—they've been sold. Didn't you know? (*Gestures in the direction of other buildings offstage.*) The crib, the barn, the springhouse—they go to a museum over in Tennessee. I got the house—from the Army Corps of Engineers.

BUDDY: I've been comin over to your house practically every day, and you never said anything about tearin this house down.

JENNINGS: I thought you knew.—I would have got the other buildings, too—if I'd known in time. I've been waiting for your Grandpa and Grandma Shelton to move out, so—

BUDDY: <u>I've</u> not moved out!

JENNINGS: Henry, your grandpa and grandma have —just this morning, over to your Uncle Hilliard's.

BUDDY: I told you, I'm Buddy! And <u>I've</u> not moved!

JENNINGS: Well, you're supposed to be. Supposed to be in school, too. What did you think to do—just sit back on your thumb and live on here with the hoot owls?

BUDDY: I'm not going to Hilliard's. That big-butt! Not going to Cordell County High School, either.

(*As WILEY appears at the side of the house, marking logs, JENNINGS gestures toward him.*)

JENNINGS: You're always wanting to work for me—you can help these fellers put it back together.

BUDDY: I want this house to be here! (*Points to the ground.*)

JENNINGS: (*Sits on a block of wood.*) Tell you what— we'll drive over to that museum sometime, when the barn's put back together—and the crib and springhouse. You can see them over there.

(*BUDDY shakes his head. Country music is heard offstage. ROMA LIVESAY enters from stage left, carrying portable tape player which is playing "Mama, He's Crazy." She does a flirtatious dance in front of JENNINGS. She turns the music off.*)

ROMA: Hi! Drove all the way over to your house before I remembered you said you'd probably be down here.

(*ROMA looks from JENNINGS to BUDDY, who has picked up a stick and in his frustration begun to beat the ground with it. She senses something.*)

ROMA: Is the fur about to fly between you two?

JENNINGS: Well, Henry here—

ROMA: Henry?

BUDDY: My name's Buddy, I've told you a hundred times.

JENNINGS: I call him Henry because he wants to live off in the woods, like Henry Thoreau.

BUDDY: He's tearin my house down!

(*JENNINGS puts arm around ROMA, walks away with her, leaving BUDDY sitting in front of the house.*)

JENNINGS: Could you talk to him, Roma? (*Puts both arms around her, kisses her on forehead.*)

ROMA: (*Crosses back to BUDDY.*) Go on down to your Uncle Hilliard's, Punkin. Stay with your Grandpa and Grandma Shelton.

JENNINGS: And get back in school—instead of growing up like a weed!

BUDDY: You're not my boss, neither one of you! (*Beats the ground with a stick.*)

(*ROMA and JENNINGS exchange glances. She crosses back to JENNINGS.*)

JENNINGS: (*To ROMA.*) How do I get into these situations? — Listen, about last night, I— I hope you don't think I —

ROMA: Why do you feel you have to explain?

JENNINGS: (*Glancing at BUDDY, who is preoccupied.*) It just— happened. I didn't—

ROMA: I'm glad it happened. On a boat. A first for me!

BUDDY: (*Suddenly looks up. Something has occurred to him.*) Hey, Jennings, how about lending me—fifty dollars.

JENNINGS: (*Taken aback by the request.*) I never took you to raise, Henry!

BUDDY: I said <u>lend</u>. I'll pay you back—or else work it out.

JENNINGS: You're crazy, Henry. You know it? If it was your Grandpa Shelton talking he'd say you need to be bored for holler-head!

ROMA: What do you need with fifty dollars, Buddy?

BUDDY: Need to buy a few things...groceries...few other things.

JENNINGS: And live in the woods, right, Henry?

BUDDY: Somewheres. —Give me twenty dollars now and I'll go start hauling that wood for you.

(*JENNINGS takes out his wallet and holds out a bill to BUDDY.*)

JENNINGS: Then go to it. (*As BUDDY starts to take the money, JENNINGS pulls it back.*) And then go on over to Hilliard's, all right?

BUDDY: All right. (*Pockets money, turns, and picks up the framed pictures he has set down earlier.*) I'll just go see Mom Shelton and Grandpa. I don't aim to stay! (*Glancing down at pictures he's holding.*) Haulers went off and forgot these when they left this morning. This here's my great Grandpa and Grandma.

JENNINGS: Go on, Henry!

(*BUDDY exits.*)

ROMA: I feel so sorry for him. He's lived in this house all his life.

(*JENNINGS sits on block of wood. ROMA sits beside him.*)

JENNINGS: I feel sorry for the boy, too. But what can I do? I'm trying to finish this book.

ROMA: You're a bookworm, Jennings Wells. You know it? — Probably just as soon I'd stay away. (*After no response from JENNINGS.*) Okay. (*Stands. Turns as if to leave.*)

JENNINGS: No, no. Sit down, Roma. (*Laughs.*) But when I came back, I never figured on you, that's for sure!

ROMA: Well, I remembered you! In an old army jacket, with a rifle in the crook of your arm, waiting for Clyde to come out of the house.

JENNINGS: (*Laughs.*) When you came down to the house that first time, I kept sitting there, wondering —

ROMA: Wondering, Who in the hell is this, right?

JENNINGS: Well, yes, for the longest time!

ROMA: Thinking, Is this some country hophead?

JENNINGS: Something like that crossed my mind, yes!

ROMA: I could tell! You came back and taught school in Cordell County a year or two—

JENNINGS: Yeah, two.

ROMA: Next thing I knew, you were teaching in a college, over in Virginia. But you still came back to Newfound lots.

JENNINGS: Oh, practically every weekend, back then. When Mom and Dad were still living.

ROMA: And when you and Roseanne Shelton were going together. (*She watches him for his reaction.*) And playing and singing in the Rockytop Festival.

JENNINGS: You do remember a lot, don't you, Roma?

ROMA: I was up in high school by then. That was about all us girls ever talked about—you and Roseanne Shelton. We thought you all were just like a lord and lady in one of those old ballads you all would sing at the Rockytop Festival.

JENNINGS: That was a good thing, Rockytop. But it played out; Roseanne went on the road with a band. Everything just—played out.

ROMA: Then you took to writing books. That one about the Rockytop Festival, and—

JENNINGS: Didn't like my books, did you?

ROMA: I never said that!

JENNINGS: Well, they made a lot of people around here mad—because I criticized strip mining. You know, even Roseanne was for all the roads and mining. Probably what we fell out over, ultimately. I figured maybe you thought the same way.

ROMA: No! You didn't make me mad. You told the truth. How America Came to Cordell County. That's a good book. I've read every one of them. Oh, I've kept up with you Jennings Wells.

JENNINGS: (*Reflecting.*) Now, I've come back home, and run into you, and Roseanne's boy.

(*BUDDY re-enters, still carrying the pictures.*)

BUDDY: Hey, Jennings, I got to thinking— I need to borrow your truck.

JENNINGS: What are you talking about, Henry?

BUDDY: There's some stuff down at the Trash 'n Treasure. (*To ROMA.*) I'm gonna live by myself, see. Hunt, fish, trap, dig some ginseng. Work around. (*Back to JENNINGS.*) If I could borrow your truck—

JENNINGS: Henry, I look at you, it's just like looking at myself when I was your age. I was just lucky old Willis Weatherford came by our school and told me about Berea College.——Why, you wouldn't last, by yourself, till the snow flies!

ROMA: I wish you'd listen to Jennings, Buddy. He knows.

BUDDY: No telling how much I can make digging sang. I know where to look for it, how to dry it, and all. I've helped Grandpa Shelton dig some. People have always dug sang here in the mountains. The old pioneers, back in the old days.

JENNINGS: Just how long do you figure, Henry?

BUDDY: Four, five hundred years, maybe.

JENNINGS: Henry, people haven't lived here that long. Indians, yes. But not the rest of us.

BUDDY: Mom Shelton told me one time about something that happened back in the old days. All these people came from all around one night in the fall to this one house for a corn shucking. Some of the women put their babies in a back room of the house, on beds. And after the corn shucking, Great-Grandma Spivey's mama went in the room and got her baby, and was half-way home, in a wagon, when she went to nurse the baby and found out it wasn't her baby she had! So they turned the wagon there in the road and started back—and met another wagon. It was another woman and her husband. They'd found out they had the wrong baby, too. So they switched babies there in the road and all went home. That was my great-grandma, Mom Shelton's mama, that was one of the switched babies. (*Holds up picture.*) I could have been switched, and nobody found out about it. No telling who I am.

JENNINGS: You're a mixed-up boy, not a mixed-up baby, Henry. Talk to your Grandma and Grandpa Shelton. —Have they not ever talked to you—about your mama?

(*BUDDY shakes head.*)

JENNINGS: Didn't your mama ever talk to you?

BUDDY: I just barely remember her. Just know who she is from her picture. (*Stands waiting.*) Is the key to the pickup in the ashtray, like it usually is?

JENNINGS: Henry, what do you think you're up to?

BUDDY: Well, when you put my house back together, over at your place, I'll live in it there. Till then, what I figure—I'll just live in that old house of yours up there in the Gudger Holler. Nobody livin in it.

JENNINGS: That's because nobody <u>could</u> live in it. Nobody's lived in it since I was a boy.

BUDDY: I'll be your renter. And if I can't pay you, I'll work it out!

JENNINGS: (*Stands.*) I've decided I'm not going to let you work for me anymore, Henry. Just now, I decided that. If I let you work around for me, at piddling jobs, I'll just be helping you stay out of school.

BUDDY: If you won't rent me that house in the Gudger Holler, I'll just go up there and live, anyway!

JENNINGS: Well, go on then! See how long you last!

BUDDY: Key in the ashtray?

JENNINGS: (*More and more put out.*) Yes. Now get out of here! (*Aside to ROMA.*) This is not a boy—more like an affliction!

ROMA: Jennings!

(*BUDDY exits.*)

ROMA: Is it all right for him to drive?

JENNINGS: (*Moving closer to ROMA.*) No, but he does have a license.

ROMA: Where did he learn to drive? (*ROMA moves closer to JENNINGS.*)

JENNINGS: (*They stand embracing.*) Seems like he was born knowing how!

ROMA: You taught him, didn't you? His Grandpa Shelton didn't have a car.

JENNINGS: Yeah. I taught him. There around home.

ROMA: And took him to get his license, didn't you?

JENNINGS: I probably shouldn't have. But there wasn't anybody else. He's a pretty good boy, but—

ROMA: (*Steps back from JENNINGS.*) And he's Roseanne's boy.

JENNINGS: He is.... But— (*Draws her close to him.*) Want to go back out on Big Ivy Lake again tonight? In the runabout?

ROMA: We could. (*Laughs.*)

JENNINGS: We could just go back down to the house. They can finish marking these logs and start knocking them down without us.

ROMA: (*Holds on to his hand.*) I know where we can go.

(*They exit.*)

SCENE FIVE

ROMA and JENNINGS enter, ROMA carrying her tape player. They sit down.

JENNINGS: Why'd you want to come up here to Rockytop?

ROMA: Thought you might want to come up here—for the memories.

JENNINGS: (*Looks around.*) This place is all grown up.

(*ROMA turns up tape player.*)

JENNINGS: This is just a guess, but you wouldn't happen to like country music, would you, Roma?

ROMA: What do you think?—I just wonder, though, if <u>you</u> do.

JENNINGS: Some of it. Why?

ROMA: Because of some things you wrote in the Rockytop book.

JENNINGS: About country music? Couldn't have been much. I don't know much about country music.

ROMA: I believe that! At least, nothing past Lefty Frizell, Kitty Wells, and the death of Hank Williams!

JENNINGS: I must have stopped listening about then.

ROMA: I don't think you ever liked country much. Even in the Rockytop Festival, all you ever sang with Roseanne was old-time ballads. Like it had to be literature, or you weren't interested.

JENNINGS: All that—Rockytop, and Roseanne—that was another country, seems like. (*Studies her.*) What difference does it make—whether I like country music or not?

ROMA: Because, I just don't see what's wrong with songs you made fun of in your book.

JENNINGS: Did I make fun?

ROMA: Yes! Put them down!—Roseanne liked country. She wanted country songs in the Rockytop Festival, and you didn't. You say so in the book.

JENNINGS: I just thought Rockytop was about something else.—Why, some of these songs you've been playing for me—they're right interesting. Like that one, "Wild and Blue," and "I Don't Remember Loving You." Love as a pathological state—which it is!

ROMA: It is not!

JENNINGS: Of course it is! But that's all right, even if it is.

ROMA: What ones <u>don't</u> you like?

JENNINGS: I suspect that's gonna take a while!

(*JENNINGS takes a flask from a backpack that has camera case and other items in it. Finds cup. Pours a drink. During conversation, they pass it back and forth.*)

JENNINGS: Hmm. What ones I don't like.—Anything with dumb puns, like "The only thing I can count on now is my fingers." Or: "Four scores and seven beers ago / I told her I'd be home."— Any song about a deck of cards. Any "Here-I-am-in-my-cups-again" song.

ROMA: Why?

JENNINGS: I hear them and just want to say: You might not be so depressed (*Raises the drink.*) if you'd lighten up on the booze.

ROMA: People get depressed, booze or no booze.

JENNINGS: Oh, sure.

ROMA: There's a lot of truth in some of those old drinking songs—barstool songs. I think.

JENNINGS: Maybe so.

ROMA: (*Takes cup from him, sips.*) I know so!

JENNINGS: I admitted I don't know much about country music.

ROMA: I'm gonna teach you! I brought you this quiz. (*She gets up and retrieves a magazine from her clutch bag. Returns to her block of wood and sits down with it, leafing through the magazine.*) This is called "The History of Country Music vs. You."

JENNINGS: Why does it have to be me <u>versus</u> country music? I'm not <u>against</u> country music.

ROMA: Hush and take the quiz! "Hello Walls" was written by Faron Young. True or false?

JENNINGS: False.

ROMA: False is right. Faron Young didn't write "Hello, Walls." Who did?

JENNINGS: I don't believe this!— I don't know. I'll look it up. I've got this book down at the house, history of country music.

ROMA: Just like you to have to get it out of a book! —Tell me what else you don't like!

JENNINGS: Truck-driving songs. Big-wheels-rolling songs. There ought to be a moratorium declared on them!

ROMA: I know what you are, Jennings Wells. You're a snob. You went off to school, became a big teacher, big writer, and now you're a snob!

JENNINGS: It's not that. It's just that there aren't that many good songs. Not that many good anythings.— For instance, take all those uxorious songs that—

ROMA: What kind of songs? Uxorious?

JENNINGS: Yes, uxorious. I-love-only-you songs.

ROMA: Like where the man sounds like he's, you know, whipped?

JENNINGS: (*Laughs.*) Well, I wouldn't put it just that way. I—

ROMA: If that's what you mean, you might as well say it! That's what "uxorious" means. Right?

JENNINGS: Well, it means— (*Grinning.*) You do beat all!

ROMA: I went to school, too, you know. Learned some words. Like "uxorious." That's the kind of word I like to be able to say—and then not say it! What else don't you like?

JENNINGS: I really despise all the thank-God-I'm-just-a-common-man-in-a-common-van songs, these glad-I'm-so-dumb-because-high-brow-people-are-crazy songs.

ROMA: (*Touches his brow.*) Proves it! Jennings Wells is a snob and a highbrow. You know, they say a hit dog hollers!

JENNINGS: Not at all. There's lowbrow crazies, too.

ROMA: Yep! Snob and a highbrow! Um-hummm! (*Runs her fingers through his hair.*) —What else?

JENNINGS: Surely you can't defend these poor-lovers-stay-together-but-let-them-get-a-two-story-house-and-the-marriage-falls-to-pieces songs.

ROMA: Sometimes that's the way it is, (*Reflects.*) With me, though, I was poor, and the marriage still fell apart—twice! Tell you about it sometime—when we've had more to drink! —Anyway, what performers do you like?

JENNINGS: I sort of like Anne Murray.

ROMA: (*Pokes a finger into her mouth.*) Lord! I can see we're not ready to dance with our eyes closed and still not step on one another's feet!— I'm gonna have to educate you, Jennings Wells.

JENNINGS: (*Picks at his pants.*) Sticktights! We're covered with 'em! Acting like a couple of teenagers.

ROMA: Good! I don't think I ever acted like a teenager when I was one. —I was fourteen when I had my first date—real date. This boy at school, John L. Freeman, asked me to go with him to a school dance. I looked forward to that dance for days! Mama and I made this green velvet dress with a big bow. And when I walked in to the dance that night—we were just kids, John L. wasn't supposed to pick me up, just be my date at the dance—when I walked in, everybody else had on jeans—and there I stood in a green velvet dress with that big bow!

That was just the first of several miscalculations I made. My first marriage, for instance. The pipes froze in the trailer Roger moved us into, and—-

JENNINGS: Roger who?

ROMA: Roger Devazier. Anyway, the pipes froze, and stayed frozen for days, and Roger wouldn't get them fixed. Kept saying they'd thaw. Went off every day, sometimes to work, I guess. There I was with no water in the house. What little I had, I carried from Mama's. Water got so precious during that cold spell—it just kept hanging on—if something stuck in a pot or pan when I tried to cook, I threw the pan away rather than waste water washing it! Had to go to Mama's to take a bath.— I didn't last the winter with Roger. (*After a pause, during which they share a drink.*) Then there was my second husband.

JENNINGS: Who was that?

ROMA: It slips my mind!

(*JENNINGS laughs.*)

ROMA: No, I just can't bring myself to call his name. —Anyway, he's not around here any longer. Roger Devazier's not, either. But I did everything but wear candypants for that son of a bitch. And he treated me like a baloney string!...I left Roger Devazier because he was no-account. When I broke up with What's-His-Name—and that didn't take as long as the first time—I was beginning to think it was me... something the matter with me. (*She looks up at him.*)

JENNINGS: You asking me for an opinion?

ROMA: Maybe.

JENNINGS: I don't think there's anything the matter with you. You've had troubles, but—

ROMA: I am trouble.

JENNINGS: No, you—

ROMA: Something's wrong—you have to admit. I mean, you have to be pretty dumb to drive your ducks to a poor pond twice.

JENNINGS: You were young, not dumb. If you'd stayed with either one of them, that would have been dumb. I'd say you've been treated bad.

ROMA: Rode hard and put up wet, that's me! But—they say this place always was hard on women and mules!

JENNINGS: Looks to me like, in spite of everything, you've done awfully well. You got out of all that, went to school, got a job, your own place.

ROMA: Never got what I wanted.

JENNINGS: What?

ROMA: I wanted to be married. Both times... I wanted a baby... Can forget about that, I guess. (*Looks around.*) You wouldn't have come up here—to Rockytop—if I hadn't dragged you—would you?

JENNINGS: Oh eventually, maybe.

ROMA: It's a lot of memories, right?

JENNINGS: Yeah. Everything's coming back fast.

ROMA: Roseanne—has she ever—? I thought maybe you—heard from her—sometimes. (*After a silence.*) Did I say the wrong thing?

JENNINGS: Oh, it's all right, Roma. That was all over years ago. She wanted to leave. I wanted to stay. We both ended up leaving.

ROMA: I thought maybe you wanted the old Shelton house because Roseanne—

JENNINGS: I wanted it because—when I first got back, I was cleaning up around home there, one of the old houses, used to be a tenant farmer house. And it had just fallen in on itself, collapsed. And it struck me—everything I remembered about home here was just collapsing, fallin' in on itself. I wanted to save something, something that was like it used to be.

ROMA: I do think you ought to get out more.— But then I take up your time. You must despise to see me coming.

JENNINGS: I like to see you, Roma. Love to see you. But—

ROMA: But I pull you away from your work.—Well, I aim to!

JENNINGS: No. You're not slowing me down, you're speeding me up. It's like—when we were down on the lake last night, I remembered reading somewhere about how lake water separates out into layers—layers of different temperatures—during the summer. Then, in the fall, when the top layer cools, a lake turns over…top layer sinks to the bottom, bottom layer rises to the top.—-Everything I've been these last years is sinking, everything I used to be is rising, coming back…

ROMA: And I'm speeding that up?

JENNINGS: Yeah. Oh, yeah! I'm usually not that fast!

ROMA: Good! (*Stands. They embrace.*) Maybe we both need to speed up—to make up for lost time!

JENNINGS: Fine—as long as we don't crash! —This coming home—it's not what I thought it would be. I've been thinking about what Buddy said—am I saving the Shelton house, or just helping to destroy it? I don't know.

ROMA: (*Pulls him to his feet.*) You've got to get into circulation.

JENNINGS: What do you mean, circulation?

ROMA: Well, ever since you've been home, you've sat down there humped up over books and papers, never get out and about, not even to see your own people!

JENNINGS: My own people?

ROMA: You wrote all those books, about roots and country life. Where were you when you wrote them? In a big university! In Europe! I believe you think Cordell County's a ballad. Maybe it did used to be. But it's a country song now, I guarantee you. —Remember Edna Rae? Used to be your favorite cousin? You've not seen her in years. Now Edna Rae's real people!

JENNINGS: Edna Rae. Gerald's sister. It's true. How many years?

ROMA: How about seventeen? That's how long Edna Rae told me it's been since you've bothered to come see her.—I'm taking you on, Jennings Wells, as a case. (*Takes his hand, starts dancing with him, stops.*) I'm taking you on—like one of the people I get assigned at the Human Resource Office. I'm gonna drive you up Green Valley Road to see your Cousin Edna Rae. Get you back into circulation.

JENNINGS: You've improved my circulation already.

ROMA: (*As she starts to lead him off.*) Edna Rae and I've been wanting to go to a Conway Twitty concert. You can take us!

JENNINGS: (*As they exit.*) A Conway what?

SCENE SIX

Jennings' house. JENNINGS is at large worktable typing. Books, papers, magazines, posters, photographs, reminders on wall above the worktable. A guitar hangs on the wall. BUDDY enters stage left with a bundle of mail—manila envelopes, business envelopes, magazines, newspapers—an armload. He drops it all on the end of Jennings' worktable.

BUDDY: I'm your renter now....Figured I'd carry your mail up from the mailbox for you.

JENNINGS: (*Without looking up from typewriter.*) What say, Henry?

BUDDY: How come you get so much mail? I never do get any.

JENNINGS: You ever write to anybody, Henry?

BUDDY: No.

JENNINGS: Maybe that explains it.

BUDDY: (*Lays his hand on the typewriter.*) Is that what you're always doing—writing to people?

JENNINGS: That's about it, Henry. (*He turns from the typewriter to the mail. Looks at a small envelope, sticks it in his shirt pocket. Finally, he pushes all the other mail to the back of the table.*)

BUDDY: That's a lie, I bet. You write books, I know.

(*JENNINGS looks at watch. Gets up, puts on jacket, takes envelope from shirt pocket and puts it into inside coat pocket.*)

BUDDY: Can we ride around? I'll drive us over to Jewell Hill.

JENNINGS: I don't want to go to Jewell Hill. I go over there, hoping things will look better. They just get worse.

BUDDY: We could check out the flea market.

JENNINGS: Always the same junk: ceramic birdbaths, flowerpots, pink flamingos standing on one leg, big pictures of wet-eyed children.

BUDDY: You remember when they had all them stuffed animals, and that big stuffed gorilla? Wonder if anybody ever bought that thing?

JENNINGS: If it stays around Jewell Hill long, they'll make it a deputy sheriff, or a school board member.

BUDDY: We don't have to go to Jewell Hill. I'll drive—and we won't talk about school! Just ride around and listen to WWJH.

JENNINGS: That station depresses me. Nothing but country music and a police blotter full of wrecks and stolen tape decks. (*He begins a mock newscast from the Jewell Hill radio station.*) "Unit 1, driven by Mr. Ernest Honnicut of Pea Ridge, Route 1, crossed the road, plunged down an embankment, and overturned. Two passengers in Unit 2, which struck a culvert in an attempt to avoid Unit 1, 18-year-old Dustin Leatherbetter and his wife, 13-year-old Chelsea Leatherbetter, were pronounced congenital idiots on arrival at the Rag Shank Infirmary. Mr. Honnicut was lodged in the Rag Shank jail on a variety of charges, including driving under the influence of an insane theology, carrying a concealed church key, and littering the public highway with his person. In addition, according to a report filed by Trooper Hooper, the arresting occifer, Honnicut's fly was unzipped." (*Dropping the mock newscast.*) —You go on and stay out of school, Henry, and you can be a part of Jewell Hill society, too!

BUDDY: All you do is make fun. If you just make fun of everything around here, why'd you come back?

JENNINGS: (*Gazes thoughtfully at BUDDY.*) Every once in a while, Henry, you ask a good question?

BUDDY: (*Grins.*) Let me ask you this.

JENNINGS: (*Glances at watch.*) I have to go.

BUDDY: Well, wait.—I've been cleaning up my pictures— the ones the haulers forgot when they took Mom Shelton and Grandpa's things? There's this picture of my great-grandpa Shelton, and I was trying to clean the glass, and took these little tacks out of the back, and I found this other picture. I don't know who it could be.

JENNINGS: I did that same thing once, Henry.

BUDDY: Did you find out who it was?

JENNINGS: No.—But there's somebody behind everybody, Henry. Depend on it.

BUDDY: I'd like to know the straight of it.—Mom Shelton's mama, my great-grandma Spivey, she almost got mixed up one time. They went to somebody's house one Saturday night, for a corn-shucking—-

JENNINGS: You told me that story once before, you know, Henry?

BUDDY: I've got this other picture—picture of my Mama. Just a little one. (*Takes a snapshot out of his wallet and shows it to JENNINGS.*) She lives in Ohio. Sometimes she goes to New York.

JENNINGS: (*Looking at the photo.*) I thought you said you never heard from your mama.

BUDDY: I don't. Mom Shelton told me my Mama lives in Ohio. She sent Mom Shelton this picture, and Mom Shelton gave it to me.

JENNINGS: (*Hands the photo back to BUDDY.*) That's you Mama, all right.

BUDDY: She's pretty.

JENNINGS: Very beautiful.

BUDDY: You got any pictures of yourself? I know you've got some. (*Looking around on the table.*) I saw some in an envelope. You got one I could have?

JENNINGS: What do you want with a picture of me, Henry? I'm right here, you can see me.

BUDDY: Put it in my billfold, with my Mama's. (*Finds envelope on the table.*) Can I have one?

JENNINGS: Go ahead.

BUDDY: (*Takes out a photo and puts it in his wallet.*) I'm writing a book, too—sort of. You know that?

JENNINGS: You're writing a book, Henry?

BUDDY: Remember you told me if I was going to live out in the woods like Henry Thoreau, I'd have to keep a journal. Well, I started writing stuff down—thoughts. But not because of Henry Thoreau. Because of something I heard down at the Trading Post. There's this man over in Granger County—his daddy got run over in the road, years ago, about dark, one Christmas Eve. Whoever did it didn't stop, and they never found out who did it. So this man started writing things down in a tablet—exactly what happened to his daddy.

JENNINGS: Yeah?

BUDDY: For a while, he figured whoever ran over his daddy lived right around there—in Granger County. Then he got to thinking, it happened on Christmas Eve, so it might have been somebody that just come home for Christmas. So he wrote down the names of everybody that used to live around there but was working up north now—in Indianapolis, or Cleveland, or Columbus. And he made another list of them that had kin living on the creek above him—because his daddy had been hit by a car that was coming down off the creek. He filled up several tablets. And he finally figured out who it had to be that ran over his daddy, and there was a trial, and they proved it.

JENNINGS: I see where you're coming from, Henry— So you figured—

BUDDY: Figured if I got me a tablet, and listened, and looked, and asked around, someday I might be able to find my Daddy!

JENNINGS: (*Studies BUDDY thoughtfully, then looks at wristwatch.*) Henry, I've got to go pick up Roma and Edna Rae.

BUDDY: Where you all goin?

JENNINGS: I'm takin them to a show in Johnson City. We're gonna have an early supper here. Why don't you have supper with us, and then, on the way down, we can drop you off to stay tonight with your Grandma and Grandpa Shelton.

BUDDY: I'm not goin to Hilliard's!

JENNINGS: If I said you could drive the pickup over there—

BUDDY: Nope. Told you, I'm your renter now. My house is right up the holler here. But I'll come to supper!

(*JENNINGS turns, exits.*)

SCENE SEVEN

ROMA and EDNA RAE are clearing the table after supper at Jennings' house, EDNA RAE is a woman in her middle-fifties. Her hair is dyed blonde and done in a 1950's fashion. BUDDY sits at the table, picking at his food.

ROMA: I told you I'd get Jennings to take us, Edna Rae. Didn't I?

EDNA RAE: Jennings is my cousin and I've known him since he was a baby. But sometimes, I just don't know if he's kiddin or what. Like when we were driving over here and he asked me, "What is a Conway Twitty, anyway, Edna Rae?"

ROMA: Oh, he was kiddin you! (*To BUDDY.*) Buddy, you didn't hardly eat anything. How come you're so mopey, Punkin?

BUDDY: Just not hungry.

ROMA: You better eat, hon.

EDNA RAE: Anyway, I can't hardly believe we're really goin! I've been crazy about Conway for years but this'll be my first Conway Twitty concert. I can't believe it's happening, hardly!

ROMA: Well, it is. Did you hear how Jennings was talking in the car, Edna Rae? He's beginning to sound like he used to. He said dry weather had just about "rurnt" some corn. And the other day, he said that old silo down there at the barn was out of whanker. Out of whanker! You don't hear people say things like that any more, not even around here.

EDNA RAE: Used to you did.

(*JENNINGS enters from stage left, putting on a tie.*)

JENNINGS: Say things like what?

ROMA: We're talking about you. (*To EDNA RAE.*) When he gets a little tired, he starts to sound like I remember—like he talked before he ever left home.

JENNINGS: (*Sitting at the table.*) You don't remember hardly anything about me. You couldn't. You were just a kid then.

ROMA: (*Reaches out and touches the tip of his nose.*) Sometimes I forget what I went to the store for, but I remember everything about you, Jennings Wells.

EDNA RAE: Why don't you just quit that school, Jennings, and come back to Newfound for good?

JENNINGS: Coming home's a tricky business, I'm finding out. I could live, I reckon. But folks around Newfound don't have much use for a two-cylinder scribbler like me.

EDNA RAE: Shoot! You come on home and we'll run you for school superintendent. Get rid of old lard-butt. He's the dumbest thing, anyway!

JENNINGS: I was told, years ago, by the Cordell County Schools, that my services would no longer be required. I believe that's still the view!

BUDDY: (*Stands to go.*) Thanks for supper.

ROMA: I thought you'd be going to the concert with us, Buddy. You're welcome to.

BUDDY: Naah.

JENNINGS: I never thought I'd see the day when you wouldn't want to go, Henry!

BUDDY: I'm goin somewhere—up to my house.

(*BUDDY exits slowly.*)

ROMA: Will he be all right up there in that old house? He acts sort of peak-ed. Didn't eat hardly anything.

JENNINGS: I tried to get him to go over to Hilliard's. He wouldn't hear it.

EDNA RAE: Are you goin to this big school board meetin they've announced, Jennings? You ought to. They want to close the Kingdom School.

JENNINGS: I know. But I may just become the Official Historian of Roma Jean Livesay.—Might as well. Can't get much else done. Try to work on other things, Roma comes by, scatters my mind like a dandelion bloom.

ROMA: You can always run me off and get your work done.

JENNINGS: No danger!

ROMA: (*Smiles.*) The Official Historian of Roma Jean Livesay. See, Edna Rae. He's been studying up. Listening to the Statler Brothers.

JENNINGS: Reading about them.

ROMA: (*Taking magazine from her clutch bag.*) He claims he's been reading up on country music. Let's see how much he really knows, Edna Rae. (*Flips through magazine.*)

JENNINGS: Oh, no. Is that that country music quiz again? Put that up. (*Glances at watch.*) We've got to get on the road if we make it on time.

ROMA: Hush. We've got plenty of time. I'll start with the same question I asked you the other day. "Hello, Walls" was written by Faron Young. True or False?

JENNINGS: I believe I said false.

ROMA: False is right. But remember, this is a two-part question. Who did write "Hello, Walls?"

JENNINGS: I still don't know!

ROMA: Guess, then.

JENNINGS: Let Edna Rae answer that part. She'll know.

ROMA: You can help him just this once, Edna Rae?

EDNA RAE: Willie Nelson wrote "Hello, Walls."

ROMA: Right. But you can't help him any more, Edna Rae. —This singer is the seventh son of a seventh son.

JENNINGS: Glen Campbell.

ROMA: Heey, that's right! I think he's been studyin up.

JENNINGS: I've read up on Conway Twitty—for this concert. All the stuff about Twitty City was in Edna Rae's brochure. There's Conway under a Twitty City banner... and his symbol... a Twitty Bird? And Conway in a green knit shirt and green baseball hat saying, "Hello, darlin'....nice to see you." Twitty City? A Twitty Bird?—I don't know, I must be missing something.

ROMA: He's slow, Edna Rae, but I'm getting him into circulation. Since I brought him up to your house that first time, I've taken him to the pool hall!

JENNINGS: I didn't know any of those guys. They all seemed to know Roma, though. She'd say: Did you get your hay in, W.J.?—How's your mama, Joe? Somebody brought her some insurance papers to help them fill out. Then there was this guy, the one with hair that curled from under a feed store hat—like a pagoda roof. Who'd you say he was, Roma?

ROMA: Oh, Clayton Pressley. He's poor potatoes, and few to the hill!

JENNINGS: (*To EDNA RAE.*) He hit on Roma!

ROMA: Oh, he didn't—

JENNINGS: There she was, bent forward at a pool table, getting ready to break, and he walks past and pats her on the bottom.

EDNA RAE: Clayton Pressley's not what you'd call right bright. If you put his brains in a cricket's head, it'd run backwards.

JENNINGS: I didn't know what might happen.

ROMA: Oh, he's nothing to—

EDNA RAE: What did happen?

JENNINGS: Why, Roma never even looked up. She just stood there with that cue stick in her hand, threatened to break some other balls with it if he did that again. I think he believed her. And she beat me, two out of three games. I never played a lot of pool.

ROMA: (*Turning a page in the magazine.*) All right. I'm gonna give you another question, Jennings. Let's see—-

JENNINGS: Let's give Edna Rae a quiz on Conway.

ROMA: She'd just make a hundred, I guarantee. She knows more about Conway than Conway's mama knows.

JENNINGS: (*Takes Roma's magazine.*) Let's try her, anyway. (*Scans. Finds something.*) You ready, Edna Rae?—Conway Twitty's real name is—fill in the blank.

ROMA: You'll have to beat that.

EDNA RAE: Harold Jenkins.

JENNINGS: He got the name, Conway Twitty from—complete the statement.

EDNA RAE: Conway, Arkansas and Twitty, Texas.

ROMA: You might as well give up, Jennings. Edna Rae <u>knows</u> Conway.

(*They get up from the table.*)

EDNA RAE: (*Looking at her Conway Twitty brochure.*) I'm sure glad you're driving us to this Conway concert, Jennings. I won't ride anywhere with Earl anymore, even if I can catch him in good enough shape to drive. Roma's helped me a lot, got me going to these meetings in Jewel Hill. I've learned something. I didn't cause Earl's problem, I can't control it, I can't cure it.

ROMA: (*Pats EDNA RAE's hand.*) The important thing for you is to have a life of your own, Edna Rae.

EDNA RAE: I've been to one concert in Johnson City before—but that was Kenny Rogers.

ROMA: Kenny don't blow Edna Rae's dresstail up, not like Conway.

EDNA RAE: That was the night Earl wrecked us on the way back to Newfound. Like to killed us both. That was the last time I ever rode anywhere with Earl.—But you're a good driver, Jennings.

ROMA: Maybe we can get him to take us to Twitty City sometime.

JENNINGS: Look, we really had better get rolling. We've got about a two-hour drive.

ROMA: (*As they exit.*) I don't think Edna Rae's gonna be able to wait two hours before she sees Conway!

EDNA RAE: Oh, honey, I guess I'll make it. But I still can't believe this is happening!

JENNINGS: I can't either, Edna Rae.

EDNA RAE: This is better than Christmas!

(*Lights dim.*)

SCENE EIGHT

Lights come up on BUDDY SHELTON on the front porch of Jennings' house. He is wrapped in a blanket, shivering.

BUDDY: (*Knocks.*) Hey, Jennings? (*Knocks again.*) Hey, Jennings? You got any aspirins? (*Peers in, then out toward the drive.*) He's gone. (*He sits down and starts writing in his notebook.*)

BUDDY: (*Voice-over.*) I'm not feeling too pert, as Grandpa Shelton would say. Feel lazy, draggy. Try to eat; things don't taste right. Had the shakes again last night. Thought I'd shake apart. Now they're coming back again. Had strange thoughts. Thoughts went by purple and orange and wavy. I'd try to hold on to one and it would pass right on by, like a horse on a merry-go-round, moving up and down to music. Throbbing in the back of my head. Aspirins help a little. But I've taken all I had. Something funny: I'm peeing orange.

(*BUDDY gets up, pulls the blanket around him, continues to shiver. Sits down again and writes in notebook.*)

BUDDY: (*Voice-over.*) Having these strange dreams, too. Dreamed I was with Jennings in his pickup, and Grandpa Shelton was with us, and it was raining, and the windshield wipers were whacking back and forth, like a heartbeat. But I couldn't see out because the windshield was all fogged up. We all had on boots and plaid shirts and denim jackets, and over that heavy overcoats, like we were going hunting. And the strange thing was, Jennings wasn't driving; Grandpa Shelton was driving—but he can't drive! We're all jammed up in the pickup and I have my head over on Grandpa Shelton's chest, but I can't feel his heart beating. I think his heart has stopped. I rub a circle with my fist on the fogged windshield and I can see the pickup's veering off the road toward this row of fence posts, and I'm trying to tell Jennings "I don't think Grandpa Shelton's heart's beating" and trying to get Grandpa Shelton's boot off the gas pedal, and him up off the wheel, but I can't move him and we keep veering off the road and start clipping fence posts, and I can't get Grandpa Shelton's foot off the gas.

(*BUDDY lets his notebook fall and pulls the blanket closer around him. Sits shivering. Images flash on the wall behind him. Quick images of photographs: his Grandpa Shelton, Grandma Shelton, Jennings, his mother, Roma, fire, a car crash. BUDDY, dreaming, hears a mix of voices: his GRANDMA SHELTON, JENNINGS, ROMA.*)

GRANDMA SHELTON'S VOICE: What's to become of that boy?

BUDDY: Grandma Shelton.

JENNINGS' VOICE: Go on over to Hilliard's.

BUDDY: No, I'm your renter now.

ROMA'S VOICE: Wish you'd listen to Jennings, Buddy.

BUDDY: He's tearing my house down.

JENNINGS' VOICE: And get back in school.

BUDDY: No.

GRANDMA SHELTON'S VOICE: She'd picked up the wrong baby.

BUDDY: I could have been switched.

JENNINGS' VOICE: You're a mixed up boy, Henry...not a mixed up baby.

BUDDY: I'm Buddy!

JENNINGS' VOICE: Somebody behind everybody, Henry.

BUDDY: I told you—I'm Buddy!

JENNINGS' VOICE: Won't last till the snow flies!

ACT TWO

SCENE ONE

The sound of car doors slamming. JENNINGS and ROMA enter arguing in front of Jennings' house, unaware of BUDDY's presence.

JENNINGS: You're not going to let up on me, are you, Roma?

ROMA: I know you must have said <u>something</u>, or done <u>something</u> to make Edna Rae cry. What did you say to her?

JENNINGS: I don't know. I can't figure it. The whole thing doesn't seem quite real to me. They call it a concert. It's not like any concert I ever attended.

ROMA: Well, what did you expect?

JENNINGS: I don't know. It was more like a carnival—or a basketball game, fireworks display, and political rally rolled into one. What is it with this "Hello, darlin'... Nice to see you?" The women went wild.

ROMA: I want to know what you said to Edna Rae.

JENNINGS: I'm trying to remember. —I'd read the lyrics to a lot of Conway's songs—thinking performance didn't much improve them. I had to laugh at "Somewhere Between Her Blue Eyes and Jeans." Then, during the break, when you were out getting something to drink, I guess I kidded Edna Rae about that song.

ROMA: "Somewhere Between Her Blue Eyes and Jeans?" What did you say about it?

JENNINGS: I said I thought the lines were dumb. (*Recites lines.*) "Somewhere between her blue eyes and jeans / There's a heart that's been broken along with her dreams."

ROMA: You think that's dumb, do you?

JENNINGS: If the location of her heart is that much in doubt, she must be an anatomical freak.

ROMA: And that's what you said to Edna Rae?

JENNINGS: Something like that.

ROMA: Well, shit, Jennings! How come you have to be such a smart-ass?

JENNINGS: I swear I didn't mean—I was just running on.

ROMA: That's what was dumb!

JENNINGS: All I did was—say what I thought about the song. The way you and I sit around and talk about songs. Say what we think about them.

ROMA: "Blue Eyes and Jeans" just happens to be the story of Edna Rae's life. Her only son, killed on a motorcycle. Two daughters who don't ever come home. Nobody but Earl, and him an alcoholic.—Why don't you stop worrying about the fine points and listen to what the song <u>says</u>?

JENNINGS: Are we going to argue about a dumb song?

ROMA: You hurt Edna Rae.

JENNINGS: I didn't put Edna Rae down. I put the song down. How did I hurt Edna Rae?

ROMA: I don't believe you, Jennings Wells!—If you don't know, I can't explain it to you. She came back there to the restroom, crying.

JENNINGS: I thought she was crying.

ROMA: She was cryin in the car on the way back.

JENNINGS: I know. Worst drive I ever had in my life.

ROMA: And I never felt so sorry for anybody in my life. She's got nothing to go home to, and you—you had to ruin the only pleasure she—

JENNINGS: I didn't mean to ruin it—to hurt Edna Rae.

ROMA: Well, you did! I'll tell you one thing, Jennings Wells, there's some things you can't study up on in two weeks. Conway knows some things you don't. I used to think you knew everything. After tonight, I wonder if you know anything.

JENNINGS: (*After an awkward silence.*) Sit down, Roma.

ROMA: (*Takes out car keys.*) No... I'm going home. (*Starts out.*)

JENNINGS: Then come by— tomorrow?

ROMA: (*Without looking at him.*) No.

JENNINGS: I'll come over there, then.

ROMA: No.

JENNINGS: You don't want to see me?

ROMA: I fell in love with you, Jennings, a long time ago. When you used to come by our house and I danced for you. I've always measured other men by you, and none measured up. I guess I've been waiting for you all this time, hoping, thinking we could still be together.—(*Turns to go.*) Guess I was wrong again.

JENNINGS: You're right about one thing: I don't belong here. I have to admit it. I don't live here any longer. Can't live here any longer. You've as much as said it. I know about as much about this place as I know about country music.

ROMA: I'm going home.

JENNINGS: Hilliard said it: "What gives you the right," he said, "to think you belong here? You've been gone. It's the ones who've stayed here," he said.— Buddy said it: "If all you do is make fun of this place, why did you even come home?" Good question. But you've showed me best of all. Thanks, Roma.

ROMA: I know what you're going to do. You'll leave now. Go on, leave. Get about two hundred miles from here, and you'll be able to like Newfound again. You can think of us as nice smooth people, no rough edges. Maybe you can write another book about us, about how wonderful it is to be part of some place, rooted. Yeah, you like that word. Kinfolks. Community. You like those words too.—Goodbye, Jennings.

(*ROMA exits.*)

JENNINGS: (*About to enter house, he calls after her.*) I guess you're right again, Roma.—I can't stay here. (*He looks down, discovers BUDDY.*) Henry? Roma? Roma, come here, it's Henry— something wrong with him.

ROMA: (*Re-entering.*) Buddy? Where?

(*BUDDY, half-sitting, half-reclining, shivers in his blanket. JENNINGS and ROMA crouch on either side of him.*)

ROMA: (*Shaking him gently.*) Buddy? Buddy?

BUDDY: (*Still reacting to his dream.*) I'm Buddy! I've told you, I'm Buddy!

ROMA: Can't you call him by his right name?—Wake up, Buddy!

BUDDY: (*Struggling.*) I said I'm—

ROMA: Of course, you're Buddy. Wake up, Buddy. Sit up.

(*BUDDY sits up, pulls blanket closer around him. Shivers.*)

ROMA: What's wrong, Buddy?

BUDDY: Sick.

(*ROMA kneels beside him and puts an index finger on his lower left eyelid.*)

ROMA: Look up. (*She puts a finger on his lower right eyelid.*) Look up again. — (*To JENNINGS.*) I should have known, when he was shivering here on the porch the other evening. And tonight at supper he wouldn't eat.

JENNINGS: Known what?

ROMA: Look! (*Holds down BUDDY's eyelid again.*)

JENNINGS: Jaundice!

ROMA: Where does he get water here? Is there water up at that old house he's stayin in?

JENNINGS: He gets water right here at the house.

ROMA: You been drinkin water anywhere else, Buddy?

BUDDY: Lots of places. Old springs, out in the woods. Wherever I happen to be, out roamin.

ROMA: Have you looked at yourself? You're yellow as a pumpkin. Open up; stick out your tongue…. Say "aaaah."

(*BUDDY does what she says.*)

JENNINGS: (*Looking.*) He's sick, all right.

BUDDY: I know that!

JENNINGS: He can't stay here, sick, by himself.

ROMA: That's pretty plain!—I'll take him in to the clinic in Jewell Hill.

JENNINGS: No, you go on, I'll take him.

ROMA: What will you do after he sees a doctor? Bring him back here? Leave him by himself?

BUDDY: (*Shivering.*) You leaving, Jennings?

JENNINGS: No, I— (*To ROMA.*) I wouldn't leave him by himself. I won't leave—just yet. I told Hilliard half of the water in Cordell County's polluted!—Come on, Henry.

ROMA: If he goes with you, I'm following.

JENNINGS: You don't trust me to take this boy to the doctor, do you? Let's not argue. (*Takes BUDDY's hand.*) Here, let's get you up, Henry. Can you walk to the car, or am I gonna have to carry you?

(*BUDDY stands up with JENNINGS' help. Pulls his blanket around him.*)

BUDDY: I can get up, but I'm not goin to Hilliard's!

ROMA: (*Moves to BUDDY's side.*) Come on, honey.

(*As they are about to exit, BUDDY turns and goes back and picks up his notebook. Clutching the notebook, he exits with ROMA and JENNINGS.*)

SCENE TWO

Local LOAFERS, on their bench, joined by LLOYD SUTHERLAND.

DELANO CRUMM: (*Finishing a joke.*) So then after you've baked your carp on that pine board, with them bacon strips across him, so that bacon grease soaks all the way down through that carp and into your pine board,—what you do is, you eat the board and throw the carp away! Yeah, eat the board and throw the carp away!

(*LLOYD SUTHERLAND enters.*)

DELANO: Howdy Lloyd. How are things over in the Kingdom?

LLOYD: Ah, Lord, kind of on the down-go, I tell you!

WILEY WOOLFORD: What's goin on, Lloyd?

LLOYD: There was talk about closin our school. We hoped it was just talk. But now the school board's called a meetin about it.

(*BUDDY enters.*)

LLOYD: How do, little Buddy.

BUDDY: Mr. Sutherland.

DEE RHODOMMER: Where you been lately, Ace? Ain't seen you around.

BUDDY: Been sick.

WILEY: You still living on Jennings Wells' place?

BUDDY: I've moved.

WILEY: You and him fall out?

BUDDY: No, I just moved, after I got sick.

LLOYD: Where is Jennings, Buddy? I've been by there twice lookin for him. Can't catch him at home.

BUDDY: I've been watchin for him, too. He's been gone.

LLOYD: I need to see him, ask him if there's any way he can help us with this school thing. We don't hardly know how to go at it. Don't know lawyer words.

WILEY: Jennings Wells ain't no lawyer, is he?

LLOYD: No, but he knows the lingo—the book way to go about it. We'd hate to lose our school.

WILEY: (*Shaking his head.*) Lloyd, if you put Jennings Wells up against Hilliard, that'll be a splatterment, depend on it.

DEE: (*To BUDDY.*) Jennings'll have your Uncle Hilliard on him, just like before, right Ace?

LLOYD: What I'm afraid of is, they'll meet over there at Jewell Hill and run something through and we won't know a thing about it. I've tried, I don't know at the times, to find out when the meetin is. They give me the run-around.

BUDDY: I bet Jennings could find out for you.

LLOYD: I'm hopin so. (*To BUDDY.*) You went to the Kingdom School—how many years, son?

BUDDY: First eight years.

LLOYD: He's a sharp tack, this feller. Puttin somethin past this boy'd be like sneakin daylight past a rooster!

DELANO CRUM: (*To BUDDY.*) You ain't goin' to school now are you, Ace? You've quit, ain't you?

BUDDY: I liked it at the Kingdom School, though.

(*BUDDY goes into Trading Post.*)

LLOYD: Some of this young generation, I'll tell you, they're comin up different. That boy of Fain's was home Christmas, from California, with his wife and Younguns. One of the younguns got to playin with a seashell there at the house. We always used it for a doorstop. I told him, I said, "Hold it up to your ear," and he did, and I said, "What do you hear?" He kindly looked at me and grinned and said, "The freeway?"— I'd always heard it was the ocean roarin in a shell. But that youngun—the freeway!

(*LLOYD goes into Trading Post.*)

DELANO: Yeah, Lloyd's right, it's different now.

DEE: Progress!

DELANO: It's been a-changin all along.

DEE: Reckon we've been too busy to notice.

DELANO: Here comes Deputy Dawg.

WILEY: With his beeper. Still wearin his deputy sheriff's hat.

DEE: Old Cecil—what you call all hat and no cattle.

(*CECIL PEDIGO enters, carrying a fishing rod.*)

WILEY: Been catchin any carp lately, Cecil? Delano here's got a good recipe for you, if you have.

CECIL: (*Sits down on end of the bench.*) Hell, I ain't caught even a carp. Only thing I snagged, any size, was a damned old needle-nose garfish. I hate them sumbitches. Tuck and drove a stick straight up and down between his jaws. Throwed him back in. He won't be jerkin nobody else's bobber under.—I'm gonna go to squirrel huntin 'stead of fishin'.

DELANO: Squirrel season's not open yet, is it, boys?

(*DELANO looks around to WILEY and DEE for an answer. They shake their heads, No.*)

CECIL: Makes no never mind to me. Game warden won't write me up. I used to deputy with him.

DEE: I hear there's not likely to be many squirrels this year. Dry weather and all.

CECIL: Said they wasn't gonna be many last year, but I got a hunnert and forty seven.

DELANO: That many, Cecil.

CECIL: I'm goin for two hunnert this year. Two hunnert—if I have to kill the last squirrel in Cordell County.

(*BUDDY comes out of the Trading Post with a soft drink and a package of crackers. Starts past the loafers.*)

CECIL: What say, Slick! (*BUDDY doesn't answer.*) Hey, Ace!

BUDDY: (*Moving past them.*) My name's not Slick, nor Ace, neither.

DEE: What is your name today?

CECIL: Who're you the daddy of?

(*BUDDY moves on past the LOAFERS, but sits down within earshot to drink his cola and eat the crackers.*)

WILEY: Old Walter Hooper's a daddy now, I reckon. One of them Shook girls has slapped a paternity suit on him!

DEE: He big her?

WILEY: Who knows? You know what they say, it's Mama's baby and Papa's—maybe.

DELANO: Who was Walter's daddy?

WILEY: You know, old Hill Hooper—the one they call Bug.

DELANO: That Walter's a funny lookin feller, I tell you!

WILEY: Musta been marked by a bulldog before he was borned.

DEE: Them Shufords musta been marked by somethin—the ones they call the Hoppin Shufords. I seen em once. Went up there with my uncle to buy two calves. They was out in the garden, choppin weeds, a boy and girl, up fifteen or sixteen year old, and didn't have any legs hardly at all, either one of em, legs just tapered off like tadpoles. Draggin theirselves along in the rows there, choppin out weeds with little short hoes. Pink Shuford, their daddy, he's plumb normal. And their mama, too, I reckon. And them other Shuford younguns was just as normal as you or me.

WILEY: Who said you was normal?

DELANO: Girl over in what they call the Kingdom, got no legs. Or maybe baby legs, like they never growed with the rest of her. I seen her once through field glasses, sittin out in a chair under a weepin willer. I believe it was over in the Kingdom—or maybe up on Lost Creek.

BUDDY: It wasn't in the Kingdom. Nobody over there like that.

CECIL: How do you know so much, Knot-head?

BUDDY: I know everybody over in the Kingdom.

CECIL: You don't even know how your hammer's hangin, so what do you know about freaks? We're talkin freaks here.

BUDDY: I know you.

CECIL: You better watch it, Ace. You fixin to get your tail twisted.—You livin up at Jennings Wells's now?

BUDDY: I never said I was.

WILEY: Jennings Wells— I recollect one time Jennings Wells come back in—years ago, when he's goin to school—and he's tellin Nelse Ledbetter about psychology. Tried to give Nelse a 'sociation test. Nelse couldn't associate nothin' with nothin'!

DELANO: That was when Jennings already had a job teachin school.

WILEY: Got his ass fired, though.

DELANO: You don't know. He mighta quit.

WILEY: Quit, shit. Cecil's boss, Hilliard Shelton, got him fired, because of the way Jennings talked about the strip minin. What I heard.

DELANO: Now he's just come back over home there and set down.

WILEY: He's been printin them things in the paper. He'll mess around and get Hilliard on his ass again. Hilliard'll sick old Cecil here on Jennings.

CECIL: (*Boasting.*) Hilliard Shelton just about runs Cordell County, you better believe that. (*Looks in the direction of BUDDY, who is still sitting half turned away from the others.*) Ain't that right, Slick? (*When BUDDY doesn't answer.*) Hey, little Shelton?

(*BUDDY looks around slowly.*)

CECIL: Ain't that right? Your Uncle Hilliard—he's got the power in Cordell County.

BUDDY: I don't know anything about him—much.

DEE: What I don't know is how old Jennings Wells makes a livin.

CECIL: He may sell dope, like some of these other high-falutin fellers that's come in here.

BUDDY: That's a lie.

CECIL: Yeah? How do you know?

BUDDY: I know he don't sell dope.

CECIL: I could tell you things, Ace. More maybe than you'd like to know. Get that Jennings Wells to give <u>you</u> one of them 'sociation tests.

(*BUDDY finishes drink, crumples cellophane wrapper in his hand, and gets up.*)

BUDDY: (*As he leaves.*) I associate you with puke.

CECIL: Hey, Ace! (*To others.*) Friggin little wood-colt! They say Jennings Wells is that boy's daddy. I could tell him things!

(*CECIL's beeper sounds.*)

DELANO: (*Throws up his arms in mock alarm.*) Lord, look out, Cecil's startin to beep!

(*CECIL stands, steps away from the others, and begins to fiddle with beeper.*)

WILEY: Better call the office, Cecil!—Boys, we're gettin' <u>modern</u> here in Cordell County!

DEE: Progress!

SCENE THREE

Jennings' house. JENNINGS sets two suitcases down by the worktable and stands gathering up books and papers. BUDDY enters.

BUDDY: Where'd you go after you and Roma took me to the doctor? It's been two weeks. Where've you been?

JENNINGS: Been off stompin out ignorance, Henry. Couldn't stomp out any around here.

BUDDY: Over in Appalachia?

JENNINGS: You're <u>in</u> Appalachia, Henry. —You'll have to get out of that old Gudger house, Henry. I'm not going to be here.

BUDDY: I'm already out. I'm not your renter anymore. After you and Roma took me to the doctor, she drove me to Hilliard's, to stay with Mom Shelton and Grandpa.

JENNINGS: That's good, Henry.

BUDDY: But I wouldn't get out of the car! I told her if she put me out at Hilliard's, I'd just come back over here and live in the old Gudger house. She said that wouldn't do.— I'm stayin at Roma's.— You leavin <u>again</u>?

JENNINGS: That's right, Henry.

BUDDY: (*Picks up suitcase and sets it closer to the house.*) You can't leave! (*Turns back to JENNINGS, agitated.*) We've got to put Grandpa and Mom Shelton's house back together. (*Trying to think of any way to keep JENNINGS from leaving.*) You've got a lot of mail, box is full. Didn't you see it? I'll run down to the box and get it.

JENNINGS: I'll pick it up on my way out, Henry.

BUDDY: No!—-Let's ride around some. They've got a whale over at the mall in Jewell Hill. A live whale. In a tank, on a flatbed truck. Heard it on the radio. We could see that whale!

JENNINGS: I don't want to see a whale!

BUDDY: I'm takin my medicine, like you told me to. Before you left. Just ask Roma.—You and her mad at each other?

JENNINGS: (*Picks up suitcase and moves it back out by the table.*) You mean me and Miss Mis-Conception? Miss Mis-Understanding?

BUDDY: She's not mad at you.—Well, a little, maybe. She talks about you, though. All the time. Got me checkin to see if you've come back home.

JENNINGS: Well, I don't guess it makes any difference.

BUDDY: (*Moves suitcase back away from the table.*) You can drive me over to Roma's. I'm not supposed to get too tired—because I've been sick.

JENNINGS: Roma won't want to see me.

BUDDY: She will! She does—I guarantee!—And you know who else wants to see you? Lloyd Sutherland.

JENNINGS: School board?

BUDDY: Lloyd wants you to help keep em from closin the Kingdom School.—I liked the Kingdom School.

JENNINGS: I went to that school, too. You know that? —Well, I wish I could help Lloyd.

BUDDY: You can. Lloyd was down at the Tradin Post a little while ago. He said you'd tell em what to do—to keep the school.

JENNINGS: Yeah. Tell em what to do! That's the bind I'm in. There's Hilliard, and his crowd. They don't have any use for a thing I think or say. Then there's Lloyd Sutherland and his people, think I have the answers to all their problems in my head. Think I can pull the answer out, a rabbit out of a hat.

BUDDY: Lloyd really wants to see you.

JENNINGS: (*Glances at the suitcase, the stacked books and papers, then at Buddy.*) Tell you what. I'll put this stuff in the car and drive you over to Roma's. On the way, we'll stop at the Trading Post, see if I can find Lloyd. (*Starts to pick up books and papers from table.*)

BUDDY: (*Comes between JENNINGS and the books and papers, his back to the table.*) Roma talks about you. All the time.

JENNINGS: What's she saying about me?

BUDDY: Just "Jennings this, Jennings that"—about every five minutes. She said you wouldn't have gone off if you'd known they were thinkin about closing the Kingdom School.

JENNINGS: She's wrong about that!—Anyway—let's go see if we can find Lloyd Sutherland. (*Turns, obviously abandoning intention of taking suitcase, books and papers with him.*)

BUDDY: (*Aware that he has won.*) Can't we go see that whale before we go to Roma's?

JENNINGS: (*Turning to go.*) No! No whale! First Lloyd, then Roma!

BUDDY: (*Steps back and shoves the suitcase back closer to the house.*) Well, you can't leave again! I'll let the air out of your tires!

SCENE FOUR

The Trading Post. LOAFERS on their bench. As DEE RHODOMMER and WILEY WOOLFORD speak, DELANO CRUM comes out of the Trading Post with a bottle drink and a package of crackers.

DEE: I was raised up in a old house like that Shelton house we moved. In dry weather, them shingles on the roof would turn up like sled runners: then when it'd rain, if you's layin up there under the roof at night, you could hear them shingles poppin, like they're sealin back down.

WILEY: Ours leaked! And I've woke up under a shake roof many's the mornin in winter when there'd be a dustin of snow on my quilt.

(*The sound of a car coming to a quick stop. JENNINGS and BUDDY enter quickly, BUDDY looking back.*)

JENNINGS: (*To LOAFERS.*) You fellers seen Lloyd Sutherland?

DELANO: He was here a while ago. Lookin for you. (*To other LOAFERS.*) Where'd Lloyd go?

BUDDY: (*Still looking back, pushes JENNINGS on past the LOAFERS.*) Now, are you gonna believe me? That Cecil Pedigo—. Rode your back bumper! Tried to run us off the road—twice!

JENNINGS: Cecil won't ever see the day he can run <u>me</u> off the road.— Did he go on past?

BUDDY: (*Looking back.*) No! He's pulled in right behind us out there. He's gettin out of his car...walkin this way. He's after you. Here he comes. What are you gonna do?

JENNINGS: Come on around here by the horseshoe pits. I'll handle Cecil. (*They walk away from loafers' bench.*)

(*CECIL PEDIGO enters, walks past LOAFERS, approaches JENNINGS and BUDDY, stands glaring defiantly at JENNINGS. LOAFERS rise from their bench and follow at a distance.*)

BUDDY: (*To JENNINGS.*) Watch him! Hilliard's sicked Cecil on you, for sure!

JENNINGS: Naaah! I'll find out what's on his mind. (*To CECIL.*) What can I do for you, Cecil?

(*CECIL moves a couple of steps closer without speaking.*)

JENNINGS: What's on your mind, Cecil?—By the way, where'd you learn to drive?

CECIL: These here articles you're putting in the paper... about the schools.

JENNINGS: Yeah, what about them?

CECIL: You're buttin in where you're not wanted.

JENNINGS: (*Laughs.*) Cecil, I didn't know you took an interest in education. What's education ever done for you?

(*JENNINGS picks up a horseshoe and, turning his back to CECIL, pitches it toward the opposite pit. CECIL steps up behind JENNINGS, taking a blackjack from his back pocket, and hits JENNINGS in the back of the head. BUDDY picks up another horseshoe and hits CECIL on the shoulder with it as JENNINGS sways but does not fall. BUDDY hits again, this time striking CECIL's head. JENNINGS, recovering, grabs at the blackjack and throws CECIL to the ground. BUDDY kicks him.*)

JENNINGS: (*To BUDDY, restraining him.*) Let him alone! (*Breathing hard a minute, picks up blackjack from the ground and tosses it in the direction of the loafers' bench.*) Get up, Cecil. Get up, get out of here!

(*CECIL gets up slowly, shuffles past astonished loafers. The sound of his car leaving is heard. DEE has stepped over and picked up the blackjack.*)

DEE: (*Holding the blackjack out to WILEY and DELANO.*) Look at this thing! (*Makes striking motion with blackjack.*)

BUDDY: (*To JENNINGS.*) I told you! He come to scare you away from that school board meeting.

WILEY: (*Taking the blackjack in his hand, making a back-and-forth motion with his wrist.*) Cecil's head-whacker. I'd sooner walk into a circle saw than get hit with that thing.

JENNINGS: (*Swaying a little, rubs back of his head, stares in the direction CECIL has exited.*) Damn! I'm ready to <u>leave</u> this place, but I'll not be <u>run off</u>! Come on, I've got to find Lloyd Sutherland.

(*DELANO takes blackjack from WILEY, looks first in the direction of CECIL's exit, then back toward JENNINGS and BUDDY.*)

DELANO: That horseshoe Cecil took on the burr of the ear'd be about as bad.

BUDDY: You going to help him now?

JENNINGS: You better believe I am!

(*JENNINGS acknowledges LOAFERS, as he exits with BUDDY.*)

JENNINGS: Boys.

DELANO: You all right, Jennings?

JENNINGS: I'm fine, boys.

(*JENNINGS exits with BUDDY.*)

WILEY: (*Wipes his brow.*) I tell you, things is pickin up around here!

DEE: Yeah, happenin, seems like, faster than they used to.

WILEY: Fellers, I reckon you know, if this comes to court, we're witnesses.

DELANO: It'll never come to court, I guarantee you. Why, that Cecil, he's been a deputy sheriff. Thinks he still is one.— But it ain't over, you can depend on that, too.

WILEY: Goes to show you, though—set in one place long enough, you'll see somethin!

DEE: Bet if we hang around that school board meetin this evening, we'll see something else!

SCENE FIVE

The Jewell Hill Community Center. ROMA LIVESAY, upstage center, with EDNA RAE, waiting for school board meeting to begin. DELANO CRUM, WILEY WOOLFORD, DEE RHODOMMER, LLOYD SUTHERLAND, others, file past them and take seats for the meeting. As EDNA RAE speaks, ROMA keeps looking off.

EDNA RAE: Aunt Velma, she'd never been further than Lexington in her life. Then she up and went with her church group to New York City. Saw all the street people. Said they didn't have any manners at all. Said she never was as glad to be back home in her life. I worry about her. She won't take her medicine like she's supposed to. Saves it, so it'll last longer. I wish you'd talk to her, Roma. She won't listen to me.

ROMA: I will, Edna Rae.

EDNA RAE: I feel sorry for Aunt Velma, but she'll drive you crazy if you let her. The other night she wanted to watch Billy Graham on TV, and her picture went out. She called me on the phone, wanted me to turn the program on and tell it to her over the phone.

ROMA: (*To EDNA RAE.*) All Jennings said on the phone was there'd been a little trouble; he's coming to the school board meeting.

EDNA RAE: He didn't say what kind of trouble, hon?

ROMA: No, I wonder what—?

EDNA RAE: Well, I just hope you all can get *your* trouble worked out...is what I hope. I told him so when he come by the house. Come to apologize, he said. I said, why, honey, you don't owe me any apology. If my feelings got hurt, I know you didn't go to do it. You should be talking to Roma, that's what I told him.

(*JENNINGS enters with BUDDY. JENNINGS has a white bandage on his head. ROMA approaches.*)

BUDDY: Hilliard's behind it all. Just ask Roma.

ROMA: Jennings! What on earth?

BUDDY: Lloyd Sutherland said Jennings looked like he'd been sackin wildcats.

JENNINGS: Thanks for coming, Roma. (*Nodding to his cousin.*) Edna Rae.

ROMA: Jennings, what's happened?

BUDDY: Been in a fight, that's what!

ROMA: Fight?

BUDDY: See, they've got this whale in a big tank in the parking lot out at the mall. Big tank on a flatbed truck.

ROMA: Whale? What's that got to do…?

JENNINGS: Nothing!

EDNA RAE: (*As she and ROMA inspect the bandage on the back of JENNINGS' head.*) And you've come to this meeting, anyway, Jennings, hurt and bandaged up?

JENNINGS: I'll be all right. I was looking for Lloyd Sutherland, to tell him I wasn't coming. But after Cecil jumped me, I changed my mind. I'm not about to be run off!

ROMA: But the bandage—where—?

BUDDY: Dick Lovell put it on.

EDNA RAE: The veterinarian?

BUDDY: We headed over into The Kingdom, to find Lloyd Sutherland, and come up behind Dick Lovell's van. He'd been somewhere doctorin cows.

JENNINGS: He didn't want to do it. Said he wasn't a doctor, he was a large animal veterinarian. I said, well, I am a large animal.

BUDDY: He fixed Jennings up, right there on the side of the road!

JENNINGS: You know what Lovell was afraid of? —Malpractice! He said, "If you tell anybody I patched you up, I'll deny it!"

(*HILLIARD SHELTON gavels the school board meeting to order.*)

BUDDY: (*As gavel sounds.*) And you know what? We never did get to see that whale!

HILLIARD SHELTON: A representative of the Kingdom community has informed me they want Mr. Jennings Wells to make a statement on their behalf.

EDNA RAE: (*Raising her hand, like a school child.*) That's Dr. Jennings Wells.

HILLIARD: (*Raps gavel.*) All right, <u>Dr.</u> Wells.

(*Snatches of JENNINGS' statement can be heard alternating with BUDDY, EDNA RAE, and ROMA's comments spoken from where they have taken seats at the back of the meeting area.*)

JENNINGS: First, I'd like to say it's wrong to think people don't value education. We do.

BUDDY: (*To ROMA.*) There's old big butt Hilliard.

EDNA RAE: Jennings is right, you know it, Roma?

ROMA: Shhh!

JENNINGS: We want better schools, schools that serve our communities. But a bigger school is not automatically a better school.

HILLIARD: A bigger school's not automatically worse, either.

BUDDY: Wish he wasn't my uncle!

JENNINGS: No, but I think it's interesting nowadays, if you look around the world, you see people everywhere rejecting collectivization—and here we are still collectivizing our schools!

EDNA RAE: Why, I think Jennings could run our schools just fine!

ROMA: Will both of you hush!

HILLIARD: I don't see your point.

JENNINGS: Another thing: our young people don't learn the history of their own place, and it's clear that the more we know about our own place, the more we're apt to care about it, and want to take care of it. But that history's ignored or obscured. Bankers and industrialists have named our towns after themselves. As if our communities didn't have names already. Look underneath these names and you'll discover the old names given by the settlers. Underneath Barton, Spring Creek; under van den Berg, Red Oak; under McEwing, Pick Britches. These industrialists robbed our region not only of its mineral wealth, but even of its names. And thus of memory, and a sense of the past.

HILLIARD: Dr. Wells, do you have children in attendance at the Kingdom School?

JENNINGS: No, I don't.

HILLIARD: Have you ever had children in attendance at the Kingdom School?

JENNINGS: No.

HILLIARD: What is your interest in the Kingdom School?

JENNINGS: The board is well aware of my interest. I'm representing people who do have children attending the Kingdom School—families who have been sending their children there for generations.— I attended the Kingdom School.

HILLIARD: Dr. Wells, are you a lawyer?

JENNINGS: Hilliard, just call me Jennings. And you know I'm not a lawyer. (*Turning to others.*) Look, we all know one another here; we know why we're here. I'd like to talk about that.

HILLIARD: I'm asking these questions for the record. It's important what the record shows. Do you agree?

JENNINGS: I agree. And I'd like the record to show that any taxpayer has a legitimate interest in the county's schools, whether he has children enrolled in those schools or not. Do you agree to that?

HILLIARD: Agreed.

JENNINGS: I'd also like the record to show you don't have to be a lawyer to take an interest in school matters, or to represent a group of parents in a matter involving their children's school. Do you agree to that?

HILLIARD: I don't believe anybody said you had to be a lawyer—

JENNINGS: But you implied it. I assume, then, that you agree—you don't have to be a lawyer to represent one side of an issue in a school board hearing.

HILLIARD: Agreed. And I'm glad to see you agree that there are two sides to this issue.

JENNINGS: We're all in such agreement here, why don't we just shake hands around and go home?

(*Applause from some MEMBERS OF THE AUDIENCE.*)

HILLIARD: (*Raps gavel for order.*) Mr. Wells, it appears you have been in an accident. You appear to be in some pain. I wonder if you feel up to continuing.

(*LLOYD SUTHERLAND, angry at this suggestion, comes up from his chair. Another MEMBER OF THE AUDIENCE restrains him.*)

JENNINGS: Appearances can be so misleading! Can't they, Hilliard? I may <u>appear</u> to have been in an accident, but I think you know (*Pats bandage on head.*) this was no accident. I may <u>appear</u> to be in pain, but I have never felt better. I certainly do want to continue!

HILLIARD: (*Hurriedly, rushing the meeting to a close.*) I don't know that anything more needs to be said. The issue is clear-cut: do we keep the Kingdom School open, or close it? Do we stand still educationally in Cordell County, or go forward, progressively, by consolidating this old school with a modern, up-to-date educational plant?

ROMA: (*Stands.*) I'd like to say something!

HILLIARD: (*Startled.*) Yes?

ROMA: I think there's a lot more to be said.

(*Nods from GATHERING, affirmative murmuring.*)

EDNA RAE: (*Stands beside ROMA.*) I went to that meeting about the landfill and everybody there had a chance to speak. Everybody got three minutes. I think everybody that wants to ought to have a chance to speak.

HILLIARD: Well, you're talking.

EDNA RAE: I just believe the Kingdom School's a good school, and always has been. People who've gone to this school, they've gone on and done right well. There's been doctors and lawyers and judges that went to school here. And it's always been more than just a school. Why, I remember we had war bond rallies here. People would put on a program, pick and sing, have a good time, and then buy war bonds.

LLOYD SUTHERLAND: (*Stands.*) I've been studyin on something. They say it'll be better for our younguns to consolidate because they've got computers at the other school. Say the children can be hauled now that we've got the roads. Well, how come the roads is just one way—to haul folks out to the big school? Why can't we haul computers up here? How come it's always a road out but never a road in?

HILLIARD: I don't see that this is gettin—

BUDDY SHELTON: (*Stands.*) I want to say something—about Cordell County High School. I'm the only one here that's ever been to it. I went a year and a half, and I quit it. I won't ever go back, either. One bunch over there just thinks about football and basketball, and the other bunch smokes dope.

(*Throughout, ROMA looks back and forth, delighted at the turn the meeting has taken.*)

EDNA RAE: I've heard it's the truth!

BUDDY: The mothers of some of the cheerleaders run the school! And grades don't make any difference, anyway! You can get these blank report cards and just fill em out. Excuse slips, too. You can't go down the hall hardly without gettin into a fight. Half the girls are going to have babies.

EDNA RAE: It didn't used to be that way.

BUDDY: One ninth grader was meetin her boyfriend out on the parkin lot. He'd been in the penitentiary. And one teacher come to school with a black eye her boyfriend gave her. Another teacher was datin a student.

LLOYD: We don't want to send younguns into a mess like that! What we ought to be talkin about is fixin Cordell County school before we think about doin away with the Kingdom School.

DELANO: (*Rises to speak.*) You know, I hadn't thought about it till Lloyd mentioned it, but he's right: a road goes in the same as it goes out.

WILEY: (*Rises to speak.*) That's right. The roads is good now, but still, in a bus, it's a good hour's ride, hour and a half, maybe, one way from over in the Kingdom. Now, that's hard on <u>little</u> kids. I don't see why—-

(*DEE rises to speak after WILEY.*)

EDNA RAE: (*Raises her hand for recognition, shakes it urgently, having thought of something else.*) Mr. Chairman! Mr. Chairman!

(*ROMA's face is bright with excitement and delight. She looks across at JENNINGS, then raises her hand too.*)

ROMA: Fox on the run, Jennings! Fox on the run!

HILLIARD: (*Raps with gavel.*) We'll carry this meeting over.

ROMA: Till when?

HILLIARD: I don't know! We'll set a date and announce it.

EDNA RAE: Let us know, because we'll all want to come!

HILLIARD: Meeting adjourned!

(*Lights down on School Board Meeting.*)

SCENE SIX

JENNINGS, ROMA, EDNA RAE, AND BUDDY enter Jennings' house.

EDNA RAE: I don't know when I've had so much fun, you all! That meeting got me all stirred up! I've been remembering so many things! Jennings, do you remember when we were gathering walnuts with Grandma Wells over there by the Kingdom School and all the butterflies lit on us?

ROMA: Butterflies?

EDNA RAE: Yes! I bet there was five hundred big orange and black butterflies. More like a thousand! We were sitting there resting, and all of a sudden they just come down out of the air and lit all over us—me and Jennings and Grandma Wells. You remember, don't you, Jennings?

JENNINGS: It sounds unbelievable, but it's the truth.

EDNA RAE: Grandma Wells whispered to us. "Don't move," she said. "Don't move." But after a while I did, and they all flew off again. Grandma Wells said it was a sign.

ROMA: Sign of what?

EDNA RAE: She never did say. But she said it was a sign.

JENNINGS: It was a sign monarch butterflies were migrating, that's what it was a sign of.

EDNA RAE: (*Embraces JENNINGS.*) Anyway, I'm just so proud of you, Jennings!

JENNINGS: Proud? Why? I didn't do anything.

EDNA RAE: You got Hilliard to put off closing the school.

JENNINGS: You all did that! I was just blundering around till you and Roma broke the whole thing open. I felt about as useless as—well, I won't say.

EDNA RAE: You <u>were</u> talking over people's heads a little. I never know half the time what you're talkin' about, but I know you do.— You got people to thinking.

JENNINGS: About all we did was buy a little time, Edna Rae.

EDNA RAE: Well, we'll be right there, every time it comes up, and just talk Hilliard's ears off. You can put things in the paper about it, and more and more people will get interested. Lord, I can't wait till the next meeting! You'll have to go with us, too, Buddy, and talk about that mess at Cordell High.

ROMA: Wasn't Buddy good, Jennings?

JENNINGS: (*Pats BUDDY on the back.*) You did fine, Henry. That took nerve, too—to get up there in front of your Uncle Hilliard.

BUDDY: That's why I did it—because it was Hilliard!

JENNINGS: But I still think, bad as it is over there, you ought to be in that school.

ROMA: Jennings, don't start!

JENNINGS: You're not hurting Hilliard by not going. You're only hurting yourself. Right now you're just like a hog under an apple tree— eat and sleep and never look up to see where it's all coming from.

ROMA: He's been sick, Jennings! He's still taking medicine.

JENNINGS: When you get well, then what?

BUDDY: I'm gonna be free. Like Grandpa Shelton says, I like to be free.

JENNINGS: You can't be free and ignorant. Anyway, you're gonna be free. Then what?

BUDDY: Get me a job. Live some place, but not at Hilliard's.

JENNINGS: (*Nods.*) So, you're free. Got a job, roof over your head. Clothes to wear, enough to eat. Then what?

BUDDY: Sounds all right to me!

JENNINGS: Sure it does. But after all that, the "then-what" days are gonna come, Henry. You'll be beatin around in a pickup with a baseball cap on top of a half bushel of hair. Then your hair will start to recede, you'll round out from drinking beer, so in your sleeveless padded jacket, you'll begin to look like a walking hand grenade. By that time some girl will have struck your fancy, and you'll have her set up in a double-wide, and you'll wake up some day and look back and won't know what happened.

BUDDY: How do you always know so much about everything?

JENNINGS: I know. I see it everywhere.

ROMA: Now hush! Both of you! Honestly, Jennings! You go off without a word. Nobody knows where you are for two weeks. Then you come traipsing back, like nothing happened... and jump down a sick boy's throat!

EDNA RAE: You hush, too, Roma. You know why you're arguing? Because you care about one another.

JENNINGS: Edna Rae's right, Henry. I do care about what happens to you.

BUDDY: Yeah. Well, maybe I know more than you think. (*Pulls a small notebook from his back pocket. Looks at ROMA, as if for advice.*)

ROMA: (Nods.) Go ahead, show it to him.

(*BUDDY hands JENNINGS the notebook, sits down.*)

JENNINGS: What's this? (*Begins turning pages.*)

ROMA: You told Jennings about the book you've been writing, didn't you, Buddy?

BUDDY: Yeah, but I doubt if he remembers.

ROMA: He's been working on it since he got sick.

BUDDY: (*To JENNINGS.*) But it wasn't till I lay sick all that time that I read the books you wrote. About how you and my mama played and sang at the Rockytop Festival, how you all went together back then.

JENNINGS: (*Leafing through the notebook.*) I know you must have heard talk. But that's all it is—talk. I loved your mama. Begged her to stay here and marry me. She wouldn't. (*Picks up a copy of How America Came to Cordell County, flips to a section of photographs, points.*) Who is that?

BUDDY: My Mama.

EDNA RAE: (*Looks at the book.*) I remember your mama, Buddy.

JENNINGS: That feller there beside her, who's that?

BUDDY: (*Grinning a little.*) That's you.

JENNINGS: Well, that feller could have been your daddy. Would've been. But wasn't.—I saw you once, when you were about six months old, up in Ohio. I went up there, after you were born, tried again to get your mama to come home. Asked her again to marry me. She wouldn't.— I'm not your Daddy, son. (*Hands notebook back to BUDDY.*)

BUDDY: (*Looking at the notebook, turning it in his hands.*) Shoot! I thought I had it figured!—If you're not, who is then?

JENNINGS: I believe your daddy was Jack Daugherty, country musician your mama joined up with after she left here. He was killed in a wreck in Baton Rouge, Louisiana. Your mama ought to have told you. Still ought to. (*JENNINGS hands BUDDY a flashlight.*) Why don't you go see if I was right about that tire?

(*BUDDY exits with flashlight.*)

JENNINGS: (*To EDNA RAE.*) You <u>are</u> right, Edna Rae. I care about that boy.

ROMA: I just wish you wouldn't jump all over him about school.

EDNA RAE: Don't be like the woman with the sick cat, Jennings.

JENNINGS: What do you mean, Edna Rae?

EDNA RAE: This woman had a sick cat, had to give it medicine. Every day she had the awfullest time getting that cat to take its medicine. The fur flew! One day she knocked the medicine over and it spilled out on the floor. The cat walked over and licked it up!

JENNINGS: (*Grins.*) I'll remember that, Edna Rae! The woman with the sick cat!

BUDDY: (*Comes back onstage, cuts off flashlight.*) Three tires! Three! Flat as biscuits! You were right, Jennings. Look here. I pulled this out of the left front with wire pliers. (*Hands JENNINGS something.*)

JENNINGS: (*Inspects a small, metal object.*) Um-hmm. (*To ROMA and EDNA RAE.*) One tire was already going down on us when we were coming up the drive there. You were coming along right behind us. You probably picked some up too, Roma. (*Turns the object in his fingers.*)

BUDDY: No her tires are all right.

ROMA: What is that thing?

EDNA RAE: That's a jack-rock.

JENNINGS: (*He drops it on the table, picks it up, drops it again.*) —Sow a bunch of these on a road, you can ruin a lot of tires.

EDNA RAE: During that last strike, the miners put em on fishing rods, and cast them down off the road bank into the road. If <u>their</u> people came up the road in cars, they reeled em in. If the <u>scabs</u> came up the road, they left em layin!

JENNINGS: I bet the road from the mailbox up is full of em.

BUDDY: (*Turns, with flashlight.*) I'll go down and see.

JENNINGS: No. Wait.

BUDDY: I bet I know who strowed em. Cecil Pedigo. I saw him one day down at the Tradin Post, rollin one around and around in his hand.

EDNA RAE: The more you know about some people, the better you like dogs!

JENNINGS: (*Staring out into the darkness.*) I wonder— (*Suddenly.*) —Cut out the lights! (*Motions to BUDDY.*) The lights. Turn them off!

(*BUDDY turns off lights. The stage darkens.*)

JENNINGS: Don't turn on that flashlight, either.

ROMA: (*Whisper.*) What is it?

EDNA RAE: What did you see, Jennings?

JENNINGS: Down on the road... car pulled over and the lights went out.—I might have known.

ROMA: Known what?

JENNINGS: Cecil's not finished with me yet.

EDNA RAE: You know he's been accused of burning down people's barns.

JENNINGS: Why, that's part of the Pedigo heritage—a Pedigo's God-given right!

BUDDY: What you gonna do, Jennings?

JENNINGS: I'll have to go down there.

(*Sounds of JENNINGS moving around, opening and closing a drawer. Metallic sound of pistol being tested.*)

ROMA: Jennings, don't—-

EDNA RAE: You're already hurt, Jennings.

JENNINGS: I'm hurt. But if that's Cecil, and I don't go down there, I'll be hurt worse: I'll be out a barn.

ROMA: I'm goin with you.

JENNINGS: No, you stay right here—all of you. I'll be all right.— Look there! See that?

ROMA: Where?

BUDDY: I saw it.

(*JENNINGS exits silently.*)

EDNA RAE: Looked like on the branch-bank—below the barn. A light... just for a minute. Then it went out. He probably had to have a little light to come up through them willows on the branch-bank—right, Jennings? Jennings? (*To ROMA.*) Jennings is gone!

ROMA: Let's be real quiet, so we can hear. (*After a silence.*) I never did see anything. Maybe there's not anything down there.

BUDDY: Bet there is—'cause I saw a light. And I bet it's Cecil.

ROMA: Oh, I hope not!

BUDDY: I might ought to go down there, anyway!

ROMA: No, you're not going.—Shhh! Listen!

(*Distant sound of a MAN talking.*)

EDNA RAE: I hear something.

ROMA: Shhh!

BUDDY: Look! There! A light, right at the corner of the barn.

EDNA RAE: It's stayin on, right in the same spot.

ROMA: Is that Jennings, or somebody else?

BUDDY: That's Jennings' big old six-cell flashlight. I know that light.

EDNA RAE: Is it Jennings talking?

ROMA: I can't tell.

BUDDY: The light went out.

EDNA RAE: Now what?

BUDDY: Maybe it'll come back on.

ROMA: (*After silence.*) I guess not. Oh, Jennings… down there in the dark… with a pistol. No tellin—.

BUDDY: Car lights!

EDNA RAE: Over on the road, looks like.

BUDDY: It's turning, right in the road… going back the other way.

ROMA: Where's Jennings? If that was his flashlight at the barn, why didn't it ever—-? Oh, Lord, let it come back on!

(*ROMA reacts to sound of footsteps on the porch.*)

EDNA RAE: Somebody! (*In the semi-darkness, she looks around for something to defend herself with. Picks up a fireplace poker.*)

ROMA: Jennings? Jennings, is—?

(*JENNINGS enters.*)

JENNINGS: Yeah.

ROMA: Oh!

(*EDNA RAE puts down the poker.*)

BUDDY: Was it him, Jennings? Was it Cecil?

JENNINGS: Yeah. That car—it turned around, didn't it?

BUDDY: Turned right in the road, looked like.

ROMA: Went back toward Jewell Hill.

JENNINGS: Good.

BUDDY: Can I turn on a light?

JENNINGS: I guess.

(*Lights come on to reveal JENNINGS, pistol in belt, holding clothes draped across left arm, in left hand a gasoline can, and long flashlight in right hand.*)

ROMA: What's all that?

(*JENNINGS holds up can.*)

EDNA RAE: Gas?

JENNINGS: Actually, number one kerosene, Edna Rae. But just as good to burn a barn.

(*JENNINGS sets down the can, holds up shirt, lays it on table; holds up pants, lays them on table; holds up cap with Cordell County Sheriff's Department lettered on it.*)

ROMA: What was he going to do, Jennings? Use those rags to start a fire?

JENNINGS: Rags? These are Cecil's clothes!

BUDDY: You made him strip!

JENNINGS: What did I want with the carcass? The hide's enough.

(*JENNINGS motions to BUDDY to help him. Picks up hammer from shelf, tacks Cecil's pants, then shirt, then hat, on the wall, so they are displayed like the skin of an animal.*)

JENNINGS: You've heard of nailing somebody's hide to the wall.

ROMA: He's out there—? Oh my God!

(*BUDDY laughs.*)

ROMA: So that <u>was</u> him, turning his car over there on the road?

JENNINGS: Yeah.

EDNA RAE: Where will he go now?

JENNINGS: To get some clothes, I'd think!

BUDDY: What about his beeper?

JENNINGS: Must have left that in the car.

BUDDY: Old Cecil, headin out in his Pontiac in nothin but his shoes, shorts, and his beeper!

JENNINGS: Just shoes and beeper, I guess. Wasn't wearing any shorts.

ROMA: Is it going to be a feud now? Are you going to have to sit up every night to see if he tries it again?

JENNINGS: If I have to, yes. Anyway, it's not Cecil. It's Hilliard. But I'm gonna fight him. He's not going to burn me out.

EDNA RAE: We'll help you, Jennings, if it comes to that. We'll take turns settin up, won't we, Roma?

ROMA: Sure.

BUDDY: I know what we could do! Let's dig a big hole and cover it over with sticks and leaves, and have big sharp sticks in the bottom of it! (*When ROMA and JENNINGS stare disapprovingly, BUDDY changes the subject.— To ROMA.*) Told you it'd be Cecil down there at the barn. Wish I'd bet you money! (*To JENNINGS.*) Can I go jack up your car and start fixing them tires?

JENNINGS: You can't see to do it. Wait till morning, Buddy.

BUDDY: I'll turn Roma's car lights on your car. (*Looks to ROMA for permission.*) Is that all right?

(*ROMA nods, looks to JENNINGS for his agreement.*)

JENNINGS: (*With a wave of his hand.*) Go on then!

(*BUDDY exits.*)

JENNINGS: (*After a moment of awkward silence.*) I want to stay, Roma. I want to stay and fight!

EDNA RAE: You do it, Jennings. We'll fight with you.

JENNINGS: (*To ROMA.*) What do you think?

ROMA: (*Crosses to him, kisses him.*) That's what I think!

JENNINGS: (*Holds her.*) I have so much to tell you, Roma!

ROMA: I have things to tell you, too!

JENNINGS: I left because I was so ashamed of myself, and you were mad at me.

ROMA: I wasn't mad at you. Disappointed. Not mad.

JENNINGS: I—felt like I couldn't stay here. Then I— I found out I couldn't stay away—from you. —So back I come. And right now, I feel like I'm really back, and it feels the way it used to feel here.

ROMA: How does it feel?

JENNINGS: Mean, and sweet. (*Gestures to Cecil's clothes on the wall.*) Mean, and sweet. This place is Cecil, and Hilliard, and that's mean, but it's you, too, and you're sweet!

ROMA: I'm not sugar, nor salt, nor nobody's honey.

JENNINGS: (*Hugs her.*) Yes you are.

EDNA RAE: You know what you said to Buddy? You said, "I'm not your daddy, son."

JENNINGS: I did?

ROMA: You said it. But you still can be, Jennings. You already act like you are.

EDNA RAE: (*To ROMA.*) Don't forget who's been actin like a mama to him since he got sick.

JENNINGS: (*Goes to window, looks out, turns back.*) I'm not leaving again, Roma.

ROMA: It used to be the smart ones left here. Now it's no trick to leave. You have to be smart to stay!

EDNA RAE: You will take us to Twitty City, won't you, Jennings?

JENNINGS: (*Grins.*) I will! — I'm home, Roma. I'm back! Remember I told you once you were speeding me up, and I felt like a lake turning over? Well, it's different now, more like—years ago, first time I went to Europe, I was on this student ship, and when it moved out of the harbor, for the first time I felt the swell of the ocean. The ship rose...and rose...and then fell, it seemed, forever. That's what it feels like now. I feel like I'm setting out for God knows where, toward something shining white, far away, on a hill. But—I've been there before...because it's this place I'm headed for. Only now it's all strange and new!

EDNA RAE: Like the song says, you can go home, you just can't go back.

ROMA: That's right, Edna Rae. You can't go back, but you can go on. (*To JENNINGS.*) Can we go with you?

JENNINGS: Go with me? You're it! You and Edna Rae and Buddy. My first, best country! You are country— you have to admit! (*Embraces her.*)

(*BUDDY enters.*)

BUDDY: Got to get them tires fixed, because I want to see that whale before it gets gone from Jewell— (*Stops when he sees JENNINGS and ROMA embracing.*) —Hill.

JENNINGS: We'll get those tires fixed, and see that whale if it's still in Jewell Hill!

BUDDY: All right!

JENNINGS: But we've got to get started pretty soon on putting your house back together. Out back here.

BUDDY: I want to bring Mom Shelton and Grandpa over to see it when we get it back together.

JENNINGS: Sure.

ROMA: (*Looks toward Jennings' guitar.*) Jennings, play something for us.

JENNINGS: (*Reaches for guitar.*) Play? Play what?

EDNA RAE: You know it. It's one of your favorites, and we've been practicing up on it.

(*EDNA RAE whispers in JENNINGS' ear, steps back, and holds hands with ROMA.*)

JENNINGS: Black Waters? It's been a long time. Let's see? (*He begins to play.*)

ROMA and EDNA RAE: (*Sing.*) "I come from the mountains, Kentucky's my home," etc....

(*EDNA RAE takes BUDDY by the arm, pulls him in beside her.*)

EDNA RAE: Come on, Buddy, you know this too.

(*The singing continues. ROMA, as she sings, reaches out and touches the tip of JENNINGS' nose with the tip of her finger. The lights fade with the last lines of "Black Waters."*)

THE END

Peggy Howell in *His First, Best Country* by Jim Wayne Miller, Horse Cave Theatre, 1992

Jim Wayne Miller

Jim Wayne Miller, a native of North Carolina, was graduated from Berea College in Kentucky and received his Ph.D. from Vanderbilt University. He was a professor of German language and literature at Western Kentucky University for 33 years. He served as a consultant to the Appalachian Studies programs in Kentucky, Tennessee, and Ohio and was a visiting Professor in Appalachian Studies at the Berea College Appalachian Center.

His honors include the Alice Lloyd Memorial Prize for Appalachian Poetry in 1967, the 1980 Thomas Wolfe Literary Award, the Zoe Kincaid Brockman Memorial Award, the Appalachian Writers Association Book of the Year Award and the Appalachian Consortium Laurel Leaves Award.

His books include *Copperhead Cane* (1964), *Dialogue With A Dead Man* (1974), *The Mountains Have Come Closer* (1980), *Vein of Words* (1984), *Nostalgia for 70* (1986), *Brier: His Book* (1988), and *Newfound* (1989). His last book, *The Brier Poems*, was published posthumously in 1997. More information on Jim Wayne Miller and his work can be found at www.jimwaynemiller.com.

Tom Williams and Rebecca Ryland in *Piggyback* by Sallie Bingham, Horse Cave Theatre, 1994

PIGGYBACK
by
Sallie Bingham

Warren Hammack and Tom Williams in *Piggyback* by Sallie Bingham, Horse Cave Theatre, 1994

Piggyback opened on June 24, 1994, with the following cast:

DORIS ULMANN	*Rebecca Ryland*
JOHN JACOB NILES	*Tom Williams*
PENCIL MARCUM	*Warren Hammack*
QUIZZIE	*Katy Edenfield*
TESSA	*Jaana Sipila*
GEORGE UBLER	*Tom Luce*

Director: Pamela White
Stage Manager: Myrle Curry
Set Design: Patricia G. Skinner
Lighting Design: Philip Hooter
Costume Design: Marty Hagedorn
Properties Master: Patricia G. Skinner
Music Director: Gabrielle Mattingly Gray
Classical Music Composition and Fiddle Improvisation: Gabrielle Mattingly Gray
Ballad Coach and Dulcimer and Piano Improvisations: Daniel Dutton
Curtain Music: Southwestern Pulaski County High School Madrigal Singers
Technical Director: Steven R. McCormick
Production Assistants: Laura Bucher, Andrea Conque

Warren Hammack, Tom Williams, Katy Edenfield and Rebecca Ryland in *Piggyback* by Sallie Bingham, Horse Cave Theatre, 1994

Characters:

DORIS ULMANN, *fifty-two, a frail, elegant figure, usually dressed in white. Although she is not physically strong, she is vibrant and charming. She speaks immaculate English yet there is a hint of woodenness as though each word is translated literally from her native German.*

JOHN JACOB NILES, *a small, handsome man, forty years old. He has escaped his Kentucky background by enlisting in the First World War and subsequently embarking on a singing career.*

TESSA, *Doris' maid*

GEORGE WEBLER, *Doris' chauffeur*

PENCIL MARCUM, *a weathered mountain man*

QUIZZIE, *his young girl friend*

Place: A Park Avenue apartment; a hotel in Whitesburg, Kentucky; the porch of a mountain cabin; and small country roads.

Time: 1932 and 1933.

ACT ONE

SCENE ONE

Early morning, spring, 1932. The living room of a smart Park Avenue apartment. The elegance of the interior may be suggested by claret-red velvet upholstery, inviting cushions, oriental bronzes, a wistful madonna, and an immaculate white polar bear rug. JOHNNY stands looking at a row of framed photographs on the wall.

Voices, off: a brief domestic discussion in German. DORIS enters. She is dressed in a long white dress and leans lightly on a bamboo cane. She carries photographs.

DORIS: I am sorry to have kept you waiting.

JOHNNY: You said to come early.

DORIS: It never occurred to me that you would take me at my word.

JOHNNY: That's a habit of mine. I'm sorry.

DORIS: It's a beautiful spring day, I was glad to be forced out of my bed earlier than usual. I was up until two A.M., developing.

JOHNNY: Here?

DORIS: Where else? I have converted a bathroom to a darkroom. I photograph during the day and develop at night. (*Showing him photographs.*) These are from Virginia. I have been more deeply moved by my mountaineers than by any of those New York faces.

JOHNNY: (*Looking at photographs on the wall.*) Awfully somber.

DORIS: My celebrities. Albert Einstein, Calvin Coolidge, Anna Pavlova... I don't photograph theatrical people, as a rule; they do not wish to show character in their faces.

JOHNNY: I am a theatrical person.

DORIS: I don't propose to photograph you, Mr. Niles.

JOHNNY: (*Looking at framed portraits.*) Is this your signature?

DORIS: A red D inside a red U.

JOHNNY: (*Pointing to one photograph.*) And this J?

DORIS: Jaeger. My married name. I don't use it now...My sitters eat sandwiches while I photograph them, drink cocktails, smoke cigarettes. Would you like something?

JOHNNY: No. No, thank you.

DORIS: Sit down, please. Do you smoke?

JOHNNY: No.

DORIS: No vices whatsoever? (*JOHNNY smiles.*) What part of Kentucky do you call home?

JOHNNY: Louisville, but I've traveled extensively in Europe—

DORIS: When I saw you last night, at the Grand Street Theater, playing Woodrow Wilson—

JOHNNY: What did you think?

DORIS: I thought, "There it is again — the voice of the mountains."

JOHNNY: Not quite right for Wilson.

DORIS: It's those little words I love — tarnation — words like that. So specific. Like a drop of water. "That woman-person" — they called me in Virginia. "She sure is a traipsing woman-person." I liked that. So clear. Like a blade of light.

JOHNNY: I sing, as well — not just the southern mountain songs. I have a full repertoire from the European —

DORIS: (*Interrupting.*) You are a troubadour. A traveling minstrel.

JOHNNY: Marion Kirby and I have engagements every season, in this country and in Europe. Would you like to hear us, one day?

DORIS: (*Laughing.*) No. I noticed your strong arms, last night. Is your back strong, too?

JOHNNY: (*Standing up.*) I've hoed corn, planted tobacco. Don't be afraid to look.

DORIS: I'm not afraid. (*She comes closer, delicately touches his shoulders.*) How old are you?

JOHNNY: I'm forty.

DORIS: You look younger.

JOHNNY: We're both...youthful.

DORIS: I don't discuss my age.

JOHNNY: What kind of work, exactly —?

DORIS: Beast-of-all-burdens. Handy man.

JOHNNY: Assistant?

DORIS: I have no assistants. I work with a very large, very heavy camera. The plates are 6 1/2 by 8 1/2 inches. Glass. Very heavy, as well. They must be packed in wooden crates. I carry a tripod, lenses, tools and extra parts. Medicines, in a special valise, and of course clothes — and food. I am very careful about my diet. Nothing fried ... I take along an electric water heater, and a large water container. So — your job, young man, will be to carry all those things.

JOHNNY: To carry things ...

DORIS: Yes. As you can see, I am not very strong.

JOHNNY: Why, what is your problem?

DORIS: I have no problem.

JOHNNY: You limp, use a cane —

DORIS: I was foolish enough to fall on the sidewalk outside this building, last winter. Very foolish. I should have seen the ice. The break did not heal properly. And then, as I told you, I must watch my diet — but none of that is what you would call a "Problem." It is simply ... a fact of my existence. I am used, very used, to such facts — and no! I do not ask for pity. Never! But I do ask for your help — and I will make it worth your while. You know the mountains, you can help me find the out-of-the-way places.

JOHNNY: I can certainly read a map, but those dim lanes are not on any map.

DORIS: Dim lanes?

JOHNNY: That's what they call them.

DORIS: You are a poet, as well as a singer?

JOHNNY: Sing — dance — collect the old songs — A little bit of everything —

DORIS: I like your honesty. Of course, you'll have new clothes. (*She writes an address on a scrap of paper, hands it to him.*) Go to this address. I want you completely outfitted for hot weather in mountainous country. Now — tell me about your poetry.

JOHNNY: I'd rather say it than talk about it.

DORIS: Very well.

JOHNNY: (*Reciting from memory.*)
Pure water is the best of gifts
That man to man can bring;
But who am I that I should have
The best of everything?
Let princes revel at the pump;
Let peers with ponds make free —
Whiskey and wine and even beer
Is good enough for me ...

They laughed at that, when I read it at the Algonquin Hotel. At the Round Table, as they called it, but that round table had a head —

DORIS: And you were not it —

JOHNNY: No.

DORIS: Your poem has a certain charm. Tell me, do you drink?

JOHNNY: Only to enjoy myself.

DORIS: I do not believe you are so moderate.

JOHNNY: I'm not! We Kentuckians take our enjoyment seriously.

DORIS: We will see! Be ready to leave in six weeks, on June thirtieth. Is it agreed?

JOHNNY: Just one thing.

DORIS: What is it?

JOHNNY: I have several singing engagements in July, with Marion.

DORIS: Who is this woman?

JOHNNY: My singing partner — very large, with a formidable temper.

DORIS: Surely you can cancel these engagements.

JOHNNY: You don't know Marion.

DORIS: Nor wish to! Take care of this matter, Mr. Niles.

JOHNNY: I'll do the best I can...What do I call you?

DORIS: People who don't know me call me Miss Ulmann.

JOHNNY: Miss... Doris?

DORIS: If you prefer.

JOHNNY: How long is this jaunt?

DORIS: Sometimes I am gone for months.

JOHNNY: I see.

DORIS: Is there something that might keep you here in New York or force you to make a sudden return?

JOHNNY: I'm footloose and fancy free.

DORIS: You're very handsome, to be so free. Very well. Till next month, then. (*She turns to exit.*)

JOHNNY: Miss Doris?

DORIS: Yes?

JOHNNY: I have a little Chevrolet — a workhorse of a car.

DORIS: George will drive us, in my Lincoln.

JOHNNY: Over those mountain roads?

DORIS: George drove a German general in the World War — on the Russian Front.

JOHNNY: I see ...

DORIS: Any more questions?

JOHNNY: Well, if I have the clothes, and the back, and the arms —

DORIS: Isn't there something else you want to ask?

JOHNNY: No.

DORIS: No?

JOHNNY: Not now.

DORIS: Very well. (*She shakes hands.*) You are at the start of a very big adventure.

JOHNNY: If I'm to be any use at all, I must have my own camera.

DORIS: None of my other assistants —

JOHNNY: How many others have gone to the back of beyond with you, Doris?

DORIS: I'm not accustomed to being called by my first name on such brief acquaintance.

JOHNNY: How many others?

DORIS: Only Tessa — my maid. And George, to drive.

JOHNNY: I'm not a maid, or a chauffeur.

DORIS: (*Quietly.*) I know that, Mr. Niles.

(*DORIS exits.*)

JOHNNY: (*Takes paper out of his pocket and reads the address.*) Lexington Avenue and Sixty-First Street. Whitman Brothers Tailor, next door to a haberdasher... She'll have ordered everything — probably her husband bought his clothes there. So I'm to be her fancy man.

(*JOHNNY puts paper in his pocket. WEBLER enters, with an envelope.*)

WEBLER: The madam left this for you.

JOHNNY: (*Taking envelope.*) I believe I know what this is.

WEBLER: The madam is very generous.

JOHNNY: How long have you known her?

WEBLER: Eleven years — in service with her and the doctor.

JOHNNY: The doctor? What sort of man —?

WEBLER: Good day, Mr. Niles.

(*WEBLER exits.*)

JOHNNY: (*Opens the envelope, reads.*) "Have faith, Mr. Niles." Faith! (*He laughs, looks around the room.*) Faith, my dear Miss Ulmann, butters no parsnips.

(*JOHNNY puts the paper in his pocket and exits.*)

SCENE TWO

Morning. Late June. The scene is the same. The stage is now cluttered with boxes, crates and trunks. JOHNNY, dressed in a heavy tweed suit, shirt and tie, is on his knees, hammering nails into the lid of a large wooden crate. DORIS, dressed in white, wearing a small hat, stands watching him, her arms folded.

DORIS: Remember, those are glass plates.

JOHNNY: You've told me three times. (*Stands, takes off jacket.*) It's hot weather for hammering. (*Carefully lays jacket on the chair.*) You don't mind?

DORIS: I prefer my gentlemen fully dressed. However, in an emergency ...

JOHNNY: Thanks. (*He finishes hammering the crate lid down as DORIS watches.*) That about it?

DORIS: I must consult my list. (*Takes long list out of pocket.*) Let me see... Food box. (*As she reads from the list, JOHNNY indicates each box.*) Tools. Where are the uninflated tires?

JOHNNY: George took them down to the Lincoln.

DORIS: Very well... Bolts of black cloth.

JOHNNY: In here.

DORIS: Claw hammer and nails in the tool box?

JOHNNY: I put them in myself.

DORIS: Now... My clothes.

JOHNNY: (*Counting trunks.*) One, two, three, four, five —

DORIS: I always wear white in summer. Dotted swiss. I hope I'll be able to find a good laundress. In Virginia, there was a fine old laundress named Queenie. She called me, "That white angel with black eyes ..."

JOHNNY: You must have tipped her well.

DORIS: She liked me. (*Returning to list.*) <u>Your</u> clothes...

JOHNNY: (*Counting.*) One. Two.

DORIS: Only two suitcases? I assume you made a list of the contents...

JOHNNY: I know them by heart... Two tweed suits. You forgot the heat.

DORIS: I want you to look decent, Mr. Niles. George wears a uniform, no matter what the temperature.

JOHNNY: George has a bee in his bonnet.

DORIS: He worries about me. Continue.

JOHNNY: Three shirts, two ties, six pairs of socks, two new pairs of shoes — one with cleated soles for mountain climbing — six undershirts... undershorts —

DORIS: How many?

JOHNNY: Eight, for some reason.

DORIS: That's the number I ordered.

JOHNNY: Two handkerchiefs, and a cap. (*He pulls cap out of his pocket, puts it on.*)

DORIS: Very becoming.

JOHNNY: Jodhpur pants — custom made — and boots. That's it.

DORIS: Now for my equipment. (*She consults the list. JOHNNY indicates each crate or box, as before.*) The Corona-view camera. Ten crates of plates. The tripod —

JOHNNY: I packed two. A large one, and a small —

DORIS: (*She picks up a small box, opens it, takes out a small camera, 4 x 5.*) I purchased this little Rollieflex yesterday. Here... (*She hands the camera to JOHNNY.*) See how it feels. (*JOHNNY awkwardly manipulates the camera.*) I'll show you how to use it. And three boxes of small plates, to go with it. That will be enough, for a start.

JOHNNY: Thank you.

DORIS: You're welcome. (*Matter-of-fact.*) It will give you a taste of the art — without my interference, or influence. At the very least, something to do. (*Returning to list.*) Where's the valise of medicines?

JOHNNY: Here. (*He continues to hold camera for another beat. Then he replaces it in its box.*) I have my own... instrument, you know.

DORIS: Where is it? It's not on my list.

JOHNNY: Here. (*He takes out a long cloth bag which has been partially concealed behind the other gear. As DORIS watches, he unties the ties on the bag and takes out a home-made dulcimer.*) Molded on the medieval rebeck, which had three strings and a bow. Mine has four strings, and no bow — I pick it. (*He plays a few chords.*) "And the jocund rebecks sound..." That's Milton.

DORIS: Let me touch it. (*She plucks the strings, a disconsolate sound.*) Strange.

JOHNNY: "Harpes, lutes, and crouddes right delycyous ..." Stephen Hawes. He was a poet, and a groom to Henry VII.

DORIS: A poet, and a groom. Useful combination. Why does it make such a doleful sound?

JOHNNY: That's its nature. Mountain people call it the sad minor. Really the minor third. (*He plays more chords.*)

DORIS: What are these woods?

JOHNNY: Kentucky walnut. Curly maple. Wild cherry. Rosewood. All held together with good French rabbit-skin glue.

DORIS: French?

JOHNNY: I found it in a little village during the war, in Normandy. I crashed a plane there. (*Continuing with his description.*) The strings are steel, covered with bronze.

DORIS: What do you call it?

JOHNNY: A dulcimer.

DORIS: Play me something. (*She sits down on one of the crates, lays her cane on the floor.*)

JOHNNY: I've been collecting ballads since I was a child. (*He tunes the dulcimer.*) When I first started collecting, people thought I was quaint and cute. Nobody had ever tried to write down the old songs.

DORIS: (*Very simply.*) You know something. (*She moves, awkwardly, to another crate closer to Johnny.*)

JOHNNY: Yes.

DORIS: Tell me.

JOHNNY: This was the first one I ever wrote down. Granny Cilla Baker sang it for me, on Red Bird Creek, near Manchester. She was 82 years old. (*He plays and sings.*)
For many years he lay lamenting,
A prisoner to the Turkish king,
The Turkish king he had one daughter,
She was of high degree.
She stole the keys of her father's prison,
Said, "They be a prisoner I must see."

DORIS: Go on.

JOHNNY: It's long.

DORIS: Never mind.

JOHNNY: (*Singing as he plays the dulcimer.*)
She took him to her father's castle,
She bad him drink the strongest wine,
I do not want Lord Bateman's siller,
I only wish that she were mine.

DORIS: Siller?

JOHNNY: Silver. Money.

DORIS: Go on.

JOHNNY: (*Singing.*)
They made a vow, they made a promise
They made hit free, so hit would stand,
He vowed he'd marry ne'er another,
She vowed she'd have no other man.

(*As JOHNNY sings this last verse, TESSA enters silently and stands listening. She is a pretty young woman, wearing a maid's uniform and cap. She carries a small silver tray with an envelope on it.*)

TESSA: (*Softly.*) Madam ...

DORIS: What is it?

TESSA: They said it was urgent.

DORIS: Bring it here.

TESSA: (*Bringing envelope to her.*) They're waiting for an answer.

(*DORIS reads the note. An expression of irritation crosses her face. JOHNNY and TESSA watch her closely. DORIS glances up, frowns. JOHNNY begins to put away his dulcimer in the cloth bag. TESSA moves closer to observe him.*)

TESSA: What is that thing?

JOHNNY: A mountain dulcimer.

(*TESSA touches the string. A single, discordant note. She laughs, looks at JOHNNY.*)

TESSA: Sounds so strange...

JOHNNY: It's got a sad voice.

DORIS: (*To TESSA.*) Come here. (*TESSA scampers to her.*) Tell them, no answer. (*She folds the note up tightly, thrusts it into her pocket.*) Why are you standing there?

TESSA: Madame, they said —

DORIS: I don't care what they said. Go.

(*TESSA glances at JOHNNY pleadingly, then exits.*)

DORIS: She's a foolish soul.

JOHNNY: Sweet, though.

DORIS: You must learn not to influence my people. I won't stand for it. (*JOHNNY does not respond. DORIS takes out her list. Her hands are trembling.*) There must be no disagreement between us, on this point. Let me see, now... (*She consults her list, frowning.*)

JOHNNY: What was in that letter, Doris?

DORIS: Apologize to me, please.

JOHNNY: What for?

DORIS: You have unintentionally hurt me.

JOHNNY: Miss Doris, I am here to help you with your trip, not with your feelings.

DORIS: Then we will discuss my trip. Get out the map. Show me your plan.

JOHNNY: (*Takes out map, spreads it on table.*) Tonight we'll be in Washington. The Raleigh Hotel. Very comfortable. You'll enjoy it. Tomorrow morning, we'll have the congressional breakfast. A dollar and seventy-five cents — everything, even the things you dream of.

DORIS: What do I dream of, Johnny?

JOHNNY: I'll tell you what my dreams are: Hot homemade biscuits, melt in your mouth. With butter. Rasher bacon. Smoke-cured. Scrambled eggs, or fried, if you prefer.

DORIS: I do not eat fried foods.

JOHNNY: Home-made damson plum jelly —

DORIS: You're always hungry.

JOHNNY: I've never had enough, since I came to New York.

DORIS: Show me the map. After Washington, where?

JOHNNY: Here. (*He traces the line of their journey with his finger.*) After Washington, we drive to White Sulphur Springs. Very elegant.

DORIS: I can't see.

JOHNNY: Come here.

(*DORIS looks for her cane. It is out of reach. She looks at JOHNNY, who returns her look steadily.*)

DORIS: I can't reach my cane.

(*JOHNNY does not reply. DORIS begins to raise herself from the crate without the benefit of her cane. She moves with difficulty. At last erect, she takes a single, staggering step towards JOHNNY. About to fall, she holds her arms out. JOHNNY leaps up, goes to her, steadies her. Then he leads her towards the table on which the map is displayed.*)

DORIS: I want to see.

JOHNNY: In a minute. What was in that letter?

DORIS: What business is it of yours?

JOHNNY: Everything is my business, now.

DORIS: It was from my husband.

JOHNNY: The doctor?

DORIS: Yes.

JOHNNY: You always call him the doctor.

DORIS: I don't like the way it sounds: ex-husband. That's not the way to describe a human being to whom one has been married for quite some years.

JOHNNY: What does he want?

DORIS: Nothing I am free to discuss.

JOHNNY: It's money, isn't it?

DORIS: Please, Johnny. Not now. Let me look at the map.

JOHNNY: Everyone wants something from you. All those people at your table, at the Grand Street Theater. Your party, you called them. Vultures, preying on you. I saw that right away...

DORIS: There are some things I can do —

JOHNNY: I want you to know one thing, Miss Doris. There is nothing you can do for me.

DORIS: Nothing?

JOHNNY: You don't believe me?

DORIS: Why should I? You are a hungry young man. Hungry for all the things of this world. I have some of them. Hungry, even, for affection — is that something to be ashamed of?

JOHNNY: I can't convince you with words — but you'll see — when we're traveling those mountain roads, together —

DORIS: With George.

JOHNNY: In the front seat of the Lincoln, with his box of uninflated rubber tires. We'll be in back, with our boxes and crates stacked around us —

(*During this speech, the light gradually brightens.*)

JOHNNY: Nobody in the mountains will ever have seen such a sight as the three of us, and all that gear, in the Lincoln —

DORIS: Now show me the map.

JOHNNY: (*Showing her.*) In Whitesburg, we'll stay at the Daniel Boone Hotel. I'll see that you're comfortable —

DORIS: One thing.

JOHNNY: What is it?

DORIS: No little flirtations. No stops by the side of the road. Nothing to embarrass me.

JOHNNY: Or George?

DORIS: I'm serious.

JOHNNY: Tell me about the doctor.

DORIS: Don't you understand, there are certain situations, where there has been so much pain. They can't be summed up, in words.

JOHNNY: No promises, then.

DORIS: No?

JOHNNY: It's better, that way. Remember the ballad? (*He sings softly.*)
They made a vow, they made a promise,
They made it free, so hit would stand —

(*As he sings, images of mountain country are appearing across their faces. Green leaves. Laurel in bloom. Mountains.*)

JOHNNY: (*Still singing.*)
He vowed he'd marry ne'er another,
She vowed she'd have no other man ...

(*JOHNNY grabs his jacket, and they exit.*)

JOHNNY: (*Still singing.*)
She took him down unto the sea sad,
She left him sailing o'er the main,
Said: "Fare ye well, my own, my true love,
I fear I'll ne'er see you again.

(*Images of the mountains fade as they exit but the light remains bright. WEBLER, in full chauffeur's uniform, enters and begins to gather up the crates and bags. When he picks up JOHNNY'S dulcimer, he looks at the bag curiously, then shrugs, with something both awed and indignant in his expression.*)

SCENE THREE

It is evening of the second day of the journey. DORIS and JOHNNY are seated in the back seat of the Lincoln, among boxes of clothes, camera equipment, etc. WEBLER is in the front seat, in his uniform, driving. NOTE: set can be conveyed with three chairs.

DORIS: (*Looking at map, with JOHNNY.*) Mullens! Welch! Cucumber! Squire! Wolf Pen! What names!

JOHNNY: When we get over from West Virginia into Kentucky, tomorrow, you'll have an even finer selection: Canada, Zebulon, Flat Lick —

DORIS: Those names... Last night at the White Sulphur Inn, I understood what we were about to leave behind.

WEBLER: Clean beds, clean water, clean food —

DORIS: Why, certainly. But that's only a part of it. We are leaving behind those smiles, the ones you see all over the good parts of the South: all teeth and lips. You never see those smiles in the north, and I think we will not be seeing them in these mountain towns.

JOHNNY: People hoard their smiles, in poor places.

WEBLER: Nothing to smile about.

DORIS: George, if it were not for you, Johnny and I would have to complain!

WEBLER: The way these people treat you, Mrs. Ulmann —

DORIS: Why, how do they treat me?

WEBLER: Like ordinary.

DORIS: I believe I prefer that. I have been special too long.

WEBLER: I am humiliated, for you, madam, if you will forgive me.

JOHNNY: Humiliated!

DORIS: Hush, Johnny. You do not understand. Of course I forgive you, George. To serve a woman who is being treated "like ordinary" is a serious diminution.

WEBLER: These people do not understand your position, in New York — the distinguished lady who makes all the portraits of celebrities.

DORIS: No, they don't understand. That is the relief of it.

JOHNNY: I believe I see what you mean.

DORIS: Do you? Or are you merely trying to outdo George?

WEBLER: Never fear, Madame. In all the years I have known you —

JOHNNY: Ah, there's the rub.

WEBLER: I believe length of service counts for something, even in this country, Mr. Niles.

JOHNNY: And I am in all ways so new, Mr. Webler — raw, almost, wouldn't you agree?

WEBLER: Whatever you say, Sir.

JOHNNY: Yet I shall outlast them all.

DORIS: Which "all"?

JOHNNY: I'll close this window. (*He starts to close the window between the front and the back seat.*)

DORIS: (*Stopping him.*) No. We have no secrets.

JOHNNY: We will.

(*Silence.*)

WEBLER: Mrs. Ulmann, if you wish to close that glass —

DORIS: I do not wish, George.

WEBLER: It would be of no consequence to me.

DORIS: But of very great consequence to me.

JOHNNY: You are always in the midst of a crowd. It's going to be solitary, though, in the mountains.

DORIS: The last refuge of real Americans. When they are over-run by the modern world, we'll lose our past.

JOHNNY: Have you noticed, Doris — your "types" never have names. You don't record them on your portraits.

DORIS: Their names are of no importance. It is what they represent —

JOHNNY: Yet your name, in all its variations, is important — the red D, the red U, the lost J. They're on all your photographs.

DORIS: Not the J.

JOHNNY: What happened to the good doctor?

WEBLER: That was a sad day.

DORIS: We were divorced.

JOHNNY: That's all there is to say?

(*DORIS nods. JOHHNY takes out his dulcimer.*)

JOHNNY: In that case, I'll sing away a few miles—

DORIS: Good.

(*DORIS leans back, smiling and relaxing, as JOHNNY tunes his dulcimer.*)

JOHNNY: (*Singing.*)
 I gave my love a cherry that hath no stone,
 I gave my love a chicken that hath no bone,
 I gave my love a thimble that hath no end...

DORIS: Do these mountain people really say "hath"?

JOHNNY: They use the king's English as it was in Shakespeare's time. (*He continues to sing.*)
 How could there be a cherry that hath no stone?
 How could there be a chicken that hath no bone?
 How could there be a thimble that hath no end?
 How could there be a baby that's no cryin'?

DORIS: That last, at least, I know to be impossible.

JOHNNY: Have babies figured in your life, Mrs. Jaeger?

DORIS: Please do not call me that, Johnny.

JOHNNY: It seems suitable, today. (*He continues to sing.*)
 A cherry when it's blooming, it hath no stone.
 A chicken when it's pipping, it hath no bone.
 A thimble when it's rolling, it hath no end.
 And a baby when it's sleeping, there's no crying.

DORIS: A fine riddle. Where does it come from?

JOHNNY: It's the second I collected. Miss Wilma Creech of Pine Mountain sung it for me, last summer.

DORIS: Take me to see her, please. With that name, she must have a face worth photographing.

JOHNNY: It'll be a hard climb up.

DORIS: I'll be equal to it.

JOHNNY: And there'll be no satin comforters and tubs of steaming hot water like the White Sulphur.

DORIS: I don't need all that.

WEBLER: Excuse me —

DORIS: What is it?

WEBLER: I believe we are lost. (*He stops the car.*) I took a right turn a mile behind, and now it seems the road has come to an end.

(*ALL peer out the windows.*)

JOHNNY: We're at the edge of a gulch. The road just drops away —

WEBLER: And night coming on. I warned you, Mrs. Ulmann —

SCENE FOUR

A room in the Daniel Boone Hotel in Whitesburg, Kentucky. Stage center, a narrow iron bedstead. DORIS, wearing a white nightgown, lies asleep. Right, a rickety wooden table, with an electric plate. JOHNNY, in shirtsleeves, is heating coffee in a pan on the electric plate. Uncurtained windows. A rocking chair, chest of drawers, and hooks for hanging clothes. A sleeping bag, unrolled. A bare light bulb hangs from the ceiling. The trunks and boxes, still unpacked, are piled in a corner. It is early morning.

JOHNNY: (*He carries a cup of coffee.*) Good morning, Miss Doris. Sun's been up an hour. You said you wanted to get an early start.

DORIS: What day is this, Johnny?

JOHNNY: Wednesday. Beauty was yesterday; this is Whitesburg. I've made coffee — black, good and hot. Wish you'd take milk. It'd be kinder to your poor stomach.

DORIS: (*Sitting up in bed.*) Hand me my wrap, please.

(*JOHNNY does so. Helps her to put it on. Hands her the coffee.*)

DORIS: Thank you...

JOHNNY: How did you sleep?

DORIS: Not so very well. That chicken, last night. It was fried.

JOHNNY: Pain?

DORIS: A little — nothing to speak of.

JOHNNY: You should have waked me.

DORIS: It was not necessary.

JOHNNY: I've arranged for us to visit Aunt Beth Holcolm and her husband, Solomon, today. It's a long way — to the Top of Turkey. You'll need your strength. If I could prevail on the kitchen to send you up some eggs —

DORIS: I never eat in the morning. Who are these people?

JOHNNY: She raises geraniums in pots on the porch. He farms, when he can. They know some of the old songs.

DORIS: How did you find them?

JOHNNY: I have my ways...

DORIS: Tell me.

JOHNNY: (*He refills her cup.*) I found me a contact-man.

DORIS: Already — this morning?

JOHNNY: Early! Ma Hibbler directed me to the Bat-Winger. Now, a bat-wing is a flat, half-pint bottle of some of the good local corn liquor... He sells it, it appears.

DORIS: How much did you offer for his information?

JOHNNY: Twenty-five cents a week, and Sunday dinner here at the Daniel Boone Hotel.

DORIS: Not bad. How will you pay him, Johnny? (*She indicates to JOHNNY that she wants to get out of bed. He helps her.*)

JOHNNY: Out of my expense account. Which dress — ?

DORIS: I must wash, first.

JOHNNY: Things are a little rough —

DORIS: I've been in more remote places. Pour some of that water into the basin, please.

(*JOHNNY pours water from jug into wash basin on the chest of drawers. DORIS takes her cane, goes to the basin, washes while JOHNNY watches.*)

DORIS: Towel, please. (*He hands it to her.*) There — that's better. Now, if you will find the white dotted-swiss in that first trunk — the one with the blue-ribbon bow —

JOHNNY: At your service, Miss Doris. (*With a flourish, JOHNNY opens a trunk and pulls out white garments.*) Which of these —

DORIS: Terrible person! I told you, the one with the blue-ribbon bow...

JOHNNY: (*Bringing her the dress.*) Why do you always wear white?

DORIS: To be fresh, and cool. (*She takes the dress.*) I am, in a way, my own icon. Have you noticed? The women here always touch my clothes.

JOHNNY: And you loan them!

DORIS: Yes...

JOHNNY: But we move on so quickly! There's no time to return the loan.

DORIS: Where is my hat?

JOHNNY: I'll dig for it.

(*While JOHNNY digs into the trunk, DORIS manages to slip the dress over her head. This is an awkward performance and she is clearly determined not to ask for help.*)

JOHNNY: This one? (*He shows her a large leghorn hat.*)

DORIS: Not that... The small hat.

(*JOHHNY finds it, brings it.*)

DORIS: Please. Would you do me up the back?

(*She turns her back to him. He begins to button a low row of buttons, whistling "Black, black, black is the color of my true love's hair."*)

JOHNNY: There... (*She turns to face him.*)

DORIS: Have you packed the plates in the holders?

JOHNNY: I managed to do it before you woke. Eighteen plates. Thirty-six exposures. Will it be enough?

DORIS: For today—perhaps... Ring for Webler, if you please.

JOHNNY: There's no bell system here. I'll go see if he's downstairs. (*JOHNNY walks towards exit.*)

DORIS: Thank you.

(*JOHNNY exits. DORIS goes to the mirror over the chest of drawers and begins to brush her hair. Then she opens a drawer, takes out an enormous purse, begins to pack it with all sorts of paraphernalia. JOHNNY re-enters, followed by WEBLER, who steps in front of JOHNNY and approaches DORIS.*)

WEBLER: Good morning, Mrs. Ulmann. At your service.

DORIS: Take this, please. (*She hands him the enormous purse.*) We are ready to start. Has Mr. Johnny told you where we are going?

WEBLER: I wait to hear from you, Madam.

DORIS: Johnny, you must explain.

JOHNNY: I'll show him as we go along.

DORIS: (*Sitting on the bed.*) Show him the map, Johnny.

JOHNNY: I have it in my head. I can't show it.

DORIS: Johnny.

WEBLER: Perhaps we can get directions from that gentleman downstairs. The... bat-winger, yes?

JOHNNY: Miss Doris. If I'm in charge, here —

DORIS: You are in charge of directions, yes.

JOHNNY: Then I must be allowed to do it my own way.

WEBLER: This... bat-winger told me he knows the roads.

DORIS: Very well, Johnny, we will do it your way, but you will have to sit in the front seat with Webler, to direct him. I had rather thought you would prefer to sit in the back with me.

JOHNNY: (*With effort.*) I will sit in the front.

WEBLER: But my extra tires —

JOHNNY: I will sit on top of the tires!

DORIS: Very well. Hand me my cane ... (*JOHNNY does so. She touches his arm.*) Thank you ... Webler, you may begin to load the car. That crate over there — be careful, it's the glass plates.

(*WEBLER loads himself up, exits.*)

DORIS: We will be down presently. Johnny, don't forget to take along your camera.

JOHNNY: I will not use that camera today, Miss Doris. Possibly never. I'll take the dulcimer — and my notebook— (*He has loaded himself up.*) Now —

DORIS: What a sight you are! But wait — we have not yet planned the evening meal. I will not be able to eat any more of that fried chicken. (*She sits down.*)

JOHNNY: (*Beginning to unload.*) Planned ... the ... evening... meal. Did you just think of that?

DORIS: Yes — the smell of bacon when Webler opened the door. I'm afraid they may be planning that for our supper...

JOHNNY: They call it dinner, here. All right. (*He sits down beside her on the edge of the bed.*) Tell me what you want Ma Hibbler to prepare.

DORIS: I noticed fresh green beans on that roadside stand, last night. Explain to this... Ma that she must boil them for a little time only in lightly salted water, and serve them with butter. If she is able to find spinach, she must boil it also, then pass it through a sieve. No white bread, no corn bread (bah!), but plain whole-wheat bread, toasted. Coffee, yes —

JOHNNY: With hot milk? *Cafe au lait*?

DORIS: I suppose it would be better for my insides... Black bean, split pea, barley or lentil soup. That I will eat. I will also take a small portion of a simple unspiced custard.

JOHNNY: We will have to pay more, of course.

DORIS: Money is of no importance, in this case. *Navare necesse est!* I have had an ulcer since girlhood. Three operations. (*She stands, with the help of her cane.*) Now. Take up your things again ... (*JOHNNY does so.*) The tripods ... (*He continues to load himself up.*) Are you ready?

JOHNNY: Ready. To sail? It is necessary to sail?

DORIS: An old saying of the doctor's. Give me your arm.

(*Formally, JOHNNY offers her his arm. They proceed towards the exit.*)

JOHNNY: So the doctor was a literary man.

DORIS: Cultivated. He loved to tell stories with the camera. Now I—as you know—I look for the images that carry history, I look for the faces that will remind us, years from now, who peopled this country at its founding.

(*Still talking, they exit.*)

SCENE FIVE

Evening of the same day, the Daniel Boone Hotel. Black cloth has been nailed over the windows, and the room is dimly lighted by a single small red bulb, hanging on the cord from the ceiling. JOHNNY, in shirt sleeves, is packing glass plates in light-proof paper, then returning them to the crate. DORIS, exhausted, sits in the rocker. JOHNNY is whistling.

DORIS: In the past I did all that for myself. Placed the plates in the holders. Replaced them in the crate. At one time, I even tried developing but it was impossible in this situation ... I am too tired, now.

JOHNNY: You looked as though you were going to faint, back there on the Holcolm's porch. Solomon whispered to give a sip of corn liquor to the "Poor tired woman-person", but I told him I was in charge of you and it wouldn't do. He asked me if you were my woman-person — I saw your funny smile.

DORIS: I saw you... gloat. Be careful — (*JOHNNY nearly drops a plate.*) Be sure to fold the corners. You were able to write down their song?

JOHNNY: Lord William's Death. I've heard it before — but not this variation.

DORIS: Sing it for me.

JOHNNY: I don't think you'll like it.

DORIS: Please.

JOHNNY: (*Still packing plates, he begins to sing.*)
Awake, ye seven sleepers,
And take a warning of me:
I will not have your eldest girl
But the wee one rides with me, fa, la, la
The wee one rides with me, fa la le,
By the little Binory.

DORIS: They argued — the woman and her husband. What was it she didn't want him to sing?

JOHNNY: Solomon wanted to put in something about a watery cross but Beth wouldn't have it. Then they fell to disputing about "Death-naming."

DORIS: Death-naming...

JOHNNY: Did you know Richard Wagner has Lohengrin warn Elsa twice not to name him during the coming battle?

DORIS: Of course. My father took me to all the Wagner operas before I was 10 years old.

JOHNNY: (*Singing.*)
She held, she held so silent,
And never shed a tear
Until she saw her brothers fall

> And the father who loved her so dear, fa la la,
> And the father who loved her so dear, fa la le,
> By the little Binory.
>
> Hold hard, hold hard, Lord William
> Your hand so strong and so sore,
> For I could have many lovers true,
> But fathers I never have more, fa la la,
> But fathers I never have more—-

DORIS: How true.

JOHNNY: So the doctor was no father. But was the father a doctor?

DORIS: Riddle me no riddles, Johnny!

JOHNNY: Did you photograph them?

DORIS: Never.

JOHNNY: Why?

DORIS: My father was of the old school. He would have considered it an impertinence. My husband had his own equipment. He was a talented amateur.

JOHNNY: And that is enough for today.

DORIS: (*Smiling.*) Quite enough.

(*JOHNNY goes to the basin, pours water, washes as DORIS watches.*)

JOHNNY: They told me downstairs they've stewed some prunes, for you, and run them through the food grinder. Shall I fetch them?

DORIS: Not just now. Tell me ... Do you understand that song? Why he died —

JOHNNY: Because she named him? I begin to understand.

DORIS: Johnny, don't blame me for not telling you things.

JOHNNY: I begin to understand your magic. It dwells in mystery!

DORIS: But we are growing closer. How does the song end?

JOHNNY: You were so busy getting poor old Beth into her Granny's linsey-woolsey dress and posing her by that busted spinning wheel —

DORIS: I like to show the things they do.

JOHNNY: The things they *did*.

DORIS: Johnny, that is my concern.

JOHNNY: But we are growing closer.

DORIS: Very well. The linsey-woolsey — is there something untrue about that dress? Beth is the same as her grandmother in many ways, no? The superstitions. The songs. The lack. The linsey-woolsey — does it show anything about her which is not true? Would her "store-boughten" calico have shown something all true — or only another part?

JOHNNY: And then you got her to drag out the cards, as well —

DORIS: The cards. And the hackle. Beautiful words. Beautiful objects. Of course they're no longer used to comb wool. But does that make them untrue?

JOHNNY: Next you'll be telling me you mess with your negatives, smear gum bichromate on your prints.

DORIS: I did that once; I outgrew it. Reality is enough for me now.

JOHNNY: Your reality.

DORIS: And your songs. You sometimes change the words, don't you?

JOHNNY: I improve them...

DORIS: We're not so very different. (*She holds out her hand.*) I don't question the way you rearrange your songs. Don't question me. We are both poets, am I correct? We are both in love with a certain light.

JOHNNY: My "rearranging", as you call it, makes the old songs more beautiful. We are both in the business of illusion, Doris.

(*DORIS shakes her head, turns away.*)

JOHNNY: Would you like a glass of buttermilk?

DORIS: I loathe buttermilk.

JOHNNY: Perhaps plain milk —

DORIS: If you insist.

(*JOHNNY turns towards exit.*)

DORIS: Would you be so kind as to make certain that Webler has eaten? I am not certain of the ways of this hotel.

JOHNNY: Miss Doris — I am not in the habit —

DORIS: Help me, Johnny. He is my people.

(*JOHNNY exits. DORIS reaches for her cane and goes from window to window, pulling aside the black cloth. She looks out, curiously, then retreats. Evening light floods the stage. She turns off the red bulb. Goes to the mirror over the chest of drawers and looks at her face. A knock.*)

DORIS: Enter...

(*WEBLER enters.*)

WEBLER: Madam, if I may speak with you a moment...

DORIS: Certainly.

WEBLER: (*With repressed emotion.*) I have served you for eleven years, Madam — you and the doctor. I have seen many changes. I have been obliged to accept... many difficulties. I could never have believed —

DORIS: What is it, Webler?

WEBLER: Madam. Forgive me. Just now, I was out there, on the street. People have gathered. These... lousy mountaineers. They are staring at your windows. They are laughing. They think indecent things were going on here, behind the black cloth.

DORIS: (*Rising, with difficulty, leaning on cane, going to the window.*) Let them see me, then. An old woman —

WEBLER: With such a young man!

DORIS: (*Standing in the bright light in the window.*) I have never cared what people say. You remember, during my divorce, the talk —

WEBLER: Madam! I never listened.

DORIS: Do not listen now. (*With a queenly gesture, she waves out the window.*)

WEBLER: As you say, Madam. (*WEBLER turns towards exit, turns back.*) But if that young man —

DORIS: Mr. Niles?

WEBLER: If he could only act a little more serious!

DORIS: I don't believe either you or I can make Johnny serious. Good night. Sleep well. You will be driving some terrible roads again tomorrow.

WEBLER: I do not call them roads. Good night, Madam.

(*WEBLER exits. DORIS remains at the window, looking out. The light begins to fade.*)

DORIS: The plates, for tomorrow ... (*She starts towards the crate, leaning on her cane. A spasm of pain halts her.*) God in Heaven.

(*She staggers to the bed, lies down. The light continues to fade. JOHNNY enters, with a covered dish and a glass of milk. He rushes to the bed.*)

JOHNNY: Doris... (*He tries to raise her. She resists weakly.*)

DORIS: Leave me. Send me George...

JOHNNY: Let me —

DORIS: Send me George.

(*JOHNNY rushes out the exit and can be heard off-stage shouting for WEBLER.*)

DORIS: I am so hideous when I am unwell...

(*WEBLER enters, followed by JOHNNY. He goes to DORIS, looks at her, begins to set to work. He opens the valise of medicines, gets out pills, etc.*)

DORIS: Hurry!

WEBLER: In a moment, Madam. (*He brings pills. JOHNNY brings the glass of milk.*) Water.

(*JOHNNY rushes to the basin, empties the milk into it, refills the glass with water.*)

DORIS: (*Taking glass, drinking water, taking pills.*) Faw... (*She lies back.*)

JOHNNY: (*To WEBLER.*) What are those pills?

WEBLER: For the pain. (*He returns the pills to the valise. Then he takes DORIS' pulse.*) Very fast. She is feverish... I must find the thermometer. (*WEBLER begins to search through the valise. JOHNNY stands helplessly.*) She was very much overtired today. The trip along that creek bed they call a road. Lousy mountaineers. How they stared. She is exhausted, poor lady. (*He brings thermometer to the bed, puts it in DORIS' mouth. They wait.*) Sing us one of your songs, Mr. Johnny.

JOHNNY: (*Singing in a mechanical way*)
They lay fair Ellen in the near churchyard,
Lord William just beside her,
And from his heart grew a red, red rose
And from her heart a briar ... (*Add verses if necessary.*)

WEBLER: (*Taking out the thermometer.*) One hundred and one. A sick lady!

JOHNNY: Ma Hibbler will know a doctor.

WEBLER: A doctor here?

JOHNNY: Doris — do you want me to get you a doctor?

DORIS: No.

WEBLER: Madam, you are very sick.

DORIS: Johnny — I must talk to you. George. Please leave us.

WEBLER: I will be just outside in the hall.

DORIS: Go, please.

(*WEBLER slowly exits, closing the door.*)

DORIS: Now. Johnny. Come here.

(*JOHNNY approaches the bed. The light is now very dim.*)

DORIS: This has not been an easy day for you.

JOHNNY: No.

DORIS: You are used to your own rules, your own life. And now I must ask you something even more difficult.

JOHNNY: Tell me.

DORIS: Take my hand... I must go back to New York, Johnny. I no longer have the strength.

JOHNNY: But I am your strength. You hired me for that.

DORIS: But I find that I cannot lean...

JOHNNY: Doris... Get rid of Webler. Lean on me.

DORIS: I cannot.

JOHNNY: In New York — when you hired me. You said — strong arms. Strong back.

DORIS: I must go back to New York. And you must go with me, to help me.

JOHNNY: But if you will not lean on me here —

DORIS: Hush. Call Webler, tell him to load the Lincoln.

JOHNNY: And me? I stand here, waiting? I watch him do what I am more than capable of doing.

DORIS: I have paid you no money, Johnny.

JOHNNY: That's not important

DORIS: I am so hideous when I am unwell.

JOHNNY: Yet George can see you. He can take your poor tired body in his arms.

DORIS: Johnny ...

(*DORIS holds out her hands. JOHNNY takes them. They hover, close together, about to kiss. DORIS turns her face away.*)

DORIS: Take me back to New York.

JOHNNY: I'll get the car.

(*JOHNNY opens the door. WEBLER rushes in.*)

WEBLER: Madam! I'll fetch the car —

DORIS: That's enough, Webler. I'll ride home with Johnny Niles, and I don't want to hear any more about it.

(*The following scene comes immediately after the above, with no break. WEBLER might arrange the three chairs for the car, then they all climb in. DORIS curls up close to JOHNNY.*)

DORIS: Sing to me, Johnny. Sing the one you took from Mrs. Combs at Puncheon Camp Creek.

(*JOHNNY sings one verse from "Black Is the Color of My True Love's Hair."*)

DORIS: Thank you... (*She is in pain.*) Help me, Johnny... Brush my hair...

WEBLER: I am taking you back to the city, to your own doctor—

DORIS: Enough. My brush is in my purse, Johnny. (*JOHNNY begins to brush her hair.*) You see, Johnny — so much better than words — the songs, the images...

JOHNNY: But where are you — how can I find you — when I know so little...

WEBLER: Spare the poor lady.

DORIS: (*Rousing herself.*) No. I don't wish to be spared. It's the money — isn't it Johnny? Always the money.

WEBLER: Ah!

JOHNNY: Yes — to begin with...

DORIS: Siler, don't they call it? Lousy siler? Yes — I got it from my father, and I gave it to my husband, and one day, Johnny, I will give it to you. It is not love. It never was love. Now — sing me a song, Johnny, sing me something to put me to sleep.

(*JOHNNY puts his arms around her, she leans back, and closes her eyes as he begins to sing, very softly, "Black, black, black...." WEBER shrugs fiercely, leans forward, driving fast.*)

ACT TWO

SCENE ONE

April of the following spring, 1933. Living room in Park Avenue apartment. Bright noon. Champagne and glasses on the table. DORIS, leaning on JOHNNY, is slowly walking around the room.

JOHNNY: Easy at the corner... That last fever has left you shaky. Now...

(*They continue the slow walk.*)

DORIS: I still feel safer with my cane.

JOHNNY: The cane may slip. It may fall from your hand. It may slide out of reach.

DORIS: And you never slip, or slide? You are never out of reach?

JOHNNY: All fall, all winter — did I slip or slide?

DORIS: Only when you and the Marion went off to sing.

JOHNNY: Did you ever lack for me when you wanted to go to the theater? When you needed a taxi? Or someone to carry that enormous purse of yours, pick it up when you let it fall, put everything back inside?

DORIS: You have been good to me, Johnny.

JOHNNY: On the snow, on the ice, at Christmastime — We even shared a Christmas card: you photographed me as Joseph and Tess as the little virgin —

DORIS: But you were gone, after Christmas, for a week — singing in Germany. I had to depend on George, or the cane.

JOHNNY: Even a donkey deserves a day off.

DORIS: Do you feel like a donkey, Johnny?

JOHNNY: Mind — here's another corner.

DORIS: Answer me.

JOHNNY: And now, on my birthday — my forty-first! You give me champagne. No, I don't feel like a donkey.

DORIS: I haven't given you your present.

JOHNNY: I don't need anything more.

DORIS: No?

JOHNNY: You've given me too much, already.

DORIS: I have something for you. (*She takes a small, wrapped box out of her purse and hands it to him.*)

JOHNNY: The theater tickets and the dinners and the champagne are more than enough, Doris.

DORIS: Open it.

JOHNNY: It's fortunate I have no shame ... (*He unwraps the package, takes out a pair of cufflinks.*) Diamonds. Doris. They'll be saying in the mountains I'm your fancy man.

DORIS: You won't wear them in the mountains.

JOHNNY: They're beautiful. Thank you ... (*He kisses her lightly.*)

DORIS: Now, Johnny, let us discuss our trip.

JOHNNY: It will be easier, the second time. I'll weed out a lot of paraphernalia we didn't use, last summer.

DORIS: Are you sure everything will fit in that little car of yours?

JOHNNY: I'll make it fit. No one will stare at the little Chevrolet. And it's a workhorse of a car, it'll go up anything.

DORIS: Will there be room for all the... what do you call it? Photography-plunder?

JOHNNY: Everything will fit into the trunk, or the back seat.

DORIS: And you're sure you won't mind the driving...

JOHNNY: Remember how frightened you were when George took those hairpin curves? Don't tell me you've forgotten.

DORIS: No... Kiss me, Johnny.

(*JOHNNY does so lightly.*)

JOHNNY: I'm always melancholy, on big occasions. Something is missing.

DORIS: Would you get my camera?

JOHNNY: There's nobody to photograph here.

DORIS: Please.

JOHNNY: So the time has come.

(*JOHNNY exits. While he is gone, DORIS carefully arranges the champagne bottle and two glasses on the tray. JOHNNY enters, with the camera and tripod; with a gesture, DORIS shows him where to set it up.*)

JOHNNY: I'll open the champagne.

(*JOHNNY does so. DORIS photographs his hands. He gives her a glass, takes one for himself, toasts her silently.*)

JOHNNY: You only photograph my hands.

DORIS: (*Softly.*) They are very fine. (*She leaves the camera.*) It may be we are making a mistake.

JOHNNY: Why?

DORIS: I am weaker now than I was last summer. I will be able to do even less...

JOHNNY: But we will not have George.

DORIS: What difference will that make?

JOHNNY: You'll lean on me. And I'll be satisfied.

DORIS: You will never be satisfied, Johnny. Even when you have stripped me to the bone!

JOHNNY: Stop that, Doris!

DORIS: (*Shocked by his tone.*) Johnny!

JOHNNY: All winter in New York, you've teased me — treats don't make up for that! Here I'm your "little assistant," the country boy your friends laugh at. They think I'm one of the "types" you photograph — nameless, a "contemporary ancestor" — at my age — and you allow them to think that — and Marion and I sing *lieder* together all over this country and in Germany and France. I know the European tradition better than my own...

DORIS: Come here.

(*JOHNNY does so, kneels beside her; DORIS puts her hands on his head.*)

DORIS: I have no types now, Johnny.

JOHNNY: We need to go back to the mountains. We need to work together. The cameras, my notebook, the dulcimer. It's no good here for us. You resist. Hold back. Shield something you think is precious. And I... I starve. Let's get started again. I'll carry your gear, I'll sing, you'll laugh... We'll work, together.

DORIS: I will never be able to do enough for you, Johnny.

JOHNNY: Doris, you're so... protected. You still won't let me in.

DORIS: What do you mean, Johnny?

JOHNNY: I mean... into your head. The rest doesn't matter.

DORIS: Because you can get "the rest" elsewhere?

JOHNNY: Yes...

DORIS: But perhaps my head is a private place...

JOHNNY: That's why the first trip didn't work. You wanted to keep me out. If we're partners, we have to let each other in. Do you want to be partners, Doris?

DORIS: I want to travel with you, yes. (*With effort.*) The doctor and I were partners — gifted amateurs. A professional works alone.

JOHNNY: How regal. But in those little mountain hotels — will you be able to hold the line? Aren't you afraid?

DORIS: Of you?

JOHNNY: No. Of letting me in.

DORIS: Then... We will not. (*She stands up.*)

JOHNNY: Not?

DORIS: Not go on together. (*She stands facing JOHNNY. Pause.*) Be so kind as to hand me my cane.

JOHNNY: (*Softly.*) No.

DORIS: You have never refused to help me before.

JOHNNY: If I hand you that cane, you will take it and slowly, slowly, you will walk out of this room.

DORIS: *Navare necesse est —*

JOHNNY: It is necessary to go on sailing. Courtesy of the doctor —

DORIS: And of my father. Hand me my cane...

JOHNNY: Let go of words, Doris! They're the broken glass on top of your wall —

DORIS: My cane!

(*JOHNNY takes the cane, breaks it.*)

DORIS: (*Calling.*) Tessa! (*She turns towards exit, tries to walk unaided, staggers.*) Tessa!

JOHNNY: (*Throwing the pieces of the cane to the floor.*) She won't hear you, Doris.

DORIS: Johnny — go.

JOHNNY: Tell me about your husband.

DORIS: You are a scavenger — (*She takes a step, nearly falls.*)

JOHNNY: Tell me!

DORIS: (*Standing, unaided, during this speech.*) Very well, Johnny — I will tell you. (*Speaking rapidly, tonelessly.*) I was nine years old when my poor mother died. She had been sick for years — ever since I was born. And finally she died. And she was buried, here, in New York, and I rode in a car to her funeral. I was a little girl. I did not know how to cry. I watched the other people, the grownups, there, at the funeral, and they knew how to cry. But Papa and I... We stood side by side, at her grave. He held my hand. Papa and I did not cry.

The next summer, Papa took me abroad. Back to Germany. We visited the great cities, the museums, the cathedrals. We ate dinner together, alone, in the restaurants. Papa poured a little wine into my glass, he fed me pieces of food from his plate. We did not talk. During the day, we looked at the great, old paintings, the works of the masters. At night, he tucked me into my bed, then sat smoking a cigar by the night table. I could not fall asleep until the cigar end stopped burning in the darkness. I wanted him to go out in the evening, to have friends...

One evening, in the hotel restaurant, a pretty young woman was passing our table, and she dropped her purse — a blue silk purse. My father picked it up. Then he stood up and offered it to her. And she spoke to us, and smiled. After that, every day, I looked for her. I thought they could go to the museums together. She would not get tired, she would know the names of the great masters. But I never saw her again...

On that trip, Papa bought me a camera. It was a fine wooden camera, handmade in Germany. He thought it would amuse me. I began to take pictures. I began to carry that heavy wooden camera about with me everywhere, until Papa grew sick of it...

Later when I was first married, my husband gave me a camera, a fine wooden camera. He was a photographer himself, it was his hobby. We joined a bicycling-and-photography club, we took trips together to the country on weekends and photographed flowers... Then one day I took the camera alone, out into the street. I took a picture of a doorway. Yes. A plain brownstone doorway. The shadow cut across it — so. There was something in that shadow. Some mystery. It was not pretty... And then I began to photograph faces...

After that, my husband gave up photography. He said I had become too serious. Later, we were divorced.

JOHNNY: Why did you never have children?

DORIS: My husband and I saw very little of each other.

JOHNNY: It doesn't take much.

DORIS: I suppose I was too solitary.

JOHNNY: Have you ever regretted it?

DORIS: You don't miss what you've never had — or even imagined. Is the cross-questioning over?

JOHNNY: Not ... quite.

DORIS: What now?

JOHNNY: Your Jewishness.

DORIS: Oh, come — surely —

JOHNNY: Tell me.

DORIS: There is nothing to tell. I come from a world where it would be inconceivable to discuss such things... We lived in a wider sphere. Literature, painting, music. Neither the question of 'being Jewish' nor the term was ever discussed. It was simply... a fact. Do you see what I mean?

JOHNNY: No.

DORIS: When you put it in words, it is all so poor.

JOHNNY: It's better than nothing, Doris.

(*A timid knock.*)

DORIS: Enter.

(*TESSA, carrying a birthday cake, and WEBLER, in uniform, enter.*)

TESSA: For Mr. Johnny.

(*TESSA places the cake on the table. WEBLER lights the candles.*)

DORIS: When was this baked?

TESSA: On my afternoon off. I paid for the eggs and flour myself.

WEBLER: Forty-two candles... (*As he lights them.*)

JOHNNY: (*Snatching off a candle.*) Forty-one!

TESSA: One to grow on, Mr. Johnny. (*She takes one candle from him, places it in the cake.*) George — we must sing.

(*WEBLER and TESSA stand side by side and sing Happy Birthday.*)

TESSA: Now you must cut the cake, Mr. Johnny.

WEBLER. You have the first slice. (*He hands the cake knife to JOHNNY.*)

JOHNNY: A slice for everyone? (*He begins to cut the cake.*)

DORIS: I am so sorry. I cannot eat white cake.

TESSA: Oh, Madam — I forgot.

DORIS: It is unimportant.

JOHNNY: Three slices, then.

(*JOHNNY cuts three slices, places them on plates. Gives a slice to WEBLER and to TESSA, who thank him.*)

DORIS: Forks, Tessa?

TESSA: Here they are, Madam. We will go, now — if you will excuse us...

(*TESSA sees the broken cane, hesitates, then picks it up with a glance at DORIS to dispose of it off stage. Note: DORIS does not use a cane after this.*)

JOHNNY: Thank you, both.

WEBLER: Mr. Johnny. Since you and the madam are leaving early in the morning... If I may offer one word of advice. Your left tire. It is low.

JOHNNY: Thank you. Will you see to it?

WEBLER: Certainly. (*To DORIS.*) Always at your service, Madam. (*He bows.*)

DORIS: You will be on hand early, to load the car?

WEBLER: Of course.

(*WEBLER and TESSA exit.*)

JOHNNY: Whew. A display of nobility.

DORIS: They know I will be back, in time.

JOHNNY: Meanwhile George can cool his heels, eat three good meals a day of Tessa's cooking, and live like a gentleman.

DORIS: He is a gentleman.

JOHNNY: And I am not. No, Doris — don't take it back. (*He puts the plate of cake down.*) It's my commonness that drew you, as they say in the mountains.

DORIS: Johnny —

JOHNNY: Have some cake.

DORIS: I do not eat white cake.

JOHNNY: You WILL not eat white cake — but you can. (*He takes a forkful and puts it to her lips.*) For my birthday, Doris.

DORIS: No.

JOHNNY: Take a bite of cake. (*JOHNNY is determined. There is an element of flirtation.*)

DORIS: (*Swallowing.*) Now — leave me —

JOHNNY: No, Doris. I will not be dismissed. Have another bite of cake. (*He takes another forkful and puts it between her lips.*) No one has ever humiliated me as you have humiliated me, Doris. A little champagne? (*He offers her the glass, she waves it away, he drinks it.*) Have another bite of cake, and then I'll help you to your bed. You need your rest. We start at six, for the mountains.

(*JOHNNY gives her another forkful of cake, leans down, kisses her on the lips. DORIS breaks free, going to her camera; she moves with some difficulty but JOHNNY does not offer to help her. She takes him gently but firmly by the shoulders, puts the cake knife in his hand, moves him to the window. Surprised, but accommodating her, he poses while she takes several shots of his hands, giving him a glass to hold, a key etc. JOHNNY is resigned, amused.*)

SCENE TWO

JOHNNY and DORIS are seated in the front seat of Johnny's small car. He is driving. There is a minimal amount of equipment in the seat with them, this time; most has been stored in the back seat and the trunk. DORIS, wearing a dark dress, sits beside JOHNNY, a map spread across her knees.

JOHNNY swerves to avoid hitting a man who is walking along the road.

JOHNNY: (*Shouts out the window.*) Roads are for CARS, mister!

DORIS: Mountaineers don't seem to care much about cars.

JOHNNY: Don't change the subject. We were talking about the doctor.

DORIS: YOU were talking about the doctor.

JOHNNY: You said he was your partner.

DORIS: For a while, with the camera — yes.

JOHNNY: And here I'd imagined love, tears, recriminations —

DORIS: Nonsense. He lost interest, I went on. Look, there's the turn for Beauty! I marked it here on the map.

JOHNNY: We're back. (*He takes the turn.*) I thought this time it would be different.

DORIS: Johnny, you can't expect —

JOHNNY: But I do. I expect everything.

DORIS: Not of me, please.

JOHNNY: Yes. Of you. I thought with George out of the way —

DORIS: He was never in the way.

JOHNNY: Simply as another man —

DORIS: I never think of George as a man.

JOHNNY: Where does that leave me?

DORIS: You are my partner.

JOHNNY: Is that all?

DORIS: All?

JOHNNY: I crave your magic, Doris.

DORIS: That's a mere matter of the angle of the light, Johnny. It comes and it goes, depending on the season and the time of day. It can no more be shared than the light. I do not control the source.

JOHNNY: You are talking in riddles.

DORIS: You are not eager to understand. Let me tell you what it would mean for my photographs — if I shared with you what you call my magic. I would change my focus, entirely. Instead of aiming the camera out, at all this we're passing — the clay banks, the face of that old man we passed back there along the road — instead, I would turn the camera inwards, towards... you. Your hands, for example.

JOHNNY: You have my hands.

DORIS: They are very fine. But I photograph them because they are fine. I see them taking the cork out of a champagne bottle, pouring wine into two glasses, touching the strings of your dulcimer as you sing a song — for me.

JOHNNY: I am flattered.

DORIS: Perhaps. But my photography won't become the tool of this passion. My camera is for the world as it exists out there — these thin roads, that sycamore tree. It's the world I want, Johnny.

JOHNNY: That puts me in my place.

DORIS: You've been asking to be put there for some time. Your discontent — put it at the service of your sad songs! We have work to do, Johnny. We are — thank God — partners.

JOHNNY: A dreary word.

DORIS: I hope you will have a higher opinion of partnership, one day.

JOHNNY: (*Mischievously.*) And the next time you wish me to brush your hair, Miss Doris, will that be partnership, too?

DORIS: I am only human, Johnny.

JOHNNY: Sometimes I wonder.

DORIS: Most of the qualities you would call human have been scalded away. I am fifty years old.

JOHNNY: You forget I've seen your birth certificate, my dear. You are fifty-one.

DORIS: Does it matter?

JOHNNY: You know the answer. Hold tight, we're about to cross the creek — Watch out, there! I almost didn't see her —

DORIS: Who?

JOHNNY: Young lady with her dress hiked up, wading in the creek. Couldn't have been more than fifteen but well-finished already. I love their innocent ways.

DORIS: You gave her a fine splashing —

JOHNNY: Shall we stop and offer her assistance?

DORIS: No.

JOHNNY: I've heard that tone of voice before, somewhere! "Don't embarrass me, Johnny. No little flirtations along the way — " But I, too, am only human, Doris.

DORIS: And a great tease. Drive on. We want to reach Ma Hibbler's before dark.

JOHNNY: I, too, am used to having what I want. (*He begins to sing from "Lady Ishbel and Her Parrot."*)
He followed her up and he followed her down
He followed her where she lay,
And she not having the strength to withstand,
Nor the breath to say him nay.

JOHNNY: First one I wrote. (*He sings.*) "Go way from my window...go way from my door...Go way way way from my bedside, and bother me no more..."

DORIS: That's yours?

JOHNNY: I heard a little scrap of a tune on my Daddy's farm. You could say I made it out of whole cloth.

DORIS: The only one?

JOHNNY: I'm a recorder, Doris. I write down what would otherwise be lost. 'Course, I do make the old songs better...

DORIS: You're the blue-eyed grass, Johnny — hollow-stemmed. Everything runs through you. You connect.

JOHNNY: Thank you. A kind of grass!

DORIS: It helps me, to know.

JOHNNY: So you don't have to think any more.

DORIS: Instead, I see...

JOHNNY: Next you'll dress me up in homespun, prop me beside a spinning wheel.

DORIS: You have that in you, too.

JOHNNY: I was raised on a farm, Doris — but it was in the Bluegrass; my father was a lawyer. I used to enjoy confusing you, with my country ways —

DORIS: I was never confused. I'm not asking you to tell me anything, Johnny.

JOHNNY: Because you're not interested.

DORIS: I don't learn anything from these accounts.

JOHNNY: I learned early, on that farm, to keep my mouth shut and my ears open —

DORIS: Stop! Stop! There's Peter Ingram! The chair-maker from Berea! Get the tripod, Johnny, and the sheet metal—

(*JOHNNY overcomes his surprise, stops the car, begins to assemble the equipment as DORIS jumps out.*)

DORIS: (*Calling.*) Mr. Ingram! Just a minute! Remember me? The photographer woman...

(*DORIS exits. JOHNNY, loaded with equipment, hurries after her.*)

SCENE THREE

A week later. The light has brightened as in the first mountain scene. The front porch of a cabin. Entrance into the house, center. Bench, stage left. Chair, stage right. Steps down. QUIZZIE, a beautiful, wild-looking young girl, wearing a calico dress, is scraping corn off a cob into a pan. She is seated in the chair. PENCIL MARCUM, wearing overalls and smoking a pipe, sits on the bench, and near him, DORIS, dressed in a dark dress, is setting her camera up on its tripod. JOHNNY, stage center, is playing his dulcimer and singing.

JOHNNY: (*Singing.*) "Black, black, black is the color of my true love's hair. Her lips are something rosy fair ..."

QUIZZIE: (*Singing.*) "She's the fairest face, and the fairest hand, that ever was seen in all my father's land ..."

(*JOHNNY lays aside the dulcimer and gets a notebook from DORIS' purse which lies on the floor.*)

JOHNNY: Wait a minute, now — (*He begins to write.*)

PENCIL: (*Taking pipe from mouth.*) It's bad luck to have yourself photographed, and I'm in a trade that's needing luck all the time.

DORIS: What is your trade?

PENCIL: Well, I'm a preacher, lady.

QUIZZIE: You ought to hear him!

JOHNNY: How come you're called Pencil?

PENCIL: Well, it's this way. I learned my reading and writing at that one-room log schoolhouse you all passed on the road up here. I used a pencil, some call it a writing stick, though one time my granny taught me how to make a tolable good ink from mixing ripe pokeberries and vinegar. I didn't go for it, though. Pencil is good enough for writing letters for them that don't know how to write, and it's good enough for my name.

QUIZZIE: He writes letters for everybody around these parts. He writ my Daddy when he moved me in here. Never did get a word back.

DORIS: I'll be sure you get a copy of your photograph.

PENCIL: Sure enough? You'll do that?

DORIS: With your name on it, too.

(*During the following speeches, DORIS is busy with her camera, does not appear to listen. JOHNNY is entranced, writing notes.*)

JOHNNY: Quizzie, sing me the next line in that little song of yours.

QUIZZIE: Oh, it ain't my song. My mama sung it, and my granny, and on back... Let's see now, where was I?

"I love the ground whereon she stands ..."

JOHNNY: (*Accompanying her on the dulcimer.*) "I love the ground ..." Why are you called Quizzie?

QUIZZIE: By rights it's Quebella but he calls me Quizzie. You best ask him.

PENCIL: It's this way. I married up with a woman years and years ago. At first it seemed like she was the right sort for a young fellow with a smallish farm and a hankering to preach the gospel, but it didn't work out. She come on up here with her house-plunder, and 'twerent much either, and a tall, mean-faced thirteen-year-old son, who was what we call around here a "come-by-chance." 'Course, anybody with any sense knows what the chance is and how a body comes by it. (*QUIZZIE laughs.*) Now this boy, his name was Elmer, wouldn't pick up the handle of a hoe to help me raise my crop, but when I passed the corn on to the Lasser boys (they made liquor out of my corn on shares) and I got my share — two five-gallon jugs — Elmer, my stepson, made hisself his own jug-thief and drank right along, till one day he drank too durned much and fell off a cliff and died ... His mama didn't stay around long after that, and I got lonesome.

JOHNNY: (*Writing rapidly.*) What's a jug-thief?

PENCIL: It's a elder stalk with the wadding dug out of the middle and it's used to poke down into a jug or a bottle, and when it's down as far as you want it to be, you jam your thumb tight on the open end and lift out the elder stalk and let the drinking whiskey dribble into a cup or a gourd or right into your mouth. Now, that's a jug-thief.

DORIS: That's why her name's Quizzie?

QUIZZIE: Tell em, Honey!

PENCIL: Don't you honey me! I call her Quizzie cause it suits me. Don't a man have the right to call his woman any durn thing he wants?

JOHNNY: I call my woman Miss.

PENCIL: Now, that beats all! Quizzie — don't you go getting any ideas!

DORIS: But I pay him back. I take beautiful pictures — of his hands.

PENCIL: My lord. Not his face?

DORIS: I like his hands better.

JOHNNY: Well, I make her tell me stories.

DORIS: Stories don't mean anything. Now, Mr. Marcum, would you be so kind as to move to the other end of the bench?

PENCIL: Sun is there. It's hot.

QUIZZIE: Here, Pappy, I'll help you off with your jacket. (*She does so.*)

PENCIL: Don't you pappy me ... (*He pinches her playfully.*) Now, you know a man-person can think and think heavy if he ain't got no woman-person asking him jack-ass questions and pawing around at him.

(*DORIS puts hat on PENCIL. He does not resist.*)

PENCIL: You sure is a pretty woman-person. Where you fetch her from, Johnny?

JOHNNY: New York City.

QUIZZIE: Where be that?

JOHNNY: About a thousand miles north of here.

DORIS: Johnny — hold the reflector. Over there in the corner. (*Johnny does so.*)

PENCIL: What you got the poor feller doing now?

DORIS: Helping me with the light.

PENCIL: Folks say if a man-person has a nice comfortable woman to love of him, he has a fair chance to live a long life... Maybe he don't want to live a long life with the woman bothermments a female brings with her. (*Softly, to JOHNNY.*) Now, I ain't much use, work-wise, to Quizzie here, but she is so useful to me, bed-wise, it turned out to be a cash crop.

DORIS: Hold perfectly still while I count...

PENCIL: Ma'am, I'll do my best... Bring me my Bible box, Quizzie.

(*QUIZZIE goes into the cabin.*)

DORIS: What's that?

PENCIL: Now, Ma'am, I tole you I'm a preacher. I handle the sarpants, too.

DORIS: Not snakes...

PENCIL: Yes, Ma'am. A fellow has to learn how to keep away from the business end of a sarpant. But in my trade a fellow has got to walk the woods. Many folks call in their small children when I pass, saying that I be teched.

JOHNNY: (*Writing furiously.*) Why teched?

(*QUIZZIE enters with a box which she hands to PENCIL.*)

PENCIL: For two reasons: I browse with the snake-beasts, and I was borned in the middle of the week so I'm continual looking both ways for Sunday.

DORIS: Now, Mr. Marcum ... (*PENCIL freezes. DORIS removes the lens cap, counts. She replaces the lens cap.*) Thank you.

QUIZZIE: I sure would like to be in a picture.

DORIS: (*She looks at QUIZZIE critically.*) I wonder if you might have something in the cabin...

JOHNNY: Now, Doris —

DORIS: An old dress of your granny's?

QUIZZIE: My granny never lived in this place. She's buried over near Mousie.

PENCIL: Now, Quizzie, do like the lady tells you. They's some old finery of my wife's laid up in the cabin. Go in and look under the bed.

QUIZZIE: I don't —

PENCIL: Now, Quizzie.

(*QUIZZIE exits into the cabin.*)

PENCIL: Quizzie's just like a cat-tail growing in a snake-doctor swamp. When the wind blows a mighty storm, she bends with the wind, and when the storm ain't got no more blowing in it, Quizzie stands up as straight as any of 'em. But suppose you had an old granddaddy oak tree in her place: if the storm ever blows him over he finds hisself sawed up into cord wood.

(*QUIZZIE enters, wearing an old dress, carrying a sunbonnet.*)

PENCIL: Oak makes powerful good cord wood.

DORIS: Good. (*She ties the bonnet on QUIZZIE.*) Now, if by chance you have a spinning wheel, somewhere, or a pair of cards —

PENCIL: Got some cards in the dog-trot.

QUIZZIE: I ain't never carded wool in my life.

PENCIL: Well, your Granny did, and your mama, too — you can bet your life on that. There ain't any harm in it. Go get 'em.

QUIZZIE: I don't know what to do with 'em.

PENCIL: I said, get 'em.

(*QUIZZIE exits.*)

PENCIL: You got to talk right to women folks!

(*QUIZZIE re-enters, with cards.*)

PENCIL: That's right... Ain't seen a bit of wool in these parts for years... used to be sheeps all over, but not no more. Just them mines, now.

DORIS: A little more this way... (*She arranges QUIZZIE in a chair, then goes to her camera.*) Please sit absolutely still while I count... (*She takes off the lens cap, counts, replaces lens cap.*) Thank you.

PENCIL: Now there's a little piece of you in that black box along side of me, Quizzie.

JOHNNY: (*He has taken out his dulcimer.*) I'm looking for more verses to this tune. Do you know it? (*Singing.*) "I wonder as I wander out under the sky....How Jesus my Savior was born for to die ..."

QUIZZIE: (*Singing.*) "I wonder as I wander out under the sky ..."

(*QUIZZIE stops singing abruptly. DORIS moves her camera to get her in range.*)

PENCIL: Sing some more.

QUIZZIE: (*Singing.*) "Why Jesus my savior was born for to die..."

JOHNNY: Don't you know any more of it?

QUIZZIE: Dressing up in these old rags — that I'll do. Standing around here in the hot sun while your woman person points that box at me. That I'll do! But singing the songs I don't even know to begin with — why, my mama never sung those songs! She was modern! Born modern! And me, too — I've been to Cincinnati —

PENCIL: All right, now, Quizzie.

QUIZZIE: And I'll go back there too, one of these days.

JOHNNY: I'm sorry.

PENCIL: Young womens is always talking when nobody wants to hear.

DORIS: What was it like in Cincinnati, Quizzie?

QUIZZIE: Tall houses, with stairs and stairs! Great wide streets. Noise, night and day... I stayed there a solid month and then I come back.

PENCIL: Home's best.

QUIZZIE: Maybe!

DORIS: (*To JOHNNY.*) Let's move on, give these good people time to recover... Goodbye, Mr. Marcum. (*She shakes hands with PENCIL.*)

PENCIL: Now, you be sure to get my picture to me.

DORIS: I'll get it to you, and if I don't, Johnny will. Goodbye, Quizzie. (*She holds out her hand. QUIZZIE hides her hand behind her back.*) Take the camera, Johnny.

QUIZZIE: Asking about Cincinnati like she ain't been there herself.

DORIS: We'll send you your picture, Quizzie.

QUIZZIE: Put my name on it. My real name!

DORIS: What is it?

QUIZZIE: Quebella Colton... Marcum!

PENCIL: Now, wait a minute, here —

(*Arguing, Pencil and Quizzie exit into the cabin.*)

DORIS: Give me your arm, Johnny...

(*JOHNNY and DORIS exit to area in front of porch.*)

DORIS: They all want to go and dress up!

JOHNNY: Not in that old homespun, Doris —

DORIS: And you, every evening in the hotel, taking out the "plain words" and putting in the "fancy words" so the songs will sell in the east —

JOHNNY: Doris — you make people look more interesting, and I make songs sound prettier —and the world is better — a little — because of us.

DORIS: A little better.

JOHNNY: Come on! I see some people watching for us over there across the creek —

DORIS: Why, they're waving at us!

JOHNNY: Word's gone out up and down the hollow — the magic-makers are here — We'll take what's homely and make it prettier than a picture —

DORIS: Three women and a child! And the women are wearing sunbonnets! I have to get over there.

JOHNNY: I don't believe you can wade Cutshine Creek, Miss Doris, not unless you're willing to hike up those long skirts.

DORIS: Carry me over, Johnny.

JOHNNY: Carry you —

DORIS: Piggyback.

(*JOHNNY turns his back, crouches slightly. DORIS with surprising agility climbs on his back.*)

DORIS: Gee Haw!

JOHNNY: Haw means left, Miss Doris.

DORIS: Then I mean gee...

(*Slowly, JOHNNY carries DORIS on his back across the stage. Stage center, they turn as though to face a camera.*)

SCENE FOUR

The hotel bedroom three days later. Morning. JOHNNY, seated at the table, is writing in his notebook, the dulcimer beside him. DORIS is brushing her hair.

JOHNNY: (*Checking his notes, reads aloud.*) Kite. Hueysville. Jackie and Garnet. Leburn, Hindman, Carrie and Dwarf. We covered a lot of ground in a week.

DORIS: And those roads...

JOHNNY: The Chevrolet does better than the Lincoln touring car! (*Picking up dulcimer, beginning to play.*)

"Oh where have you been, Jimmy Randal, my son?/ Oh where have you been, my oldest dear one?"

(*DORIS stops what she is doing, comes closer.*)

JOHNNY: "Oh Mither, oh Mither, go make my bed soon,/ 'cause my courting has sicked me and I fain would lie doon..."

DORIS: Johnny ...

JOHNNY: (*Singing.*) "What would you your sweetheart, Jimmy Randal, my son?/ What would you your sweetheart, my oldest dear one?/ Bullrushes, bullrushes and them all parched brown,/ Cause she gave me the pizen that I did drink down..."

DORIS: Johnny ... Get the camera.

JOHNNY: Too early to go to work, Miss Doris!

(*JOHNNY gets the camera, sets it up on the tripod as DORIS directs.*)

DORIS: Take the dulcimer and sit over there on the floor.

(*JOHNNY does so, begins to play and sing. DORIS takes several photographs.*)

DORIS: (*Teasing.*) Look at me the way you looked at that little mountain girl in the stream a week ago.

JOHNNY: Who, the unwilling bride?

(*JOHNNY assumes a romantic, yearning expression; DORIS takes another photograph.*)

JOHNNY: (*Singing.*) "Oh, I married a wife and I tuck her to home/ As the gentle fair jenny, the rosemary tree..."

DORIS: That's the look...

JOHNNY: (*Singing.*) "But I many times wished I'd left her alone/ As the doe skims over the green valley ..." (*Imitating old woman's voice.*) "Now, take a case right here on Cutshine. About seven or eight years ago there was a young couple here, married just a few months when the husband ups and almost beats the daylights out of the young wife... He used a tobacco stick."

DORIS: I have that old woman — Mrs. Green —

JOHNNY: (*Reading from notes. Imitating Mrs. Green.*) "There was a certain amount of bawlin and carryin on in the cabin and then it was quiet. But the next mornin when the young husband was sitting at the breakfast table, the young wife crept up from behind and beat the tar out of him before he could set down his coffee cup."

DORIS: Can we make up, Johnny, without the tobacco stick?

JOHNNY: I wasn't aware we'd fallen out ... (*Singing.*) "But I, being young, I tuck me to wife,/ As the gentle young jenny, the rosemary tree ..."

DORIS: You haven't looked at me for three days.

JOHNNY: Busy, Doris — just like you. (*Singing.*) "A woman who plagued me out of my life/ As the doe skims over the green valley."

DORIS: Look at me, Johnny.

JOHNNY: (*Singing.*) "Oh, for fear of her spoilin her pretty cloth shoes/ The pots in the kitchen she never would use."

DORIS: (*Taking his hand.*) When you rode me piggyback over Cutshine Creek three days ago — I felt you in my bones.

JOHNNY: (*Singing softly.*) "Oh, first day so weary I come from the plow/ Said, "Wife, dearest wife, can I eat a bit now?"

DORIS: I'll do whatever you say, Johnny.

JOHNNY: Whatever?

DORIS: There's not much, is there? I'm not a young girl anymore, and I'm not well.

JOHNNY: (*Singing.*) "Lay a piece of stale pone on yon highest shelf/ If you want more for dinner, go git it yourself..." I must go down and see if they've remembered to poach two eggs, for you.

DORIS: Perhaps I could try going down to breakfast.

JOHNNY: Rest, Miss Doris. You know what happens when you overextend yourself. (*He stands up.*) Maybe a piece of white toast, with your eggs?

DORIS: I don't want food, Johnny.

JOHNNY: I'll be right back.

(*JOHNNY exits. DORIS takes off her dress and her shoes. Unpins her long hair. JOHNNY reenters, carrying a covered dish.*)

JOHNNY: These were laid this morning...

(*JOHNNY stops, stares at DORIS, who is sitting on the bed in her petticoat and camisole, her hair loose over her shoulders.*)

SCENE FIVE

Evening, two days later. The hotel room. The stage is empty. JOHNNY, supporting DORIS, enters. He wears evening clothes and she is elaborately dressed. He half-carries her across the stage to the bed.

DORIS: Johnny ...

JOHNNY: Are you in pain?

DORIS: I wanted to leave in the middle of that awful supper. They're doing good things at Berea — but I would have preferred my plain mountain faces.

JOHNNY: They have their vices too, my dear.

DORIS: Sing me a little song, Johnny.

JOHNNY: (*Fetching dulcimer, drawing up chair to bedside.*) What do you want to hear?

DORIS: The one from yesterday, from the old granny woman at the mill... "The Seven Sorrows"

JOHNNY: (*Tuning dulcimer. Singing.*) "The very first blessing that Mary had/ It was the blessing of seven/ To think her little Jesus/ Was on the way to heaven..."

DORIS: The plates we exposed today — they need to be wrapped and packed.

(*JOHNNY lays aside dulcimer, takes out plates, begins to wrap them in lightproof paper as DORIS watches.*)

JOHNNY: You sat on the orange crate and told me what to do. I set up the camera. Took off the lens cap —

DORIS: I counted.

JOHNNY: I never thought you'd let me set up your camera. Ten plates —

DORIS: We didn't have the strength for more.

JOHNNY: Tomorrow we'll head for Brasstown, get Mrs. Hensley and her baby.

DORIS: I won't be able to go with you tomorrow.

JOHNNY: Let me call you a doctor.

DORIS: No. No doctors.

JOHNNY: Doris — be sensible. A doctor may be able to do something to relieve your pain.

DORIS: Sing to me, Johnny. That'll do more than a doctor...

JOHNNY: No, Doris — no singing. I'm going downstairs and tell Ma Hibbler to fetch us a doctor.

DORIS: I won't see him.

JOHNNY: I'm responsible for you, young lady —

DORIS: Johnny... Just for tonight. Leave it be, and sing me the song you took down yesterday at Hindman, from the pretty little girl with the black eyes...

JOHNNY: The... Unquiet Grave? (*He begins to sing softly.*) "The wind blew up, the wind blew down,/ It brought some drops of rain;/ My own true love is the only one,/ And she in the grave has lain,/ And she in the grave has lain."

(*As JOHNNY continues to sing, DORIS sinks back on the pillows. The light fades.*)

JOHNNY: (*Singing.*) "Ah weep your tear and make a moan,/ As many a gay youth may,/ And sit and grieve upon her grave,/ For a season and a day ..."

(*As he sings, slides of the mountain faces are projected across the rear of the stage.*)

JOHNNY: (*Singing.*) "And when the season's past and gone,/ The fair young maid did say,/ "What man is weeping on my grave,/ The night and most the day?"

DORIS: Did it never occur to you... Once I gave in...

JOHNNY: What's that you say, Doris?

DORIS: Once I gave in, there would be nothing left of me.

JOHNNY: That's morbid.

DORIS: Perhaps. But true.

JOHNNY: (*Singing softly.*) "See there, alas, the garden green,/ where often we did walk./ The fairest flower that e'er was seen/ is withered at the stalk."

DORIS: The spring is broken.

JOHNNY: "Our own hearts, too, must die, my love/ and like the stalk decay,/ so all that you can do, my love,/ is to wait your dying day."

DORIS: Johnny ... I have to go home.

SCENE SIX

The Park Avenue apartment, a few days later. It is early morning. DORIS lies on a sofa in the living room. JOHNNY sits beside her, holding her hand.

DORIS: Coffee...

JOHNNY: Not till the doctor comes.

DORIS: Then sing to me.

JOHNNY: I was in such an allfire rush to get you up here last night and into your bed, I left the dulcimer in the car.

DORIS: I'll ring for George... (*She fumbles.*) I can't seem to find the buzzer, Johnny —

JOHNNY: Here... (*He rings.*)

DORIS: My eyes are beginning to fail. Turn on a light.

JOHNNY: But it's morning —

(*A knock.*)

JOHNNY: Enter ...

(*WEBLER enters, in his uniform, and stands at attention near the exit.*)

WEBLER: You rang, Mrs. Ulmann?

DORIS: Johnny, tell him.

JOHNNY: George, would you bring up the dulcimer, from the car?

WEBLER: I have it in the hall, I did not wish to leave it on the seat of the car. (*Aside.*) The doctor said she should sleep.

JOHNNY: She'll fall asleep when I sing to her.

WEBLER: Very well.

(*WEBLER exits.*)

DORIS: I hear you whispering.

JOHNNY: It's nothing, darling. Rest, if you can.

DORIS: Every muscle has a sort of stitch in it, yet when I try to stretch out, I can't.

JOHNNY: Let me rub your poor tired feet.

DORIS: No, Johnny. I am so hideous when I am ill... Send for Tessa.

JOHNNY: What can she do for you —

DORIS: I want her to brush my hair.

JOHNNY: I have brushed your hair every morning for a month.

DORIS: Please, Johnny.

JOHNNY: (*Ringing.*) I won't leave, Doris — you know that.

DORIS: I don't want you to leave.

(*TESSA enters.*)

DORIS: Please, brush my hair. Brush it, and braid it, the way you used to do when I was ready to sleep.

TESSA: Yes, Madam. (*She takes brush out of her apron pocket, approaches the bed, begins to brush DORIS' hair. DORIS sighs.*) There, Madam — it will pass —

DORIS: Yes, it will pass.

(*WEBLER enters with dulcimer.*)

WEBLER: Here you are, Mr. Johnny. (*He hands the dulcimer to JOHNNY.*)

JOHNNY: Thank you, George. I've finished one of the old songs — for you, Doris.

DORIS: Before you begin... I have something to say, to all of you.

WEBLER: Now, Madam —

DORIS: No, George, I can't rest until I have made a certain matter clear. My will —

JOHNNY: No, Doris.

DORIS: Tessa, brush with a little more vigor, I am not dead yet —

TESSA: Oh, Madame —

DORIS: Johnny, you must know — and George, and Tessa — I have been thinking about this for a long time. I left everything to you, Johnny. With provisions, for their lifetime, for Tessa and George —

JOHNNY: Doris, we have never discussed money.

DORIS: You need only to listen.

JOHNNY: Don't you remember saying, "You're a poet, Johnny, and poets don't need anything"?

DORIS: I want you to be able to travel, to sing your songs. I want audiences here and abroad to hear them. You will need money for that. Don't argue with me, Johnny. And then, I am leaving all my plates to you, my equipment, everything. You'll need to find a place for them, where the photographs will be preserved. All of this will take time, Johnny. You will earn your keep.

JOHNNY: We'll talk about this later —

DORIS: No false shame, Johnny — it has never been a problem for us before... Tessa, you will have a small annuity. And with your references, you should be able to find a good steady job.

TESSA: Oh, Madame —

DORIS: Now, no tears. George, you are approaching an age when you should think about retiring. I have left you the Lincoln touring car —

WEBLER: I am not ready to retire.

DORIS: It should fetch a good price... You will also have a yearly income, enough to pay the rent of that little apartment uptown you're so fond of —

WEBLER: Pardon me, Madam — but is this written somewhere?

DORIS: The paper's in my desk. Why are you all so sheepish? We have lived together, closely, for years. There is nothing to be ashamed of, in accepting money. Do you think I believe you worked for me for money?

JOHNNY: Doris, when I first saw you, at the Grand Street Theater, I thought perhaps my life would be easier, if —

DORIS: If you met an older woman with a certain amount of resources.

JOHNNY: Yes. It burned away, Doris.

DORIS: I know. Do you think I could have been fooled? Play me your new song.

(*The sun is rising and the light is brightening.*)

JOHNNY: (*Plays and sings, as much as is feasible.*) "I wonder as I wander..."

DORIS: I can see the mountains, and their faces.

(*WEBLER and TESSA turn toward the exit.*)

DORIS: Stay. (*To JOHNNY.*) Don't forget to take the photographs to Pencil and Quizzie.

JOHNNY: I won't forget. (*Singing.*) "If Jesus had wanted for any wee thing,/ A bird in the sky or a bird on the wing..."

(*DORIS lies quietly on the couch during the remainder of the song. ALL listen to JOHNNY. At the end of the song, ALL THREE look at DORIS and realize that she has died.*)

THE END

Tom Williams and Rebecca Ryland in *Piggyback* by Sallie Bingham, Horse Cave Theatre, 1994

Barbara Brandt in *The Dancers of Canaan* by Ron Mielech, Horse Cave Theatre, 1995

THE DANCERS OF CANAAN
by
Ronald A. Mielech

Mimi Rice, Barbara Brandt and John Sterling Arnold in *The Dancers of Canaan* by Ron Mielech, Horse Cave Theatre, 1995

The Dancers of Canaan opened on July 7, 1995, with the following cast:

ELDER JACOB	*John Sterling Arnold*
ELDERESS EMMANUEL	*Mimi Rice*
PETER SCROGGINS	*Peter Bisgaier*
REBECCA WESTCOTT	*Barbara Brandt*
SARAH	*Meredith Hagedorn*
CHILD	*Phoebe Digges-Elliott*
SHAKER WOMEN	*Elaine Digges, Peggy Holbrook, Siobhain Meyer, Julie Tisdale, Amber Lynn Turner*
SHAKER MEN	*Brad E. Burton, Drew DiCostanzo, Caleb Humphreys, Donald L. Johnson, Kevin Jones, Kip London, Tom Luce, Joey Stocks*

Director: Pamela White
Stage Manager: Judith Waltz
Set Design: Patricia G. Skinner
Lighting Design: Gregory Etter
Costume Design: Marty Hagedorn
Properties Master: Patricia G. Skinner
Sound Design: Billy Gooch
Music Composition: The Shakers
Choreographer: Melanie Asriel
Musical Consultant: Randy Folger
Other Consultants: John Campbell, Tommy Hines
Vocal Coach: Byron Craft
Dance Captain: Joey Stocks
Technical Director: Jeremy Artigue
Production Assistants: Gregory John Romero, Amber Lynn Turner

I have had the good fortune of working with an outstanding playwright and two exceptional teachers of playwriting. John Gassner was a wise and avuncular leader to a very frightened novice. Jerome Lawrence of *Inherit the Wind* fame was the most inspirational teacher I have ever had. But I have never had a better all-around mentor than Warren Hammack. Little did I realize when *Canaan* was first read at Horse Cave that our relationship would become so important to me.

After the Horse Cave production, I wrote to Warren and his wife, Pamela White, who directed the play so beautifully: "After carrying the idea around with me for some time, I decided to take a crack at entirely rewriting the ending of *Canaan*… In light of the reaction from some quarters, I thought it worth a try to explore alternatives…"

A few years later, the new version of the play was performed at Ohio Dominican College in Columbus, Ohio, to a most enthusiastic response. The changes not only tied up loose ends but made for a more organic conclusion. Once again, the old adage, "Plays aren't written; they're rewritten" held true.

The current economics of the theater allows little opportunity for such development to occur. And that is the priceless gift that Horse Cave Theatre has given to Kentucky and her playwrights – a gift that must not be allowed to die in the years ahead.

– Ron Mielech

The Dancers of Canaan

Characters:

ELDER JACOB

ELDERESS EMMANUEL

PETER SCROGGINS

REBECCA WESTCOTT

SARAH

CHILD

REBEL SOLDIER

YANKEE SOLDIER

SHAKER WOMEN

SHAKER MEN

Place: Pleasant Hill, Kentucky – a Shaker community in the central, Blue Grass area of the state.

Time: From September, 1859, to November, 1860.

Songs:

Act One

   "A People Called Shaker"

   "The Followers of the Lamb"

   "The Shepherdess' Song"

   "The Gift to Be Simple"

   "A Mother Ann's Song # 1"

   "My Carnal Life I Will Lay Down"

   "Who Will Bow and Bend Like a Willow"

   "Come Life, Shaker Life"

Act Two

   "Followers of the Lamb" (Reprise)

   "Now My Dear Companions"

   "Zion's Kingdom"

   "Hop Up and Jump Up"

   "The Gift to Be Simple" (Reprise)

The music is authentic Shaker music.

ACT ONE

The setting suggests a Shaker meeting hall.

Upstage center is a large window in the form of an archway – a Palladian window without side panels. Directly in front of the window is a small balcony-like platform, perhaps four feet in height. Access to this area is by a short set of stairs to the left and rear of the balcony.

The balcony itself sits on a lower platform which is about 6 to 8 inches off the stage floor. This platform has a blunted pie-shape and is just large enough to hold scenes of two or three people. There are exits left and right of this platform. When the Shakers enter as a group, the men will enter and exit on the left and the women on the right.

The rest of the stage, which is by far the largest area, is open except for a row of benches left and right which face each other across the width of the stage. All of the dancing and most of the scenes will take place in this open, downstage area.

Everything is made of wood – the platforming, the benches, the flooring. There is a stark, clean, simple beauty to it all.

A young woman, REBECCA WESTCOTT, is kneeling downstage center. She appears to be drawing water from a stream into an oaken bucket. She wears a simple homespun dress. Her appearance is frail and willowy but unmistakably attractive. Suddenly, behind her, the setting is bathed in a blood red light. We hear the loud crackling of a roaring fire. REBECCA drops her bucket and rushes offstage, shouting.

REBECCA: Mary! Mary!

> *(The lights go to black for an instant, and then a single spotlight reveals a girl-child, dressed in white, standing in the window up center. Once again, the lights go to black. After a moment the lights come up full. A sturdy man in his mid-fifties, ELDER JACOB, dressed in Shaker attire and holding a broad-brimmed hat, stands at the front of the small platform. At the entrance ways, upstage left and right, a chorus of men and women stand in their lines ready to come forward into the main area. ELDER JACOB comes forward to address the audience.)*

ELDER JACOB: Good evening and welcome to our Shaker community here at Pleasant Hill. It is in our tradition to welcome visitors to our worship services. Perhaps what you see will be different than you experience in your own places of worship. But we ask you please to accord our services the same respect as you do your own.

> *(ELDER JACOB retires again to the upstage platform. The SHAKERS come forward singing the opening song – "A People Called Shaker.")*

CHORUS: *(Singing.)*
A people called Shaker – how many things they tell
About a land of Canaan, where saints and angels dwell.
But sin that dreadful ocean
Encloses them around
With its tides, still divides them from
Canaan's happy ground.

> *(As the song is repeated several times, the SHAKERS circle about the stage, leaving..... the MEN stage left, and the WOMEN stage right. It is important to note that <u>at no time</u> (unless otherwise stated) <u>do Shaker men and women touch</u>. The lights go out; the singing dies softly in the darkness.)*

> *(When the lights come up, two of the benches have been placed in the up center area, opposite each other at about a 45 degree angle. ELDERESS EMMANUEL, a keen and compassionate woman in her fifties, stands beside ELDER JACOB upstage of the benches. On the edge of the light, the LITTLE GIRL enters from up right. She crosses down center and stands, waiting, in a soft pool of light. REBECCA also enters up right. She is dressed as before but carries a humble bouquet of wildflowers and a small canvas bag which contains her few earthly possessions. She gives the appearance of following the CHILD without in any way seeing her. As*

REBECCA comes forward, the CHILD leaves the light and exits left. REBECCA stands down center until ELDERESS EMMANUEL speaks.)

ELDERESS EMMANUEL: Come in, Rebecca.

(*REBECCA steps forward into the upstage light as the downstage pool of light is extinguished.*)

ELDERESS EMMANUEL: I'm Elderess Emmanuel... This is Elder Jacob.

(*ELDER JACOB nods.*)

REBECCA: (*Softly.*) Hello.

ELDER JACOB: Please, sit down, Rebecca.

(*REBECCA sits on the bench right.*)

ELDERESS EMMANUEL: I understand from Brother Caleb and Sister Elizabeth that you wish to join our Society of Believers here at Pleasant Hill.

REBECCA: Yes, Ma'am. I come clear across the state to do that very thing. Lived my whole life over in Lynch. You folks know where that is?

ELDER JACOB: (*Smiling.*) I know Lynch.... "Squat down" on the Virginia border, as they say.... Coal minin' country.

REBECCA: Yes, sir. That's right.... Just plain mountain folks.

ELDERESS EMMANUEL: Tell me, child, how did you come to hear of us in Lynch?

REBECCA: From Abigail Stoker. She was a nurse at the hospital where they took me after the accident.... (*Pause.*) Did Sister Elizabeth tell you about the accident and my baby dyin' the way she did?

ELDERESS EMMANUEL: Yes, dear, she did.

REBECCA: I was in the hospital not carin' whether I lived or died.... 'Bout as down on this life as a body could get.... Feelin' like God had no use for me neither.

ELDERESS EMMANUEL: We've all felt that way at one time or another, Rebecca. But God is always with us... God never stops loving us.

REBECCA: Yes, ma'am. That's sort of what Abigail told me, too. But I was feelin' like I killed my baby with my own two hands.... Only I didn't, of course... But I kept thinking there must have been somethin' I could o' done to save my baby... Somethin' I <u>should</u> o' done... I still think about that sometimes – over and over.

ELDER JACOB: If it was God's will, my child, there was nothing anyone could have done.

REBECCA: (*Absorbed in the recollection.*) ...Thought maybe I should have took her with me to the crick when I went to fetch the water... But it was dog cold outside... Snow on the ground... If I'd o' looked up at the roof of my shack, I reckon I'd o' seen them chimney-embers already startin' to burn... 'Cause when I got down to the crick and looked back to the house, the whole place was burnin' like it was made out of paper... And little Mary inside... I started screamin' and runnin' like a wild thing through the woods... I don't remember anything after that... They found me a time later up on the ridge – all in a heap. Probably would have froze to death if they hadn't found my tracks in the snow... And as I was lyin' in that hospital, I was wishin' they hadn't. (*REBECCA pauses, struggling with the memory.*)

ELDERESS EMMANUEL: (*Crosses and sits beside her, taking her hand.*) ...Are you all right, Rebecca?

REBECCA: Yes, ma'am... I'm fine... Anyway, that's how Abigail come to tell me about you folks.... She said she spent some time here when she was a little tyke.

(*ELDERESS EMMANUEL looks at ELDER JACOB, trying to recall.*)

ELDERESS EMMANUEL: Abigail??

REBECCA: Stoker... Oh, she said as how you wouldn't remember her... She was only here a short time... Her folks was just passin' through... But she remembered Pleasant Hill all right... Said it was the most beautiful and peacefullest place on earth. Told as how the Brothers and Sisters sang and danced to the Lord God Almighty, and was about as close to Jesus as a body could be.

ELDERESS EMMANEUEL: (*Smiles.*) Thank you, dear.

REBECCA: Abigail said when I heard that, it was the first bit of life I took an interest in in weeks... So she give me this little blue book on the life of Mother Ann... And that was the most beautiful book I ever read. I cried and cried for days. And I fell in love with Mother Ann like she was my own mama. And I knew what I wanted to do right then... I wanted to come to Pleasant Hill and live an upstandin' Shaker woman for the rest of my days... (*Suddenly, with alarm.*) Elderess Emmanuel... Elder Jacob... I just don't know what I'd do if you wasn't to take me in.

ELDERESS EMMANUEL: That shouldn't be a problem, Rebecca... (*She glances at Elder Jacob, who nods.*) You are welcome here with us.

ELDER JACOB: But I must warn you, child: Our ways are hard. We demand <u>much</u>, but God gives us <u>much</u> in return.

REBECCA: I ain't scared of hard ways... Known hard ways all my life.

ELDERESS EMMANUEL: We rise at four-thirty in Summer. An hour later in Winter... As one of our sisters, you will be given a different work assignment each month – cooking, washing, basket-making, perhaps... or weaving -

REBECCA: ...Excuse me, ma'am, but I ain't never done up a basket nor weaved a thread since I come tumblin' out of mama the day I was born.

ELDERESS EMMANUEL: (*Smiling.*) We will teach you, my dear... We have many here who are, as we say, "hand-minded".

ELDER JACOB: Here, we live each day as if we will die tomorrow; but we work as if the products of our hands will endure forever.

REBECCA: "Hands to work; hearts to God." Ain't that what Mother Ann say?

ELDER JACOB: Good for you, Rebecca. She did indeed.

REBECCA: I remember as how she say <u>that</u> in the little blue book Abigail Stoker give me. But the part I liked best was the tellin' of the miracle.

ELDER JACOB: (*Testing.*) Which miracle was that, Rebecca?

REBECCA: The one where she was on that big ocean ship comin' to America. There was her and her brother, William, and her husband, Abraham Stanley – only she weren't no longer sharin' his bed – and Mary Partington and -

ELDERESS EMMANUEL: (*Surprised.*) You know <u>all</u> their names, dear?

REBECCA: Yes, ma'am... Surely do... Don't you?

(*ELDERESS blushes and drops her head. ELDER JACOB tries to hide a smile.*)

REBECCA: (*Continuing on, innocently.*) Every single one... 'Course there was only nine of them, all told... Anyway, they took to singin' and dancin' and praisin' the Lord on the deck of that big old ocean ship, until the man in charge - I think his name was Captain Smith of New York City - say as how they should stop it, or he was gonna toss 'em all off right there where they was... in the middle of the At – lantic Ocean. But they kept right on at it and that's when that big storm come up and knocked some old boards loose 'long side of that boat... Down she was goin'! Till Mother Ann allowed as they should all pray to the Lord God Almighty... And wouldn't you know? Along come a big old wave, smacked them loose boards right back into shape and they sailed right on over to America. Even Captain Smith of New York City allowed as how

Mother Ann and the Lord Almighty saved his leaky old boat.

ELDERESS EMMANUEL: You have quite a fine memory.

REBECCA: Never had much schoolin' though, ma'am... But I stayed at it long enough to learn me to read... That's how I come to be able to read that little blue book Abigail Stoker give me.

ELDER JACOB: It seems you know many of our ways already, Rebecca.

REBECCA: I do... I know about how everybody shares everything, and women are thought to be as upstandin' as men – 'cause of Mother Ann – and everybody lives together as brothers and sisters and nobody has husbands... And even the children belong to everybody... I know lots more too, if you was to quiz me.

ELDERESS EMMANUEL: That won't be necessary, child. You have learned your lessons well... You will live at the end of the lane in Westhouse, sharing quarters with Sarah Dunleavy. She's a good girl and will help you to learn more of our ways.

ELDER JACOB: And this evening in assembly we will introduce you to your new Brothers and Sisters. After a time of trial, you may sign the Covenant, making you an official member of the Society... Even then, however, should you wish to leave us, you will be free to go.

REBECCA: I won't never leave Pleasant Hill... I know that for certain. Just like I knew in my heart of hearts that you was goin' to take me in to be a Shaker lady.

ELDERESS EMMANUEL: Really, child, how did you know that?

REBECCA: Mother Ann told me...

(*ELDER JACOB and ELDERESS EMMANUEL look at each other.*)

REBECCA: She had <u>four</u> babies die... She knew as how they died on account of her sinful ways... But the Lord God Almighty forgive her anyway... That's why he made the miracle. So Mother Ann and all the world would know as how He forgive her.

ELDER JACOB: He must love you very much to have sent you to us in this way... Welcome to our Gospel Order, Sister Rebecca.

ELDERESS EMMANUEL: (*Kissing her gently on the cheek.*) God bless you, child.

(*The lights go to black for a moment. Then a spotlight picks up ELDER JACOB downstage center.*)

ELDER JACOB: Today, my Brothers and Sisters, another lost sheep has come to our fold.

(*ELDER JACOB begins to sing "The Followers of the Lamb." The lights come up full revealing the SHAKER WOMEN standing at their benches stage right and the SHAKER MEN before their benches stage left. REBECCA and ELDERESS EMMANUEL stand together down right. As ELDER JACOB sings, he is joined center stage by the MEN who perform the first section of the song.*)

ELDER JACOB: (*Singing.*)
O, brethren ain't you happy
O, brethren ain't you happy

MEN (*All.*)
O, brethren ain't you happy
Ye followers of the Lamb

Sing on, dance on, followers of Emmanuel
Sing on, dance on, followers of the Lamb

(*Repeat refrain.*)

(*At this point, the MEN and WOMEN take over. ELDERESS EMMANUEL also joins in, leaving*

REBECCA *standing alone down right.*)

WOMEN:
O, sisters ain't you happy
O, sisters ain't you happy
O, sisters ain't you happy
Ye followers of the Lamb

Sing on, dance on, followers of Emmanuel
Sing on, dance on, followers of the Lamb

(*Repeat refrain.*)

(*The MEN join the WOMEN – MEN to left; WOMEN to right. REBECCA is swaying to the music.*)

TOGETHER:
I'm glad I am a Shaker
I'm glad I am a Shaker
I'm glad I am a Shaker
Ye followers of the Lamb

I mean to be obedient
I mean to be obedient
I mean to be obedient
Ye followers of the Lamb

Sing on, dance on, followers of Emmanuel
Sing on, dance on, followers of the Lamb

(*Repeat refrain.*)

(*At the conclusion of the song, the SINGERS are standing with hands and eyes upturned to heaven, all but REBECCA and a YOUNG MAN stage left. They are looking at each other, accented by soft rings of light. The stage lights go out except for the spotlight on the young man, PETER SCROGGINS. The SINGERS retire in the darkness, softly singing the last line of the song a time or two. PETER speaks. Note: When PETER speaks these periodic monologues, there is no attempt to make them "addresses" to the audience. Rather they are spoken mostly straight ahead, as if he were reading from a journal or remembering intimate thoughts.*)

PETER: (*Monologue.*) Today, a new sister came to us from the World. Her name is Rebecca Westcott. Her eyes are the clearest blue, and she has not yet learned to keep them cast down upon the ground. She has soft brown hair, and she moves with the grace of a willow wand in the breeze.

(*The light goes out on PETER. When the stage lights come up again, two benches are situated upstage in the main acting area. They are parallel to each other; but on a diagonal to the footlights. They represent beds in Westhouse. SARAH DUNLEAVY kneels beside her "bed" upstage, and REBECCA kneels beside her "bed" upstage. There is a long pause during which SARAH looks back several times at REBECCA.*)

SARAH: ...Sister Rebecca?... You still sayin' your night prayers?

REBECCA: Lordy, no! I been finished with my prayers loads ago. I just been kneelin' here thinkin' about all that happened today... I'm so excited. I don't think I can sleep at all tonight.

SARAH: Four-thirty comes mighty early.

REBECCA: Wisht it was here right now... I sure am fond of bein' here... Folks are right friendly, I'd say. (*SARAH nods... Pause.*) Where you from, Sarah?

SARAH: You mean originally?

REBECCA: Uh-huh.

SARAH: Second floor. (*REBECCA laughs. SARAH blushes.*)

REBECCA: No, child, I mean where was your home?

SARAH: Oh... Lancaster County.

REBECCA: Where's that?

SARAH: Pennsylvania... (*Trying to extend the conversation.*) We were neighbored to some Amish folk. There are lots of Amish in Lancaster County.

REBECCA: What are Amish?

SARAH: They're <u>sort</u> of like Shakers... Only they marry and don't use machinery and things... They were nice folks. Kept to themselves mostly. But me and my friends made fun of 'em 'cause they was different. I'm sorry we did that now.

REBECCA: I know what you mean. Folks used to make fun of James Ketchins 'cause he couldn't hardly walk with but a limp.

SARAH: Who's James Ketchins?

REBECCA: He were my baby's daddy... Just shows what folks don't know. James Ketchins could mine more coal than two men his size, boss say. (*Pause.*) You sure don't talk much, do you?

SARAH: Sisters say I'm real shy till I get to know a body. Then I speak right up... sort of.

REBECCA: Well, if you was to talk more early on, maybe you'd get to know folks quicker... That a-way you could get right on to sayin' what was on your mind.

SARAH: I guess.

REBECCA: I'd say you and me was about of the same age... I'm twenty years old.

SARAH: I'll be twenty-two come Christmas Day – the same day Jesus was born. I like having the same birthday as Jesus.

REBECCA: My yes!

SARAH: ...I don't normally like to be different. I'd just as soon most people didn't even notice me.

REBECCA: My, you sure are shy, ain't you child... Well, I expect you and me is gonna be real good friends.

SARAH: I don't ever want to leave Pleasant Hill. There's a pretty white oak tree in the cemetery – next to where Sister Elizabeth Meachem lies. I'll show you tomorrow. I want to be buried under that oak tree and rest there forever with Jesus and Mother Ann.

REBECCA: You sure have it all studied out, all right.

SARAH: I guess... (*Pause.*) ... Might as well go to sleep.

REBECCA: You go right on... I couldn't sleep a particle right now.

(*SARAH swings her feet up on the bench and sits "in bed." REBECCA hums a bit of "Followers of the Lamb" and hop-steps across the room.*)

REBECCA: ...I sure was fond of the singin' and dancin' too. Will you teach me to dance that-a-way, Sister Sarah?

SARAH: You'll learn... Every Wednesday evenin' we practice dancin'.

REBECCA: There was a fine lookin' boy out there among the brethren - seemed to have a sprightly step, too.

SARAH: You mean Peter Scroggins, I reckon.

REBECCA: I don't know, but he sure is a fine lookin' critter.

SARAH: Shame on you, Sister Rebecca. You ain't never to say such things.

REBECCA: What's wrong with just sayin'...? Seems natural.

SARAH: Natural don't matter... It ain't proper talk, and it sure ain't proper thinkin'... Don't you let the sisters hear you talkin' that way.

REBECCA: (*Completely sincere.*) ...Oh... All right... (*She crosses up the steps to the balcony.*) I'm sure glad to have you to help me, Sister Sarah... Elderess Emmanuel say as how you'll teach me all the things proper to a Shaker lady.

(*REBECCA stands now with her back to the audience, looking out the window... There is a long pause...The sound of a wind rising is heard. The lights begin to dim.*)

REBECCA: Sarah... You hear that?

SARAH: Hear what?

REBECCA: The wind... Don't you hear that wind risin' up out there?

SARAH: There ain't no wind out there... Why, I can see the tops of the trees right here from my bed. Branches ain't stirrin' a little bit.

REBECCA: (*Surprised.*)... You're right... They ain't... (*Listens.*) But there's wind stirrin' up out there just the same... Wind like I never heard before.

SARAH: (*With some urgency.*) Sister Rebecca, please come back to bed.

(*The wind grows louder still.*)

REBECCA: Shhh!... (*Listening intently.*) Lord Almighty, Sarah, I can hear my name on the wind...

SARAH: There ain't no wind, honest!

REBECCA: There is, I tell ya... I can hear my name on that wind – clear as anything.

(*REBECCA runs down the steps and rushes toward the upstage exit.*)

SARAH: (*Jumping out of "bed."*) ...Where are you goin', Sister?

REBECCA: Outside.

SARAH: You can't go out there... It's after prayer-time... And there ain't nothin' nor nobody out there.

REBECCA: There is, Sarah... There's a storm comin' up... And somebody out there is callin' my name on the wind.

(REBECCA *runs off up right.*)

SARAH: (*Fairly screaming.*) Please, don't go out there, Rebecca! Please!

(*The wind reaches a crescendo and then begins to subside somewhat. The lights go out on the scene upstage. Down left, the LITTLE GIRL, carrying a rag doll, appears in a strange light. From the darkness, we hear the voice of a WOMAN singing "The Shepherdess' Song."*)

SINGER:
How beautiful are those and how blessed they be
Who in deep tribulation daily follow me.
I have a robe divinely fair for such children to wear.
And a crown shining bright they shall wear with delight.
When done with the fading things of time.

(*Toward the end of the song, REBECCA enters down right. She sees the CHILD and approaches her cautiously.*)

REBECCA: Who are you, child? ... Was that you callin' my name on the wind?... What on earth you doin' out here this hour without your mama?

(*Note: When the CHILD speaks, she does not move her lips. Her voice is recorded.*)

CHILD: ... Seth...

REBECCA: Seth?... Who's that, child?

CHILD: Seth...

REBECCA: Seth some kin of yours, child?... What's the matter, baby... I'll help you if I can.

CHILD: Come... to... Seth.

REBECCA: Where is he?... Is he hurt somewhere?

CHILD: ... Seth needs us... Please come.

REBECCA: All right... I'll fetch Sister Sarah... You come with me?

(*The CHILD shakes her head.*)

REBECCA: You stay here, then.... Sarah and me gonna be right back. (*REBECCA starts to exit, stops and turns back to the CHILD.*)... Is Seth hurt? Does he need a -

(*But the light has gone out on the CHILD and she has disappeared.*)...

REBECCA: (*Tense.*) ... Baby!.... Where are you, child?

(*The ending of "The Shepherdess' Song" is heard once more from the darkness.*)

SINGER: (*Offstage.*)
And a crown shining bright
They shall wear with delight
When done with the fading things of time.

(*As the SINGER's voice dies away, the wind rises with sudden and violent intensity.*)

REBECCA: (*Shouting above the wind.*) Where <u>are</u> you, child?... Possum Baby!... There's a storm comin' up.... Sarah!... Sarah!!

(*REBECCA turns and dashes off stage left... The sound of the wind suddenly stops... When the lights come up, ELDERESS EMMANUEL and ELDER JACOB stand upstage center side-by-side. The "beds" have been removed and the area is clear. The SHAKER WOMEN stand before the row of benches stage right. The SHAKER MEN are in a line before the benches stage left. The MEN and WOMEN face each other across the room.*)

ELDER JACOB: My dear Brothers and Sisters, today let us give thanks for the blessings God has given us – for the love and mercy of Jesus Christ and Mother Ann... who help us in our trials and deliver us from the temptations we receive.

ELDERESS EMMANUEL: Let us give thanks to Jesus Christ and Mother Ann for the good and simple life they have called us to... With their help, let us labor to attain our perfection in the spirit of true humility.

(*A VOICE begins the most famous of all the Shaker songs, "Simple Gifts." The MEN and WOMEN close ranks at center stage as they sing and move to the song.*)

GROUP: (*Singing.*)
'Tis the gift to be simple, 'Tis the gift to be free.
'Tis the gift to come down where we ought to be.
And when we find ourselves in the place just right,
'Twill be in the valley of love and delight.

When true simplicity is gained,
To bow and to bend we will not be ashamed
To turn, turn will be our delight.

Till by turning, turning we come round right.

(*The lights go out except for a single spotlight on PETER down right.*)

PETER: (*Monologue.*) Today, I spoke to Rebecca Westcott for the first time, though it was not in the presence of another Brother or Sister... She asked me several times to leave and I expect I should have respected her wishes. And yet she did not seem to mind my bein' there and we spoke for some time.

(*The light goes out on PETER. When the lights come up again, the stage is alive with activity. On a bench stage right, TWO YOUNG WOMEN sit side-by-side. The one holds yarn between her outstretched hands as the other winds the yarn into a ball. Stage left, a YOUNG MAN sits on a bench weaving the seat of a chair with strips of caning or fabric; next to him sits ANOTHER MAN gathering thatch into handfuls for the making of brooms. After PETER finishes his monologue, he sits next to the BROOM MAKER, and joins him at his task. A WOMAN has been sweeping the upstage platform. She is joined by REBECCA, who kneels and begins scrubbing the floor. The music to "Simple Gifts" stays under the action. REBECCA has picked up the melody, and is humming along. One by one the BROTHERS and SISTERS leave the stage. Finally, only REBECCA remains alone on stage, scrubbing. After a short time, PETER appears behind her in the upstage entrance way.*)

PETER: (*Softly.*) Rebecca.

REBECCA: Lordy, how you frightened me, Peter Scroggins!

PETER: ...You know my name?

REBECCA: 'Course I do. I know the names of almost all the brothers and sisters by now... What kind of rusty you doin' comin' up here top of Westhouse? You ain't supposed to be up here.

PETER: I know... But I just <u>had</u> to talk to you... Please. It's mighty important.

REBECCA: Oh well, if it's important, I reckon... What is it you want, Peter Scroggins?

PETER: I need you to tell me of the World, Rebecca.

REBECCA: Can't say as I know much about the World... Didn't spend much time in it myself.

PETER: Know more than me. 'Bout all I know has come rollin' down that little stretch of road out there.

REBECCA: Was you brung up a Shaker baby?

PETER: Aye... I didn't know my ma... And I just turned 19 last week.

REBECCA: ... So's you got to settle your mind on leavin' or stayin', is that a fact?

PETER: That's it... And here <u>you</u> are just come from the World, if you see what I mean.

REBECCA: Sure, I can't settle your mind none, Peter Scroggins.

PETER: But you can tell me of the World some... What's it like, Rebecca?

REBECCA: (*Shrugs.*)... I reckon most folks see the World as how the World treats <u>them</u>... Some days to me it was sweeter than a berry... Some days it was stone hard... Stone hard is how it was mostly, I guess.

PETER: Is that why you come to Pleasant Hill?

REBECCA: Had my reasons.

PETER: I know about your baby dyin'... Is that why you come here?

REBECCA: It were one reason... But there were others... Mostly 'cause I didn't want to be a sinner no more. Wanted to give my life to the Lord God Almighty.

PETER: People are always talkin' about sinnin'. I don't think folks sin near what they think they do.

REBECCA: Who told you that?

PETER: Nobody... It's just what I <u>think</u>.

REBECCA: Old Pa say I was a sinner... Say as how one day God was gonna punish me hard... I guess maybe He has, too.

PETER: Why did your Pa say that?

REBECCA: 'Cause of James Ketchins.

PETER: Who's he?

REBECCA: He were my baby's daddy.

PETER: Oh... (*Pause.*) Did you love him?

REBECCA: Oh, I sure did... He was the sweetest, gentlest boy I ever knew... Met him at a church sociable back home.

PETER: What church was that?

REBECCA: I don't know. Never said, as I know of... Anyhow that's where I met James Ketchins... Met him at a church sociable on a Saturday night... Folks was dancin' how they do... Only James Ketchins was born with a bad leg... Couldn't hardly walk with but a limp, so he never took to dancin' as you might expect. And, since I never learned how, we just got to talkin' about things... He sure could put a body to ease with his talking, though. Before long we was seein' one another every chancst we got. And though it was wrong havin' the baby like we did, we was fixin' to marry... Then what happened at the mine changed all that.

PETER: What was that, Rebecca?

REBECCA: Cave in... Tunnel number four... Buried alive under all that coal and earth... It's wrong, I guess. But I still think about that boy and my baby... (*Pause.*) Oh, God! They was the two most precious things I ever had in my life. (*She is struggling to hold back her tears.*)

PETER: Thinkin' on them, isn't wrong, Rebecca... That's no sin... Even Elderess Emmanuel and Elder Jacob will tell you that.

REBECCA: (*Resuming her work.*) I think you better go now, Peter. We ain't supposed to be talkin' together this-a-way.

PETER: What's wrong with just talkin'? Brethren are allowed to visit Sisters in their rooms some times.

REBECCA: You know that ain't the same. Brethren and Sisters are <u>together</u> such times... sittin' four feet apart with clean white hankies in their laps and hands folded proper into 'em.

PETER: It's still talkin', as I see it. (*Crouching down beside her.*) Rebecca, do you know that out in the World, young men my age can go to Colleges?

REBECCA: What are them?

PETER: A college is like a school. You go there to learn things. Folks study on bein' doctors and lawyers and writers... You can say what you think and even write it down into a book, if you've a mind to.

REBECCA: Sounds like a busy place, all right.

PETER: (*Sitting beside her on the floor.*) ... Rebecca, do you know what fiction is?

REBECCA: (*Thinks.*) I expect I don't.

PETER: 'Course you don't, 'cause it's a kind of writing not read here or made by us. It's looked upon as worldly and not of a truth. But <u>I</u> don't think it's that way at all.

REBECCA: You read that kind of writin'? ...Biggest book I ever read was a little blue book about Mother Ann.

PETER: If you weren't to tell anyone, I could let you read a book of such fiction.

REBECCA: I don't think so... (*With sudden eagerness.*) What's it about?

PETER: It's of a kind known as novel... Written by Mr. Charles Dickens, an Englishman. It's called Oliver Twist.

REBECCA: That's a strange name for a book, I'd say.

PETER: It's the name of a boy.

REBECCA: I reckon that's even stranger.

PETER: He was an orphan boy. And Mr. Dickens tells of the hard life of this boy and the ways of the poor folks in London.

REBECCA: And there weren't no such boy?

PETER: No, but probably hundreds of such boys just like him. See how I mean?

REBECCA: No.

PETER: Well, though the people named in the book may be no such people and the happenings, no such happenings, still the hard way of bein' poor is of a truth. Same kind of truth you can read in a newspaper.

REBECCA: Then why you want to read on it in Mr. Dickens' book?

PETER: 'Cause he makes things come alive in your head – just like you was there in London, England.

REBECCA: Just like Mother Ann on that leaky old boat?

PETER: That's right.

REBECCA: How did you come by your book, Peter Scroggins? Abigail Stoker give me mine.

PETER: Over to Danville.

REBECCA: Where's that?

PETER: Short ways south of here... Went over there one day last fall with Brother Daniel to sell our vegetables. I was sittin' in the wagon waitin' for him to return from the Countin' House, when a young student of Center College come right up to me. I must have appeared in need of deliverance from my idleness, 'cause he asked me would I like to have the book.

REBECCA: What did Brother Daniel say when he come back?

PETER: Nothin'. I tucked that book inside my coat till we got home. Then I hid it in a hollow log over by the sheep pen. That's where it lies yet today, no doubt – I can show you where it is if you'd like to see it.

REBECCA: No... I expect I know enough about bein' poor... (*Pause as she reflects.*) And you don't think what you done was wrong?

PETER: If knowin' of the world be sinful, I can't see how a God who made all the world would punish a believer for his interest in it.

REBECCA: Peter Scroggins, I'd say as how you've a powerful urge to look this old world right square in the eye.

PETER: (*Kneeling excitedly.*) I won't rest content till I do. I want to go to the cities and see the new factories... I want to board a mighty steamship and sail off to see Mr. Dickens' London, England... (*Pause.*) And even if war is to come, as some folks are sayin', then I want to see that, too... I want to see it all, Rebecca – the beautiful and the terrible.

REBECCA: You're sure a strange boy, Peter Scroggins... But I know you're gonna do the right thing... Now I think it's time you head on out of here before Sister Sarah comes back.

PETER: (*Rising.*) All right. You fixin' to tell on me bein' here?

REBECCA: No... I wouldn't do that.

PETER: That world out there must sure be a funny place... Here it is callin' me like a will-of-the-wisp, and then bringin' somebody as pretty and sweet as you to Shaker ways... Wouldn't seem right somehow if we was to pass one another lickety-split... 'Bye, Rebecca.

REBECCA: 'Bye Peter.

PETER: Thank 'ee.

(*PETER exits up right. REBECCA stands for a moment staring after him. Faintly, we hear the sound of the wind. It begins to build and then fades away.*)

SARAH: (*From off.*)... Sister Rebecca? You up there in the loft?

REBECCA: (*Returning to her work.*) I am, Sister Sarah.

SARAH: (*Appears up left.*) Was Brother Scroggins up here?

REBECCA: (*Pause.*) Not as I know of.

SARAH: I could o' swore I saw him goin' down the Brother's stairs just now.

REBECCA: Maybe he had business on the third floor.

SARAH: I guess.

(*Softly the wind begins to rise.*)

SARAH: Better finish up here quick... Sister Ann Harkins says she's gonna need you to help serve in the refectory tonight. Old Prudence ain't up to it again.

REBECCA: (*Listening intently.*)... Sarah!... Listen!... There it is again!

SARAH: (*Nervously.*) There's what, Sister?

REBECCA: The wind... I hear it just like before... Same as it was on that first night I come here.

SARAH: I expect you ought to finish your chores and get yourself on down to the kitchen straight away.

REBECCA: Maybe that little girl-baby's out there again.

SARAH: So what if she is... No concern of yours, I expect.

REBECCA: The wind keeps a-risin' that-a-way and not a branch stirrin'... (*With sudden urgency.*)... That little girl-baby's out there, Sarah... She's callin' to me again. I know she is.

SARAH: Don't you go out there. You hear me?

REBECCA: I got to, Sarah... The wind -

(*REBECCA starts to run off up left.*)

SARAH: (*Shouting.*) Rebecca! ... <u>I hear the wind!</u>

(*REBECCA stops and looks at her.*)

SARAH: I hear it as I heard it that first night you was here.

REBECCA: Then why'd you say -

SARAH: I didn't know if I was to tell you.

REBECCA: Tell me what, Sarah?

SARAH: I asked Elderess Emmanuel, and she said if we heard the wind again I was to tell you... About the child, I mean... If that's <u>what</u> she be.

REBECCA: You tryin' to tell me she be some kind of spirit-baby?

SARAH: I am... That's what folks say... Except not a child, maybe.

REBECCA: Tell me about the spirit-baby, Sarah.

SARAH: Folks say maybe she's the spirit of a long ago Shaker lady... Followed her husband here. But never took to Shaker ways... After a time, she begged him to go back to the World... But havin' found the Lord, he wouldn't leave... Then one day, they found her body floatin' in the river.

REBECCA: (*Softly.*)... In the river?

SARAH: Right down at the landin'... But the strangest part was, weren't more than a day or two later – found him, too... drowned right there in the river.

REBECCA: But why anybody think that spirit-child had a way in it?

SARAH: Seems like years later, there was another Sister, new-come from the World, told as how she saw the same little girl you did... Callin' to her queer-like on the wind... holdin' onto a rag doll just like you told me... <u>There</u>... And then gone... Wasn't long after a mighty storm come up and that young Sister set after lookin' for that child... Old river was runnin' hard that night... Near took her body half way to Tennessee when they found her.

(*Pause.*)

REBECCA: Ain't nobody else ever seen that child?

SARAH: Nobody claimed to it, if they did... Not till about a year 'afore you come to us.

(*Pause.*)

REBECCA: Say on, Sister.

SARAH: As I heard it told, Old Sister Prudence McCann, up in years almost to ninety, was on her death bed over to Easthouse. Seems like all at oncst she set to ravin' and talkin' queer-like. Spoke as how years before, when she was a young sister, she was thinkin' on leavin' Gospel Order for the World... Then one stormy old night, she said as how she saw that same girl-child come to her on the wind... Had that rag doll with her too... Come to her on the wind like an angel of the Lord... Told her everything was gonna be all right... Told as how she was gonna live out her days to a ripe old age right here at Pleasant Hill. And that's what she done all right. But nobody knew for sure if it was just the ravin' of a sick old woman or what.

REBECCA: Spirit-baby real, Sarah...

SARAH: I guess.

(*Pause.*)

REBECCA: What else folks say about that girl-child, Sister?

SARAH: Nothin', I know of.

REBECCA: Then come down to it: ain't nobody clear nor certain of the ways of spirit-baby, is that right, Sarah?

SARAH: I reckon.

REBECCA: Ain't nobody sure who she be or why she come.

SARAH: Elderess Emmanuel says: best way is to pray to the Lord God Almighty and leave old spirit-baby be. That be the best way by far, she says.

(*There is a long silence... Suddenly REBECCA looks up.*)

REBECCA: Sarah... Sarah, listen.

SARAH: The wind... It's stopped... Praise the Lord, Sister... Praise the Lord Almighty.

REBECCA: Oh, Sarah... (*She suddenly breaks down and begins to cry.*)

SARAH: (*Holding her.*) It's all right, Rebecca... Spirit-child can't hurt you now.

REBECCA: I ain't afraid... I just feel so awful... Like I want to cry forever.

SARAH: I know how you feel... I was the same way when I first came here... I didn't think spring would ever come... But it did.

REBECCA: I want to be a good girl, Sister Sarah... I wanna give up my sinful ways and live in the love of the Lord God Almighty.

SARAH: Lord loves you, Rebecca... Though lovin' <u>Him</u> sometimes is hard... But spring is comin'... And everything will come fresh and new...

(*REBECCA dries her eyes and smiles.*)

SARAH: Here now, come look for yourself.

(*SARAH takes REBECCA's hand and leads her up the balcony to the window.*)

SARAH: See the top of that ol' maple tree over there. Look at them little green buds just fillin' up with life.

REBECCA: Oh, Sarah, them buds is gonna be poppin' quick as anything... Spring'll be here no time – fillin' up the hills and fields... Look, Sarah, what's that over yonder?

SARAH: Where?

REBECCA: Over there... Patch with the funny little fencin' about it.

SARAH: That's Holy Ground... Won't be long we'll be havin' Spring Picnic over there.

REBECCA: (*Ecstatic.*) Oh, Lordy, Sarah. I do so love a picnic... We used to have lovely picnics back home – down along the Cumberland River.

SARAH: (*Hesitantly.*)... Well, it – it ain't a <u>real</u> picnic.

REBECCA: (*Disappointed.*)... What kind of picnic is it?

SARAH: It's a Shaker picnic... We <u>call</u> it a picnic... 'Cause we go there to Holy Ground and eat a spiritual meal... And we dance, and we gather up baskets of spirit-seeds and plant 'em all over our land... As far as it goes... All the way to the river... Plant seeds of Love and Hope and Truth... Makin' the ground ready for God to plant His seeds and ours, too – so we'll have good crops come harvest... It's a wonderful time, Rebecca, and the dancin' is such fun... It lasts almost the whole day over.

REBECCA: (*Smiling*)... You're sayin' true, Sister Sarah. Spring is comin' on quick, and it's gonna make everything sweet and fresh and new... Praise the Lord God Almighty!

(*The lights go out on the scene. We hear the rousing strains of "Mother Ann's Song # 1" played instrumentally. When the lights come up, a mimetic dance is in progress which should have all the vigor of an old-fashion barn dance.*)

(*The scene is Holy Ground. An empty barrel has been placed upstage center. The WOMEN, as usual, are to the right; the MEN to the left. There are bright table cloths spread out on the ground and the MEN and WOMEN are finishing their spiritual meal. ELDER JACOB moves upstage of the barrel as the WOMEN gather up their baskets. They skip-dance to the music passing ELDER JACOB as he fills up their baskets with imaginary seeds. Then the WOMEN weave a variety of patterns in and out among the MEN. The WOMEN toss the "seeds" from their baskets in all directions. The MEN join in the dance by whirling the table cloths about in splashes of color. Suddenly the song stops. The MEN and WOMEN drop their heads in silent prayer and then, with shouts of joy, rush off in various directions to plant their spirit-seeds.*)

(*The stage is empty for a moment and then REBECCA enters slowly with her basket. She looks off in the direction of the dancers but makes no effort to join them. SARAH enters down right, also carrying a basket.*)

SARAH: Rebecca?... What's troublin' you, girl? Your stomach turn sour on you?

REBECCA: Oh, Sarah, I do wisht it had been a real picnic. With sweet cider and fresh bread... Down 'long the river... (*She notices SARAH's disappointment.*) ... Oh well, I expect maybe I am a bit peaked-feelin' today. You run along. I'll catch up in no time.

SARAH: All right... You go on back to Westhouse. Old Prudence'll fix you up with some of her sassafras tea... Sure to get the winter blood out, right now.

REBECCA: I will, Sarah... You run along now.

(*SARAH exits. REBECCA turns and crosses down stage. She kneels and takes a green maple leaf from her basket. She holds the leaf to her cheek and begins to cry softly. Now, holding the leaf in her lap, she begins to rock rhythmically back and forth... PETER enters upstage. He looks closely at REBECCA.*)

PETER: Rebecca?

REBECCA: Peter.

PETER: Are you all right?

REBECCA: Yes... I'm fine. Please go away.

PETER: Why are you cryin'?

REBECCA: No reason.

PETER: Folks don't cry for no reason.

REBECCA: Don't matter... Just go away... I pledged to God in my prayers not to talk to you this way no more.

PETER: (*Ignoring her.*)... I'd like to help, if I can... Sometimes just talkin' can help.

REBECCA: You can help by just movin' yourself out of here. Right now.

PETER: ....I ain't goin' till you say what's troublin' you.

REBECCA: It's just a silly old nothin', is all.

PETER: Are you thinkin' on James Ketchins and your baby, again?

REBECCA: Maybe... If I was to tell you, would you go and leave me be?

PETER: Aye... I will.

REBECCA: But you ain't to tell a livin' soul.

PETER: Never tell anybody the things we say to each other.

REBECCA: I cry now every time I see the first green leaf on a maple tree or the first leaf turn red and gold come autumn... (*Looks at him.*)... Well now, ain't that just silly woman's doin's?

PETER: I expect you have your reasons.

REBECCA: (*Pause.*)... I cry 'cause James Ketchins would fetch me home the first green leaf he'd see in spring and the first leaf to turn red and gold come autumn... Kept 'em all, too... Pressed in a old bible preacher give us... Kept every one in that old bible.

(*Pause.*)

PETER: Rebecca, I come to tell you I made up my mind to leave Pleasant Hill.

(*REBECCA turns quickly to look at him.*)

REBECCA: Oh... (*Pause.*)

PETER: I reckon that ain't much of a surprise to you though, is it?

REBECCA: No... You fixin' on leavin' soon?

PETER: Lots of work to do here till summer's over. I'm no Winter Shaker... I'll stay for the work and get on out before the first snowfall.

(*Pause.*)

REBECCA: They say ever since that trouble over to Harper's Ferry, there's sure to be a war.

PETER: I expect if it's to come there's no stoppin' it. Maybe it's the only way some folks is ever gonna be free.

REBECCA: Shaker ways don't allow killin'... You'll hold hard to that won't you, Peter?

PETER: Don't know what a man'll do till he's pushed right to it... Maybe it ain't right either for some folks to stand aside and let others do the killin' for 'em.

REBECCA: Elder Jacob say ain't no reason for one livin' soul ever to kill another.

PETER: Lot's of ways one livin' soul ought not be treatin' another. Black man ought not be sold and whipped and treated like a no account. Our black Shakers would tell you that, and Elder Jacob would preach it.

REBECCA: What if – what if the war was to take you?

PETER: I ain't afraid of dyin', Rebecca... Least ways I think not.

REBECCA: James Ketchins weren't afraid of no coal minin' slide neither... But he's lyin' under ten ton of mountain side, just the same.

PETER: All I know is the Lord will be with me in the paths I choose to go. Other than that – what I'll feel or what I'll do – won't know till the World out there takes its measure of me and I of it.

REBECCA: Then God be with you, Peter Scroggins. I'll pray for you every night – same as I pray for James Ketchins and my little possum baby... (*Pause.*) I reckon it's time for you to put your tracks in the dust now. We'll just say our goodbyes here.

(*PETER tries to say something more but can't. They stand looking at each other for a moment, then PETER turns and begins to leave up let. Suddenly, he stops and whirls back to her.*)

PETER: I can't... I can't just turn my back and walk away like this.

REBECCA: (*Apprehensively.*)... Peter -

PETER: I came to say more... I been studyin' on how to say it for days... But there's no way of sayin' but straight out.

REBECCA: Please, Peter... Please leave me be.

PETER: When my time comes, Rebecca... Before the first snowfall... When I leave Pleasant Hill... I want you to come with me as my wife.

REBECCA: No, Peter... I can't do that.

PETER: I love you, Rebecca... I love you as deep as a man can love a woman.

REBECCA: (*Putting her hands over her ears.*) Stop it!... Stop it!

PETER: And if you was to look into your heart, I think you'd find a tiny seed of love for me, too.

REBECCA: Peter Scroggins, you are a devil-boy... That's what you are. You are a devil-boy come straight up out of hell.

PETER: It's not wrong for a man and woman to love each other. You loved James Ketchins, didn't you?

REBECCA: Stop it!

PETER: Was that wrong? What was wrong about your love with James Ketchins? Said yourself that him and your little baby were the two most precious things of your whole life.

REBECCA: (*Screaming.*)... They're dead!... They're dead!... They're dead!

(*REBECCA drops to the ground sobbing. There is a long pause. PETER stoops beside her.*)

PETER: (*Gently.*) That's right, Rebecca, they're dead and restin' with the Lord... And you are alive... You are young and beautiful and full of God's life... And you can make more babies to love – just like your little possum baby.

REBECCA: (*Looks at him coldly.*) Oh, you are a cruel and heartless boy, Peter Scroggins... You want to run to that World out there? You get runnin'... You run to your war or anything you've a mind to. I turned from that World, and I ain't goin' back to it for you nor nobody.

PETER: If that's what you want... (*He stands.*) But it won't stop me from lovin' you... And it won't stop me from askin' you to think on it till the time comes.

REBECCA: If you don't leave me alone this instant, I'm callin' out for Elder Jacob... Callin' out and tellin' what we been doin'.

PETER: (*Angrily.*)... Go on!... Go on and call out for Elder Jacob! Call out for whoever you please! Ain't nothin' in this world we been doin' to be ashamed of in the eyes of God or anybody else.

REBECCA: I aim to be an upstandin' Shaker lady... Follow the ways of Jesus Christ and Mother Ann.

PETER: You can run from the World, but you can't run from yourself.

REBECCA: Mother Ann lost four of her babies and God still forgive her.

PETER: God isn't punishin' you, Rebecca.

REBECCA: I'm a sinner in the eyes of the Lord.

PETER: God is love and forgiveness. And not just for Shaker folks – for everyone.

REBECCA: I killed James Ketchins in the eyes of the Lord.

PETER: No, Rebecca! No, not the Lord... You... It's you been punishin' yourself like you was holdin a serpent to your heart.

REBECCA: (*Crying out at the top of her voice.*) Sarah!... Sarah!!

(*Complete silence and stillness. Tension hangs in the air.*)

PETER: (*Softly.*)... I ain't ashamed... I ain't ashamed of the love I hold for you.

(*SARAH rushes in. She stops short as she sees PETER.*)

SARAH: Peter?

REBECCA: (*Very calmly.*)... Sister Sarah, you go get Elder Jacob... Bring him here. Tell him I need to confess my sins straight away.

(*SARAH rushes off. REBECCA and PETER stand looking at each other over an endless void.*)

PETER: I love you Rebecca. I'll hold you in my heart forever.

(*PETER bends down and picks up the maple leaf. As he extends it to her, the lights go to black. From the darkness we hear the SHAKERS singing "My Carnal Life I will Lay Down."*)

CHORUS: (*Singing.*)
My carnal life I will lay down
Because it is depraved.
I'm sure on any other ground

The Dancers of Canaan

I never can be saved.

My haughty spirit I'll subdue.
I'll seek humiliation
And if I'm true my work to do
I know I'll find salvation.

(*When the lights come up, the MEN and WOMEN are lined up at the benches opposite each other. At the top of the lines are PETER and REBECCA. ELDERESS EMMANUEL and ELDER JACOB stand side-by-side on the small platform center.*)

ELDER JACOB: Brother Scroggins. Stand forward.

(*PETER does, several paces.*)

ELDERESS EMMANUEL: Rebecca, is it true that Peter Scroggins has broken silence with you in secret and has expressed a love for you of carnal nature?

REBECCA: (*Faintly and hesitantly, her eyes cast downward.*)... Aye.

ELDER JACOB: Peter, what say you to this charge?

PETER: ... I love her as a man loves a woman... To say otherwise is to say untrue.

ELDERESS EMMANUEL: Rebecca, do you agree that Peter Scroggins attempted to lure you from Gospel Order for the purpose of living as man and wife.

REBECCA: ... Aye.

ELDER JACOB: And do you, Peter Scroggins, agree to such intent?

PETER: Aye.

ELDERESS EMMANUEL: You may return to your place, Rebecca.

(*REBECCA joins the line.*)

ELDER JACOB: Do you, Peter Scroggins, wish to remain a true and obedient member of the Society of Believers?

PETER: (*Pause.*)... Aye.

ELDER JACOB: Do you agree to the punishment that shall be given you before this assembly?

PETER: I do.

ELDER JACOB: Then so long as you remain in Gospel Order, you are never to speak to Rebecca Westcott or to any of your Sisters except in the presence of another Brother or Sister and then only of necessity... (*Pause.*) For a period of three months you are restricted to your quarters except as you are required to take meals, labor at your work in the fields, and join this community in worship service... Do you so agree, Brother Peter?

PETER: I do.

ELDER JACOB: Then you are to retire to your room forthwith – to begin a period of three days of fasting and prayer... Go now, Peter. And may God have mercy on your soul.

(*PETER looks longingly at REBECCA, whose eyes remain cast down. PETER exits up right.*)

ELDER JACOB: The devil has clearly stolen among our flock. Let us pray for Brother Peter and let us "labor" to purge us of our sins.

GROUP: Amen!

(*A SINGLE VOICE begins "Who Will Bow and Bend Like a Willow." The singing begins slowly and gradually* OTHERS *join in. The song will continue to grow in speed and intensity, taking on the energy and excitement of a full-scale revival. Perhaps, at some point, someone might drop to his/her knees, speaking in tongues; another worshipper falling into convulsions.*)

SHAKERS: (*Singing.*)
Who will bow and bend like a willow
Who will turn and twist and reel
In the gale of simple freedom
From the power of union flowing.
Who will drink the wine of power,
Dropping down like a shower
Pride and bondage all forgetting
Mother's wine is freely working.

Oh ho! I will have it, I will bow
And bend to get it.
I'll be reeling, turning, twisting
Shake out all the starch and stiff'ning.

MAN: Forgive me, O Lord, for my failure to accept my duties with a grateful spirit!

(*The* GROUP *now takes up the song, "Come Life, Shaker Life," at a very rapid pace.*)

GROUP: (*Singing.*)
Come life, Shaker life! Come life eternal!
Shake, shake out of me all that is carnal!

(*A* WOMAN *shrieks and falls to her knees.*)

WOMAN: Forgive me, my Brothers and Sisters, for lusting after the things of this world!

(*Another* WOMAN *dropping to her knees.*)

OTHER WOMAN: Forgive me for holding in my heart a jealousy toward my Brothers and Sisters who surpass me in holiness and zeal!

(*The song has been continuing to the frenzied movements of the* WORSHIPPERS.)

GROUP: (*Singing.*)
Come life, Shaker life! Come life eternal!
Shake, shake out of me all that is carnal!
I'll take nimble steps, I'll be a David
I'll show Michael twice how he behaved
I'll take nimble steps, I'll be a David
I'll show Michael twice how he behaved!

(*Suddenly the song stops. The lights dim except for an intense spotlight on* REBECCA. *She drops to her knees, center stage. The* DANCERS *freeze and there is absolute stillness.*)

REBECCA: In the name of Mother Ann... In the name of Jesus Christ... In the name of the Lord God Almighty, I confess the sin I hold in my heart of hearts... I share the sin of Peter Scroggins... I love him as I loved my Pa who turned me from his door; I love him as I loved my poor possum baby who died in the fire; I love him in the way I loved James Ketchins who lies buried in the bowels of the earth... God have mercy on my sinful soul!

(*There is a final burst of sound and movement from the* WORSHIPPERS.)

GROUP: (*Singing.*)
I'll take nimble steps, I'll be a David
I'll show Michael twice how he behaved!

(Then the stage goes to silence and blackness.)

ACT TWO

When the lights come up, ELDERESS EMMANUEL and ELDER JACOB are standing up center on the little platform. The rest of the SHAKERS have placed themselves downstage in straight lines facing the audience. As usual, MEN are to the left and WOMEN to the right. They are singing in unison.

ENSEMBLE: *(Singing.)*
O brethren, ain't you happy
O brethren, ain't you happy
O brethren, ain't you happy
Ye followers of the Lamb

Sing on, dance on, followers of Emmanuel
Sing on, dance on, followers of the Lamb.

(Perhaps the ENSEMBLE continues to hum or sing softly under the following bits of dialogue.)

ELDER JACOB: *(As if, once again, addressing an assemblage of visitors.)*... My dear friends and neighbors: not only do we Shakers strive to be pleasing in the eyes of God, but to be pleasing in the sight of each other as well. We strive to conform our behavior to the precepts laid down for us in our <u>Manual of Good Manners</u>.

(As each SPEAKER delivers a tenet from the <u>Manual</u>, he or she comes forward, speaks and then returns to his or her place.)

WOMAN: "It may be known whether a person is well bred or not, by seeing him eat <u>one</u> meal; it is, therefore, highly necessary to observe the rules of decency and good behavior while eating."

MAN: "Always sit erect at table."

REBECCA: "The body should lean a little forward when eatin', to avoid droppin' food on your clothes."

MAN: "Never gaze at a person when he is eating, for it looks as though you covet his victuals."

WOMAN: "Always pick your bones clean. Shaker your plate."

PARTICULAR MAN: "Never throw nothin' under the table."

(The GROUP looks at him askance. He shrugs slightly and steps back into his place.)

ENSEMBLE: *(Singing.)*
O sisters, ain't you happy
O sisters, ain't you happy
O sisters, ain't you happy
Ye followers of the Lamb

(Clapping.)
Sing on, dance on, followers of Emmanuel
Sing on, dance on, followers of the Lamb.

(Again the GROUP speaks severally.)

REBECCA: "Always be willin' to take your share of disagreeable chores."

MAN: "Never play mean, dirty tricks upon anyone; it shows meanness of heart and an ugly disposition."

WOMAN: "Jests and jokes are edge tools, and very dangerous to use, as they wound the tender feelings of our friends."

SAME PARTICULAR MAN: "Never stand on the sides of your feet; it runs down your shoes."

(Once again, he is looked at with disapproval; he sheepishly steps back into place.)

ENSEMBLE: (*Singing.*)
I'm glad I am a Shaker
I'm glad I am a Shaker
I'm glad I am a Shaker
Ye followers of the Lamb.

(*Clapping.*)
Sing on, dance on, followers of Emmanuel
Sing on, dance on, followers of the Lamb.

(*The GROUP speaks severally a third time.*)

WOMAN: "Never hang about in company where you are not wanted."

MAN: "Be careful not to slam doors hard, not walk heavy up and down stairs; it shows a noisy sense."

WOMAN: "The wicked borrow and never return; but Christians and well bred people make it a rule to return whatever they borrow, as soon as is convenient."

(*The PARTICULAR MAN steps forward. This time everyone looks at him hard before he speaks.*)

PARTICULAR MAN: "Never make fun of anyone on account of his form, features – or lack of intelligence – for it is <u>very</u> mean." (*He smiles smugly and steps back into place.*)

ENSEMBLE: (*Moving vigorously as they sing.*)
I mean to be obedient
I mean to be obedient
I mean to be obedient
Ye followers of the Lamb:

(*Clapping.*)
Sing on, dance on, followers of Emmanuel
Sing on, dance on, followers of the Lamb.

(*The singing trails off as the stage darkens.*)

Followers of the Lamb
    Followers of the Lamb
        Followers of the Lamb.

(*The lights come up once again in the center area. We are now in Rebecca and Sarah's bedroom. The two benches which substitute for beds are in place. REBECCA, however, is in the center of the room. She clutches a small blue book to her breast as she sings softly to herself.*)

REBECCA: (*Singing softly.*)
When true simplicity is gained
To bow and to bend we won't be ashamed.
To turn, turn will be our delight
Till by turning,
Turning we come round right.

(*As REBECCA has been singing, she has been slowly and simply acting out the lyrics. As she finishes singing, she kneels in an attitude of prayer. After a time, ELDERESS EMMANUEL enters up left.*)

ELDERESS EMMANUEL: .... Sister... (*No response.*).... Sister Rebecca?

REBECCA: (*Looking up.*).... Yes, Elderess?

ELDERESS EMMANUEL: You weren't at breakfast this morning. And you haven't been to your work station... Are you ill?

REBECCA: No... I'm fine... How's Sister Sarah this mornin'?

ELDERESS EMMANUEL: ... She's had another bad night... Her fever's worse. We've sent for a doctor in Harrodsburg.

REBECCA: (*Incredulously.*) Worse?... Her fever got worse?

ELDERESS EMMANUEL: <u>Much</u> worse, I'm afraid.

REBECCA: But she's gonna be better. I been prayin' to Mother Ann and Jesus Christ all night long.

ELDERESS EMMANUEL: You must understand, dear, Sister Sarah is very ill.

REBECCA: But she <u>is</u> gonna be better... I <u>know</u> she is! Long as I keep prayin'; God is gonna make Sarah better.

ELDERESS EMMANUEL: Still we must go on, Rebecca -

REBECCA: I know you can send me to my work station. But I need to stay here. If I don't, Sister Sarah's gonna die.

ELDERESS EMMANUEL: (*Pause.*)... How do you know that Sister?

REBECCA: I just know is all.

ELDERESS EMMANUEL: Rebecca, I too pray for Sister Sarah. We all do. But we must be prepared to accept God's will in these matters.

REBECCA: That's just what it is – God's will, all right... It's God's will I keep on prayin' here in my own way – just as long as it takes to make Sister Sarah better again.

ELDERESS EMMANUEL: (*Long pause.*)... All right, Rebecca. (*She starts to go; stops.*) I think Sister Sarah is very lucky to have such a good friend.

(ELDERESS EMMANUEL *exits.* REBECCA *drops her head again in prayer. As the lights fade, we hear a section of "My Carnal Life I Will Lay Down" played instrumentally through the black out. The lights come up on the bedroom again.* SARAH *is seated on "her bed", her legs covered by an afghan. She is recovering from her illness.* REBECCA *enters carrying a bowl of soup.*)

REBECCA: Evenin', Sister Sarah!

SARAH: 'Lo Becca.

REBECCA: My, my! Don't you look fine this hour. Fit as a old bullfrog sittin' wide-eyed on a lily pad. (SARAH *smiles faintly.*) Getting' stronger every day... Brung you another bowl of Sister Martha's herbal stew.

SARAH: (*Accepting it.*)... You ever try this stuff?

REBECCA: (*Cautiously.*) N-o-o-o.

SARAH: Well, don't... Best just to go ahead and die of natural causes. (*She shovels a spoonful into her mouth and makes a terrible face.*)... Ugh!

REBECCA: (*Laughing.*)... My! And downright sassy, too! You <u>must</u> be feelin' better.

SARAH: (*Changing her mood.*)... Rebecca, could you stay with me a spell?

REBECCA: Surely could.

SARAH: I've had somethin' on my mind that I need to talk to you about powerful bad.

REBECCA: (*Sitting opposite her.*) I can give you more lovin' than wisdom, I expect. But if that's what you're lookin' for, you just say on.

SARAH: Well... you know how sick I was. Sicker, I guess than I ever imagined a mortal could be... On fire with the fever... Knowin' I could die quick as anything.

REBECCA: I guess we all knew that for sure. Thought we might lose you straight away.

SARAH: Oh, Becca... I think I done somethin' terrible wrong!

REBECCA: What are you sayin', child?

SARAH: Lyin' there in the fever like I was... Close as a heartbeat to bein' with Jesus... I was gonna be with Jesus, and Mother Ann and Momma... And that's when it come over me.

REBECCA: What, Sarah?

SARAH: I didn't want to die, Becca. I was afraid. In my heart of hearts, I prayed that Jesus wouldn't take me... I wanted to stay right here with you and all the others... Wasn't that hateful of me?

REBECCA: Hateful?

SARAH: Jesus come to take me to Heaven forever and there I was holdin' on to this old life for all I had in me? (*Pause.*)... Becca?... It's all right. You can tell me what you think. I know you'll tell me true.

(*REBECCA sits behind SARAH on the bench and holds her tightly in her arms.*)

REBECCA: (*Slowly and deliberately, as if trying to comprehend fully the meaning of her own words*)... Sarah, I never prayed so hard in my life as I did to the Lord Jesus on the subject of makin' you well again. Think that was wrong of me, child? ... Prayed hard as I knew how so's He'd let you go right on <u>livin'</u> ... And that's when it come to me, too, Sarah: life can't be right just some time... or just for some folks... There must be somethin' awfully important about what it <u>is</u>.

SARAH: I don't think I understand, Rebecca.

REBECCA: Well, I don't mean God Almighty made us an easy world to live in. He sure didn't do <u>that</u> exactly. But you can't make a pot out of clay either.... less'n you knead it first and fire it after. Then it can turn into somethin' beautiful.

(*Pause.*)

SARAH: But the world ain't all pain and sufferin', Becca. God made us lots of good things, too.

REBECCA: I guess that's part of what I'm tryin' to say too, child.

SARAH: ... Gave us warm sun and cool breezes and rich, black earth...

REBECCA: And some days, a sky so blue you want to take off your shoes and go wadin' in it.

SARAH: Then you don't think I was wrong not wantin' to meet Jesus right now?

REBECCA: (*Smiling.*) Like you say, Sarah – if God Almighty went to all this trouble to fix us up so fine a spot as this ol' world, seems the least we can do is stay put till our time comes. I think that's what Elderess Emmanuel would say, too... Fact is, your time just ain't come yet, girl... Why, looks to me like we're gonna grow old together, right here at Pleasant Hill.

SARAH: Oh, Becca, do you think so?

REBECCA: I surely do... Why, we'll be so old we won't be able to climb to the top of Westhouse to scrub on those floors any more!

SARAH: (*Laughing.*)... So old Sister Martha will have clean forgot how to make her herbal stew!

REBECCA: So old we won't have nothin' to do all day but sit rockin' in the sun!

SARAH: Hurrah! (*She forgets and tosses a spoonful of soup in the air, sprinkling it all over herself. Shocked.*) Oh, Rebecca!... Now look what I done... What am I gonna tell Sister Martha?

REBECCA: You just tell her you're a pioneerin' woman.

SARAH: What?!

REBECCA: Reckon everybody knows what a bellyful of Sister Martha's stew can do for your innards, but up until now, ain't nobody thought of spreadin' a little around on top! Turns out: maybe rubbin' it in is a whole lot better than slurpin' it down.

SARAH: Oh, Becca!

(*They embrace. Blackout. From the darkness, we hear a section of "Simple Gifts" played instrumentally. A single spotlight now picks up PETER standing down left.*)

PETER: (*Monologue.*).... Harvest time has come and gone. Most days now there's a chill in the air. A body can tell it isn't long off to first snowfall. My time to leave Pleasant Hill has come.

I remember one time reading in a science book – a big red book kept under lock and key in the school house – about how Nature disdains a void... I reckon that means that when I go – in my absence – something else will come along to take my place. Only, I'm a mite scared of what it is that's on its way... Sometimes, even now we can hear the cannons roarin' off in the distance. And once I saw what looked to me like Yankee reconnaissance in the hills across the river. No doubt about it, the War is on its way to Pleasant Hill.

And one more thing: I haven't spoken to Sister Rebecca since that day at Holy Ground. Kept my word as I said I would. But I aim to keep my word on another matter as well. Come leavin' time, I'll be askin' Rebecca to join me as my wife – just as I told her I would. Even before I heard about her confession at meetin' house, I knew she loved me – as I love her – man to woman. And I know somethin' else for certain: Ain't a heart inside a woman can hold more love than Rebecca's can... Just now – I'm hopin' that little ol' heart of hers has a stickin' place for a whole bunch of courage.

(*The light is extinguished on PETER. After a moment, the lights come up on ELDERESS EMMANUEL and ELDER JACOB in the upstage area. ELDER JACOB is entering with a bundle wrapped in tarpaulin. ELDERESS EMMANUEL is seated on a bench reading from a small book.*)

ELDER JACOB: Everything's in order... He should be by shortly. (*He places the bundle carefully on the floor.*)

ELDERESS EMMANUEL: I'm going to miss him.

ELDER JACOB: I miss them all, Sister – everyone that has ever left us.

ELDERESS EMMANUEL: I know... (*Pause.*) It's just that Peter has always seemed special – such a bright young man.

ELDER JACOB: An agile mind is not always a blessing, I'm afraid.

ELDERESS EMMANUEL: I remember one afternoon – going with my father to Dr. Emerson's house in Concord, Massachusetts. There was a young man there by the name of Henry David Thoreau. He was full of life and curiosity – the room fairly sparkled from his energy. In some ways, Peter has always reminded me of young Mister Thoreau.

ELDER JACOB: (*Smiling softly.*)... May I also remind you, Sister -

ELDERESS EMMANUEL: I know, Brother – a Shaker's past is best left where it lies... But you needn't worry – I never felt a deep attachment to an Oversoul. (*She smiles.*)

ELDER JACOB: I've gotten his provisions together – a change of clothing, a good piece of tarpaulin to keep off the weather, some meal and a bit of salted meat. That ought to get him as far as Louisville, I should imagine.

ELDERESS EMMANUEL: (*Pause.*)... Have you tried to talk to him?

ELDER JACOB: Have I counseled him to stay, do you mean?

ELDERESS EMMANUEL: If it were possible perhaps -

ELDER JACOB: No, Sister, I have not. Our ways demand more than simple belief. We seek nothing less than perfection. You know as well as I: doubt does not rest comfortably with commitment. It is best that Peter discover the world for himself – best for him and best for our community of Believers.

ELDERESS EMMANUEL: It is, after all, the others we must think of, isn't it?... You're a good man, Brother Jacob... Your hurt is no less deep... But you always do what is best for the others.

(*PETER enters up right.*)

PETER: May I come in?

ELDER JACOB: Yes, please.

(*PETER enters the playing area.*)

PETER: (*With nods of acknowledgement.*)... Elderess Emmanuel... Elder Jacob... I came for my things as you told me.

(*ELDER JACOB indicates the bundle on the floor.*)

PETER: I been studyin' on what to say as partin' words... Only now that I'm here, everything's sort of a jumble in my head. Don't mind tellin' you though, my heart feels somethin' terrible.

ELDER JACOB: Sometimes words aren't important, Peter. I don't think Elderess Emmanuel and I would do a very good job of putting our feelings into words just now either... Do you have your uncle's address in Louisville?

PETER: Yes, sir... Elderess Emmanuel gave it to me last week.

ELDER JACOB: He seems like a good man, Peter. He's agreed to take you in for a spell and help you get a start in the world.

PETER: ... Did he mention of my mother? Is she alive, did he say?

ELDER JACOB: I'm afraid we didn't speak of your family. I'm sure your uncle will tell you what he can when you get there.

(*PETER nods... A pause.*)

PETER: ....I – I expect I better be getting' on down to the landin'... Don't want to miss the boat up river. (*PETER starts to pick up the bundle.*)

ELDER JACOB: Peter, there *is* something I'd like to say -

PETER: Yes, sir. (*He lets the bundle lie.*)

ELDER JACOB: ... I'm now in my fifty-fifth year. I came to Community when I was thirty-eight years old. I had been a successful business man in the world – a grain merchant. What I saw in my life distressed me greatly – men professing to be followers of Christ, following only the ways of Man – greed, hypocrisy, the quest for power over others – these were their gods... You're a good boy, Peter. Stay that way.

PETER: I'll try surely... You and Elderess Emmanuel are the only mother and father I ever knew. If, in the world, I'm to have children some day, I'll teach them the things you taught me. I'll teach 'em about livin' simple and workin' hard and about all men bein' brothers. I'll tell 'em of Jesus and Mother Ann, too... I expect there will always be a part of me that'll be a Shaker, no matter what.

ELDER JACOB: Bless you, Peter.

ELDERESS EMMANUEL: I thought perhaps you'd like to have this book.

(*She extends it to PETER who takes it from her.*)

PETER: Mother Ann's little book.

ELDERESS EMMANUEL: I've marked a passage I thought you might like to carry with you.

(*PETER opens the book and reads softly.*)

PETER: ... "Do not go away and report that we forbid to marry, for unless you are able to take up a full cross, and part with every gratification of the flesh, for the Kingdom of God, I would counsel you, and all such, to take wives in a lawful manner, and cleave to them only, and raise up a lawful posterity, and be perpetual servants to your families... Mother Ann."

ELDERESS EMMANUEL: I've something else for you, Peter. Something I think you will treasure. (*She takes a small package wrapped in brown paper from the pocket of her apron. She gives it to PETER.*) Your mother gave this to me the day she brought you to Pleasant Hill. She knew as Shakers, we hold all things in common. But I promised her if you ever chose to leave Gospel Order, I would see that it was given to you.

PETER: (*Having opened the package.*) ... A comb – shiny as a pearl.

ELDERESS EMMANUEL: I watched her take it from her hair that day... She looked tired and her features were drawn... But, as I watched her soft, dark hair fall gently about her face, I thought how very beautiful she was... It was all she had to give you, Peter.... She loved you very much.

(*PETER struggles a moment with his emotions, and then he suddenly embraces ELDERESS EMMANUEL. She instinctively raises her arms to return his embrace. But then, slowly, she allows her arms to fall to her sides. But she makes no reprimand; nor does ELDER JACOB who looks away.*)

PETER: Thank you... Thank you both for everything.

ELDER JACOB: Come, Peter, your Brothers and Sisters are waiting to bid you farewell... God be with you, my son.

(*PETER picks up the bundle from the floor as the lights go to black. In the darkness, we hear the ENSEMBLE singing, "Now My Dear Companion." When the lights come up again, the bench up center has been removed. ELDERESS EMMANUEL and ELDER JACOB are once again standing side by side on the small platform upstage.*)

(*PETER stands far downstage, his back to the audience, facing ELDERESS EMMANUEL and ELDER JACOB. The SHAKERS enter from upstage left and right. The MEN and WOMEN meet and move downstage in pairs. PETER shakes hands with the MEN – or embraces close friends – and bows slightly to the WOMEN who return a curtsy. Then the MEN move off to the left and the WOMEN to the right. They face away from PETER, never to look back on him. PETER moves gradually upstage as he encounters each couple. It is important to note that REBECCA is not present.*)

ENSEMBLE: (*Singing.*)
Now my dear companion
Is the time to start anew
Anew, Anew for the Kingdom of Heaven
With faith and zeal and courage strong
We will ever be marching on
Toiling on, struggling on, for a perfect Heaven.

We will not be hindered
While we walk the narrow way.
Narrow way, narrow way with Our Gospel Kindred
But every foe that comes in view
In ourselves we will subdue
And be true to subdue the way that leads to glory.

(*When PETER has moved to the top of the line, he stands before ELDERESS EMMANUEL and ELDER JACOB. They exchange bows, and then ELDERESS and ELDER split to right and left. PETER, bundle in hand, steps between and beyond them into the upstage area. He looks back one last time at his <u>family</u>. All backs are to him. As he turns to leave, the lights go to black on the dying strains of the hymn.*)

(*From the darkness, we hear SARAH's voice.*)

SARAH: (*Calling out.*) Rebecca!... Sister Rebecca!... Will you come on!

(*When the lights come up, SARAH is standing down stage left, holding a large empty laundry basket. She is calling to REBECCA who is offstage left.*)

SARAH: Sister Rebecca!

(*REBECCA enters down left.*)

SARAH: We're gonna be in a heap of trouble if we're not over to the Wash House before this storm comes in.

REBECCA: Probably ain't gonna rain a drop. By the time we take all the beddin' down, we'll have to turn right around and hang it all back up again.

SARAH: Don't matter which way – however Sister Joshua tells us... Where have you been, anyway?

REBECCA: Over to the Old Mill.

SARAH: What on earth were you doin' over there?

REBECCA: Remember that little rose slip I planted by the stone fence last spring?... Well, it's doin' right hearty, I'd say. Appears now it'll surely bloom come springtime.

SARAH: I declare!... Don't you ever get tired of stickin' things in the ground?

REBECCA: Watchin' things grow is fun... Like watchin' God paint a picture.

SARAH: Sounds like Peter Scroggins talkin' now –

(*There is a pause. REBECCA drops her head. SARAH is upset with herself.*)

SARAH: I'm sorry, Rebecca. I didn't mean to say that.

REBECCA: I know... That's all right... That's Peter's gift.

SARAH: (*Impatiently.*) Come on, Sister – please!

REBECCA: (*Holding her ground.*).... Sarah?

SARAH: What, now?

REBECCA: What was it like? When you signed your name into the Covenant book, I mean?

SARAH: .... I don't know – you just write down your name and say some words is all.

REBECCA: I mean – how did you feel inside yourself? Did you feel different somehow?

SARAH: ... Sort of... 'Course, I guess everybody feels it different somehow.

REBECCA: How did *you* feel it, Sarah?

SARAH: Hard to say... Strange, I guess... Like a dream I had one time.

REBECCA: Tell me of the dream, Sarah.

SARAH: Well... I was – I was in this big room, all dark and shadowy – with windows way high up on the walls, only there was no light comin' in hardly at all... And then, this big iron door closed behind me. But it weren't scary or anything... It closed real gentle like – soft and without a sound – like the fallin' of a snowflake... And when I turned around again, there was all this white light streamin' in from everywhere... And it was real peaceful – like I was meant to be there forever.

REBECCA: Oh, my, yes, Sarah!... That's just how it ought to be. Things feel different here than any place I've ever been.

SARAH: What do you mean by that?

REBECCA: Like when I first come to Pleasant Hill.

SARAH: I remember – you said we'd be best friends, and that's just how we are, best friends.

REBECCA: I was feelin' real bad 'cause I had nothin' to bring with me to Community – on account of the fire and all.

SARAH: That's all right. Lots of folks come that way.

REBECCA: Just last week, Brother Daniel Cummins brought three Hampshire sheep and a brand new carriage harness... And when Sister Charity come, she brought a bedstead and two bolts of fine linen... And you was able to give that mixin' bowl your dear Gran'mama give you one Christmas... But all I had was the clothes on my back and thirty-seven cents I had left over that Abigail Stoker give me for my passage. So I give Elderess Emmanuel and Elder Jacob thirty-seven cents and a bunch of wildflowers I picked on the road down to the river. And they blessed me as if I had given them a king's ransom. In my heart, I knew they were pleased with my gift, and they seemed right pleased about my comin' on to stay... I never felt so welcome anywhere before... And all I brought to Community was thirty-seven cents and a bunch of silly ol' wildflowers.

SARAH: Don't matter what you give. It's what's in your heart that matters.

REBECCA: Sarah?

SARAH: Yes.

REBECCA: ... Do you suppose that's the way God loves us?

SARAH: Yes, Sister... I surely do.

REBECCA: (*Smiling.*)... Sister Lucy Almonds say I'm doin' right well at bein' a Shaker lady... She say, come springtime, I can sign into the Covenant Book if I've a mind to... Maybe I'll sign the book the very day my little rose slip puts out its first blossom.

SARAH: Well, it ain't gonna do that anytime soon. And standin' around talkin' about it ain't getting' the bed sheets took in.

REBECCA: (*Laughing.*) You know, Sarah, when we first met, you was a shy little critter by your own tellin'... But since you got me to scold after, you've turned into a right forceful young lady.

(*SARAH joins in the laughter.*)

SARAH: Come on, Sister Rebecca... I'll race you to the Wash House.

(*They turn to run off when PETER suddenly appears upstage in their path.*)

SARAH: (*Startled.*)...Peter!!

PETER: Sister Sarah... Rebecca...

REBECCA: (*Quietly.*) Hello, Peter.

(*They stand their ground at some distance.*)

PETER: Been lookin' everywhere for you, Rebecca. I missed you over to Meetin' House just now.

REBECCA: ... Figured we'd said our goodbyes a long time back, Peter... Dared not to have the hurt of watchin' you leave.

SARAH: I better get on down to the Wash House... I'll just tell Sister Joshua, I couldn't find you.

REBECCA: No, Sarah... I want you to stay right here.

PETER: Rebecca's right, Sister... Gave my word I'd never speak to Rebecca again except in the presence of another... Besides there's nothin' I ever said – or aim to say now – that I'm ashamed of.

(SARAH *stays uncomfortably in the background.* PETER *moves closer to* REBECCA.)

PETER: You know why I come, don't you, Rebecca?

REBECCA: (*Softly.*)... Yes.

PETER: Just like I spoke it: The day I was to leave Pleasant Hill was the day I'd come to ask you to be my wife.

(REBECCA *says nothing.*)

PETER: I love you, Rebecca... Loved you from the first day I saw you.

REBECCA: Peter -

PETER: Before you say on, I'd just like to try to speak as I feel... Truth is, I'm as scared of the world out there as you are... Scareder, maybe... But I know one thing: if we was together, there'd be no trouble we couldn't get through... and no day so awful there'd be no joy in it... There's a part of me, Rebecca, that's all unfinished somehow... Like a fine Shaker box with nothin' to put inside... There's a part of me I need to make me feel whole that ain't even mine... It's you, Rebecca... You're the part of me I need to make me whole... Just as I pray there's a part of me you need in the very same way. As I see it, that's how the Lord Almighty made most men and women to be... And, if you was to come with me, Rebecca, I'd love you and honor you till my last day on this earth. I truly will.

REBECCA: There's no finer man than you, Peter Scroggins. And that's a fact. You honor me with the askin' – sin or no sin, as my brothers and sisters might see it... It's just that things happen sometimes, Peter – things that nobody even expects or makes plans for.

PETER: Things like what, Rebecca?.... Like losin' your little possum baby?

REBECCA: No, not that... Not _just_ that... Peter, do you remember what you said to me that first day we spoke – up top of Westhouse... when you was about to leave?

(*Pause.*)

PETER: I said as how it seemed you was takin' up a Shaker life quick as I was runnin' from it and, if we wasn't careful, we'd be passin' one another "lickety split."

REBECCA: Don't you see, Peter? That's what happened... With no blame or meanin' to it – we just passed one another "lickety split."

PETER: Say it how you will, Rebecca. But I'll tell you straight out – you don't belong here. And I'll hold to it, if you marry me or no.

REBECCA: _You_ can't judge a thing like that...

PETER: I say I can and do. These are fine people here, Rebecca, and I love 'em the same as you do. Some fit in like they was born to it – Sister Sarah here, for one.

REBECCA: Peter, I do, too.

PETER: And I say not. I've seen brothers and sisters come and go, Rebecca. Studied 'em all my life... Some come dead to the world and find new life here and that's a fact... And some come tryin' to hide from life, like they was afraid to let it touch 'em... Hidin' ain't livin', Rebecca... There's a whole bunch of life in you, girl, and it ain't meant to be shut away at Shakertown.

REBECCA: (*Gently.*) I'm sorry... But you don't understand -

PETER: Answer me one question, Rebecca... One question and swear it's of a truth... Do you love me?... Do you love me the way you loved James Ketchins?... Do you?

REBECCA: I do, Peter... I love you as I loved James Ketchins. And I expect if we was to live together as man and wife I'd love you even more.

PETER: Then come with me, girl... Come with me as my wife.

REBECCA: I can't.

PETER: In heaven's name, Rebecca – WHY?

REBECCA: Because I promised Mother Ann, if she made Sarah better, I'd never leave Pleasant Hill.

(*There is a long pause. PETER is stunned and unsure of what to say or do.*)

REBECCA: ... It's all right, Peter... I'm happy here... Really I am.

PETER: (*Almost in despair.*) Rebecca... Rebecca, prayin' for Sister Sarah that way was as fine and beautiful a thing as... as a body could do. But God didn't let Sarah live because of your promise... <u>God</u> wanted Sarah to live... Just as He wants you to live, too.

REBECCA: How do <u>you</u> know what God Almighty wants of me, Peter?

PETER: Rebecca, this might be our one and only chance to live the blessings of a full life together... Maybe the very life you and I was put on this earth to live.

REBECCA: Maybe God Almighty doesn't decide things like that <u>for</u> us, Peter... Maybe our life is more like a gift – and each one of us has to decide who gets what part of it.

PETER: Shakers come and go all the time. If this is where your heart is, it will draw you back like a loadstone. And I won't stop you, I promise... Just don't throw away the one chance we might have together.

(*A boat whistle is heard plaintively in the distance.*)

REBECCA: Your boat's in, Peter... You better hurry on now, or you'll miss your boat up river.

PETER: ... It won't be leavin' soon. Lots of provisions to take on. Plenty of time for you to change your mind.

REBECCA: ...Goodbye, Peter... God be with you. (*She turns away down right.*)

PETER: (*Slowly, hesitantly.*)... Seems I got me an uncle down in Louisville I didn't know I had... I aim to make sure he'll always know my whereabouts... So folks can get hold of me, if they've a mind to... I wrote down where he lives on this paper here, Rebecca... (*He offers the paper.*)... If you was just to take it... I mean, if you was ever to change your mind...

(*REBECCA has remained still throughout, her back turned to him. PETER decides it is pointless to continue.*)

PETER: I'll never stop lovin' you, Rebecca... I'll wait for you forever, if I need to... (*He turns to SARAH.*) Bless you, Sister Sarah.

SARAH: 'Bye, Peter.

PETER: ... 'Bye, Rebecca... God bless you.

(*He turns and runs off up left. There is a long pause. REBECCA continues to stand motionless.*)

SARAH: Storm's movin' in now... I better go, Becca. I'll tell Sister Joshua I couldn't find you.

(*She exits up right. REBECCA stands staring off. After a moment, she lifts her eyes to heaven.*)

REBECCA: Mother Ann?... Give me the light to see my way.

(*A gun shot rings out stage left.*)

REBECCA: (*Screaming.*) ... Peter??!!

(*As she dashes stage left, a young CONFEDERATE SOLDIER stumbles on stage in front of her.*)

REBEL SOLDIER: (*Wide-eyed with disbelief*)... My God, ma'am, I – I been shot... (*He stumbles toward her.*)... Don't let me die.

(*Instinctively, she backs away from him to center stage. He falls at her feet. VOICES are heard off left.*)

VOICES: (*Off.*)... You hit him sure... He's gotta be around here somewheres... Looks like he might have stumbled off into the brush over yonder.

(*A young YANKEE SOLDIER enters with a rifle. He and REBECCA make eye contact. She drops to her knees and holds the young CONFEDERATE BOY in her arms protectively.*)

YANKEE: (*Crying out.*)... I found him! He's over here!

VOICE: (*Off.*) Can't let the Rebs know we're about. If he ain't dead, Private, finish him off, you hear?

(*Pause. The YANKEE raises his rifle and holds the wounded BOY in his gun sight. REBECCA draws the BOY closer to her.*)

YANKEE: (*Finally lowering his gun. Calling out.*)... He's dead, Captain!... Let's get out of here!

(*He exits left. Pause.*)

REBEL SOLDIER: Thank you, kindly, ma'am... Appears I found me my very own guardian angel.

REBECCA: I'll go fetch help, now... They won't be back soon.

REBEL SOLDIER: (*Holding tightly to her hand and pulling her back to him.*)... Please don't leave me, ma'am!

REBECCA: But you're hurt bleedin' bad... You need help straight away.

REBEL SOLDIER: No, Ma'am... I don't think so... I was a farm boy back in Alabama... Looks to me like I found me the last good piece of earth I'm likely to see... Suppose I ought to know what place this is, after all.

REBECCA: This here is... is called Pleasant Hill... We're Shaker folks hereabouts.

REBEL SOLDIER: I heard of you folks, all right. (*He begins to cough.*) Maybe I came to the right place after all... (*He coughs, violently, spitting blood.*)... Jesus, help me... I'm scared ma'am. I don't want to die.

REBECCA: I know... I know... (*She holds him closer.*)... It'll be all right, boy... Just like Elder Jacob read to us in the Bible: This day you'll be with the Lord Almighty in Paradise.

REBEL SOLDIER: But I'm a sinner, ma'am.

REBECCA: Shh! ... Be still now, boy... Lord loves you just the same.

REBEL SOLDIER: But I killed a man in a fire fight down around Jellico... Maybe two men... Maybe three...

(*REBECCA is rocking him now. She is softly humming the "Shepherdess' Song" to him.*)

REBEL SOLDIER: (*Long pause.*)... Tell me, ma'am... If I was sorry... I mean, sorry as I truly am for the killin' of my fellow man... Do you think the Lord could forgive me such a sin as that?

REBECCA: Yes, boy... I surely do.

REBEL SOLDIER: (*Looking steadily into her eyes.*)... How do you know that, ma'am? How do you know God could even forgive me such a sin as that?

(*Something is slowly dawning on REBECCA. She looks up and listens carefully to her own answer.*)

REBECCA: Because <u>I</u> can, soldier boy... Because I can.

REBEL SOLDIER: Ma'am?

REBECCA: (*Smiles down at the boy in her arms.*)... All I know for sure is that the Lord Almighty wants to hold you in his arms and rock you like a baby from this day on.

REBEL SOLDIER: (*Smiles.*)... Then I ain't scared no more, ma'am... (*Pause.*) It's getting' dark all around now... What's your name, ma'am?

REBECCA: ... Rebecca... Sister Rebecca.

REBEL SOLDIER: .... That's a pretty name for an angel... Tonight, when you say your prayers, Sister Rebecca, will you remember to pray for me? (*He coughs again.*)

REBECCA: I surely will and every day and every night... Just like I pray for my Papa and James Ketchins and little Mary... and dear, dear Peter...

REBEL SOLDIER: My name's Seth, ma'am... Seth - (*He tries to form a last name. It doesn't come and on his last breath, he repeats.*) ... Seth...

(*REBECCA stares dumbly at the dead soldier cradled in her arms. Suddenly, the wind begins to rise again with great intensity. The lights dim and the LITTLE GIRL appears once more in her strange light.*)

CHILD: Thank you, Becca... (*The CHILD turns to exit.*)

REBECCA: Spirit baby! (*The CHILD pauses.*)...I'm frightened.

CHILD: I'll be with you, Becca... I'll be with you.

(*The wind reaches a fever pitch and the lights go to black. When the lights come up, we are again at Meeting House. A jubilant spirit prevails among the SHAKERS as they fill the stage with song and dance. The song is "Zion's Kingdom."*)

SOLOIST: (*Singing.*)
I've set my face for Zion's Kingdom
Holy, bright and glorious
Oh...

GROUP: (*Joining in.*)
I've set my face for Zion's Kingdom
Holy, bright and glorious
Oh...
Though boist'rous winds may often blow
Oh...
To that bright home I'm bound to go
Oh...

(*As the song is being repeated a second or perhaps a third time, REBECCA enters upstage. She is stunned and bloody. The singing gradually stops as the GROUP notices her.*)

ELDERESS EMMANUEL: Rebecca?!... Sister, are you all right? (*ELDERESS goes to her side.*)

REBECCA: (*Quietly.*) Yes...

ELDERESS EMMANUEL: But your clothing, Child... You're blood and mud head to foot.

REBECCA: I just now buried a soldier boy... A young Confederate boy...

(*The CROWD reacts.*)

ELDERESS EMMANUEL: (*Softly.*) God rest his soul.

REBECCA: ... Over in the field by the sheep pen.

ELDER JACOB: (*Simply.*) Then the war has come at last.

ELDERESS EMMANUEL: (*Holding Rebecca.*)... We thought you had gone off with Peter.... There's still time, Child... You're free to go if you wish... Perhaps with the war coming —-

REBECCA: No, ma'am... I wish to stay... Maybe Peter was right after all... Maybe I did come here for all the wrong reasons – with a heart full of guilt for all the bad things that happened to me – tryin' to hide from the world just like he said... But – I - come... And I found somethin' else. I found a peace like I've never known... A deep and healin' peace like this land's gonna need to stop the bleedin' of this awful war... And I found somethin' more, too.

ELDERESS EMMANUEL: What's that, Sister?

REBECCA: It's the part I don't understand neither... Much as I love Peter... All I know is there's somethin' different inside me now... Somethin' I can't even say what – as strange as Sister Sarah's dream and bigger than all the love in the world – strange and real and beautiful as the stars in the sky on a coal dark night.

ELDERESS EMMANUEL: I understand, child. I surely do.

ELDER JACOB: ... My dear brothers and sisters... The time of our trial is at hand... The War has come to Pleasant Hill. But long after the cannons grow still, the spirit of this place – the simpleness of our ways – must be left behind to remind the World of a better way... Come now, my children, let us not be afraid... Let us dance to the Lord with hope and with joy... Let us dance as Mother Ann would have danced... Let us dance to the wonder and mystery of life...

(*The simple, delicate strains of "Hop Up And Jump Up" are heard. Slowly, the CONGREGATION begins to dance.*)

(*REBECCA comes forward and stands center stage. She does not join in the dancing. A faint light begins to grow around her. Then we hear the final boat whistle in the distance – low and insistent. REBECCA turns upstage. She looks for an instant as if she would follow. Instead, she turns again and faces forward, lowering her head in prayer. The DANCERS are moving slowly around her in the deepening shadows.*)

(*The music changes now to the haunting strains of "Simple Gifts." From the shadows, the CHILD enters and crosses to REBECCA. She looks up and smiles at the CHILD. Then, in the brightening circle of light, they dance together in love and final triumph.*)

THE END

Ron Mielech

Ron is a retired Professor of Drama at Thomas More College in Northern Kentucky where he directed over 40 major productions. As a playwright, his work has been seen on college, community, and professional stages, including the Barter Theatre in Virginia, The Mazur Theatre in NYC, Horse Cave Theatre, and most recently The Ensemble Theatre of Cincinnati.

Thomas Baird and Pamela White in *Desert Flower* by Betty Peterson, Horse Cave Theatre, 1996

DESERT FLOWER
by
Betty Peterson

Greg Bernet and Thomas Baird in *Desert Flower* by Betty Peterson, Horse Cave Theatre, 1996

Desert Flower opened on July 12, 1996, with the following cast:

GLENDA EVERSON	*Pamela White*
ROY EVERSON	*Thomas Baird*
MARILEE	*Pam Pendleton*
TEAK	*Greg Bernet*

Director: Warren Hammack
Stage Manager: Matt Jackson
Set Design: Sam Hunt
Lighting Design: Lynne Chase
Costume Design: Marty Hagedorn
Sound Design: Ben Haffner
Properties Master: Patricia G. Skinner
Technical Director: Jeremy Artigue
Resident Production Assistant: Kip London
Production Assistant: Heather Lyn Davis

I arrived at Horse Cave Theatre without any formal training or experience as a playwright, and the reason I had begun writing those first scenes of *Desert Flower* was that the material had seemed to want them.

Warren Hammack and Pamela White worked closely with the playwrights in preparing for the readings of their scripts in the Kentucky Voices program, and I learned how valuable these public readings are for the playwright. Horse Cave Theatre audiences knew good plays, and they knew when something the playwright was attempting to do was simply not working. The playwrights who participated in the workshops offered valuable input of their own as we struggled to refine our scripts.

When *Desert Flower* received its world premiere at Horse Cave Theatre in the summer of 1996, it was a magical experience – the dynamics of writer, director, cast, crew, and audience all coming together to create something that at that moment had never before existed.

I have continued to write plays, and some have seen production elsewhere, but there will never be another experience as wonderful as that first production. It is a great honor to have *Desert Flower* appear in this anthology along with the many other marvelous plays written by playwrights I admire, some of whom I have come to know and love as well. We have all shared in these unforgettable experiences with the wonderful people of Horse Cave, and the anthology is a fitting tribute to those who made these experiences possible for all of us.

– Betty Peterson

Desert Flower

Characters:

GLENDA EVERSON, *attractive woman, thirties, married to Roy*

ROY EVERSON, *handsome, well-built and rugged, late thirties*

MARILEE, *Glenda's friend since grade school*

TEAK, *Marilee's ex-husband, friend to both Roy and Glenda*

Place: *A modest home in a small town in Kentucky. Cooking/dining area, sitting area, and bedroom, with bathroom concealed off bedroom, but in such a way as to allow for voices to be heard by audience. Furnishings are in Early American decor, some of which has been handed down from another generation. Cooking/dining area has a refrigerator, a stove and oven, a counter for canister set, coffeepot, etc., a sink, and a telephone. There is also a wall clock and a small radio. A set of salt and pepper shakers is on the table. A door in cooking/dining area leads to outside, and an archway implies other rooms and serves as another entrance. A coat rack stands by the door. Sitting area has a sofa, a coffee table, a TV, and a trophy case. Pictures of children, etc. are arranged on top. Several popular magazines are arranged neatly on coffee table. A bed, a chest of drawers, a chair, and a clothes closet make up the bedroom. (Some small items will be noted in scenes as needed.) Although children are never seen, there should be ample evidence of their presence, such as a basketball, a Cub Scout uniform, tennis shoes, etc.*

Time: *1990-1991 during the months of Desert Shield/Desert Storm.*

ACT ONE

SCENE ONE

Callings

As lights go up, GLENDA is seen sitting at a table in dimly-lit dining area drinking coffee. She is wearing a housecoat and slippers. Lights are focused on bedroom. The empty bed has a slept-on, wrestled-on look, and so does GLENDA. Her hair is partially gathered up and pinned on top. A man's clothes and other items have been carefully lined up across the bed: pants, shirt, underwear, socks, belt, and a small brown bag such as one might carry shaving supplies in for a trip. Old work shoes spattered with paint are on the floor beside the chair. Water is heard splashing.

ROY: (*From bathroom.*) Glenda!

GLENDA: (*Taking coffee with her, she walks slowly toward bathroom.*) I'm coming.

ROY: Glennn-daaa!

GLENDA: (*Enters bathroom.*) I said I was coming, Roy. You don't have to wake up the whole house.

ROY: What took you so long? Scrub hard down the middle. That's where it itches the worst. (*Pause.*) Ain't you got no more power than that?

GLENDA: I do the best I can.

ROY: I wonder.

GLENDA: What's that supposed to mean?

ROY: Nothing. (*Pause.*) You got my work clothes laid out? Remember I have to have my Monday pants...all swole up after the weekend.

(*Water is heard splashing as GLENDA rinses ROY's back.*)

GLENDA: I remembered. I laid out your other things too, and the bag with your deodorant and cologne in it. (*Emerging from bathroom.*) I don't know why you can't just put your stuff in the medicine cabinet like anybody else. I get tired of dragging that bag out every time. (*She grabs Roy's underwear from bed and goes back to bathroom.*)

ROY: I have to keep my stuff hid from the boys.

GLENDA: Now, step out on this towel.

(*Water splashes as ROY steps out of the tub.*)

ROY: Did you ever think I might get tired of some things too?

GLENDA: Like what?

ROY: Like I get tired of having to clean out this tub every morning before I can take my bath. Them two boys of yours leave a ring at night as wide as the tires on a Mack truck. Looks like you'd clean that out for me.

GLENDA: (*Emerges from bathroom, coffee in hand.*) They're your boys too. (*Stops, turns toward him.*) Besides, I'm trying to teach them to clean up after themselves.

ROY: You ain't doing too good a job.

GLENDA: I could use a little help from you.

ROY: I make the money. Rest is up to you. Restoring cars for a living ain't much, but I do it all for you, mama. Ain't that enough?

(*GLENDA, leaning against wall, doesn't respond.*)

ROY: Glenda? Where'd you run off to? Looks like if you cared about me, you'd stay with me.

GLENDA: You know what I was just thinking, Roy?

ROY: No telling.

GLENDA: I was just thinking about how we sneaked off to Mobile, Alabama that spring before we got married. And how it was so cold, and we rolled up in that army blanket and went to sleep there by the ocean. And a ship went by and sounded its horn and woke us up, and we just snuggled up closer and went back to sleep. Remember that?

(*ROY emerges from bathroom. He is dressed in underwear and has a towel draped around his neck.*)

ROY: It was a boat, Glenda, it wasn't no ship.

(*BOTH move to bed. GLENDA sits on the bed, one leg tucked under her, still sipping her coffee. ROY sits on the side of the bed and begins wiping the bottoms of his feet with the towel.*)

ROY: Don't you ever vacuum?

(*GLENDA ignores him.*)

ROY: (*Reaching for his socks.*) Why'd you lay out brand new socks?

GLENDA: All your old ones are in the dirty clothes.

ROY: Ain't that what you got a damned washing machine for?

GLENDA: I didn't wash them because you had these new ones you could wear.

ROY: (*Groans.*) I start wearing my new socks to work in, first thing you know, they'll be wore out just like the old ones.

GLENDA: (*Laughs.*) It's only for one day, Roy.

ROY: (*Tosses socks to her.*) The least you could do is take the tags off for me.

(*While GLENDA removes the tags, ROY examines his toenails.*)

ROY: Look at that. I could be Howard Hughes.

GLENDA: I'm not your mama, Roy.

ROY: Oh, yes you are. (*Taking her in his arms, he kisses her lustily.*) Sung me a real sweet lullaby last night, didn't you? (*Releases her.*) I just like having you close to me.

(*GLENDA looks at him seductively then, moves up close behind him and puts her arms around him.*)

GLENDA: Hey. Why don't we go back to Mobile sometime? We could be close there. Real close.

ROY: I can't just go running off to Mobeel. (*Continues to dress.*) And a trip like that costs money. You need to grow up, Glenda.

(*ROY puts way too much deodorant in his armpits, spreading it partially up his arms and down his sides.*)

GLENDA: I told you a long time ago I could get on at the sewing factory to help us out, but you wouldn't let me. (*Moves to chair.*) How come you always use so much of that stuff?

ROY: When a man sweats, he don't fool around. The women in that factory are wild. You can't even take care of what little there is to do here, much less hold down a job.

(*GLENDA glares at ROY.*)

ROY: (*Chuckles.*) It's true, and you know it. Did you pick up the furnace filters like I told you to?

GLENDA: (*Hesitates.*) No.

ROY: See what I mean?

(*ROY splashes on too much cologne. GLENDA starts to leave.*)

ROY: Where you going?

GLENDA: To wake up the boys for school.

ROY: Don't wake them up yet. I can't stand all that racket early of a morning. You need to fix my hair before it dries out looking like this. You should've cut it this weekend. Hair and toenails grow out together.

(*ROY is fully dressed now except for his shoes, and is putting on his belt. GLENDA stands as though she is still about to leave.*)

ROY: Glenda? You hear me?

(*GLENDA picks up the hair dryer from the bed. She turns it on and stands rubbing the attached brush back and forth across her hand. ROY looks at her like she's lost her mind.*)

ROY: What are you blow-drying?

(*GLENDA moves close to him. She watches his hair fly for a moment before touching the brush to it.*)

GLENDA: Maybe we could move to the country. Grandma had eight kids out like that, and she always seemed happy. They worked hard, but they had fun too, Mama said. And they made all their own clothes, sometimes out of feed sacks and-

ROY: (*Laughs.*) -You want a feed-sack dress? I can get you a feed sack over at Jackson Milling this very day. Watch what you're doing there! My ear's getting awful hot!

GLENDA: (*Smiles.*) I just mean the old days seemed better. They didn't have much, but they had fresh water from the spring, and they breathed fresh air. And at night they'd all gather around the fireplace and tell stories until the little ones fell asleep, Mama said.

ROY: Ain't that a pretty picture? It's just a picture, Glenda, it ain't real.

GLENDA: My mama wouldn't lie!

ROY: I didn't say she was lying. She just ain't remembering too good. People have a way of prettying up the past. You got a lot to learn.

GLENDA: How do you know so much?

ROY: I just do. Shut that dryer off. You already scorched my hair. Is it laying down on the sides like it's supposed to? Sticks out like wings when it needs cutting.

(*GLENDA turns the dryer off and stands picking at the brush.*)

GLENDA: I don't see why we couldn't just find a nice quiet little place in the country, let the boys run barefoot through the woods and-

ROY: -Ain't you heard a word I said? The boys wouldn't run through the woods without their Nikes on.

(*ROY looks at GLENDA to see if she will laugh at his little joke. She doesn't.*)

ROY: What's got into you lately? You got everything a woman could want. A good house, two good kids, and a old man that loves you and don't ask for much. You ought to be the happiest woman alive.

GLENDA: I guess you're right.

(*GLENDA sighs and begins putting his things back in the brown bag.*)

ROY: Aye god, you know I'm right. You're always talking about your precious grandma, why can't you just be happy like her?

GLENDA: I guess I should be happy.

ROY: Damned right, you should. (*Looking around the room.*) What've you done with my shoes?

GLENDA: (*Gets them for him.*) But she had something I don't have.

ROY: And what's that?

GLENDA: I don't know exactly.

ROY: Then what'd you bring it up for? (*Tightening laces.*)

GLENDA: Maybe she really loved what she was doing, or maybe she just didn't know any better, but I'll bet it never entered her mind to do anything else. It was like her calling.

ROY: I don't know why it has to be any different with you. (*He stretches and yawns.*) I'm your calling, mama.

(*ROY laughs, picks up towel and throws it at GLENDA. She catches it.*)

GLENDA: But it *is* different with me.

ROY: Marilee's been putting ideas in your head again, ain't she?

GLENDA: What are you afraid of, Roy?

ROY: (*Stands abruptly.*) Nothing! Roy Everson ain't afraid of nothing. I just know when she's been putting ideas in your head. (*Starts to pace.*)

GLENDA: Are you saying I couldn't possibly know how I feel unless Marilee tells me?

ROY: No, that ain't what I'm saying.

(*GLENDA starts to say something, but changes her mind.*)

ROY: (*Stands over her.*) Look, all I know is, we was doing just fine until she come back and started running her mouth. You been acting different ever since. Can't you see she's just trying to stir up trouble? She wants you divorced like her and that's the whole reason she moved back here.

GLENDA: Her mother is the whole reason she's back here. After her daddy left, her mother just couldn't- Marilee's trying to encourage me to do what I want, that's all.

ROY: And what is it you want, Glenda?

GLENDA: I want- (*Stands.*) I want to...go to college.

ROY: Go to college? Good god, Glenda! You talk plum crazy sometimes.

(*ROY walks away from GLENDA to dining area. GLENDA takes coffee and follows him.*)

GLENDA: You're probably right. It is a crazy idea.

ROY: Go to college.

(*ROY takes his keys and billfold from top of refrigerator. Hooks keys onto belt.*)

GLENDA: Want me to cook you some breakfast?

ROY: (*Looks at clock.*) Hell, I ain't got time for that now.

GLENDA: I wish you wouldn't cuss so much.

ROY: I'll cuss if I want to. (*Takes cap from top of refrigerator and puts it on.*) Looks like if you cared about me you would've cooked me something when you first got up. What do you do anyhow, getting up so early every morning here lately?

GLENDA: I just sit and drink coffee.

ROY: Is that all?

GLENDA: And think.

ROY: You what?

GLENDA: I just sit and think.

ROY: (*Laughs.*) What for?

GLENDA: I guess I'm just crazy like you say.

(*ROY pulls GLENDA to him and wraps his arms around her.*)

ROY: Ummm. You're so soft. You don't know what it's like to hold you after working with metal all the time.

(*GLENDA looks up at him and smiles.*)

ROY: Do you think you can remember to pick up the furnace filters today?

GLENDA: I guess I can.

ROY: Do you love me?

GLENDA: I guess I do. (*She leans her head against his chest.*)

ROY: Then kiss your old man goodbye.

GLENDA: I guess I could.

SCENE TWO

Old Shoe Prints

GLENDA is in dining area preparing to bake cookies, tearing off wax paper and placing it on the table, getting out cutters, etc. She is wearing a skirt and blouse and flats. Her hair is pulled back from her face and held with a clasp.

Television is on in sitting area, and GLENDA occasionally stops to listen as news of the situation with Desert Shield is heard: "Less than eighteen hours after the Security Council authorized the use of force against Iraq if Saddam Hussein fails to comply with the UN's call for an unconditional withdrawal from Kuwait by January 15, President Bush made a surprise announcement. Iraq's Foreign Minister would be welcome at the White House during the week of December 10, and Secretary of State James Baker could meet with Saddam in Baghdad later. The Iraqi government today issued a statement agreeing to the proposed meetings, while referring to Bush as 'arrogant' and an 'enemy of God.' Sources close to the White House say if Saddam remains true to character, he may see Bush's diplomatic move as further proof of our weakness, and this being the case, war may be inevitable."

Meanwhile, the U.S. troops practice in the desert...and wait. More news in a moment." CNN signature music is heard.

GLENDA sighs and turns off TV with remote, and turns on radio. She begins singing along as she takes cookie dough out of refrigerator. MARILEE comes bursting through door. She is wearing a bodysuit and an oversized shirt that covers her to mid-thigh. She has a short, easy-care hairstyle. Everything she does is with great enthusiasm and self-assurance.

GLENDA: (*Almost drops the cookie dough.*) Marilee! I wish you'd learn to knock before you come barging in like that. Why can't you just knock?

(*GLENDA turns off radio.*)

MARILEE: Sorry, kiddo. Knock. Knock. (*Knocks on table.*)

GLENDA: (*Shrugs.*) Who's there? (*Puts dough on table and begins to flatten it.*)

MARILEE: Myya.

GLENDA: Myya who?

MARILEE: Myya sure are testy today.

GLENDA: Just busy, Marilee.

MARILEE: Oh, you're always busy. Leave that stuff alone a minute, will ya? I got something I wanna show ya.

GLENDA: What?

MARILEE: Just come with me. (*Takes GLENDA by the arm.*)

GLENDA: What, Marilee?

MARILEE: Now close your eyes.

GLENDA: Why?

MARILEE: Just close your eyes, dang it!

GLENDA: Okay, okay.

(*MARILEE turns GLENDA to face the door, then opens door.*)

MARILEE: Now, open your eyes.

GLENDA: Marilee? A jeep?

MARILEE: Not just a jeep! A Suzuki Samurai. Black interior and exterior, manual five-speed transmission, and soft top, which, as you can see, is down and ready.

GLENDA: You trying to sell it or something?

MARILEE: No, silly. I just bought it. So whatta ya think?

GLENDA: I uh...I think it looks just like you. (*Goes back to dough.*)

MARILEE: What's wrong? You don't like it, do you? (*Closes door.*)

GLENDA: Why do I have to like it?

MARILEE: You don't. (*Cools.*) What's this for?

(*MARILEE points to cookie dough GLENDA is now rolling out.*)

GLENDA: Cookies for the PTA bake sale tomorrow.

(*MARILEE chuckles and shakes her head.*)

GLENDA: What?

MARILEE: Nothing. What kind of cookies?

GLENDA: Peanut butter crunch. My mama's recipe. I like your jeep, Marilee, really.

MARILEE: No, you don't. (*Pinches off some dough and tastes it.*)

GLENDA: Do, too.

MARILEE: Then put that stuff up and come go for a ride with me—feel the wind on your face—live a little!

GLENDA: (*Using the cookie cutters to make a variety of shapes.*) These have to be done now.

MARILEE: Now is for today. You're working on tomorrow. Come on, let's take the jeep and go to the Kroger Deli and buy the cookies.

GLENDA: Marilee...you're supposed to bake the cookies.

MARILEE: So who'd know?

GLENDA and MARILEE: (*In unison.*) I would!

MARILEE: (*Sits at table.*) Still the same as when we were in school. You wouldn't cheat on a test even if the teacher left the room, cause *you'd* know. Where did you get such an overdeveloped sense of right and wrong?

(*MARILEE drums on table with her hands.*)

GLENDA: I wouldn't call it overdeveloped, really. Right's right, and wrong's wrong, you know? Will you stop that?

MARILEE: Well, sorreee! Why are you so edgy? (*Pause*). I need a beer.

(*MARILEE goes to refrigerator and helps herself. Gets one for GLENDA and opens it for her.*)

GLENDA: You know I don't like beer.

MARILEE: Start cultivating a taste, then, cause you need to loosen up. I've never seen you so uptight. And you won't go for a ride with me cause your face is all pinched up for motherhood and cookies. You're no fun at all.

(*MARILEE flops in a chair and takes a long drink. GLENDA takes a drink of her beer and makes a face.*)

GLENDA: Jeeps are dangerous.

MARILEE: See?! (*Gestures in defeat.*)

GLENDA: No, really. Roy calls them a death trap. Has to do with the narrow...narrow something or other.

MARILEE: Wheel base?

GLENDA: Yeah, that's it.

MARILEE: That's just Roy talking. I swear, he's got you thinking he knows everything.

GLENDA: He knows a lot about cars.

MARILEE: Maybe. (*Pause.*) Is he mad at me or something?

GLENDA: Why would you ask that?

MARILEE: It just seems like he brushes me off lately. I called to talk to you the other day, and he was downright rude.

GLENDA: How do you mean?

MARILEE: He said he'd tell you I called if he thought about it then hung up on me. He was just hateful, you know—the way he did it.

GLENDA: (*Drinks more beer.*) Don't know what his problem is.

(*GLENDA slides cookies in the oven. The phone rings.*)

MARILEE: I'll get it.

(*As MARILEE is talking, GLENDA cleans her hands and begins cleaning up the table.*)

MARILEE: Hello...Oh, hi. (*Turns to GLENDA with hand over mouthpiece.*) It's your mama. Yeah, this is Marilee. (*Pause.*) Just fine, and you? Umhum. (*Holds phone out away from her ear, looks at GLENDA, smiles and rolls her eyes.*) Oh, I just came by to take Glenda for a ride in my new jeep. (*Pause.*) No, it's not an army jeep. It's a black- Yeah, she's right here. (*Puts hand over mouthpiece.*) Wanna talk?

(*GLENDA rolls her eyes and takes the phone from MARILEE, who begins to finish cleaning up the cookie mess.*)

GLENDA: Hi, Mama. (*Pause.*) Yes, jeeps can be dangerous, but- (*Pause.*) I know why you called, and the answer is no, I haven't been to pick up your hamburger meat for you yet. I said I would pick it up, and I will, when I get time. (*Pause.*) Mama, it will be on sale all week. As soon as I get a chance, I'll- (*Pause.*) I'm making cookies for the bake sale tomorrow, okay? (*Pause.*) No, I don't think they'll run out of ground beef. (*Pacing.*) Mama, this is the third time you've called to- You don't need to call again about it. Bye.

(*GLENDA hangs up quickly. MARILEE has been trying to keep from laughing aloud during their conversation.*)

GLENDA: I shouldn't have been so short with her. But she just drives me crazy.

MARILEE: (*Moves to sitting area.*) I thought your mama finally got her license?

GLENDA: (*Putting finishing touches on cleanup.*) Oh, she did. Bless her heart, she was determined. And it's a wonder she'd had the nerve, with Daddy right there telling her she'd never pass the test. He always did put her down.

MARILEE: Yeah, I remember. (*Seated on sofa.*) What made her wanna get her license after all these years?

GLENDA: Daddy's eyes got to where he couldn't see well enough to drive, and then she felt like she had to pass the test, not just so she could drive, but so she wouldn't have to hear Daddy say, "I told you so!" for the rest of her life.

(*GLENDA opens oven and checks cookies. Moves to sitting area.*)

MARILEE: Now that she has her license, why doesn't she just get her own ground beef?

GLENDA: Because it's on sale at a store she's not used to. She just has this little *path* (*Makes a path with her hands.*) she takes; anything she wants that's not along that path, I have to pick up for her.

(*MARILEE laughs.*)

GLENDA: I really don't mind doing it, to keep her from having to be on a road she's not used to. But she just drives me crazy with something once she gets it on her mind. Drives Roy crazy too, and then he gets on me about it: "Can't you do something about that mama of yours?" So I not only have to deal with her, I have to deal with him about her—double trouble.

(*GLENDA sits beside MARILEE, one leg drawn up under her.*)

MARILEE: You know, Glenda, I can't understand why you'll stand up to your mama and me, but when it comes to Roy, you've got his big old shoe prints all over you.

GLENDA: That's not fair, Marilee.

MARILEE: Why not? I've seen the way you cater to him—afraid to do anything without his okay.

GLENDA: He just needs to feel like he's in charge, so I let him. He's not a bad person.

MARILEE: And you even defend him!

(*GLENDA gets up and moves toward the oven.*)

GLENDA: Listen, Marilee. I defend him because I love him. Thanks! You just made me realize that.

MARILEE: Oh, yeah?

GLENDA: Yeah. Sometimes I get confused about the way I feel. (*Looks in oven.*)

MARILEE: I can understand why. What I can't understand is why you stay with him.

GLENDA: Maybe I have a harder time walking away than you do.

MARILEE: And why do you think that is?

GLENDA: Because life isn't that simple for some of us.

MARILEE: Well, sorreee! I didn't mean to sound simple.

GLENDA: You know what I mean. At least he's faithful to me. How many men can you say that about?

MARILEE: Not many, I guess, least of all Teak.

GLENDA: I'm sorry. (*Moves toward her.*)

MARILEE: No, don't worry about it. I'm past that.

GLENDA: Really? Sometimes I get the feeling you still love Teak, but won't admit it.

MARILEE: (*Laughs lightly.*) You're such a romantic. (*Pause.*) But let's say I do still love him. Love isn't always enough, Glenda. When I first came back I thought he had changed. I even considered- But like I said, I'm past it. Getting on with my life. Speaking of which, have you thought anymore about going to college like you said?

GLENDA: (*At the end of the sofa.*) I've thought about it. I even mentioned it to Roy.

MARILEE: And what did he say?

GLENDA: Nothing, really. (*Grabs throw-pillow and cradles it to her.*)

MARILEE: Come on, Glenda, it's me, remember? What did he say?

GLENDA: He thinks it's crazy.

MARILEE: That figures.

GLENDA: I think Roy's just afraid of what might happen to us if I did go to college.

(*GLENDA sits beside MARILEE.*)

MARILEE: Well, look at you. He can see you're not happy living like this. Listen, there are plenty of men out there who would treat you right, if you gotta have one.

GLENDA: But I...sometimes he can be so sweet and....besides, even if I ever did want to leave, I couldn't.

MARILEE: What makes you say that?

(*GLENDA looks away.*)

MARILEE: What is it? Come on, Glenda, you can tell me. Why do you say you couldn't leave?

GLENDA: Because...because he said if I ever left he would kill himself.

MARILEE: Kill himself?

(*GLENDA buries her face in the pillow.*)

MARILEE: Look, men say crap like that all the time to get you to do what they want. You don't really believe him, do you?

GLENDA: (*Looks up from pillow.*) I didn't, but then the first time we got into it and I threatened to leave, I mean really leave, he sat in there at that table loading his gun and begging me not to make him do it, and me crying and pleading with him not to do that to me, and- It went on for hours until finally I promised him I would never leave him.

MARILEE: Was this after I divorced Teak and moved away?

GLENDA: No. This was before.

MARILEE: How come you never told me?

GLENDA: It's not something you go around telling people.

MARILEE: So, you never thought about leaving after that?

GLENDA: Oh, I thought about it lots of times. But every time we argued he would punch a wall or kick something. It was scary. I didn't know what he might do. Then after Roy Dean came along, and Jason, I didn't want them seeing that, and I didn't want to break up our family, so I just-

MARILEE: (*Concerned now.*) -Did he ever hit you, you know, or hurt you physically?

GLENDA: No, not like that. I was just afraid-

MARILEE: -Glenda, that's bondage!

GLENDA: (*Folds her arms over her head.*) Don't, Marilee. (*Drops her arms*) Maybe it is...kind of...but it's so hard to- (*Moves to TV. Picks up one of the boys' sweaters that has been left on top and holds it to her.*) If I...left, and he really did kill himself, how could I possibly live with that? How could I do that to our boys?

MARILEE: (*Grabs sweater from her and throws it angrily on sofa.*) Roy would be doing that to the boys, not you!

GLENDA: No, it would be me, just me, don't you see? And I can hear the boys saying to me: "Mama, why did you have to leave him? Daddy would still be alive if only you had"- Oh, Marilee, how awful! I don't want Roy to die! I want us to be together. I just want us to be a family.

MARILEE: I know. (*Puts her arms around her.*)

GLENDA: (*Steps back.*) Tell me, Marilee, what does "for better or worse" mean but staying together even when things don't go the way you'd hoped? The only difference between couples who stay together and those who don't, is they never stop trying to make it work. It's not because they never had problems. Look at my mama and daddy.

MARILEE: Yeah, look at your mama in particular, what it's done to her. Is that what you want?

GLENDA: No, I don't want to live like that. I just keep hoping he'll change.

MARILEE: (*Returns to sofa.*) How long are you prepared to wait?

GLENDA: I don't know. I just know I've got to keep trying to make it work, Marilee.

MARILEE: You both have to be trying, don't you think?

GLENDA: Roy does try. There are just some things he can't seem to get past.

MARILEE: I don't know what to tell you, Glenda, except sometimes, to find a solution to a problem you have to look in your gut. Besides, I think Roy's just full of hot air, you know?

(*BOTH look at each other and sniff.*)

GLENDA and MARILEE: (*In unison.*) The cookies!

GLENDA: I forgot to set the timer!

(*BOTH rush to the oven. MARILEE grabs a towel and begins fanning the cookies as GLENDA takes them out.*)

GLENDA: Oh, they're burned already! Why are you fanning them, Marilee?

MARILEE: Danged if I know! (*Throws down the towel.*)

GLENDA: Oh, what the heck. Maybe we'll just go to Kroger after all. Come on, you can drive me in your new jeep.

MARILEE: Atta girl!

(*BOTH exit.*)

SCENE THREE

Roosters and Hens

ROY is talking on the phone.

ROY: I been home for over a hour. No sign of her. No supper. No nothing. All I found was empty beer cans and burnt cookies. (*Pause.*) You're her mama, ain't you? I just thought maybe you'd- Yeah, her car's still here. (*Pause.*) Jeep?! I better get off here in case she tries to call. (*Pause.*) I told you, she was gone when I got home. How would I know what time she left? I better get off here and- (*Takes cap off and throws on table.*) Yeah, maybe they went to get your ground beef. Yeah, I'll tell her to call you. Yeah, I promise. (*Slams receiver down.*) Stupid move calling that woman.

(*Car doors slam. Roy starts toward door. GLENDA enters.*)

ROY: Where the hell have you been?

(*MARILEE and TEAK enter.*)

TEAK: Aw, this crazy ex-wife of mine cleaned out a ditch line showing off in her new jeep.

(*ROY goes to GLENDA and puts his arms around her.*)

ROY: You all right?

(*GLENDA nods.*)

TEAK: They're just a little shook up, is all. Marilee called me. I went and picked them up. (*Puts arm around MARILEE.*) Yeah, she can't stand being married to me, but let her get in trouble and ole Teak's the first one she thinks of. I swear, Roy, you can't get rid of them.

MARILEE: (*Shrugs off his arm.*) I'm sorry we had you worried, Roy.

ROY: Main thing is nobody got hurt. Them jeeps got a narrow wheel base.

MARILEE: I need a bathroom.

GLENDA: Me too.

(*BOTH exit through archway.*)

MARILEE: I wish you could have seen the look on your face when we went in that ditch!

(*BOTH are now laughing. The men look at each other and shake their heads.*)

ROY: Lucky they didn't get hurt. A jeep?

TEAK: You know Marilee.

(*They sit at the table.*)

ROY: Any damage to it? (*Eating the burned cookies.*)

TEAK: Don't know yet. I'm just glad I was around today when she called. Been awhile since I'd seen her.

ROY: You still got it for her, don't you?

TEAK: I'd take her back in a heartbeat if she'd have me, but Marilee knows better.

ROY: How're things over at the airport? You still flying them plant hotshots around?

TEAK: Business as usual. Gets kind of interesting when they take women up with them though. Air's the best place to be with a woman. (*Pause.*) By the way, I ran into a guy the other day who said he was at the car show last month. Said you won another trophy with that '63 Impala you restored.

ROY: Yeah!

TEAK: What did you say that car has in it? A 409?

ROY: Four hundred and twenty-five horses.

TEAK: Man-oh-man! Four in the floor, right?

ROY: Yeah.

TEAK: This fellow said it was the prettiest red convertible he'd ever seen.

ROY: People are always after me to sell her to them. Right buyer comes along, I will.

TEAK: Right money, you mean.

ROY: No, I mean the right buyer. Somebody who'll care about her and treat her right.

TEAK: This guy said you were an artist, so maybe he would appreciate the car. I gave him your phone number. Hope that's all right.

ROY: Yeah. Won't do him no good to call though, if he ain't the right-

TEAK: -I hear you. Hey, let me see that trophy.

(*BOTH move to sitting area. ROY points to one of the trophies.*)

ROY: That's the one.

TEAK: Man! That's a beaut. (*Pause. Points to another one.*) And look at that one. I remember when you got it. It was while I was still married to Marilee, and we all went to the Charlotte Auto Fair with that...what was it...Camaro?

ROY: '69 Z-28.

TEAK: We ought to do that again sometime. That was a real blast.

ROY: You and Marilee was really thick that weekend. Too bad you had to go and screw it up.

TEAK: I thought I could stop fooling around, Roy, but it's like, you know, when somebody brings in a big tray with all these different kinds of food on it, you've got to have some of all of it. Risky business these days though. Man's got to be careful.

ROY: Way I see it, there are some things you just don't do, and fooling around is one of them.

TEAK: That's because you're a one-woman man.

(*GLENDA and MARILEE enter through archway.*)

GLENDA: You remember. It's the quilt my grandmother gave me.

ROY: Took you long enough.

MARILEE: Just talking, Roy.

ROY: You're good at that, ain't you?

MARILEE: So, what if I am?

TEAK: We better go get that jeep out of the ditch, Marilee.

(*ALL moving to door.*)

ROY: Need any help?

TEAK: We can manage.

ROY: If there's any damage, bring it by the shop. Won't cost you.

TEAK: Hey, thanks man. Come on, Marilee. (*Opens door. Looks at GLENDA and winks.*) Take it easy, Glenda. No harm done.

(*GLENDA smiles. TEAK and MARILEE exit.*)

GLENDA: (*Rushes words.*) I'm sorry there's nothing to eat. And I burned the cookies for the bake sale. That's where we went—to get more cookies. And now I still don't have any. When I go pick up the boys I'll get some and bring us back a Big Mac or something. I don't know why I-

ROY: (*Takes her in his arms.*) -You could've been hurt, you know that?

GLENDA: I'm sorry, Roy.

ROY: I just don't want something happening to my baby.

(*Kissing her, ROY begins backing GLENDA to the edge of table. He lifts her onto it, and begins kissing her again, making moves up her skirt. She responds to him. Door opens.*)

MARILEE: Glenda, I just wanted to tell you I'll get the cookies and- Oops! Sorry.

(*MARILEE closes door and leaves. ROY has jerked away from GLENDA. GLENDA has come off the table.*)

ROY: Why is it that woman never knocks? Can't you teach her better than that?

GLENDA: (*Thinks it's funny. Begins discarding cookies in trash.*) I guess not.

ROY: She ain't nothing but trouble. And now, she drinks my beer and almost kills my wife. Some friend you got there. (*Looks in refrigerator.*) She left me some, didn't she?

GLENDA: There's plenty of beer, Roy. And Marilee's been my friend since before we bought our first training bra.

ROY: (*Repeats flatly.*) Training bra.

GLENDA: Besides, I drank one of the beers myself.

ROY: You did? You don't even like beer. What made you go and do that?

GLENDA: She thought I was too tense and opened one for me, so I drank it.

ROY: And why'd you take off with her in that death trap? You know better than that.

GLENDA: I know. It was stupid.

ROY: Stupid ain't the word for it. It was more like ignorant.

(*ROY brushes past GLENDA to the sitting area. He grabs a newspaper from the coffee table, slaps it across his hand, sits and opens it.*)

GLENDA: (*Follows him.*) You know what, Roy?

(*ROY ignores her.*)

GLENDA: Marilee was right. I do have your big old shoe prints all over me!

ROY: (*Looks at her.*) You what?

GLENDA: She told me that today, and I defended you. But she's right.

ROY: (*Returns to paper.*) She's a troublemaker, Glenda. I told you, she just wants you divorced like her.

GLENDA: (*Looking over his shoulder.*) Remember how you used to laugh and tell me about funny things you did on the farm, like putting a piece of paper around a hen's neck just to see her run backwards and squawk and act crazy?

(*ROY laughs.*)

GLENDA: And remember how you said the rooster would flog her, and jump on top of her and peck her when she started doing that?

ROY: (*Laughs.*) Yeah, I reckon it turned him on.

GLENDA: Well, I feel like that poor hen must have felt. I already feel awful about what happened, and you come along and jump on me and start pecking me.

ROY: Aw, Glenda, it ain't the same thing. (*Reaches for her, pulls her around beside him on the sofa.*) I'm sorry if I jumped on you. You know I didn't mean nothing by it. (*Kisses her.*) Speaking of jumping on something....

(*ROY pushes GLENDA back on the sofa. Phone rings. GLENDA tries to get up to answer it.*)

ROY: Let it ring. It's just your mama checking on you. I told her you'd call her.

GLENDA: (*Sits up.*) Roy, you didn't?

ROY: I was so worried about you, I made the mistake of calling her.

GLENDA: Oh, great. Now she'll have to call me two or three times before she gets it all straight in her mind.

ROY: I know. It was stupid.

GLENDA: Stupid ain't the word for it. It was more like ignorant!

ROY: Hey, wait a minute, now. Who's the rooster here, huh?

(*ROY pushes GLENDA back down on the sofa and tries to pin her arms. They wrestle.*)

SCENE FOUR

Testosterone

Sitting room: ROY, in work clothes, is seated at one end of the sofa, TV remote in hand.

Someone is being interviewed on television: "Congressman, you've been quoted as saying you oppose a land attack in the Middle East. Would you elaborate on that for us?" Congressman: "I just don't think our boys should be sent into Kuwait by land. If a move is made that brings on a war, then our planes from the carriers in the Persian Gulf and those based on land should be used to bring Iraq out of Kuwait. I believe the economic embargo has dealt a serious blow to Saddam and the Iraqi economy; I think it's working, but the deadline for withdrawing their troops from Kuwait is almost here, so there's no turning back now."

GLENDA enters through archway during the interview carrying a basket of clothes. She sits on the sofa and begins folding and stacking towels and wash cloths, etc.

ROY: Hot damn! I hope we bomb 'em all to hell!

(*ROY bangs the coffee table with his fist, startling GLENDA. He turns the TV down, so that words are not audible.*)

GLENDA: Why would you want us to start killing people?

ROY: Somebody's gotta do it. That Saddam what's his name-

GLENDA: -Hussein.

ROY: Insane, if you ask me. Any man who would act like that, killing his own people, don't deserve to live, much less be in charge.

GLENDA: It's not about that. He was killing people before oil came into the picture, and we didn't care. It's about oil, Roy. That's what the ultimatum is all about. If they exported oysters this wouldn't even be happening.

ROY: Since when do you know about oysters?

GLENDA: I read that in the newspaper. But I know one thing, if I could, I'd be up there in Washington right now carrying one of those signs that says NO BLOOD FOR OIL.

ROY: (*Laughs.*) You're crazy, you know that?

GLENDA: I would!

ROY: You just don't understand how this all works, do you? You'd think again if you had to start paying thirty dollars a gallon for gas, now wouldn't you?

GLENDA: I'd manage.

ROY: Not with my money, you wouldn't. (*Stretches out one leg on top of some of the piles of clothes.*)

GLENDA: (*Lifts his leg.*) Don't do that, Roy. These are clean you know.

ROY: A man can't even relax in his own house. Why didn't you do that before I got home?

(*GLENDA flashes him a look.*)

ROY: The least you could do is fold them somewhere else.

GLENDA: Maybe I'd like to watch the news too.

ROY: Why would you want to watch something you don't understand?

GLENDA: Oh, I understand it alright. I just don't happen to agree with what President Bush is doing.

ROY: If you understood, you'd agree with it. Them boys have waited out there in the desert long enough for something to happen. They need some action.

GLENDA: That's what's so stupid about war. You'll have all these innocent people in danger, and no telling how many will die. All because of one man. Why can't they just use reason?

ROY: You can't reason with a man like that.

GLENDA: (*Pause.*) What would you do if I did go to Washington and carry a sign?

ROY: Don't push me, Glenda.

GLENDA: I've got a right to do whatever I want!

ROY: Not as long as you're married to me, you don't.

GLENDA: (*Pause.*) You know what I think, Roy?

ROY: No telling.

GLENDA: It's the testosterone in men that makes them want power and control—makes them violent.

ROY: (*Laughs.*) Test-toaster-what?

GLENDA: You know. The sex hormone. If all men were castrated we wouldn't have war.

ROY: (*Pulls legs together and turns them away from her.*) Good god, Glenda. You want me to be castrated?

GLENDA: Oh, Roy, you know what I'm saying.

ROY: The trouble with you, Glenda, is you don't understand men. (*Turns back to TV.*) Go get me a beer, will you?

(*GLENDA leaves off folding and gets up to go get him a beer. When she gets to the refrigerator, she stops and comes slowly back toward him.*)

GLENDA: Why don't you just get it yourself, Roy?

ROY: What?

GLENDA: Why don't you just get up and get your own beer?

ROY: You always bring me a beer when I want one. Why, all of a sudden, do I need to get it myself?

GLENDA: It's power and control, right? You want to control me.

ROY: Oh, here she goes. It's got nothing to do with that stuff. Looks like if you cared about me, you'd want to do that much for me.

GLENDA: That's not the point.

ROY: (*Jumps up.*) Then what is the point, Glenda?

GLENDA: The point is, I was busy, and you could have respected me enough to get up and get it yourself.

ROY: Well, maybe you've spoiled me, huh? How come I don't feel spoiled? How come I feel like you don't want to do nothing for me here lately? (*Challenges her.*) Now that you're up, why don't you just go ahead and get it for me?

GLENDA: No. (*Walks to end of sofa.*) I'm busy.

ROY: Busy? Folding clothes is keeping you busy? Here, I'll give you something to keep you busy! (*Begins knocking and throwing stacks of clothes to the floor.*) That'll keep you busy for awhile.

(*ROY pushes the remote to turn off television, then throws it down, hard, on the sofa. Goes to refrigerator.*)

GLENDA: See! There you go again. If you don't get your way you get violent.

ROY: Violent? Ha! You ain't seen violent. I could turn this refrigerator over without even thinking. (*Grabs it on both sides.*)

GLENDA: Oh, I know—how well I know. (*Begins picking up clothes and putting them in the clothes basket.*) I remember how you used to punch the wall when you got mad at me, and kick and throw stuff.

(*ROY has heard all this before. He gets his beer and leans against the refrigerator as he drinks it, watching her.*)

GLENDA: (*Voice is wavering.*) And the way you took parts off the car so I couldn't go anywhere. And the times I threatened to leave and you-

ROY: (*Stands erect, more intense.*) -Yeah, and I don't do that stuff no more. Have you got a recorder for a brain? That was a long time ago. I said I was sorry about all that. But that ain't enough, is it? You got to keep bringing it up. Let's wrap ole Roy's past around his neck and choke the living hell out of him, is that it? (*Knocks a tray from the counter top to the floor.*)

GLENDA: (*Stands, holding the basket of clothes.*) Things like what you just did, remind me of the past, that's all. The only reason you stopped doing those things was because I started giving in to you.

ROY: (*Calms a bit.*) I could be out here chasing women like all these other men. Instead, I love you, and only you, Glenda. Don't that count for nothing?

GLENDA: Of course it does. I just wish you would-

(*Phone rings. They look at each other without making a move to answer it. After second ring, ROY, who is standing closer to it, moves away from it.*)

ROY: You get it. I ain't in no mood to talk, especially not to your mama.

GLENDA: How do you know it's her?

ROY: Oh, it's her all right.

(*ROY takes the salt shaker from table, sprinkles some in his hand and licks it. GLENDA sets the basket down and answers the phone.*)

GLENDA: Hello. Yes, he's here. Sure. (*Places hand over phone.*) Someone wants to ask you about a car.

(*GLENDA hands ROY the phone and exits with clothes basket through archway.*)

ROY: Yeah. Umhum. Ummmhumm. Well, I been offered more than that for her and turned it down. (*Pause.*) I see. What is it you plan to do with her if you buy her? I mean, this baby ain't never seen rain. I keep her in a controlled environment, and nobody touches her but me. (*Laughs.*) Yeah, that's right. (*Pause.*) Yeah, we can talk about it some more. Are you here in town? Why don't I meet you there, and you can go take another look at her? Okay.

(*ROY hangs up. As he turns away, the phone rings again.*)

ROY: That's got to be her. Glenda! (*Waits. Decides he has to answer it.*) Yeah. Hey, scout! (*Pause.*) Daddy'll come and get you. Your mama ain't feeling too good. Is Roy Dean with you? Okay. Listen, how would you two boys like to go with me to show off the Chevy to a man that might buy her? All right! Stay put. I'll be there in a minute.

(*ROY hangs up. GLENDA enters with a stack of dish towels and cloths to put away. She doesn't look at ROY. He goes and grabs her from behind and starts nibbling her on the neck.*)

ROY: Ummm...

(*GLENDA doesn't respond.*)

ROY: You ain't still mad at me, are you?

GLENDA: I just wish you'd try to understand how I feel sometimes.

ROY: (*Caressing her shoulders, then down her arms.*) You feel good to me.

GLENDA: I'm serious, Roy. I love you and the boys, but I need- I don't know why I can't just go take some classes and-

ROY: (*Backs away.*) -Is that what this is all about? You going to college? Why is that so damned important to you all of a sudden?

GLENDA: Well, maybe it would give me.... (*Hesitates.*) Maybe I could get a good-paying job and help out.

ROY: Like, what kind of job?

GLENDA: You know, like I could be a nurse or something. I could go for two years and be a registered nurse. How about that?

ROY: They make good money all right. But you can't handle all that, and you know it.

GLENDA: I can too! And I could get a grant or a loan to help pay for it so you won't-

ROY: -Hell no! We ain't taking no handouts and we ain't going in debt. No sireee bob-o-link! I got the money. Roy Everson's got the money. (*Takes out billfold, starts pulling out bills and throwing them on the table.*) How much do you need, huh? Here, take all the pieces to the Boss Mustang I'm restoring, and here, take my new truck tires too!

GLENDA: Roy, don't be this way. Just forget about it. Just forget I said anything.

ROY: No, if that's what it's gonna take to make you happy, aye god, that's what you're gonna get! (*Takes cap from top of refrigerator and puts it on. Grabs coat off coat rack.*)

GLENDA: Where are you going?

ROY: (*Opens door.*) What difference does it make? You don't care about me anyhow.

GLENDA: Just tell me where you're going.

ROY: To find a rope and hang myself!

(*ROY goes out the door, slamming it. GLENDA throws up her hands, then grabs a stack of potholders and throws them.*)

ACT TWO

SCENE ONE

Playing Games

Car doors slam. GLENDA and MARILEE enter. MARILEE is dressed as usual. GLENDA is wearing a dress and heels as for church, and a coat. BOTH are carrying books and school supplies.

GLENDA: I can't wait to get out of these clothes!

MARILEE: I told you, you didn't need to dress up to go to the college, Glenda.

(*BOTH dump the books and supplies on the table.*)

GLENDA: I know. I felt so stupid. Thanks for taking off work at the fitness center to go with me. (*GLENDA removes her coat and hangs it on the rack.*) Can you believe where the holes were in that boy's jeans, the one in front of us in line?

MARILEE: Really!

(*MARILEE laughs and plops down at the table. GLENDA moves to the table and stares at materials.*)

GLENDA: I can't believe how much all of this stuff cost. I shouldn't have done it, Marilee. Let's just take it all back and cancel my registration.

MARILEE: Will you stop that? What's wrong with you? I thought this was what you wanted?

GLENDA: Oh, I want it! I want it more than even *you* know, Marilee. Do you think I can do it? (*Drops in chair.*)

MARILEE: Well, of course you can, silly. You were always at the top of our class. (*Drumming out a rhythm on the table with her hands.*)

GLENDA: (*Separating and stacking the books and supplies.*) Funny. I don't seem to have the old confidence anymore.

MARILEE: (*Goes to refrigerator.*) You can blame that on Roy boy!

GLENDA: Do you have to start on him again?

MARILEE: He's brought you down, and you know it. (*Surveys contents of refrigerator.*) You should've gone on to college right out of high school, instead of marrying your mister stud muffin and having babies. I tried to tell you, but you wouldn't listen. (*Helps herself to a beer and returns to table.*)

GLENDA: You didn't go to college either, you know.

MARILEE: But I hated school. You loved it. That's why I think he had some kind of control over you even then.

GLENDA: Was that the last beer?

MARILEE: Why? Did you want one? I'm sorry, I should've asked.

GLENDA: Not me! (*Goes to look.*) It was the last one, Marilee. Roy always wants a beer when he gets home.

MARILEE: I don't believe you, kiddo. Worrying about a little thing like that.

GLENDA: Sometimes it's the little things that are important. My mama always said: "If a high wind comes and you're out in it, hold onto a little sapling."

MARILEE: Say what?

GLENDA: (*Laughs.*) Anyway, marriage is about being able to bend without breaking. Compromise, you know?

MARILEE: With the woman doing all the compromising. No thanks.

GLENDA: I hate to say this, but if you had given in to Teak a little, maybe he wouldn't have run around on you.

MARILEE: You're wrong, Glenda. He had the red eye from the beginning, and men never change. (*Pause.*) Are you still worried about Roy's beer? I can go get him one at my house.

GLENDA: No. The beer is nothing compared to....

MARILEE: Compared to what? Keeping Roy in toilet paper?

GLENDA: He didn't know I was going to the college to register today and buy books.

MARILEE: So surprise him. I thought you said he told you to go on to college if that's what you wanted.

GLENDA: He did. But he didn't really mean it.

MARILEE: So work him, if that's how you want to play it.

GLENDA: I don't work him. I just give in to him, and usually that satisfies him.

MARILEE: And that's the part (*Slams beer down on table.*) that makes me want to throw up. It's power, Glenda, that's all it is!

GLENDA: (*Stands.*) I know it's power, and I've told him so, but of course he denies it. (*Picks up one of the books.*) Why do you think I went ahead and registered today and bought these? (*Throws book back on table, hard.*)

MARILEE: Don't get your ovaries inflamed. I think it's great! It's about time you stood up to him.

GLENDA: (*Drops back in chair.*) But I know what will happen. He'll just get furious with me and throw a big fit, and then I will have to cancel everything.

MARILEE: Let him throw ten fits. You don't have to cancel anything!

GLENDA: That's easy for you to say. (*Stands.*) I need to get out of these clothes.

MARILEE: Whatever, kiddo.

GLENDA: (*Sits back down.*) Marilee...oh, what's the use. (*Looks at clock.*) I better start supper first. Roy will be home in an hour.

(*GLENDA gets up and begins getting out pans and setting them on the stove, then selecting some potatoes to peel. MARILEE gets up to help her.*)

MARILEE: I can't remember the last time I actually cooked something.

GLENDA: It must be nice.

MARILEE: Yeah, but it gets old sometimes, eating out or else nuking something quick in the microwave.

GLENDA: This gets old too. Do you like being divorced, Marilee?

MARILEE: It's okay. Gets lonely sometimes. (*Holds up a potato.*) This potato is starting to sprout. Is it still good?

GLENDA: You don't cook much, do you? (*Takes potato from her and examines it.*) Yeah, it's still good. Those new sprouts look like little mice feet, don't they?

MARILEE: (*Laughs.*) You're totally warped, you know that?

GLENDA: (*Laughs with her. Pause.*) Roy says you want me divorced like you.

MARILEE: Maybe he thinks I want us to run off together and become Amazon women.

(*MARILEE flexes her arms. They laugh and sit at the table to peel.*)

MARILEE: So tell me, how are you gonna break the news that you registered for classes today? I mean, it's just hard for me to see how-

GLENDA: -Why'd you have to bring it back up? Now my ovaries really are starting to hurt.

MARILEE: You see? You make yourself sick worrying about what move you have to make next, just to satisfy a man who I bet doesn't spend five minutes worrying about how you feel.

GLENDA: I don't know, Marilee. Sometimes I think he does worry about how I feel, but somehow, when he connects the dots, he gets a different picture from the one I get. (*Pause.*) You really are a good friend to me, but don't worry, I'll work through this one just like I always do. And maybe there'll come a time-

(*Truck door slams.*)

GLENDA: What was that?

MARILEE: Sounded like a door slamming—a truck door.

GLENDA: (*Glances at clock.*) Marilee?! Quick, help me get rid of these things!

(*BOTH gather up books and supplies. MARILEE opens oven door and begins tossing hers in, then takes the ones GLENDA is holding and does likewise. A notebook is thrown in bottom of oven. GLENDA remembers she still has on the dress, and clutches it.*)

GLENDA: And look at this! You better leave, Marilee.

MARILEE: No, I'm staying. I'm not gonna let him hurt you!

GLENDA: Oh, he's not going to hurt me, for crying out loud, but seeing you will put him in a bad mood. You can go out this way. (*Motions toward archway.*)

MARILEE: Yeah, okay. Roy boy's all yours! (*Grabs beer and starts to leave, but too late.*)

(*ROY enters, wearing work clothes and cap and coat. Looks at MARILEE in surprise.*)

MARILEE: I was just leaving. (*Holding beer behind her.*)

ROY: Good. Bye, Marilee! (*Removes coat and throws it over chair. Keeps cap on.*)

MARILEE: Later, kiddo.

(*MARILEE keeps beer hidden as she moves toward door and exits.*)

GLENDA: Later.

ROY: How long has she been here?

GLENDA: Not long. You're home early. (*Continues to prepare their meal.*)

ROY: Maybe. (*Opens refrigerator.*) What happened to my beer?

GLENDA: Maybe you drank it.

ROY: There was a beer in here when I left for work this morning.

GLENDA: Are you sure?

ROY: Quit playing games, Glenda. You give my last beer to her, didn't you? (*Slams refrigerator door.*)

GLENDA: She just took it.

ROY: Why didn't you stop her?

GLENDA: It's just a beer, Roy. I can get more.

ROY: That don't help me now. Why'd you let me get down to just one, anyhow? Ain't you ever heard of a store? (*Sits at the table.*) What kind of trash did she fill your head with this time?

GLENDA: I wish you wouldn't talk about her like that. You always say the same thing.

ROY: That's because I know how she is. Always trying to stir up trouble. She's just jealous because you got a man and she don't. (*Takes salt shaker, sprinkles salt in hand, and licks it.*)

GLENDA: No, I don't think she wants another man.

ROY: Well, she needs one to put her in her place.

GLENDA: And where's that, Roy? Under his thumb?

ROY: Naw, just under him.

(*ROY laughs. He takes cap off and puts it back on.*)

GLENDA: You think that's all any woman needs.

ROY: What she really needs is to learn how to treat a man. This women's lib crap has ruined more marriages than anything else. You can't have two people trying to run things. Somebody's gotta be in charge.

GLENDA: And why does it always have to be the man?

ROY: (*Pause.*) It just does. What're you cooking there? We still having Shake and Bake chicken like you said?

GLENDA: (*Quickly turns to face him and backs up to oven door, guarding it.*) Actually, I thought I'd deep-fry it. It's quicker.

ROY: Aw, I wanted that barbecue kind.

GLENDA: It takes too long. And I'm getting a late start.

ROY: Come to think of it, what *have* you been doing? Why are you all dressed up like that?

GLENDA: I went out.

ROY: Out where?

GLENDA: (*Returns to cooking.*) To the college to register for classes.

ROY: (*Stands abruptly, causing chair to fall backwards to floor.*) You what?!

GLENDA: (*Turns, startled.*) I just said that to see what you would do.

ROY: Well, are you satisfied? Look what you made me do! (*Picks up chair.*) You ain't gonna let up on this college business, are you?

GLENDA: Roy, what would you have done if I had gone ahead and registered for classes without you knowing?

(*ROY stares at her.*)

GLENDA: Well?

ROY: What makes you think I would've done something?

GLENDA: Because I know how you are.

ROY: If you know so damned much, why'd you even bother to ask?

GLENDA: You know I wouldn't do anything you didn't really want me to, so you'll be happy to know I'm not going to bother you about it ever again.

ROY: What changed your mind?

GLENDA: You did.

ROY: How's that?

GLENDA: What have we just been talking about? You've made it clear you don't want me to go to college, so I'm not going.

ROY: You'd do that for me? (*Smiling.*)

GLENDA: Don't I always do what you want?

ROY: Yeah. You're a good woman, Glenda. (*Puts his arm around her waist and kisses her on the neck.*) Ummm! (*Pause.*) Naw, I've decided you ought to go on to college.

GLENDA: I told you, I'm not going.

ROY: You want me to beg you to go now, is that it?

GLENDA: No, Roy, I'm just not going.

ROY: Aye god, you'll go if I tell you to! And I say you're going!

GLENDA: You mean it? (*Tries to offer him a look of surprise.*)

ROY: Yeah, I mean it.

GLENDA: You're sure you mean it?

ROY: You better shut up before I change my mind.

GLENDA: (*Reaches up and takes off his cap and kisses him lightly.*) Thanks, Roy. (*She's disgusted with herself.*)

ROY: You always get what you want, don't you? But mark my words, Glenda, you'll be sorry.

GLENDA: Why? Are you going to make me sorry?

ROY: Naw, I wouldn't do that to you. (*He's smiling.*) All I mean is, you don't know what you're getting into. And you've got to remember one thing. You're still my wife, and you're still a mama to our boys, no matter what.

GLENDA: (*Puts his cap back on his head. Gets chicken out of refrigerator.*) So how did work go today?

ROY: Not too good. I killed half a day trying to figure out what was wrong with the damned computer.

GLENDA: What happened?

ROY: Don't know. It just wouldn't read out for me. All I know is my head ain't felt right since.

(*GLENDA laughs.*)

ROY: It ain't funny, Glenda. I can't afford to go out and buy a new one if it's tore up.

GLENDA: I know.

(*A knock is heard at the door.*)

ROY: (*Opens door.*) Well, if it ain't the beer thief.

MARILEE: Ooooh, Roy! Is you the law?

GLENDA: Oh, he's the law, all right.

MARILEE: (*Goes over to table and sets bag on table, then pulls out one beer, and then another.*) I'm paying you back, with interest.

ROY: You didn't hafta do that.

MARILEE: I know I didn't hafta, but I didn't want Glenda to be in trouble over it.

GLENDA: Am I in trouble, Roy?

ROY: (*Opens one of the beers and sits at the table.*) What made you think Glenda would be in trouble?

MARILEE: Because she was worried about it.

ROY: What'd you tell her, Glenda?

MARILEE: She said you were a bad-ass bear without your beer, Roy.

(*MARILEE grabs ROY's beer and takes a drink of it. He looks at her in astonishment.*)

MARILEE: Is that true?

ROY: Yeah, I'm a bad-ass all right. Tell her what a bad-ass I am, Glenda.

GLENDA: I think he wants me to tell you he's letting me go to college.

ROY: Yep. I've decided to let her go, if it's what makes her happy.

(*MARILEE has begun stirring in one of the pots on the stove. She looks at GLENDA, who is washing the chicken.*)

MARILEE: Soooo, you're <u>letting</u> her go to college, are you? Well, that's just real big of you, Roy.

GLENDA: Don't, Marilee.

ROY: Let her talk, Glenda. (*Gets up.*) I'd kinda like to hear what she's got to say. You got a lot to say, don't you, Marilee? Always saying it to somebody besides me. Well, here's your chance.

MARILEE: (*Turns to face ROY.*) I just don't think it's right for Glenda to have to get permission from you to do something like this—something this important to her.

ROY: That's why she's got a husband, and you don't.

MARILEE: Oh, really? Well, if having a husband means putting up with that kind of crap, no thanks!

ROY: Aw, come on, Marilee. Glenda always gets what she wants, and you know it.

MARILEE: But she shouldn't have to grovel to get it.

ROY: Did you grovel, Glenda?

GLENDA: Why, no, Roy. I just said I'd decided not to go to college, and you said I would go if you told me to, so I'm going.

ROY: (*Gesturing toward GLENDA.*) See?

MARILEE: God!

ROY: Look, Marilee. What Glenda and me does is our business. You been filling her head with trash ever since you moved back here, and I'm getting fed up with it if you want to know the truth.

GLENDA: Roy!

MARILEE: It's okay, Glenda. Roy, I don't give a big rat's ass what you think of me, but take a good, long look there! (*Points to GLENDA.*) If you don't get real smart real fast, you just might lose the best thing that ever happened to you! (*Grabs extra beer from table to leave.*) And I'm taking back my interest.

ROY: Aw, get over it, Marilee.

(*As MARILEE is about to leave, she runs into TEAK, who was about to knock at the door.*)

MARILEE: What do you want? (*Upset with all men now.*)

TEAK: I thought I might find you here. I need to see you.

MARILEE: (*Brushes past him and exits.*) Well, you've seen me!

TEAK: Marilee? (*Follows her and exits.*) Wait up.

GLENDA: Roy, how could you say those things to her?

ROY: Hell, it was easy. (*Sits on sofa.*)

GLENDA: You know what I mean. She's just trying to stand up for me because she thinks I won't stand up for myself. (*Has chicken laid out on paper towels.*)

ROY: What's to stand up for? I aggravate you a lot, but I don't mean nothing by it, you know that. You never did tell me where you been today.

(*GLENDA is silent.*)

ROY: I know where you been, Glenda.

GLENDA: (*Warily.*) You do?

ROY: (*Laughs.*) Yeah.

(*GLENDA looks at him in wonder. Telephone rings.*)

GLENDA: Get that, Roy. It's not Mama. She's pouting and won't call.

ROY: (*Answers it.*) Yeah. Yeah, I'll come and get you. Where's your brother? (*Pause.*) Okay. Be there in a minute. (*Hangs up.*) Roy Dean. Needs to be picked up at the gym.

GLENDA: You know, I said something to him the other day about wanting to go to college, and you know what he said?

ROY: Probably said you couldn't hardly take care of what little there is to do around here, much less go to college.

GLENDA: That's exactly what he said.

ROY: (*Laughs. Takes cap off and puts it back on.*) 'At's my boy!

GLENDA: It's not funny, Roy. One day he's going to marry some girl and talk to her the same way. He's going to be just like you.

ROY: And what's wrong with that?

(*TEAK knocks once and enters.*)

TEAK: Could I see you for a minute, Roy.

(*GLENDA and ROY look at each other.*)

GLENDA: I'll go get Roy Dean. Chicken'll wait until I get back. Can you keep an eye on things?

ROY: (*Exaggerates, hands shaking.*) Do you think I can handle that?

(*BOTH men laugh, as GLENDA grabs her coat and exits.*)

TEAK: (*Sees chicken.*) Glenda fixing this chicken for tonight?

ROY: She said something about frying it. I kinda like Shake and Bake myself. That barbecue kind.

TEAK: You got any of that stuff? I know how to make it. We'll surprise her.

ROY: Why, yeah!

(*While ROY gets the Shake and Bake, TEAK reaches over and turns on oven. ROY hands the box to TEAK.*)

ROY: So what's up?

TEAK: (*Tears open box.*) Nothing, thanks to you. I got tickets to the game in Lexington on Saturday. I thought I might talk Marilee into going with me, but she's pretty upset right now.

ROY: Aw, she's just mad at me for telling her to butt out.

TEAK: I don't know, I couldn't get her to say much, but I think she's worried about Glenda.

ROY: What makes you think she's worried about Glenda?

(*TEAK puts contents of envelope in plastic bag and begins coating [shaking] the pieces of chicken in it.*)

TEAK: She said something about Glenda trying to go to college and- Is she really going?

ROY: Yeah, I reckon so. I tried to tell her she didn't know what she was getting herself into, but you know how women are.

TEAK: Yeah, but I think Marilee's really- (*Drops one of the pieces of chicken to the floor.*) Man, I'm sorry.

(*ROY picks it up, looks it over, knocks something off it with his finger, and hands it to TEAK.*)

ROY: Little dirt won't hurt it. I'll eat that one myself.

TEAK: What I'm trying to say is, I believe Marilee's thinking you won't be able to handle Glenda's going to college.

ROY: You don't say? (*Pause.*) Oh, I can handle it all right. I don't like it, though. What man would?

TEAK: I don't know, Roy. Think about it like this: If it makes her happy—makes her feel good about herself, that'll benefit you. There's nothing more ex-cit-ing than a woman who feels good about herself—you know, has that ole confidence. (*Gives him an elbow and a knowing look.*)

ROY: Think so, huh? I don't know. I kinda like Glenda the way she is.

TEAK: Yeah, of course you do. I'm just saying she'll be even better if- (*Sniffs.*) Something burning?

(*ROY goes to the stove and checks pots.*)

ROY: No. Everything's fine.

TEAK: Smells like paper.

(*TEAK goes to stove, looks around. ROY sniffs, then realizes where it's coming from and opens oven door. Smoke pours out.*)

Roy: Holy shit! (*Turns off oven.*)

TEAK: Man-oh-man-oh-man!

(*TEAK looks around for something to help. ROY reaches in the oven and pulls out a notebook and throws it to the floor, stomping it to put out the fire. Picks it up.*)

ROY: Aw, Glenda!

TEAK: What is it?

ROY: (*Starts to laugh.*) That crazy Glenda, trying to hide her school stuff from me.

TEAK: Why would she try to hide her school stuff?

ROY: Oh, she was just playing one of her little games.

TEAK: What?

(*ROY holds up charred notebook, letting it swing back and forth between his thumb and forefinger.*)

ROY: You see, Teak, I don't need a more ex-cit-ing Glenda.

(*BOTH laugh.*)

SCENE TWO

Break Point

Two months later. Stage is in general disarray, strewn clothes, paper cups, paper plates. Enter GLENDA, ROY right behind her. GLENDA is wearing a serape, jeans, and calf-length boots. Hair is hanging loosely about her face. She wears a backpack. ROY is dressed in his usual work clothes and cap.

ROY: Well, what've you got to say for yourself?

GLENDA: (*Takes off backpack and slams it down on the table.*) You wouldn't like what I have to say!

ROY: Try me.

GLENDA: How dare you treat me like a child! Come barging in the library and dragging me out like that!

(*GLENDA begins to put on coffee, making as much noise about it as she can.*)

ROY: (*Pacing.*) Oh, now you're gonna turn this all around and make me the bad guy, huh? I was just worried about you, that's all. No woman needs to be out after dark by herself these days.

GLENDA: It was the library for crying out loud, not some smoky bar. I told you I had research to do and I'd be late. That's why I took the boys over to Mama's for the night. No, you weren't worried about me, you were just checking up on me to see if I was really there. I hope you're satisfied.

ROY: I ain't a damned bit satisfied. Way you been acting lately, wouldn't nothing surprise me.

GLENDA: And just what do you mean by that?

ROY: Look at you! Running around here looking like some damned hippie, letting everything go to hell on a paper plate. (*Making sweeping motion with his arms to indicate the mess. Lifts lid from pot on stove.*) And a man can just take so much "Hamburger Helper."

GLENDA: Why can't you try helping me out instead of causing trouble?

ROY: Me? (*Looks at her.*) What're you doing?

GLENDA: (*Settling herself at the table. Getting papers out of backpack, prepares to type.*) I've got to get this paper ready for class tomorrow.

ROY: That's all you ever worry about is your damned classes. What about me, Glenda? Don't I count no more? I'm just a peon that gets in your way, is that it?

(*Glenda ignores him and begins to type.*)

ROY: I asked you a question, Glenda!

GLENDA: (*Stops typing.*) You do count, but right now I've got to work on this paper. I have to set priorities.

ROY: Priorities my ass. How's this for a priority? I say you quit college and stay home where you belong. (*Is pacing.*)

GLENDA: I'm not quitting. (*Goes back to typing.*)

ROY: If I say you quit, you quit.

GLENDA: Not anymore, Roy. (*Stops typing.*) And another thing, I've decided to major in psychology instead of being a nurse, and that's going to take a long time, so you may as well get used to it.

ROY: (*Throwing his arms in the air.*) Let's just get up on our high-horse, why don't we. Before you get too high, just remember, I'm paying, so if I quit paying, you quit going.

GLENDA: (*Goes back to typing.*) Whatever you say, Roy.

ROY: Oh, no you don't. We ain't playing that game no more. I want my wife back.

GLENDA: And I just want to finish this paper.

ROY: What about what I want? You could care less what I want!

GLENDA: It's couldn't care less.

ROY: What?

GLENDA: If you could care less, it means you care some. People always get that wrong.

ROY: You think you're so damned smart, don't you? I let you go to college and all of a sudden you're smarter than me, is that it? That's why a man can't be good to a woman, she starts taking advantage of him.

(*GLENDA continues to type. ROY puts both hands on the table across from her, and leans into her face.*)

ROY: Look at me when I'm talking to you!

(*GLENDA continues to ignore him.*)

ROY: (*Rakes papers and books to floor.*) I said look at me, dammit!

GLENDA: (*Stands.*) Roy! You had no right to do that!

ROY: I got a right to do whatever the hell I want, and don't you ever forget it!

GLENDA: I don't know why I stay and put up with you! (*Begins picking up papers.*)

ROY: What is it, Glenda? I'm not good enough for you now? Huh? Found somebody smarter than me? Some college professor maybe? Maybe you're just using me to get through school so you can dump me! Is that it?

GLENDA: That's not it, and you know it.

ROY: The hell I do! Which is more important to you, college or me and the boys? Huh? (*Pause.*) Which is it? (*Pause.*) Answer me, Glenda.

GLENDA: That's not fair, Roy.

ROY: (*Mocking.*) That's not fair, Roy. I'll tell you what is fair. If I ain't the man of this house no more, then I got no business being here.

(*ROY glares at GLENDA then charges to the bedroom. GLENDA tries to put papers back in order. ROY jerks his clothes from closet. He carries a load in each hand, still on hangers, to the sitting area and slings them on the sofa. Goes back to bedroom and gets luggage from closet, throws it on the bed and starts emptying drawers into it, pulling drawers out of dresser and dumping contents, then throwing drawer aside. GLENDA goes to bedroom.*)

GLENDA: What are you doing?

ROY: What does it look like I'm doing? I'm leaving!

GLENDA: Oh, this is a new one!

ROY: You think I won't? You watch me, Glenda. A man can just take so much!

GLENDA: Well, here, let me help you! (*Pulls out a drawer and dumps contents on the bed. Reaches under the bed and drags out his brown bag and throws it on the bed.*) I wouldn't want you to forget this stupid bag! And here! (*Jerks curtains down and throws them at him.*) Take the curtains too! You might have a window where you're going! (*Screaming.*) I've had it with you, Roy, you and your damned ego and stupid threats. Do you hear me? I've had it. Had it!

(*ROY, stunned, watches helplessly. Follows GLENDA as she leaves bedroom.*)

ROY: Come back here, Glenda!

(*GLENDA grabs some of the clothes from the sofa and drags them to the door. ROY follows behind her.*)

ROY: Here now, what're you doing?

(*GLENDA opens door and throws out clothes. Turns and sees ROY. Explodes.*)

GLENDA: Damn you! Damn you!

(*GLENDA grabs canisters one by one and attempts to throw them, with ROY either catching them or taking them from her as she picks them up.*)

ROY: Stop it, Glenda. I said stop it!

(*GLENDA lets out a cry of frustration and begins pounding his chest with her fists. ROY stops her, holding her arms. He suddenly releases her and hands her the canister marked TEA, which really has money in. Change is heard clinking.*)

ROY: Here! Throw this!

(*GLENDA takes it. Suddenly realizes what she's doing and starts backing away from him. Still holding the canister, she turns and runs to the bedroom, crying. She places canister on dresser, clears the bed of suitcase, etc. and gets beneath the bedspread, sitting cross-legged with it pulled over her head, rocking back and forth and sobbing. ROY follows and stands watching her. He moves toward her.*)

ROY: Glenda?

(*GLENDA doesn't respond. ROY moves to her side.*)

ROY: You all right?

(*ROY reaches out and touches her. GLENDA jumps, startled. She pulls the bedspread away from her face, but it still covers her head like a scarf. She puts her hands over her face. ROY sits beside her and puts his arms around her.*)

ROY: Don't feel bad, mama. It ain't nothing.

GLENDA: Nothing? (*Grabs covers and pulls them to her and starts to rock again.*)

ROY: Oh, it was something all right!

(*ROY's laughing about it, but the laughter is strained. Puts his arms around her. GLENDA continues to rock back and forth, taking him with her.*)

ROY: Would you quit rocking? You're making me drunk. Why are you rocking?

GLENDA: I don't know. I don't know why I do anything anymore.

ROY: You thought I was leaving and you went a little crazy, that's all. You know I couldn't leave you, mama.

GLENDA: Would you stop calling me "mama"? And I wish you would leave.

ROY: You don't mean that, now.

GLENDA: Don't tell me what I don't mean!

ROY: Okay. Okay. But I'll tell you what you need.

(*ROY presses her back on the bed, and lets himself down on top of her. GLENDA pushes him off and jumps up.*)

GLENDA: No, Roy! That's the trouble with us. We have sex and the problem is supposed to just disappear. Well, not this time!

(*GLENDA exits to bathroom. ROY follows her quickly, trying to get there before she shuts the door. He is too late. He tries the door. It is locked. He knocks.*)

ROY: Glenda. Come on, Glenda. Aw, mama, don't do me like this. Come on. Come to daddy.

(*ROY listens. Slaps wall and moves to dining area, where he re-orders the canisters. Turning to survey the mess of books and papers, he decides to pick them up. As he does so, he stops to read from one of the papers. GLENDA emerges from bathroom. ROY looks up from his reading in anticipation of her coming to him, but instead, she goes to the bed and throws herself across it. ROY tosses the paper aside and heads to the bedroom to confront her.*)

ROY: All right! Just what is it you want from me, Glenda?

(*GLENDA ignores him.*)

ROY: Talk to me.

(*GLENDA continues to ignore him. ROY sits on bed and pulls her up by one arm.*)

ROY: Damnit! I said talk to me!

GLENDA: (*Yanks free of his grasp and stands.*) I can't talk to you, Roy. You know why? Because you don't listen. I've been talking and talking, and you don't hear me!

(*GLENDA starts to cry again. ROY is disconcerted by her crying.*)

ROY: (*His anger diminished.*) I'll ask you again. What is it you want from me?

GLENDA: I want- (*Takes a deep breath, calms.*) I don't want to keep living like this. I can't.

ROY: What's so bad about it? At least I don't beat you.

GLENDA: Well, thank you!

ROY: Look. All I ever wanted was for you to love me like I love you.

GLENDA: (*Moves away from him.*) I don't think you know what love is.

ROY: I may not know what love is, like you say, and I don't claim to have it all figured out like you do, but I know what love feels like, and I don't feel any from you right now. Look at me and say you love me. (*Pause.*) You can't do it, can you?

GLENDA: (*Looks at him.*) I love you, Roy.

ROY: No you don't. You're just saying that because you know that's what I want to hear.

GLENDA: Well, isn't it?

ROY: Yeah, but I want you to say it like you mean it. You never loved me, did you?

GLENDA: I did love you, Roy.

ROY: Did love?

GLENDA: You said I never loved you, and I just said I did, that's all.

ROY: Then, you're saying you don't love me now, is that it? Go on. Say it.

GLENDA: (*Turns away from him.*) There are times when I think I love you, but when you get demanding and start acting crazy...I hate it when you get like that...hate you. (*Turning to him.*) And all our married life you've done that to me. I can't live like that anymore. I won't! (*Sits in chair.*)

ROY: Has it really been that bad, Glenda? Because if it has, I might as well go ahead and kill myself and get it over with.

(*ROY gets up and goes to closet and takes down the box that holds his handgun. Takes it out.*)

ROY: This way you won't have to put up with me no more.

GLENDA: (*Jumps up.*) Oh no you don't! Don't pull that on me now—not now! (*Starts to leave the room, then turns.*) If you decide to kill yourself, that's your choice, not mine. The hand that picks up the gun can lay it down!

ROY: (*Turning the gun over in his hand.*) You see, Glenda, if you don't care about me I got no reason to go on living.

GLENDA: And what about our boys, Roy? Don't you care about them? Do you want them to have to grow up without you?

ROY: They'll be better off without me.

GLENDA: You know that's not true! How can you say that?

ROY: (*Desperate to reach her.*) You don't love me.

GLENDA: I never said I didn't love you. I'm just trying to get you to understand some things. Look at me! God! If you want to kill yourself I can't stop you. I just can't!

(*GLENDA runs from bedroom. Stops in archway, covers her ears, closes her eyes, and waits fearfully. ROY raises the gun to his temple, hand trembles, then he relaxes and lets his arm fall to his side, standing there defeated. GLENDA, not hearing anything, lowers her hands from her ears and opens her eyes. ROY, in frustration, suddenly throws the gun down hard, causing it to discharge. GLENDA screams and drops to the floor on her knees. Rocks back and forth, moaning.*)

GLENDA: No! Oh, God! No! No!

(*ROY jumps when the gun discharges. GLENDA's scream causes him to run to her. All of this happens so quickly it overlaps.*)

ROY: Glenda! It's okay! It's okay, baby.

(*ROY pulls her up from floor, thrusts her against him, stroking her. GLENDA is trembling.*)

ROY: The gun just went off. I'm sorry, baby. The damned thing just went off.

(*ROY moves with GLENDA to one of the chairs, sits down, holding her in his lap and rocking her as though she were a small child.*)

ROY: I'm sorry...I'm sorry.

(*GLENDA's emotions have gone from terror to numbness. ROY's emotion draws her out of herself, and instinctively, she begins to comfort him. She puts her arms around him, stroking him. ROY has pressed his face into her shoulder. He pulls back to look at her.*)

ROY: You're still shaking.

GLENDA: It's just that I thought you really had- and- (*She stands, pressing a hand to her forehead.*) Oh, you don't know how cold and awful that feels. (*She faces him.*) You did that on purpose, didn't you...to scare me...to make me think you really had killed yourself? Oh, Roy, how could you?

ROY: (*Stands and grabs her.*) God, no! I could never even think of doing something like that. I slammed the gun down. It went off.

GLENDA: Oh, Roy, you really could have been killed!

ROY: I know it! Listen, I know I'm crazy. Always have been. And I ought to be locked up in a institution just like you said.

GLENDA: What? What are you talking about?

ROY: I read it in your paper there, Glenda. (*Motions to her paper.*) You said sometimes he is violent against hisself and others and needs to be put in a institution.

GLENDA: Oh, Roy! That's not about you. (*Starts to laugh*). I can't believe you thought- (*Breaks into another fit of laughter.*) I had to do a profile of a paranoid schizophrenic for psychology. And you thought.... (*Laughs some more.*)

ROY: (*Begins to see the humor in it.*) Well, it sounded just like me!

GLENDA: (*Laughs again and puts her arms around him.*) Oh, Roy, I really do love you.

ROY: Tell me how I can make it better, Glenda. Help me....

GLENDA: You just need to remember that I want us to be a family just as much as you. And just because I want something else too, doesn't mean I don't love you and our boys.

ROY: Yeah, I guess I know that.

GLENDA: (*Looks around at the mess.*) I'm sorry I went ballistic earlier. I can't believe I actually stooped to that level.

ROY: Yeah, that's usually my job. Maybe you got some of that test-toaster stuff in you too, huh?

(*GLENDA laughs. ROY helps her pick up.*)

ROY: I'm sorry I said you had to quit college. I don't want you to quit.

GLENDA: And what happens next time I have a paper due or exam to study for?

ROY: I'll probably pack up and threaten to leave again.

GLENDA: Roy!

ROY: Aw, Glenda, I'm just messing with you.

GLENDA: But I think there is hidden hostility there.

ROY: You take a psychology class and all of a sudden you're a shrink. Do you have to spend so much time on your classes?

GLENDA: I just want you to be proud of me.

ROY: (*Goes to her.*) Proud of you? I'm proud of you when you're being a good mama to our boys, and a good wife to me. That other stuff don't matter.

GLENDA: It matters to me, Roy.

ROY: I know it does, but...when you start working on a paper or something, it's like...you go away from me.

GLENDA: I'll try not to do that, but you'll have to try too.

ROY: So does this mean you'll still wash my back once in awhile?

GLENDA: (*Smiles.*) Will you wash mine?

ROY: (*Looks her up and down.*) Hell, I'll wash you all over!

(*GLENDA laughs. Goes to door and bends over to pick up clothes she threw out.*)

ROY: (*Taking in the way she looks in her jeans.*) You know, I kinda like my new little hippie wife with the test-toasterone. But you better be careful bending over like that. Could be trouble!

GLENDA: Roy!

ROY: Oh, lord. It ain't been five minutes, and I already screwed up. Leave it to the country boy.

GLENDA: Hey, I first fell in love with that country boy, remember? That was part of your charm.

ROY: Oh, I was charming was I? And all this time I thought it was the hay in my barn.

GLENDA: (*Laughs.*) That too!

(*ROY takes clothes from her and they move to bedroom. In bedroom, they hang the clothes in the closet and replace drawers that were removed.*)

GLENDA: You know, we keep saying we've got a right to do anything we want, but we don't really. I mean, when you're married, you can't just do whatever you want without considering the other person, because... what you do affects that person too, right?

ROY: Yeah.

GLENDA: You're not even listening, are you?

ROY: Yeah, I'm listening. You said you had me whipped and I better get used to it.

GLENDA: Oh, I did not.

ROY: That's what you said.

GLENDA: You know I wouldn't like it if I could push you around. I wouldn't be attracted to a man like that.

ROY: You wouldn't, huh? Now let me get this straight. I'm supposed to let you push me, but not too far, is that it?

GLENDA: Something like that.

ROY: You're crazy, you know that?

GLENDA: Yeah, I know that.

ROY: (*Pushes her playfully.*) Just how far can I push you now, Glenda, huh? (*Pushes her again.*)

GLENDA: (*Backs away from him.*) Roy, don't.

ROY: Come on now, how far is too far?

(*ROY starts to push her again. GLENDA crosses over to the other side of the bed. He moves around to grab her. Presses her down on the bed and kisses her passionately. GLENDA suddenly rolls him over and sits astride him, pinning his arms over his head.*)

GLENDA: I think you just went too far, country boy, way too far.

SCENE THREE

Wanting it All

A few months later. GLENDA is barefoot and stretched out on the sofa reading a book. She is wearing jean shorts (cut-offs). A knock is heard at the door.

GLENDA: (*Over her shoulder.*) Come on in!

(*TEAK enters. He is wearing shorts and sandals.*)

TEAK: Hello in there!

GLENDA: Teak! What are you doing here?

TEAK: Roy not here?

GLENDA: He had to go pick up something in town. He should be back any time if you want to wait.

TEAK: Yeah, I'll just wait around a few minutes. What're you up to?

GLENDA: I just got back from taking the boys to their Saturday doings. Picked up this book and can't put it down, even though I've read it before. Ever have that happen?

TEAK: What is it you're reading?

GLENDA: <u>Sibyl</u>.

TEAK: Sibyl? Oh, yeah. That was the woman with all the different personalities.

(*TEAK sits on the end of the sofa. Reaches for GLENDA's feet to kiss them.*)

GLENDA: (*Sits up quickly.*) Behave, Teak. You've read it?

TEAK: Yeah, back in college. I saw a movie once about another one, Eve, was it?

GLENDA: "The Three Faces of Eve."

TEAK: That was it. Fascinating stuff. I wouldn't mind having a woman like that. One day she's this sweet little wife, and the next day she's this little whore ready for action.

GLENDA: That probably is the only kind of woman you'd ever be faithful to.

TEAK: I don't doubt it. By the way, I heard about you winning the Psychology Scholarship. Congratulations.

GLENDA: Thanks. Roy's happy about it. Now he won't have to lay out so many of those big bucks he's always complaining about.

TEAK: Yeah, that Roy's something else.

GLENDA: (*Puts down her book.*) Want some coffee?

TEAK: Yeah, that sounds good.

(*BOTH move to kitchen. TEAK watches the way GLENDA walks.*)

TEAK: You know, a woman like you needs to be treated special. Needs to have a big house with a pool, and maybe a chauffeur to drive her wherever she wants to go.

GLENDA: Lord, Teak. It was a scholarship, not the Nobel Prize.

TEAK: Yeah, but you're that kind of woman, don't you know?

GLENDA: (*Pours coffee, laughing at his talk.*) Black, right?

(*TEAK nods. Sits at the table.*)

GLENDA: I don't want all that stuff, Teak. (*Sits at the table with him.*)

TEAK: Yeah, you do. (*Raises his cup to hers.*) To women of the nineties. I love them all!

GLENDA: What I really want is to discover whatever it is in me that's calling out for form...for expression. I don't know. I can't explain it. I want my family, but I want that too. Is that so wrong?

TEAK: Nothing wrong with that.

GLENDA: I don't know, Teak. I feel awfully guilty sometimes. (*Takes a sip of her coffee.*) Crazy, huh?

TEAK: Not crazy. You just think too much. (*Pause.*) Well, maybe you are crazy!

GLENDA: (*Laughs lightly. Grows more intense.*) Did you know that you only use a small portion of your brain, Teak?

TEAK: Yeah, Marilee always told me that.

GLENDA: (*Laughs.*) No, I mean all of us do. And wouldn't it be great to learn how to use all of it? All that power and energy! We could probably heal our own bodies and minds, and- (*Smiles.*) Well, anyway, I used to dream about stuff like that, but I kind of stopped dreaming after I married Roy and ran smack into reality, you know?

TEAK: Yeah, I know. By the way, how did you get so smart?

GLENDA: Smart? I'm just determined. I get that from my mama. She just never had the chance to do what

I'm doing. I'd like to go on to graduate school after I get my degree, and then I'd like to teach and maybe even- I guess I still can dream, can't I?

TEAK: Sure, you can. (*Touches her chin.*) You just bloom when you talk like that. Hey, you ought to go flying with me sometime. I could show you places I'll bet you've never seen. And up there in the air, man-oh-man! It's great!

GLENDA: Go flying with you, Teak? Never.

TEAK: You mean you don't trust me? Come on, I'd be flying. What could I do?

GLENDA: (*Deadpan.*) Automatic pilot. I know how your mind works.

TEAK: (*Laughs.*) Oh, I'd like to all right. We sure could do one hot number together, you and me.

GLENDA: (*Smiles.*) You don't just have sex with everyone you're attracted to.

TEAK: Works for me!

GLENDA: Teak! I used to think there was hope for you and Marilee, but-

TEAK: I'm just kidding. But it is too late for Marilee and me.

GLENDA: It doesn't have to be.

TEAK: Afraid so.

(*Phone rings.*)

GLENDA: (*Gets up.*) Hello. Yes, he's here. How did you know? (*Puzzled, hangs up, and sits back down.*) Marilee. She just wanted to know if you were here.

TEAK: (*Stands.*) Thanks for the coffee, sweet thing.

(*TEAK kisses GLENDA on top of her head and moves for the door.*)

GLENDA: What's going on around here, anyway?

TEAK: Not a thing. (*Opens door. Looks back at her.*) Oh, but there could be. If only you'd-

GLENDA: -Teak! You're hopeless.

(*TEAK laughs and exits. GLENDA takes another sip of coffee. She gets up and goes to the phone and dials.*)

GLENDA: Hello, Mama? (*Sits down.*) I was just thinking about you and decided to give you a call. Enjoying my time off from classes. (*Pause.*) I know you're proud of me, Mama, and yeah, the scholarship will really help out. (*Pause.*) Why would you say that? You know where I got the spunk. I got it from you. And, Mama...I just wanted to tell you...I'm sorry...I'm sorry you never had the chance to- (*Tears have filled her eyes and her voice.*) Nothing is wrong. I'm just feeling a little emotional today, that's all. Yeah, I'll be all right. I'm sure. Okay. I will. I love you too, Mama. Bye.

(*GLENDA sits with phone still to her ear, eyes closed, then goes back to her book on the sofa. ROY, TEAK, and MARILEE enter. ROY is dressed in jeans, tee shirt, and tennis shoes. Wears cap. MARILEE has on cut off sweat pants and top with arms and neck cut out. She is wearing tennis shoes without socks.*)

ROY, TEAK and MARILEE: (*In unison.*) Surprise!

(*GLENDA, startled and genuinely surprised, jumps up. ROY, TEAK, and MARILEE put boxes on the table.*)

ROY: Computer and printer. All for you, baby.

GLENDA: Roy!

(*GLENDA runs and throws her arms around ROY. TEAK is keeping his distance from MARILEE. They exchange a long look as ROY and GLENDA enjoy the moment. GLENDA drops away from ROY and goes over to open one of the boxes.*)

GLENDA: How could you afford to buy it for me, Roy?

ROY: (*All smiles.*) I sold the Impala!

GLENDA: Oh, Roy! You didn't tell me.

ROY: I was saving it as a surprise.

(*GLENDA struggles with the tape on the box. ROY whips out pocket knife and cuts it right open.*)

ROY: I got it.

GLENDA: What made you decide to buy me a computer?

ROY: (*Glances at TEAK.*) Anybody wins a scholarship deserves something, don't you think?

MARILEE: Yeah, that's great kiddo. I'm real proud of you.

TEAK: Yeah, Glenda. (*Winks at her.*)

GLENDA: You all are so sweet to do this. But where will we put the computer, Roy?

ROY: I got it all figured out. That room where I keep all my junk is going to be cleaned out and fixed up into a room just for you. That way you can go in there and work on your stuff in peace, instead of having to be out here.

GLENDA: Well, you're just full of surprises.

MARILEE: (*To GLENDA.*) Come on. Let's go check out the possibilities for that room!

GLENDA: Okay!

(*GLENDA gives ROY another hug. She and MARILEE exit.*)

TEAK: Glenda know how to operate one of these things?

ROY: Reckon so. She took a class on computers. One thing about Glenda, if she don't know, she'll learn.

TEAK: Proud of her, huh?

ROY: Of course I'm proud. What man wouldn't be? Want a beer? (*ROY gets a beer from the refrigerator.*) How about chips?

TEAK: Just beer. I deserve one after that.

ROY: Come on, let's put our dogs up.

(*They sit on the sofa and put their feet on coffee table.*)

TEAK: Marilee never would let me do this at home.

ROY: Ah, you just don't know how to handle women, that's all. You gotta show 'em who's boss and give 'em what they need, if you know what I mean? (*Adjusts cap.*)

TEAK: Yeah, I know what you mean, and you're a lying stack of shit, too.

(*TEAK throws a pillow at ROY. Both laugh. ROY picks up remote and turns on TV.*)

(*CNN signature music is heard, then the following: "For the third time this week Iraq has sought to block U.N. representatives from inspecting nuclear weapons components, actions President Bush is calling a 'flagrant breach' of Resolution 687 establishing the cease-fire. Though Pentagon officials expressed confidence that enough forces remain available in the Persian Gulf to accomplish any mission ordered, Bush has indicated he will continue pursuing diplomacy."*)

ROY: Looks like Saddam's up to his old tricks. I don't reckon he's learned a thing. What'd you make of that war?

TEAK: What war? We just went in there and, BAM, it was over. Man-oh-man! What I wouldn't give to be able to fly one of those stealth bombers.

ROY: Yeah, there wasn't no fight to it. Hell, me and Glenda's had better fights than that one was. But looks like it ain't over yet. There'll be more trouble.

TEAK: (*Laughs.*) Between you and Glenda?

ROY: (*Smiles.*) Yeah, that too.

TEAK: You're lucky you and Glenda are still together. Don't too many make it these days. Hard trying to work everything out.

ROY: Yeah, it's hard all right. But if it means enough to you-

(*GLENDA and MARILEE return from back room.*)

MARILEE: (*To GLENDA.*) And I've got a table you can use to set your printer on. It'll fit right in that one corner. (*Calling toward sitting area.*) Come on, Teak. We gotta go.

(*ROY and TEAK get up and move to them, beers in hand.*)

TEAK: (*To ROY, with a knowing look.*) I guess we had better leave.

MARILEE: That room's a good idea, Roy. I'll have to admit I'm impressed.

ROY: Not too impressed, I hope. I'm still a bad-ass, Marilee.

GLENDA: (*Moves next to ROY.*) Yeah, I guess Roy's always gonna give me trouble.

MARILEE: You two kill me. Come on, Teak, let's leave them to fight or make love or whatever it is turns them on.

TEAK: Yeah. Hey, Glenda. Roy got your mama to keep the boys at her house tonight. Soooo! (*Makes a clicking noise with his tongue and gives her a knowing look.*)

MARILEE: Come on! (*Drags him toward the door.*)

ROY: Appreciate the help.

GLENDA: Yeah, thanks. You two are great.

(*TEAK and MARILEE exit.*)

GLENDA: You arranged all this and got my mama to keep the boys, too? Ummm! You're all right.

(*GLENDA still has her arms around ROY. She presses herself up against him. ROY takes her to him. GLENDA moans softly against him.*)

GLENDA: (*Pulls away slightly.*) And you sold the Impala! Wow!

ROY: Yeah! Ain't that something? (*Pause.*) Hey, I nearly forgot the best surprise of all.

GLENDA: Another one? For crying out loud, Roy.

(*ROY leads her to bedroom, where he reaches beneath the pillow and pulls out a box, wrapped so the lid will lift off, a ribbon on top. Hands it to her.*)

ROY: For you.

GLENDA: (*She smiles at him.*) You're so sweet. (*She lifts the lid.*) Oh...it's...what is it? (*Lifts out a feed sack, puzzled.*)

ROY: You remember that feed sack I promised you?

GLENDA: Feed sack? I don't-

ROY: Yeah, I want you to make you one of them feed-sack dresses like your grandma used to make.

GLENDA: (*Laughing, somewhat bewildered.*) Oh, Roy.

ROY: (*Laughing heartily, fully enjoying his little joke.*) I reckon you got just about everything a woman could want now, don't you?

(*GLENDA looks at him, then looks back at the feed sack.*)

GLENDA: Well, I reckon I do.

THE END

Pam Pendleton and Pamela White in *Desert Flower* by Betty Peterson, Horse Cave Theatre, 1996

Betty Peterson

Betty Peterson is currently Professor of English at Somerset Community College in Somerset, Kentucky. Her short stories, poems, and articles have seen publication in national and regional journals and magazines, as well as in anthologies.

Her first full-length play, *Desert Flower,* was produced in 1996 at Horse Cave Theatre. Other production credits followed: *Real Daddy* (one-act), Riverstone Gallery and McCreary Heritage Festival (2000); *The Dollmaker*, an adaptation of the novel by Kentucky native Harriette Simpson Arnow, commissioned through a grant from The National Endowment for the Arts, performed at the first annual Harriette Arnow Conference (2003); *The Good Daughter*, Festival of Kentucky Women Playwrights, Artists Collaborative Theatre (2005); *River Dreams*, an adaptation of noted Kentucky author Billy C. Clark's autobiography, J.B. Sowards Theatre (2007).

She is a Virginia Center for the Creative Arts Fellow and received the Kentucky Arts Council's Al Smith Fellowship for Playwriting in 2007. Peterson is a member of The Dramatists Guild of America, Inc.

Peggy Holbrook and Liz Bussey in *Raven's Gift* by John Howell, Horse Cave Theatre, 1997

RAVEN'S GIFT
by
John Howell

Brian C. Russo and Mary Suib in *Raven's Gift* by John Howell, Horse Cave Theatre, 1997

Raven's Gift opened on July 11, 1997, with the following cast:

BRIAN LINDGREN	*Brian C. Russo*
ALANA LINDGREN	*Liz Bussey*
CARLA	*Peggy Holbrook*
SEAMUS GRAHAM	*David Owen*
IRENE WORTH	*Mary Suib*
PAUL WORTH	*Ron Marr*
PETE FILCHOCK	*Ronald J. Aulgur*
CAROL FILCHOCK	*Virginia Wagoner*
ANDREW DAILEY	*Nathan White*
DAVID GOLD	*William Bruner*
GLORIA HOLBROOK	*Pam Feicht*
JODI DeGEORGE	*Naomi Buck*
BOY at DOOR	*Joseph McKinney*

Director: Warren Hammack
Stage Manager: Rachel Dockal
Set Design: Tom Tutino
Lighting Design: Lynne Chase
Costume Design: Marty Hagedorn
Sound Engineer: Michael Vaughan
Properties Master: Patricia G. Skinner
Technical Director: Jeremy Artigue
Production Assistant: Kip London

Long before I thought about being involved in the Kentucky Voices program or trying my hand at playwriting, I was a fan of Horse Cave Theatre. I always found it to be a very pleasant experience to drive down from my home in Louisville to see a play at the theatre, and was always impressed by the productions there. Whether it be a Shakespeare play, a farce, or a modern drama, the play was well-executed.

The Kentucky Voices program and playwriting classes at Horse Cave provided me a coherent and deeper perspective on what I was trying to accomplish. The feedback from other participants was always helpful, and the instructor, Warren Hammack, invariably was able to identify and clarify issues in the work which I had only dimly sensed.

Having *Raven's Gift* produced at the theatre was exhilarating. I was able to see how a production was put together, interact with the actors to provide insight into the characters in the play, and rewrite as necessary during the rehearsal process. It was most gratifying to talk with theatre patrons about the play after it was produced.

I have been fortunate to have had many wonderful experiences in my life, both personal and professional. The process at Horse Cave and in the Kentucky Voices program blended these two aspects together and ranks close to the top in terms of proud moments. I am not aware of any other venue in the state of Kentucky where I could have had a comparable experience.

– John Howell

Raven's Gift

Characters:

BRIAN LINDGREN, *surgeon*

ALANA LINDGREN, *his wife*

CARLA, *Brian's nurse*

SEAMUS GRAHAM, *Brian's mentor*

BOY at door

LITTLE RAVEN

Patients and their family members:

IRENE WORTH

PAUL WORTH

PETE FILCHOCK

CAROL FILCHOCK

ANDREW DAILEY

Legal Personnel:

DAVID GOLD, *defense attorney*

GLORIA HOLBROOK, *plaintiff's attorney*

JODI DeGEORGE, *court reporter*

Place: Various locations in a suburb of a Midwestern city: the Lindgrens' dining area, Dr. Lindgren's office, the cemetery.

Time: Mid-1990's.

ACT ONE

SCENE ONE

The Lindgren's dining area – morning. BRIAN and ALANA LINDGREN, a professional, affluent couple in their early forties, are sitting silently at their breakfast table. She is working a crossword puzzle; he is reading the newspaper. ALANA is in a robe. BRIAN, in a suit, is about to leave for work.

BRIAN: I'd like you to be here when I get home tonight. We need to talk about the suit – the deposition is coming up.

ALANA: A five-letter word meaning "limber"? It ends in an "e".

BRIAN: I'm going to be wiped out, but I need...

ALANA: "Loose"? No, that won't work.

BRIAN: Could you answer me?

ALANA: I've already told you. Sandy and Karen and I have plans. We won't be back until late. The play won't be over until close to eleven, then the drive back from the city... It'll be late.

BRIAN: You've always got a reason. I've been trying to talk to you about this for weeks. Months!

ALANA: Oh, I'm the one who doesn't talk. Sure. You're the talker, Brian, if that's what you want to believe.

BRIAN: Please, it's not every day I go through something like this.

ALANA: I've been here most evenings, but tonight's been planned for a month. I'm not going to change it.

BRIAN: You know this could change our lives, don't you? If I lose...

ALANA: You've got insurance. An "a"?

BRIAN: It'll triple; it'll go through the roof... When <u>would</u> be a convenient time? (*ALANA doesn't respond. BRIAN stands, puts on his suit coat.*) And it's not just the money... I don't know if I'll feel the same about medicine again. Hell, I can take only so much. Inevitably, something...

ALANA: "Dodger's PeeWee". It's a five letter word, starting with "R".

BRIAN: (*Resigned voice.*) Reese.

ALANA: That's it! That works.

BRIAN: Alana.... I don't ask much of you anymore, since Jeffrey, but this....

ALANA: (*Looking up from her crosswords for the first time, glaring.*) No! I won't be here! And it has nothing to do with Jeffrey! How dare you!

BRIAN: I'm sorry. I shouldn't have... but... do you care at all?

ALANA: (*Attention back on her puzzle.*) Sure I care, it's...

BRIAN: I've got people scheduled back to back today. And it's my on-call day. (*Aside.*) Man, why didn't I just get a job driving a beer truck?

ALANA: Quit feeling sorry for yourself.

BRIAN: I could use a little encouragement once in a while.

ALANA: Couldn't we all?

BRIAN: (*Checks his watch.*) I've got to go.

ALANA: (*Still focused on the puzzle.*) Wear your seatbelt.

BRIAN: Yeah.

ALANA: "Agile!" I got it, it fits!

SCENE TWO

Dr. Lindgren's office – that afternoon. BRIAN's nurse, CARLA, is looking through records on his desk, separating them into various stacks. She and BRIAN have worked together for years, and interact with the ease and naturalness that familiarity promotes. Being slightly older than BRIAN, CARLA occasionally plays a "big sister" role with him, a liberty that he accepts and both secretly enjoy. BRIAN enters, wearing a white clinic coat, carrying another, smaller stack. He is smoking a cigarette. It has been a long day and both are a bit fatigued.

CARLA: Are you finished with these?

BRIAN: Yes.

CARLA: Smoking again?

BRIAN: How many more out there?

CARLA: Three. This place smells like some seedy beer joint. Really, Brian...

(*CARLA waves her arm to fan the smoke. BRIAN takes a deep drag on his cigarette, and puts it out in an ashtray already overflowing with used butts.*)

BRIAN: Who's next?

CARLA: (*Hands him a chart.*) Andy Dailey. Second follow-up post knee surgery.

BRIAN: (*Scanning the record.*) Right. Would you mind...? (*Gesturing toward the ashtray.*)

CARLA: (*Picks it up with an exaggeratedly long-suffering look.*) Don't you think you should get a grip? It's not good for you, it isn't exactly the model of healthy behavior for our patients, and it isn't professional.

BRIAN: You're right, Carla, as always. How fortunate I am to have not only a top-notch nurse, but a relentlessly critical conscience, as well.

CARLA: (*A stern look.*) You need it.

BRAIN: How about a compromise?

CARLA: Such as?

BRIAN: (*Brightly.*) A smoke-eater!

CARLA: A what?

BRIAN: A smoke-eater. Little gadgets you can buy that absorb the smoke or something. Clean the air.

CARLA: (*Smiles despite herself.*) Seriously, it's time you cut down, doctor. I don't mean to be nosey, but....

BRIAN: Good, send Andrew in.

(*CARLA opens the door, calls ANDREW, a teenage boy, into the office. He wears an ace bandage on his right knee and limps noticeably.*)

ANDREW: Hi, doc.

BRIAN: Hi, Andy. How 'bout sitting up on that table?

ANDREW: Sure.

BRIAN: Let's take a look at that ol' knee. (*BRIAN unwraps the bandage, examines the knee.*) How's it feeling?

ANDREW: No problem.

BRIAN: No pain?

ANDREW: A little... usually at night or after I've been on the bike for twenty minutes.

BRIAN: Remember now, what I said. Don't try to do too much. Take it gradually, give the tissues time to heal. It's looking fine. Go ahead with the exercises I gave you, maybe increase them a little each day. Be sure and stretch gently first.

ANDREW: OK.

BRIAN: When does basketball practice start? (*BRIAN is flexing ANDY's knee.*)

ANDREW: Three weeks tomorrow.

BRIAN: You're not going to be quite ready by then, but you should be at full strength in, oh, five or six weeks.

ANDREW: Damn!

BRIAN: (*Patiently but forcefully.*) You partially tore the anterior cruciate ligament and we've repaired it. If it had torn completely, you'd be out for the season. You're very lucky, but you've got to let it heal.

CARLA: It's a long season, Andy. You'll be in there before too long. It's better not to rush things.

ANDREW: Yeah, I know.

BRIAN: Keep up the good work. Set up another appointment with the nurse in about a month. Maybe we can give you the go-ahead then. We'll see.

ANDREW: OK, doc, thanks.

BRIAN: Who's....?

CARLA: The Filchocks. (*Hands him another chart.*) I'll bring them in.

(CARLA *exits with* ANDREW. BRIAN *busies himself with organizing some items on his desk, entering a note in Andrew's record.* CARLA *ushers in a middle-aged couple,* PETE *and* CAROL FILCHOCK. *She touches* MRS. FILCHOCK *on the arm, smiles reassuringly, then exits.* BRIAN *opens* MR. FILCHOCK's *record.*)

BRIAN: (*Reviewing the record.*) How's it going, folks?

PETE: About the same, doc.

CAROL: He was up all last night, Doctor Lindgren, pacing and smoking.

PETE: Yeah, I felt real restless, antsy. Couldn't even sit still. And the damn headaches just won't go away.

BRIAN: Have you thought about what I said last week?

PETE: What, you mean see that other doctor?

BRIAN: Yes, Dr. Nordstrom, in Cleveland.

CAROL: I've tried to discuss it with him, sir, but he just won't talk about it.

BRIAN: Why not, Pete?

PETE: Oh, I don't know... I...

BRIAN: He's a specialist in kidneys and adrenal surgery. We're going to run some additional tests, but everything we have is consistent with a tumor in your adrenal gland.

CAROL: Oh, no!

PETE: You mean cancer?

BRIAN: No. There's a very low probability of malignancy, but there is a moderate to high risk of going into shock from the anesthesia, or for a dangerous post-surgical drop in blood pressure.

PETE: But... can't you... handle it?

BRIAN: This can be a tricky situation, Pete, and Dr. Nordstrom is known throughout the region for his experience with it... You want the best.

PETE: Hmmmm, I....

BRIAN: What's holding you back from contacting him?

CAROL: I think he's afraid for some reason.

PETE: No, I ain't.

CAROL: Why then?

PETE: I got my reasons.

(BRIAN *and* CAROL *wait for him to elaborate on this, but he does not.*)

CAROL: That's what he always says. I just run into a stone wall with him. (*Pulls out a hankie, dabs at her eyes.*) He's so bullheaded.

BRIAN: You realize that this could be extremely serious, don't you?

PETE: Yeah.

BRIAN: The tumor has to be removed, and soon. You're running the risk of a stroke or a heart attack.

CAROL: He gets upset so easy. The other day a branch fell on the roof and he acted like it was the end of the world. Screaming, his face got real red.... It was terrible.

PETE: Damn it, Carol, stop that exaggeratin'.

CAROL: It's true!

BRIAN: Your systolic blood pressure has shown significant elevation under stress, Pete. (*Scans the record.*) Cholesterol levels look good, the thyroid profile was normal.

CAROL: <u>Please</u>, honey. Something could happen.

BRIAN: I'm going to schedule some more tests. We need to be on top of this.

(*The couple nod in agreement. BRIAN talks on the phone intercom with CARLA.*)

BRIAN: Could you come in please?

(*CARLA enters.*)

BRIAN: Schedule Pete for an MRI – I don't believe we'll need a provocative histamine. And we need updated blood and urine for the lab.

CARLA: OK.

BRIAN: I'll be in touch when the results come back.

PETE: OK, Doc.

BRIAN: Would you like me to contact Dr. Nordstrom for you?

CAROL: Please, Pete, he's only trying to do what's best for you.

PETE: Let me think about it some more.

BRIAN: We might need to move quickly, Mr. Filchock.

PETE: Yeah, I know. Thanks, Doc.

(*PETE shakes BRIAN's hand. CARLA leads the couple out. BRIAN jots some notes in the chart. CARLA sticks her head back in, hands him another record.*)

CARLA: Oh, by the way, David called. He's having difficulty setting up the deposition. Apparently the other attorney is waiting on a report from her expert. He'll be in touch as soon as he hears something.

BRIAN: Ok.

(*CARLA exits. As he looks through Irene's record, BRIAN shakes his head. He looks toward the waiting room, braces himself, then goes to the door.*)

BRIAN: Mrs. Worth? Irene? Come in.

(*IRENE WORTH, an elderly, frail woman enters the office.*)

BRIAN: How's it going today?

IRENE: I was sort of hoping you would tell me that, Doctor Lindgren.

BRIAN: (*Smiles.*) Yes, what I meant was, how are you feeling?

IRENE: Not too well, sir. Not well at all, to be honest.

BRIAN: The pain?

IRENE: No better. I doubt if I ever sleep more than an hour or two at a time. I'm always tired, and the pain's pretty constant.

BRIAN: Staying busy? Keeping active?

IRENE: As best I can.

BRIAN: How do you spend your time?

IRENE: Oh, piddle around the house, listen to the radio some, music, you know. Not much TV. All those soap operas and game shows. It all seems so silly, so pointless.

BRIAN: But you've been taking your walks, I hope?

IRENE: I don't have any choice on that. I have to take care of my dog. He has to be fed and walked. So, I exercise whether I feel like it or not.

BRIAN: A dog? I didn't remember....

IRENE: I might not have mentioned him before.... (*As BRIAN looks through the chart.*) Do you have a dog?

BRIAN: Me? No, not since I was a kid. I don't think my wife...

IRENE: I suppose a dog would....

BRIAN: Cause complications?

IRENE: Yes, they do that. No doubt about that.

BRIAN: I'm pleased you're walking, getting some exercise.

IRENE: Even if I'm dying?

BRIAN: (*Taken aback.*)....

IRENE: It's ok, doc. A person knows when it comes. Only nobody'll talk about it with me. Not that there's anybody who's particularly interested.

(*Without thinking, BRIAN lights a cigarette.*)

BRIAN: We need to discuss the lab results from last week.

IRENE: Could you just give me the gist? All the details, you know, it's too overwhelming.

BRIAN: It doesn't look good.

IRENE: No, I didn't expect it to be.

BRIAN: The growth is back, it's larger, the white cells are way up.

IRENE: Uh, huh.

BRIAN: It's metastasized. Spread. Your kidneys and pancreas show signs of abnormal cells.

IRENE: I see.

BRIAN: We're about out of options, Irene.

IRENE: Don't feel bad. You've done your best. And Carla's been wonderful. (*Approaches tearfulness.*)

BRIAN: We could try another....

IRENE: No! I mean.... I'm so tired... I'd rather just... let... go.

BRIAN: Is the medicine helping at all?

IRENE: A little. It pushes the pain back some, for a while.

BRIAN: You are getting some relief?

IRENE: Some.

BRIAN: You could take more.

IRENE: Oh, I know, but if I take too much it just knocks me out. Once or twice I couldn't take Raven for his walk.

BRIAN: Raven?

IRENE: My pooch. He's black, like a raven. Ben named him, before he died.

BRIAN: Raven means a lot to you.

IRENE: Oh, yes, he's my buddy. Took me a while to warm up to him — he was really Ben's dog. But now....

BRIAN: Tell me something, Irene. I probably shouldn't ask this.

IRENE: Go ahead, I'm past being embarrassed.

BRIAN: If Raven felt the way you do now, what would... you... want to happen?

IRENE: That's a tough one.

BRIAN: I shouldn't have asked.

IRENE: Oh, come off it, doc. I don't want to be coddled. (*BRIAN is unsure how to proceed.*) I guess you see a lot of pain.

BRIAN: Yes.

IRENE: And you have to watch it happen, be there.

BRIAN: It goes with the territory.

IRENE: And it'll happen to you someday, Doctor Lindgren.

BRIAN: Yes, I know.

IRENE: I wonder if you <u>really</u> think so. There was a part of me that never believed I would die until... it became obvious. Like I was special or something. It's crazy, but down deep inside, a person doesn't think it'll happen to them.

BRIAN: It's always a shock, no matter....

IRENE: But as far as Raven goes, I guess as long as he still liked his food, still wanted his walks, still wanted to be touched... I'd want him to live.

BRIAN: I see.

IRENE: I guess that means I ain't ready to go yet.

(*BRIAN surreptitiously checks his watch.*)

BRIAN: You enjoy your music?

IRENE: Oh, yes. Mostly WMXT.

BRIAN: I'm not...

IRENE: No, you wouldn't be familiar with it. They play the old songs, from when Ben was courting me. Jo Stafford, Bing Crosby, the Dorsey Brothers, you know.

BRIAN: Not many current hits, I take it.

IRENE: Oh, hell no. Turned on my radio the other day and thought it was broke, sounded like static. Then I figured out my granddaughter had switched stations. Never heard such noise.

BRIAN: Does it, the music, bring back some memories?

IRENE: Oh, yes! Wonderful spring evenings. Walks in the woods. Going to dances with the gang.

BRIAN: (*As he leafs through the file.*) How many children do you have, Irene?

IRENE: Two now. Steve died in an automobile accident.

BRIAN: I'm sorry.

IRENE: It was a long time ago. It was horrible at the time but we got through it. Our love got us through it.

BRIAN: And the others?

IRENE: Cathy lives in New York. She visits a couple of times a year.

BRIAN: Is she aware of your... condition?

IRENE: I haven't told her a whole lot. She's very busy, works for some book publisher, in marketing. I don't want her to worry.

BRIAN: Perhaps she'd want to know.

IRENE: And then there's Paul. He's got three kids and a ton of bills. He doesn't have much time to spare, either.

BRIAN: So it comes down to you and Raven and the music.

IRENE: Doesn't sound like much, does it? But when you stop taking things for granted, you'd be surprised how little you need. The trick is to appreciate things, the sun, the flowers — while you still don't <u>have</u> to.

BRIAN: (*Begins to disclose his feelings.*) I wish I could do that, appreciate things. Most days it's dark when I get in and dark when I leave. I go days without noticing anything.

IRENE: But you help people.

BRIAN: Well... at least that's what I tell myself.

IRENE: Don't let things pass you by, doc. (*Realizes the subtle shift.*) You don't need me telling you how to live. I'm taking up all your time. I'm sorry.

BRIAN: (*Resuming the professional role.*) Anything else, Mrs. Worth? Any other sources of stress?

IRENE: Well, only...

BRIAN: Yes?

IRENE: It's Raven. He's got me in a hell of a mess.

BRIAN: How so?

IRENE: Well, remember I told you he still likes his food and walks?

BRIAN: Yes?

IRENE: That's not all he still likes.

BRIAN: (*Smiles.*) Uh-Oh.

IRENE: A few weeks ago he was gone for a couple of days. I was scared to death, but he came back looking sheepish. I guess he finally got hungry.

BRIAN: Did you....?

IRENE: And now there's this pretty little Sheltie down the street that's....

BRIAN: Expecting?

IRENE: Her owners are mad as hell. They were wantin' to breed her with another Sheltie, but now it looks like they're gonna have a litter of mutts.

BRIAN: And Raven's the guilty party?

IRENE: He's not sayin', but the evidence looks pretty strong to me.

BRIAN: A neighborhood squabble. That's all you need.

IRENE: It's not going to do them much good to harass me, is it?

BRIAN: What'll happen to Raven?

IRENE: Paul's gonna take him, thank God. His kids love him.

BRIAN: And the pups?

IRENE: I don't know, doc. They keep telling me it's gonna be my responsibility, but I don't know if I'll be able... it'll take more energy than I got. Raven's last gift to me and I'm not going to be able to enjoy it.

BRIAN: Yes, placing them would be quite a job, I imagine.

IRENE: That reminds me. I been meaning to ask... what are we talking about with time, you know?

BRIAN: Roughly two months. Maybe ten weeks. Three months at the outside. And it won't be fun.

IRENE: Don't let me suffer too much, Dr. Lindgren. Please.

BRIAN: No, I won't. (*BOTH sit silently for a few moments.*)

IRENE: Could you help me up? I better be leaving.

(*BRIAN helps IRENE out of her chair.*)

BRIAN: Is there anything else I can...?

IRENE: What was his name?

BRIAN: Who?

IRENE: Your dog. When you were a boy.

BRIAN: Higgins.

IRENE: (*Smiles.*) Nice name. What happened to him?

BRIAN: Oh, we moved into a "better" neighborhood, nicer house. My dad decided there wouldn't be room for him, I guess. He just left him behind. (*At this BRIAN seems unexpectedly affected, having difficulty controlling his feelings.*)

IRENE: (*Sensing his sadness.*) I'm sorry.

BRIAN: It happened so long ago. (*Aside.*) How could he do that?

IRENE: It must've been sad for you, a little boy.

BRIAN: Yes, I guess it was.

IRENE: Well, I'm going. I'll be counting on you now, Dr. Lindgren.

BRIAN: I know. Stay in close touch. I'll do... all I can.

(*BRIAN opens the door. As IRENE moves through it, she places her hand on his arm for a moment, then exits. BRIAN returns to his desk, writes a note in her chart. He then takes out a cigarette, lights it, takes a drag. Suddenly, he angrily stubs it out, buries his face in his hands.*)

SCENE THREE

Dr. Lindgren's office – three weeks later. CARLA is in BRIAN's office going over some forms with Irene's son, PAUL. He is disheveled, wearing soiled work clothes, having responded to an emergency call from Carla about his mother.

CARLA: Irene listed you with us as next of kin, so we need you to sign some forms, Paul. Just in case. You're her oldest child, correct?

PAUL: Yes, ma'am.

CARLA: Now this one is your...

(*They are interrupted by a knock on the door. Without waiting for it to be opened, ALANA enters.*)

CARLA: Alana!

ALANA: Hi, Carla, where's Brian?

CARLA: He was called to Pines Memorial on an emergency. (*Checks her watch.*) He left about 45 minutes ago.

(*ALANA shows her disappointment, slumping into a chair.*)

CARLA: Were....? Did you....?

ALANA: (*Sighs, as if it is an overwhelming task to respond.*) I had asked him to take the afternoon off. We had planned to go to lunch.

CARLA: I'm sorry, Alana. We had to reschedule several patients. He must've...

ALANA: (*Cuts in.*) Yes, he "must've." (*Resentfully.*) He could've called.

CARLA: Alana, if you could wait just a minute until I finish here, I'll...

PAUL: Are you the doctor's wife?

ALANA: (*Without looking up.*) Yes.

PAUL: He's a wonderful doctor, ma'am. My mother... she never stops sayin' how nice he is, what a good doctor he is.

ALANA: (*Offhandedly.*) Does she?

PAUL: It's her that he went to see, over at Pines. Mom's neighbor found her on the back porch this morning. She was unconscious. I guess she'd be dead now if it wasn't for that dog of hers. Kept barking until Mrs. Shepherd went and checked on her.

CARLA: Is that who called the ambulance?

PAUL: Yeah.

ALANA: Well, I'll be... (*Starts to stand.*)

CARLA: Please, Alana, wait just a minute. (*ALANA slumps back down.*)

PAUL: (*To ALANA.*) I'm sorry, ma'am, but.... I wouldn't want anybody else looking after my mother.

CARLA: This one needs to be witnessed by you, Paul. It allows Dr. Lindgren to release information if necessary, to other doctors. (*He signs.*) This one is your permission for him to treat your mother, Irene, with whatever medical procedures he deems necessary and warranted. (*He signs.*) And this one... your mother asked that she not be kept alive artificially, if it comes to that. I've stapled her written request to that effect to the top of the form. Your signature acknowledges that her wish is supported.

PAUL: OK. (*He signs and prepares to leave.*) Is that it?

CARLA: Yes, thanks for coming by, Paul.

PAUL: Thank *you* for all you've done for Mom. (*PAUL shakes CARLA's hand.*) Well, I'll be getting over to Pines. Maybe....

CARLA: Let's hope for the best. Your mother was in good spirits when she was in a few weeks ago. I believe she still has some fight in her.

PAUL: Bye. (*Turns to ALANA.*) Bye, ma'am.

(*ALANA nods to him as he moves past her. He exits.*)

CARLA: Alana, the way he went out of here....

ALANA: In a rush as usual, for everyone else.

CARLA: I'm sure he didn't mean to disappoint you.

ALANA: (*Sarcastically cheerful.*) No need to give solace, Carla. I'm used to disappointment. I'm an expert.

CARLA: (*Tentatively.*) He seems under a lot of stress lately.

ALANA: Does he?

CARLA: Maybe it's the lawsuit, I don't know....

ALANA: (*Casually.*) He mentions it.

CARLA: (*Trying to make conversation.*) Was it something special today?

ALANA: In a way, yes. (*Subdued.*) It's been three years now. .. Today....

CARLA: Jeffrey? Has it already been that long?

ALANA: I wanted us to be together, maybe visit the grave. Just the two of us, a quiet remembrance.

CARLA: Did he know what you had planned?

ALANA: I was going to suggest it at lunch. (*Stands, attempts to regain the superficial cheerfulness.*) Well, I better....

CARLA: I'm sorry, Alana.

ALANA: (*Suddenly in a rage.*) Stop saying that! I don't need your pity!

CARLA: I mean about Jeffrey.

ALANA: I know what you mean! Keep your smarmy sentiments to yourself! I don't want them! (*Silence. ALANA is torn between a need to avoid her pain and a need to stay now that she has broached something powerful.*) You believe I'm the cause of his death, don't you? He wouldn't have died if I'd been there, isn't that right?

CARLA: No, of course not!

ALANA: If I had been a better mother, if I had watched him more closely! Isn't that what you think?

CARLA: Accidents happen, Alana, you couldn't....

ALANA: They say one thing to my face and what they really think when I'm not around....

CARLA: Who?

ALANA: Everybody! You! Brian! My mother! Everybody!

CARLA: (*Placating, but becoming irritated.*) That's just not true. Not at all!

ALANA: I can't... I... miss him so much, Carla.

CARLA: He was a beautiful child, a wonderful little boy.

ALANA: (*Falls back into the chair.*) I want to die. (*A shriek explodes out of her, followed by heaving sobs.*)

CARLA: Oh, Alana, honey.

(*CARLA cautiously extends her hands, kneels in front of ALANA, holds her. ALANA, continuing to sob, grasps her in desperation.*)

SCENE FOUR

Two months later – Dr. Lindgren's office. ANDREW enters with CARLA.

CARLA: I told you the time would pass quickly, Andy.

ANDREW: Seemed like forever.

CARLA: But you're back at practice now, right?

ANDREW: Yeah.

CARLA: How's the jumper?

ANDREW: Hittin' nothin' but net.

CARLA: And the lateral movement?

ANDREW: Defense ain't never been exactly my best point, but it's comin' along.

CARLA: You're here for a medical statement of your injury for the school's files?

ANDREW: Coach said it had to do with the insurance or somethin'.

CARLA: Here you are. Doctor Lindgren prepared this earlier.

ANDREW: Thanks, ma'am.

CARLA: Good luck, Andy. And watch out for Springfield Wilson – they're going to be tough this year.

ANDREW: Yeah, I know.

(*CARLA shows ANDREW out, calls Brian's attorney in.*)

CARLA: Mr. Gold?

(*DAVID GOLD enters. He is young, well-dressed, overweight, very anxious.*)

CARLA: Doctor Lindgren should be here momentarily, David. Can I get you a cup of coffee?

DAVID: I believe I'm "coffeed" out for the day, Carla. Thanks anyway. Was he delayed?

CARLA: Always. He called a few minutes ago on his car phone, asked you to wait if you could.

DAVID: OK. (*Checks his watch.*) I've got to leave for court in about 20 minutes. I hope…

(*BRIAN enters, looking harried.*)

BRIAN: I'm sorry, David. Things got complicated — had a hard time getting away.

(*The two men shake hands.*)

DAVID: A physician's work is never done, I suppose. (*They sit down.*)

BRIAN: You need coffee?

DAVID: No, I'm fine.

BRIAN: Carla, could you get me a cup?

CARLA: Sure. (*CARLA exits.*)

BRIAN: Where do we stand, as you see it?

DAVID: I'll know more after the deposition. But they're not going away.

BRIAN: I didn't expect them to.

DAVID: No, they usually don't, but sometimes….

BRIAN: How does it look?

DAVID: I really don't know, Brian. We've gone over the records carefully and nothing unprofessional jumps out at us. It looks like you've covered all the bases, but….

BRIAN: But what?

DAVID: You could still lose. It's impossible to predict what a jury might do, particularly once Gloria

Holbrook goes through one of her presentations.

BRIAN: Is she dramatic?

DAVID: I guess that's the right word, histrionic maybe, but she's good. There won't be a dry eye in the courtroom when she finishes. She'll leave them wanting retribution from you, surely from the insurance company. I've seen her in action.

BRIAN: I thought this had something to do with truth.

DAVID: The truth is what the jury decides, Brian.

BRIAN: Even if there's distortion? What is this — some Vonnegutian charade?

DAVID: It's the system. Whoever puts on the best show. Our side is more boring than hers, so she has the advantage.

BRIAN: You've got to be as good as she is, David. This is my life she's affecting.

DAVID: I'll be prepared, but I don't have all that righteous indignation going for me.

BRIAN: (*Massaging his eyes.*) So what's our strategy?

DAVID: Have you thought about settling?

BRIAN: Yes, I have. But I don't want to — it doesn't seem right.

DAVID: We either settle or we put on our case and hope for the best at the trial.

BRIAN: That's it?

DAVID: As I say, maybe after the deposition we'll have more to go on.

BRIAN: Do we have a firm date yet?

DAVID: Oh, yes, thanks for reminding me. (*Looks in his appointment book.*) The 11th, at 2:45. That was one of the times you gave me.

BRIAN: About three weeks away.

DAVID: (*Stands, prepares to leave.*) One other thing, Brian.

BRIAN: (*Follows him to the door.*) Yes?

DAVID: You have any problem with Dr. Graham looking over the entire case, the records, the statements, whatever?

BRIAN: Seamus?

DAVID: He's the master. If he finds nothing, you're in a stronger position. If he finds something amiss, it'll help us know what to do next.

BRIAN: No.... it's fine. I'd feel better if he did review it all — I'd like to know what he'd say.

DAVID: OK. Got to go. See you on the 11th.

BRIAN: It'll be here, right?

DAVID: Yes. (*The two men shake hands again.*)

BRIAN: See you then.

(*DAVID exits, BRIAN returns to his desk. CARLA enters, hands BRIAN a cup of coffee and a chart.*)

CARLA: Mr. and Mrs. Filchock are waiting.

BRIAN: Oh, yes, almost forgot.

CARLA: Last one of the day, doctor.

BRIAN: Send them in.

(*CARLA leads the couple in. They are arm in arm, smiling, although PETE is slightly favoring his right side.*)

PETE: Hi, doc.

BRIAN: Have a seat, folks. Let me review this. (*Scans the record as the couple settles in.*)

CAROL: He's doing wonderfully, Dr. Lindgren.

BRIAN: The tests look very good.

CAROL: He's more relaxed than I've seen him in a long time. It's a miracle.

BRIAN: You doing <u>that</u> well, Pete?

PETE: Yeah, I'm feelin' great. Ready to get back to work.

BRIAN: No more headaches?

PETE: No headaches, no dizziness, no pain, none of those damn palpitations. And my energy's coming back.

BRIAN: That's great. I'm very pleased. Your blood pressure is stable and back in the normal range. The surgery went well, but you never know.

CAROL: We can never thank you enough, Dr. Lindgren. (*Dabs at her eyes.*)

PETE: Come on, honey, you're gonna embarrass the doctor.

CAROL: I'm sorry, it's just....

BRIAN: It's enough to see your husband feeling better, Mrs. Filchock. I know you appreciate it.

CAROL: You'll never know....

BRIAN: Do you have a target date to return to work, Pete?

PETE: We're talking two weeks from yesterday, if you have no objections.

BRIAN: I have none, except that I would ask you to phase in gradually.

PETE: Oh, yeah, half-time for a least a month. Got to build my mental endurance up.

BRIAN: You're right. Let's keep the medications where they are a bit longer, then we'll begin tapering off.

PETE: Whatever you say, doc. Honey, could I have a minute alone with the doctor?

CAROL: Yes, of course.

PETE: I want to say something to him, private-like.

CAROL: Fine, I'll wait outside. Take your time.

(*As CAROL exits, the two men stand.*)

PETE: Doc, I.... please tell me if this ain't none of my business, but....

BRIAN: OK.

PETE: I saw the lawyer leave here.

BRIAN: Did you?

PETE: Yeah, an' I heard about this lawsuit against you.

BRIAN: Word gets around.

PETE: Back a couple of months ago when I was having my problems, you wanted me to see a doctor in

Cleveland. Remember?

BRIAN: Right, Dr. Nordstrom.

PETE: An' I wouldn't agree, right?

BRIAN: Yes, that's right.

PETE: The reason I wouldn't is... I trust you. I knew you'd do your best. I didn't want another doctor, no matter how good he's supposed to be.

BRIAN: Well, thank you, Pete.

PETE: My point is... don't let them beat you. You got a lot of patients countin' on you. Fight them, doc. Don't give in. If you need me to do anything, to testify or anything, I will. You're a good doctor; you just stand your ground and you'll be ok.

BRIAN: (*Moved.*) Thanks, Pete. Thanks.

PETE: I been wantin' to say it for a good while. Well, I got to be goin'. Taking Carol to dinner. (*Conspiratorial tone.*) Like I say, my energy's comin' back. Bye, doc.

BRIAN: Goodbye, Pete.

(*PETE exits. BRIAN sits down, begins to record some notes in the chart. CARLA enters.*)

CARLA: Brian?

BRIAN: Yes?

CARLA: Irene's son just walked in – he'd like to see you for just a minute.

BRIAN: Irene Worth's son?

CARLA: Yes.

BRIAN: OK.

(*CARLA ushers PAUL in. He carries a small covered picnic basket with him. BRIAN stands to greet him.*)

BRIAN: Nice to meet you, ... uh, Paul, isn't it?

PAUL: Yeah, nice to meet you, doc.

BRIAN: Your mother spoke of you. (*The two men shake hands - BRIAN gestures to a chair.*)

PAUL: No, doc, I don't want to take your time. I just wanted to thank you for everything you did for mom.

BRIAN: Thank you. I wish we could've given her a few more good years. That last episode... if we could've gotten her to the hospital sooner, maybe...

PAUL: Well, I know you did what you could. But she, uh, left something for you.

BRIAN: Left something?

PAUL: Yeah, just a second, sir.

(*PAUL reaches into the basket and pulls a small black puppy out.*)

PAUL: She said to tell you that this would make up for Higgins.

(*PAUL hands the puppy to BRIAN, who accepts it a bit stiffly.*)

BRIAN: One of her dog's puppies?

PAUL: Yeah, one of Raven's litter.

BRIAN: Raven, that's right.

PAUL: We been callin' him Little Raven. He's jus' like his old man. Coal black, mischievous, frisky.

BRIAN: Well, uh... thanks, Paul.

PAUL: Have fun, doc. And thanks again for mom.

BRIAN: Yes... you're welcome.

(*PAUL exits. CARLA enters.*)

CARLA: Well, well, what do we have here?

BRIAN: What's Alana going to say about this?

CARLA: Maybe she'll like the company.

BRIAN: Somehow.... I don't see that.

CARLA: Well, good luck. Remember now, I'll be late tomorrow.

BRIAN: I think I can manage.

CARLA: The records are on my desk... in order. Bye.

(*CARLA exits, leaving BRIAN alone with the puppy.*)

BRIAN: Little Raven, huh? Well, Little Raven, I don't know what kind of deal you got here. I'm not too good with the people and things I love, but we'll give it a try. We'll give it a try.

SCENE FIVE

That evening. BRIAN enters the dining room of his home. ALANA, setting the table, does a double take when she sees him with the dog.

ALANA: What's that?

BRIAN: A dog.

ALANA: I know it's a dog. Why the hell are you carrying it?

BRIAN: A patient gave it to me. Bequeathed it, actually.

ALANA: A patient gave it to you?!! What are you planning to do with it?

BRIAN: I want to keep it.... him.

ALANA: (*Becoming angrier.*) Oh no, you're not. Who do you think would take care of it? You're never here.

BRIAN: I could see that he goes out in the morning and feed him. And I would take him out when I got home... in the evening.

ALANA: And guess who would look after the beast during the day?

BRIAN: It wouldn't require that much. Just...

ALANA: Anything is too much. No!

BRIAN: Please, Alana. It's, he's a gift. We can put him in the garage until we fence a part of the yard for him. He'd be no trouble, really.

ALANA: No! Absolutely not!

BRIAN: Why not?

ALANA: Why not? How many reasons do you need? I don't want to be bothered – I don't have the time, or the inclination to look after it, him.

BRIAN: How much time do you think it would take?

ALANA: And he'll shed. We'll have dog hair on the furniture, our clothes, everywhere.

BRIAN: Please, be reasonable, give him a chance.

ALANA: First thing tomorrow, I want you to place an ad in the paper for him. He can stay until someone buys him. That's it, that's as far as I'll go.

BRIAN: His name is Little Raven. Would you like to pet him?

(*ALANA makes eye contact with the dog. It looks back innocently, expectantly.*)

ALANA: No.

BRIAN: Oh, come on, it won't hurt.

ALANA: You promise to call the paper in the morning?

BRIAN: Yes.

(*ALANA tentatively touches the dog, then pets him. It responds to her.*)

BRIAN: See... he wants you to be his master.

ALANA: (*Drawing back her hand.*) Now, Brian, stop that. As soon as someone responds to the ad, it's ..... he's gone. Agreed?

BRIAN: (*Resigned.*) Agreed.

(*ALANA, shyly, hesitantly, pets it again, then returns to what she was doing.*)

BRIAN: (*To LITTLE RAVEN.*) Let's check out the back yard, buddy. Use it while you can.

(*BRIAN exits with LITTLE RAVEN, leaving ALANA alone onstage. She stops her activity and looks in the direction of Brian's exit.*)

ACT TWO

SCENE ONE

The cemetery. ALANA approaches her son's grave, carrying a bouquet of flowers. She stands silently for a moment before the grave, then gently places the bouquet on it. After several beats, she speaks.

ALANA: Hi, honey. It's me, mom.... Your daddy was going to come with me, but... well, you remember how busy he always is. Maybe this weekend I'll bring him back with me.

I saw your buddy Kevin at the grocery last Friday, with his mom. He's eight now. In the third grade. We talked about the time the whole gang went to the Outer Banks together. Us and the Wright's and the Blackburn's. Wasn't that a wonderful time? I remember it like it was... You and Kevin and, what was that little girl's name, the Blackburn's daughter? Was it Cassandra? Yes, I believe that was it, or... Anyway, she and her family moved to Oregon last year. Doctor Blackburn took a job at the medical school there. But I'll always remember you and Kevin and her running into those waves and laughing. Running up and down that beach the whole week. We were so happy. (*She starts to choke up but catches herself.*)

Grandma Katherine was over yesterday, complaining about all her aches and pains, how her medicine just doesn't help her, how nobody understands her. She's about to leave on a cruise with her friend, but you'd think she was...

Oh yes, your father brought home a little black puppy, a little mutt last week. One of his patients gave it to him. You can probably guess who gets to clean up after him and make sure he has water. But we put an ad in the paper, so he shouldn't be with us much longer. He'll be leaving, so I can't get too attached. You never had a puppy, did you? They say that all little boys and girls should have a pet, but I don't remember us ever discussing it. For some reason, that seems odd to me. Well, Jeff, I'll be going now. I'll be back soon with your dad. I love you.

(*ALANA crouches, puts her hand briefly on the flowers, then stands, pauses a second, then exits.*)

SCENE TWO

Dr. Lindgren's office. CARLA is in Brian's office, organizing files, straightening his desk. A knock on the door, followed by the entrance of SEAMUS GRAHAM, an elegantly dressed silver-haired man carrying a briefcase.

CARLA: Dr. Graham?

SEAMUS: Dr. Graham, is it? Come now lass, not so shy! It's old Seamus, your favorite charlatan.

CARLA: You're here, thank God! (*The two hug, CARLA breaks into tears.*) Everything's going to be okay now.

SEAMUS: Of course it is, bonnie Carla. Why wouldn't it be?

CARLA: I've been so worried.

SEAMUS: Now, now, it can't be all that bad. (*They separate.*) Is the boss about?

CARLA: He'll be here shortly. He's expecting you, he wants to talk to you, of course.

SEAMUS: But you're looking splendid, my girl. How long has it been?

CARLA: Several years, at least, Seamus. Since...

SEAMUS: I know! The conference in Santa Fe, right?! I would've remembered if I had gazed on your beautiful face since.

CARLA: Same old Seamus, alright. Oh, it's wonderful to hear that blarney again. That's been four years ago.

SEAMUS: The blink of an eye, that's all it is. The blink of an eye.

CARLA: I don't know about that – the last year's been like an eternity around here. I've been worried about Brian.

SEAMUS: The lawsuit's taken the wind out of his sails, I presume.

CARLA: It's been on his mind constantly – he's showing stress. Smoking more, distracted... And of course you heard about his little boy, what happened.

SEAMUS: Ah, yes. The drowning. Tragic. Horrible. A neighbor's pool, as I understand.

CARLA: Yes. I don't think things have been the same with Brian or his wife since it happened.

SEAMUS: You never quite get over something like that, I'm afraid.

CARLA: Oh, it's so good to hear your voice. (*They hug again.*)

SEAMUS: Perhaps I should come around a bit more often. (*They both chuckle.*) Well, let me get myself a tad organized here, lass. (*Begins removing papers from his briefcase.*)

CARLA: How's it look?

(*BRIAN enters.*)

BRIAN: Seamus!

SEAMUS: Brian! (*The two men shake hands warmly.*) You look as busy as ever, lad.

BRIAN: I can't complain about that, sir.

CARLA: If he was any busier, I don't know what we'd do, Dr. Graham. We'd have to clone him.

BRIAN: How about something to drink?

SEAMUS: Surely, surely.

BRIAN: Coffee?

SEAMUS: Would you have any....

CARLA: No Scotch, I'm afraid, but we do have some tea steeping. With a slice of lemon, right.

SEAMUS: (*Genuinely moved.*) You remembered that? I am touched, dear Carla.

CARLA: What about you, Brian?

BRIAN: I'll join Seamus. It'll be like old times.

(*CARLA exits.*)

BRIAN: How are things at the University? I'm always reading about the research your staff is doing. Makes me envious, particularly at the end of a long day. <u>Particularly</u> recently.

SEAMUS: I've got some good men, but all I do is fight the bureaucrats for them, barter with politicians over funding, and the like. Not the most rewarding way to spend my time, but necessary, I suppose. Somebody's got to wrestle the demons.

BRIAN: It takes someone of stature to fight those kinds of battles.

SEAMUS: Kind of you, Brian, but you better watch out. I might show up here some lovely morning and want to be your partner.

BRIAN: Anytime, sir. I'd love it.

(*CARLA returns with the tea. BRIAN serves them both.*)

BRIAN: Did we get the x-rays on Mrs. Morgan, yet?

CARLA: I'll check.

BRIAN: If they haven't arrived, give the clinic a call. Occasionally they need a goose.

CARLA: Sure. (*She exits.*)

SEAMUS: I hope, Dr. Lindgren, that every night before you tuck yourself in, you thank the good Lord for Carla. She's a jewel.

BRIAN: I'm not sure I could function without her.

SEAMUS: Yes. Well, you've got a deposition scheduled for this matter of the breech delivery, do you?

BRIAN: Next Tuesday.

SEAMUS: I see. I've scanned the hospital records, the patient's history, your records, her statement (*Pointing to the stack of papers.*), and I note that three months prior to the delivery you advised Mrs. Hollis to consider a caesarian section in light of the probable nature of the presentation.

BRIAN: That's right.

SEAMUS: It looked strongly like the fetus would present in a breech position.

BRIAN: Yes.

SEAMUS: And she declined, as I understand it.

BRIAN: She said she needed to think about it. She wanted to wait as long as possible before deciding.

SEAMUS: Ah, yes, but nature has a way of taking the choice out of our hands, don't you agree?

BRIAN: She had no history of....

SEAMUS: Exactly! Her two previous deliveries were normal, predictable, without incident. There was no reason, based on her history, to expect an overly rapid labor on this occasion. The combination of a breech position and precipitous delivery is a dangerous medical circumstance. As I can glean what the hospital records offer, you managed it as well as anyone could have. Mother and child survived, but the fetus suffered a brief anoxia.

BRIAN: That's it in a nutshell.

SEAMUS: It's necessary to understand one basic, often overlooked fact, Dr. Lindgren, and undoubtedly you've heard me say this many times before, but Nature Can Be Unkind!

BRIAN: Yes, I have heard you say that before.

SEAMUS: This is a perfect example of a situation where no one is to blame. No one misbehaved. Untoward possibilities were anticipated. But not all negative outcomes can be prevented! Like any other profession, we have our bad apples, but you are most certainly not an example. On the contrary, it is highly likely that your medical skill in this situation saved this child's life.

BRIAN: I'm pleased that you see it that way, but I'm still looking at a potentially huge judgment against me.

SEAMUS: It's come to the point in this culture that people feel entitled to payment whenever anything unfortunate happens to them. Someone, by god, has to pay. Don't be intimidated, lad. If lawyers had to live by the same standards they would impose on us, they'd never get out of court. Was it Bierce who defined a lawyer as "one skilled in the circumvention of the law"? As it is, hardly a week goes by without seeing a barrister led away in shackles, with a wide, toothy grin, exclaiming that he did nothing wrong.

BRIAN: (*Laughing.*) At least it seems that way.

SEAMUS: If greed is the rot of this society, these attorneys who make their living suing good people are the cockroaches feeding off of it. They pander to the pain of poor, grieving souls.

BRIAN: What do you recommend that I do?

SEAMUS: (*Shouting.*) Stand your ground! You've done nothing wrong! Don't let your attorney settle with them. Make them prove what they allege. I don't see how they can.

BRIAN: Thanks, Seamus, I feel better.

SEAMUS: Now, lad, let's pour a bit more tea and peruse some minor details in this matter.

(*The two men prepare to review the material in more careful detail. SEAMUS removes a flask from his briefcase and pours some of its contents into his tea.*)

SCENE THREE

The Lindgren's dining area – morning. ALANA is seated in the dining area, working on a crossword puzzle. BRIAN speaks to her from offstage.

BRIAN: (*Off.*) Have you seen the black and silver striped tie?

ALANA: Look in the second drawer. (*Waits a few beats, returning her attention to the puzzle.*) Find it?

BRIAN: (*Off.*) Yeah.

ALANA: Want some coffee?

BRIAN: (*Off.*) Yes, please.

(*ALANA puts down her puzzle, pours Brian a cup of coffee. BRIAN enters, straightening his tie, putting on his suit coat.*)

ALANA: Uh-oh, the black suit.

BRIAN: Funerals and court appearances. (*Puts cream and sugar into the coffee, stirs it.*)

ALANA: That tie looks nice with it, Brian.

BRIAN: Let's hope the plaintiff's attorney thinks so. Maybe she'll be nice to me.

ALANA: How are you feeling about today?

BRIAN: Scared to death, but I'm glad it's finally here. It reminds me of high school, before a big game. Afraid you just might be destroyed, blown out, not knowing if you're up to it.

ALANA: What time is it scheduled?

BRIAN: Two forty-five.

ALANA: Hmmm.

BRIAN: I won't have time to worry about it - I'll be in surgery all morning.

ALANA: Maybe it's better not to dwell on it.

BRIAN: We'll see, I guess. How about you? What'll you be doing today?

ALANA: Karen and I are working out this morning. Of course then I have to take your dog to the vet for his shots.

BRIAN: Thanks, Alana, I....

ALANA: Then I want to look at some sofas. The one in the den has seen better days. They're having a sale at Alexander's on some really nice ones.

BRIAN: Could we put the old one in the basement?

ALANA: I was going to donate it to the....

BRIAN: But it fits all my indentations perfectly! It's so comfortable.

ALANA: It's ten years old.

BRIAN: Just getting its second wind. Please hold off on its execution for awhile.

ALANA: Oh, Okay. For a while. What time will you be home?

BRIAN: I'll have to call you. After the deposition I'll make rounds, but it should be earlier than usual.

ALANA: But you will call?

BRIAN: Yes, as I leave Pines, I'll call you. (*BRIAN stands, takes a last sip of coffee.*) Well......

ALANA: Brian, good luck. I know you'll do fine.

BRIAN: Keep your fingers crossed. (*BRIAN walks to the door. ALANA follows him.*)

ALANA: I know I haven't been as supportive as you wanted, but I'll be thinking about you. I don't know why, it's been hard for me to ....

(*BRIAN turns, ALANA embraces him tightly. He responds.*)

BRIAN: Thanks, Alana. That'll help. (*He gives her a kiss on the cheek, exits.*)

ALANA: Call now! Bye! Wear your seatbelt!

(*ALANA sits down to resume her crossword puzzle. There is an offstage bark. She looks up toward the bark momentarily, then resumes her puzzle. Another couple of barks, more insistent this time. After a few beats she rises, exits briefly. She then returns carrying LITTLE RAVEN, resumes the puzzle while holding him on her lap.*)

SCENE FOUR

Dr. Lindgren's office – that afternoon. BRIAN is at his desk, looking over the records one last time. CARLA enters.

CARLA: Both attorneys are here, but the court reporter hasn't arrived yet. Do you....?

BRIAN: Send them in. We can get situated so that when the reporter arrives, we'll be able to start right away.

CARLA: You need anything?

BRIAN: How about a quick flight to Aruba?

CARLA: I was thinking more along the lines of a cup of coffee.

BRIAN: Carla, if I have one more cup, I'll probably break the state record for peeing in one day. You might ask the attorneys, though.

CARLA: Okay.

BRIAN: Are we squared away on our patients?

CARLA: I rescheduled Mr. Fowler and Leonard Furman. Dr. Fischer will be handling your calls until tomorrow at 8:00.

BRIAN: Hey!

CARLA: Even depositions have an upside, I guess.

BRIAN: Well, let the firing squad in, and be ready with the blindfold.

CARLA: Now Brian, no gallows humor, if you don't mind.

(*CARLA ushers in the attorneys. GLORIA HOLBROOK enters first, followed by DAVID GOLD. She is flamboyantly dressed, sweeping into the room as if she is walking onto a stage. Everything about her is exaggerated, dramatic.*)

GLORIA: My, what a nice, cozy office.

DAVID: Brian, this is Gloria Holbrook. Gloria, this is Dr. Brian Lindgren.

GLORIA: I've heard _so_ much about you, Dr. Lindgren. I'm honored to finally meet you.

(*GLORIA extends her hand. BRIAN is a bit taken aback. He manages a weak handshake with her.*)

GLORIA: I bet your patients feel comfortable here, sharing their confidences with you.

BRIAN: I hope so, Ms. Holbrook.

GLORIA: Gloria! Call me Gloria, please.

CARLA: Can I get anyone something to drink?

DAVID: I'll have a cup of coffee, black, Carla, if it's no trouble.

CARLA: Sure.

GLORIA: Would you possibly have any Jasmine tea?

CARLA: No, I'm sorry, we don't. I believe we might have a package or two of Lipton's, but that's it.

GLORIA: Well, then, sweetie, could you bring me a glass of ice water?

CARLA: I think I can manage that.

GLORIA: Thank you _so_ much, hon.

(*CARLA rolls her eyes to BRIAN as she exits.*)

DAVID: The reporter is on her way – I saw her downstairs. She should be here in a few minutes.

BRIAN: Any idea how long this might take?

DAVID: Mine should be brief, Brian. Your credentials, experience, your point of view on this situation.

GLORIA: I just have a few questions. For clarification, you understand.

(*The door opens, and the court reporter, JODI DeGEORGE, enters.*)

JODI: Sorry I'm late.

DAVID: We were just chatting, introductions and so forth.

JODI: I'm Jodi DeGeorge, sir.

BRIAN: Brian Lindgren. (*The two shake hands.*) I take it you know these two.

JODI: Oh, yes. We've crossed paths a time or two. Let me set up my recorder, and we'll be ready to get started.

BRIAN: Sure.

(*The ATTORNEYS pull their notes out of their respective briefcases while JODI readies her equipment. CARLA leans in the door.*)

CARLA: Brian, Alana is on line 2. She insists on speaking with you. She's extremely upset.

BRIAN: Now?

CARLA: She says it's an emergency.

BRIAN: (*Sighs.*) Okay. (*Picks up receiver.*) Hello. No, we're just about to start. What's the.... oh, no! Alana, I can't.... try to calm down. You're at the vet's? What happened?... was he hit or run over? But you were able to get him to Dr. Murphy's office.... unconscious.... was he breathing? No blood? That's good... no, no, you did everything you could. It's not your fault, these things can happen. Yes. You'll be staying until you hear something? Good – tell the doctor to do whatever is necessary. No, I'm glad you called. I would've wanted to know. I'm sorry, Alana, but.... no.... right.... okay. I'll talk to you later. (*BRIAN hangs up the receiver, stunned.*) My dog... he was hit.

DAVID: Sorry, Brian.

GLORIA: Are we ready to begin?

JODI: Dr. Lindgren, please raise you right hand. Do you solemnly swear or affirm that the testimony you are about to give is the truth, the whole truth, and nothing but the truth, so help you God?

BRIAN: (*Softly.*) I do.

(*CARLA brings in the drinks for the attorneys, then exits.*)

DAVID: Brian, could you please state your full name and credentials for the record?

BRIAN: Brian Lawrence Lindgren, M.D.

DAVID: Tell us about your education and training.

GLORIA: I'm willing to stipulate the doctor's credentials.

DAVID: You don't want to review his educational background?

GLORIA: I'm aware the doctor has a medical degree. His current functioning is the issue.

DAVID: Ok, then I'm including his résumé as part of the record for this deposition. (*DAVID hands copies of the résumé to JODI and GLORIA.*) We'll save it for the trial, Brian.

BRIAN: Sure.

DAVID: Dr, Lindgren, would you say that you have considerable experience with the issues and problems of pregnancy and delivery?

BRIAN: Yes, I would.

DAVID: Could you elaborate?

BRIAN: After my residency, I worked for three years in a group surgical practice in Philadelphia. While I was there, I spent two days a week in an ob-gyn clinic for low-income patients. During that time, I delivered, I don't know, probably between 600 and 700 children, and was responsible for both prenatal and postnatal care of the mothers.

DAVID: Did any patient that you served during that time ever bring a lawsuit or action of any kind against you?

BRIAN: No.

DAVID: Did your experience in obstetrics end when you moved to this community?

BRIAN: No, it didn't.

DAVID: How, so?

BRIAN: I took a position here which primarily involved surgery, but while I was building my practice, I continued to deliver babies and care for their mothers.

GLORIA: Excuse me, Miss DeGeorge, but you did get the comment about his <u>primary</u> responsibility in his position here?

JODI: Yes, he said it primarily involved surgery.

GLORIA: Thank you.

DAVID: Why did you continue in the obstetrics area when you moved here, Dr. Lindgren?

BRIAN: Several reasons. The need was there, I wanted to fill my schedule as much as possible, and....

DAVID: You're good at it, isn't that so?

BRIAN: Yes, I am.

DAVID: In fact, isn't it true that you received a state-wide award for your work in the clinic in Philadelphia recognizing your skills?

BRIAN: Yes, that's true.

GLORIA: Please record my objection to this as irrelevant.

DAVID: Irrelevant? How can....?

GLORIA: Past performance is not necessarily an indicator of present competence.

DAVID: So, Dr. Lindgren, after setting up your practice here, your time was divided between your specialty by training in surgery and your secondary specialty of obstetrics?

BRIAN: If you looked at my schedule six months after I arrived, it would have been about 25% surgery and 75% obstetrics. As time has passed, my surgical practice has grown, and I've been progressively less involved with obstetrics. At this point, it's about 90% surgery.

DAVID: But you still work with pregnant women, including delivering their children?

BRIAN: Yes, at this point, they are entirely patients I've had for years, they're comfortable with me, and don't want to change to another doctor. But it's less and less. I don't accept new patients in the obstetrics area.

DAVID: So, if I understand it correctly, you might have delivered a given woman's baby or babies in the past, and although your practice now involves a higher percentage of surgery, should that woman become pregnant again, she might turn to you for her care.

BRAIN: Yes, exactly. I've not taken any new obstetrics patients in probably six years.

DAVID: And you've referred.....

BRIAN: I've referred as many of my former clients as possible to Dr. Lehman and Dr. Fitzgerald.

DAVID: Let the record indicate that these are physicians who have opened practices in this area during the past five years.

BRIAN: Both specialists in obstetrics.

DAVID: Now, Dr. Lindgren, was Angela Hollis one of those women whose older children had been delivered by you?

BRIAN: Yes, she was.

DAVID: Could you....?

BRIAN: I've known Mrs. Hollis for at least twelve years, since shortly after I first opened my office here. I delivered her two oldest children, and she insisted that I care for her during this pregnancy.

GLORIA: Object to the characterization of her request for service as "insistence".

DAVID: Brian... Dr. Lindgren, is that an inappropriate way of describing her attitude toward your management of her pregnancy?

BRIAN: Well, I tried to refer her, as I've done with many other patients, but she wouldn't hear of it. She was adamant.

GLORIA: Please note for the record that the words "insist" and "adamant" are unduly harsh and pejorative.

DAVID: Could you expand a bit on why you chose those words, sir?

BRIAN: Yes. As I said, I initially tried to refer Mr. Hollis to Dr. Fitzgerald when she informed me of her pregnancy.

DAVID: This may seem redundant to you, but could you tell us why you attempted that?

BRIAN: The same as what we've been discussing here. I have less and less time for that type of work and wanted to connect her with someone else.

DAVID: But she demanded that you see her through the delivery?

GLORIA: Objection. Counsel is leading.

DAVID: You can respond, doctor.

BRIAN: Yes, she wouldn't consider a referral. She said that she trusted me, that this would be her last child, and that she didn't want to start over with a new doctor.

DAVID: Was she a difficult patient?

GLORIA: Objection. We are not here to criticize my client.

DAVID: Go ahead, Brian.

BRIAN: I wouldn't say she was "difficult", at least she hadn't been in the past. She is an assertive person, the type who wants a strong say in her medical care. She was knowledgeable, intelligent. I liked her.

DAVID: There were no adverse incidents during her previous pregnancies?

BRIAN: No.

DAVID: Of any kind?

BRIAN: None. Completely uneventful, successful deliveries.

DAVID: But problems developed with this one?

BRIAN: Yes.

DAVID: Could you describe them?

BRIAN: It became apparent during her pregnancy that it would likely be a breech delivery.

DAVID: Does that pose insurmountable problems?

BRIAN: Not at all. The situation has to be recognized, acknowledged, and planned for. A common way of handling it is through c-section, caesarian, rather than a vaginal delivery.

DAVID: In your notes of March 4th and again on April 17th, there are entries documenting your discussion of the situation with her and advising a recommended strategy, are there not?

BRIAN: Yes, there are.

DAVID: Could you scan these copies and state whether this is your handwriting?

BRIAN: (*Looks it over.*) Yes, it is.

DAVID: Counselor? (*Hands copies to Ms. Holbrook.*) Jodi, here are your copies for the record.

GLORIA: Thank you.

DAVID: Tell us how it went from there, Dr. Lindgren?

BRIAN: Mrs. Hollis didn't want a c-section if it was possible to deliver vaginally. As in the past, she wanted to experience the birth naturally, not to have to resort to anesthetics. So she asked to hold off as long as possible in the hope that the fetus would either drop into a normal position, or it could be turned for a normal delivery.

DAVID: But that never happened, isn't that true?

BRIAN: No, it didn't.

DAVID: What other problems occurred?

BRIAN: She had an overly rapid labor.

DAVID: Explain that for us, in layman's terms, if you could.

BRIAN: Her other deliveries were normal in terms of progression through the stages of labor, predictable from initiation to completion of the process. In this case, Mrs. Hollis moved almost immediately from the first signs of labor to imminent delivery.

DAVID: Is that necessarily a problem? An insurmountable one?

BRIAN: Not in itself. But in combination with the breech position of the fetus, it created a very tricky situation.

DAVID: In what way?

BRIAN: It didn't leave us with sufficient time to turn the infant or deliver it prior to some oxygen deprivation occurring.

DAVID: The child was delivered alive, was it not?

BRIAN: Yes, a breech extraction was ultimately necessary, with relatively minor adverse consequences. It could have been much worse.

DAVID: In your opinion, did you and the hospital staff do everything medically indicated, reasonable, and necessary in this matter?

BRIAN: Yes, we did.

DAVID: If Mrs. Hollis had agreed earlier to a caesarian delivery, would it have made a significant difference?

BRIAN: It's impossible to know. If we had been able to plan for the delivery and acted at the first sign of contractions, we might have been able to avoid what happened, but there is no guarantee to that.

DAVID: Thank you, doctor. No further questions. Your witness, counselor.

GLORIA: Thank you, Mr. Gold. Dr. Lindgren, you've indicated that your work with pregnant women has declined dramatically over the past five to ten years. Is that true?

BRIAN: Well, it has declined as my surgical practice has increased. I would describe it as a gradual change, rather than a dramatic one.

GLORIA: You're uncomfortable with the word "dramatic", and yet you estimate that it has dropped from 75% of your practice to around 10% at this time. Isn't that a dramatic change?

BRIAN: I think that....

GLORIA: Yes or no, sir.

DAVID: He has the right to explain his response, Ms. Holbrook.

GLORIA: He can't give a simple, direct answer?

DAVID: He's allowed to...

GLORIA: (*To JODI.*) Please indicate that the doctor was unable to directly respond to my question.

BRIAN: It was a gradual shift in emphasis, completely my choice.

GLORIA: Is that so, Dr. Lindgren? But isn't it true that the less you do something, the less you practice.... the duller your skills become?

BRIAN: Doesn't that depend on what you're specifically talking about?

GLORIA: Surely you've heard the saying "Use it or lose it"?

BRIAN: Yes, but....

GLORIA: As you did less and less obstetrics, isn't it a reasonable presumption or conclusion that your skills and sensitivity in the area correspondingly were less acute?

BRIAN: No.

GLORIA: Why not? Are you not subject to the same conditions of life as the rest of us?

BRIAN: I believe I was still sufficiently active in the area to maintain my skill level.

GLORIA: You do? I see. Of course, that is a point which might be open to question, alternate opinions, don't you think?

BRIAN: Perhaps. You could probably obtain three different opinions on the color of that wall if you paid enough.

GLORIA: Was your shift in professional focus <u>completely</u> a matter of choice, doctor? Or did it reflect other factors?

BRIAN: It was completely my choice. I prefer doing surgery and wanted the bulk of my practice to reflect that.

GLORIA: What about other factors?

BRIAN: What factors? Could you be specific?

GLORIA: I would rather you enumerate them for us.

BRIAN: Since there are none, other than my preference, I can't enumerate them.

GLORIA: I would note for the record that Dr. Lindgren is not being fully forthcoming in this matter.

DAVID: (*Heatedly*) I object to this imputation. Counsel is implying conditions without fairly considering that the doctor's response is a valid and full one.

(*GLORIA and DAVID's comments overlap.*)

GLORIA: This is his opportunity to make an accounting.

DAVID: You're not allowing him to do so.

JODI: Please, one at a time. I can't get everything unless I can hear it.

(*GLORIA leafs through her notes.*)

GLORIA: According to records from the State Medical Board, you've attended only one continuing education seminar in obstetrics during the past five years, Doctor Lindgren.

BRIAN: But I've attended four others in surgical practice.

GLORIA: True, but that's not really the point, is it? More evidence that you've not kept up with the field, wouldn't you say?

BRIAN: I don't believe you could necessarily conclude that.

GLORIA: Perhaps other experts would see it differently. Isn't that possible?

BRIAN: Anything's possible.

GLORIA: Now earlier, when you talked about Mrs. Hollis, you sounded angry when you mentioned her unwillingness to immediately agree to a c-section.

DAVID: Object to the characterization.

GLORIA: Doctor, were you annoyed with her delay, as you alleged, in making a decision about that matter?

BRIAN: At the time we initially discussed it, I wasn't annoyed.

GLORIA: Not at all?

BRIAN: No. She had always been a reasonable patient, and I expected her to be on this occasion. As we moved closer to the projected delivery date, though, I became more concerned, maybe more anxious or frustrated about her delay. It was taking an unnecessary risk from my point of view. As the records indicate, I discussed this with her, but she didn't seem to appreciate that it could be dangerous.

GLORIA: Are you blaming her for what happened?

BRIAN: I'm responsible for clearly providing the necessary medical information and her alternatives and dealing with the situation as it presented itself, but she is responsible for allowing it to develop, against my recommendations.

GLORIA: You had options, didn't you?

BRIAN: Such as?

GLORIA: Referral. Insisting that she decide.

BRIAN: I was trying to work with her. I don't believe it would have been ethical for me to refer her at that late stage. Still, everything would have been okay had not the delivery been an unpredictably precipitous one.

GLORIA: Should that have been anticipated?

BRIAN: There was no reason to expect it. By definition, you don't expect the unexpected. You might consider the possibility, but you don't expect it. Mrs. Hollis' procrastination had led to a situation in which, if anything went other than perfectly, her child would be at risk.

GLORIA: And you discussed this with her?

BRIAN: Yes, I did.

GLORIA: Are you referring to the entry of April 17th?

(*BRIAN and DAVID look through their material.*)

BRIAN: Yes.

GLORIA: Could you read it, please?

BRIAN: It says "Possible complications of breech delivery again explained to patient. Advised her to decide as soon as possible regarding c-section. Mrs. Hollis hesitant, still hopeful of normal delivery."

GLORIA: Is that it?

BRIAN: That's the entry. Obviously it's a summation of a 15 minute discussion.

GLORIA: Isn't it equivocal? Couldn't that entry be interpreted differently than you imply? A jury would be in a position of accepting your explanation or other possible expositions wouldn't they?

BRIAN: I don't believe it's equivocal.

GLORIA: (*Voice beginning to rise.*) You persist in not looking at this situation clearly and fully, doctor.

BRIAN: I've gone over this in my mind a thousand times.

GLORIA: But from your own biased perspective.

DAVID: Object. You are being argumentative, counsel.

GLORIA: (*Dramatically.*) What about this child? What about his parents?

BRIAN: Could you be specific?

GLORIA: That little boy might never be able to play basketball with the other kids; he may never have the coordination to learn to dance. There are many things he'll never be able to do as well as other boys. Isn't that true?

BRIAN: We don't really know at this point what the long-range consequences will be, but he's really very fortunate. Any damage he sustained was quite mild. Furthermore, I did not cause it to happen. I'm not perfect, I've made mistakes, but this isn't one.

GLORIA: (*Ignoring his response.*) And his parents! They will face increased costs throughout his lifetime. Every day they will re-experience the loss. <u>It will never end.</u> (*BRIAN is silent.*) Do you have no shame, Dr. Lindgren? You're a physician; you've taken an oath to treat your patients to the best of your ability. And yet, you've allowed this child and his family to suffer needlessly. It could have been prevented. You have killed this family! How can you live with this? (*BRIAN is still silent.*) Please answer me! Behave like a man! I need a response from you, for this family.

(*BRIAN is taken aback by the viciousness and intensity of GLORIA's attack. For the first time, he looks beaten, on the verge of submitting to her view. Suddenly there is a knock on the door. CARLA enters.*)

CARLA: I'm sorry to interrupt. Brian, Alana just called. She wanted you to know that Little Raven is fine.

(*CARLA exits. BRIAN nods.*)

GLORIA: I'm waiting for an answer!

(*BRIAN throws down a pen that he's been holding, stands, begins to move about.*)

BRIAN: I'll give you an answer.

DAVID: Brian, wait....

BRIAN: It's okay, David. I want to respond to Ms. Holbrook fully and thoroughly, so that there will be no possibility of misunderstanding. She deserves it.

DAVID: Caution, Brian, don't..... (*BRIAN shrugs off his attorney's suggestion.*)

BRIAN: Three hours ago I was covered with blood, operating on a 19-year-old girl brought into the emergency room following an automobile accident. I had to remove her spleen. There was no margin of error. She could have died. She still might. I suppose if she does, some lawyer will be requesting the records. I did my best, but it might not be good enough. But what were <u>you</u> doing at about that time, Ms.

Holbrook? Chatting amiably with your colleagues over a martini, discussing who to sue next?

Aside from Mrs. Hollis and her husband, no one feels the pain of what happened more intensely than I do. Your amateur theatrics notwithstanding, I'm sure you have no true feeling for this family. I'm not claiming that my feelings approach those of Mrs. Hollis or her family, or that they are for the same reason. On the contrary, my sadness is that it did not have to happen. I pride myself on my competence, and it hurts when I see less than the best outcome.

I did nothing wrong in this matter, and yet my life has been disrupted for months because of it. Most probably, it will continue to be so for months or years more. I've suffered and so have my patients. It's been a distraction and a source of stress to me. Do you, in your pretended "caring" appreciate that? I think not. You only care about one thing, Ms. Holbrook, and that's the money you might make out of this. Strip away all your phony concern and your crocodile tears, and we find dollar bill signs. You're hoping to make a quick buck out of your hustle, that's all.

But I have some advice for you Gloria. You want me to address you that way, don't you? After all, we're such good friends. I have a response for you that you might want to convey to anyone in your life who's important to you. Clue in your hairdresser. Send a message to your stockbroker. Inform your astrologer. Whoever. And the message is: (*Exaggerated whisper.*) You are in a fight to the death. Got it? Would you like a translation? The meaning is: I'm not going to settle. I'm going to fight this as long as necessary, through as many appeals as it takes until I'm vindicated. And then do you know what I'm going to do? I'm going to sue you, Gloria, for frivolously bringing this action against me. You know there are precedents, don't you, of physicians or medical societies suing specific attorneys or legal firms? That bothers you, doesn't it? You're not sure just how an overview of your professional activities would look, are you? How much scrutiny do you think your life and practice can bear?

I did nothing wrong or unprofessional in this case, and all the hollow rhetoric and word games won't change the facts. That's the bottom line, and that's all I have to say. For now.

(*BRIAN sits back in his chair. There is no sound in the room, other than JODI's machine. Finally, GLORIA clears her throat and speaks.*)

GLORIA: No further questions.

(*GLORIA sweeps out of the room without a word to anyone. DAVID slowly stands. JODI begins closing up her equipment.*)

DAVID: Well, Brian, I don't know if you helped yourself, but it was fun to watch. I'll call you in a day or two and we'll see where things stand. (*BRIAN stands. The two men shake hands.*)

BRIAN: Thanks for you help, Dave. I'd say you *more* than held your own.

DAVID: Yeah. See you, Miss DeGeorge.

JODI: Bye.

(*DAVID exits. BRIAN goes to the door, to open it for the reporter.*)

BRIAN: Did I make a fool out of myself?

JODI: No, I wouldn't say that. I'd say you reamed her good. Real good.

(*JODI exits. BRIAN sits down again heavily. CARLA enters. BRIAN takes out a cigarette. Surprisingly, she lights it.*)

CARLA: Can I join you?

(*BRIAN gives CARLA a cigarette. She lights up.*)

BRIAN: Coming over to the enemy?

CARLA: Sometimes mercy overrides discipline, Brian. Guess who called while you were in the deposition?

BRIAN: Gee, I don't know. Who?

CARLA: Seamus.

BRIAN: Seamus? Why would.... he knew about the deposition, didn't he?

CARLA: He knew. Can you think of any other possible reason he might call here?

BRIAN: I'm sorry, Carla, my brain is dead about now, I can't...

CARLA: (*Barely able to contain herself.*) He wants to see me.

BRIAN: See you?

CARLA: Socially, silly. He asked me out.

BRIAN: (*Finally it registers on BRIAN.*) Wonderful, Carla. That's great! (*The two spontaneously and warmly hug.*) He's not going to take you away from me, is he?

CARLA: I'd say that would be jumping to conclusions, Brian.

BRIAN: Or maybe you could recruit him.

CARLA: We'll see.

BRIAN: Carla....... thanks.

CARLA: What? For what?

BRIAN: For everything. I'm not going to get all schmaltzy and embarrass both of us, but... you know.

CARLA: Oh... okay. (*Changing the subject.*) How did it go?

BRIAN: Let's just say that the scotch will taste extra good tonight.

CARLA: Pretty rough?

BRIAN: Yes, unless your idea of fun is a crucifixion. But for the first time in months, I feel relaxed. At peace.

CARLA: Is it over?

BRIAN: No, I strongly doubt that. I don't know if these things are ever over. Who knows?

CARLA: Well, at least....

BRIAN: Want to hear something weird?

CARLA: Love to.

BRIAN: If Little Raven is okay, I really don't care what else happens.

SCENE FIVE

The Lindgren's dining area – that evening. BRIAN enters the dining area. ALANA is setting the table. As she sees him, the two embrace.

ALANA: It's been a horrible day.

BRIAN: Tell me about it. How's Little Raven?

ALANA: They're keeping him overnight, but Dr. Murphy saw no broken bones or serious injuries. They x-rayed him and ran some blood tests. He was alert and moving around when I left, trying to con the vet out of some food.

BRIAN: Wonderful.

ALANA: I'm sorry, Brian. The leash just slipped out of my grip.

BRIAN: Lannie, I know it was an accident. But he's alive, that's the important thing.

ALANA: Yes. Oh, how was the deposition?

BRIAN: I think I did okay. I don't know.

ALANA: But did you answer all their questions?

BRIAN: Yes, and then some. They can always develop more, but it feels great to have it over and be home early for once.

ALANA: I haven't had time to fix dinner, being at the vet's all afternoon and all.

BRIAN: Relax. Please. I really didn't expect anything. How about if I put something on the grill?

ALANA: We still have a couple of those strip steaks left, I think.

BRIAN: Let me change first.

ALANA: You don't have to take calls tonight?

BRIAN: I'm covered until 8:00 tomorrow morning.

ALANA: Wonderful! Maybe, we....

(*The doorbell rings. BRIAN goes to the door, leads in a young boy.*)

BRIAN: He's here about the ad.

ALANA: What.... ?

BOY: (*Holds up the ad from the newspaper.*) I come for the dog, ma'am.

ALANA: The dog?

BOY: Yeah, it says, "Little black mixed breed needs a good home."

BRIAN: You remember. You asked....

ALANA: That dog has a home.

BOY: Huh?

ALANA: We've changed our minds. We're going to keep him.

BOY: You sure? I got a big yard and....

ALANA: Yes, I'm sure. He <u>has</u> a good home. Here, with me and my husband.

BOY: Uh, okay, then.

BRIAN: (*Hands the boy a $5 bill.*) I'm sorry, son, here's for your trouble. The ad ran longer than we expected.

BOY: Thanks, sir.

(*BRIAN leads the boy out. Returns.*)

BRIAN: So, you've changed your mind.

ALANA: Yes.

BRIAN: Why didn't you tell me?

ALANA: I don't know. Things just.... snuck up on me, I guess.

BRIAN: You're sure about it?

ALANA: Yes, I'm sure. Brian, I've been thinking about a lot of things. Jeffrey and .....

BRIAN: Yes.

ALANA: I loved him so much.

BRIAN: I know.

ALANA: I've been dead since he died. But I can feel myself coming back to the way I used to be. Something's changed inside.

BRIAN: That's great, Alana. I've been hoping....

ALANA: I want us to.... be able to be what we were, together.

BRIAN: That's exactly what I want....

ALANA: If I can't love, I might as well not be alive. Today, when I picked that little dog off the street, I realized how dead I've been. Selfish, wrapped up in my misery. But <u>he</u> mattered, more than anything since Jeffrey. All those feelings came back. I thought, "No, God, not again, please." And then when the vet told me he was not hurt badly, I felt for the first time in a long time that I did something right. I saved him.

BRIAN: You sure did.

ALANA: Do you still love me?

BRIAN: Yes, Alana, I love you. I've never stopped. I never blamed you for Jeffrey.

ALANA: You mean that?

BRIAN: Hey, you're my girl. That's never going to change.

ALANA: Oh, Brian. (*The two embrace, kiss passionately.*) We've both had a rough day. Fix yourself a drink, and let me take care of the food. We can spend the evening talking, really talking, like we used to do.

BRIAN: Sounds wonderful.

(*The two kiss again, playfully this time. ALANA exits. BRIAN is thoughtful for a moment, then goes to a cupboard, pulls out a bottle of Scotch, pours himself a small drink. He then lifts it, as if he is offering a toast.*)

BRIAN: Thanks, Irene. Thanks, Raven. (*He swallows the drink and exits.*)

THE END

Brian C. Russo, Peggy Holbrook and Nathan White in *Raven's Gift* by John Howell, Horse Cave Theatre, 1997

JOHN HOWELL

After attending several one-act plays produced by Actors Theatre of Louisville, I came to the belief that I could write plays as interesting as the ones I saw there. This proved to be an erroneous judgment, however, as my early attempts to do so were unsuccessful. This led me to participate in an adult education class in playwriting taught by William Thomas, former dramaturg at Actors Theatre, and eventually to classes at Horse Cave Theatre taught by Warren Hammack. Eventually I did create plays which were produced by theatre groups in Louisville, Southern Indiana, and Central Kentucky.

Raven's Gift was produced by Horse Cave Theatre and *Selling Shiloh* received a staged reading in the theatre's Kentucky Voices program. *So Many Roads* won first place in a nationwide playwriting contest organized by the University of Louisville African-American Theatre Program. Other plays which have been produced include one-acts *Safe Ground*, *The Kringle Account* and *Shades of Blue*, along with the full-length *Agony of Thatch*. Additional unproduced plays include *Omega Air*, *Queen of the Hop*, and *Strange Fire*.

Nathan M. White and Rebecca Minton in *Just Taking Up Space* by Nancy Gall-Clayton, Horse Cave Theatre, 1998

JUST TAKING UP SPACE
by
Nancy Gall-Clayton

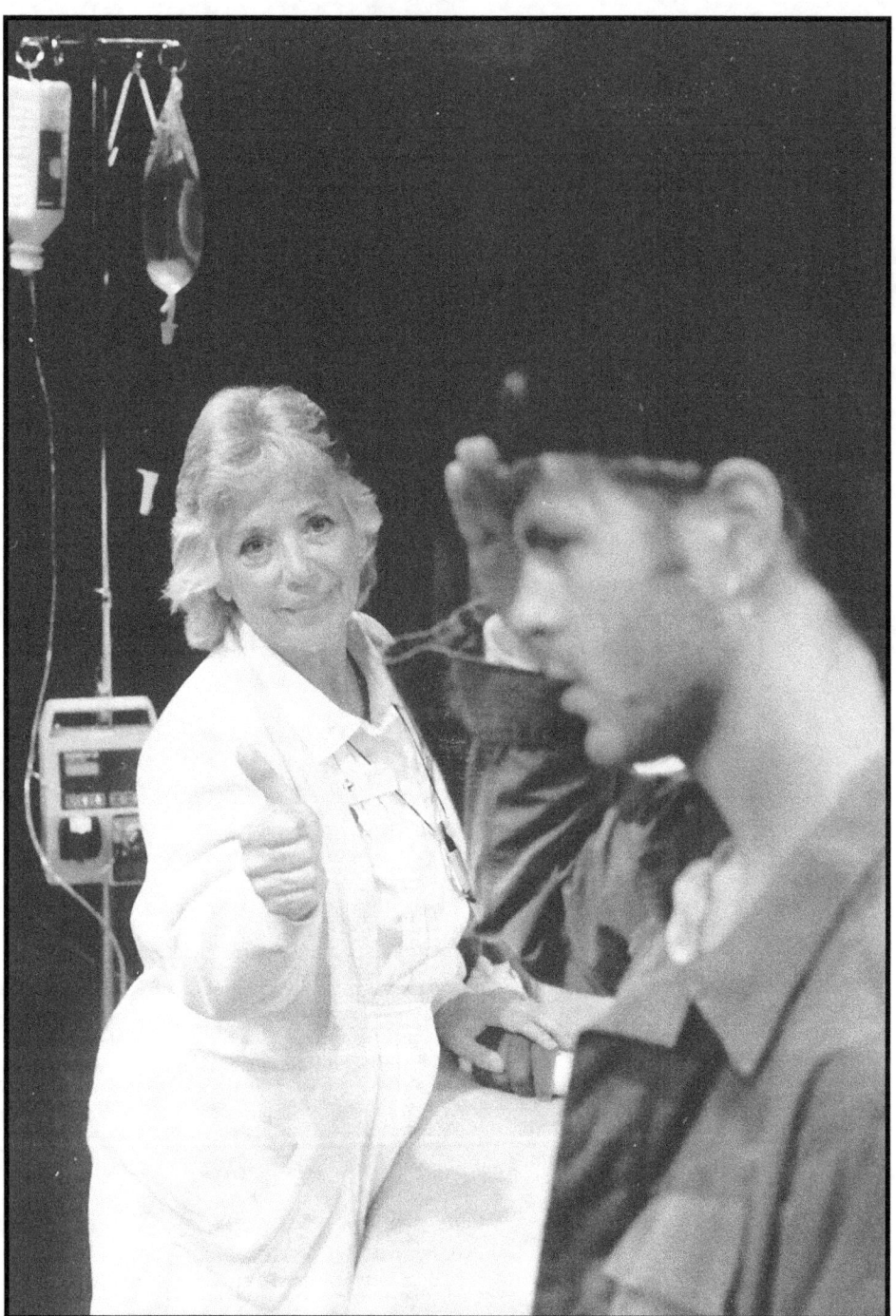

Mimi Rice and Nathan M. White in *Just Taking Up Space* by Nancy Gall-Clayton, Horse Cave Theatre, 1998

Just Taking Up Space opened on July 10, 1998, with the following cast:

FRANK OWEN	*Nathan M. White*
JENNY BRADFORD	*Rebecca Minton*
ARNIE TALBOTT	*George Pendleton III*
CHRIS ELLIOT	*Robert F. Brock*
HARRIET ARTHUR	*Nora Buttram*
MAGGIE TALBOTT	*Comika Griffin*
JANET CALDWELL	*Mimi Rice*

Director: Liz Bussey
Stage Manager: Rachel Dockal
Set Design: William W. Laing
Lighting Design: Lynne Chase
Costume Design: Marty Hagedorn
Sound Engineer: Ryan Newton Harris
Properties Master: Patricia G. Skinner
Technical Director: Jeremy Artigue
Production Assistant: Laurel Sisler

I was lucky. Although I came to playwriting late in life, I quickly found a mentor in the person of Warren Hammack. I wrote two bad plays under his tutelage and one good one, the last of which, *Just Taking Up Space,* had its world premiere at Horse Cave Theatre in 1998. In the 15 months between its selection and first performance, I revised my play many times with Warren's guidance. Our first meeting was a revelation. His copy of the script had dozens of lightly penciled cross-throughs. He never added or changed a word, but he showed me that much of my dialogue was unnecessarily wordy. He also suggested that I give real names to my Nurse, Attorney, and Judge. "Actors need to know their names," he explained. Warren was right about these and numerous other points, so why did I have qualms when he told me that Liz Bussey Fentress would be directing my play? Because I knew her as the woman in the chic white suit who knocked on corporate doors. How could she direct my masterpiece? It turned out that Liz was extremely talented at both fundraising *and* directing, and I loved her respectful, wise treatment of my script. I attended nearly every performance with a notepad and pen. "Plays are rewritten, not written," Warren had told me. I kept revising after the play closed and after Smith and Kraus published several excerpts. A decade later, I'm still revising. Since *Just Taking Up Space* premiered at Horse Cave, my work has garnered numerous awards and productions, all of which I credit to my beginnings as a playwright at Horse Cave Theatre.

– Nancy Gall-Clayton

Characters:

FRANK OWEN, *age seventeen in the first scene, eighteen thereafter, tough*

JENNY LEE BRADFORD, *Frank's seventeen-year-old girlfriend, a junior in high school, smart*

ARNIE TALBOTT, *thirties, a police officer, good guy*

CHRIS ELLIOT, *forties, Frank's public defender, true advocate*

HARRIET ARTHUR, *fifties, juvenile court judge, innovative*

MAGGIE TALBOTT, *thirties, Arnie's wife, five months pregnant in Act One and seven months pregnant in Act Two, compassionate*

JANET CALDWELL, *forties, nurse at Grandview Nursing Home, wise*

Place: Various locations within a medium-sized Southern city: "The Wall," an abandoned brick building at the edge of town, a courtroom, a hospital room.

Time: Late March through early July in the late 1990's.

ACT ONE

SCENE ONE

FRANK has just finished spray painting "FRANK + JENNY" on "The Wall." JENNY is tucking in her top as she looks on. A man's jacket is on the ground.

JENNY: Do you love me?

FRANK: Look what I just painted!

JENNY: Why "plus"? Why not "Frank loves Jenny"?

FRANK: Don't go weird on me.

JENNY: I'm not your first, am I?

FRANK: I'm almost eighteen.

JENNY: Not for that, for love.

FRANK: Love?

JENNY: We've been reading love poetry in English.

FRANK: You're still paying attention in English?

JENNY: English is my favorite subject.

FRANK: I know some of the guys like to look at Miss Evans, but–

JENNY: I like Miss Evans. And poetry. I want you to listen to something I memorized. It's by Elizabeth Barrett Browning. Even her name sounds like poetry to me. Elizabeth Barrett Browning.

FRANK: I like your name.

JENNY: "Jenny Lee Bradford" is ordinary!

FRANK: Not to me.

JENNY: Maybe you do love me.

FRANK: Huh?

JENNY: This lady, Elizabeth Barrett Browning, she lived over a hundred years ago, and her father was so cruel he wouldn't let her get married until she was forty-one years old. Forty-one!

FRANK: There's plenty of mean fathers around.

JENNY: Not everyone's like your stepfather.

FRANK: He's trying to get in every lick he can before I turn eighteen. And don't call him my stepfather!

JENNY: He didn't hit you again, did he?

FRANK: He caught me taking some chicken out of the fridge. Said it was his.

JENNY: Was it?

FRANK: How would I know?

JENNY: Your temper's going to get you in trouble, Frank.

FRANK: Go on, say it. Like Danny.

JENNY: Not like Danny.

FRANK: Can we change the subject?

JENNY: Sure. I was telling you about Elizabeth Barrett Browning and the poem she wrote for her husband.

FRANK: You're going back to school in the fall, aren't you? You're going to do senior year and graduate, aren't you?

JENNY: Probably, but listen to this poem, will you?

FRANK: What's so great about graduating?

JENNY: "How do I love thee? Let me count the ways, I love thee to the depth and breadth and height / My soul can reach." Well?

FRANK: Well, what?

JENNY: Isn't it beautiful?

FRANK: What was that word that sounded like bread? I love thee to the bread?

JENNY: "Breadth." It's an old fashioned word. It means width. She loved him every way she could – up, down, sideways.

FRANK: Poetry is a girl thing.

JENNY: Her husband was a poet, too.

FRANK: Yeah, and didn't you say they lived in the Middle Ages?

JENNY: Oh, Frank!

FRANK: Drop out, Jenny. We'd have more time together.

JENNY: Spring break starts in a couple of weeks. That's nine days in a row.

FRANK: I want to move out when I turn 18, but it'd be a lot easier if we both had jobs. We could rent a place together — maybe even a little house. We can look during spring break.

JENNY: Maybe after I graduate.

FRANK: You could be on your own!

JENNY: I want to finish school.

FRANK: School's like prison. Rules, rules, rules. I heard Mrs. Clark tell the principal I was nothing but a dumb kid with an attitude. A dumb kid with an attitude!

JENNY: You don't get it, do you?

FRANK: I get that I didn't belong in school. The last math test I ever took, I couldn't solve a single problem! There was a big zero on the top of my test.

JENNY: Solving problems with your fists isn't any good.

FRANK: Wayne starts it.

JENNY: You don't have to react.

FRANK: Yes, I do.

JENNY: I'm staying in school.

FRANK: No one cares if you finish—

JENNY: I care.

FRANK: You could get a job, and the two of us could–

JENNY: Doing what? Cleaning toilets? Flipping burgers? No, thanks! The only reason you got that job at the factory is you lied about your age.

FRANK: I had to if I wanted to make more than minimum wage. You can lie about your age, too. Maybe we could work the same shift.

JENNY: I want to finish high school! Aren't you listening?

FRANK: I'm thinking about us. Tonight was special!

JENNY: For me, too.

FRANK: That's my girl!

JENNY: I knew right away that we'd be good friends—

FRANK: The second day of school two years ago.

JENNY: First day.

FRANK: I spent the first day in the emergency room.

JENNY: It was the first day, and your cast is what knocked my books all over the floor. Then we bumped into each other when we were picking them up ... on the first day of school, sophomore year.

FRANK: Second day.

JENNY: We both were carrying a bunch of books, and we crashed into each other coming around the corner by the office.

FRANK: Upstairs by the lockers.

JENNY: Downstairs by the office right before last period.

FRANK: Does it matter?

JENNY: What matters is I was scared, and you were nice to me.

FRANK: You were nice to me, too — probably a little like Elizabeth What's-Her-Name.

JENNY: You might like poetry if you gave it half a chance.

FRANK: I do know one poem.

(*FRANK begins to spray paint "Roses are red," speaking aloud. JENNY interrupts.*)

FRANK: "Roses are red..."

JENNY: If there's enough paint in the can, I'll write my poem when you're done.

FRANK: Sure.

JENNY: I'm going to borrow your jacket, okay?

(*JENNY picks up and puts on the jacket.*)

FRANK: Sure. It's Wayne's actually.

(*JENNY discovers a knife in a pocket.*)

JENNY: Hey! What's this knife doing in here? Is it Wayne's?

FRANK: Willie sold it to me.

JENNY: The Willie who got caught stealing?

FRANK: Not everyone grew up in the country like you where no one ever stole or lied or did anything bad.

JENNY: I never said that.

FRANK: He needed what he took.

JENNY: Is that why people take things?

FRANK: I guess. ... I love you. ... Well, isn't that what you wanted me to say?

JENNY: Not till you mean it.

FRANK: Do you love me?

JENNY: I don't even know what love is. I thought we could talk about it tonight.

FRANK: Going weird again.

JENNY: Does Wayne know you have his jacket?

FRANK: I didn't steal it if that's what you mean.

JENNY: He'll give you a hard time if he finds out.

FRANK: Wayne always gives me a hard time. That's why it'd be so great to move out. With you. (*Pause.*) I'm <u>your</u> first, aren't I? I know you're seventeen, but you never mentioned a boyfriend down in the country.

JENNY: I'm not asking about your past.

FRANK: I'm not the first?

JENNY: The first I care about.

FRANK: You have secrets from me.

JENNY: Just private things.

FRANK: I want to know.

JENNY: It shouldn't make a difference.

FRANK: Exactly! So, how many?

JENNY: What do you want me to say, Frank?

FRANK: The truth.

JENNY: You're sure?

FRANK: Tell me.

JENNY: One! I didn't like him, and I didn't want it to happen. Are you satisfied?

FRANK: I should have known a girl as pretty as you—

JENNY: Don't say that! That's what he used to say—

FRANK: You are pretty.

JENNY: I tried to make myself look bad when he was around.

FRANK: To scare him off?

JENNY: Can we go now?

FRANK: It didn't work?

JENNY: <u>I'm done talking about it, Frank.</u>

FRANK: How'd that poem go again? "How do I love ... ?"

(*FRANK begins spray painting "How ..." as ARNIE enters, startling FRANK and JENNY.*)

FRANK: Where'd you come from?

JENNY: It's not past curfew, is it?

ARNIE: You're good on curfew, but I'm going to write up a citation for the graffiti.

FRANK: It was covered with graffiti before we got here.

ARNIE: That's not the point.

FRANK: What is the point?

ARNIE: I need to see some ID.

FRANK: Artists don't carry ID.

ARNIE: Your name then. Let's start with that.

FRANK: What's <u>your</u> name?

ARNIE: Officer Arnie Talbott. You look familiar: Do you ever stop by the Boys Club?

FRANK: Never.

ARNIE: You might enjoy it.

FRANK: I'm not a boy.

ARNIE: We have all ages.

FRANK: Get to the point, will you?

ARNIE: We have a good time. Basketball, volleyball, baseball, even a pool table.

FRANK: What crime have I committed?

ARNIE: Defacing public property, and I need your name.

FRANK: This old building is public property?

ARNIE: It sure is. Your name or your ID. Please.

JENNY: Tell him your name!

FRANK: Let me handle this.

ARNIE: It's a minor offense, but I don't have a choice since I saw you committing it.

FRANK: There are always choices.

ARNIE: The mayor just appointed a committee to clean up this neighborhood.

JENNY: Frank, I wish you'd—

ARNIE: (*Writing in his citation book.*) First name, Frank. Last name?

FRANK: Jenny, who wrote that thing about breadth again?

JENNY: Tell him your last name, but Officer, arrest us both. I was going to spray paint, too. I'm Jenny Lee Bradford.

ARNIE: You haven't broken the law.

FRANK: Let me handle this, Jenny! Go home.

ARNIE: I'd like for the young lady to stay also.

FRANK: Since when is writing poetry a crime?

(*JENNY removes the jacket and offers it to FRANK.*)

JENNY: You better take Wayne's jacket before things get more complicated.

FRANK: Nothing's complicated. Yet.

(*FRANK surreptitiously removes the knife and puts it behind him as he hands the jacket back to JENNY. She tries to hand it back to FRANK, but it falls to the ground.*)

FRANK: You said you were cold.

JENNY: Think, Frank!

ARNIE: You'll have to paint over the wall, maybe do some community service. Not a big deal. What comes after "Frank"?

FRANK: Don't you have to give me my rights?

ARNIE: Not unless your name will incriminate you, which would be a new one on me, and I've been in this line of work a long time.

FRANK: I don't want your life history, man.

ARNIE: You can answer here, or you can answer downtown.

JENNY: Do what he says, Frank! Please!

ARNIE: Downtown then.

FRANK: This is between him and me.

(*FRANK pulls out the knife.*)

JENNY: No, Frank!

ARNIE: Hand it over, and I'll forget everything but the graffiti.

JENNY: Do what he says!

FRANK: Not a chance.

JENNY: Please, Frank!

FRANK: Self defense is not a crime.

ARNIE: You're only making things worse.

FRANK: Things were just fine before you got here.

(*ARNIE reaches for FRANK's wrist in an attempt to make FRANK drop the knife. They struggle. ARNIE falls, hitting his head on the brick wall. ARNIE lies motionless.*)

JENNY: His head hit that wall! Is he ...

FRANK: Let's go!

JENNY: We can't just leave!

FRANK: Come on! Hurry! He'll come to in a second!

(*FRANK grabs Jenny. JENNY pulls away to go back for the jacket.*)

JENNY: The jacket!

FRANK: No time!

(*FRANK pulls JENNY. They rush out.*)

SCENE TWO

One month later. FRANK, with a red mark on his face, and CHRIS ELLIOT sit before JUDGE HESTER ARTHUR.

CHRIS: That's fine, Your Honor, but let me explain it to my client.

JUDGE: Certainly.

CHRIS: Frank, in the hearing before the other judge, you were found responsible for defacing public property and assaulting Officer Talbott. Judge Arthur wants to ask you a few questions to help her decide what punishment, if any, is appropriate. Do you understand?

FRANK: Yeah.

JUDGE: Don't I know you?

FRANK: No.

JUDGE: I haven't seen you before today?

FRANK: I never had a lady judge.

JUDGE: But you've been in Juvenile Court before?

FRANK: Well, yeah.

JUDGE: For?

FRANK: Truancy.

JUDGE: What else?

FRANK: It's my brother you're thinking of.

CHRIS: Your Honor, if there is a brother, he's irrelevant to the disposition of this case.

JUDGE: Right now I'm trying to find out what else brought your client to Juvenile Court. That is relevant.

CHRIS: I didn't see anything in the file except the truancies, Your Honor.

JUDGE: Think back, have you been in Juvenile Court for anything besides truancy? Remember, you're under oath.

FRANK: I might have been in court for assault before.

CHRIS: Assault? I didn't see that, Judge. May I look at the file?

JUDGE: "Might?" Did you say "might"? (*To CHRIS.*) You should have looked before, Counselor.

CHRIS: I did look before, Your Honor. Files are not always complete. Things get lost, misfiled, put in upside down. I apologize if there's something there I overlooked. May I—

JUDGE: I'll find it myself.

FRANK: I was in court for assault, but you weren't the judge, and it was all a big mistake anyway.

JUDGE: Assault is always a mistake. Assault One? Two?

FRANK: Assault Four.

JUDGE: No, it was more serious than that. Part of this file is missing!

CHRIS: Not necessarily. Frank could be mixed up. Maybe he was stopped, but no charges were filed.

FRANK: It's my brother you're thinking of. We look alike.

JUDGE: Don't tell me what I'm thinking of.

CHRIS: Frank, don't speak unless you're spoken to.

JUDGE: Here it is! Oh, it was Assault Four, and it was dismissed.

FRANK: Like I said!

CHRIS: What did I just—

JUDGE: Let's see ... here it says Frank had to repeat sixth grade and ... here that his longest truancy was when he and his mother were visiting the older brother who's serving 20 to life.

FRANK: The car broke down, and we were there a whole week. I didn't even want to go.

CHRIS: Your Honor, it appears you might have had my client confused with his older brother.

JUDGE: Are you still missing school?

FRANK: I quit. (*To CHRIS.*) I'm eighteen now, so should I even be in this Kiddie Court?

CHRIS: We've gone over this before. (*To JUDGE.*) Sorry, Judge.

JUDGE: You're following right along in your brother's foot steps, aren't you?

FRANK: I'm not! He killed someone. All I did was spray paint a junky old building.

JUDGE: I knew the brother pretty well before he graduated to adult court. Frank is eighteen?

CHRIS: He turned eighteen a few weeks after the incident.

JUDGE: So you escaped circuit court by the skin of your teeth?

FRANK: I'm not what you think.

JUDGE: You're lucky; that's what I think. (*To CHRIS.*) No remorse.

CHRIS: Your Honor, I've filed a Memorandum for your reference in sentencing. Also, I'd like to remind you that only those punishments authorized for juveniles can be ordered since Frank was a juvenile at the time of the offense and he didn't fit the profile for waiver.

JUDGE: We're wasting time, Counselor. Please notice which one of us is wearing a black robe.

CHRIS: Yes, Your Honor. Do you want any further information?

JUDGE: No, I've made my decision. One of this city's finest has been lying in a coma for two months, first at City Hospital and now in the skilled nursing unit at Grandview Nursing Home. Arnie Talbott was a frequent witness in our juvenile and criminal courts. Police work was more than just a job to him. He cared deeply about people, especially young people. We happen to go to the same church, and he volunteers with the youth group there. He stops by the Boys Club whenever he can. He's a good man. You obviously never knew him, or you wouldn't have hurt him.

CHRIS: Excuse me, Your Honor. If I had known you had a relationship with the victim outside the courthouse, I would have asked you—

JUDGE: To recuse myself?

CHRIS: Ineffective assistance of counsel is a serious charge.

JUDGE: I know every officer outside of court. I consider it my job.

CHRIS: Thank you.

FRANK: It was an accident! He took me by surprise!

CHRIS: We're past that. You need to listen.

JUDGE: Are you aware that you can be held in contempt of court, young man?

FRANK: For what?

JUDGE: These outbursts. For disrespect.

CHRIS: She means it. You can be locked up.

JUDGE: This is my last — Juvenile Court's — last chance to have an impact. Your case was placed on our expedited docket for violent offenses involving juveniles. The justice system acted swiftly, but the officer's recovery is going slowly. He may never come out of the coma. Justice would be served if I ordered your client to pay the medical bills, but our tax dollars pay those bills, and it's unrealistic to think your client could pay them anyway. I'd also like to order your client to go back to school. The social worker's note says that Frank dropped out of school with his father's permission.

FRANK: My mother's boyfriend signed.

JUDGE: It wasn't done according to law.

FRANK: I don't want to go back to school.

JUDGE: Don't interrupt!

CHRIS: There will be no further outbursts from my client, Judge Arthur.

JUDGE: I wish someone were available to work with your client one-on-one, but the waiting list for a tutor is more than two years long. If I sent him back to regular school, he couldn't keep up. It wouldn't be fair to the school or to him. He'd just be taking up valuable space.

FRANK: "Just taking up space"?

CHRIS: Your Honor, I object!

JUDGE: So noted. I could order your client to talk to other young people to tell them it's a mistake to get involved in crime, but I'm not sure he believes it is a mistake. I don't want to lock him up because he's liable to make new friends.

CHRIS: Your Honor, you're assuming the worst, predicting the worst. I would like to think that what this young man hears today will guide him on a better path.

JUDGE: Wouldn't we all? May I continue, Counselor?

CHRIS: Yes, Your Honor.

JUDGE: If I sound harsh, it's because life is harsh, and it has harsh results when people break the law!

CHRIS: Judge, may I speak to his family life?

JUDGE: I've read your Memorandum about your client's childhood, which was far from ideal, but he's not a child anymore. Maybe it wasn't his fault when he was three years old, Mr. Elliot. Maybe it wasn't his fault when he was six or nine or even twelve, but he's grown now. He made a very poor decision two months ago.

FRANK: It wasn't a decision; it was an accident.

JUDGE: If it had happened when you were an adult, the legal outcome would have been very different. Do you understand?

FRANK: Yeah.

CHRIS: "Yes, Your Honor."

FRANK: Yes, Your Honor.

JUDGE: I assume you have advised him that he will be in front of a circuit court judge for any future criminal behavior?

CHRIS: He is well aware of that.

JUDGE: Good. Now, my order has two parts. You've figured out the first part, I'm sure. You must paint over the graffiti. My clerk will give you a packet of information telling you where to buy the products you need. You have twenty-four hours. Do you understand me?

FRANK: Yes.

JUDGE: The second part of my order may strike you as unusual. I have discussed this at length with the police officer's wife, and she agrees. What your client must do, what I order him to do, is spend a full hour each and every day sitting with Officer Talbott at the nursing home.

FRANK: What!

CHRIS: This *is* quite unusual.

JUDGE: Unusual, but certainly not the most difficult of punishments. That's every day, from eleven o'clock till noon for the next twelve months. Those are the hours the staff at Grandview prefers. I am ordering your client to sit in Room 326 at Grandview Nursing Home. He doesn't have to talk. He doesn't have to do anything except sit in the presence of Officer Talbott. And he better not do anything inappropriate.

FRANK: Is she crazy?

JUDGE: I'm going to pretend I didn't hear that.

CHRIS: Calm down, Frank.

FRANK: Twelve months?! That's a whole year!

JUDGE: Officer Talbott is not the first police officer to wind up in a coma due to an impulsive act by a lawbreaker. A police officer in Tennessee was in a coma for more than seven years. Are you listening?

FRANK: I'm listening! ... Your Honor.

JUDGE: Perhaps by looking at Officer Talbott, your client will reflect on how a dispute over a minor offense led to what could be the end of a man's life. If and when the officer comes out of his coma, your client must <u>still</u> visit the nursing home unless the officer objects. If the officer dies, the prosecutor may well bring new charges.

FRANK: (*To CHRIS.*) Can't you do something?

JUDGE: The staff will be able to observe Frank by closed circuit television, and they will be taking a variety of other precautions as well. Your client is ordered to do nothing that might be harmful to the officer. Severe consequences will follow, not could, but will. And, as always, disobedience of a court order can result in a contempt finding and incarceration. Do you wish to make a closing statement, Mr. Elliot?

CHRIS: I don't believe a closing statement is necessary. However, I repeat my objection to the Court's remarks about Frank's brother. I further object to this form of punishment which appears nowhere in our state's statutes. I also wish to remind the Court that the young man has sworn that he had no intent to harm the officer.

JUDGE: So noted. Perhaps I should remind you that I don't want to hear that he's committed another offense.

CHRIS: None of us want that, Your Honor.

JUDGE: The law gives juvenile judges a great deal of discretion, but I'll note your objection. The appellate court has never had a problem with my sentences in the past, Mr. Elliot. I believe you have some familiarity with that.

CHRIS: Yes, Your Honor.

JUDGE: Any questions?

CHRIS: When do the visits begin?

JUDGE: What time is it? ... Today! It begins today. You won't get in a full hour today, but it begins today.

CHRIS: May I go to Grandview with my client?

JUDGE: It might be helpful to have an intermediary today, but otherwise, no. Your client may, of course, talk with you as often as he wishes about his experience. If you believe you have reasonable grounds for a modification in the order, file a motion with a supporting affidavit.

CHRIS: Yes, Your Honor.

JUDGE: Anything else?

CHRIS: No, Your Honor.

JUDGE: That will be all.

SCENE THREE

A short time later. At the nursing home, JANET is tending ARNIE, who is comatose in a hospital bed. FRANK and CHRIS enter.

JANET: May I help you?

CHRIS: I'm Chris Elliot from the Public Defender's Office, and this is Frank Owen.

JANET: Oh, yes! We had a briefing about this ... arrangement yesterday, but I was only expecting the young man. I'm Janet Caldwell, one of the day nurses.

CHRIS: Hello, Miss Caldwell. Frank will come alone after today.

JANET: Glad to meet you, Mr. Elliot. Hello, Frank.

FRANK: Hello.

JANET: You can sit, you can stand, you can walk around in this room, but don't touch him or any of the equipment. Do we understand each other?

FRANK: Yeah.

CHRIS: The judge made it clear that he's to do nothing that might hurt the officer.

JANET: If you need anything or have a question, come ask at the nurses' station across from the elevator where you came in. And Frank, that closed circuit camera — and I — will be watching this room from eleven to twelve.

FRANK: I thought he was in a coma.

JANET: That's just why he needs so much care. He has to be turned every two hours, or he could develop bedsores. He has to be suctioned, or he could choke. We have to keep up with his IV. We have to check his vital signs. We have to exercise his limbs ... just to give you an idea.

FRANK: Oh.

CHRIS: He understands there'll be severe consequences if there are problems.

FRANK: I think this guy and the judge are friends.

JANET: She's stopped by a few times, and it wouldn't surprise me if she shows up during your visitation.

FRANK: "Visitation"?

CHRIS: It's only a word. Do you understand what the nurse is saying?

FRANK: I'm going to obey the order!

JANET: This facility provides excellent care, and you will see a lot of me.

CHRIS: We were expecting that, weren't we, Frank?

FRANK: Sure.

JANET: A lot of people care about this man, and to be honest, the staff is worried about how this is going to work out.

FRANK: I bet.

CHRIS: Let me give you my card. Will you call me if you have any concerns?

JANET: I'll leave this at the nurses' station. By the way, Frank, you could do some good while you're here. It might help if you talked to Officer Talbott when you're in the room.

FRANK: You want me to talk to him?

JANET: To him, to yourself, to an imaginary friend. What you say is less important than your tone. Keep it low and calm. The human voice can be very soothing. We encourage people to talk in the presence of patients in comas.

CHRIS: I'll discuss it with him. Frank, do you want to ask the nurse anything?

FRANK: Nah.

CHRIS: He's a little overwhelmed by the judge's order.

JANET: It's unusual.

CHRIS: Yes, it is. Thank you for your help.

(*JANET exits. FRANK slouches into a chair. CHRIS goes to ARNIE.*)

CHRIS: Hello, Officer Talbott. I'm Chris Elliot from the Public Defenders' Office, and this is Frank Owen. I ... uh ... last night, I took my son to a baseball game. See, it's not hard. Say anything or just sit. But whatever you do, don't—

FRANK: What time is it?

CHRIS: About 11:45.

FRANK: Can she really do that? Order me to be here from 11 to 12 every day?

CHRIS: She <u>did</u> order it.

FRANK: Community service, sure, but I never heard of being sentenced to visit a nursing home! It's a good thing I'm not allergic to flowers.

CHRIS: Actually if you were, we might have a shot at getting the order changed.

FRANK: I just remembered! I'm allergic.

CHRIS: I objected in court for the record, but your judge knows what she's doing.

FRANK: Don't call her "my" judge!

CHRIS: I'm on your side, remember?

FRANK: So far, you haven't done me much good, have you?

CHRIS: Harriet Arthur likes for kids to have contact with their victims.

FRANK: I was writing a love poem! Why didn't you say that in court!

CHRIS: You could have been writing John 3:16, and it wouldn't have made a difference.

FRANK: What's that, some big important Supreme Court case?

CHRIS: A Bible verse about love—

FRANK: Love!

CHRIS: It wasn't the graffiti that got you in trouble. Don't you understand that?

FRANK: I understand that the judge is nuts.

CHRIS: Judge Arthur has a reputation for creativity.

FRANK: So how come I never heard of her? None of my friends ever had her.

CHRIS: Judges rotate in and out of Juvenile Court.

FRANK: Will you make sure this is legal?

CHRIS: Juvenile judges have a lot of discretion.

FRANK: I'm going to lose my job.

CHRIS: You're working? You didn't tell me that.

FRANK: Going on two years.

CHRIS: Maybe I can get the time of the visit changed. When do you get off?

FRANK: Three.

CHRIS: Would you want to stop by on your way home from work — if the nurses and the police officer's wife and the judge agree?

FRANK: Maybe I'll ask for another shift. Maybe I'll quit. There's other ways to make money than the box factory.

CHRIS: You're not supposed to work in a factory until you're 18.

FRANK: I _am_ eighteen.

CHRIS: But you just said you'd worked there going on—

FRANK: I'll stick with the time the judge said.

CHRIS: You're sure?

FRANK: I'm sure!

CHRIS: Not so loud! Remember what the nurse said.

FRANK: The guy's vegged out.

CHRIS: You shouldn't say something like that in front of him. Some people who come out of comas—

FRANK: This guy ain't "some people," and he ain't coming out of it. Not after one year and not after seven. That judge had it in for me because of my brother, and this cop is going to die on me. I can feel it.

CHRIS: There's no reason to think he's going to die, Frank, but people in comas sometimes do register what's being said.

FRANK: What are you, a lousy lawyer or a lousy doctor?

CHRIS: Would you rather be in jail? Do you want to be locked up?

FRANK: No.

CHRIS: The judge said you can't do anything inappropriate.

FRANK: I heard her.

CHRIS: You're pretty smart—

FRANK: I guess I forgot to show you my last report card.

CHRIS: Street smart, you're a survivor.

FRANK: Huh?

CHRIS: I think the judge felt the same way.

FRANK: Right, that judge was in love with me!

CHRIS: She doesn't come down hard on kids unless she thinks it's worth it. She gave you a message loud and clear. Don't screw up.

FRANK: It makes me mad.

CHRIS: And that's your main problem, do you realize that? Your temper.

FRANK: That shows how little you know.

CHRIS: Anger won't change the court order. Anger won't get you anywhere.

FRANK: Thanks for the advice. You can leave now.

CHRIS: Will you call me if you want to talk?

FRANK: About what?

CHRIS: That mark on your cheek, for example. You managed to keep it out of my line of vision this morning, and I'm guessing the judge didn't see it either.

FRANK: Wayne spilled coffee on himself this morning and got hacked off at me.

CHRIS: Your stepfather?

FRANK: My <u>mother's boyfriend.</u>

CHRIS: He hit you because he spilled coffee on himself?

FRANK: And me having to go to court today reminded him that I lost his jacket that night.

CHRIS: He assaulted you. You could press charges. I can get someone to take a picture of your face.

FRANK: What am I, your Cause of the Month?

CHRIS: Just call me if you want to talk, okay?

FRANK: Yeah, sure.

CHRIS: You can do this.

FRANK: Good bye!

(CHRIS exits and FRANK addresses ARNIE.)

FRANK: If you're waiting for me to apologize, forget it! People have a right to defend themselves; even cops know that. Of course, the judge didn't exactly see it that way. You all help each other out, don't you, the cops and the judges and the attorneys?

(*FRANK reads cards on flowers haltingly.*)

FRANK: Got a lot of friends, don't you? "Thinking of you, your fellow officers." ... "The Boys Club" ... "Love always, Mom and Dad" ... and on and on and on! Why doesn't your wife take some of these home? You sure aren't smelling them, are you? You're not doing anything except "taking up space." It's like a funeral home in here. If you're planning on dying, why don't you just get it over with! I might be better off if you did die, you know that? I don't think she'd make me visit the cemetery, do you? I could keep my job back, get away from that jerk Wayne, get an apartment with Jenny.

(*FRANK looks at a pink arrangement.*)

FRANK: Pink is Jenny's favorite.

(*FRANK starts to remove a flower, glances up at the closed circuit TV, and replaces the flower.*)

FRANK: People watching me. That's the story of my life. Danny watching me, Wayne watching me, <u>you</u> watching me.

(*JANET rushes in.*)

JANET: We can't hear you on that thing, but it's obvious you're not talking in low, quiet tones. Maybe you shouldn't talk at all right now. Maybe I should sit here with you.

FRANK: Maybe he shouldn't have talked to me that night.

JANET: And maybe I'll just call Mr. Elliot.

FRANK: It's not my fault if he fell and hit his head.

JANET: You need to stop talking or change your tone.

FRANK: Yeah.

JANET: I am responsible for this patient. He's what matters. His comfort and safety. Can you lower your voice, or do I need to call your lawyer? He's probably still in the building. I can page him right now, or I can call the judge.

FRANK: Okay.

JANET: "Okay, I'll keep my voice in normal tones." Go on, say it.

FRANK: Okay, I'll keep my voice in normal tones.

JANET: Thank you. I'll be gone for a few minutes, but other people are watching you.

(*JANET exits.*)

FRANK: It's noon anyway. Twelve months! (*To ARNIE.*) You've ruined everything for me!

(*FRANK rushes out, colliding with JANET.*)

JANET: Slow down, and work on sounding calm at 11 o'clock tomorrow.

FRANK: Fine.

(*JANET is tending ARNIE when MAGGIE enters.*)

JANET: Hello, Mrs. Talbott.

MAGGIE: Is everything all right?

JANET: He's doing fine, about the same as yesterday.

MAGGIE: And last night?

JANET: He had a good night. The notes say he was very peaceful all night.

MAGGIE: Has the doctor seen him today?

JANET: Oh, yes, he was here early.

MAGGIE: And he didn't say anything new about when, about when—

JANET: No, Mrs. Talbott. It's like he said the very first day. He could wake up anytime.

MAGGIE: Or never.

JANET: Yes.

MAGGIE: I don't know why I keep asking.

JANET: It's perfectly all right. Ask as often as you want. The young man came today.

MAGGIE: Oh, my! I'll have to be more aware of what time I come. What was he like? No, don't tell me. I don't want to think about it.

JANET: All right. Say, I just made a fresh pot of coffee.

MAGGIE: Maybe later.

JANET: All right then.

(*JANET exits.*)

MAGGIE: He's a little punk; that's what he is, even if you hate the word, Arnie. ... But I have to stay calm or it's bad for the baby. Oh, Arnie! I almost forgot to tell you! Guess what Joe just told me. I'm getting a raise. Not a big one, but a raise, a vote of confidence, and with me in line for a maternity leave in September! Your check is still coming in, too, so there's nothing for you to worry about. Your only job right now is to get well. I heard the heartbeat again yesterday, He's doing just fine. Or she, whichever we're going to have. (*Making a joke.*) You need your rest, Arnie, but it'd be so much more convenient if you could have gotten it the way other people do. The doctor and your captain and I are all going to be keeping a close eye on you when you come out of this. No more double shifts! I know you're there, inside somewhere, honey. One of these days, I'll come in here, and you'll open your eyes and look at me and you'll say, "Maggie, you owe me a smile," like you used to say every time you walked in the house. "Maggie, you owe me a smile."

(*MAGGIE removes a worn poetry book from her purse.*)

MAGGIE: It's time for your poem.

"The heart that has truly lov'd never forgets, / But as truly loves on to the close; / As the sunflower turns on her god, when he sets, / The same look which she turn'd when he rose."

I love that and I love you, Arnie. I'll be back tonight after supper.

(*MAGGIE speaks as she exits.*)

MAGGIE: A little punk!

SCENE FOUR

Later that afternoon. FRANK is painting over the graffiti. JENNY enters, carrying a book bag.

FRANK: Hey, Jen! Is it that time already?

JENNY: Last bell at three, like always.

(*JENNY goes to FRANK. As they exchange a quick kiss, JENNY notices the mark on his face.*)

JENNY: Wayne?

FRANK: Who else?

JENNY: I brought you an apple.

FRANK: How'd you know I'd be here?

JENNY: All the judges do the same thing with graffiti.

(*JENNY starts to toss the apple to FRANK.*)

FRANK: Hey! My hands are full.

(*JENNY holds the apple up for FRANK.*)

JENNY: We'll eat it together.

FRANK: That's all I want.

JENNY: Okay.

FRANK: I wish I could write a poem for you like that lady did for her husband.

JENNY: Maybe you will some day. Maybe I'll write one for you.

FRANK: I'm betting you'll write yours first.

JENNY: Did you ever think about a GED?

FRANK: For what?

JENNY: For you. For your future.

FRANK: Nah.

JENNY: What did the judge say about the officer? What's your punishment for that? They're not going to lock you up, are they?

FRANK: The judge is making me go to the nursing home.

JENNY: Community service.

FRANK: I have to sit with him! An hour a day!

JENNY: I thought he was in a coma.

FRANK: He is! I'm supposed to feel guilty when I look at all those tubes coming out of his body. They probably want me to get down on my hands and knees and beg him to forgive me, but I'm not going to. He's got a real mean nurse, too.

JENNY: An hour a day?

FRANK: Unless he wakes up and doesn't want me to.

JENNY: How long do <u>you</u> have to do it?

FRANK: A whole year – unless he dies.

JENNY: Is he supposed to die?

FRANK: No one told me anything except "don't touch this," "don't do that," "don't be late," and "don't forget we're watching you."

JENNY: What did Tommy get when he got in that fight with Mr. Wills last year?

FRANK: Community service.

JENNY: And Jimmy, when he took that radio?

FRANK: Restitution. And he's not allowed to go back to Wal-Mart ... but nothing simple like that for me. I got a crazy lady judge who likes to be creative. That's what my attorney said — creative.

JENNY: It could be worse.

FRANK: How?

JENNY: Do you want me to go to the nursing home with you?

FRANK: Nah.

JENNY: Got another paint brush?

FRANK: For all I know, the judge has got some big telescope, and she's watching me right now. If you help, she might throw me in jail. She said she could if I don't follow the order.

JENNY: You're going to follow it, aren't you?

FRANK: I don't want to become my brother's cell mate. ... Can you sneak out tonight?

JENNY: My mom is catching on.

FRANK: I can borrow John's truck.

JENNY: I don't know.

FRANK: You like being with me, don't you?

JENNY: It's not that.

FRANK: What then?

JENNY: I don't exactly know how to tell you.

FRANK: Just say it.

JENNY: I'm late.

FRANK: For what?

JENNY: My period's late.

(*FRANK whistles.*)

JENNY: It might be nothing.

FRANK: It might not be.

JENNY: Exactly.

FRANK: Which do you think it is?

JENNY: I don't know. I feel, you know, like I have an upset stomach, but maybe I'm getting the flu.

FRANK: Pregnant. Oh, Jenny!

JENNY: I'm not positive.

FRANK: I am.

JENNY: I don't want to be pregnant.

FRANK: You don't want the baby growing up without a dad, do you? I'll try to work a different shift.

JENNY: What's that got to do with anything?

FRANK: I have to quit or change shifts, so I can do this stupid thing at the nursing home.

JENNY: It has to be at a certain time?

FRANK: They don't want me to run into his wife. So let's get married. Your mom would sign.

JENNY: That's your proposal? "So let's get married. Your mom would sign." I was hoping for something a little more romantic.

FRANK: If you want a poet for a husband—

JENNY: I don't think I want a husband period. Not yet.

FRANK: I love you.

JENNY: You say those words so easily — now.

FRANK: Now there's a reason to say them.

JENNY: Don't.

FRANK: You'd make a good mom, and I'd like to try being a good dad.

JENNY: It'd be weird in school.

FRANK: You'd have to drop out.

JENNY: I don't think we should have a baby right now.

FRANK: You wouldn't have an abortion, would you?

JENNY: One thing at a time. I just want you to know that I <u>might</u> be pregnant, and if I'm not, I don't want to be.

FRANK: Can you sneak out tonight?

JENNY: Do I have to draw you a picture?

FRANK: Of what?

JENNY: No, Frank, I don't want to go out in the truck.

FRANK: To talk, I want to talk. That's all!

JENNY: Not tonight.

FRANK: Okay, Jen.

JENNY: I'm going on home while you finish up, okay? More apple?

FRANK: No, thanks.

FRANK: I'll call you.

JENNY: Okay.

FRANK: Jenny, shouldn't you be taking vitamins or something?

(*JENNY exits.*)

SCENE FIVE

Two weeks later. A calmer FRANK is at ARNIE's bedside.

FRANK: In the two weeks I've been coming, not a thing has changed in this room except the flowers, and oh yeah, whether Miss Caldwell has you facing right or left.

(*FRANK goes to the flowers.*)

FRANK: Jenny would probably know the names of every one of these. She wants me to go on a hike with her on Memorial Day to look at flowers in the woods. Sounds nuts to me, but I'll probably do it. Sometimes she picks a flower and presses it between the pages of a book. And she has this book full of flower pictures with their names and where they grow and all. She might come up to the hospital with me someday. She wants to see what goes on between us. "Not much," I tell her. "I do all the talking. " Jenny thinks it's all my fault what happened— all! You had something to do with it though. If you hadn't fallen and hit your head, I'd be working now. You'd be working, too, I guess. But why would someone want to spend his life stopping people and telling them they broke a law? Why anyone would want to be a cop? That's a good question, isn't it?

(*JANET enters.*)

JANET: That is a good question.

FRANK: Hey, Miss Caldwell.

JANET: Hey yourself.

FRANK: I guess he's not going to answer it.

JANET: Not today. Listen, I appreciate how you've been trying to keep your voice in normal tones.

FRANK: What are you, my guidance counselor? I'm not a kid! I'm eighteen.

JANET: It wasn't meant as a putdown.

FRANK: So, do you have to do something to him, or are you just checking on me?

JANET: I need to turn him.

FRANK: I can leave.

JANET: No, you can't. Just stand back out of my way, will you?

FRANK: (*Playfully*) Yes, madam.

JANET: Thank you, sir.

SCENE SIX

A few weeks later. FRANK enters ARNIE's room.

FRANK: Hey, how's it going?

(*FRANK goes to the flowers.*)

FRANK: A new one from your parents. "Love always, Mom and Dad." Another one from The Judge. No Father's Day cards though. I guess I'll have to be the one to wish you a happy Father's Day, Officer Arnie. I wonder what happened to those homemade cards I made for my dad. He would keep them on his bureau for months. I'm a pretty good artist, believe it or not. My one and only A in school was in third grade art. Dad took me to the zoo as a reward.

(*JANET starts into the room; stops to listen. FRANK doesn't notice her.*)

FRANK: I was so little I could barely see out the front window of that old beat up car we had. Usually, I had to sit in back with Danny. He had a mean streak, my brother. He'd reach over and pinch me without looking in my direction. My dad could never figure out what I was hollering about.

JANET: Excuse me, I don't mean to interrupt.

FRANK: Oh, hello! I was just talking to him. About nothing, really.

JANET: It's good for him.

FRANK: You're here on a Sunday?

JANET: I volunteered. Father's Day isn't important to me.

FRANK: Your dad and you don't get along?

JANET: He passed away a few years ago.

FRANK: Oh.

JANET: You're here every Sunday.

FRANK: I didn't volunteer.

JANET: How many weeks now?

FRANK: Eight or nine.

JANET: "Eight or nine?"

FRANK: 63 days counting today; 302 to go.

JANET: And talking to him like he was an old friend. Does he remind you of someone?

FRANK: It's not that.

JANET: What then?

FRANK: It's ... it's like he listens.

JANET: It's just possible.

FRANK: So what's he need?

JANET: His vitals and a general look. You go ahead and talk.

FRANK: I'll wait.

(FRANK watches JANET take ARNIE's blood pressure. FRANK looks at a bouquet.)

FRANK: "Love Always, Mom and Dad."

JANET: They send one every week.

FRANK: I know.

JANET: They call almost every day to see how he's doing.

FRANK: How is he doing?

JANET: His blood pressure and pulse seem fine.

FRANK: Is he going to wake up?

JANET: He could.

FRANK: Soon?

JANET: You'd have to talk to the doctor about that.

FRANK: Could he die?

JANET: All of us could die.

FRANK: You're not allowed to tell me.

JANET: Not just you, anyone who's not family.

FRANK: Yeah.

JANET: Are you worried about him — or you?

FRANK: Do you need to do anything else?

JANET: Not right now.

(JANET exits.)

FRANK: So, where was I? Oh, yeah. When we got to the zoo, my dad bought me some popcorn, and then we walked. And walked. And walked. We saw every single animal. I kept trying to decide which was my favorite, but I never could. It was almost closing time when we left. I was thinking to myself that I'd had the best day of my life but then, while we're driving home, my dad says, "I'm not sure what I think of zoos," but he says it like he's talking to himself, like he's forgotten I'm in the car, like he's forgotten my A in Art. "I don't like cages," he says, "not even for wild animals. Take the lion, for instance. It has food and water and a place to sleep, but it can't run or kill. It's lost its nature somehow, and it might as well be in prison." Was <u>he</u> feeling trapped? Is that why he left? Was it my fault? Was it something I did?

(*A piece of medical equipment bleeps. JANET rushes into room and collides with FRANK.*)

JANET: Move, Frank! Out of my way! (*She quickly checks ARNIE.*) I don't believe it! Not the ventilator!

FRANK: What's wrong? What is it?

JANET: How did this happen?!? (*She grabs the call button.*) I need a respiratory therapist stat! I need a doctor! (*She goes to the door and looks in both directions.*) Where is everybody? (*She rushes back to the bed, pushes call button again, takes ARNIE's pulse.*) The chart said he'd been suctioned. It'd be better if a doctor could take a … Frank, what happened in here? I need to know!

FRANK: Nothing happened!

JANET: Nothing?

FRANK: I was just standing here, and the equipment started to make that sound.

JANET: Did you touch him?

FRANK: No!

JANET: The medical equipment, did you touch it? Answer me!

FRANK: I haven't touched anything!

JANET: He needs this equipment to stay alive, do you understand that? To breathe!

FRANK: I haven't touched it!

JANET: Not even by accident? I need to know!

VOICE: (*Over intercom.*) May I help you?

JANET: I've got a Code Blue in here! I need some help! Where is everybody?

FRANK: I can look for a doctor.

VOICE: (*Over intercom.*) Code Blue, Room 326. Repeat, Code Blue, Room 326.

JANET: Why don't you just leave so I can think straight?

(*JANET pushes FRANK toward the door.*)

JANET: You're in the way!

FRANK: But—

JANET: Go on, I said! Can't you see I'm trying to save his life?

FRANK: His life?

JANET: Get out, I said!

(*FRANK rushes out and the lights dim.*)

ACT TWO

SCENE ONE

Two weeks later. FRANK enters ARNIE's room. There are only a few bouquets now, one of which is a blue carnation and spray of baby's breath.

FRANK: Hey, Officer Arnie, how's it going? (*FRANK goes from bouquet to bouquet, reading haltingly.*) "Your friends at District Five." Ha. Wish I had a friend down there. "Love always, Mom and Dad." And here's one from the judge. Hmm, this little one's brand new. "To Dad with love from your son?" What son? That puny thing, that lousy excuse for a bouquet is from your son! Why hasn't he sent one before? He must be one fine human being. "Your son." "To Dad with love from your son." Nah. It's probably a mistake, probably got put in the wrong room.

(*ARNIE shifts noticeably in bed and a blanket at the foot of the bed slips off.*)

FRANK: What was that? You've never done that before!

(*FRANK picks up the blanket, looks out into the hall, waves at camera, then refolds the blanket awkwardly.*)

FRANK: You know I didn't mean it about your son, don't you? (*Pause.*) One Friday night when I was eleven or so, my dad came in, handed my Mom a twenty and said he'd be back later, but he wasn't. Not that night, not the next day, not the next month. She turned him into Welfare, thinking maybe she could get some child support, but they couldn't find him, and it wasn't long before the live-in boyfriends started. She gets lonely. That's what she says, and they help pay the bills. And she likes Wayne. I don't know why.

My real dad, he was all right until near the end. Oh, he always had a temper, but at the end something went wrong. It was like he turned into a different person. Before that, we had some good times. A lot of good times. He'd take me fishing practically every Saturday in the summer. Danny couldn't sit still long enough to fish, so it'd end up just me and my dad down at the riverbank. There's this really big rock down there, big enough for two people to sit on and just lean back and relax and not think about a thing except the ripples in the water. Do you like to fish? One time, I tried catching a mess of catfish for a birthday gift for my dad—

(*JANET enters with a syringe.*)

JANET: Hello, Frank. So you're a fisherman?

FRANK: I was. ... You told me it was normal for him to move, didn't you?

JANET: Small movements are normal. He moved?

FRANK: Yeah.

JANET: Was it small?

FRANK: I guess so, but it seemed big because I never saw him move before, not on his own.

JANET: Everything seems in order – except this blanket.

FRANK: When he moved, it fell off. I'm not a very good blanket folder.

JANET: He seems fine.

(*JANET injects the syringe into the IV.*)

FRANK: What's in that thing?

JANET: Medicine.

FRANK: I knew that!

FRANK: Does he feel it when it goes in?

JANET: I don't think so.

FRANK: I've been wanting to ask you — do you think he knew all that stuff was happening on Father's Day?

JANET: Probably not, but he was fighting for his life. An unconscious person can do that just like anyone else.

FRANK: He wants to live?

JANET: I never met the man, but most people do. All I'm saying is that the systems in his body are working around the clock to keep him alive.

FRANK: But he almost died! That's why you kicked me out.

JANET: I had to, Frank. I had to take care of my patient. Eight hours a day, his life is in my hands.

FRANK: But what really happened on Father's Day? Or is it one of the deep dark secrets that you can't tell me?

JANET: You really want to know, don't you?

FRANK: Yes.

JANET: You remember what a ventilator is for, right?

FRANK: It breathes for him.

JANET: Right, only his was dislodged.

FRANK: Dislodged?

JANET: Knocked out of place.

FRANK: But why?

JANET: Different things can cause it. Mucous could block it, the patient could have a seizure, someone could bump the ventilator — accidentally or on purpose.

FRANK: I didn't do anything, I didn't touch anything.

JANET: I believe you, Frank.

FRANK: And he's okay now, the same as he was when he got here three months ago?

JANET: Officer Arnie is doing just fine.

FRANK: Does he ... does he have a son?

JANET: Not that I know of.

FRANK: Because if he had a son, he would've sent flowers on Father's Day, right?

JANET: Some do, some don't. Some don't even visit — Father's Day or otherwise.

FRANK: Well, look at this, will you?

(FRANK gets the card from the "Son" bouquet.)

JANET: Oh, that!

FRANK: Apparently he does have a son, or this is in the wrong room.

JANET: Could be. Frank. I'm afraid I'm needed elsewhere.

(JANET exits.)

FRANK: See ya. "Frank, I'm afraid I'm needed elsewhere." Let's see, I was telling you about my dad's birthday. I was nine or ten. It was about a year before my dad disappeared. I got every fishing pole out of the cellar and managed to get them down to the riverbank. I laid those poles out on the big rock where we fished and put little rocks on top of them so the poles wouldn't roll in. Then I waited and waited. Figured I'd have a mess of catfish for my dad. Surprise him real good, only, guess what? I fell asleep, and while I was asleep, a breeze came up, and those lines got all tangled up and not one of them with a fish on it!

I woke up with my dad standing over me hollering. He said my mother was worried about me and no one knew where I was and why did I think I could take other people's fishing poles?

Then he tells me, "Franklin," — he always called me "Franklin" when he was mad. "I'm going back for my birthday supper but you, you stay right here until you untangle those fishing lines!" And he left in a big huff. It was hard to do, real hard, and by the time I finished, my stomach was growling, my fingers were bleeding, and it was almost dark.

When I got home, no one was there. I found out later they'd gone to a drive-in movie. The cellar door was open, so I put the poles down there, and then I went into the kitchen. The cake plate was sitting next to the sink, but there wasn't a single piece left. I scraped some frosting off with my finger, but the dirt and the blood got mixed up with it, and I had to spit it out. Then I washed real good and went to bed in that empty house.

You know something? I've never told anybody that story, not even Jenny. In fact, I never even told my dad that I was trying to catch the fish for a birthday gift. For him.

(FRANK gives the officer a hug and exits in a rush.)

FRANK: What am I doing?!?

SCENE TWO

Later the same day. MAGGIE, seven months pregnant, is looking at the "Son" bouquet. JANET is tending ARNIE. JENNY comes to the door.

JENNY: Excuse me. Is this Room 326?

MAGGIE: Yes.

JENNY: Officer Talbott's room?

MAGGIE: Yes. I'm Mrs. Talbott.

JANET: Can I help you?

JENNY: I'm looking for my boyfriend.

MAGGIE: Why would your boyfriend— Oh! He must be —

JANET: Mrs. Talbott, you don't have to—

JENNY: I'm Jenny Bradford, and I'm awful worried about Frank.

JANET: He should have been here at eleven, but he didn't come.

MAGGIE: The one who did this?

JENNY: Yes, ma'am.

JANET: If I see him, I'll ask him to call you. You should leave.

JENNY: But do you have any idea where he might be?

MAGGIE: You have a real nerve coming in here!

JANET: You better go.

JENNY: Okay.

MAGGIE: No, on second thought: Don't! (*To JANET.*) I have some questions for her.

JANET: You're not going to upset yourself, are you now?

MAGGIE: I'm fine.

JANET: I need to check on another patient, but I'll be back in a few minutes.

(*JANET exits.*)

MAGGIE: All right. Now, tell me your name again.

JENNY: Jenny Lee Bradford.

MAGGIE: And Frank Owen is your boyfriend?

JENNY: Yes, but he's not like you're thinking.

MAGGIE: What I'm thinking is that my husband could be dead. I'm thinking that this baby might grow up without a father. I'm thinking that he's a danger to society. I'm thinking this visitation business was a bad idea.

JENNY: But you agreed! It was the judge's idea. Frank only came because he had to. Well, that was the way it was at first. Now, oh! I don't know, it's so confusing.

MAGGIE: "Confusing" is not the word I'd use.

JENNY: Ma'am, I'll just go. I was only looking for Frank. I don't mean to bother you.

MAGGIE: I don't want you to go. I want to understand. How many other kids are there like Frank Owen?

JENNY: He's had a rough life.

MAGGIE: That excuses what he did?

JENNY: No, but there's more to him than you think.

MAGGIE: I bet.

JANET: (*Entering.*) You're not calm.

MAGGIE: I'm fine.

JANET: You can talk in the lounge.

MAGGIE: I'm exactly where I want to be.

JANET: Please, don't upset yourself, Mrs. Talbott.

JENNY: Are you Miss Caldwell?

JANET: Yes.

JENNY: Frank talks about you all the time. He's been doing a good job, hasn't he? Tell her!

JANET: She's here to visit her husband.

MAGGIE: Frank Owen has been doing a good job, Janet?

JENNY: You know what he's like now, how he's been changing.

MAGGIE: Changing to what?

JENNY: Tell her!

MAGGIE: It's all right, Janet. I want to know.

JANET: I had my doubts at the beginning.

MAGGIE: He doesn't want to go to jail!

JENNY: It's more than that. Maybe it wasn't at first, but it is now.

JANET: He might be in the lobby. He always walks around the lobby after his visits. Why don't you go look for him while I talk with Mrs. Talbott? But don't let him come up here now.

MAGGIE: I've seen him! He's the boy pacing in the lobby when I come on my lunch hour! I can't believe it!

I've actually seen him.

JENNY: He's upset that your husband hasn't recovered. That's why he paces.

MAGGIE: He's upset because the judge is making him visit.

JANET: Mrs. Talbott, are you sure you want her to stay? I have to go help with an admission. Maybe I can find someone to come in while I'm gone.

MAGGIE: I don't need anyone, you go ahead.

JANET: If you're sure.

(*JANET exits.*)

JENNY: Frank's not a mean person; he's really not. It was just a bad combination of circumstances that night.

MAGGIE: Is that what he says? "A bad combination of circumstances"?

JENNY: No, that's how I see it. If just one thing had been different, maybe nothing would have happened.

MAGGIE: Just "one thing"?

JENNY: Not a particular thing, but if Frank and I had been there five minutes earlier — or later — of if he hadn't brought the knife with him — or if your husband had come before Frank started painting — or if—

MAGGIE: If life could be rewritten, do you think my husband would still be in a coma?

JENNY: Frank was wrong. I've told him so more than once.

MAGGIE: What's wrong is that Arnie's been unconscious for more than three months. He was working overtime that night because he was needed. That's the kind of man my husband was. He thought about others, and he gave of himself. What kind of man is Frank? That's what I want to know. What kind of man is Frank?

JENNY: We were at this place called "The Wall." Kids like to go there to talk, to have some privacy. We'd just … we'd, well, believe it or not Frank was telling me he loved me—

MAGGIE: Love!

JENNY: We thought we were alone, and your husband startled us. He said he was going to arrest Frank for writing on the wall.

MAGGIE: So your boyfriend pulled out a knife and attacked him.

JENNY: He just happened to have the knife with him. He'd just bought it. But the knife didn't even touch your husband.

MAGGIE: Does that matter?

JENNY: I guess not.

MAGGIE: I sit here, day after day, talking to someone who looks like Arnie. When I touch him, it feels like Arnie, his skin, his hand, his hair. But when I talk to him, he doesn't answer. When I hug him, he doesn't hug back, and when I kiss him, he just lies there. Some days it seems he might as well be in a coffin except his body's warm.

JENNY: I'm so sorry.

MAGGIE: You're "sorry." You were discussing "love." There was "a combination of circumstances." Words are cheap, but life has no price tag.

JENNY: I don't know another way to say it. I AM SORRY.

MAGGIE: You're probably worth ten Franks. How old are you? Sixteen? Seventeen?

JENNY: Sixteen.

MAGGIE: When I was sixteen—

JENNY: Being pregnant must make it harder.

MAGGIE: You have no idea.

JENNY: Do you have other kids?

MAGGIE: No.

JENNY: He's really not violent.

MAGGIE: Oh?

JENNY: Except that night. He lost his temper. There was a struggle. Your husband fell and hit his head.

MAGGIE: You make it sound like it was Arnie's fault. One, two, three.

JENNY: All I mean is Frank didn't plan it. It wasn't something he meant to do. He panicked. He thought the judge's order was stupid, but he's been coming every single day until today. Now he's going to blow it and get in trouble with the court. He was doing so well.

MAGGIE: "Well" at what?

JENNY: Talking to him, talking to your husband. Miss Caldwell can tell you. Frank tells him private things. He calls him "Officer Arnie."

MAGGIE: That's about all I can handle. Will you go now?

JENNY: Sure. I'm sorry.

MAGGIE: Just go.

(*JENNY exits.*)

MAGGIE: Young people! Don't they ever think about anyone except themselves? (*She looks at ARNIE. Long pause.*) Yes, Arnie, I'll do it. Where is that call button anyway? (*MAGGIE pushes call button.*) I know just what you'd say, just what you'd say!

JANET: (*Over intercom.*) Yes?

MAGGIE: Has the young lady gotten on the elevator yet?

JANET: (*Over intercom.*) She's still waiting for it.

MAGGIE: Would you mind sending her back?

JANET: (*Over intercom.*) Are you sure?

MAGGIE: I'm sure.

JANET: All right then.

MAGGIE: Yes, Arnie, I know. "You have to listen to kids to get them to listen to you."

(*JENNY enters.*)

JENNY: You wanted me?

MAGGIE: It was my husband's idea.

JENNY: What?

MAGGIE: I want you to tell me about Frank

JENNY: I thought you had him figured out.

MAGGIE: I'm willing to listen to a little more.

JENNY: Well, sure then. ... It probably sounds strange, but Frank is the only real friend I've had since my mom and I moved here. We used to live down in the country. I wasn't used to cities or sidewalks or neighbors close by or much of anything about a place like this. I didn't fit in at all. I missed everything about the country, and there was no one to talk to. My mom works second shift, and lots of days we don't even see each other.

MAGGIE: No brothers or sisters?

JENNY: They're all much older. There was some trouble right before we moved here, and they didn't see things my way, and we weren't that close to begin with.

MAGGIE: What kind of trouble?

JENNY: Just trouble, and when we moved here, I met Frank the first day of school, and we hit it off. I had the wrong clothes and the wrong hairstyle and all that, but he didn't care. He cares about me, me the person. And I care about him. I know he's not perfect, but who is? He's a friend. (*Looking at the flowers and cards.*) I guess your husband has plenty of friends.

MAGGIE: Right after it happened, there were so many flowers, it practically looked like ... like a funeral home.

JENNY: (*Approaching the "Son" bouquet.*) This one's baby's breath, isn't it?

MAGGIE: From our son.

JENNY: You already know you're having a boy?

MAGGIE: I know, but Arnie doesn't.

JENNY: Baby's breath grew wild near our house in the country.

MAGGIE: Why don't you take it?

JENNY: I couldn't! Not that one!

MAGGIE: Arnie would like the idea of me giving it to you.

JENNY: You're sure?

MAGGIE: I'll just keep the card for him to read later.

JENNY: Thank you. A son. I wonder what I'll ... I ... I might be pregnant, too.

MAGGIE: The man who did this to my husband is going to be raising a child? I'm sorry, I didn't mean that. You surprised me. You're not sure?

JENNY: I throw up every time Mom fries eggs.

MAGGIE: Have you tried eating a couple saltines before you get out of bed in the morning?

JENNY: That would help?

MAGGIE: It helped me.

JENNY: I better be going. I didn't mean to say anything about that. I need to find Frank.

MAGGIE: Kids always talk around Arnie.

JENNY: Yeah. Well, Good bye, Mrs. Talbott.

MAGGIE: Not so fast. What grade are you in?

JENNY: A senior — if I go back.

MAGGIE: If?

JENNY: Frank doesn't want me to, but I like school. I got straight A's in English.

MAGGIE: My favorite subject. Do you like poetry?

JENNY: Yes! We studied Elizabeth Barrett Browning junior year. The night ... that night ... you know—

MAGGIE: Go on.

JENNY: That night I'd been telling Frank about her.

MAGGIE: You were discussing Elizabeth Barrett Browning that night?

JENNY: Trying to. Her poem that starts "How do I love thee" because we were talking about love and all.

MAGGIE: I have a book you might enjoy.

(*MAGGIE finds it in her purse and hands it to JENNY.*)

JENNY: It looks really old.

MAGGIE: My grandmother gave it to me when I was about your age. The poetry of Thomas Moore.

JENNY: I've never heard of him.

MAGGIE: He was an Irishman who lived about 200 years ago.

JENNY: (*Leafing through book.*) He wrote a lot! Are there any love poems?

MAGGIE: Plenty. Let me find the one I always read to Arnie.

(*JENNY hands the book back. MAGGIE locates the poem but recites by memory.*)

MAGGIE: "The heart that has truly lov'd never forgets, / But as truly loves on to the close; / As the sunflower turns on her god, when he sets, / The same look which she turn'd when he rose."

JENNY: Is that what love is? Caring about someone forever, no matter what?

MAGGIE: That's one definition.

JENNY: You and your husband: you're in love, right?

MAGGIE: Of course we are. Would you like to borrow the book?

JENNY: But you just said you read it to him every day.

MAGGIE: I've memorized that poem, and now that I think of it, Arnie would like the idea. I'm counting on you to return the book though. It's a loan, not a gift.

JENNY: You're giving me flowers and loaning me a poetry book. I wish Frank thought like you!

MAGGIE: He doesn't like poetry?

JENNY: No, but he still has dreams. He wants a house and a yard where I can grow flowers like we had in the country. He wants lots of kids and especially a son he can take fishing. He wants our kids to learn to swim and he wants all of us to take family trips.

MAGGIE: It sounds like a fairytale.

JENNY: He's been saving money ever since he quit school—

MAGGIE: He dropped out?

JENNY: He said the teachers made him feel dumb. But the day after he quit, he went right out and got a job. Never missed a day. In a couple more years, he might have made line supervisor.

MAGGIE: If he'd had a diploma?

JENNY: If he was still there. He had to quit to fit in his visits here.

MAGGIE: I didn't know.

JANET: (*Looking in doorway.*) Is everything all right, Mrs. Talbott?

MAGGIE: Yes, thank you, Janet.

JANET: All right.

(*JANET exits.*)

JENNY: Frank hopes to go back to work when your husband gets well. He's on a waiting list for a different shift right now.

MAGGIE: I'm glad we talked.

JENNY: Me, too. I'll take good care of your book.

MAGGIE: And now you need to talk to your mother. You need to pay attention to what you eat, you need to be taking vitamins, you need plenty of sleep, and you need to see your doctor!

JENNY: I don't have a doctor.

MAGGIE: A clinic, then. Ask your mother to take you.

JENNY: She doesn't know.

MAGGIE: Make an appointment with one of the Health Department clinics. And ask your mother to go with you. You need to tell her.

JENNY: I'm scared.

MAGGIE: Of your mom or of being pregnant?

(*Sexual assault victims often survive emotionally by dissociation. JENNY's story should be told in a matter-of-fact fashion.*)

JENNY: I had an abortion two years ago.

MAGGIE: You've already been pregnant?

JENNY: No one was supposed to know, but then I talked about it afterwards. That's part of why my mom and I moved. My dad wanted it to stay a secret. He drove me to a little cinder block building miles from where we lived, and a man in a lab coat, I don't think he was a doctor, he did it, the abortion.

MAGGIE: Are you saying your father arranged for you to have an illegal abortion?

JENNY: A real doctor from a big city like this will be able to tell, I'll get in trouble or my mom will. The doctor will give me a lecture. He'll say I'm too young to be a mother, and then my baby will be taken from me, and I'll never see it again. I can't go to a doctor!

MAGGIE: It doesn't have to be like that. I know a doctor, a lady doctor, who would be very kind. But why an illegal abortion? Right or wrong, it's been legal for years, and you said your father wanted you to have one. Why wouldn't he just take you to a clinic?

JENNY: He was afraid of the law. (*Pause.*) Do you know what I'm saying?

MAGGIE: (*Pause.*) Your dad?

JENNY: Yes.

MAGGIE: Did anybody try to help you? Did anything happen to him?

JENNY: Child protective services tried, but one of my sisters told them I lie a lot, and my mom told them she didn't know what to think. There wasn't enough evidence to do anything; that's what they said. So they closed the case.

MAGGIE: How did they know to check on you in the first place?

JENNY: I missed so much school that my English teacher reported it. The worker who came to the house took me aside and asked if anything was wrong, and I told her. That was a big mistake. Her supervisor came out and then the police. They took all of us off in different rooms and asked us questions, but they said there just wasn't enough evidence.

MAGGIE: They didn't even have a doctor examine you?

JENNY: A doctor checked me, but he said he couldn't tell anything for sure, and of course, my dad denied everything.

MAGGIE: That's unbelievable. Did your dad uh—

JENNY: He never touched me again.

MAGGIE: You sound so calm about it — like you're telling a story about someone else.

JENNY: That's what it's like, like it happened to someone else. I thought I was going to get help by telling it, but the best help was moving here where nobody knows about it. Oh, and my mom decided to leave my father, so it was the two of us moving up here and then I met Frank when I really, really needed a friend.

MAGGIE: And your friend has gotten you pregnant!

JENNY: Maybe.

MAGGIE: I really want to understand — and then I see Arnie. Arnie, who could wake up any day — or never. (*Pause.*) This didn't have to happen!

JENNY: I've got to find Frank.

MAGGIE: You tell Frank he's only to come between eleven and twelve.

JENNY: He may not come at all. That's why I have to find him.

MAGGIE: Do you want the name of the lady doctor?

JENNY: No, but thanks.

MAGGIE: You should call a clinic then. And tell your mother.

JENNY: Can I still have the flowers and the book?

MAGGIE: Yes. Now go.

(*JENNY exits. MAGGIE leans over ARNIE and gives him a tearful hug.*)

MAGGIE: How'd I do, honey? How'd I do?

SCENE THREE

Four days later. JENNY and FRANK enter, he with a picnic basket and she with a blanket. JENNY spreads the blanket, and they sit.

FRANK: What's all this, Jenny?

JENNY: Chocolate cake, paper plates, forks, napkins, coffee in a thermos, cups, cream, sugar.

FRANK: That's not what I meant.

JENNY: It's a picnic. And I want you to be comfortable.

FRANK: This isn't about poetry, is it?

JENNY: Something much more important.

FRANK: More important than poetry?

JENNY: Yes, it is.

FRANK: I missed four days, but I'm going back tomorrow. I'm going to call my lawyer Monday morning and explain. I told you that when I called this afternoon.

JENNY: Open this thermos, will you?

FRANK: Sure. You're really something, you know that? Oh! I almost forgot. I want to give you something.

JENNY: I'm not in the mood for an engagement ring, Frank Owen. If that's a ring, you're going to have to take it back.

FRANK: Aren't you the girl who wants more romance in her life?

JENNY: No rings.

FRANK: Will you keep this for me?

JENNY: Your knife? I'll keep it.

FRANK: I've been thinking about some other things, too, like both of us working at the factory.

JENNY: I'm not going to.

FRANK: That's fine.

JENNY: I found out about this school program for pregnant teens, and …Did you say "that's fine"?

FRANK: I don't want you to work at the factory.

JENNY: Really?

FRANK: I've been thinking about how you have to stand up all day, and your hands get scratched from the cardboard. It might be better if you just finished school — that teen school if you want.

JENNY: Where are you getting all these ideas?

FRANK: Promise you won't think I'm crazy?

JENNY: I promise.

FRANK: I talked it over with Officer Arnie in my mind. That's one reason I want to go back to the nursing home — so I can keep figuring things out with him.

JENNY: That's great!

FRANK: You don't think I'm nuts?

JENNY: I've been figuring out some things, too. I met Mrs. Mrs. Talbott, and—

FRANK: You met Officer Arnie's wife?

JENNY: I was at the nursing home looking for you that first day you missed your visit, and we started talking.

FRANK: I don't believe it!

JENNY: She loaned me a book, and when I took it back, we talked some more. She called me again today.

FRANK: Officer Arnie's wife called you!

JENNY: She's pregnant, they're going to have a little boy.

FRANK: A son?

JENNY: Their first.

FRANK: You're sure about that?

JENNY: She's huge. I don't think there's any doubt.

FRANK: About the son, about the baby being their first son?

JENNY: That's what she said.

FRANK: So that little bouquet was really from … He's not dead, is he? Officer Arnie's not dead?

JENNY: He woke up yesterday!

FRANK: No!

JENNY: Yesterday afternoon. He just opened his eyes and called out for his wife. The nurses heard him and came a-running.

FRANK: I really thought he was going to die. Was Miss Caldwell there?

JENNY: She was.

FRANK: She could have called me.

JENNY: Maybe it's against the rules.

FRANK: She could have called anyway. What happened after he woke up?

JENNY: The nurses told him he was in a nursing home and why and his doctor came in, and I don't know — ordinary stuff for someone who wakes up from a coma.

FRANK: Did they mention me? Did they tell him about my visits? What did _he_ say?

JENNY: They called Mrs. Talbott, and she came right over. She says he seems exactly the same except tired, like he's been taking a very long nap. He hasn't forgotten anything.

FRANK: Not anything?

JENNY: He knows his name and who he is and what his job is. That stuff.

FRANK: He's normal? Healthy? He's okay?

JENNY: They can't say for sure yet, but he seems fine.

FRANK: Has he gone home? Is he home yet? Will I be able to … Will I have to … What's the judge going to say? … He remembers everything?

JENNY: He'll be at the nursing home a while, to build up his strength and make sure he's all right. That's what Mrs. Talbott says.

FRANK: Jenny, think of all the stuff I've told him!

JENNY: I know.

FRANK: So what do I do now?

JENNY: You visit him. You said you were going back. What do you mean, "What do I do now?" You talk with him. We're invited to go tomorrow.

FRANK: Both of us?

JENNY: Mrs. Talbott asked me to come along with you, but if you'd rather go alone, that's okay.

FRANK: No.

JENNY: Then we'll both go. They're expecting us at eleven, your regular time.

FRANK: He's going to hate me.

JENNY: No, he's not.

FRANK: What do you know about it?

JENNY: He likes kids.

FRANK: He's going to hate me!

JENNY: Frank! Think!

FRANK: I am thinking! I can't go.

JENNY: You have to go!

FRANK: You don't understand; you just don't understand!

(*FRANK exits running.*)

SCENE FOUR

Next day, 11:30 a.m. ARNIE is sitting up in bed as JANET takes his blood pressure. MAGGIE and ARNIE are listening to JENNY.

JENNY: I hope he comes, but he's scared.

ARNIE: I don't bite.

MAGGIE: I told her confrontation wasn't your style.

JENNY: It's the idea of seeing you awake. He wanted you to wake up, but I guess it was easier to talk to you before.

ARNIE: No one to interrupt.

JANET: The first day was very rocky. So was the second and the third. I told him and his attorney that talking in your presence was good — and eventually he did that. And did that. And did that some more. Eventually, he talked nonstop from the minute he arrived till the minute he left.

MAGGIE: Young people are hard to figure out.

JANET: That's the truth. (*To ARNIE.*) Your blood pressure is just fine today.

MAGGIE: Let's keep it that way.

ARNIE: I'll do my best.

JANET: Did you turn in your dinner order yet?

ARNIE: It's right here. What else can I do for you?

JANET: Keep getting better.

ARNIE: I'm planning on it. See you later, Janet.

JANET: You can't get rid of me that easily. I have a few instructions for you: first and most important: don't wear yourself out! Tell everyone to leave if you get tired. Use the call button if you need anything. Don't overdo it!

ARNIE: This isn't going to be much of a party.

JANET: That's the idea.

MAGGIE: I'll keep an eye on him.

JANET: All right, then.

(*JANET exits.*)

ARNIE: So, your boyfriend is scared?

JENNY: Scared mostly of what you'll think of him. He thinks you're going to hate him.

ARNIE: It'd be a lot easier to sort out if he'd come up here.

JENNY: It worries him that he was talking to you so much. He was thinking he might be crazy—

ARNIE: A man who couldn't possibly respond?

JENNY: Yes.

(*JUDGE HARRIET ARTHUR enters.*)

JUDGE: Arnie, it's good to see you! How are you, Maggie?

MAGGIE: Great, now that Arnie's getting better.

ARNIE: This is a surprise, Harriet!

JUDGE: Maggie gave me the news yesterday, and I thought I'd just stop in for a few minutes. A lot of people have been worried about you. People at the courthouse ask me about you every single day.

ARNIE: Tell them I appreciate it, will you? And all the flowers and cards, too.

JUDGE: I sure will.

ARNIE: Tell them I'm doing fine, and I'll be back very, very soon.

MAGGIE: He'll be back when the doctor says he can go back and not before. He's not ready for lots of company yet either.

ARNIE: I'm not?

MAGGIE: You're not.

ARNIE: Aw, Maggie.

JUDGE: I'll let everyone know.

MAGGIE: Thank you, Judge.

ARNIE: I hope not too many cases had to be delayed while I was here, Harriet.

MAGGIE: Oh! I'm sorry. Jenny, this is Judge Arthur. Harriet, this is Jenny Bradford.

JUDGE: Glad to meet you.

JENNY: How do you do, ma' am.

JUDGE: Another one of your young fans?

ARNIE: In a way.

MAGGIE: Jenny's a special girl.

ARNIE: So, Judge, did you need my testimony on the Carruthers case? I was really looking forward to taking the stand on that one.

JUDGE: Carruthers is right where he should be. We used Fred Johnson's testimony, and the jury was only out two hours.

ARNIE: Glad to hear it.

JUDGE: He got the maximum, too. You're not the only police officer in the jurisdiction.

MAGGIE: I tell him the same thing, but he won't listen. He can't wait to get back in his blues.

ARNIE: Why shouldn't I?

MAGGIE: Because you could have been killed, that's why. Because you're going to be a father soon, because I need you.

ARNIE: It's all I know, Maggie. It's who I am.

JUDGE: You are one of those people who only looks like himself in uniform. But Maggie's making a lot of sense, Arnie.

ARNIE: Don't gang up on me.

JUDGE: I'll tell everyone that I saw you and that you're doing great, how's that?

ARNIE: Don't leave yet. We're expecting someone any minute, someone you might be interested in seeing, Judge — only he seems to be running late.

JENNY: Very late.

JUDGE: Who would that be?

JENNY: Frank Owen, ma'am.

JUDGE: Frank Owen is coming?

JENNY: It was your order.

JUDGE: (*To ARNIE.*) You don't have to see him, you know. It's up to you now.

MAGGIE: What? The man who cheerleads for the people he arrests? He wants to see him, Judge, and I'm kind of curious myself. I've gotten a different impression of Frank over the past few days.

JENNY: He's not coming.

MAGGIE: Don't give up on him yet.

ARNIE: She says he's scared.

JUDGE: That's better than angry.

JENNY: He's trying to not be angry.

ARNIE: Good.

MAGGIE: He could come in that door any minute.

JUDGE: Are you sure you want to be involved with someone like Frank?

MAGGIE: She doesn't have a lot of choice right now.

(*ARNIE clears his throat with an "ahem" sound.*)

ARNIE: Maggie!

JENNY: That's okay. I told my mom.

JUDGE: You're pregnant?

JENNY: Yes.

JUDGE: It's a familiar story. Is this the first visit he's missed? (*Pause.*) Well, is it?

JENNY: He didn't miss any until four days ago, five now.

JUDGE: His older brother is in prison—

JENNY: Frank doesn't want to be like Danny. In fact, he's scared to death of being like Danny. Oh, why doesn't he come?

MAGGIE: Honey, maybe we're asking too much, expecting too much too soon.

JENNY: I think I'll go. It was nice meeting you, Officer Talbott and Judge Arthur.

JUDGE: Good luck, Jenny.

JENNY: *(To ARNIE.)* Thanks for being willing to see Frank today.

ARNIE: I'd still like to meet him. Will you tell him that?

JENNY: If I see him.

MAGGIE: Call me, okay?

JENNY: I will.

   (JENNY exits.)

MAGGIE: A shame, isn't it?

JUDGE: The pregnancy or the boyfriend?

MAGGIE: How mixed-up kids always seem to find each other.

JUDGE: Who else would they find?

ARNIE: Me! At the Boys Club. Or a teacher or a Scout leader or a minister.

MAGGIE: She's such a sweet girl — and bright, too.

ARNIE: Change never comes easy.

JUDGE: Once a boy goes bad, he usually stays bad.

ARNIE: Harriet, you should get off the bench if you believe that!

JUDGE: I see what I see.

MAGGIE: Jenny thinks Frank learned a lot by coming up here.

JUDGE: That was my hope, but not necessarily my expectation.

ARNIE: There's always hope.

   (FRANK enters timidly carrying a bouquet. JENNY is behind him.)

ARNIE: Ah, what have we here? What did I just say?

JENNY: He came, Mrs. Talbott! He came!

FRANK: I'm Frank Owen, Officer. I need to apologize to you.

ARNIE: Yes?

FRANK: I'm sorry about what happened back in March. You were just doing your job. I see that now. I'm ... I'm sorry I hurt you. It was my fault, <u>all</u> my fault. *(FRANK hands the officer the bouquet.)* These are for you.

ARNIE: Thank you. That's nice of you.

FRANK: Are you Mrs. Talbott, ma'am?

MAGGIE: Yes, I'm Maggie Talbott.

FRANK: I owe you an apology also. I'm sorry for what I've put you through.

MAGGIE: It's been difficult; that's for sure.

ARNIE: Come over here and shake my hand.

   (ARNIE and FRANK shake hands.)

FRANK: *(To MAGGIE.)* Will you accept my apology, too?

MAGGIE: *(Long pause.)* Yes. But there's someone else you need to apologize to.

FRANK: Oh. I ... um, hello, Judge Arthur. I wasn't expecting to see you here.

JUDGE: Hello, Frank. I'm glad you finally made it, but I think Mrs. Talbott was referring to Jenny.

FRANK: Jenny?

JENNY: You were more than twenty minutes late. I'd given up on you.

FRANK: I've been in the lobby trying to figure out what to say.

JENNY: You've had since last night to figure that out.

FRANK: You're right. I'm sorry, Jenny, for causing you so much worry.

JENNY: Thanks, Frank. Judge Arthur, he might be going to jail for missing visits, isn't that true? (*To FRANK.*) You might be in jail when I go to the hospital to have the baby! What about jail, Judge Arthur?

JUDGE: Call your lawyer first thing Monday. He'll get you a hearing date.

FRANK: Okay.

JUDGE: Jail is not automatic.

FRANK and JENNY: It's not?

FRANK: I can be there for the baby!

JUDGE: Call your attorney first thing. We can't discuss it here.

ARNIE: Tell your attorney to give me a call, too, Frank.

JUDGE: I guess I don't need to remind you that public defenders are the <u>other</u> team?

MAGGIE: You're not going to court to testify, Arnie Talbott, do you hear me?

ARNIE: I can give a sworn statement. I bet the nursing home has a notary. Or Frank's lawyer could take my deposition. We could even have court right here in this room, couldn't we, Judge?

MAGGIE: Absolutely not! Frank, have your attorney call <u>me</u>, okay?

JUDGE: Not a bad idea. (*To MAGGIE referring to ARNIE.*) He's like a kid waiting for Christmas.

MAGGIE: Tell me.

ARNIE: All right, Maggie, we'll do it your way.

MAGGIE: As long as you're in that bed attached to all those tubes, we will.

JUDGE: Maybe I can come up with some kind of restraining order.

ARNIE: You wouldn't!

JUDGE: No promises. Arnie, take care of yourself.

ARNIE: Call me if you need me, will you? I'm going to get bored here.

MAGGIE: Arnie!

JUDGE: You'll have Frank's visits every day, if you want them.

ARNIE: I'm looking forward to them.

JUDGE: Good. Well, so long. Take care, Maggie.

(*JUDGE exits to chorus of good-byes.*)

FRANK: Officer, can I ask you something?

ARNIE: Why not call me Officer Arnie? Isn't that the name you used when I was unconscious?

FRANK: (*To JENNY.*) I told you! He knows everything I said!

ARNIE: Jenny told my wife that you called me "Officer Arnie."

MAGGIE: And I told him. I don't think my husband heard a word you said during your visits.

FRANK: That's just what I was going to ask you.

ARNIE: That's between us. We'll talk about it later. Will you come back tomorrow?

FRANK: You really want me to?

ARNIE: Just the two of us. Will you come?

FRANK: I'd like to.

ARNIE: When I get out of here, maybe we'll schedule ourselves a little fishing trip.

FRANK: You like to fish?!

ARNIE: Every now and then.

FRANK: I know a really nice spot.

ARNIE: We'll check it out when the doctors – and Maggie – say it's okay.

MAGGIE: It's really happening then.

ARNIE: Of course, it's happening. Come over here, Maggie. You owe me a smile!

(*MAGGIE goes to ARNIE, takes his hand and smiles.*)

FRANK: You owe me one, too, Jenny.

JENNY: Yes, Frank, I think I do.

(*JENNY smiles and takes FRANK's hand. They start out the door. FRANK looks back.*)

FRANK: I'll see you tomorrow.

THE END

Nancy Gall-Clayton

Nancy Gall-Clayton won the Streisand Festival of New Jewish Plays, the Eileen Heckart Drama for Seniors Contest, and Heritage Festival XIII. She has been a finalist for Actors Theatre of Louisville's Heideman Prize, the New Harmony Project, the Getchell Prize, and the Kernodle New Play Competition. Nancy has been a Visiting Artist at Ohio State University and a Tennessee Williams Scholar at Sewanee Writers' Conference. Her writing has been published by Dramatic Publishing and others. The Kentucky Foundation for Women and Pleiades Theatre Company have supported her work. She belongs to the Dramatists Guild and the International Centre for Women Playwrights.

Robert F. Brock and Pamela White in *Someday's Gone* by Frank Schaefer, Horse Cave Theatre, 1999

SOMEDAY'S GONE
by
Frank Schaefer

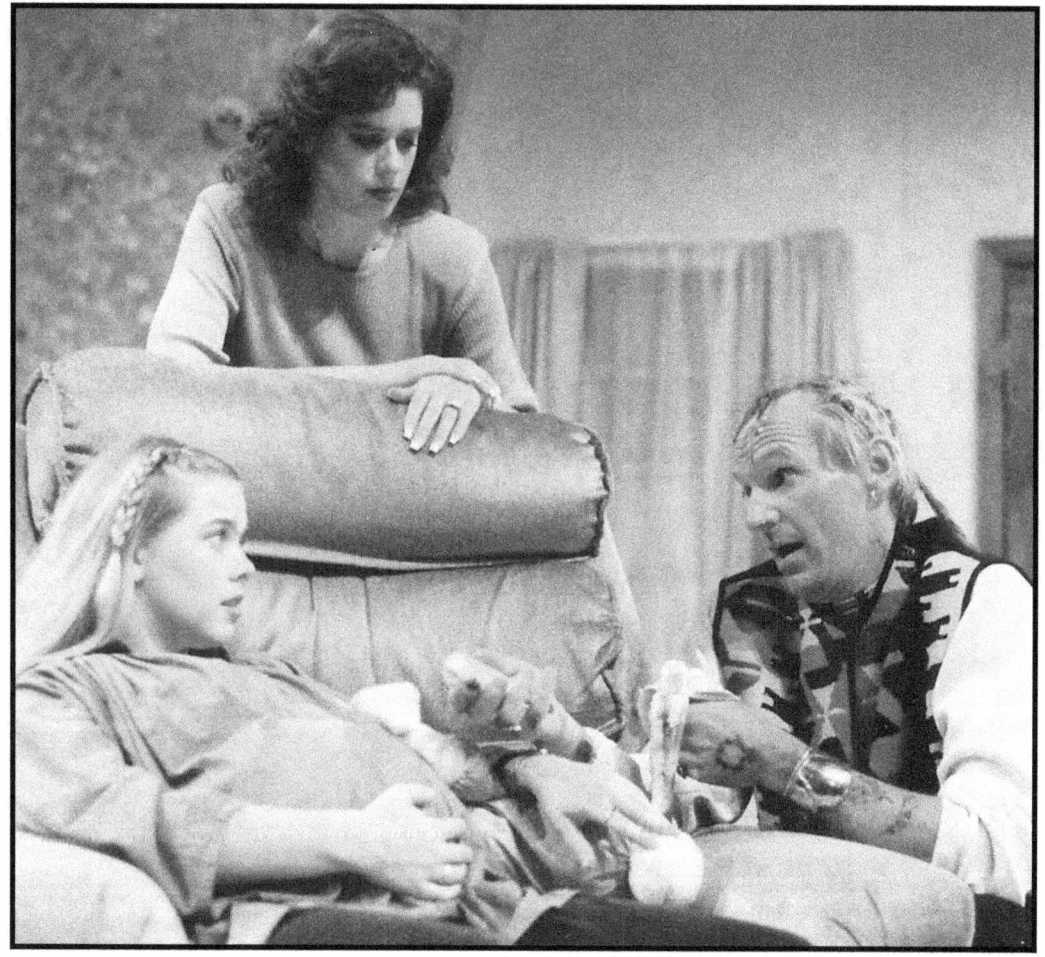
Amber L. Walker, Tina E. McGhee and Alex Cherington in *Someday's Gone* by Frank Schaefer, Horse Cave Theatre, 1999

Someday's Gone opened on July 9, 1999, with the following cast:

EDDIE FORTMAN	*Robert F. Brock*
MICHELE MAXWELL	*Pamela White*
CERISE POWERS	*Tina E. McGhee*
JONI CANTRELL	*Amber L. Walker*
SATURN	*Alex Cherington*

Director: Carey Upton
Stage Manager: Ryan Newton Harris
Set Design: Jeremy Artigue
Lighting Design: Lynne Chase
Sound Design: Andrew M. Bartlett
Costume Design: Marty Hagedorn
Properties Master: Jean Burch
Technical Director: Jeremy Artigue
Assistant Director: Mark Christopher Baer
Production Assistant: Laurel Sisler
Assistant Production Assistant: Jennifer Barclay

Horse Cave, Kentucky, has to be one of the most improbable places to find a thriving repertory theater. Especially one that's over thirty years old.

I remember my first visit to Horse Cave in 1980 mainly for the stench that emanated from the cave and hung over the town. People wanted to live there?

But things changed, as they do. The cave is now cleaned up and odor-free. I next returned in '92 or '93, I suppose, to visit Warren. I was living then in Allen County. A refugee from Dallas, I was finishing a novel while caretaking the ancestral home/farm of a Dallas friend. One thing led to another, as things do, and I soon began to wonder if I could make my way around a stage again and talked Warren into hiring me for a season. It so happened that I was working on a play at the time, and I soon heard about the Kentucky Voices readings.

Well, we read it, and the next year – or year after that – darned if it didn't open right there on that stage in that improbable town in that improbable theater!

I'd long known, after twenty novels and about sixty editors that there's no such thing as a golden word, so the process of having my work fiddled with neither shocked nor fazed me. It was more fun with a play, really, because I got to see those bare words on a page take shape in ways beyond those I had imagined.

That day's long gone, now, but I cherish it. Thanks, crew.

– Frank Schaefer

Characters:

EDDIE FORTMAN, *a lady's man and would-be "player," early to mid-thirties*

MICHELE MAXWELL, *Eddie's childhood sweetheart and ex-wife, the same age as Eddie*

CERISE POWERS, *a wealthy businessman's daughter and Eddie's fiancé, around thirty*

JONI CANTRELL, *a very pregnant sixteen-year-old, Michele's niece*

SATURN, *a spaced-out friend of Michele, anywhere from thirtyish to fiftyish*

VARIOUS CHARACTERS (*Voices only, on answering machine.*)

Place: Eddie Fortman's apartment in any large city.

Time: Late August.

ACT ONE

SCENE ONE

Eddie Fortman's bachelor apartment in a large and moderately prestigious apartment complex. It may be as upscale as budget permits, but should be tastefully decorated, all very clean and neat, as befits an up and coming hard charger.

A couch, coffee table, recliner, dining room table with chairs, and a telephone with an answering machine are required. A door upstage opens to the exterior. A door stage left leads to the kitchen and laundry room, and a third at stage right leads to a corridor giving access to bedrooms and bathroom. Curtains cover one or two upstage windows.

A poster-type photograph of a cliff face is prominently displayed somewhere. Part of another wall is outfitted as a climbing wall with foot and hand holds, a pipe for chinning and dangling, etc. Again, this may be as simple or fancy as budget allows, but in any case, little of it need be practical.

A Friday afternoon in late August. Light enters the apartment through curtained windows. After a beat, the front door opens and MICHELE MAXWELL enters. MICHELE is dressed casually, her hair is done plainly, and she wears little (if any) makeup. She carries a cardboard box and a sack loaded with groceries.

MICHELE: Eddie? (*No answer.*) Well, rats. (*Leaving the door open, she deposits box and sack on the dining room table, and pats a cat figurine on the table.*) Hi, you. (*Heading back to open door.*) Any minute, now. One way or the other. How you can be so <u>calm</u> about this is beyond me. (*She exits briefly and returns glancing through a handful of mail that she tosses onto the haphazard pile already on the table, upon which, a burglar alarm shatters the silence.*) Darn! (*She runs to the alarm keypad and punches in the code, which turns off the alarm.*) Idiot alarms, anyway. (*She deposits the box on a small pile of similar boxes.*) What're they gonna steal, Eddie? Your socks?

(*MICHELE picks up the grocery sack and starts to the kitchen, but is stopped by the phone. She replaces the sack and hurries to the phone.*)

MICHELE: Ed Fortman's residence. May I?—... Of course, I'm supposed to be here. I had the number, didn't I? .... What do you want me to do? Cross my heart? ... Henderson. His mother's maiden name was Henderson. I went through this with you people Wednesday. The alarm thing doesn't warn you when you come in the door and I'm not used to these idiot things, so if you'd <u>please</u> fill out a repair order, I'd appreciate— ... Yes, Henderson. ... Yes. Thank you very— (*Looks at phone.*) You have the manners of a goat!

(*MICHELE slams down the phone and, adding a bunch of bananas to a tray of fruit and munchies already on the table, exits to the kitchen with the rest of the groceries. When the phone rings again, she enters on the run and grabs it.*)

MICHELE: Hello? ... No, he said he'd be here by five, but he hasn't— ... This is his ex-wife, Michele. May I—

... Oh, hi, Cerise. Nice to meet you. ... Oh, yes. (*A harder tinge to her voice.*) And I'm looking forward to meeting you too. ... Right. I'll tell him the minute he— ... Right. Bye.

(*She hangs up, heads for the kitchen. The phone rings.*)

MICHELE: Hello? ... No, he hasn't— ... I know he's late. I'm his ex-wife, Mi— ... Well, I can't exactly show you my driver's license, now, can I. Will you settle for his mother's maiden name? ... I'll tell him you called, Tiffany. Bye... Tiffany... Jeez, Eddie...

(*MICHELE exits to the kitchen. The phone rings.*)

MICHELE: (*Offstage, calling.*) He's on his way! Call back later. I'm putting away groceries.

(*After four rings, EDDIE's machine picks up.*)

EDDIE: (*On machine.*) Hi. This is Ed Fortman...

MICHELE: (*Head out of kitchen, over machine.*) Is that you, Eddie?

EDDIE: (*On machine.*) Sorry I'm not here to take your call... (*MICHELE snorts in disgust and disappears into kitchen.*) ....but if you'll leave your name and telephone number, I'll get back to you shortly. Thank you.

MICHELE: (*Offstage, and over the end of the message.*) I hate those things! Doesn't anybody know how to call back?

(*The front door opens and EDDIE, dressed expensively and stylishly, and carrying expensive luggage, enters in time to hear...*)

DEBBIE: (*On machine, seductively.*) Hi, Eddie. This is Debbie. My husband's out of town this weekend...

(*EDDIE closes the door, puts down his bags, and hurries to the phone, noting Michele's presence, off, as...*)

MICHELE: (*Offstage, calling.*) That's disgusting, Eddie.

DEBBIE: (*On machine as EDDIE listens.*) ... and I'm so lonely... You said you'd be home by five, but, well, call me when you get there, huh? Maybe we can—

EDDIE: (*Picks up.*) Debbie! ... How's my little light at the end of the tunnel? ... Yeah. Just this minute walked in the door. How are you?

MICHELE: (*Offstage, calling.*) Eddie? Is that really you?

EDDIE: (*To MICHELE, with hand over mouthpiece.*) Yeah. Gimme a sec, huh? (*Into phone.*) I know what you mean...

(*MICHELE enters from kitchen. EDDIE gives her the high sign: quiet.*)

EDDIE: (*Into phone.*) Tonight? I can't. My ex is camping out here for a few days until she finds a place of her own, so ... Your place? You sure that's safe? ... Well, maybe around ten, say? ... Mmm. I'll call first. ... Yeah! ... Bye. (*Hangs up, looks fondly at MICHELE.*) I'll be damned. Look at you!

(*This is the first time they've seen each other for four years, and their conversation, at first, is awkward.*)

MICHELE: Look at yourself. (*A beat.*) I guess I messed up your night, huh?

EDDIE: Are you kidding?

MICHELE: Mr. Popularity. All the world's women are looking for you.

EDDIE: Sure. (*A beat.*) You found everything?...

MICHELE: Oh, yeah. Towels, and... you know... (*Picks up the cat figurine.*) This little guy.

EDDIE: You like him?

MICHELE: He's perfect for my collection. Thanks. That was sweet of you.

EDDIE: Well, I saw him and remembered you liked cats, so... (*Not letting things get too sentimental.*) You look great. It's good to see you.

MICHELE: Just frowsy, pushy old me.

EDDIE: Frowsy? You? (*Moving quickly to his luggage, and exiting right with it.*) Better put my bags in my room, huh?

MICHELE: I feel frowsy... (*Calling after him.*) Barging into your life again. (*A touch of bitterness.*) As if there were any room there.

EDDIE: (*Off.*) Always room at Eddie's inn.

MICHELE: Yeah. Well... (*Not for EDDIE's ears.*) This is so ridiculous! (*A beat. With forced cheer.*) So, then! You're really engaged?

EDDIE: (*Off.*) Well, halfway, sort of.

MICHELE: That sounds tentative.

EDDIE: (*Off.*) Isn't it always, until you walk down the aisle?

MICHELE: I suppose. Pretty fancy name, Cerise.

EDDIE: (*Off.*) Pretty fancy family. Her father's Wade Powers, the developer.

MICHELE: Should I be impressed?

EDDIE: (*Off.*) Most are.

MICHELE: Rich, huh?

EDDIE: (*Off.*) Only a fool marries poor.

MICHELE: Thanks a lot. But you know what?

EDDIE: (*Enters.*) What?

MICHELE: I love you anyways.

EDDIE: And I still... Now, damn it Mick! Cut it out!

MICHELE: You mean that, Eddie?

EDDIE: Yes. No! Ah, hell, I don't know what I mean.

MICHELE: Isn't it about time to figure that out?

EDDIE: (*A beat.*) I haven't changed, Mick, if that's why you're here. Sometimes I miss...the way things were, but I'd probably just mess us up again. I'm sorry.

MICHELE: Silly me. Thought I'd check it out...

EDDIE: Can't we just let bygones be bygones? Just be friends?

MICHELE: (*A sigh. Resigned.*) Okay, Eddie. Bygones are bygones.

EDDIE: Aw, Mick...

(*They embrace. After a moment, EDDIE steps back and regards her with affection.*)

EDDIE: What a sight. I had no idea I missed you so much.

MICHELE: Sure. Tell me another, huh?

EDDIE: I did. Big time.

MICHELE: Right, but Cerise, Tiffany, Debbie, and who knows how many others were admirable substitutes.

EDDIE: Forget substitutes. (*A beat. Deadly serious.*) You were a hard act to follow, you know. I really did miss you.

MICHELE: An act... Oh, never mind. Yeah, I suppose you probably did... (*Pokes his chest.*) The big city must agree with you. You look great. (*Indicates climbing "wall."*) That rock climbing stuff has done you some good.

EDDIE: (*Breaks away to check his mail.*) You better believe it. You find a place yet?

MICHELE: Eddie! We've barely said hello!

EDDIE: (*Separating junk mail.*) I didn't mean it <u>that</u> way. But you did interview and get the job, right? Sign a contract?

MICHELE: Yup. Teen Pregnancy Outreach, here I come.

EDDIE: Teen Pregnancy?...

MICHELE: Arrived in town Monday, signed the contract Tuesday, started Wednesday, and had my first client yesterday. My own niece, would you believe?

EDDIE: Harvey's and Alison's kid? Joni?

MICHELE: Only niece I have. I called her to say hello, and guess what?

EDDIE: You mean she's?... Oh boy. Is she married?

MICHELE: Of course not.

EDDIE: Ah. I forgot. That's the way it's done these days. (*Exasperated.*) How could she do that?

MICHELE: The usual way, I assume. It happens every day.

EDDIE: But she's just a kid! What? Fourteen? Fifteen?

MICHELE: Sixteen.

EDDIE: I can't believe Harvey didn't tell me.

MICHELE: It's supposed to be a big secret.

EDDIE: He's your brother-in-law. (*Looking at a bill.*) I thought I paid this!

MICHELE: Alison must be turning in her grave.

EDDIE: (*Absent-mindedly.*) I'll bet... (*Another bill.*) Damn!

MICHELE: Anyway, what a mess. And I thought it was bad in Guatemala.

EDDIE: (*Interested in the mail.*) Uh-huh...

MICHELE: (*Shooting from the hip.*) So I instituted a new policy. We find the fathers, and castrate them.

EDDIE: Mmm. That's good.

MICHELE: Yup. That teaches the horny little boogers. One strike and they're sopranos.

EDDIE: Makes sense to— You <u>what</u>?

MICHELE: We were married nine years, Eddie. You didn't listen to me then, and you still don't.

EDDIE: I heard, I heard. The boys are guilty, and the girls are victims.

MICHELE: I didn't say that.

EDDIE: But that's what you meant. We were married nine years, and I listened.

MICHELE: You are so—

EDDIE: On the other hand, that would limit them to one apiece. (*Tearing open another envelope.*) Ah! Here we go!

MICHELE: What's that?

EDDIE: (*Pulls out airline tickets.*) Tickets to Vermont. (*Points to the photograph hanging on the wall.*) My first big climb. Leave Wednesday. (*Holds up a handful of bills.*) Would you look at this crap? Visa, American Express, Discover… They're <u>killing</u> me!

MICHELE: So, don't use them.

EDDIE: Are you kidding?

MICHELE: Plastic, my beloved, will drive you crazy.

EDDIE: Hah!

MICHELE: Shrivel your gonads, too. Which in your case would be a catastrophe. It's a proven fact. (*She pats his cheek, heads for stage right exit.*) Don't go away. I brought you a present, too.

EDDIE: Shrivel my… What do you mean, talking like that?

MICHELE: (*Exiting.*) It's no worse than, "My husband's out of town this weekend." A married woman!

EDDIE: So? That's different. (*At table.*) Pumpkin seeds? Malted yogurt balls? What <u>is</u> this garbage?

MICHELE: (*Off.*) I had to eat something.

EDDIE: What was wrong with the food in the freezer?

MICHELE: (*Off.*) Hah!

EDDIE: (*On his way to the climbing wall.*) I don't listen, you don't read labels. It's all high carb or protein, and low fat.

MICHELE: (*Off.*) Right. Factory made, with a shelf life of pig iron. (*Entering.*) Plus you nuke it which everybody <u>knows</u> destroys all the vitamins and natural goodness—

EDDIE: (*As he does a chin-up.*) Yipes! Look, Ma! No vitamins.

MICHELE: I am <u>thinking</u> of your well-being.

EDDIE: My well-being's healthy as a horse, thank you very much.

MICHELE: Oh, yeah. Now I remember. (*Exits to bedrooms.*) The whole concept's decadent. Jeez, can't you do <u>any</u>thing for yourself? Is it that hard to cook a meal?

EDDIE: You know I don't cook. I'm a salesman, not a housewife.

MICHELE: (*Off.*) Big deal. Just what the world needs. More computers.

EDDIE: Newer, bigger, smaller, faster, and I'm just the boy to peddle them. (*Going to boxes.*) What's in the boxes?

MICHELE: (*Returning with present.*) Goodwill goodies for my new place, when I find it.

EDDIE: Glad to see you spared no expense. (*Holds up something that looks real used.*) Used but cheap.

MICHELE: They're good enough for who they're for. Which reminds me. Cerise called.

EDDIE: Really? I talked to her just before I got on the plane.

MICHELE: Checking up on <u>me</u>, most likely. Tiffany called, too.

EDDIE: Yeah, yeah.

MICHELE: (*Hands him a present.*) She said you had her number. Go on. Open it. Which I don't doubt for one second.

EDDIE: (*Feels present, which is oddly shaped.*) What is it? A bone?

MICHELE: You'll see.

EDDIE: (*Opening present.*) Any calls on the machine?

MICHELE: I don't know. I just walked in the door myself.

(*EDDIE hits the play button.*)

MACHINE: You have...one...message.

MICHELE: I wonder what <u>her</u> name is.

EDDIE: Shhh!

MACHINE: Harvey, Eddie. Don't say I didn't warn you, but you just lost your shirt on that Hopper Brown Bag deal—

EDDIE: Crap!

MACHINE: —you liked so much, and you're going to have to come up with forty thousand by the 10th. Give me a call Monday and we can talk. Sometimes shit happens, pal.

EDDIE: Damn!

MICHELE: Rats!

EDDIE: The bastards! The rotten, conniving bastards! What do you mean, rats? You been talking to Harvey?

MICHELE: Only about Joni. I was hoping it was my friend, Saturn, is all.

EDDIE: Oh. (*Relieved, he finishes unwrapping the present.*) Saturn, huh? The car or the planet? (*He stares at a wooden relaxer that's built somewhat like a dumb bell.*)

MICHELE: A relaxer. Made by an Indian tribe in Guatemala. And a guy I roomed with for a while down there.

EDDIE: Wouldn't want to be too lonely too long, would you.

MICHELE: Oh, my. Is the pot calling the kettle black? We were friends, okay?

EDDIE: Whatever you say. So anyway, this Saturn guy helped the Indians—

MICHELE: Saturn was my roommate. An Indian made the relaxer. His mother was kind of a free spirit, I take it.

EDDIE: The Indian's mother was a free spirit?

MICHELE: No, the Indian's mother was an Indian. Saturn's mother was the free spirit.

EDDIE: Why am I not surprised? And his father?

MICHELE: I don't know. I don't think they get along.

EDDIE: (*A touch of bitterness.*) Maybe he's a barber.

MICHELE: More like old money, I think, but Saturn doesn't talk about him.

EDDIE: He must have said <u>something</u>.

MICHELE: Just...little things. He runs deeper than he lets on.

EDDIE: Don't we all. (*Holds up relaxer.*) What do I do with it?

MICHELE: You stick it... Oh, never mind. Here. Give me your coat.

(*EDDIE removes his jacket and gives it to MICHELE, who carelessly tosses it to one side. EDDIE hurriedly retrieves it and carefully drapes it on the back of a chair.*)

EDDIE: Hey! Careful! That's an Armani you're treating like a rag.

MICHELE: Is that a status symbol or something?

EDDIE: At fifteen hundred bucks, you'd better believe it.

MICHELE: Fifteen hundred!... That's obscene. Sit.

EDDIE: It's a necessity. This isn't Lubbock.

MICHELE: More's the pity.

EDDIE: Lubbock's where they load the turnip truck. And if you like it that much, why don't you go back?

MICHELE: It's a coat. A lousy coat. Sit, I said. (*MICHELE positions him where she can work on his back.*) Now relax. (*After a moment, sings as she works.*)
Shine on, shine on, harvest moon,
Up in the sky.
I ain't had no lovin'
Since January, February, June or July...

EDDIE: Boy. Haven't heard *that* for a while.

MICHELE: Bring back old times?

EDDIE: You bet. (*A play for her.*) Mmm. Feels good. Should I take off my shirt?

MICHELE: (*Swats him playfully.*) That's not the old times I was thinking of. (*To change the subject.*) So you're doing stocks and stuff. And Harvey's your broker?

EDDIE: Takes real good care of me, too.

MICHELE: He should take real good care of his daughter.

EDDIE: He's probably doing the best he can.

MICHELE: Did you know he wanted her to have an abortion?

EDDIE: Harvey? You sure about that?

MICHELE: According to Joni.

EDDIE: Whatever, he's helped me make a bundle.

MICHELE: "Lost your shirt" is making a bundle? I can't even imagine losing forty thousand dollars.

EDDIE: Wasn't his idea. Either way, win a few, lose a few. I'll make it back. (*Doesn't want to talk about it.*) How were your folks?

MICHELE: But forty thousand...

EDDIE: I said, how were your folks?

MICHELE: (*Her turn to go along.*) Same as ever. Daddy tyrannical, as usual, doing deals and making money. He asked about you. Still thinks I was a fool for leaving you.

EDDIE: I'll bet your mother doesn't.

MICHELE: You'd win, too. Anyway, I mostly saw his backside on the way out the door, except for Saturday night when he tore himself away long enough to take Mama and me to dinner. Mama cowed, as usual, and bored stiff.

EDDIE: That's hardly news. What your mother needs is a hobby.

MICHELE: What she needs is a life.

EDDIE: What she <u>needs</u> is to put a plug in the jug. Some people just don't know when they've got it good.

MICHELE: And you do, I suppose.

EDDIE: You're durn tootin'. I'll pull down three hundred in commissions this year, and fifty more with my investments.

MICHELE: After that Brown Bag stuff?

EDDIE: So I write it off. You gotta rub it in?

MICHELE: Sorry. Still, that's a far cry from our tuna fish casserole and hamburger helper days.

EDDIE: Onward and upward. See what you're missing?

MICHELE: Missing? I'd go crazy. See what I <u>escaped.</u>

EDDIE: Have it your way. That about it?

MICHELE: Just relax, okay?

EDDIE: I <u>am</u> relaxed.

MICHELE: Oh, yeah? (*She digs.*) What's this?

EDDIE: Hey! (*Escaping.*) Damn! Wha'd'ya think you're?—

MICHELE: Knots. That's not relaxed.

EDDIE: It's my back, and I say—

MICHELE: You're as bad as Daddy.

EDDIE: Who's doing a hell of a lot better than <u>my</u> father ever did.

MICHELE: He's a mess. A 61 year old—

EDDIE: The man makes five, six hundred grand a year. You should be such a mess.

MICHELE: Money isn't everything.

EDDIE: It beats hell out of tuna fish casseroles. Or rice and beans, for that matter. How much did you make in Guatemala?

MICHELE: Enough to live on. Plus two hundred a month in a savings account for when I got out.

EDDIE: Forty-eight hundred for two years? Holy megabucks! Move over world!

MICHELE: A Single Step is a labor of love. Money isn't the point.

EDDIE: Wrong, Mick. Money's the <u>only</u> point.

MICHELE: If you're a leech. What ever happened to putting in a little more than you take out?

EDDIE: (*Coldly retaliating.*) I've done that a time or ten.

MICHELE: (*Hurt.*) You have to throw it in my face? Brag about it? All right! You want to make me feel bad, you succeeded. Happy?

EDDIE: No more than I was when you walked out. What was Prince Charming's name?

MICHELE: Dylan was a friend I could talk to.

EDDIE: I was your husband. You could have talked to me.

MICHELE: I tried. You were too busy, too angry with Mr. Stoner, to listen.

EDDIE: You're damned right I was angry. The son of a bitch called me a flunky in front of the whole office. And the worst part is, he was right!

MICHELE: This is so silly!

EDDIE: Silly, hell. Four years in the same stupid job, going nowhere. No wonder you ran off to nursing school. Someone in the family had to make a decent living.

MICHELE: That's <u>not</u> why... At the time, you thought it was a great idea. You encouraged me.

EDDIE: I didn't encourage you to stick your nose in a book and forget I existed.

MICHELE: I didn't. And you didn't have to...screw...Stoner's wife.

EDDIE: Two birds with one stone. Paid back Stoner, and what the hell, I sure wasn't getting any at home.

MICHELE: That's an obscene lie!

EDDIE: "Not tonight, Eddie. I have to study. I'm too tired."

MICHELE: And that was it? Sex?

EDDIE: Okay, okay. I take it back.

MICHELE: That's not... take-backable! I thought I'd <u>die</u> when I divorced you!

EDDIE: Then why did you?

MICHELE: You want their names? (*From tears to anger.*) Sharing you with every woman you could lay your hands on wasn't my idea of the storybook marriage.

EDDIE: It wasn't every, and they weren't important. You were the only one I loved...who counted.

MICHELE: You're darn right I counted. All six, plus probably a few I missed.

EDDIE: You exaggerate. Wildly.

MICHELE: You still don't get it, do you? One would have been too many. Even one.

EDDIE: They didn't <u>matter</u>, damn it!

MICHELE: They did! A whole marriage worth!

EDDIE: Okay. I'm the bad guy. Please, <u>please</u>...

MICHELE: No! None of your guilty little boy crap. We had something wonderful, Eddie! And all of a sudden you were this new person I didn't even know, screwing every woman you could get your hands on—

EDDIE: Will you quit saying that? I told you—

MICHELE: If the shoe fits—

EDDIE: The shoe doesn't fit, because it's not true!

MICHELE: It's close enough, plus hell bent on wheeling your way to the top of the pile. Anything you wanted, any time you wanted it. Are you <u>ever</u> going to give back more than you've been given?

EDDIE: I wasn't <u>given</u>. I started with nothing as you damn well know. I worked hard and took risks. I <u>earned</u>.

MICHELE: Boy! Horace Algernon himself.

EDDIE: Horatio Alger, for crying out loud.

MICHELE: Whatever. I'm proud of you. Proud.

EDDIE: Gimme a break. I gave at the office.

MICHELE: I'm sure.

EDDIE: Through the nose. They call them taxes which, among other things, pay all that foreign aid to support the peasant hordes you love so much.

MICHELE: And the peasant hordes are grateful. <u>Eternally</u> grateful!

EDDIE: (*On the verge of attacking, but backs off.*) Look. It's been almost four years. Can we cut each other a little slack?

MICHELE: No! Because you haven't seen how desperately they live, and then come back here to stores with more food for <u>dogs</u> than the people I worked with even know how to dream about for themselves, and alarm systems and answering machines and fifteen hundred dollar arm and hammer coats and—

EDDIE: <u>Armani.</u>

MICHELE: What<u>ev</u>er, and nobody gives a damn.

EDDIE: Says you. (*A beat. Gently.*) I didn't write the rules, Mick. I just play the game, try to make a living and get ahead, same as everybody else.

MICHELE: They aren't rules. They're choices! (*Dropping it with an effort.*) Oh, never mind... Never mind...

EDDIE: Okay, they're choices, and it's either make them or get lost in the dust. But that still doesn't make me a monster.

MICHELE: I suppose not... (*Looks at self in a mirror.*) Gaawd! Look at me. Miss Sniffle. Miss Save-the-World. I swore I was <u>not</u> going to pull any of this culture shock crap.

EDDIE: Wouldn't be you.

MICHELE: That's what Daddy says.

(*MICHELE is interrupted by the doorbell. EDDIE freezes, glances at his watch. He and MICHELE whisper loudly.*)

EDDIE: Damn! That'll be Sandy. She lives upstairs. Yell "Just a minute."

MICHELE: Are you?...

EDDIE: She's always bugging me.

MICHELE: You're using me!

EDDIE: Just do it, okay? Please?

MICHELE: Oh... (*Calls out.*) Just a minute!

EDDIE: (*Whispers.*) "Be right there."

MICHELE: How'd you fight them off before I got here? (*EDDIE gestures wildly.*) I'll be right there!

EDDIE: (*Heads for stage right exit.*) I'll be in the shower. Tell her I'll call her.

MICHELE: Anything else? Like you've got a hot date with Debbie?

EDDIE: You do, and you're outa here <u>tonight</u>.

MICHELE: You wouldn't—

EDDIE: Try me. You're not my wife, and I don't have to be nice to you.

MICHELE: You weren't nice to me when I <u>was</u> your—

(*EDDIE raises a warning finger. Points to the door.*)

MICHELE: Coming!

(*EDDIE smiles, gives her an after-you-Alphonse gesture, and exits.*)

MICHELE: (*Heading for door in a stage whisper.*) You're a bum, Eddie. You hear me?

(*MICHELE opens the door for CERISE. CERISE is in her late twenties, not necessarily particularly pretty, but expensively dressed and made up. Insecure and dependent on men, she is also a smart businesswoman and an archly condescending daughter of a wealthy man.*)

MICHELE: Hi. May I help you?

(*CERISE is relieved to find MICHELE so unglamorous. Still, however terrified of and threatened by her, she takes control with a condescending, even bubbly, friendliness.*)

CERISE: You must be Michele.

MICHELE: That's right. And you?—

CERISE: I'm Cerise.

(*MICHELE's knees turn to jelly, but she recovers quickly and puts on a good face.*)

MICHELE: Oh...

CERISE: May I come in? Thanks.

MICHELE: Be my guest. (*An awkward beat.*) So we meet at last.

CERISE: Yes. Eddie's told me so much about you, I feel I know you already. He is here, isn't he?

MICHELE: Yes, but I'm afraid he's—

(*CERISE has noted Michele's garage sale goodies, and leaves no doubt that she considers them trash.*)

CERISE: Isn't he wonderful?

MICHELE: (*Closing the door.*) That's not exactly how I'd put it.

CERISE: Of course. He told me all about you being in Mexico working with the natives.

MICHELE: Guatemala. I was—

CERISE: Whatever. I think that's so wonderful! I'm a naturally giving person, but brrrr, I mean, living in a jungle just wouldn't fit my lifestyle.

MICHELE: Actually, I was in the mountains.

CERISE: Really. I love the mountains, of course. Where else would one ski? (*A beat.*) But I don't believe Mexicans ski, do they?

MICHELE: I wouldn't know. I was too busy running a women's clinic... In Guatemala.

CERISE: Of course. Eddie said you were a nurse or something. Still, with all those snakes and the people so primitive... Well where would you shop? Is that your car in Eddie's visitor space?

MICHELE: (*Starting to get dangerously sore.*) Kind of ratty, right?

CERISE: Oh, no! Not that...exactly...

MICHELE: Not like yours. I'll bet you have a really neat car, with your lifestyle and all.

CERISE: A 450 SL sports model. I wanted a Mitsubishi like Eddie's, but Daddy said the Mercedes was more businesslike. At least it's red.

MICHELE: Imagine that! Just like your name!

CERISE: Of course. Red's my favorite color. Luckily, I'm an autumn.

MICHELE: That's luck if I've ever heard it.

(*CERISE picks up on MICHELE's tone and responds with a haughty coolness reserved for social inferiors who challenge her.*)

CERISE: Yes. And now, if you don't mind, I'd like to see Eddie for a moment?...

MICHELE: Fine with me. (*The devil makes her do it.*) You'll find him in the shower.

CERISE: I beg your pardon?

MICHELE: Practically ran in there the minute he came in the door. He had a bad day.

CERISE: Really? I spoke to him before his flight, and he was in wonderful spirits.

MICHELE: A bad flight, then. Came rolling in here and the first thing he tells me— hardly even said hello— was he had this sore on his yeah-yeah.

CERISE: You mean, on... But how would he get?...

MICHELE: Who knows? Anyway, it was just a little bitty red spot, so teensy I had to look real close to see it.

CERISE: He showed you?—

MICHELE: Well, it isn't like I hadn't seen it before.

CERISE: Of course, but...

MICHELE: Oh! Silly me! Not his you-know-what. I've seen it before. I mean almost every day for years and years.

CERISE: Well, sure!

MICHELE: And just because we used to be married doesn't mean we can't be friends, and to see that poor, sad little shriveled up thing with a sore on it...

CERISE: Please...

MICHELE: I mean, if I can't put our differences behind me and support him in his hour of need...

CERISE: But you should! That's so...caring?...

MICHELE: Oh, no more than Eddie would be. He'd want to see if I had—

(*The phone interrupts her.*)

MICHELE: 'Scuse me... (*Answering phone.*) Hello?... Saturn! Where are you? When'd you?— But a taxi would cost a fortune! Hold a sec, okay? (*Hand over phone, to CERISE.*) It's this friend I roomed with in Guatemala. Poor guy is totally broke, but he has these great tattoos, and rings everywhere, and this funky hair... (*A bright idea.*) Golly! Maybe you?... I told Eddie I'd go with him to the Doc-in-a-Shop on our way to dinner, and I don't see how I can get to the airport, so maybe if you don't have anything to do you could pick him up?

CERISE: Well, actually...

MICHELE: I mean, it's not like he's weird, really. Just seriously funky, you know?

CERISE: I don't know...

MICHELE: I'm sure you'd like him. He's a very sweet guy once you get used to the artwork and hardware.

CERISE: (*Edging toward door and escape.*) I'm sure, but I have a... this appointment, so I just dropped by to say hello, and I...I have to change and eat a sandwich or something, you know, and well...

MICHELE: Saturn would love to meet—

CERISE: So if you'd just tell Eddie I came by?... And we can talk tomorrow?

MICHELE: (*Laughing as CERISE exits.*) You still there, Saturn?... Eddie's future wife, poor thing. Where are you? ... Delta, huh? Got it. You still going to Charlie's? ... Oh, we'll find it. He still have that clunker you can use? (*EDDIE, wearing a robe, pokes his head into the room.*) Great! ... Yeah, it'll take me a while 'cause it's pretty far and I've only been there once, so... Right. See you out front, then.

EDDIE: (*Entering cautiously.*) She gone?

MICHELE: In a cloud of dust. Said to tell you she'd just dropped by to say hello.

EDDIE: Sure. Who was on the phone?

MICHELE: Saturn. He's at the airport. I told him I'd pick him up.

EDDIE: I thought we were going to eat together.

MICHELE: I'll munch on something in the car. (*Exiting to kitchen.*) 'Nother time, okay? We've got the whole weekend.

EDDIE: Stood up by my own ex-wife. That's a hell of a note. (*Suddenly suspicious.*) You coming back?

MICHELE: (*Off.*) Yup. After I take him to a friend's. You think I'd bring him here?

EDDIE: The thought occurred.

MICHELE: (*Entering with fruit, graham crackers, etc.*) And drive all three of us crazy?

EDDIE: Too bad. You could share a sleeping bag. Happy campers, both.

MICHELE: Give it up, okay? Read my lips. We are not lovers.

EDDIE: Just curious.

MICHELE: Just pushy. Unlike some whose name I won't mention, I don't sleep with just anybody.

EDDIE: What's that supposed to mean?

MICHELE: Don't ask stupid questions.

EDDIE: Then don't jump to stupid conclusions. Because neither do I.

MICHELE: (*Packing a plastic bag with food.*) Right. Let's see. Debbie, Tiffany, probably Sandy, and God knows who else in addition to Cerise, of course. That sounds like anybody to me.

EDDIE: Hey! These are class ladies.

MICHELE: They're class ditzes. Including Cerise.

EDDIE: Really? And how would you know?

MICHELE: I've talked to her, remember, and she has the personality of a frozen quiche. She's the one you picked to replace me?

EDDIE: Why not? I love her deeply. She's sharp, she's hip, she—

MICHELE: Lets you wrap her around your little finger?

EDDIE: Let's just say she doesn't have to wear the pants in the family.

MICHELE: That qualifies her, okay.

EDDIE: Plus, she's one of her father's top leasing agents.

MICHELE: One of her father's .... My, my. And there you have it, don't you. Eddie Fortman the gold digger.

EDDIE: Her pedigree, my drive. A tried and true tradition, Green Eyes.

MICHELE: Green eyes, my... (*A sigh of resignation.*) Yeah. I guess so. You're a jerk, Eddie. A jerk and a two-timing son of a bitch, but you aren't...easy to get over.

EDDIE: (*Indicating food in bag.*) You call that supper?

MICHELE: I'm the best deal you ever had. Too bad you blew it. Too bad for both of us. West on the freeway and follow the signs, right?

EDDIE: Right. Watch for speed traps when you get inside the airport. They lie in wait there.

MICHELE: Thanks. (*Pausing at door before exiting.*) Oh, yeah. She's gullible, too. Happy days! (*She exits.*)

EDDIE: Drive careful! (*He heads for the telephone.*) <u>Best</u> deal? Maybe you were, <u>but</u>... (*Dials.*) Debbie. Eddie. My ex just left for the airport to pick up a friend. You up for a little early? ... Mmm. ... Right. You bet. I'm starved. Anything good to eat there? ...Mmm. With bells on.

SCENE TWO

Approximately 8:00 p.m. Monday, three days later. Eddie's mail is gone. The cat figurine and the fruit basket, with bananas, remains. The apartment has been neatened. EDDIE, alone, works on his computer.

EDDIE: Microsoft. Can't sell Microsoft. Be stupid...

(*The doorbell rings.*)

EDDIE: It's open!

(*The door opens to reveal CERISE, who is dressed casually in skirt and blouse, and carries a large purse. She's on edge, a little too bright.*)

CERISE: Hi, Eddie.

EDDIE: Hey, Babe...

CERISE: (*Closing door behind her.*) Sorry I'm late. What are you doing?

EDDIE: Trying to figure out how to cover that forty thousand if I have to. You eat yet?

CERISE: Way too much finger food. I'm stuffed.

EDDIE: Good. (*Up from computer.*) Well, don't just stand there. Come see me.

CERISE: Okay...

EDDIE: Are you all right?

CERISE: (*Laying purse on table, and going to him.*) Sure! I can't believe it's almost eight, is all.

EDDIE: I expected you earlier.

CERISE: I know, but Mr. Anton and Johnny showed up for cocktail hour, and the time got away.

EDDIE: Who's Johnny?

CERISE: A new "aide." It turned out to be kind of fun. I did my Marilyn, and even Daddy laughed.

EDDIE: I'm sure everyone had a wonderful time.

CERISE: Don't <u>be</u> that way. Johnnie is Mr. Anton's latest professional pretty boy, and I wouldn't touch him with a ten foot pole. Even if he'd let me.

EDDIE: But you hung around half the night.

CERISE: It's only eight. I changed and got over here as soon as Daddy let me go. Oh! (*She turns to show off her—red—earrings.*) Well?

EDDIE: They look great. You like 'em?

CERISE: (*Goes to him.*) They're wonderful. (*Embracing him.*) Thank you.

EDDIE: I like buying presents for my baby, making her feel good...

CERISE: Awww, Eddie... (*The embrace becomes an intense kiss. At kiss's end...*) Wow!

EDDIE: (*Strokes her breast.*) Anybody ever tell you how smart and beautiful you are?

CERISE: (*Stopping him.*) Don't, Eddie. What if Michele?—

EDDIE: She's at the clinic tonight. All night.

CERISE: Still, I mean... You know how I feel about that.

EDDIE: I just want to make you happy, baby.

CERISE: I know, and I want to, but... (*She breaks away from him and goes to her purse, extracts an envelope and thrusts it at him.*) Here.

EDDIE: What's this?

CERISE: The proposal you asked about.

EDDIE: (*Opens envelope.*) Hey! That's my girl! Are you something or what? (*Scanning contents.*) He gave you this?

CERISE: Not exactly. It's from one of his personal files that I'm not supposed to have the password for.

EDDIE: (*Finding what he wants.*) He and Anton are merging, all right. This is stone cold?

CERISE: Almost, I'm told.

EDDIE: What do you mean, almost?

CERISE: Mr. Anton hasn't signed off on it yet.

EDDIE: He will.

CERISE: Probably, but Daddy's fingers are still crossed.

EDDIE: He will, damn it! He has to!

CERISE: I suppose, but even if he does... (*A deep breath.*) I don't want you to buy it.

EDDIE: What?

CERISE: I don't want you to buy it.

EDDIE: Why in the hell not? That stock's going to double, maybe even triple—

CERISE: It's illegal, to begin with, and ...unethical.

EDDIE: Unethic... Now there's a good one. I guarantee your father's buddies have been buying Wade Powers Inc. illegally, and unethically, for a couple of weeks.

CERISE: I know that, and—

EDDIE: So this boy's joinin' the game, and spreading the wealth while the spreadin's good.

CERISE: —and I'm glad you have aspirations, but Daddy wants it kept secret, and if he thinks I...

EDDIE: He won't know I've bought it, so he won't think anything.

CERISE: I'm serious about this, Eddie.

EDDIE: Great. Then you'll no doubt have a forty thousand dollar ethic handy to bail me out.

CERISE: You have assets you can sell.

EDDIE: And gut my portfolio? No way. (*Running his con.*) This'll put me back in the black, Baby, maybe even over the magic number. And you know what that means.

CERISE: You mean that?

EDDIE: So close I can taste it. Mr. and Mrs. Edward R. Fortman.

CERISE: Oh, Eddie! (*An impetuous kiss, but then a pull back.*) Still...

EDDIE: Ba-abyy...

CERISE: I just wish there was another way.

EDDIE: It's worked for your father and his friends. Many times.

CERISE: That doesn't make it right.

EDDIE: You're saying he's one of the bad guys?

CERISE: No, but there are better ways. I signed a new client for three floors last week. No strings, no tricks. We'll make money, they'll be happy.

EDDIE: What is this? A test?

CERISE: Yes. I want to marry you. Not a magic number.

EDDIE: (*A beat. chastened.*) You know what? You're right.

CERISE: Forty thousand is nothing. We can make that back, and more.

EDDIE: We, huh?

CERISE: You'll see. I promise.

EDDIE: What can I say? No strings, no tricks... (*He tears the documents in half, and tosses them aside.*) Whatever makes my baby happy.

CERISE: Oh, Eddie, I love you so much!

EDDIE: Yeahhh... (*A passionate kiss. This time, when EDDIE touches her breast, she doesn't stop him. When the kiss ends...*) You think we ought to drink a toast or something?

CERISE: Mmm-hmmmm...

EDDIE: Wait here... (*Starts out, stops.*) You won't go away?

CERISE: Not in a million years. (*EDDIE exits.*)

EDDIE: (*Off. Sings.*)
Shine on, shine on harvest moon,
Up in the sky,
I ain't had no lovin' since...

(*Alone, CERISE hugs herself and spins with delight. She removes her shoes and wriggles out of her hose, which she dangles impishly from two fingers as EDDIE reenters with an open bottle of wine and two glasses.*)

EDDIE: Oh, ohhh...

CERISE: See? I didn't go away...

EDDIE: (*Sets down wine and glasses.*) Ba-abyyy...

CERISE: (*Drapes her hose over his shoulder and starts to undo his shirt buttons.*) Mr. ...and ... Mrs. ... Edward...R...Fortman...

EDDIE: You and me, Cerise. Just the two of us...

CERISE: Oh, Eddie!....

(*CERISE kisses EDDIE fiercely. Just as the kiss is well underway, the doorbell rings. EDDIE and CERISE freeze. They speak in urgent whispers.*)

EDDIE: Damn!

CERISE: Nooo... (*The doorbell rings again.*) What do we do—

JONI: (*Off.*) Aunt Michele? Is this the right place? It's me. Joni.

CERISE: Who's Joni?

EDDIE: Michele's niece... How did she?—

JONI: (*Off.*) Are you there, Aunt Michele? Uncle Eddie?

EDDIE: I knew I never should have let Mick—

JONI: You gotta let me in! I'm gonna be... Please?...

(*CERISE breaks from EDDIE, stares fearfully at the door.*)

CERISE: She did this, didn't she!

EDDIE: (*Starts for door.*) I have no idea, but we'll soon find out.

CERISE: Don't answer it! (*Runs to EDDIE, grabs her hose, then calls.*) He'll be right there.

EDDIE: (*Making himself presentable.*) Just a minute. I'm on my way...

(*While CERISE frantically stuffs her hose in her purse and puts on her shoes, EDDIE goes to and opens the door for JONI CANTRELL. JONI is sixteen, and very, very pregnant.*)

JONI: Hi, Uncle Eddie. Remember me? I guess I was just a little kid the last time you saw me.

EDDIE: Sure, but...

JONI: (*Nervous, so her sentences tend to run together.*) Gollee, it's good to see you. But this complex is so big I thought I'd never find your apartment. Is Aunt Michele here?

EDDIE: No. She's working tonight.

JONI: I know, but she said she'd meet me here. Can I come in? Please?

EDDIE: (*Unsure, but stands a little aside.*) Well, I was...

(*JONI enters, carrying an overnight bag and BUNNY, an old and tattered stuffed rabbit, and goes immediately to a chair.*)

JONI: Thanks. I've got to sit down... (*Sees CERISE.*) Oh. Hi. Gee, did I interrupt?—

CERISE: No, we were just...talking...

JONI: (*To EDDIE.*) I didn't know you had company.

EDDIE: Maybe if you'd called first...

JONI: I only had forty cents. I'm sorry, Uncle Eddie.

EDDIE: Well, don't cry. It's not the end of the world.

JONI: But you don't know! I'm pregnant!

EDDIE: Really!

JONI: It's not funny!

CERISE: She's just a kid, Eddie.

EDDIE: More like two kids, you ask me.

CERISE: (*Daggers to EDDIE.*) That was uncalled for. (*To JONI.*) But we don't understand. Why aren't you with your husband?

JONI: I don't have one.

CERISE: Oh, dear. You poor—

JONI: And my father just kicked me out, so—-

EDDIE: He what!?

JONI: Kicked me...

EDDIE: He can't do that!

JONI: Well, he did.

CERISE: But that's terrible!

JONI: So I called the shelter since I didn't have any money for a cab and Aunt Michele said I could walk here since it was only two blocks and she would pick me up. Could I have a glass of water, please?

CERISE: Sure, honey. Eddie'll... (*Gestures toward kitchen. EDDIE throws up his hands in disgust and exits.*) What about your mother? Didn't she say anything?

JONI: Mama died six years ago. In a car wreck.

CERISE: Oh, you poor kid. I'm so sorry. Still, your father must've known a long time ago.

JONI: Yeah, but I didn't tell anybody and kept out of sight, so he let me stay.

CERISE: Why'd he kick you out now?

JONI: Because I said I'm going back when school opens again Monday even if he doesn't want me to. (*EDDIE returns with water.*) Man, I've never seen him so pissed. Thanks. (*JONI drinks.*) I was really thirsty. Anyway, what's the big deal? People get pregnant all the time, don't they?

EDDIE: People hold up banks all the time, too.

JONI: Yeah?...

EDDIE: I'd be pissed, too. And so would Alison. Were you crazy?

CERISE: Come on, Eddie...

EDDIE: Come on, Eddie, hell. She's gonna have a baby!

JONI: What'd you <u>want</u> me to do? Kill it?

EDDIE: I didn't <u>want</u> you to do anything.

CERISE: (*To JONI.*) Don't be talking that way.

JONI: How am I supposed to talk? I mean, he sounds just like my father. You think I <u>like</u> being pregnant? You think I don't know how <u>stupid</u> I was? That I did it on purpose so I could... that I <u>want</u> to be... (*Clutches abdomen and winces.*) I'm so scared...

CERISE: (*Going to her.*) Now see what you've done?

EDDIE: Me! I haven't even <u>seen</u> her. For years!

CERISE: She can't help it if she's pregnant.

EDDIE: Can't help!... It's not like being struck by lightning. Pregnancy is participatory.

CERISE: Don't listen to him. He's just a grouchy old bear. Everything's going to be all right.

JONI: I want Michele! I just wish she'd hurry and—

(*The doorbell rings.*)

CERISE: There she is, now—

EDDIE: It's open!

(The door opens and SATURN enters. SATURN is weirdly dressed and coiffed, and richly adorned with hardware and tattoos. Contrary to initial impressions, though, he is not a total freak; he just marches, very honestly, to his own very different drumbeat.)

SATURN: Yo, crew! *(A take.)* Hey! The famous Eddie! *(Puts out a hand to shake.)* Heard a lot about you man.

EDDIE: *(Ignores SATURN's hand.)* Who in the hell are you?

SATURN: Me? I'm Saturn.

EDDIE: Ah! An answer at last. The planet! Rings and all!

SATURN: *(To CERISE.)* Did I miss something here?

EDDIE: 'Cause he's definitely in orbit. I suppose you're looking for Michele, too.

SATURN: Not really. Are you?

EDDIE: You betcha. Nothing would please me more than to see her walk through that door right now.

CERISE: Calm down, Eddie.

EDDIE: Calm down? Whose side are you on, anyway?

CERISE: Yours. Because you're upsetting her, and—

EDDIE: I'm upsetting <u>her</u>?

CERISE: Yes, and she's liable to have her baby right here if you don't calm down.

JONI: Oh no!

EDDIE: She'd better not.

JONI: I can't! Not here!...

EDDIE: *(To JONI.)* You'd better not! You hear me? Don't you <u>dare</u>—

JONI: I want Mich-elllle....

(SATURN has made his way to the table and helped himself to two bananas, one of which he partially peels immediately. The other he stashes in a shirt pocket or elsewhere for action as indicated in dialogue. On the way to JONI, he nearly collides with EDDIE.)

SATURN: 'Scuse me, man.

EDDIE: Feeding time a little late at the zoo tonight?

SATURN: How'd you guess? *(The old monkey with the banana bit, which CERISE thinks is funny.)* Oof-oof-oof-oof... *(Seriously to JONI.)* You must be Joni, right?

JONI: Yes

SATURN: Well, hold tight, Joni, 'cause Michele will be along in a minute. Her car broke down and a wrecker's towing her in. Soon as they get here, we're on our way to the shelter.

JONI: She's really coming?

SATURN: Any minute now. *(Offers her the banana.)* You want a banana?

JONI: No thank you.

SATURN: Loaded with potassium.

JONI: I don't <u>like</u> bananas.

SATURN: To each his own. I mean, hey! I don't like dead cow parts. (*Offering the banana to EDDIE as JONI gags and clutches her abdomen.*) What about you, man? Real good for stress.

EDDIE: Her car broke down where?

SATURN: Somewhere between here and the shelter, must be. (*He notes the climbing exercise paraphernalia and the enlarged photo.*) Whoa! You a rock climber?

EDDIE: I'm learning.

SATURN: Superior! Small world, man!

EDDIE: You're a climber?

SATURN: When there's a rock, and when I'm in the mood. (*Indicates rock face poster.*) Old Flatface, right?

EDDIE: How did you know that?

SATURN: It's on the tour. You climb it yet?

EDDIE: I suppose you have.

SATURN: (*Heads for the wall.*) A few hundred feet of it four or five years ago. Too much rock for me.

EDDIE: I can beat it.

SATURN: You don't "beat" a rock, man. You can climb it, but you can't "beat" it.

EDDIE: Michele didn't tell me you were a climber.

SATURN: Must not've mentioned it. Neat lady, huh?

JONI: I think she is.

EDDIE: (*To JONI.*) Haven't been around her much, recently, have you.

JONI: She sure stood up to my father. For all the good it did. (*To CERISE.*) May I use the restroom?

    (*SATURN tests a foothold, and climbs. He peels and eats banana, hangs from wall in various positions. CERISE helps JONI stand.*)

CERISE: Sure. Come on...

JONI: That water, you know..

SATURN: (*To EDDIE.*) Brings back old times.

CERISE: I know. I hated that tiny bladder business.

JONI: You have a baby!?

CERISE: (*Escorting JONI off.*) <u>Had</u>. A little girl.

EDDIE: You what?

SATURN: Yup, call me a climbing fool.

CERISE: (*On her way out, to JONI.*) Ten years ago. My daddy made me give it up for adoption.

EDDIE: You never told me... (*CERISE and JONI are gone. To SATURN.*) She never told me she'd had a baby.

SATURN: Maybe she forgot.

EDDIE: Having a baby isn't something you forget!

SATURN: You ever ask her?

EDDIE: Of course not.

SATURN: There you have it. This is so cool! I never knew anybody who had his own climbing wall.

EDDIE: It isn't <u>that</u> great...

SATURN: A wall's a wall. I'm impressed, man.

   (*There's a knock on the door.*)

MICHELE: (*Off.*) Eddie? (*The door bursts open as MICHELE enters. Sees EDDIE only.*) Thank God you're here. Where's Joni?

SATURN: (*Still on wall.*) She had to go.

MICHELE: (*Spins to see SATURN.*) Go? She couldn't have! Where?

SATURN: (*Points with partially peeled banana.*) To the can. (*The old monkey bit again.*) Oof-oof-oof-oof.

MICHELE: It's not funny, Saturn. (*To EDDIE.*) Is she all right?

EDDIE: Oh, <u>she's</u> fine. But I've got a major problem.

MICHELE: Like?...

EDDIE: This is not a maternity ward!

MICHELE: I get the point.

EDDIE: It's my apartment. I don't need babies being born—

MICHELE: They're not.

EDDIE: They could be! She could pop any second, and I want her out of here before she does.

MICHELE: As soon as I—

EDDIE: And you and your planet, too. You sign that lease yet?

MICHELE: This afternoon. I'll be gone by the time you come home from Vermont.

EDDIE: You'd better be. Come next Sunday, I want to walk through this door and find the place mine again. (*CERISE enters.*) Where is she?

CERISE: Give her a minute, huh? (*To MICHELE.*) Will she be glad to see you! The poor kid's a wreck.

MICHELE: (*To EDDIE.*) That's what I was trying to tell you. Do you have fifty dollars?

EDDIE: I'm supposed to pay to get her—

MICHELE: The wrecker! He wants sixty dollars, cash only. All I have is ten—

EDDIE: Tough luck.

MICHELE: He'll take my car to the pound if I don't pay him, and if he does... I'm warning you, Eddie...

EDDIE: (*Pulls out wallet.*) Okay. Okay! Six. I have six dollars. I use credit cards! You know that.

MICHELE: Saturn!

SATURN: Don't look at me. Paint and a futon cleaned me out. What about Joni?

MICHELE: She'd have taken a cab if she had any.

   (*Horn blows offstage.*)

MICHELE: Darn him! (*A desperate idea.*) Cerise!

EDDIE: (*Looking for CERISE's purse as MICHELE runs to door.*) Yeah! Cerise!

MICHELE: (*Yells out door.*) Just a minute! I'm on my way!

CERISE: Gosh, I don't know. Let's see. I got money from the machine yesterday, and I bought gas and lunch and two pair of hose... That was twenty-two and twenty-five, with the tip, and...

JONI: (*Enters and runs to MICHELE.*) Aunt Michele!

EDDIE: (*Starts rummaging through CERISE's purse.*) Forget the balance sheet, will you?

MICHELE: There, there. Everything's going to be all right. Just calm down...

CERISE: (*Sees EDDIE going through her purse.*) Eddie! That's my purse!

EDDIE: She needs fifty dollars. (*EDDIE pulls CERISE's hose out of the purse, throws them to one side. SATURN catches them.*

CERISE: No!

(*Everyone stares at SATURN, who holds the hose away from him.*)

SATURN: (*To MICHELE.*) Two dollars, tops. (*With a shrug.*) If the driver's kinky.

CERISE: (*Grabbing her hose.*) Give me those. (*To MICHELE.*) Does he do this all the time?

MICHELE: What's yours is his.

CERISE: (*Stalks to EDDIE and grabs her purse.*) My purse... (*Looking for wallet.*) And my fifty dollars that I'll give her.

EDDIE: I was just—

CERISE: Because I know what it's like to be where she is and...

(*Horn sounds offstage. MICHELE starts for the door.*)

CERISE: ...it isn't very much fun, and...

MICHELE: (*Calling out door.*) I said I'll be right there!

EDDIE: You act like it was a federal offense.

CERISE: ...and you're treating her like a criminal or a freak...

EDDIE: I was only looking for your wallet!

CERISE: (*Finds wallet, and as if nothing had happened.*) Here we are. There should be three twenties in here... You have ten, you said?

MICHELE: (*Digging in own purse.*) Actually eleven. (*Finally finds it, counts out.*) Yeah. Five...six seven eight nine... (*Rummaging.*) Well, darn!

EDDIE: You trying to drive me crazy? Give her the nine! Take the nine for... It's a lousy dollar! Here... (*Pulls out own wallet.*) Take my one, that makes ten...

MICHELE: (*Takes dollar bill from EDDIE.*) We're handling this perfectly fine, Eddie, so go fall off a cliff, why don't you.

SATURN: I offered him a banana.

MICHELE: He hates bananas.

CERISE: I didn't know that.

JONI: So do I.

CERISE: (*Finds money and hands it to MICHELE.*) Oh. Here they are.

MICHELE: (*Takes twenties, and hands change to CERISE.*) Thanks. I'll get the rest back to you. (*On way out door.*) Back in a flash.

JONI: (*To CERISE.*) Thanks. You're really neat, too.

CERISE: (*A quick hug.*) We girls gotta stick together, but thanks for the compliment, honey.

JONI: Yeah, except I've been thinking about what you said? And I guess I'd kind of like to keep my baby, if I can.

CERISE: I wish I'd done that. Every day of my life, I wish… (*Breaking off, then too brightly.*) If you do—and you <u>will</u>—may I come see him?

JONI: Sure, except he's a girl, and I'm going to name her Alison, after my mom.

CERISE: What a pretty name! And I can come see her?

JONI: Sure.

CERISE: And if you ever need help, or want to see a movie or something, I'd love to watch her for you.

JONI: Well, once I'm set up and know where I'll—

CERISE: I'm so excited! I'll bet she's going to be so beautiful! (*To EDDIE.*) You hear that? You could come with me and help.

EDDIE: How? Burp the baby? Wipe her little bootie?

JONI: I don't need your help.

EDDIE: Too bad. And here I was, standing by—

MICHELE: (*Enters.*) All right, crew, as Saturn would say.

EDDIE: (*Ignoring her.*) What about the kid's daddy? You gonna sign him up for a shift or two?

MICHELE: Eddie…

EDDIE: Like when you go to the movies, or out to cruise the mall?

(*JONI shrinks into herself. MICHELE and CERISE turn on EDDIE.*)

MICHELE: Stop this <u>now</u>.

CERISE: She's doing the best she can, Eddie.

EDDIE: Who could ask for anything more? Let 'em <u>all</u> do their best! Another few million illegitimate kids, who cares any more?

MICHELE: A lot of us, darn it. I work my <u>butt</u> off—

EDDIE: And they tax <u>my</u> butt off.

MICHELE: Taxes, my foot. You probably cheat on them as—

EDDIE: Don't say it. Don't push me too far.

SATURN: Ah, crew?

CERISE: Don't say what?

MICHELE: You'll find out soon enough, sweetie.

(*Only SATURN is paying attention to JONI, who is obviously going into labor.*)

SATURN: Better listen up, crew.

EDDIE: Don't change the subject.

CERISE: I don't even know what the subject <u>is</u> anymore.

JONI: Michele!

SATURN: That's easy. She's going to have her baby.

(*Stunned silence. All heads turn to JONI, who has started the breathing routine she's been taught. Everyone speaks at once.*)

MICHELE: What?

JONI: Michele!

EDDIE: No!

CERISE: Quick! Help her lie down!

EDDIE: Not in my recliner! (*MICHELE remains calm and takes charge.*)

MICHELE: (*To JONI's side.*) Don't stop breathing, baby…

JONI: I won't. I'm breathing…

MICHELE: Saturn? You know the way to a hospital?

SATURN: No.

JONI: I'm breathing…

CERISE: I do, but my car's too small for—

MICHELE: (*To CERISE as she starts to door with JONI.*) We'll take Saturn's. I'll ride in back with Joni and you can navigate.

EDDIE: Now wait a minute. She's—

JONI: The pain stopped.

SATURN: How far is it?

CERISE: I'm not sure.

MICHELE: Good. Just relax a minute…

CERISE: Pretty far…

SATURN: Well, I'm on fumes and broke, so—

EDDIE: (*Grabbing for his wallet.*) No problem, Saturn. Here's five.

SATURN: That's okay, man.

CERISE: I have ten dollars. We can use—

EDDIE: (*Tucks five in SATURN's shirt pocket.*) No, I insist. Buy gas, Saturn. <u>Please</u> buy gas.

MICHELE: (*Pointing to bag and steering JONI toward door.*) Cerise will bring him. Come on, now…
 (*CERISE gets overnight bag and BUNNY, and follows them.*)

SATURN: (*On way out.*) I'll get this back to you, man.

EDDIE: No need. Buy gas, buy bananas, buy a new ring for your nose! What's five dollars between fellow climbers?

(*The door closes behind SATURN, leaving EDDIE alone.*)

EDDIE: What a zoo!

(*He goes to the table, pours himself a glass of wine, and drinks with a sigh of relief. He notes, then, the documents he earlier tore up. He picks them up, considers, and, making up his mind, finishes the glass of wine, sets down the glass, and heads for his computer.*)

EDDIE: Nothing ventured, nothing... (*Brings up screen, clicks mouse, types.*) And what she doesn't know, won't hurt her. (*He finds what he wants*)... Here we are. Wade Powers, Inc., six and three eighths... (*Considers again, and, his mind made up*)... Don't fail me, Anton. Just sign those papers... Don't you <u>dare</u> fail me...

ACT TWO

SCENE ONE

The next Friday. JONI has had her baby. The apartment is a shambles, with MICHELE and JONI attempting to leave before Eddie's scheduled return Sunday evening.

MICHELE: (*Enters, obviously tired.*) Joni? You here?

JONI: (*Offstage, in bedroom.*) Hi, Aunt Michele.

MICHELE: Look at this place!

JONI: (*Enters stage right.*) How are you?

MICHELE: Thank God it's Friday. House calls all day. Never even got close to the shelter. How was school?

JONI: Great! I'm glad I went back, even if it was only for a half day. (*Shows off new hairdo.*) See?

MICHELE: You did your hair!

JONI: We did each other's. They call it mental health and attitude. You like it?

MICHELE: I like your <u>mood</u>. What happened to Miss Gloomy?

JONI: Like you said, I decided to feel better.

MICHELE: And?...

JONI: Oh, nothing, really.

MICHELE: Okay. (*Starts for kitchen.*) Boy, I am starved.

JONI: Except Alison's doing so well, they told me maybe I can take her home next week!

MICHELE: No! Yes! (*Embracing her.*) That's wonderful! I'm so happy for you!

JONI: I wish my father and Uncle Eddie were, too.

MICHELE: They will be. You wait and see. You know they love you.

JONI: They used to. Remember how Eddie used to ride me on his shoulders and take me on the rides and buy me cotton candy at the fair?

MICHELE: That <u>was</u> fun, wasn't it.

JONI: And now, he's so grumpy and mean...

MICHELE: Aw, he's just real...<u>busy</u> these days.

JONI: It's more than just busy.

MICHELE: Maybe it seems that way now, but don't give up on him yet, okay? He'll change his tune once he gets home and sees Alison.

JONI: Maybe. Except... Except where's <u>my</u> home?

MICHELE: Joni...

JONI: What if the state makes me give her up?

MICHELE: The state pays indigent fifteen-year-old drug addicts to keep their babies. Believe me, they'll be delighted to let you keep yours.

JONI: But they <u>could</u> take her. I never should have had her.

MICHELE: You never should have been having sex in the first place, but it's nine months too late to worry about that. <u>Now</u> you're going to move in with Saturn and me and get on with your life—sensibly—with your daughter.

JONI: If you say so. I just wish mama could see her.

MICHELE: I wish it too, honey. Maybe she does.

JONI: I mean "be here" see. Maybe my father wouldn't be so mean, then, too.

MICHELE: Harvey will come around. I guarantee.

JONI: Ha! He'll <u>never</u> take me back.

MICHELE: Joni, I am tired, I am hungry, and I am fed up with this negative energy. Are you packed?

JONI: No.

MICHELE: Then I am going to fix something for supper, and you are going to finish packing. Now!

JONI: (*Starting off right.*) Okay.

MICHELE: And quit feeling sorry for yourself.

JONI: That's easy for <u>you</u> to say. You don't have to—

MICHELE: Go! Finish. Before Saturn gets here. (*JONI flounces off.*) Kids having kids. Sheesh! (*Exits to kitchen.*) Joni! I thought you were going to wash the dishes.

JONI: (*Offstage right.*) I was, but I was so tired all I could do was lie down, and then I had to start history because it's going to <u>kill</u> me, and I have a makeup quiz Monday over the first four chapters.

MICHELE: (*Off.*) No more excuses, Joni. In here now and do them so I can start supper. I want to be out of here tonight so we can come back and clean tomorrow.

JONI: (*Offstage right.*) Pack, wash dishes, pack, wash dishes. You sound like my father.

CERISE: (*Offstage, outside front door.*) I don't know why her car's here, Eddie. I told you, she never returned my call.

(*The front door opens and CERISE helps EDDIE in. EDDIE's right arm is in a sling. He is in pain from a pair of cracked ribs, a broken collar bone, and a broken arm, and walks gingerly. When he moves too fast or talks too excitedly, the ribs remind him. Upon their entrance, EDDIE stares in shocked anger at his trashed out living room. CERISE is upset when she hears MICHELE's voice.*)

MICHELE: (*Off.*) <u>Now</u>, Joni.

JONI: (*Offstage right.*) <u>Okay</u>.

EDDIE: Damn!

CERISE: Now, Eddie…

JONI: (*Carrying BUNNY, enters from right, stops abruptly when she sees EDDIE.*) Uh-ohhh… (*She ducks back out of sight.*)

EDDIE: (*Spotting JONI.*) What the!… Wait a minute, you.

CERISE: You know what will happen if you yell.

MICHELE: (*Off.*) Eddie?

EDDIE: What?

MICHELE: (*Off.*) Is that you?

EDDIE: No, it's the Pope.

JONI: (*Entering.*) Hi, Cerise. Hi, Uncle Eddie.

CERISE: Hi, honey. You did your hair!

JONI: Uh-huh. You like it?

CERISE: It's wonderful!

(*EDDIE snorts his disgust as he goes to the answering machine.*)

MICHELE: (*Entering.*) Oh, boy...

MACHINE: You have...twelve...messages.

CERISE: Hello, Michele.

(*EDDIE pushes a button on the answering machine.*)

MICHELE: Hi.

DEBBY: (*On machine.*) Hi, Eddie—

(*EDDIE quickly turns off answering machine.*)

MICHELE: (*To EDDIE.*) What are you doing here?

EDDIE: I live here.

MICHELE: Not going to listen to your messages?

EDDIE: (*Avoiding CERISE's look.*) Later. What are you doing here?

MICHELE: It's only Friday. You're not supposed to be here until Sunday.

EDDIE: It's my apartment. I can be here Friday if I want to be here Friday. (*His voice rises.*) I can be here Saturday or Sunday or Monday or Tues—- (*His ribs remind him they're broken.*) Aghhh....

(*MICHELE rushes to EDDIE, who staggers toward the recliner, which is covered with stuff ready for MICHELE's and JONI's move.*)

MICHELE: Whatever?... You're hurt!

EDDIE: Sharp eye, Nurse. (*He stares at the recliner.*) What's all this stuff?

MICHELE: (*To CERISE.*) What?—

CERISE: I left a message at the shelter.

MICHELE: I was out in the field, and nobody told me when I called in.

EDDIE: Would you people mind if I sat on my own damn recliner?

MICHELE: Sure. I mean, of course not. Just throw that stuff on the floor (*Back to CERISE.*) What in heaven's name did he do?

(*CERISE has rushed to help EDDIE. MICHELE notices JONI in the stage right entrance, and emphatically points to the kitchen. JONI, keeping as far from EDDIE as possible, crosses and exits to kitchen.*)

CERISE: Let me, honey. It's too heavy for you... (*Helps him sit.*) There you go. You want to lean back a little?

EDDIE: Not too far. Ribs hurt too much...

MICHELE: I'm sorry, Eddie. If I'd known... What happened?

EDDIE: I fell.

MICHELE: Oh, no!

(*JONI peeks in from the kitchen and listens.*)

EDDIE: Broke my arm, collar bone, and two ribs.

MICHELE: That's awful.

EDDIE: I thought you'd be tickled pink.

MICHELE: Why would you think?—

EDDIE: (*Quoting her.*) "So go fall off a cliff, why don't you?"

MICHELE: I didn't mean it <u>that</u> way.

EDDIE: Sure, sure...

MICHELE: I mean, literally.

EDDIE: (*To CERISE.*) Where are my pills?

CERISE: I don't know.

EDDIE: They're in my small bag. (*Tries to get up.*) I gotta get my bags.

CERISE: You stay there, honey. Michele and I... (*A questioning look, and a nod from MICHELE.*) ... will get them.

(*CERISE and MICHELE exit at front door. Behind them, JONI enters tentatively from kitchen.*)

JONI: I'm sorry I'm here, Uncle Eddie. I know you don't want me, but I don't have any place else to go yet. (*Picks up a pile of mail on her way to him.*) We saved your mail. (*Hands it to him.*) You want to see it?

EDDIE: Not especially.

JONI: My father works for the one on top.

EDDIE: (*Awkwardly opening envelope.*) I know that. He's my broker.

JONI: Really? I'm sorry you got hurt.

EDDIE: So am I. (*Reads.*) Aha! Bingo!

JONI: What's that?

EDDIE: Just some stock I bought. Nothing important.

JONI: Oh. (*Not really interested.*) I had my baby. (*Turns to show off her abdomen. Holds out BUNNY.*) See?

EDDIE: (*Glances up.*) That's nice. What'd ya call it? Bugs?

JONI: Huh?

EDDIE: Never mind.

JONI: Oh. (*Not giving up.*) I thought you'd be happy that she's normal and... healthy and everything.

EDDIE: I am. I'm ecstatic. Her father is too, I trust?

JONI: Actually, I don't think he knows yet.

EDDIE: Responsible little fart, isn't he. He have a name?

JONI: Sure. Jimmy.

EDDIE: So where is good ol' Jimmy?

JONI: In Connecticut. He wanted to be here, but his education's real important so his parents sent him off to private school.

EDDIE: Nothing like keeping your priorities straight.

JONI: That's what his mother said, and since he's only seventeen… I just didn't think it could happen to me. And now, I mean, I love her and all, but everything's so messed up.

EDDIE: He going to pay child support?

JONI: I guess we didn't talk about that.

EDDIE: You'd better. If his folks can afford private school, they can afford child support.

JONI: That's what Michele said. Anyway her name's Alison after Mama, and she weighed five pounds and four ounces, and I can bring her home when she weighs six pounds.

EDDIE: Bring? Home?

JONI: Not here.

(*MICHELE and CERISE enter with EDDIE's bags.*)

JONI: Gollee…

MICHELE: Gollee, what?

JONI: He thinks I was going to bring Alison here.

MICHELE: Not a chance, Eddie.

EDDIE: A reasonable fear, Mick. Here you still are, after all.

MICHELE: Look. I'm sorry you hurt yourself, but we'd have been long gone if you'd arrived on schedule.

EDDIE: Ah! Of course! It's *my* fault that you're here.

MICHELE: Don't start that—

EDDIE: That my apartment is full of… Oh, damn, that hurts.

CERISE: Here's your bags, Eddie. Which small one?

EDDIE: The *small* small one, of course. (*To MICHELE.*) And a glass of water.

(*Neither MICHELE nor CERISE appreciate his peremptory manner, but he is hurt, after all, so they let it pass. CERISE opens the smaller of the two small bags to find the pill vial. MICHELE exits to kitchen.*)

JONI: Does it hurt bad?

EDDIE: Of course not. It's all in my head.

JONI: That's what the doctor said when I had Alison.

EDDIE: If your doctor can't tell the difference between your head and—-

CERISE: Eddie!…

EDDIE: Okay, okay. Anyway, get a new doctor. Better yet, don't _need_ a new one.

(*CERISE opens vial, shakes out pill.*)

JONI: I know. Still, the pain won't last forever.

EDDIE: Define forever.

CERISE: (*Handing pill to EDDIE.*) Here you are.

EDDIE: The other one, too.

CERISE: (*Shakes and checks vial.*) There isn't another one.

EDDIE: That can't be! (*CERISE hands the vial to him.*)

MICHELE: (*Entering with water.*) One glass of water coming up. (*EDDIE takes the water from MICHELE and swallows the pill.*) You're welcome.

EDDIE: (*To CERISE.*) What happened to the other one? There were two left.

CERISE: Don't look at me. I didn't take it.

EDDIE: Refill. It says "one refill." (*Hands vial to CERISE.*) Here. Take it to a drugstore.

CERISE: But I…

MICHELE: And that's an order.

EDDIE: (*Glares at MICHELE. To CERISE.*) I'm sorry, Baby. Please. The pain…

JONI: My doctor said just ride the wave and everything will come out all right.

EDDIE: I'm not having a baby, Joni.

MICHELE: You'd think you were.

CERISE: I need to be at that reception.

EDDIE: And I need my pills.

CERISE: But all our top clients—-

MICHELE: Dishes, Joni.

EDDIE: Just do it, okay? (*CERISE hesitates. Ominously.*) Okay, Cerise?

CERISE: Well…

JONI: (*Starting for kitchen.*) Oh, yeah. I forgot. Sorry.

CERISE: I suppose, if you really need them…

EDDIE: (*To CERISE.*) Kiss before you go?

JONI: Huh?

CERISE: Eddie…

JONI: Oh.

EDDIE: Can't make it without a kiss from my baby.

    (*CERISE tries to give EDDIE a peck on the cheek, but EDDIE gets his good hand behind her head and gives her a real kiss.*)

MICHELE: (*To JONI, shooing her out.*) And something to eat. Can't make it without something to eat.

CERISE: (*Breaking from EDDIE.*) I swear, you can be so…

JONI: (*On her way out.*) Like what?…

    (*CERISE grabs her purse and the vial, and heads for the door.*)

MICHELE: I don't care. Anything.

CERISE: (*Exiting.*) I'll be back…

MICHELE: (*As door closes.*) Congratulations, Eddie. Three minutes, three women, three put downs.

JONI: (*Off.*) Aunt Michele?

Someday's Gone

MICHELE: What?

JONI: (*Off.*) There isn't anything.

MICHELE: Of course there is. Doctor up last night's sauce, and put some water on to boil for spaghetti.

EDDIE: Enough for me, too. I haven't had anything to eat since last night.

JONI: (*Off.*) But I don't know how to doctor sauce.

MICHELE: Figure it <u>out</u> Joni. I swear teaching these kids to think is like trying to teach turkeys to talk.

EDDIE: You're the one who took the job. What are you doing? Moving her in with you?

MICHELE: She's my niece, and the shelter's packed. There's a spare bedroom.

EDDIE: Good ol' Mick. Still picking up strays.

MICHELE: Some people pick up strays, some pick up women.

EDDIE: Which are preferable to teenage mothers. They leave in the morning. Earlier, with a little luck.

MICHELE: What do you know? A talking turkey.

EDDIE: It was a joke, okay?

MICHELE: It wasn't funny.

EDDIE: I noticed you weren't laughing. (*A beat.*) I'm tired, Mick. I hurt too much to fight.

MICHELE: You started it. You can stop any time you want.

EDDIE: And you can... (*He relents.*) You're right. I started it. Truce? I won't even say anything more about you still being here.

MICHELE: Mr. Magnanimous himself! Heart as big as a... (*Her turn to relent.*) Ahhh, I'm sorry. Bad habit, this bickering. (*A beat.*) You really are hurt, aren't you.

EDDIE: (*Trying to get comfortable.*) More like embarrassed, which is worse.

MICHELE: (*Going to help him.*) What. You're the first person to fall off a rock?

EDDIE: No, but—

MICHELE: Then let it go. Here. (*She massages his temples.*) Relax. Let the pill kick in.

EDDIE: We didn't used to, did we.

MICHELE: What?

EDDIE: Bicker. Mick and Eddie, Eddie and Mick, walking the halls, cracking jokes, debating... some team we made, huh?

MICHELE: Even that horrid apartment on Rock Street...

MICHELE and EDDIE: (*In unison.*) Dinosaur roaches!...

EDDIE: Soaking together in that old bathtub, Sunday morning paper and coffee in bed... Not a care in the world.

MICHELE: Some of my most favorite memories. I still dream about those days.

EDDIE: Don't get maudlin on me, Mick.

MICHELE: I'm not. Just vaguely sentimental. Still, it was the best time of my life.

EDDIE: Not mine.

MICHELE: Really? I thought—

EDDIE: I'm not talking about you and me.

MICHELE: Who... what else was there?

EDDIE: Poverty sucked, Mick.

MICHELE: We weren't poor.

EDDIE: What else would you call it? (*A yawn.*) That broken down old Falcon had poor written in rust all over it.

MICHELE: It took us to work and home again.

EDDIE: What a thrill. Home to the roach palace.

MICHELE: Home to each other!

EDDIE: (*Terminating the massage.*) That wasn't the point.

MICHELE: What was?

EDDIE: Working eight-to-five keeping other people's books, counting other people's money? That was a life?

MICHELE: A fine life! Plenty of—

EDDIE: It was a dead end street! Forty years of day in and day out, staring me in the face.

MICHELE: (*A beat. With controlled anger.*) Your father's a good man, Eddie.

EDDIE: My father's a flunky, and doesn't own a pot to piss in.

MICHELE: I don't remember you ever going hungry. He's also the salt of the earth.

EDDIE: So what? Shampoo, sir? This about right over the ears? A little mousse, maybe? A dash of cologne? (*Another yawn.*) That's a life? (*Sleepily.*) Keep their own damn books. Nobody's flunky...

(*The front door opens and SATURN pokes his head in.*)

MICHELE: I don't need this, I don't need this...

SATURN: (*Entering.*) Hey, crew!

MICHELE: Hi, Saturn.

SATURN: Why so bummed? Don't need what? (*He sees EDDIE's bags, but not EDDIE.*) Oh-ohhh.....

MICHELE: What?

SATURN: Another stray? Eddie is going to be seriously wanked if he finds out.

EDDIE: (*Sleepily.*) You're smarter than you look, Saturn.

SATURN: (*Peers over recliner.*) Eddie? You mean it's Sunday already? Whoa! Far out!

EDDIE: I take it back. You're not smarter than you look. Plus you have bad manners. You ever hear of knocking?

SATURN: What are you doing here? You aren't supposed—

EDDIE: Don't say it. I fell. The rock beat me.

SATURN: Rock doesn't care who climbs it, who falls.

EDDIE: It does too.

SATURN: First rule. Don't fight it. Paper wraps rock.

EDDIE: What does that mean?

SATURN: Scissors cut paper, paper wraps rock, rock dulls scissors. (*EDDIE stares at him.*) It's a game.

EDDIE: I don't play games. Go away. Disapppear.

SATURN: You beat yourself, man.

EDDIE: I took a chance, and I fell. Go pierce something. Get a new tattoo.

SATURN: (*To MICHELE.*) How's Joni?

MICHELE: She did her hair today.

SATURN: Cool. Bad news, by the way.

EDDIE: Good. Serves you right.

MICHELE: Thanks loads. (*To SATURN.*) What now?

SATURN: The house won't be ready until Tuesday or Wednesday.

EDDIE: What!?

SATURN: The breaker box overheated and the city says it has to be replaced before anyone can live there.

EDDIE: Now wait a—

MICHELE: Great!

SATURN: Actually it was lucky I was there and turned off the power, or the whole place could have burned. We can finish moving in, though. (*To EDDIE.*) How far'd you fall?

EDDIE: A lousy eight feet. (*To MICHELE.*) I suppose that means you'll want to stay until—

MICHELE: I don't have much choice at this late date.

JONI: (*Off.*) Michele?

SATURN: You're lucky it wasn't eighty, man.

EDDIE: If I'd been lucky, I wouldn't have fallen, period.

MICHELE: If you'd been lucky, you'd have landed on your hard head.

EDDIE: If I'd been lucky... (*Yawns.*) ... I'd have come home to an empty apartment.

SATURN: (*Wanders to the table, where he picks up a banana.*) Man, I bet you two were a thrill a minute when you were married.

JONI: (*Off.*) Aunt Michele? Help!

EDDIE: Who asked you?

MICHELE: (*Heading for kitchen.*) On my way. (*Over her shoulder, a parting shot.*) Thrill barely scratches the surface.

EDDIE: (*Struggles to sit up. To MICHELE.*) Up yours. I didn't ask to run a homeless shelter. (*Falls back in pain.*) Damn, that hurts. If I could just get comfortable, fall asleep or something...

SATURN: (*Eating banana.*) Ribs?

EDDIE: Two. And my collar bone and arm. (*A sigh of relief.*) Oh boy. Just having her out of the room... Why can't we get along, Saturn?

SATURN: I don't know. I guess I just rub some people the wrong way.

EDDIE: That's for sure. But I was talking about Michele. I mean, what do women want, anyway? You ever ask yourself that?

SATURN: No.

EDDIE: I swear, they ought to come with warning labels, like…ladders, or bug spray… Yeah. That's it. (*A big yawn.*) …like Bugs and Elmer Fudd. Elmer always chasing Bugs and shooting at him. Bugs always getting away, thinking he's so smart… But no matter how smart he is, next time around there's old Elmer taking a bead on him again. You know what I think?

SATURN: I got no clue.

EDDIE: One of these days, Elmer's gonna, blam, drop that bunny in his tracks. (*Yawning, fading fast.*) Won't that be something?

SATURN: Yeah. For Elmer. Problem is… (*He realizes EDDIE is asleep, so gently…*) Problem is, Elmer better be careful of what he asks for. 'Cause Bugs is the one thing in his life he…

MICHELE: (*Off.*) You want garlic bread, Eddie?

SATURN: (*On his way to kitchen door.*) … And what's he gonna do when that wabbit's gone? (*At door, and offstage to MICHELE.*) He's asleep.

MICHELE: (*Off.*) What about you? Spaghetti with veggie sauce?

(*The front door opens, and CERISE pokes her head in.*)

CERISE: Eddie?

SATURN: (*Shushing CERISE. Quietly to MICHELE.*) Sure. Lot's of garlic on the bread.

(*SATURN watches as CERISE enters.*)

CERISE: I'm back.

SATURN: He's asleep.

CERISE: Thank goodness!

SATURN: What's wrong?

CERISE: I don't know what to do. He sent me for a refill of his prescription, but the pharmacy says it's a controlled substance and they can't fill it because it's written by an out of state doctor, and when he finds out…

SATURN: Not your fault.

CERISE: What difference will that make? He'll get crazy and yell at me, anyway.

SATURN: Then get crazy and yell back.

CERISE: I couldn't do that.

SATURN: Why not?

CERISE: He might…you know…

SATURN: Dump you? No way. You're his trophy. Guys like him don't throw away trophies.

CERISE: Eddie might.

SATURN: Then ask your doctor for a prescription. Or slip the druggist an extra hundred.

CERISE: Bribe him? That would be illegal.

SATURN: Money makes its own laws. You know that.

CERISE: I'd be too scared.

SATURN: Of what?

CERISE: Everything! Oh, I don't know. I'm just always frightened of anything that isn't regular. Like your tattoos? I had a friend with a beautiful pink rose on her shoulder, and I wanted one, too, but if Daddy or one of my husbands, or Eddie, saw it, they'd... Well, you know...

SATURN: How many husbands have you had?

CERISE: Eddie will be my third. And I love him and all, and want to be a good wife and make him happy, but... I don't know, it's just I...well... (*A look to make sure EDDIE is asleep.*) Sometimes I wish I could be more like you and Michele.

SATURN: More what?

CERISE: You know. Free to be myself.

SATURN: You already are.

CERISE: That's what you think. Having money, being Wade Powers' daughter...

SATURN: Best reason I can think of for pretending you don't have it.

CERISE: I couldn't do that.

SATURN: Why not? You want to be Wade Powers Junior for the rest of your life?

CERISE: No. Not really.

SATURN: Then get out while the getting's good. Before it's too late.

CERISE: But how would I?—

SATURN: Leave. Go somewhere where no one knows you and wait tables. Get a job on a cruise ship and bum around. Learn to do without.

CERISE: You did that?

SATURN: (*A finger to his lips.*) Dirty family secret.

CERISE: I don't understand... Why?

SATURN: (*Points to EDDIE.*) Need I say more?

CERISE: It's not that easy for a woman.

SATURN: Not that hard, either. Plenty have.

MICHELE: (*Off.*) Everything's ready, Saturn. Come and get it. (*EDDIE stirs.*)

SATURN: (*To MICHELE, careful not to disturb EDDIE.*) Keep it down, huh? There enough for Cerise?

MICHELE: (*Off.*) She's back? Sure.

SATURN: On our way. (*To CERISE.*) Plenty for three, plenty for four.

CERISE: Could I? (*Almost immediately.*) No. There's a big reception tonight to celebrate Daddy's merger, and he'll be furious if I'm late.

SATURN: Whatever Daddy says?

CERISE: (*On way to door, loud enough to disturb EDDIE.*) You don't have to rub it in. (*Quickly hushed.*) Sorry. Would you tell Eddie... you know...

SATURN: Will do. Hey...

(*CERISE stops at the front door. SATURN takes the bunch of bananas from the table and offers them to her.*)

SATURN: Here you go. Take these with you.

CERISE: I'm not really hungry...

SATURN: To eat at the reception.

CERISE: Are you crazy?

SATURN: Blow their minds!...

CERISE: I couldn't... You'd do that?

SATURN: In a New York minute.

CERISE: (*Shyly, accepting the bananas.*) You're really goofy, you know that?

SATURN: (*The old monkey bit.*) Oof-oof-oof.

CERISE: (*Impulsively kisses him on the cheek.*) And kind of sweet, too.

(*CERISE exits. SATURN shrugs, grimaces as EDDIE threatens to wake. SATURN hurries toward the kitchen.*)

SATURN: (*Exiting.*) Joni, where's Bunny?

JONI: (*Off.*) Right here. What do you?...

(*SATURN reappears almost immediately. He carries BUNNY who, as JONI appears in the door and watches, he takes to EDDIE.*)

SATURN: He needs a binkie.

JONI: Eddie? Are you kidding?

(*Careful not to disturb him, SATURN places BUNNY in EDDIE's arms.*)

SATURN: Even tough guys need binkies every once in a while. They just don't know it.

(*EDDIE cuddles BUNNY, and sleeps again. SATURN shushes JONI'S giggle with a finger to his lips, and steals away from EDDIE.*)

SATURN: There you go, Elmer. Sleep tight. Don't let them wabbits bite.

SCENE TWO

The time is 5:30, the next Tuesday afternoon. Michele's backpack and a few stray articles of clothing lie on the floor. A very wispy, sexy teddy lies unnoticed on the couch. The stage is empty, the front door is ajar. After a moment, the front door swings open to reveal CERISE, who carries a bag of groceries and a fancy paper gift bag.

CERISE: Hello? (*Entering and kicking the door closed.*) Door's open. You here, Michele? (*There is no answer. CERISE deposits the gift bag on the couch and notices the teddy, which she picks up and...*) My, my, Michele.

(*CERISE tosses the teddy onto the pile of MICHELE's clothes; exits to the kitchen with the bag of groceries. MICHELE enters through the hall door with some items which she stuffs into her backpack.*)

MICHELE: Going... (*She notices the teddy, holds it up.*) My, my, Cerise. (*And tosses it back onto the sofa.*) ... going, gone.

CERISE: (*Entering behind her.*) Hi, Michele.

MICHELE: (*Startled.*) Why don't you tell a person?

CERISE: That's what I was doing.

MICHELE: I'm sorry. I didn't mean to snap, but you startled me. I expected to be gone before you got here.

CERISE: I'm glad you weren't. (*Looks around.*) Where's Joni?

MICHELE: Who knows? Saturn said he'd pick her up, so almost anywhere, I suppose.

CERISE: That sounds like Saturn. He's so...strange...

MICHELE: For sure, there's only one of him.

CERISE: Does he really have money, do you think?

MICHELE: Could be, if he needs it. A new generator was delivered to the clinic in Guatemala three weeks after the old one gave up the ghost.

CERISE: He'd bought it?

MICHELE: I don't know. The space for the purchaser's name on the invoice was blank.

CERISE: But you think it was him.

MICHELE: I asked. "Whoa!" he said. "You been 'shroomin'?"

CERISE: What's 'shroomin'?

MICHELE: Eating hallucinogenic mushrooms. They grow down there.

CERISE: But that wasn't an answer, was it.

MICHELE: It was Saturn's answer. And who was I to ask again?

CERISE: You were right about one thing. He does grow on you.

MICHELE: He's a good friend.

CERISE: He's different from everyone else I know. Kind, gentle. Sort of sweet, really.

MICHELE: Don't let Eddie hear you talk like that.

CERISE: He does make it difficult to have friends, doesn't he. (*An awkward pause.*) You're about ready?

MICHELE: Yup. Empty the washer and dryer, kiss the place goodbye, and that will be all she wrote. End of chapter umpty-ump.

CERISE: I thought you didn't care.

MICHELE: I thought I didn't, too, but your first love...

CERISE: I know. Mine was... Well, never mind. But I know what you mean.

MICHELE: Don't we all. When I remember the Eddie I grew up with, sometimes I just...

CERISE: I wish I'd known him then.

MICHELE: You'd have liked him. He was sweet, considerate... a little goofy, actually. Kind of like Saturn, if you can believe that. Always giving me presents...silly little things.

CERISE: I'm sorry. I didn't—

MICHELE: Not your fault. Anyway, he's all yours, now, so to speak.

CERISE: Still, I didn't want you to think... I mean, it isn't as if I came along and...

MICHELE: I know. And no hard feelings, okay? Sometimes, things work out...different than I expected.

CERISE: I guess, but... (*A little nervous.*) I was wondering, what?—

MICHELE: (*Checks time.*) Darn! Five thirty-five!

CERISE: What happened?

MICHELE: What <u>didn't</u> happen? Saturn ran out of gas so I had to take Joni to school this morning, I got a flat tire... (*Sags wearily.*)...and I processed a fifteen-year-old kid who's six months pregnant, who's on crack, and whose twenty-four-year-old "boyfriend" beat her up.

CERISE: That's so depressing. I can't imagine even talking with people like that. How do you stand it?

MICHELE: There are days when I wonder. And shit, but I feel like shit.

CERISE: What I—

MICHELE: Maybe I should switch to something more cheerful, like geriatrics.

CERISE: I know it's private, but... (*A rush.*) I just wondered why you and Eddie...you know. I mean everybody must have thought you were the perfect couple and couldn't believe it when... What happened?

MICHELE: When?

CERISE: You don't have to tell me. I know you pretend to like me to be polite and I don't blame you because I'm this self-centered ditzy rich bitch who lets men run all over her and never does anything to help people the way you do, but I have feelings, you know, and... Well, I do.

MICHELE: I know. And I like you just fine. (*A wry chuckle.*) Surprise, surprise.

CERISE: I know what you mean. And here I was, so jealous and scared of you!

MICHELE: Of me? That's what I was of you. "I'm Cerise," and my knees turned to jelly. I figured you were this... this... Anyway, I apologize for telling you that awful story that afternoon.

CERISE: You mean he didn't really show you?...

MICHELE: Heavens no!

CERISE: I didn't know what to think.

MICHELE: What did he say when you asked him about it?

CERISE: I didn't.

MICHELE: You didn't?

CERISE: I didn't dare.

MICHELE: You mean you just... thinking he might have something?...

CERISE: Oh, no. We don't do that.

MICHELE: You're kidding.

CERISE: No. Some women can't get pregnant, I can't not get pregnant. I was on the pill when I had my baby, and then I was on the pill and used a diaphragm both, and still got pregnant twice more.

MICHELE: You've had three?...

CERISE: No. (*Near tears.*) The other two, my husbands made me...you know...

MICHELE: That's terrible!

CERISE: I know. I guess I'm just a terrible person.

MICHELE: I didn't mean you! I meant them! No man has that right!

CERISE: That's what I thought, but Mama told me I should do what my husbands said if I wanted to keep them. Except I didn't. Keep them, I mean.

MICHELE: Goes to show you Mom's not always right.

CERISE: It works for her with Daddy.

MICHELE: For mine, too. But not for me, thank you very much.

CERISE: I wish I could be that strong.

MICHELE: You can be, if you want to badly enough.

CERISE: That's kind of what Saturn said. But anyway, what I wondered was, since you don't have any babies, did Eddie make you?...

MICHELE: That would have been my decision. And if he'd tried to make it for me... Pow! Right in the kisser. Or something lower.

CERISE: You wouldn't have.

MICHELE: Want to bet? Which is what you... Oh, no! You <u>were</u> kidding. And you're pregnant and Eddie...

CERISE: No, really. I told him at the start that I couldn't until we were married.

MICHELE: And Eddie went along with that?

CERISE: I guess he really does love me, huh?

MICHELE: Eddie <u>Fortman?</u>

CERISE: Uh-huh.

(*The front door opens and EDDIE, in an expansive mood, enters. He still wears the sling, and he must still favor his ribs. He sees CERISE first.*)

EDDIE: You're here early. Great!

MICHELE: <u>That</u> Eddie Fortman?

EDDIE: (*Sees MICHELE.*) Oh crap!

CERISE: Hi, Eddie.

MICHELE: Fancy that! Eddie Understanding Fortman!

EDDIE: Don't mess with me, Mick, because I'm suddenly in a very lousy mood.

MICHELE: And here I was going to say something nice to you.

EDDIE: Like goodbye?

MICHELE: Close enough. I'm out the door the second Saturn and Joni show up.

EDDIE: Which can't be a second too—

(*The front door opens, and SATURN barges in. He's accompanied by JONI.*)

SATURN: Yo, crew.

EDDIE: How about that! Wishes do come true!

SATURN: Sorry I'm late.

JONI: It was my fault. I was so excited I went to the wrong door and he couldn't find me.

EDDIE: All's well that ends well. Glad you made it, Saturn. See 'ya.

MICHELE: Excited about what?

JONI: Tomorrow! I can take Alison home tomorrow!

MICHELE and CERISE: Wonderful! That's great! Etc.

JONI: (*To CERISE, who embraces her.*) I'm so scared, but I paid real close attention in my classes, and you just <u>have</u> to come see her.

CERISE: When?

JONI: I don't know. Tomorrow night? Wednesday?

CERISE: Tell me where, and I'll be there! (*Remembering present.*) Oh my gosh!

EDDIE: Second's up! Time to hit the old road!

CERISE: Just a minute, Eddie. I almost forgot. (*Hands present to JONI.*) A baby present. It's from Eddie and me.

JONI: Gollee...

EDDIE: From whom?

MICHELE: Shut up, Eddie.

JONI: Can I open it?

CERISE: Of course.

MICHELE: Don't mind him. He's just so giving he can't keep track.

JONI: I wonder what it is...

EDDIE: Gollee, so do I.

CERISE: It's nothing fancy...

JONI: Wow!

CERISE: Just practical stuff every baby needs.

JONI: Boy... baby oil, and powder, and wipes, and shampoo... And look! Little pink ribbons for her hair!

CERISE: She'll be so cute!

EDDIE: What about a father? Got one of them in there?

JONI: How come you're so mean?

EDDIE: A father would be practical.

(*MICHELE pokes EDDIE, who freezes in pain.*)

MICHELE: It's the pain, honey.

JONI: No, it isn't! (*To EDDIE.*) You used to be almost my favorite person in the whole world, but now you've gotten mean and hateful, and I can't stand you!

EDDIE: Would someone please tell me what happened to leaving?

(*The faint sound of a buzzer is heard from the kitchen.*)

MICHELE: Clothes are dry. Wash should be done, too. (*On way to kitchen to EDDIE.*) Oh yeah. Harvey called.

EDDIE: Great! When?

MICHELE: Half an hour ago, maybe. He wants you to call him back.

(*EDDIE starts for the phone, then remembers CERISE, and abruptly turns and heads for his bedroom. Exiting.*)

EDDIE: It's a private call.

MICHELE: (*Exiting to kitchen.*) Come on, Joni. Let's hop to it.

JONI: Aren't you just so excited?

CERISE: Yes! Yes!

(*JONI follows MICHELE and exits.*)

CERISE: (*To SATURN.*) You ever see anybody so happy?

SATURN: Not recently.

CERISE: I know what you mean. (*Almost shyly.*) I want to thank you for the bananas. That was nice of you. To give them to me, I mean.

SATURN: Did you eat one at the reception?

CERISE: Uh-huh. Mr. Anton did too.

SATURN: O-kay.

CERISE: Sorry. He's one of those super-suave CEOs who has his nails manicured and wears makeup, and Daddy's and his companies just merged. Anyway, Daddy almost popped when I pulled the bananas out of my purse, and when Mr. Anton asked if <u>he</u> could have one... Well, I guess you had to be there.

SATURN: I wish I had been.

CERISE: So do I. But I wouldn't have done it if it wasn't for you.

SATURN: Ah, you just needed a little push in the right direction.

CERISE: No. More than that. You made me feel like I could do what <u>I</u> wanted to do, not just what Daddy or Eddie or any other man in the world said.

SATURN: I, uh...

CERISE: Why are you so nice to me?

SATURN: Because you're you.

CERISE: (*Impulsively, she hugs him.*) And I like you because you're you, too.

(*EDDIE, obviously in a good mood, appears in hall doorway, but stops short when he sees CERISE and SATURN together.*)

CERISE: You make me feel like—

EDDIE: How touching. (*CERISE slides away from SATURN; EDDIE advances on them.*) Makes you feel like what?

(*MICHELE enters carrying a plastic bag, heavy with wet clothes. JONI follows with a pillow case stuffed with dry clothes.*)

MICHELE: These are wet, Saturn, so we'll have to stop at a Laundromat.

EDDIE: (*To CERISE.*) A hot tamale?

MICHELE: Last minute check, everybody.

CERISE: Eddie!...

EDDIE: A real man eater, like Michele, here?

CERISE: What did I <u>do</u>? We were just talking!

EDDIE: Oh-ho! I've heard <u>that</u> one before.

JONI: Aunt Michele?

MICHELE: None of our business, Joni.

JONI: Can we leave?

MICHELE: We're on our way out the door.

EDDIE: Is there an echo? Is this where I came in?

MICHELE: I love you too, Eddie. (*Scooping up everything that's left over and stuffing it in her backpack.*)

Check the couch, somebody. I lose things in couches.

(*EDDIE freezes as CERISE holds up the teddy.*)

CERISE: There's this.

MICHELE: Not mine. I thought it was... Oh-oh.

CERISE: (*Becomes deathly still. Finally, in a small voice.*) Joni?...

MICHELE: (*With a high sign to JONI.*) Of course! I thought you had everything.

JONI: I never in my life owned anything like that.

MICHELE: Oh, boy...

EDDIE: (*He is in deep trouble.*) Don't look at me. It's not mine.

CERISE: Aw, Eddie...

EDDIE: Now, look...

MICHELE: (*To EDDIE.*) Nice. Real nice.

EDDIE: What do you mean, nice?

CERISE: How could you do this to me?

EDDIE: (*Thinking quickly.*) What? Buy you a present? I buy you presents all the time! (*Going to her, absolutely sincere.*) I hit the jackpot, saw it in a window, and just...went in and bought it for you.

CERISE: (*Almost taken in.*) How sweet. And left it where I'd find it for a surprise?

EDDIE: Great idea, huh?

CERISE: <u>And</u> put my favorite perfume on it?

EDDIE: You know me. All the way!

CERISE: I wouldn't be caught <u>dead</u> wearing Jungle Gardenia!

EDDIE: I didn't know that. How was I supposed to?...

JONI: I have homework, everybody.

CERISE: (*To MICHELE.*) I don't understand when. He was at work every day, and you and Joni were here every night...

SATURN: (*To EDDIE.*) That was a mistake, Man.

EDDIE: (*Turning to SATURN.*) You never made a mistake?

MICHELE: Except for last night, when we slept at the shelter. He said you two were... Oh-oh...

SATURN: Not a fatal one.

CERISE: It was other women, wasn't it.

JONI: I have to read <u>Romeo and Juliet</u>, Act one...

CERISE: You could have told me that.

EDDIE: You mean she didn't? All the gory, embellished details?

MICHELE: (*To CERISE.*) No thanks. When it comes to Eddie, it's every woman for herself.

CERISE: It's probably my fault, anyway.

JONI: I have six <u>long</u> algebra problems...

MICHELE: Yeah. You threw Miss Jungle Gardenia at him.

CERISE: I guess I should have taken a chance. Men need that, you know.

MICHELE: The Testosterone Kid here does, that's for sure

JONI: Plus I have a chemistry quiz, so can we <u>please</u> leave?

EDDIE: Right, Mick. Why don't you and your planet orbit her on out of here.

CERISE: No! Don't leave me alone. Not now.

EDDIE: Cerise. Baby. All I wanted was one lousy night to myself, and— (*Gives it up.*) Aw, crap. I told you about Sandy being after me, and, well, I didn't mean to. I just lost control, and couldn't help myself.

MICHELE: That's it! His gonads made him do it.

EDDIE: I didn't even <u>want</u> to...

MICHELE: Naughty, naughty gonads!

EDDIE: ...But it had been such a long time, and I just...

MICHELE: Bad testosterone. Bad, bad....

EDDIE: Do you damn it to hell <u>mind</u>?

CERISE: I trusted you, Eddie...

EDDIE: I'll make it up to you, Baby. I promise...

CERISE: (*To SATURN.*) I <u>trusted</u> him. "My one and only Baby," he said... (*Turning on EDDIE.*) You...you...

JONI: Oh, no! Alison's picture! And Bunny!

CERISE: ... lousy <u>bum</u>!

SATURN: Easy now. Let's not get crazy here.

CERISE: Maybe I <u>want</u> to get crazy.

JONI: Where are they?

MICHELE: (*To JONI.*) I thought you had everything.

JONI: I know, but I forgot... (*To EDDIE.*) Have you seen them?

EDDIE: Who?

JONI: (*Running to bedroom.*) The bedroom!

CERISE: You gave me your word! I trusted you.

EDDIE: I trusted you, too, and look where it got me. I can't even walk out of the room!

MICHELE: That's dirty pool. You know darn well she hasn't—

EDDIE: What I <u>know</u> is that I hit it big, it's supposed to be a great day, and here I am dodging the artillery and she's making it with the freak!

CERISE: A hug isn't <u>making</u> it.

EDDIE: (*To SATURN.*) Stick with her, pal. She's a gold mine.

CERISE: And he's not a freak!

EDDIE: A rich daddy here, a stock tip there, you could have more rings than Ma Bell.

SATURN: (*To MICHELE.*) There's a Laundromat a block from the house. You about ready?

MICHELE: More than. (*Calls.*) Joni?

CERISE: I don't appreciate this, Eddie.

EDDIE: Today's hot tip, stock market junkies, is Wade Powers Properties, Inc. Should go up a few more points before it evens out. Can't lose.

CERISE: Stock market?... You didn't!...

JONI: (*Entering from bedroom holding BUNNY and photo.*) I found them! (*She puts down BUNNY in order to put photo in the bag of presents.*) They weren't lost after all.

CERISE: You bought Daddy's stock behind my back. After you said you wouldn't!

MICHELE: Am I missing something here?

(*This is between CERISE and EDDIE, who might as well be alone in the room.*)

EDDIE: I'm sorry, Baby. Look...

CERISE: (*Mocking imitation.*) "Whatever makes my baby happy." You lied!

EDDIE: I changed my mind. There's a difference.

CERISE: It's the same thing!

EDDIE: Okay, I apologize. Can we let it go now?

CERISE: No strings, no tricks.

EDDIE: I said I'm sorry.

CERISE: "I love you so much I'll tear this up and forget it."

EDDIE: (*Loses it.*) The opportunity of a lifetime? Even you can't be that dumb.

(*With a cry of pain, CERISE is stunned into momentary silence.*)

JONI: Michele?

MICHELE: Hush, baby.

EDDIE: (*Has gone too far, and immediately tries to recover.*) I mean... I didn't mean...

JONI: I want to leave here. Can we please go?

SATURN: Easy, kiddo...

CERISE: That...dumb?

EDDIE: It was a slip of the—

CERISE: Believing you was "dumb"?

MICHELE: You better believe it...

EDDIE: No. No!

CERISE: (*Coldly to MICHELE.*) This is between Eddie and me.

MICHELE: Sorry.

CERISE: (*To EDDIE.*) Well?

EDDIE: I didn't mean you were dumb, Baby. Just that...one little...thing...

CERISE: Don't tell me "one," Eddie. Don't tell me "I didn't mean."

EDDIE: But I didn't!

CERISE: Then why'd you <u>say</u> it?

EDDIE: (*Blowing up.*) Because I meant it, damn it! I told you I had to come up with forty thousand. You really think I could pass up a sure thing like that?

CERISE: Right now, I don't know <u>what</u> I think.

EDDIE: Well, then, figure it out, because I'll be damned if I spend my life on the bottom of the pile.

CERISE: That's what this is all about? You weren't on the bottom.

EDDIE: I was! I am! I was born on the bottom, I know bottom. You can ask Michele.

MICHELE: That wasn't the bottom, Eddie. You don't have the foggiest idea of bottom.

EDDIE: What is this? Girls gang up on Eddie Day?

CERISE: I am not a girl!

EDDIE: Then stop acting like one. I'm talking money here, not popsicles. What is <u>wrong</u> with you people? (*To CERISE.*) Okay, I'm a lousy bum, but you think your daddy made his pile by being a boy scout?

CERISE: I don't <u>care</u> about Daddy's pile.

EDDIE: You sure as hell care about those credit cards and that red Mercedes. (*Turning to MICHELE.*) And what about you and the thousands your father spent for your college and nursing school. You think—

MICHELE: I didn't ask for that.

EDDIE: You sure as squirrels climb trees took it with no questions asked. (*To JONI.*) And what about you, Innocence? And I use the term loosely.

JONI: My father won't even <u>talk</u> to me.

EDDIE: Maybe not, but who else is gonna pick up your and the kid's hospital bill? The tooth fairy?

MICHELE: Okay! We were misinformed. You're a saint.

EDDIE: I didn't say that. (*To SATURN.*) Did I say that?

SATURN: Actually, no.

CERISE: Saturn! Whose side are you on?

SATURN: Yours. But he didn't say it.

EDDIE: And I've never pretended to be a saint, either. So get off my damn <u>case</u>!

CERISE: (*A beat. Icily.*) You mean that, Eddie?

EDDIE: Yeah, I mean it.

CERISE: Okay. (*Exiting to kitchen.*) I have quiche, pasta salad, and a bottle of really nice white wine. We could eat at your new place.

EDDIE: Now, wait a minute...

MICHELE: (*Calling after CERISE.*) Sounds good to me.

CERISE: (*Off.*) Saturn?

SATURN: Super!

EDDIE: What do you think you're doing?

MICHELE: (*Getting her back pack, etc.*) Ride with Saturn, Joni. And bring the dry clothes.

(*JONI picks up the pillow case filled with dry clothes.*)

EDDIE: Talk some sense into her, Saturn. This is crazy! I never thought she'd... (*Desperate, now, and at a loss for words.*) I mean, I didn't think...

SATURN: There you have it, man.

CERISE: (*Enters from kitchen with groceries.*) Is everybody ready?

EDDIE: Listen, Cerise, I—

CERISE: (*To SATURN.*) May I follow you?

SATURN: I'll drive slow. (*Picks up wet laundry and starts for door.*) Come on Joni.

CERISE: (*On way to front door, to JONI.*) Don't forget your present, honey.

(*JONI grabs her present, but with both hands full, forgets BUNNY.*)

CERISE: (*Returning to EDDIE to hand him the ring she removes from her finger.*) I'm not my mother, Eddie. The engagement's off. Enjoy your life.

EDDIE: Big deal. You think I can't find someone else... (*Snaps fingers.*) ...like that?

CERISE: You probably can. And that's... (*Snaps fingers.*) ...how much I care! (*Pauses at front door.*) My big claim to fame. I did not sleep with Eddie Fortman.

(*CERISE and JONI exit. SATURN pauses by the climbing wall.*)

SATURN: (*To EDDIE.*) Neat wall, man. Oh, yeah. (*Takes $5 bill from his pocket and stuffs it in EDDIE's shirt pocket.*) Here's your five. Thanks.

EDDIE: I don't need...

SATURN: (*Turns from him. To MICHELE.*) You coming?

MICHELE: In a minute.

(*SATURN exits, leaving MICHELE and EDDIE alone.*)

EDDIE: Well, you happy?

MICHELE: No.

EDDIE: I'll bet.

MICHELE: You know what's crazy?

EDDIE: Yeah. Everything, now, thanks to you.

MICHELE: What's crazy is that I taught myself to get used to being without you. It wasn't easy. First I cried a lot. Then I was mad—really angry. Then I had a lover—truly nice guy—for almost a year until I joined "A Single Step" and went to Guatemala... One thing and another, I worked at it and made a good life for myself. But all that time, the thought would strike me at the oddest moments, that maybe, just maybe, someday, we would...

EDDIE: We still could, Mick. I could—

MICHELE: No, it's too late. No more tuna fish casseroles, no more dinosaur roaches, and fresh out of maybes. (*Collects her backpack.*) Someday's come, and someday's gone. (*Wistfully, perhaps even touching him.*) I'll miss you, Eddie.

EDDIE: Mick, I—

MICHELE: (*A finger to her—or his—lips.*) Shhh! (*A beat.*) Sandy and forty thousand dollars. Wow! Move over, world. (*A wan smile as she pauses at front door.*) Have a nice climb to the top, Eddie. I hope the view's worth it.

(*MICHELE exits, leaving EDDIE alone. Hesitant momentarily, he calls after her.*)

EDDIE: You're damn right, it's worth it. You don't see me on any damn turnip truck, do you? (*He spots BUNNY, and moves, too quickly, to pick it up.*) And your stray left her damn—Ahhhhh!...

(*Doubled over in pain, EDDIE clutches BUNNY to his ribs, sinks gratefully into the recliner, and sighs in relief. After a beat, and now cuddling BUNNY, he begins to sing in a cracked and fading voice as the lights begin slowly to dim.*)

EDDIE: (*Singing.*)
Shine on, shine on, harvest moon,
Up in the sky...
I ain't had no lovin' since...

(*The phone rings. EDDIE stops singing, gets up and starts for the phone, then stops and looks at it. On the fourth ring, the answering machine picks up, and we hear...*)

EDDIE: (*On machine.*) Hi. This is Ed Fortman. Sorry I'm not here to take your call, but if you'll leave your name and telephone number, I'll get back to you shortly. Thank you.

BOOM-BOOM: (*On machine, seductively.*) Hi Eddie. It's Boom-Boom. I'm back from Lake Charles, finally. Two <u>great</u> sales, and two looong, boooring weeks. And who better to bring a foxy lady back to life than Mr. Magic?

(*EDDIE moves quickly to the phone and picks up to cut off BOOM-BOOM's following line.*)

BOOM-BOOM: (*On machine.*) Call me soon, lover. I've got a positively <u>sinful</u> yummy new recipe for whipped cream and maraschino cherries we should try out...

EDDIE: Boom-Boom! How's my little light at the end of the tunnel!...

THE END

Pamela White amd Robert F. Brock in *Someday's Gone* by Frank Schaefer, Horse Cave Theatre, 1999

Frank Schaefer

Frank is a Kentucky transplant from rural upstate New York through urban Texas, mainly Dallas. His theatrical background is with the Dallas Theater Center.

He made his living as a novelist for some twenty years, with some twenty books to his credit. He moved to Allen County, Kentucky, in 1992.

His introduction to Horse Cave was a visit to renew a friendship with Warren, with whom he had worked back in the '60s at the Dallas Theater Center.

He now works with and lives next door to his son in Austin, Texas.

Will Miller, Joseph McKinney, Walter May and Alex Eversoll in *Beating the Varsity* by Larry Pike, Horse Cave Theatre, 2000

BEATING THE VARSITY
by
Larry Pike

Alex Eversoll, Will Miller, Alex Cherington, Rick Cox, Walter May, Joseph McKinney, Chris O'Carroll and Robert F. Brock in *Beating the Varsity* by Larry Pike, Horse Cave Theatre, 2000

Beating the Varsity opened on July 14, 2000, with the following cast:

MIKE	*Chris O'Carroll*
BEN JONES	*Rick Cox*
JAY ROGERS	*Robert F. Brock*
STEVE HAMILTON	*Alex Cherington*
COACH	*Walter May*
DEBBIE	*Vickie Rogers*
YOUNG BEN	*Joseph McKinney*
YOUNG JAY	*Alex Eversoll*
YOUNG STEVE	*Will Miller*

Director: Warren Hammack
Stage Manager: Ryan Newton Harris
Set Design: William W. Laing
Lighting Design: Lynne Chase
Sound Design: Ryan Newton Harris
Costume Design: Marty Hagedorn
Properties Master: Pamela Happy Sisler
Technical Director: Jeremy Artigue
Production Assistant: Laurel Sisler
Assistant Production Assistant: Charles Eric Baldwin

I am not by nature a nervous person. But when I entered the Horse Cave Theatre auditorium for what I expected to be a dress rehearsal three nights before *Beating the Varsity*'s premiere, my anxiety spiked. The word *chaos* came to mind.

Set builders were hammering. Director Warren Hammack and Lighting Designer Lynne Chase were experimenting with lighting cues. Costume Designer Marty Hagedorn was double-checking measurements for an outfit that still needed sewing. Sound levels for music were being adjusted. The actors were fidgeting, eager for their time on stage.

Amazingly to me, no one seemed the least bit concerned.

Turns out, I shouldn't have been worried, either.

Opening night's sell-out crowd saw a beautiful – and completed – set (though I heard after the performance that the last paint was applied ninety minutes before curtain). All the costumes fit. Everything worked. The cast's timing was sharp, especially on the funny lines. The young actors hit "the shot" at the end of the play on the first try.

Wonderfully talented theatre professionals brought *Beating the Varsity* to life. They took care of the rookie playwright – on opening night and for each of the show's twenty performances. I saw them all. And as is particular to live theatre, each performance was unique, sometimes due to an actor's interpretation of the material, sometimes because of the audience's reaction to it. At every performance I learned something about one of my characters I hadn't known before. I grew as a writer.

Beating the Varsity enjoyed, in the sports vernacular, a Cinderella season. During the play's run I had the enthusiastic support of my family and many friends. Those who mounted the production – Warren, the cast, crew, and theatre staff – earned my appreciation and admiration. I was honored to share the experience with each of them.

– LARRY PIKE

Characters:

MIKE, *third-generation owner of The Lick, age forty-five*

BEN JONES, *a short, roundish man, age forty-five*

JAY ROGERS, *a handsome, fashionably dressed man, age forty-four*

STEVE HAMILTON, *a tall, handsome man, age forty-four*

COACH, *an aging man in his late-sixties or early-seventies*

YOUNG BEN, *1968 alter-ego of BEN JONES; dressed in basketball uniform of the period, white high-top canvas Converse All-Stars are essential*

YOUNG JAY, *1968 alter-ego of JAY ROGERS; dressed in basketball uniform of the period, white high-top canvas Converse All-Stars are essential*

YOUNG STEVE, *1968 alter-ego of STEVE HAMILTON; dressed in basketball uniform of the period, white high-top canvas Converse All-Stars are essential*

DEBBIE, *an attractive black woman in her late-thirties or early-forties*

REFEREE (*Offstage voice.*)

Place: The interior of "The Lick," a vintage but worn hot dogs and ice cream parlor favored over the years by students from the former high school across the street and the sprawling state university that encroaches on The Lick's corner location.

Up left, a dirty but expansive plate glass window overlooks the street. Painted in a gentle arch on the glass, wrong-reading to the audience, are the words, "Eastside Ice Cream Co." In script underneath the name is the slogan, "Lick it up!" The entrance to The Lick, double swinging doors with large glass panels, is upstage center. The lower half of the windows is fogged with condensation. A metal, industrial-grade trash receptacle is near the door. Downstage left, the serving area of the shop is dominated by a large semi-circular corner booth. The plastic tabletop is chipped, the vinyl of the bench torn and duct-taped. A restaurant-grade napkin dispenser, salt and pepper shakers, and squeeze bottles of mustard and catsup are on the table, as is a tent card that says, in neat block letters: Reserved – Varsity Only! Upstage of the booth is a counter. Behind the counter are swinging doors to the back to The Lick's freezer and beyond. Between the counter and front door sits an ancient jukebox and a large, scratched soft drink cooler. Several worn cardboard boxes and a large picnic ice chest are stacked next to the cooler. Mementos (a yearbook, a basketball jersey, an old leather basketball, a pair of worn white high-top Converse All-Stars, etc.) are arranged on the cooler and on available spaces around the shop. There are many items. Hanging above the cooler is a colorful banner hand-lettered on butcher paper. It reads in two lines, "30-Year JV Reunion! 'Any Given Day Arrives!' Go Rinks!" Various advertising signs, including a clock, hang on the wall; some are decades old and represent products that no longer exist. On the countertop, upstage left, are an old cash register, ice cream cone rack with cones, milk shake maker, and small lidded onion and relish bowls. A section of newspaper is spread on the counter. On the wall behind the counter is a cheap menu board, listing a dozen or so flavors of ice cream, and hot dogs, with prices for various ways to get them (e.g., all the way, with onions and chili, etc.)

From up right to roughly down center, overlapping the interior of The Lick, is part of a basketball court. Lines marking the baseline and upstage sideline and free throw lane are painted on the stage floor. A backboard and goal hang at regulation height up right. A wooden bench is close along the stage right sideline. Three young players, all high school freshmen, sit on the bench in basketball uniforms (with numbers only – no school name), as if eager to enter a game. They are joined by their coach, who sits at the end of the bench; he is dressed in a shirt and pants that he could have worn while teaching school, and basketball shoes like his players'. A whistle is around his neck. On a folding chair are draped a sport coat and an overcoat. The coach's worn wingtips are underneath the chair. For the most part, this portion of the stage is in "dreamier" light, except for the scenes in which action occurs on the basketball court.

Time: About 8:00 p.m., February 1998.

ACT ONE

About 8 o'clock in the evening. MIKE is behind the counter reading the newspaper. He reads slowly, and turns pages deliberately. He is dressed in a white T-shirt or other uniform shirt, white uniform pants, and a white paper food service cap. BEN is seen through the plate glass window carrying a large, worn cardboard box, tape reinforcing its corners. He wears a cheap navy blazer and gray slacks that ride low on his waist. He is not wearing a tie, and his dress shirt is open at the throat. He is paunchy, and the shirt fits snugly. BEN enters The Lick and crosses to the soft drink cooler. He sets the cardboard box down on top. MIKE does not look up from his paper.

MIKE: How many more boxes you gonna bring in?

BEN: Next to last one.

   (*BEN begins taking things out of the box, placing them on the cooler.*)

MIKE: (*Continues reading.*) Right.

BEN: Maybe two more.

   (*BEN, holding an item from the box in each hand, turns to survey The Lick, searching thoughtfully for the right place to display each. MIKE looks up from his paper, observing BEN's considerations.*)

MIKE: The Guinness Book know about you? Never known anyone to keep this much stuff from high school.

BEN: High school? This is my freshman year stuff.

   (*BEN picks out the spot for one of the mementos, and crosses to place it. He tilts his head to examine the item. Satisfied, he turns to look for a spot for the remaining piece, a yellowed copy of a school newspaper.*)

BEN: Really, just my freshman year basketball season stuff.

MIKE: You're kidding.

BEN: Nope.

MIKE: You're living in the past.

BEN: I am? Look at this place. When I started coming in here thirty-three years ago, it looked just like this. No, sorry. I take that back. Your dad kept it looking a lot better than this.

MIKE: Just like home, he used to say.

BEN: It was home to most of us. This looks like somebody's attic. Mine, maybe. What style is this, circa nineteen-what?

MIKE: Ooo, circa. I'm impressed. You take up reading?

   (*MIKE folds up the paper, and places the section with the others.*)

BEN: Not since my brief college career—

MIKE: How many weeks was it?

BEN: Would've been a whole semester but my instructors all said there wasn't any reason to take finals.

MIKE: So your reading skills are suspect?

BEN: All I read are letters from my mom, which she writes once a week even though I just live six blocks from her and she calls every day, and Sports National. Jay's bound to mention us in one of his articles sooner or later.

MIKE: Jay is not going to write about his junior varsity basketball team from thirty years ago. Not the two-time national basketball writer of the year. Jay's not likely to admit he ever played JV. Ruin his image.

BEN: B.S. Our story is what sport's all about. (*He points to the old newspaper he holds.*) Jay said so himself right here.

MIKE: Cute school news then, rub the varsity's noses in it, but that was then. This is now. Nobody'd be interested.

BEN: I would. I've never forgotten it. Not one minute of it. I remember it all.

MIKE: But it was just a practice game.

BEN: Just practice? Uh-huh. It was real, we played for real. Best we ever played. Me, anyway. I peaked at fifteen.

MIKE: Didn't think you'd gotten any taller.

BEN: If you'd played that year, you'd know what I mean.

MIKE: Knew there wasn't any point in sitting on the JV bench two years in a row. Besides, somebody had to be here to keep you guys in hot dogs and ice cream. (*He nods toward the corner booth.*) And keep unauthorized personnel out of the varsity's booth. Especially all you rinky-dinks.

BEN: That was part of it, always being second class. Like not being able to sit in the corner booth.

MIKE: What's the point of being varsity if there're no JV to abuse?

BEN: Absolutely none. And that's what made it so sweet, a whole year of crap – two years for some guys – wiped out in one afternoon.

MIKE: It was still just a practice game.

BEN: You're not listening. There was *one* moment.

MIKE: What?

BEN: It runs through my head in slo-mo. I holler out the special Duke play and Steve picks off Armstrong and Jay cuts around him just like Coach taught us. Jay looks back for my pass just as I make it, and the ball bounces up and catches him in full stride already going up to the basket, knowing the ball would be here, and he lays it in just before the buzzer. Between the ball dropping through the net and hitting the floor and us realizing we'd beat the varsity – before the varsity realized we'd beat them – it was so quiet it seemed to last forever. That moment, that was sweet. (*Beat.*) Varsity coach was so mad, he made us run laps. We didn't care. We ran 'em and raced down here.

MIKE: You make it sound like a religious experience.

BEN: If Jesus had called me right then, I'd have gone without a peep, like that Old Testament guy, Elijah.

MIKE: Whoever. I don't remember much from Sunday School. Anyway, Sports National's not exactly folksy. Not some local newspaper. (*He picks the newspaper off the counter and waves it at BEN.*) Doesn't even look like our local paper's interested. Don't believe your little reunion's gonna be page one tomorrow. Judging by the team of reporters and photographers they sent to cover it, it won't be back page, either. Of course, you can try to convince me they're just fashionably late – like all your other guests.

BEN: A thousand comedians out of work, and I'm stuck with you. If they don't show, I'll take the pictures myself.

MIKE: But who'll write the story?

BEN: (*He gives MIKE the finger.*) You're so funny.

MIKE: By the way, I much prefer garage to attic, especially yours. Don't need anymore leftovers from high school. If you'd broaden your horizons a little bit, you'd recognize that this place is National Historic Register material.

BEN: You're just too cheap to fix it up.

MIKE: Cheap's got nothing to do with it now.

BEN: Think that CLOSED sign will be enough by itself? It is Friday, and all.

MIKE: You see a line forming outside? Not exactly SRO.

BEN: Whatever. (*Realizing he is still holding the old paper, BEN reaches it toward the counter.*) You mind? I gotta get the box out of my car before the guys get here.

MIKE: Just keep it out of the relish.

(*BEN places the school paper on the counter next to MIKE's newspaper, then hurries out of The Lick and down the street the way he entered. MIKE takes a rag from behind the counter and rubs at a small area.*)

MIKE: It'll be amazing if any of those guys show up thirty years after a practice game.

(*MIKE rubs the spot harder for a moment, then gives up and tosses the rag down. He picks up the newspaper, and exits through the doors behind the counter. The Lick is vacant. JAY is seen coming down the street in front of The Lick from the direction opposite of BEN's departure. JAY reaches the doorway and enters The Lick. He is a handsome man, almost pretty, and is a stylish dresser. It is evident that he is fastidious about his appearance. He wears a camel-colored cashmere overcoat with a muffler draped around his neck. His sport coat is a muted houndstooth over gray flannel slacks. His shirt is severely starched. Its collar and French cuffs are white; the body, French blue. His tie is loud but appropriate to his attire. His Italian loafers are shined to a high-gloss gleam, and he wears thin silk socks that do not sag at his ankles. His hair is perfectly combed. He wears a tasteful but noticeable pinky ring on his right hand. His nails are manicured. He shoots his cuffs frequently, and checks his reflection in the plate glass window. He carries himself in a way that seems designed to insure that his shirt doesn't get wrinkled. JAY walks over to the drink cooler to examine the mementos on display; he picks up a few and examines them.*)

JAY: Got to be Bennie's. Only one who'd keep this stuff.

(*JAY picks up the basketball, and dribbles it a few times, between his legs, if possible. He doesn't notice MIKE come in behind him.*)

JAY: Man's got it bad.

MIKE: He may be terminal.

JAY: Mike. Hey.

MIKE: Good to see you, too.

JAY: You surprised me.

(*JAY crosses to the counter and extends his hand. JAY and MIKE shake hands somewhat formally.*)

JAY: Same old place, huh?

MIKE: Some things never change. The Lick, for example.

JAY: (*He sniffs.*) Same onions for sure.

(*JAY and MIKE laugh.*)

MIKE: Ones my grandfather used, I think, or maybe my dad changed 'em once. (*He leans on the counter.*) Surprised you showed.

JAY: (*Beat.*) I hadn't been home in a while. Bennie's little reunion seemed like a good excuse.

MIKE: He's Ben now.

JAY: He's been what now?

MIKE: His name. He goes by Ben now.

JAY: All grown up? About time. Good thing he didn't hear me. Where is Ben, by the way? (*He looks around.*) It's obvious he has been here.

MIKE: Getting another load of souvenirs from his car. The last one, he said.

JAY: I'd hate to see his house.

MIKE: (*He gives JAY a look as he speaks, gauging JAY's reaction.*) Pity his wife.

JAY: Wife? Bennie – Ben – is married?

MIKE: You didn't know?

JAY: When did it happen?

MIKE: He didn't tell you?

> (*JAY removes his muffler and overcoat to avoid looking at MIKE – and to regain his cool. He drapes the coat and muffler over the back of the varsity booth's seat.*)

JAY: Okay to put my things in this booth now?

MIKE: Enough years have probably passed, but might ought to check with Ben when he gets back. Can't believe he didn't tell you.

JAY: When did it happen?

MIKE: Six, seven months ago. He and Crystal eloped.

JAY: Please. Crystal? You're not serious.

MIKE: About killed his mother. From them eloping, I mean, not him marrying someone named Crystal, but I'm not a hundred percent sure.

JAY: Nobody could be good enough for her Bennie.

MIKE: She's pretty well over it. Most of it, anyway. Crystal's turned out to be real good for Ben. She's okay. For a blond. Maybe especially for a blond.

JAY: Blond? Real or bottled? Crystal's bound to be bottled.

MIKE: I don't think the carpet matches the drapes.

JAY: Duh.

MIKE: Crystal and Ben's mom get along great. But I get the impression his mom's still sore about not having a big church wedding.

JAY: This Crystal married before?

MIKE: Not that I know of.

JAY: Ben probably realized dear old mom would invite all his old bosses. (*He mimics a deep, TV- announcer's voice.*) "There are eight million jobs in the naked city. Ben Jones will try to hold them all." (*He reverts to his own voice.*) A regular church wouldn't be big enough, and somehow a wedding up in the old gym - (*Jerks his head toward the outside.*) - lacks a certain romance.

MIKE: For the bride. Ben would've felt right at home. Considers it a holy place. Coach would've said, "Bennie, you gotta hit both ends of the one-and-one before you get to kiss the bride."

JAY: Yeah. Coach. (*Pause.*) The way Bennie shot free throws, the poor girl would still be standing at the altar. (*Beat.*) Could this Crystal have worn white?

MIKE: Bennie could have worn white. Can't believe he didn't tell you.

> (*BEN approaches with a large box. He tries to peer around its side to make his way. MIKE points BEN's entry out to JAY. JAY turns to watch BEN enter The Lick. BEN backs in through the door.*)

BEN: Hey, Mike, you don't even have to come in from the fresh air to really get a whiff of the onions. The smell's sort of like a force field around the building.

JAY: How can anyone possibly have so much junk left over from high school?

(*BEN whirls about, looking around the box. When he sees JAY, he drops the box; there is a muffled clanking sound.*)

BEN: Hey, hey, hey, Jaybird! I knew you'd be here!

(*BEN goes to JAY, and gives him an enthusiastic embrace, clapping him on the back; JAY returns BEN's greeting in a more subdued manner.*)

BEN: (*To MIKE.*) Didn't I tell you? Didn't I say ol' Jay would make it?

MIKE: (*To JAY.*) Your name may have been mentioned.

JAY: (*He shoots his cuffs.*) I don't think I appreciate the "old" Jay bit, but, hey, I was in the area. Thought I'd drop by.

BEN: In the area! You're covering the State game Sunday, I bet.

JAY: I may be at the game, but I don't "cover" games anymore. I'm a senior writer. I do features, witty pieces – not box scores and summaries.

BEN: You could do a feature on our reunion, then. This is a great story.

JAY: I don't think so. It's not, uh, appropriate for a reporter to write a story in which he's a key figure.

MIKE: Mr. Integrity.

BEN: Then don't write about yourself.

JAY: But if I don't hit the shot, there is no story.

MIKE: (*To BEN.*) Jay here won those big awards. He can't write about just anything.

JAY: Never let 'em see you sweat.

MIKE: Speaking of which, when was the last time you interviewed some jock in a locker room?

JAY: Three, four years. Senior writers don't actually have to go in locker rooms.

MIKE: (*To BEN.*) He doesn't have to actually see the game to write something sarcastic about it, either.

JAY: With the right platitudes and an adroit use of the cliché, a skillful writer like me can file a good column <u>before</u> the game, sometimes even from another city. Lots of advantages to this, especially if there's a woman in the other city.

MIKE: Kind of hard to file an expense report that way, isn't it?

JAY: The editors and publisher tag team the accountants. The publisher just cares if advertisers buy space. And the editors just care about whether people read the column. People do, and that attracts the ad buyers. Ultimately, nobody cares where I write. Or under what circumstances. Don't ask, don't tell.

(*BEN appears enthralled by this brief account. MIKE shakes his head.*)

JAY: I've got a file full of blank receipts from restaurants and clubs all over the country. Wherever there's a hoop, I could be having dinner there right now, according to my records. Just think of me as a free agent looking for a team. (*Gives BEN a look.*) Could even be entertaining a few old friends with me. (*Shoots cuffs again.*) It all adds up. These shirts don't come from Penny's catalog.

BEN: (*To MIKE.*) Didn't I tell you Jay would be here. Isn't this great?

MIKE: (*Busies himself behind the counter. To JAY.*) Why do you think you don't have to play by the rules?

JAY: Why should I?

MIKE: Expense fraud, for one thing.

JAY: The liberal use of an expense account is part of the creative process.

MIKE: You'd know about the creative process if you had to pay the bills and meet a payroll.

JAY: But I don't. Just one of the differences between us.

MIKE: And you wouldn't want to "be like Mike," would you?

BEN: Hey, c'mon, this is a party – a celebration! Thirty years ago today the varsity got theirs! So everybody be nice.

JAY: It was today?

(*BEN crosses to the picnic ice chest.*)

BEN: Actually, it was three days ago, but Tuesday didn't seem like such a great night for a party. Besides, Mike didn't think he could close up for a big private bash like this in the middle of the week with the college students in town.

JAY: Clearly no problem tonight.

BEN: No, not tonight. (He *digs in the ice in the chest.*) Here, what do you want to drink, Jay? Beer? Soft drink, just to get you started?

JAY: Wouldn't happen to have any Woodford Reserve in there, would you?

BEN: Woodford Reserve?

JAY: Only reason I can think of to go anywhere near Rupp Arena. Great bourbon.

BEN: No, just the beer and soft drinks. I'm, uh, I'm sorry, I forgot... it, I guess....

JAY: No, you didn't. I only recently acquired a taste for it. That was just a test. But I don't go near Rupp if I can help it. Not particularly welcome there after that series I did on Eddie Sutton and Dwayne Casey and the NCAA's interest in Kentucky's recruiting practices. And if I get a package from a certain air express company, well, I let someone else open it.

MIKE: That was years ago.

JAY: Not in the Bluegrass State. Only Christian Laettner's less welcome in Lexington. (*To BEN.*) Beer's okay.

BEN: Yeah, sure, what kind? Light or regular?

JAY: Unleaded, of course. (*Pats his stomach.*) Got to watch my weight. ESPN doesn't want some guy with a gut doing guest commentary.

BEN: (*Chuckles self-consciously, and hitches up his pants as he sucks in his stomach.*) No way.

MIKE: You been on ESPN?

JAY: My agent's working on it. Feinstein writes all those books, gets on "The Sports Reporters" and NPR. Mike Lupica, for crying out loud, snooty little weasel. I just want what I'm due.

MIKE: If ESPN considers Digger an expert, you'd think they could find a spot for you.

BEN: Absolutely. It'll happen. How about it, Mike? You want a beer?

MIKE: I'm on duty. Maybe later. You guys want something to eat, – (*He points toward the menu board.*) – you know what we got.

BEN: Maybe later.

(*BEN reaches into the ice chest and pulls out a longneck bottle. He wipes the ice from it, twists off the cap, and hurries the bottle to JAY.*)

BEN: Here you go, Jaybird, ice cold.

(*BEN returns to the chest and lifts out another bottle for himself. BEN and JAY drink in silence. A few moments pass. JAY puts his bottle down and goes to the counter walk-through.*)

JAY: (*To MIKE. Pointing to the door behind the counter.*) The can still back there?

MIKE: Yeah.

(*JAY passes through the door.*)

MIKE: Sure, go ahead, help yourself. (*Wipes the countertop some more. To BEN.*) Why do you let him needle you like that? Always have.

BEN: He's just mouthing. He's got a big job.

MIKE: What? He already told you he can do it from some other city.

BEN: You get a chance to say anything about Crystal?

MIKE: He was pissed you hadn't told him. You're going to catch a rack of crap.

BEN: (*Grins.*) Probably.

MIKE: When are you going to tell him?

BEN: Later. When everybody's here she's going to stop by. (*Sees JAY returning.*) Shhh! Here he comes!

(*JAY returns.*)

JAY: Can see why the public's not allowed back there. You manage to keep the health inspector out, too?

MIKE: A free gallon or two of chocolate chip, he looks the other way.

JAY: He could hold out for a lot more. (*Checks his watch.*) Who's coming to this gala?

BEN: Steve said he was coming. Ought to be here any minute now. And I called most of the other guys I could find. Not sure who'll make it. Couldn't locate Spooner.

JAY: Did you invite Larson?

BEN: Ineligible. He got moved up halfway through the season.

JAY: But he never played any varsity.

BEN: Not my problem. He wasn't JV when we beat the varsity.

JAY: How about Van...Van what? Dad was a cop. I saw him last year at the Midwest Regional in San Antonio.

(*BEN looks impressed at the mention of the Regional.*)

BEN: Van Gilbert. Didn't invite him. He was a wuss.

JAY: An s.o.b. too. Played dirty, when he could get away with it.

BEN: How'd you recognize him?

JAY: He recognized me. Saw me on press row, came down between games, hollered at me. Security almost ran him off.

BEN: Who was he following?

JAY: Clemson. Said that's where he went.

BEN: Lost to Minnesota in double O.T.

JAY: You say so.

MIKE: You played dirty when you could get away with it, too. I saw you grab a guy's jersey once as he went by you on the way to the basket.

JAY: That would be the standard. If I do it, that's playing smart. Did I get a foul?

MIKE: Missed the elbow too. Ruined my faith in referees.

JAY: Misplaced, anyway.

BEN: (*To MIKE.*) Don't forget, Jay fouled out in the first quarter against Northwest.

JAY: In six minutes, forty-three seconds, to be exact. At home.

MIKE: Vengeance is mine, thus saith the Lord.

JAY: Probably still a record.

MIKE: I hope so. I still remember that cheap little nutcracker you gave me that time – in PE. Wasn't sure I'd take a deep breath again.

JAY: Me? Must have been some other, lesser-skilled player – though it would've been a little nutcracker, if you got it.

(*BEN laughs.*)

JAY: That why you didn't play your sophomore year? You could've worn a cup.

MIKE: A cup? You mean that was for protection there? I thought that thing was a gas mask.

BEN: You're kidding?

(*MIKE and JAY look at BEN. After a beat, BEN laughs, pretending he got it all along.*)

BEN: Gas mask, that's good. Oh, yeah, and Coach may be by for a while later.

JAY: Coach?

BEN: Yeah. Coach.

JAY: You sure?

BEN: Pretty sure. Said he'd try to drop by.

JAY: When's he coming?

BEN: I don't know. A little later.

JAY: I'm not sure if I'll be here then. I can't stay too long.

MIKE: What's the rush? I can fix you a receipt if you're worried about your tab.

JAY: I'm sure I've got one somewhere. I'll just follow my nose to the onions to find it. (*Checks his watch again.*) I told, uh, Mom I'd be in early. She still worries about me.

MIKE: She should.

BEN: Mom? Mom! You devil! Got "Mom" waiting up for you? You don't have to be sneaky around us. Mom!

MIKE: That's right, you don't have to be coy with us. Take Ben with you. Show him what it's like out in the world.

BEN: Oh, no. No way. Crystal – (*He stops suddenly, then continues quietly.*) – would kill me.

JAY: Who's Crystal?

BEN: She's . . . . She's my. . .wife.

JAY: Wife? You got married and didn't tell me?

(*BEN doesn't answer.*)

MIKE: Hey, Jay, I already –

(*JAY waves MIKE quiet.*)

BEN: It happened kind of fast. I was going to call you.

JAY: Fast? Is she pregnant? Did you get her pregnant?

BEN: No!

JAY: Well, is she dying, then? Is that why you married her so quickly – a mercy marriage?

MIKE: Ben's the one dying here.

JAY: She's not dying?

BEN: No.

JAY: When did you marry her?

BEN: A couple months ago.

JAY: A Christmas wedding?

BEN: More like a pre-Labor Day special. Or post-Fourth of July, depending.

JAY: You've been married over six months –

BEN: Seven, late next week.

JAY: Seven months, and you haven't called me? I am hurt.

BEN: I was going to, but after we eloped –

JAY: I'm sure your mother appreciated that.

BEN: You don't even want to know. It never was the right time to call you.

MIKE: Ben was just concerned about what you'd think, Jay, your being the poster child for marriage vows, and all.

JAY: (*To MIKE.*) Just having a little fun with Bennie. (*To BEN.*) You could've called. I've got voice-mail. I had to hear it from Mr. Happy here. Just like old times. Jay gets the drop on everyone.

MIKE: Just like old times. Everyone stills seems to be in ninth grade.

JAY: Be nice. This is a big party. And I think it's just about to get a little bigger.

(*JAY points to the window, and moves away, "hiding." STEVE is about to enter The Lick. STEVE is tall and trim, a handsome man. His graying hair is well cut but not impeccably combed, in contrast to Jay's. STEVE is dressed in a conservative suit and a white button-down collared Oxford cloth shirt. The collar is open and his stylish, but muted, tie is loosened. He wears fashionable glasses. He is not wearing an overcoat, and has his hands in his pants pockets, hunched over against the chill air. STEVE sees BEN through the window and waves. BEN is excited by STEVE's arrival.*)

BEN: (*Mimics a public address announcer as STEVE enters The Lick and waves at MIKE.*) An-n-n-d now, num-m-m-ber thirty-four in your program, but num-m-m-m-ber one in your hearts, Ste-e-e-e-ve Ham-m-m-m-m-il-ton!

(*BEN and STEVE shake hands and give each other a quick, brotherly hug.*)

STEVE: What's in the box?

BEN: Just a few things I brought. Souvenir stuff from our team.

(*BEN gathers the box, and unloads some of the new items.*)

JAY: (*Moving toward STEVE.*) I thought I was number one in the fans' hearts.

STEVE: (*He embraces JAY.*) Gimme my moment of glory, you big whiner. We didn't have programs. How the hell are you? How long's it been?

JAY: Too long. I'm good. You're looking good, I'll say that for you. Dropped some weight since I saw you last. As for me, I'm a little lighter around the marriage, but okay. How's, uh...?

STEVE: Carol. Great. And the boys are growing up. (*To BEN.*) All that stuff yours?

BEN: Oh, yeah.

JAY: I was going to ask about the boys. What are they now, about sixteen and twelve?

STEVE: Try eighteen and fourteen. Two freshmen.

JAY: Stevie is in college already?

STEVE: Just plain Steve now. (*To BEN.*) You can't call anybody by their nickname anymore.

JAY: So I heard.

(*A cell phone rings. JAY and STEVE both pat their coat pockets, trying to find their phones. Each finally extracts a small phone from a pocket. STEVE realizes he doesn't have an incoming call, and points to JAY as JAY answers the call.*)

JAY: Jay Rogers. . . .Helen! I'm . . .working. . . . (*Turns away from STEVE.*) Out of town, baby. I can't come drive you to Heather's. . . . Like another time zone. . . . I don't know if you can sleep over at Heather's. . . . Well, I don't remember meeting her. Maybe it was your mother who met her. . . . Where am I? With some guys I know. . . . Just guys. Look, we'll talk about it when I get back, okay? Now's not the – (*He looks at the phone.*) Good-bye to you, too.

(*JAY puts the phone away.*)

STEVE: (*Ignoring the awkward exchange.*) What grade is Helen in?

JAY: Tenth. Somedays we should have just called her "Hell," for short. A little more descriptive.

BEN: (*To MIKE.*) You know, we should have had programs. Maybe just a sheet with our names and numbers on it.

MIKE : (*He rolls his eyes, and wipes the counter.*) Please.

STEVE: It's a phase. They all go through it.

JAY: I haven't made it any easier on her.

STEVE: Not your style.

JAY: Or hers. I've worn out my welcome.

STEVE: You and Jill are calling it quits?

BEN: (*To MIKE.*) And team stats. That would have been good for the fans.

JAY: For real, this time.

STEVE: What happened this time, you don't mind my asking?

JAY: Nothing very original. Jill's best friend.

STEVE: Good planning there, man. Thought you were more creative than that.

JAY: Tell me.

STEVE: You used to be more creative than that.

JAY: You're right. I hadn't noticed I was slipping. (*Beat.*) You know, my first marriage was, I don't know, a little starter marriage. Hardly ever think about Terri. But I really like Jill. You know how hard it's always been for me to be a one-woman man. I'm allergic to commitment. (*Pause.*) It's been, uh. . . hard for me since high school, since. . . well, since high school. (*Another pause, then lighter.*) And there are just too many temptations on the road.

STEVE: You get about the same amount of trust you give. You could have gotten off the road.

JAY: But I like it.

(*MIKE brings a bowl of pretzels to JAY and STEVE. BEN gets a diet drink from the ice chest and brings it to STEVE.*)

MIKE: (*To BEN.*) Good thing you didn't go out and hire a sports information director. The varsity didn't have many fans. You guys didn't have any.

BEN: Our folks were always there.

MIKE: They probably would have recognized you without a score sheet.

JAY: <u>Your</u> folks were there.

BEN: And the varsity watched us play. And we had the JV cheerleaders.

STEVE: The varsity had to watch until halftime when they went to dress out. And I hate to burst your bubble, but Jay's the only one who "had" the cheerleaders. Of course, I'm only speaking figuratively. I think. He was the one they were there for.

JAY: What else would you expect, bunch of losers like you? But my lips are sealed. I'll never kiss and tell.

MIKE: Now that's a scoop. Stop the presses! Call <u>People</u>. (*The group laughs.*)

BEN: Jay wasn't the only one. Gail Williams was hot for me once.

(*The others hoot.*)

JAY: Crystal know about this?

(*STEVE looks quizzically at MIKE, and mouths "Crystal?" MIKE shakes his head quickly and puts a finger to his lips. JAY doesn't notice.*)

JAY: Gail Williams was hot for you for ten minutes. Gail Williams was hot for everything in pants for ten minutes! Hitting that prayer at the buzzer from the other foul line to win that game at Ward County was what made you the man of the moment.

STEVE: That shot was supposed to be a pass to me. I was open under the basket, having, unlike my lesser-skilled lazy teammates, actually run the floor like I was supposed to. Gail Williams should have been hot for me.

JAY: It was such a bad pass, he overthrew you and the ball banked in. (*To BEN.*) She was all over you on the bus ride home, right?

BEN: Bus ride home lasted longer than ten minutes.

JAY: Odds are you didn't!

STEVE: Cut him some slack. If the varsity hadn't lost their game that night, we wouldn't have got to sit in the back of the bus on the way home, and Gail Williams would still be just a fantasy to Ben.

BEN: I still think about her. (*Everyone laughs. STEVE wanders over to the display of memorabilia on the cooler.*)

MIKE: Might interest you guys to know that Gail Williams is the state N.O.W. president in Montana. Blurb was in the paper couple of weeks ago.

BEN: Now? Now what?

JAY: Where you been, man, living in a cave? N.O.W. – National Organization for Women. A very dangerous group. But Montana? Quite an effect you have on chicks, Bennie.

MIKE: "Chicks"? There's the renowned Rogers' sensitivity.

JAY: Mikey, Mikey, you know I'm a feminist when it comes to chicks.

MIKE: That'll win 'em over.

STEVE: Looks like you brought everything, Ben. (*He picks up the yellowed school newspaper on the counter.*) Here it is, right here on page one of <u>The Warriors' Record</u>, which proves it was another slow news week at our dear old school, the article that launched our friend's award-winning journalistic career, if his particular brand of wit and overworked use of the alliterative style may be called journalism. Here. Listen. "The nature of sport suggests – "

JAY: (*He steps over quickly to snatch the paper from STEVE.*) We don't need to hear that. I'm just a sportswriter, which is not the same thing as a "real" journalist. Used to hear that all the time when I got my first big job in '81. The political flacks on the city desk at the <u>Journal-Constitution</u> in Atlanta. They were the first guys, though, to call about scoring extra Falcons tickets, or Tech tickets, especially when Carolina was coming in. (*To STEVE.*) Didn't know you accountants knew about alliteration.

STEVE: Most of us even read. Sometimes we have to point at the words with a finger, but we read.

BEN: What's wrong with that?

STEVE: That what?

BEN: Pointing.

(*The others exchange glances.*)

JAY: (*Still reading the article.*) It's a bit heavy-handed, but it works. With a few variations, I've probably used it thirty, forty times. Pretty eloquent for a ninth grader. (*Flips the paper over and scans the back page, then opens it, quickly glancing over the inside pages before closing it again.*) Funny thing is, it took me so long to write this lead, it's all I wrote. Not one word describing the game, no play-by-play at all. Nothing. Paper ran it anyway. Only deadline I've ever missed. (*He puts the paper down on the memorabilia display.*)

STEVE: (*At BEN's display, he picks up the basketball and holds it out to BEN.*) And this is it, I presume, the very ball with which I hit the shot that beat the varsity. What's left in your attic?

MIKE: You hit the shot?

STEVE: I hit the shot.

MIKE: Ben said Jay hit the shot.

STEVE: Then I'm happy to set the record straight.

BEN: Jay hit the shot. He broke around your screen, took my pass and laid it in at the buzzer.

JAY: Who else could hit such a shot?

STEVE: Mr. Clutch here took your pass, all right, but it's a good thing I did all the fundamental things so well, like rolling after I set a pick. If I hadn't, I wouldn't have been in position to rebound his miss, and we wouldn't have won. Or be having this little get-together. (*To JAY.*) Who taught you to shoot lay-ups? (*He chest-passes the ball to JAY.*)

BEN and JAY: (*In unison.*) No way!

BEN: You got it wrong, Steverino. You set a helluva pick, and rolled just like you said, but there was no rebound. The shot went in.

STEVE: (*He takes this without argument, and shrugs.*) Didn't realize Alzheimer's was contagious. Believe what you want. I know who hit the shot.

JAY: (*He twirls the ball on his fingertip.*) I did. I hope your self-esteem hasn't been wrapped up all these years in this bogus memory of yours.

STEVE: (*He waves JAY off with a smile.*) Whatever you say. You're the scribe.

MIKE: He sure is, and Ben's been working on him to scribble out something on your story.

STEVE: My story?

MIKE: The team, beating the varsity, this reunion.

STEVE: (*To JAY.*) Are you?

BEN: He's thinking about it.

(*COACH, YOUNG BEN, YOUNG JAY and YOUNG STEVE rise from the bench. COACH watches the young players as they begin "shooting" jump shots, without a ball, of course. They do not speak aloud, but may be seen mouthing words and shouts as they practice.*)

JAY: Bennie thinks I'm thinking about it. I don't think I could, uh, sell it to my editor.

STEVE: It's kind of compelling.

JAY: Like, "Don't give up, don't ever give up."

STEVE: Be flip. It was important to me. But it's a miracle we lived long enough to even play the varsity, much less beat 'em, the way Coach ran us in practice. I break out in a rash if I hear the word laps.

BEN: And the bleachers. Up and down, up and down! You expect that during conditioning, but every day, even late in the season? I don't know how I made it through practice.

JAY: Laps? We could dog those –

STEVE: Which you did. (*BEN and MIKE laugh.*)

JAY: And bleachers were nothing if you didn't act like you were running for your life. I'll tell you what was bad, though –

BEN: (*He feigns fright.*) Don't say it!.

JAY: – they strike fear in the hearts of ballplayers everywhere at every level!

BEN: (*With exaggerated pleading in his voice.*) Please don't say it!

(*JAY throws the ball across the sstage to YOUNG JAY who has turned toward The Lick as if chasing down a loose ball. YOUNG JAY catches the ball and pivots back toward the basket.*)

JAY: Suicides!

(*BEN and STEVE, and even MIKE, shriek in mock terror, and freeze. The lighting on stage changes, emphasizing the basketball ccourt. The chatter of YOUNG BEN, YOUNG JAY and YOUNG STEVE can now be heard as they pass the ball around, taking a few shots, having fun, not worrying about whether or not the shots go in the basket. COACH paces the sideline.*)

YOUNG STEVE: Shoot the ball, man.

YOUNG BEN: Gimme the ball, you can't shoot.

YOUNG JAY: I'm the only one who can shoot.

COACH: On the line now! Suicides!

(*YOUNG BEN, YOUNG JAY and YOUNG STEVE stop. Whoever has the ball when COACH calls for suicides, drops it. The boys walk, heads bowed and shoulders drooping, toward the baseline. The BOYS take their places on the baseline, ready to run.*)

COACH: (*Voice still booming.*) All right, foul line back, half court back, other foul line back, baseline back. Thirty seconds. If you're slow, you go again. Ready!

(*COACH blows his whistle, and the boys run the drill, pounding up and down the court. YOUNG STEVE is clearly in front of the other two; he is giving 100% effort. YOUNG BEN obviously struggles. YOUNG JAY* runs just hard enough to stay in front of YOUNG BEN. As they run, COACH moves up and down the sideline with them, shouting "encouragement" to them.)

COACH: Move, Jones! I said thirty seconds, not thirty days! . . . Rogers, you're dogging it! Hamilton can't beat you! Pick 'em up! . . . Hamilton, you let Rogers catch you, you'll do bleachers after practice! . . . Jones, I said move!

(YOUNG STEVE and YOUNG JAY finish the drill just before COACH blows the whistle again, signaling the thirty-second time limit, but YOUNG BEN is too late.)

COACH: You're too slow, Jones! You gotta ru-u-u-n! You charge up and down my beautiful floor like a mother elephant! Lay off the damn Twinkies! Let's go, everybody goes again!

(The BOYS move to the baseline again, bent over, holding their shorts, though YOUNG JAY does not appear to be breathing as hard as the others.)

YOUNG STEVE: (Quietly, to YOUNG BEN, supporting him.) You can do it. We don't want to have to go again. Suck it up.

(YOUNG BEN bobs his head, gulping air.)

YOUNG JAY: Yeah, Twinkie, get the lard out! Move your ass, or we'll be running all day!

YOUNG BEN: (Spitting out the words between breaths.) Don't call me Twinkie! Run your ass in the ground!

YOUNG JAY: Gotta catch me first. (He laughs.)

COACH: You think this is something funny, Rogers? We'll let you go again by yourself!

YOUNG JAY: No, sir. (Under his breath.) Asshole. (To YOUNG STEVE.) You don't have to act like an Olympic sprinter. You're killing us.

YOUNG STEVE: You pick it up. I'm just trying to be ready to play.

YOUNG JAY: Gimme a break.

COACH: Rogers, if you worked as much as you run your mouth, you'd be a heckuva ballplayer. All of you, on the line! Ready! (He blows the whistle.)

(The trio runs the drill again.)

COACH: (Shouts to PLAYERS as before.) C'mon, Spooner! Keep up! . . . That's the way, Van . . . Van . . . Van the Man, you are the man! . . . Way to lead the pack, Randall! You're the only one in shape!

(The PLAYERS finish, with the same results. YOUNG BEN runs harder, but still finishes last, just after COACH blows the whistle at the end of the 30 seconds. They hold their shorts again, struggling for breath along the baseline.)

YOUNG JAY: Dammit, Bennie! If you can't make it, pretend like you sprained an ankle or something, so he'll call this off.

YOUNG BEN: Shut up!

YOUNG STEVE: Leave him alone! You barely made it!

YOUNG JAY: (He replies too loudly.) All I gotta do! (He picks up the basketball.)

COACH: I heard that, Rogers! Get over here!

(YOUNG JAY's demeanor changes; he becomes "smaller." He drops his head and half-runs over to COACH, carrying the ball with him.)

COACH: "All you gotta do"!

(The two continue speaking, "quietly." COACH puts his hand on YOUNG JAY's shoulder. YOUNG JAY shrinks back, whereupon COACH deftly grabs YOUNG JAY by the jersey, pulling him close. YOUNG JAY pulls back; he doesn't look COACH in the eye.)

YOUNG BEN: Coach sure talks to Jay a lot. What do they talk about?

YOUNG STEVE: I don't know. Practice stuff.

COACH: (*To YOUNG JAY.*) All you gotta do . . . is see me in my office after practice. We need to discuss your . . . attitude . . . again. All right?

(*YOUNG JAY gives a nod, hanging his head, again trying to escape COACH's touch on his shoulder. COACH continues talking to YOUNG JAY.*)

COACH: Get on back out there. (*Now louder, to the rest of the team.*) Again! 'Til you get it right! On the line!

(*YOUNG JAY, still carrying the ball, hurries back to YOUNG STEVE and YOUNG BEN.*)

YOUNG BEN: (*Leaning over, hands on his shorts, breathing heavily.*) You going to have to see Coach after practice again? He going to adopt you?

(*YOUNG JAY doesn't reply.*)

YOUNG STEVE: Bennie, just shut up! We gotta run!

COACH: (*Gives a short whistle blast.*) Let's go, ladies!

(*YOUNG JAY hurls the ball out of the way. It goes across the stage to JAY, who catches it just as COACH blows the whistle again in a long note that trails off to silence. The lighting changes. The Lick is emphasized now. COACH, YOUNG BEN, YOUNG JAY and YOUNG STEVE return to the bench. YOUNG JAY keeps his head down, isolating himself from his teammates. MIKE comes down to clear tables, etc., moving among young players.*)

STEVE: God, what I'd have given for a TV timeout back then. Needed Vitale to holler at Coach, "Get a tee-oh, bay-bee, get a tee-oh!"

JAY: That would have meant we'd have had Vitale back then, too.

MIKE: Please.

BEN: You know Vitale?

JAY: You work around college hoops, you can't help it. Man's everywhere there's a camera and a crowd. Enough to make you want to cover the NBA.

BEN: Nothing's that bad.

STEVE: I talked to Al McGuire at the airport once.

BEN: The Al McGuire?

STEVE: He looks old on TV, but he looks good in person. You'd think it'd be the other way around.

MIKE: What'd you talk about?

STEVE: Civil War toy soldiers.

BEN: Not basketball?

STEVE: Hardly a word. Al collects toy soldiers. Asked if I knew of any antique shops that might have some.

MIKE: "Al"?

STEVE: We'd be best friends now if I could have steered him to some soldiers. (*To JAY.*) How many games do you see a year?

JAY: Many as I want to go to. Then there are the games on the dish. (*Beat.*) Sports trivia quiz.

BEN: (*Sits up straight.*) All right!

JAY: Remember the varsity coach? Olaf Sundstrom? (*He points at STEVE.*)

STEVE: Only here our freshman year.

JAY: Point for you. Two years ago, guess which high school coach had the most active players in the Atlantic Coast Conference?

MIKE: Get outta here.

JAY: Olaf Sundstrom. Seven kids at five schools. Not a redshirt or Prop 48 in the bunch.

BEN: Unbelievable.

JAY: Heard it on a game I caught on the dish. Talk about Morgan Wooten at DeMatha if you want to. Sundstrom is the man.

STEVE: (*To JAY.*) If the school had stayed open, that could have been you. You had the potential.

JAY: Too early in his career. Who knows if Sundstrom could have developed potential back then?

STEVE: Somebody had to be the first. After the school was closed and you transferred across town, you practically started for a state champion senior year.

JAY: I was sixth man. And we lost in the title game.

STEVE: I was trying to give you a compliment. That's what I meant by practically. Where would you have gone? Duke? IU? Been one of Dean's boys?

(*JAY frowns, starts to answer, but is cut off.*)

BEN: (*To JAY.*) How many games you get on the dish?

JAY: Four hundred? Four-fifty? I don't keep track. The magazine pays for the services.

STEVE: My wife would leave me if I tried to watch that many games.

JAY: Mine did, both of them. A few other reasons were involved, too, but the dish doesn't encourage conversation. And you can't watch that many. I don't even bother taping them anymore. Either I'm at the big games, or I get accounts off the 'net when I need them.

MIKE: (*To STEVE.*) Your wife might like it if you watched that much ball. (*In falsetto.*) "Not tonight, honey, you have a ballgame to watch."

STEVE: Do all things in moderation, that's her motto.

BEN: Who cares about sex when you got basketball?

MIKE: Duh!

JAY: Hello!

(*JAY slings the ball at BEN, who just knocks it down, ball slapping his palm, then picks it up.*)

BEN: Remember the first time we played Ruffin? That old bandbox gym?

STEVE: Our first road game.

BEN: No hot water in our locker room.

STEVE: The Ruffin Panthers. They wore black high-top "Chucks."

MIKE: So did Eddie Brown in phys ed.

BEN: Eddie Brown was a pervert.

JAY: He wasn't a pervert, he just wore Keds.

BEN: P. F. Flyers.

JAY: (*Walking about.*) Worse. But Eddie Brown was just a little weird, and poor.

BEN: I don't care. Guy can't wear P. F. Flyers and expect people to think there's nothing wrong with him.

JAY: It doesn't make you perverted.

MIKE: Never known you to protect the rights of the weak and oppressed.

JAY: Just that you guys don't know what you're talking about.

MIKE: And you do?

(*JAY doesn't reply, turning away from MIKE.*)

BEN: I hate homos.

MIKE: You ever met a gay person?

BEN: Not knowingly.

MIKE: You should expose yourself to one sometime.

(*BEN sticks a finger down his throat, pretending to gag. STEVE joins MIKE in laughter.*)

JAY: (*To BEN.*) You especially don't know what you're talking about. (*Pause.*) You know, I almost didn't get to make the trip, to Ruffin.

STEVE: You went. You played. Part of the game, anyway, as I recall.

JAY: I had to do a make-up report for science. Mrs. Rist said I had not done my best work. She was right.

BEN: What a bitch.

MIKE: Science or Mrs. Rist?

BEN: Yeah.

STEVE: How can you remember that?

JAY: I even remember the report. Hypnosis. Like I knew anything about it.

STEVE: So why was that going to keep you from making the road trip?

MIKE: If we'd only given reports that we knew something about, none of us – hell, no one – would ever graduate from high school.

JAY: She said I had to re-do the report or she'd keep me from playing in the game.

STEVE: If she'd gone to Coach, he'd have just made you run a few laps to put her off. No way he'd have held you out of a game.

BEN: He taught geography and civics. What did he care about science?

STEVE: What did he know about science?

MIKE: What did he know about geography and civics?

JAY: You couldn't be sure with Coach, ... what he might be thinking ... or do. I remember it because Mrs. Rist is the reason I became a writer.

STEVE: Mrs. Rist?

JAY: She called me to her office one day right in the middle of class. We were doing some kind of dinky experiment, and Beverly Clendenin was my partner. She had on this loose sort of sweater-blouse thing, and one of the buttons was undone – I think on purpose – and I kept trying to get her to lean over so I could get a better view. She knew what she was doing, and was making me work for it.

BEN: If Beverly Clendenin had been my lab partner, I'd have given my body to science. She could have experimented with me.

MIKE: Science would have given you back.

BEN: You're killing me.

JAY: Let's focus here. While I'm trying to get Beverly at the right angle, Mrs. Rist booms out across the room, "Mr. Rogers, I'll speak to you in my office."

BEN: That little room where she kept all the chemicals?

JAY: One and the same.

BEN: Lucky you got out alive.

JAY: She pretty much sucked the air right out of the room. She was a big woman, eyes flashing, tight little hairdo, a little heavy on the Evening in Paris. She launches into how disappointed she is in my general lack of interest in schoolwork. She'd talked with my other teachers, she said, yadda-yadda-yadda. Then she said, "You're just lackadaisical and indifferent."

BEN: So?

JAY: So, exactly. I didn't know what she meant. I'd never heard those words before. I remember standing there, feeling really stupid, but I couldn't stop thinking how great those words sounded. "Lackadaisical and indifferent." I offered some weasly little, "Yes, ma'am," and hustled out of there. I get back to Beverly, and she's fixed the button, hiding the evidence –

STEVE: So to speak.

JAY: So to speak, in case Mrs. Rist calls her in, and I ask her if she knows what lackadaisical and indifferent mean. Of course, she doesn't. Who in the ninth grade would?

MIKE: So what did you do?

JAY: I was pissed and embarrassed. I looked them up.

STEVE: You looked them up.

JAY: Read my lips. I looked them up. In the dictionary. And that's how I became a writer. Can't tell you the first damn thing about the periodic table, but the power of words I learned that day in science. Every now and then, I think I should find Mrs. Rist and thank her.

MIKE: So, sports journalism has a frumpy ninth grade science teacher to thank for you?

JAY: She wouldn't leave me alone. Kept on me about using my potential.

BEN: I wouldn't know how to look 'em up.

JAY: La. La. La-lackadaisical.

BEN: L?

MIKE: You're not the sharpest nail in the bucket, are you?

BEN: Well, I'm glad to know what letter to look under, but I didn't bring this up to talk about perverts, or science class. (*To JAY.*) The Ruffin game was the one you got tossed out of for fighting with their big black center. (*BEN cuts a sideways glance at MIKE.*)

(*COACH gets up and moves to the chair or bench on which his other clothes are located. He begins changing from his practice attire into his game attire. He changes shoes and removes his whistle, laying it on the bench. He takes a tie from the pocket of the sport coat, and slips it over his head, fixing the knot around his neck. He needs to have finished changing by the time the scoreboard buzzer sounds to signal the start of the Ruffin game flashback.*)

STEVE: Forward, I thought.

BEN: Forward, center, whatever. Only black guy we played against all year. (*Attempts to twirl the ball on his fingertip, but without much success.*)

STEVE: No wonder you were always MIA on defense. You didn't know which position was which.

JAY: Center. It was a cheap trick. Not the highlight of my career.

STEVE: None of our careers.

MIKE: What goes around, . . .

(*As the conversation among the principals continues, COACH, YOUNG JAY, YOUNG STEVE and YOUNG BEN rise and huddle in front of the bench. They listen intently to COACH, who has his arm across YOUNG JAY's shoulders. They nod frequently. YOUNG JAY stands straight once and looks down the court toward the other bench, but COACH pulls him back into the huddle.*)

STEVE: I thought you started it with him.

JAY: Me?

STEVE: So his attack was unprovoked?

(*A scoreboard buzzer sounds. The YOUNG PLAYERS clasp their hands together in the center of the huddle, shout, "Warriors, battle!" then break. YOUNG JAY hustles to the corner of the court up right, where he takes his position. YOUNG STEVE is diagonally across the court from YOUNG JAY. YOUNG BEN waits near the bench for the ball, ready to make the in-bounds pass. COACH watches expectantly from the sideline, hands on his knees.*)

JAY: We exchanged a variety of discreet physical and verbal pleasantries, and then he. . . then he, in today's vernacular, took the game to another level, and things got a little more overt.

BEN: "A little more overt!" You got that right!

(*BEN bounce-passes the ball to YOUNG BEN. JAY, STEVE, BEN and MIKE freeze. The lighting changes, emphasizing the basketball court. YOUNG BEN, standing in front of bench, holds the ball over his head and slaps it to signal the start of the in-bounds play. YOUNG STEVE fakes to the baseline, then breaks toward YOUNG BEN, who throws a chest pass to YOUNG STEVE. YOUNG BEN sprints to a spot down from YOUNG JAY and sets a hard pick. YOUNG JAY seems to be locked up with the imaginary defender guarding him, and has difficulty freeing himself. At the moment of "impact" with YOUNG BEN's screen, YOUNG BEN is knocked a half-step or a whole step backwards. This does not have to be rushed; it will be all right for the young characters to "run the play" a while. COACH waves at them and hollers instructions. YOUNG JAY is pushing off – hard – with his forearm, creating some distance with the defender. YOUNG STEVE looks at YOUNG JAY, but doesn't pass YOUNG JAY the ball as he curls around YOUNG BEN's screen. When YOUNG JAY reaches the foul line, he pivots sharply back to YOUNG STEVE. YOUNG JAY is in a strong position, his man on his hip, and he calls loudly for the ball, arms reaching eagerly out to YOUNG STEVE, who is keeping the ball away from his man, turning on his pivot foot, yet watching for the opportunity to pass the ball in to YOUNG JAY. YOUNG JAY knows his opponent cannot steal a good pass without fouling. YOUNG STEVE bounces a perfect entry pass. YOUNG JAY catches the pass deftly, dribbles once to the right, faking a turn toward the basket, then starts to wheel to the left to the basket. Suddenly, YOUNG JAY drops the ball – in the middle of the play – and lunges at his opponent, pushing him with both hands. The ball rolls toward YOUNG STEVE and YOUNG BEN who are momentarily frozen, watching their irate teammate.*)

YOUNG JAY: (*Up on the balls of his feet, fists clinched. He is in his opponent's face.*) You pervert! You like my ass?

(*There is the sound of sharp whistle bleets.*)

YOUNG JAY: Yeah? Touch me again, I'll beat your nigger ass, faggot!

(*More whistle blasts. YOUNG JAY and his opponent appear to scuffle, then YOUNG JAY takes an imaginary punch to the jaw, and drops to the floor. YOUNG STEVE and YOUNG BEN finally move to his aid. Constant whistles. YOUNG BEN is kicking at a foe, and YOUNG STEVE grabs him up around the waist from behind and drags him away from the fray. YOUNG BEN is flailing about, still trying to fight. YOUNG JAY is crawling toward them, out of the middle of the brawl.*)

YOUNG STEVE: Bennie, stop, it's me! You gotta stop! We're gonna get thrown out!

(*COACH moves onto the court as if to help break up the melee.*)

COACH: (*To YOUNG BEN and YOUNG STEVE.*) Bennie, help Jay before he gets hurt!

YOUNG BEN: Lemme go. I'll kill him, kill the nigger.

YOUNG STEVE: (*Still holding YOUNG BEN back.*) Shut up, Bennie! Shut up!

YOUNG BEN: (*Slumps.*) Nigger.

(*YOUNG JAY, still crawling, has reached their feet. YOUNG BEN and YOUNG STEVE look down at YOUNG JAY, dumbfounded. YOUNG JAY lays on the floor, breathing heavily. Another whistle blast.*)

REFEREE'S VOICE: (*Offstage.*) Give me the ball, gentlemen.

(*YOUNG STEVE picks up the ball and tosses it as if to the referee; the ball bounces across the stage to STEVE. Lighting changes, emphasizing The Lick again. COACH, YOUNG STEVE and YOUNG BEN help YOUNG JAY to his feet, check his jaw, etc. They return to their seats on the bench. COACH sits on the bench next to YOUNG JAY, talking closely to him, his arm on YOUNG JAY's shoulders. After a while, YOUNG JAY slips out from under COACH's arm.*)

BEN: A wonder we all didn't get whipped. Their crazy fans coming out of the stands. Took the refs quite a while to restore order.

STEVE: Plenty of technical fouls to go around. Some people – (*Turns to JAY.*) – even got seconds.

JAY: Yeah, me and Kareem each got a pair. I got to take a long shower, think about the state of race relations in high school basketball, while you blew our lead.

STEVE: No wonder there was no hot water. What did that guy do to you?

JAY: Pinched my ass.

STEVE: Really, what'd he do?

JAY: Really.

STEVE: You started a fight in a game we were winning because you thought the guy eating your lunch on defense pinched your butt?

JAY: He did.

STEVE: In your next life forget all that stuff about basketball being a non-contact sport. Look at the scoreboard first.

JAY: I didn't want anyone touching me.

(*COACH takes YOUNG JAY from the bench and they exit.*)

BEN: Coach sure didn't like you starting that fight. He had you in his office a long time after we got back to the gym. I stood by the door and tried to listen – figured you'd be getting ripped a new one. Thought he'd be on you like white on rice.

JAY: He was.

BEN: But I couldn't hear anything. You were still in there when my dad picked me up. I was going to offer you a ride, but my dad was ready to go, and you were still in there.

JAY: Coach made sure I got the point.

BEN: What?

JAY: Nothing. When did you say he's supposed to get here?

BEN: I don't know. Later.

(*JAY checks his watch.*)

STEVE: What sheltered lives we lived. School wasn't integrated, hardly ever saw blacks, much less played against any. Now, two of my partners and three of our junior accountants are black. Good guys. We've got three women in the firm – and it's a good thing. They've got the best clients.

BEN: (*To JAY.*) The guy you called "Kareem"? Name's Roland Barnes. Been a stock broker in town for about twelve, thirteen years. Blew out a knee playing juco ball in Indiana somewhere. Came home to rehab, ended up at State. Got a degree in finance.

JAY: Like you know him.

(*Unseen by JAY, BEN and MIKE exchange a "knowing" look. STEVE sees them, and takes a step toward BEN and MIKE, with a quizzical expression, but BEN waves him off.*)

BEN: We go to the same doctor. I was in for a check up couple of years ago, he was in the waiting room. I kept thinking he looked familiar, so I finally went over and said something. It took a few minutes, but we put it together. Turns out we were at State together a semester.

MIKE: Part of a semester, in your case.

STEVE: You ask him if he pinched Jay's young butt?

BEN: Didn't have to. Said he remembered me, called me the little fat honky who kept yelling I was going to "kill the nigger."

STEVE: How about another word?

BEN: That's what I said.

JAY: That's how he acted.

STEVE: You talk that way in front of Helen?

JAY: You ought to hear how she talks around me.

STEVE: Surprise. Just use another word.

JAY: Will if I want to.

BEN: Sure, no problem, sorry. Roland thought it was funny. He could laugh. He was in better shape than when we played against him. Put on a few pounds, added a few inches, like he needed them. Still looks carved out of rock. He remembered you too, Jay.

JAY: Probably remembered how lucky he was I didn't kill him.

STEVE: Which would have been something. You were crawling off to safety while he was tossing the rest of our team out to the paramedics.

BEN: Roland mentioned luck, but it wasn't his he was talking about. He was surprised you went ballistic when he pinched you. Said he was just trying to get in your head. Never expected it'd practically start a riot.

STEVE: I thought the National Guard might have to be called out.

BEN: He thought you over-reacted, especially your threatening to beat his ni – (*Glances at STEVE.*) – uh, his black behind. Said it would not have happened. Wasn't sorry about it, though, since you got ejected and they pulled out the win.

JAY: He got tossed, too.

MIKE: The end justifies the means.

BEN: Huh? Anyway, Roland likes your work. Thinks it's "interesting" that you always write what he says are "brother-friendly" stories, considering your "youthful ideas about the races," he said. I said, yeah, you were a pretty fair guy.

JAY: A trick of the trade. Write what your readers identify with.

MIKE (*To JAY.*) You always this cynical?

BEN: He said you were a hothead who wouldn't play defense, but said you're a good writer, gets a kick out of your stuff. Likes the biting, sarcastic humor, or something like that.

STEVE: Couldn't play defense.

MIKE: (*Puts a finger to his lips, alerting STEVE to be quiet.*) You should have invited him. Sounds okay.

BEN: Thought about it.

JAY: He a friend of yours?

BEN: Run into him every now and then.

JAY: So now, except for poor alleged perverts, of course, you're a regular equal opportunity kind of guy? You'd be doing life without parole somewhere if Steve had let you go after . . . what's his name?

BEN: Roland. You live and learn. I don't feel the same about minorities now as I did then.

JAY: You've gone from wanting to "kill the nigger" to having "feelings" for minorities. You're becoming as wussy as . . . Van . . . shit!

MIKE: Van Gilbert.

BEN: I have not become a wuss.

STEVE: Hey, this trip down memory lane's got me feeling like rattling a few rims. Think we can sneak in the gym and shoot a few? I feel like dunking on you.

JAY: Dream on. You couldn't touch the rim then, probably can't reach the net now.

STEVE: Don't be talking smack.

JAY: You can't jump, but you're slow.

MIKE: I don't think –

BEN: I can probably still jimmy the girls' locker room door.

MIKE: I don't –

JAY: Then let's go! Grab the ball, Steve-o. Let me get my coat. (*He goes to retrieve his overcoat and muffler from the corner booth.*)

BEN: Who's a wuss, now? You won't freeze going across the street.

JAY: (*Putting on his coat and adjusting his muffler.*) Can't have a cold when my agent calls. (*A riff of the ESPN "SportsCenter" theme music.*) Da-da-daa-da-da-daa.

MIKE: Listen. Before the testosterone kicks in –

STEVE: (*Interrupts MIKE.*) Yeah, come on, Rogers, you can do the commentary on our exciting play.

(*STEVE picks up the ball, dribbles it once or twice, and he, BEN and JAY head for the door.*)

MIKE: I'm trying to tell you guys –

(*BEN and STEVE are already outside.*)

JAY: (*Stops and turns back to MIKE.*) Mikey, chill. We won't get caught. We're just going to shoot a few. Keep the beer cold, and get some hot dogs ready. We'll be back in a few minutes. (*He turns quickly and exits. He can be heard off-stage.*) Hey, wait up!

MIKE: I don't care if you get caught. You just can't go home again.

(*MIKE checks a couple of bins in the ice cream cooler, makes a note on his hand with a pen, then goes through the doors behind the counter.*)

ACT TWO

Shortly before 9:00 p.m. The Lick is well lit, while the basketball court area of the stage is subdued. A light snow has started to fall and can be seen through the window. MIKE is behind the counter preparing hot dogs. He stirs the chili pot and puts some buns in the steamer. His back is to the door. YOUNG BEN, YOUNG STEVE and YOUNG JAY are in their places on the bench. A song from the late Sixties is playing on the juke box. BEN, JAY and STEVE enter The Lick's front door; they are sullen. STEVE is carrying the basketball under his arm. MIKE glances over his shoulder at them, but doesn't turn around or greet them, and they don't speak to him. BEN's shirttail is half out of his pants, and he stuffs it back in haphazardly. JAY brushes the snowflakes off his shoulders. STEVE crosses to BEN's memorabilia display and places the basketball back in its place, while JAY removes his overcoat. STEVE starts to slide into the varsity's corner booth, checks himself, and slips instead into the next booth; his back is to the door. BEN is about to say something to STEVE to stop him from sitting in the varsity's booth, then is relieved when STEVE sits in the other booth. BEN sits opposite STEVE. JAY sits down next to STEVE. They sit and stare at their hands as if in a state of shock. MIKE continues with his preparations.

MIKE: Who won? Anybody get dunked on?

BEN: Can't say.

MIKE: You play in the dark? Good way to get hurt, old guys like you.

BEN: Had lights.

MIKE: So why do you look like you just lost your last game?

JAY: Cubicles.

STEVE: Best floor I ever played on.

BEN: I loved the way it squeaked when you made a cut. You could even squeak P. F. Flyers.

STEVE: They didn't even cover it to protect the wood.

JAY: You can still see part of the Warrior emblem painted in the center-jump circle. Nobody had an emblem painted on the court back then. That stoic Greek.

MIKE: Yo, Homer, you want to return from the Odyssey? What cubicles?

BEN: Department of Environmental Science and . . . something.

STEVE: Waste Management. The university's turned the gym into office space.

MIKE: No.

BEN: They think they can take over everything? This isn't a police state.

MIKE: It's called eminent domain.

JAY: The backboards are still hanging, nets on the rims.

STEVE: Bleachers are just pushed back.

MIKE: You make it sound like someone has desecrated a church.

BEN: When could they have done this? I was just in there three weeks ago.

MIKE: I tried to tell you.

BEN: What?

MIKE: Before you charged out into the cold night air.

JAY: About not getting caught?

MIKE: You told me you weren't getting caught. Didn't matter to me. I wasn't going to bail you out.

STEVE: And I was going to nominate you for the Nobel peace prize.

BEN: You knew about this?

MIKE: Yes.

JAY: (*Pause.*) You don't have to act like a hostile witness.

MIKE: Started hauling dividers and desks and stuff in last Monday. Took all week. (*Beat.*) I thought they'd have taken the goals down, too.

BEN: Can't believe you didn't tell me.

JAY: That's the pot calling the kettle black.

(*STEVE looks at MIKE. MIKE quickly puts his finger to his lips.*)

MIKE: What would you have done if I had?

BEN: Taken the university president hostage.

STEVE: You'd have released her in about an hour. She's a terrible caffeine addict.

MIKE: Save yourself the trouble. Just kill her.

BEN: It'd be justifiable homicide.

STEVE: Better not risk it.

BEN: But they've blasphemed one of roundball's holy places!

STEVE: Let the Lord deal with them, then. You aren't a Navy SEAL. No hostage-taking tonight.

BEN: I thought it was the Navy Midshipmen.

(*JAY makes an exaggerated, exasperated gesture.*)

STEVE: Let's eat. Breaking into cubicle hell has made me hungry. Hot dogs ready?

MIKE: Always.

BEN: I could eat something.

JAY: We're going to smell like onions for days. Might as well eat some. I'll take a couple of hot dogs all the way.

MIKE: Coming up. Ben? Steve? What about you?

BEN: Two sounds good to me.

MIKE: Extra chili?

BEN: The usual.

(*BEN goes to the ice chest to get drinks.*)

MIKE: (*To STEVE.*) You?

STEVE: Usual for me, too.

MIKE: One hot dog, mustard and onions, hold the dog.

(*MIKE starts preparing the food and continues with his work until the hot dogs are served, which may occur anytime during the following exchange.*)

JAY: What's up with that?

(*STEVE holds up his right wrist, displaying a Medic Alert bracelet.*)

JAY: What's that?

STEVE: Medic Alert bracelet. I'm diabetic. The hot dog's no good for me. Too many calories, too much fat.

BEN: Not to mention fly-wing parts and red dye number one.

MIKE: We only use whole fly wings, not parts.

JAY: Bummer. You have to give yourself shots?

STEVE: Just diet and exercise.

JAY: That's lucky.

STEVE: I had some bad habits.

BEN: A regular couch potato. Made me look pretty good.

STEVE: And that was on my good days. But if you don't treat it, the side effects are unpleasant.

JAY: Like what?

STEVE: Kidney failure, circulatory trouble. Blindness. Doc tells me this and I think, I already wear glasses, I've got high blood pressure, and I have to get up four, five times a night to pee, so what am I giving up ice cream and Big Macs for?

JAY: You're kidding.

STEVE: Big Macs aren't good for you, either.

JAY: I mean about having to take a leak five times a night.

BEN: He was literally pissing his life away.

STEVE: Close to it. Doc said I was in danger of getting dehydrated. But what clinched it was when he said the other real common side effect is . . . impotence.

JAY: Whoa.

STEVE: Gets your attention. I said, "Why didn't you tell me about this first?" He said, "I didn't want to hit you with too much all at once." And I said, "Doc, I'm motivated now."

JAY: What did Carol say?

STEVE: Oh, she said, "Honey, you just eat whatever you want."

(*The group cracks up.*)

STEVE: But I'm onto her, she can't trick me. (*Points to the hot dogs.*) But diabetic or not, I don't need to eat these things. (*To MIKE.*) How long they been cooking?

MIKE: Dad put 'em in with the onions.

JAY: How long have you had this?

STEVE: Found out a year ago, on my birthday, no less.

JAY: Some present.

STEVE: Maybe a pretty good one. I backslide some, but I'm bettter off now than I was then. Makes you take stock. And count your blessings. (*Pause.*) Ever wonder what happened to the rest of the guys, the ones who moved away or went to work somewhere else after college?

MIKE: I do. If they were still here, business would be better.

JAY: I don't have to wonder. They always seem to find me, like Van –

MIKE: Gilbert.

JAY: – Van Gilbert. I remembered this time.

MIKE: Just trying to help.

STEVE: Our famous friend protests too much. I think about those guys a lot. Somebody'll do something at work, or a broadcaster will make a comment during a game, or one of the boys says something at dinner, and it takes me right back.

BEN: Best time of my life.

JAY: You need to get a life.

MIKE: (*To JAY.*) You were pretty eager to run up to the old gym. You looked pretty disappointed when you got back.

STEVE: You can't say it wasn't a good time.

JAY: It was high school, just high school.

STEVE: You're so full of it. You're too cool to admit you had fun in high school? With your job, it's like you get to keep living in high school.

JAY: I work hard.

MIKE: That's the double entendre of all time.

JAY: Bite me.

STEVE: Maybe you do, maybe you don't. All I know is playing on that team was the first time I began to feel like a man.

JAY: You're the one who's full of it. Feel like a man. We were boys, just young boys, naïve kids, so easy to manipulate.

STEVE: Who was manipulated? We were high school freshmen. We seemed worldly, that's all that mattered to me. Playing ball gave us purpose, like a job or something.

JAY: You don't know what it was like.

STEVE: Tell me then.

JAY: Forget it.

(*JAY slides out of booth, taking his beer with him, and moves toward center stage.*)

STEVE: (*Follows after JAY.*) No. I like remembering. Everything, practices, the practical jokes, playing. Made me part of who I am.

JAY: Yeah, me, too. (*Mostly to himself.*) Maybe I learned things I didn't need to know.

BEN: You got to remember giving Randall hot roasted nuts before the St. Thomas game?

STEVE: Surely you remember that. You did it.

JAY: Amazing how high a guy can jump when someone spreads a layer of Cramergesic in his jock.

STEVE: How long's it been since I've thought about Cramergesic?

MIKE: (*To JAY.*) You didn't.

BEN: He did.

STEVE: Not among the manufacturer's recommended uses for the deep-heating rub, but it certainly loosened up ol' Randall that night.

BEN: Kept tugging at his crotch. All that adjusting made it worse, really rubbed the stuff in. Coach couldn't figure out what his problem was.

JAY: I'm sure he was fascinated.

BEN: I bet so. Randall must've grabbed about twenty rebounds that night. St. Thomas couldn't keep him off the boards.

STEVE: He couldn't wear underwear for about three days.

BEN: (*To JAY.*) Never forgave you.

JAY: Never could take a joke.

BEN: He could go all day in practice. Randall worked harder than anybody.

STEVE: Other than me.

BEN: You didn't go like Randall. I'd be dying, he'd just be getting warmed up.

STEVE: Randall never seemed to mind conditioning. Unlike the rest of us.

BEN: Coach said we'd hate him, he drove us so hard.

JAY: He was right about that.

STEVE: But said at the ends of games we'd be in better shape. Fatigue would get the other team, not us, and we'd love him for it.

JAY: Well, he was wrong about that.

BEN: No, he wasn't. We never lost because we ran out of gas.

JAY: We lost because we weren't that good. He rode you all the time.

BEN: He was just trying to make me a better player.

JAY: He liked getting on you. He knew you'd take whatever he dished out.

STEVE: (*To JAY.*) He rode Bennie because he knew you couldn't take it.

JAY: He got on me, too.

BEN: Just when you were too obvious about loafing on laps, or something. Nothing serious. Nothing about how you played.

STEVE: He knew you'd sulk, wouldn't play well. Maybe wouldn't even play. You were high maintenance.

JAY: I always played.

BEN: That's what he wanted. There was nothing slick about Coach.

JAY: You don't know. He knew what to say.

STEVE: He really knew the game. Might've made it to the college level, if Xs and Os were all that mattered.

JAY: We're talking about a high school JV coach here.

STEVE: Everyone starts somewhere. You started with our high school newspaper.

BEN: Everybody develops.

MIKE: (*To BEN.*) Almost everybody.

BEN: (*Gives MIKE a look, parroting.*) "Almost everybody."

JAY: Yeah, he might've done all right. He could turn on the charm. He could've talked his way into some dumb recruit's head – and his mom's heart before she ever knew what happened to her son. She would've invited him to Thanksgiving dinner. (*He goes to the ice chest and opens the lid.*) I need a beer.

BEN: Me too.

(*JAY gets two beers out of the ice chest.*)

JAY: What we've got now deserves someone like him.

MIKE: And what would that be?

JAY: Kids who constantly refer to themselves in the third person. You guys ever hear me talk about myself in the third person, kick my ass.

MIKE: Happily. Anything to the fact that the majority of the players you dis for being verbally-challenged are black?

JAY: You trying to make a point? They can't make a complete sentence and still want respect?

MIKE: (*Inclines his head at BEN.*) Lot of white guys have bad grammar.

JAY: They leave school after a year or two for a couple of mil per and a shoe contract.

MIKE: And this is stupid? That the sort of argument that won you those writing awards?

BEN: Don't forget Rodman.

JAY: Don't remind me about Dennis Rodman. Guys like Rodman have no respect for the fundamentals.

STEVE: Rodman rebounds like he invented it.

JAY: Look at his tattoos, the piercings. No respect for how a ball player should look.

STEVE: Tight shorts and knee socks like we wore looked better?

MIKE: (*To JAY.*) I don't know what's worse, you being a racist snob, or so conventional.

JAY: That's rich. Look at *this* dump.

MIKE: I could fix it up. But why?

(*COACH approaches The Lick. COACH now is aging, with graying or thinning hair. His worn cloth topcoat doesn't offer much protection as he hunches over against the cold. His wingtips are in need of a shine. He hesitates at the door, until he recognizes that MIKE has seen him. MIKE waves COACH in.*)

BEN: Can you imagine what Coach would've done if one of us had come to practice with our hair dyed? Or an earring?

(*All except JAY laugh.*)

MIKE: Ask him.

(*BEN looks up and breaks into a wide grin when he sees COACH. STEVE and JAY turn to look over their shoulders.*)

BEN: Coach, Coach! How're you doin'? Good to see you!

(*BEN and COACH embrace as men do, pounding each other lightly on the back. STEVE pushes JAY out of the booth and steps toward COACH. JAY moves to the fringe of the group.*)

COACH: Good to see you, too, Bennie. (*COACH turns to STEVE, extending his hand, which STEVE shakes.*) Life seems to be treating you very well, Steven.

STEVE: (*He pumps COACH's hand.*) Yes, sir. Glad you could join us.

COACH: It was nice of Bennie to call me. I'd about forgotten about our greatest victory. (*Looks at JAY.*) And here's our prize journalist. The famous Jay Rogers, still making his old coach proud. Good to see you, son.

(*COACH steps toward JAY to shake hands, but JAY moves away.*)

JAY: I'm a little old to be called "son."

COACH: I still think of all my players as sons.

MIKE: Something to eat, Coach? Ben's got soft drinks and beer.

COACH: A beer would be good.

BEN: I got it. (*Scurries to the ice chest and pulls out a bottle of light beer.*) Here you go. Ice cold. (*He hands the beer to COACH.*)

COACH: How'd you know I needed a light beer? (*Struggles briefly to remove the bottle's cap.*) Was someone going to ask me something?

MIKE: Ben had a question.

COACH: What is it, Bennie?

BEN: We were just comparing basketball now to when we played.

COACH: Much more physical today. Too physical.

MIKE: And the way some players look and act. That's changed, too.

BEN: Jay was saying that Dennis Rodman has no respect for the fundamentals of the game.

COACH: What's not to like about a guy who rebounds like Rodman? Are you not watching the games you cover?

JAY: I don't cover the NBA. I meant the tattoos. The technicolor hair. He wears a dress sometimes.

COACH: This is the late nineties, son. I'd think that a guy who gets around as much as you would recognize an act when you see it. I might have dyed my hair and worn a dress, too, if I could've averaged sixteen boards a game. Worn that dress all the way to the bank.

(*STEVE, MIKE and BEN enjoy a good laugh. JAY smiles thinly.*)

BEN: I might look good with a tattoo. (*Flexes a biceps.*) Maybe a basketball right here?

STEVE: How about a big target with the words "kick me here" on your butt?

BEN: Maybe I'll just have "I hate Steve" done instead. (*To COACH.*) You ain't serious about the dress?

COACH: Sixteen boards, Bennie. You didn't have sixteen boards your whole career.

(*The group laughs.*)

BEN: Would've had exactly sixteen, but the stupid ref called me for a lane violation my last game.

COACH: Who else has been here? Have I missed anyone?

MIKE: The gang's all here.

COACH: Randall couldn't come?

BEN: He lives in Iowa. Sent his regards – to everyone 'cept Jay – but said he couldn't make the trip.

COACH: (*Lost in thought for a moment.*) I remember one game he really got on the boards. Don't know what got into him. (*Beat.*) What about Spooner? Or Larson?

BEN: Wasn't able to locate Spooner. His folks are dead; no one around here to call. And Larson wasn't, uh, eligible for this reunion. He got moved up to varsity halfway through the season. He wasn't JV when we beat the varsity.

COACH: He never played any varsity.

BEN: Don't matter.

COACH: Well, it was good of you boys to get together.

STEVE: Hard to believe that was thirty years ago. Have you heard about the old gym?

COACH: What about it?

BEN: Not a gym anymore.

COACH: It's not?

BEN: The Department of Environmental Science and . . . what?

STEVE: Waste Management.

COACH: Waste Management?

BEN: Cubicle City.

COACH: What about the floor?

STEVE: Didn't cover it or anything. Street shoes – and worse – all over it.

COACH: Some administrator ought to be running laps.

BEN: Suicides.

STEVE: Don't even mention suicides. But since the floor's not covered, I need to get back in there and mark the spot where I hit the basket that beat the varsity.

BEN: Don't start that again. Jay hit the shot.

STEVE: Good thing you got here, Coach. You can straighten out these guys. Tell them I hit the shot.

COACH: (*To BEN.*) Who do you think hit the shot?

BEN: Jay.

(*COACH turns to look at JAY, but JAY is looking toward the memorabilia collection.*)

BEN: We ran the Duke play just like you taught us. Jay laid it in at the buzzer.

COACH: (*To STEVE.*) That's not how you remember it?

STEVE: Ben's got everything right except Jay's lay-up going in. It rolled off, and I was there for the rebound. Tapped it in at the buzzer.

BEN: The shot went in.

(*COACH doesn't answer. BEN, STEVE and MIKE anxiously await COACH's response. Even JAY has turned slightly to listen.*)

STEVE: It was a day just like tonight. Snow flurries. We ran our laps and raced down here to get the varsity's booth. Didn't even take showers. About froze our butts off. Ben had to break us back in later to get our clothes.

BEN: It wasn't like tonight. It was <u>warm</u> for February. I didn't even wear a jacket to school that day. You think we'd have run down here in our shorts in a full sweat in the snow?

MIKE: (*To COACH.*) Looks like you're the Supreme Court, sir.

COACH: You boys will have to settle it.

BEN: Why?

COACH: I was yelling at Spooner and Van . . . Van . . . hell, what was his name? Dad was a cop.

MIKE: Van Gilbert. The unknown player.

COACH: Right, Van Gilbert. He was a pain, but he could play dirty better than anybody I ever coached. Anybody except you, Jay. I was yelling at him and Spooner. I didn't see the shot. Just heard the buzzer and you guys shouting, Sundstrom screaming at you guys to run laps.

BEN: For pity's sake.

COACH: Sundstrom ran the varsity off the court, followed them into the locker room to chew them out. (*He pauses to look at them.*) I remember staring out at center court a long time, thinking beating the varsity was a lot of fun, even if I did miss the last play.

STEVE: You can still see a little of the Warrior logo at center court.

COACH: We were one of the first with our logo painted on the court.

BEN: Backboards are still up. Nets on the rims.

COACH: (*After a short pause.*) I always hated it when we had to share the court with the girls' team. They didn't even play basketball then. Just three dribbles and a pass, three dribbles and a pass. Those six-man teams.

MIKE: Not exactly six-<u>man</u> teams.

COACH: Good point. God-awful games. Eighteen to thirteen, forty-two turnovers. Twenty to seventeen.

BEN: Shouldn't have let 'em play.

COACH: Then, maybe. As usual, Coach Wooden is right.

BEN: He doesn't like girls' basketball, either?

COACH: To the contrary. You seen Tennessee or UConn? You got to be a man to play women's basketball these days. Coach Wooden said recently he'd rather watch the women play today than the men.

BEN: Why?

COACH: They play a purer game. Below the rim. Passing and defense are more important than sensational plays.

BEN: That explains why the tickets are cheaper, too.

COACH: That explains more about the attention span of the average fan than it does about the quality of play. I agree with Coach Wooden. I'd rather watch the women play too, these days.

JAY: Never thought I'd hear him say he'd rather not watch boys.

(*JAY moves toward the bench area. COACH jerks his head to JAY.*)

BEN: What?

COACH: You, uh, you remember how he used to get in practice. Needed extra attention. I'll just go over and, uh, do a little, uh, coaching.

(*COACH crosses to JAY, and puts a hand on JAY's shoulder. JAY jerks away.*)

BEN: (*To STEVE.*) He's still Coach's favorite.

(*For some seconds COACH and JAY talk in a whispered conversation. Every time COACH touches JAY's shoulder or puts a hand on JAY's back or arm, JAY pulls away.*)

COACH: We don't need to do this here.

JAY: What's wrong with now?

COACH: We can settle this.

JAY: I never could settle it.

COACH: We can talk this out later.

(*COACH places an arm across JAY's shoulders. JAY reacts violently.*)

JAY: Quit touching me!

(*JAY pushes COACH away with his forearm. COACH stumbles back and falls. BEN and STEVE rush to assist COACH.*)

STEVE: (*To JAY.*) What's the matter with you? Are you nuts? Settle what?

(*JAY does not answer.*)

STEVE: Coach?

(*COACH is disoriented as he gets to his feet. He brushes off his clothes. He sits, but not in the varsity's booth.*)

COACH: This is Jay's.

BEN: (*To JAY.*) What's going on?

JAY: Ask him.

BEN: What?

JAY: Ask him!

BEN: Ask him what?

JAY: Ask him what he did to me!

(*COACH drops his head.*)

BEN: Did what?

JAY: What do you think?

BEN: What do you mean?

JAY: Always ... taking me aside, talking to me .... (*To BEN.*) You saw him. You had to.

BEN: Saw what?

JAY: Touching me, patting at me. Taking me to his office – that little coach's office next to the locker room ....

BEN: (*To COACH.*) What's he saying?

(*COACH doesn't answer.*)

BEN: Jay?

COACH: (*To JAY.*) Stop.

JAY: (*To COACH.*) You stop! (*To BEN.*) He wouldn't leave me alone ... he ... he molested me!

BEN: (*After a silence. To JAY.*) I get it. This is another one of your jokes. You're just trying to get us going. (*Beat.*) This one's not very funny.

(*JAY makes no reply. COACH doesn't move.*)

BEN: (*To STEVE and MIKE.*) Tell him. This is over the line, even for the ol' Jaybird.

COACH: (*Without looking up.*) It's no joke.

BEN: Sure, it's a –

COACH: No, Ben.

BEN: Jay?

JAY: This isn't beyond you. Ask him why he coached.

BEN: What do you mean?

JAY: Ask him, you idiot!

COACH: I loved the game.

JAY: Why else?

COACH: It was because of the game.

JAY: Tell him why else!

COACH: Don't.

JAY: You liked giving your players the lingering, encouraging pat on the butt. You liked being in the locker room, didn't you, the one-on-one sessions in the locker room? Pull a muscle, you'd want to rub it down.

(*COACH shakes his head.*)

JAY: You liked seeing boys, didn't you? You liked touching – (*Turns away.*) I trusted you! All these years, how I've hated you! What you took from me!

BEN: What . . . are you saying?

JAY: Why me?

(*When COACH does not respond, JAY rushes to COACH, grabbing him by the lapels, pulling him up from his seat.*)

JAY: Why me? Why me, you bastard?

(*JAY is crying. He holds onto COACH. He continues to repeat his question – "Why me?" – eventually lowering COACH. STEVE removes JAY's hands from COACH's lapels and moves him away.*)

JAY: Why me?

COACH: There was something about . . . you were so . . . there was something fragile about you. I couldn't get on you like the others, like Bennie. I had to yell at him to get you to play harder. There was something . . . needy about you. (*He looks up at JAY.*) You reminded me . . . of me.

JAY: I was fifteen. I would have responded to . . . anything.

COACH: I couldn't help it. (*Beat.*) I knew your home life, only child, mom busy, dad always gone, nobody around.

JAY: You leave my parents out of this.

COACH: You needed the attention. You were easy to reach.

JAY: I wanted your approval. I just wanted to play ball.

COACH: You wanted contact. So did I.

JAY: You were my coach! I trusted you, and for what? You called me back over and over, reasons I had to see you after practice, reasons I had to come to that office. You preyed on me!

COACH: I was . . . fascinated with you.

JAY: God Almighty.

COACH: (*Beat.*) You could've said no.

JAY: (*Turns.*) I couldn't.

COACH: Why not?

JAY: Because I couldn't.

COACH: Why not?

JAY: Because I was afraid!

COACH: Of what?

JAY: Of... of not playing.

COACH: I had to play you. We had no chance without you.

JAY: It was all I had.

COACH: If you'd said no, what could I have done? If you'd stopped coming to the office, what could I have done?

JAY: I was afraid!

COACH: Of what?

JAY: I was afraid I liked it!

(*There is a silence.*)

BEN: (*Finally, to STEVE.*) Jay was queer?

STEVE: Not Jay.

COACH: (*Wheels to STEVE and BEN.*) Not me either!

BEN: You were... married. You had a daughter.

COACH: Leave my family out of this!

JAY: How many others were there?

COACH: Nobody younger than you.

JAY: Don't lie to me.

COACH: I couldn't risk what I loved, being around the game.

MIKE: What about that it was wrong? It was criminal!

COACH: I think about that now. But not then.

(*JAY has moved to the varsity's booth where he sits, his back to the others.*)

BEN: (*To COACH.*) Why did you come here?

COACH: I hoped Jay would be here.

BEN: I would've cut off my arm for you. My entire life I've worshipped you. (*Beat.*) You pervert!

COACH: I don't need you to lecture me –

BEN: Shut up! You can't tell me anything. How could you come here?

COACH: I wanted to see you boys – speak with you, be with you again.... Maybe I thought I could make things right with Jay.

BEN: You choked that. (*Beat.*) You make me sick. Get out of here. (*He starts pulling on COACH to move him along.*) Get out!

STEVE: Ben, leave him alone.

BEN: Shut up! I want him out of here! I want him gone!

STEVE: He's going. Let him go. (*To COACH.*) You'd better go.

(*COACH slowly gets up. With effort, he straightens his clothes.*)

COACH: This isn't what I wanted, not what you wanted. You were a fine group. Beating the varsity was special.

(*BEN turns away. He looks toward JAY, who still has his back to the group.*)

COACH: You had such potential, Jay. You could've been great.

(*COACH turns, makes his way to the door, and exits. After a significant pause, BEN runs to the door of The Lick. He steps outside.*)

BEN: Coach! Coach, wait!

(*There is no reply. COACH has returned to the bench. COACH should look younger again. He removes his coat, tie and street shoes, and puts on his basketball shoes and whistle.*)

BEN: (*Not as loudly, mostly to himself.*) Beating the varsity was special to me, too.

MIKE: Ben ... Bennie ... come back in and close the door. It's cold.

(*BEN does what MIKE asks. STEVE meets BEN and embraces him. In the varsity's booth, JAY takes a pen and a small notepad from his coat, and begins making notes. STEVE guides BEN over to the counter to MIKE. STEVE notices JAY's note-taking, goes to the varsity's booth, and sits opposite JAY.*)

STEVE: You all right?

JAY: Never better. (*He continues writing.*)

STEVE: We never knew.

JAY: He was careful. He was so ... likeable.

STEVE: There were signs. We should've seen.

JAY: Don't. We were kids. You didn't know to look.

STEVE: Why did you come tonight?

JAY: He might be here.

STEVE: I would think that might have kept you away.

JAY: You'd think. I finally just wanted to confront him. See if I could. (*Beat.*) I thought about killing him.

STEVE: I guess. (*He points at JAY's notes.*) What are you doing?

JAY: I've lived with it so long. This is my therapy.

STEVE: You never told anyone?

JAY: I couldn't.

STEVE: Why not?

JAY: He said not to. Said it was "our secret."

STEVE: I wish you'd told somebody.

JAY: Who? What was I going to tell them? I thought it was my fault.

STEVE: You told us tonight.

JAY: I should have told you then.

STEVE: That's giving us a lot of credit.

JAY: You'd have done the right thing. You weren't just anybody.

STEVE: (*He points again to JAY's notepad.*) This on the record?

JAY: My new editor heard me mention getting Bennie's invitation. Thought there might be a story here.

STEVE: Was he right?

JAY: She.

STEVE: She?

JAY: Journalism at Texas, MBA at Northwestern. She also played two years as a reserve for the Lady Longhorns. Knows her basketball. And her business. A lot tougher on expense reports.

STEVE: Was she right?

JAY: I can't write it. (*Indicates the notepad.*) Somebody else might be able to make sense of it.

STEVE: Somebody should. (*Beat.*) Something to drink?

JAY: Beer would be good.

(*STEVE slips out of the booth. Instead of going right to the ice chest and extracting a light beer and a diet soda, he stops at the counter to check on BEN. In the booth, JAY puts his notepad aside, and takes his cell phone from his coat pocket. He looks at the phone, makes like he is going to punch in a number, hesitates, then touches the numbers. He puts the phone to his ear and listens.*)

JAY: Jill . . . it's me, . . . Jay. . . . Wait, don't hang up. . . . just lis – (*He pauses to collect himself, finds his resolve.*) Please listen just a minute. . . . Some things have happened . . . no, I mean, there are some things I need to – want to tell you – things I've never told you. Maybe they help explain – I don't know. . . . I'm not trying to talk you into taking me back. Just hear me. I'll be ho – I'll be back day after tomorrow. Can we talk then? . . . That's fair. I'll call you. . . . Jill? Thanks.

(*JAY ends the call and puts the phone away. He starts making another entry in the notepad. STEVE disengages from BEN and gets the light beer and diet cola from the ice chest. He also picks up the copy of the school paper off the memorabilia collection. STEVE sits, handing the beer to JAY. He and JAY open their beverages and drink. JAY makes another note or two, then puts away his notepad. STEVE reads the article about the game.*)

STEVE: This really was good.

JAY: I think you're right.

STEVE: (*Calling to BEN and MIKE.*) Hey, listen to this.

(*BEN and MIKE make their way to the booth.*)

STEVE: "The nature of sport suggests –"

JAY: Don't read it.

STEVE: Cool it. This is good. (*To BEN and MIKE again.*) "The nature of sport suggests that when two rivals meet in a contest the stronger, more talented team prevails. But it is the essence of competition – the reason we play – that on any given day, any team can win. And this happens just often enough to represent genuine hope; just often enough to remind us that some peculiar laws are loose and at work in the universe – subtle assurances that soul can subdue strength, that determination can defeat preparation, that a sure thing is a sucker's bet. One of these mysterious laws enforced its own particular brand of justice last Wednesday afternoon in the school gym. The JV basketball team edged Coach Sundstrom's stronger, more talented varsity squad 56-55 in the weekly practice game. 'Any given day' actually arrived."

(*As STEVE reads, YOUNG STEVE, YOUNG JAY and YOUNG BEN huddle around COACH. Their huddle continues for a while as COACH appears to be giving instructions.*)

BEN: (*Picks up the basketball.*) That's what it was all about. It was the game.

MIKE: You say so.

STEVE: (*To JAY.*) Maybe you did make the shot. I don't know.

JAY: I'm not sure I remember.

BEN: I do. I was off the lane, you – (*To JAY.*) – were near the top of the key, and you – (*To STEVE.*) – were on the opposite wing. You picked Armstrong, Jay rolled around you, and I hit him with the pass. He laid it in at the buzzer. You rolled off the pick, but there was no rebound.

(*STEVE and JAY get out of the varsity's booth—this is important.*)

STEVE: I don't know. . . .

(*YOUNG BEN, YOUNG STEVE and YOUNG JAY leave the bench and take their positions on the court. COACH is up beside the bench. YOUNG BEN goes down right, away from the free throw lane; YOUNG STEVE moves up right, opposite YOUNG BEN, near the upstage sideline; YOUNG JAY is down center, at a position that would be near the free throw line. They wait, bent over, hands on their knees, ready for play to begin.*)

JAY: I'm not sure about the shot.

BEN: I'm telling you. Caught Jay in full stride – didn't have to put the ball on the floor. Best pass I ever made.

JAY: That part is right.

BEN: A perfect pass.

(*As BEN says, "A perfect pass," he makes one across the stage to YOUNG BEN. The lighting changes, focusing on the basketball court area. YOUNG BEN, YOUNG JAY and YOUNG STEVE are in the game of their lives. YOUNG BEN takes a few dribbles at his spot, surveying the floor. YOUNG JAY and YOUNG STEVE are jockeying for position.*)

YOUNG JAY: Call the play, call the play!

(*YOUNG BEN looks over to COACH at the bench. COACH waves YOUNG BEN nearer. YOUNG BEN dribbles a step or two toward COACH, who cups his hands and "shouts" to YOUNG BEN.*)

COACH: Duke, Bennie! Run Duke!

YOUNG BEN: (*Barks out the call.*) Duke! Duke!

(*YOUNG STEVE fakes a step to the basket, then cuts toward YOUNG JAY. As YOUNG STEVE reaches YOUNG JAY he sets a hard pick. YOUNG JAY immediately breaks close around YOUNG STEVE upstage toward the basket. When YOUNG JAY clears YOUNG STEVE he looks over to YOUNG BEN, who has picked up his dribble. YOUNG BEN fires a beautiful bounce pass across the lane, leading YOUNG JAY right to the basket. As the pass goes to YOUNG JAY, COACH turns to the bench, gesturing animatedly, appearing to be giving important instructions to other players. He doesn't turn around until the buzzer, signifying the winning shot has been made, is heard. YOUNG JAY catches the ball and goes to lay it up. <u>The following is critical</u>. YOUNG STEVE <u>must</u> roll toward the basket after the pick. If YOUNG JAY's shot <u>goes in</u>, the buzzer sounds. If YOUNG JAY <u>misses</u> the lay-up, YOUNG STEVE <u>must</u> rebound it and put the ball back up. If YOUNG STEVE's follow shot goes in, the buzzer sounds. If YOUNG STEVE misses the follow, repeat the rebound-and-shoot sequence, alternating between YOUNG JAY and YOUNG STEVE, until the shot is made. It doesn't matter which player makes the shot <u>as long as the buzzer does not sound until the ball goes in the hoop</u>. Once the shot is made and the buzzer sounds, YOUNG BEN, YOUNG JAY and YOUNG STEVE erupt in a wild celebration. They run a jubilant lap or two around the basketball court, YOUNG BEN picks up the loose basketball, then they exit the gym area to backstage, and enter The Lick through the "street" entrance.*)

(YOUNG STEVE *is the first in;* YOUNG BEN, *the last. Lighting changes, emphasizing the basketball court* and *The Lick, too, now.* YOUNG BEN *flips the ball to* BEN *as he runs past him. The* YOUNG PLAYERS, *still whooping it up, slide into the* varsity's *booth! The young players and their present-day counterparts do not "see" one another; at this point, their actions are independent. This does* not *include* MIKE, *who interacts with the youthful characters. Note: the* YOUNG PLAYERS *are energetic, loud, and a little "winded" from their exertion, making them sound a little "off voice" for a bit. Their adult alter-egos are also energetic here, but their energy is nostalgic, not rambunctious.*)

If YOUNG <u>JAY</u> makes the lay-up:	If YOUNG <u>STEVE</u> makes the lay-up:
YOUNG BEN: Oh, man, what a play! If I die right now, I've had a complete life. (*To* YOUNG JAY.) Way to go to the basket!	YOUNG BEN: (*To* YOUNG JAY.) God, what a choker. I thread the needle with the pass, and you blow the lay-up.
BEN: It was a helluva play. Just like Co – (*He refuses to acknowledge* COACH *now.*) Just like it was drawn up.	BEN: You really went to the hole on the play. But you cost me an assist, blowing the lay-up.
STEVE: We were perfect that day. We could've run that play in our sleep.	YOUNG JAY: Good thing one of us knows to roll after setting a screen. (*To* STEVE.) Way to rebound and put the shot back up.
YOUNG JAY: Couldn't have made it without that great pass!	YOUNG STEVE: I go to sleep at night running that play in my head. First thing I remember learning about basketball. Pick and roll. Pick and roll.
JAY: We did.	
(*All laugh.*)	
YOUNG JAY: And, man, what a pick. Armstrong's probably still wondering what he ran into!	JAY: Lucky for us Steve remembered how to follow the cutter to the basket. Probably dreamed about that rebound. Of course, he was such a loser then, he didn't have anything else to dream about.
YOUNG STEVE: What'd you expect, that I wouldn't set a good pick? Every team's got to have a guy that's fundamentally solid. On this team, that's me.	
	YOUNG BEN: (*To* STEVE.) How many rebounds did you have today?
YOUNG JAY: I hope you rolled in time to see my shot fall into the net.	STEVE: Funny thing is, the only one(s)* I got all afternoon was/were* on that play.
YOUNG STEVE: Of course I rolled. Odds were pretty good I'd have to rebound your miss.	YOUNG STEVE: The one that counted.
STEVE: (*To* JAY.) You really went hard to the hole. That was something to watch.	YOUNG BEN: You're not kidding. I can die a happy man!
YOUNG JAY: No way I was missing that shot.	
BEN: You were the man.	*Use one/was or ones/were based on how many times YOUNG STEVE has to attempt the shot.

(MIKE *turns to the varsity booth, and goes over to the boys.* STEVE, BEN *and* JAY *stand motionless.*)

YOUNG JAY: I believe I could sit in this booth forever. Today, we own The Lick.

MIKE: Actually, I think I still own The Lick.

YOUNG BEN: (*Looks over his shoulder.*) Yeah, and forever's gonna be over ten seconds after the varsity gets here.

YOUNG JAY: It'll be a while before Sundstrom gets through yelling at 'em.

MIKE: Yeah? I imagine they're going to want to know why you rinks are in their booth.

YOUNG JAY: They don't deserve it today.

MIKE: No?

YOUNG STEVE: We beat 'em today. In the weekly practice game.

MIKE: Get out!

YOUNG BEN: No, really. Jay (*Or Steve, as appropriate.*) put one in at the buzzer. Beat 'em by one!

YOUNG JAY: Yeah, we stomped 'em!

MIKE: JV beating the varsity. Well, you're safe, then. No varsity in this booth today.

YOUNG BEN: All right!

MIKE: Calls for a celebration. Hot dogs okay? My treat.

YOUNG JAY: All right!

YOUNG BEN: I'll have two!

YOUNG STEVE: Make mine all the way!

MIKE: Coming up.

(*MIKE goes behind the counter, and prepares four hot dogs and three soft drinks – the six-ounce Coca-Cola bottles – and puts them on a tray, which he takes over to the varsity's booth.*)

YOUNG BEN: We beat the varsity.

YOUNG STEVE: Can you believe it?

YOUNG JAY: Don't pinch me. (*Then, he plays the sage.*) But, you know, boys, that's the reason we play. Sometimes, if you really want it, you can beat a better team. It happens. You know what they say, on any given day, any team can win. (*Beat.*) And now that we have, I have to write about it.

YOUNG STEVE: What're you talking about?

YOUNG JAY: Mrs. Rist.

YOUNG BEN: What a bitch.

YOUNG JAY: Yeah.

YOUNG STEVE: You got to write about our game for science class?

YOUNG JAY: No, dip wad. She asked me to be a sports writer for <u>The Warrior's Record</u>. She's the advisor.

YOUNG BEN: How's the science teacher get to be the advisor for the student newspaper? Even one as crappy as ours.

YOUNG STEVE: (*To YOUNG JAY.*) What do you know about sports writing?

YOUNG JAY: Nothing. But when Mrs. Rist tells you to do something, you don't say no. I think I can write about the game. I just don't know how to start the article. Almost takes the fun out of winning.

YOUNG BEN: Yeah, almost.

(*They all laugh. YOUNG BEN looks over his shoulder again at the door.*)

YOUNG BEN: If the varsity comes in here and beats our butts, that'll take the fun out of it.

(*MIKE arrives with their food.*)

YOUNG STEVE: Well, I can't wait to read it. As long as it's not full of clichés like you were spouting off a minute ago.

YOUNG BEN: What do you mean, clichés? What?

YOUNG JAY: You're dangerous. Can't believe your mother lets you out alone.

YOUNG STEVE: She doesn't worry about him as long as he's with us.

YOUNG BEN: What clichés?

(*The young characters eat in silence. MIKE joins BEN, JAY and STEVE. The basketball from the game is on the table.*)

STEVE: (*Checking his watch.*) Even with everything, I'm glad Bennie got us together. It was . . . I'm glad he did it. But I've got to go. Carol'll be sending out a posse.

MIKE: You sound a little posse whipped.

JAY: You're a nonstop riot, aren't you?

STEVE: So, Ben, you going to get us together for a fortieth?

BEN: Yeah, all my stuff'll keep.

MIKE: I'm sure it will. But you'll have to meet somewhere else.

STEVE: You already booked ten years from now?

JAY: No way we couldn't meet at The Lick.

BEN: We'll pay you next time, if you want.

MIKE: No can do. There'll have to be a change of venue.

JAY: Why?

MIKE: Damn eminent domain. University president's master plan. In six months they'll be putting up a home ec building right on this spot.

STEVE: You're kidding? When did you find this out? (*He sits again.*)

MIKE: Got the condemnation order Tuesday.

BEN: The thirtieth anniversary of the game. You could've told me.

MIKE: And ruin this night for you?

JAY: You were right. We should go kill her.

MIKE: This is a prime spot – the last spot on the street the university didn't already own. Lucky they left us alone as long as they did. And the buyout's pretty good. Tell you the truth, I'm tired of it. The Lick's not The Lick anymore. The college population doesn't appreciate it. We don't serve Tex-Mex or fuzzy navels or have six TVs over the bar. Hot dogs and ice cream are too simple for people today. I'm going to take the university's money and move to the beach. That'll be my revenge.

JAY: Going to open another place?

MIKE: Haven't thought about it. If I do, it won't be The Lick. Not at Hilton Head.

JAY: Hilton Head?

MIKE: Got an option on a condo.

JAY: (*He whistles.*) Can you afford that?

MIKE: Yeah, thank you for asking. Steve here has done my books for years, and recommended some investments. I'm in good shape. With the buyout, I'll be even better.

JAY: Well, great. I got a place there, too.

MIKE: At Hilton Head?

JAY: Right on the water.

MIKE: Then maybe I'll live up near Myrtle.

(*All laugh. BEN nudges MIKE, pointing to the window. DEBBIE, an attractive black woman, nicely dressed, approaches The Lick. As she enters, JAY gives her a lingering appraisal.*)

JAY: I'm sorry, miss, this is a private party. But we might be able to find a place for <u>you</u>.

(*DEBBIE smiles at JAY. She nods, first to BEN, then to MIKE and STEVE.*)

DEBBIE: (*She moves to JAY.*) You must be Jay. Debbie Barnes. A pleasure.

(*DEBBIE offers her hand, which JAY takes uncertainly.*)

JAY: Pardon?

DEBBIE: Ben and Mike and Steve have told me all about you. I've been very eager to meet you.

JAY: I don't. . . .

DEBBIE: Oh, my. Ben hasn't told you.

JAY: Told me?

BEN: Jay, I'd like to introduce you to my fiancée.

(*Debbie shows JAY her impressive engagement ring.*)

JAY: But I thought. . . .

(*JAY looks to MIKE for help, but MIKE is beaming.*)

JAY: What about Crystal?

BEN: Crystal?

DEBBIE: Crystal?

JAY: (*To BEN.*) Crystal! Your wife! The blonde!

DEBBIE: (*To BEN.*) Your wife? You lying, two-timing. . . .

(*BEN, STEVE, MIKE and DEBBIE all stare at JAY for a beat, then explode with laughter. BEN makes a motion like casting a fishing rod, complete with a high-pitched "Wheeee" sound, hooks a big one and reels it in.*)

JAY: You aren't married, are you?

BEN: (*Giving DEBBIE a hug around the waist.*) Looks like you've lost a step, buddy.

JAY: There is no Crystal, is there?

(*BEN grins broadly, and slowly shakes his head. It is his moment.*)

JAY: I'll be damned.

BEN: Not exactly like old times, is it? Ben gets the drop on Jay!

(*BEN and MIKE exchange high-fives.*)

JAY: I guess . . . congratulations. I wouldn't have believed you'd marry a . . . uh – anyone as charming as Debbie.

DEBBIE: (*She takes BEN's arm.*) It was practically love at first sight.

JAY: (*Spreads his hands.*) I don't. . . .

BEN: Remember Roland Barnes? "Kareem"? Bumped into him at the state high school tournament last year. Debbie was with him.

DEBBIE: I'm his sister. Roland introduced us.

BEN: One thing just led to another.

JAY: What about your mom?

BEN: She's pretty cool with it.

DEBBIE: She thinks I'm really good for Ben. Me, too.

JAY: This is definitely a wrap for me. Nothing can top this for Jay Rogers.

MIKE: There is a God after all!

(*MIKE steps over quickly and gives JAY a pretty good kick in the butt.*)

JAY: What the hell?

MIKE: You said if you ever referred to yourself in the third person to kick your ass.

(*BEN and STEVE laugh at JAY, pointing fingers. The present day characters begin making preparations to leave The Lick.*)

STEVE: (*He embraces JAY quickly.*) Great to see you. Hang in there.

JAY: Thanks. We've got to keep in better touch. You got a card?

(*Both men pull business card cases from their coat pockets and exchange cards.*)

STEVE: (*Reading from JAY's card.*) "Jay Rogers. Senior writer. <u>Sports National</u>." I knew you when. (*He flips the card over.*) "Ginger. Chapel Hill." This a good phone number?

(*JAY makes a grab for the card, but STEVE is too quick for him.*)

JAY: Let me swap that one for a fresh card. I may need that one later.

STEVE: Uh-huh, I think I'll keep this one. (*He pockets the card.*) Better than having your autograph, though I guess this is sort of like your signature, isn't it?

JAY: Trade back if I can get you a pass to the ACC tournament?

STEVE: Whooo! This one must be really hot to open with a bid like that! I'll have to see the pass first.

JAY: I'll call you.

STEVE: You do that.

(*JAY retrieves his overcoat and muffler and puts them on.*)

MIKE: (*To the young characters in the varsity's booth.*) We're outta here, guys. Bus the table.

(*YOUNG BEN, YOUNG JAY and YOUNG STEVE begin to gather up their trash and carry it to the receptacle near the door.*)

YOUNG STEVE: (*While they are cleaning up.*) I bet everybody's out of the gym. How're we going to get our clothes?

YOUNG JAY: Anybody know a way in?

YOUNG BEN: I can probably get the girls' locker room door open. Have before.

YOUNG STEVE: You have? Why didn't you say something?

YOUNG BEN: Can't tell everybody that kind of secret.

YOUNG STEVE: We're not "everybody." We're us.

YOUNG JAY: Who cares, as long as we get in. I've got to get the instructions from Mrs. Rist for my article out of my locker.

YOUNG BEN: What a bitch.

YOUNG JAY: Maybe she's not so bad.

YOUNG BEN: And I'm LBJ. (*To MIKE.*) Thanks for the hot dogs, Mike.

YOUNG JAY: Yeah, thanks.

YOUNG STEVE: We appreciate it, Mike.

MIKE: Glad to do it. Congratulations on the great win.

(*Everyone has moved near the door, the young characters standing next to their present-day selves. MIKE surveys The Lick.*)

MIKE: Anyone forget anything before I turn out the lights? (*He reaches for the switch next to the door.*)

JAY: Wait a sec.

(*JAY picks up the basketball off the table and shoots/bounces it toward the cooler and one of BEN's cardboard boxes of memorabilia.*)

If JAY "makes" the "shot":	If JAY "misses" the "shot":
(*BEN and STEVE react with comments like, "Hasn't lost the touch," "Count it," "Wish you'd done that more often 30 years ago," etc. YOUNG BEN, YOUNG STEVE and YOUNG JAY react similarly – but in silence among themselves. JAY and YOUNG JAY both act like the shot was nothing, just routine.*)	(*BEN and STEVE offer appropriate negative commentary – "The iron was unkind," "Never could shoot," etc. STEVE, (particularly if YOUNG JAY missed the shot at the buzzer during the depiction of the game) says, "Looks like I got one more rebound to get," etc. Again, the YOUNG PLAYERS act similarly, only silently.*)

(*Hit or miss, amid the laughter and comments, JAY starts to retrieve the ball.*)

BEN: Just leave it.

YOUNG BEN: (*To YOUNG JAY.*) We'll be back.

(*YOUNG STEVE and YOUNG JAY murmur assent as JAY returns. MIKE turns out the lights. These lights remain on: over the basketball court area one light shines on COACH, who looks out where center court would be, then lowers his head; the other, a security light, shines on the memorabilia display. The group exits The Lick, present-day and younger alter-egos together. MIKE holds the door for DEBBIE and they exit together so the principal pairings are kept intact. After the group exits The Lick, the light fades out over COACH, then, after a few more seconds, over the memorabilia display.*)

THE END

Larry Pike

Glasgow, Kentucky, playwright and poet Larry Pike won the 2003 Joy Bale Boone Poetry Award. His play *Beating the Varsity* was produced by Kentucky Repertory Theatre in 2000. Two other plays, *Newsroom* (2005) and its sequel *Full Moon* (2009), also received staged readings during the theatre's Kentucky Voices showcases.

His poetry has been published widely.

A graduate of Mars Hill College, Purdue University, and Kentucky Repertory Theatre's playwriting workshop, Larry is human resources manager for a large manufacturer and is active in civic affairs. His wife, Carol, is a guide at Mammoth Cave National Park. Their family includes sons Daniel and David; Daniel's wife, Amy; and beautiful granddaughter Anne Rhoades.

Larry's dedication for *Beating the Varsity* reads: *For Carol, Daniel and David, with thanks to Warren.*

Liz Bussey Fentress in *Liz's Circus Story* by Liz Bussey Fentress, Horse Cave Theatre, 2001

LIZ'S CIRCUS STORY
by
Liz Bussey Fentress

Liz Bussey Fentress with Loo-kah in *Liz's Circus Story* by Liz Bussey Fentress, Horse Cave Theatre, 2001

Liz's Circus Story opened on August 3, 2001, with the following cast:

    LIZ   *Liz Bussey Fentress*

Director: Robert F. Brock
Stage Manager: Laurel Sisler
Set Design: Sam Hunt
Lighting Design: Lynne Chase
Sound Design: Ryan Newton Harris
Costume Design: Marty Hagedorn
Puppets: Marty Hagedorn
Properties Master: Pamela Sisler
Technical Director: Jeremy Artigue
Assistant Sound Designer: Kevin McCoy
Production Assistant: Brad Seal
Assistant Production Assistant: Matt Kovar

Like several playwrights who had world premieres at Horse Cave Theatre, I developed *Liz's Circus Story* in Warren Hammack's playwriting class. Unlike the others, I was writing an autobiographical play for one actor—which I intended to perform myself. Warren instructed me to read the first draft aloud for a small audience in my living room. Still acting my heart out after three hours while a friend's husband slept soundly on the couch, I learned playwriting lessons fast and furiously.

Later that spring, Robert Brock directed a revised, two-hour version of *Liz's Circus Story* for the Kentucky Voices staged reading series. Robert and I began the process of creating the play's physical life with only a bench and a stool on a bare stage. Mainly, we needed to know how an audience would react: Was the story clear? Was it funny? Was it sad? Would the audience care about the characters? At the conclusion of the reading, recognizing I still had work to do, I knew I had a play.

Robert also directed the world premiere of *Liz's Circus Story* which opened August 3, 2001; the 90-minute script was now in full color. Robert had asked the production staff to create "a circus!" And so Sam Hunt, the set designer, built a big top complete with a blue and white, candy-striped center pole, and a circus ring trimmed with red and yellow stars. Marty Hagedorn, the costumer, made a dazzling, red satin ring mistress jacket. When Robert said the show needed circus animals, Marty produced a supporting cast of puppets for me to operate: a horse, an elephant, and a tiger. Ryan Harris filled the auditorium with classic circus music, and Lynne Chase aimed a spotlight center stage.

In the curtain speech that evening, Warren said, "Liz performs the play by herself. There are no other actors; she is without a safety net." Except, I did have a safety net—it was Warren.

– Liz Bussey Fentress

Liz's Circus Story 593

Characters:

NARRATOR

LIZ, *21 at the beginning of the play, 44 at the end*

PAUL, *Liz's childhood friend, a circus clown*

MOTHER, *Liz's mother*

WAYNE, *a school teacher who starts a circus*

BUCK, *an obstreperous horse*

JOANNE, *Wayne's wife*

DAY, *a small goat*

KATHY, *Wayne's deaf sister*

GRANDPA BUSSEY, *Liz's imaginary grandfather*

SOPHIE, *Wayne's first tiger*

KILLER, *a circus worker*

OKHA, *Wayne's elephant*

MISS MARLENE, *a female aerialist*

MR. BOB, *a male aerialist*

LOO-KAH, *a tiger born on the show*

KILLER'S DAD

HAL, *a community theatre director*

TOM, *Liz's actor-friend*

LIZ'S CIRCUS STORY is performed by one actor: a 44-year-old female Narrator. The Narrator plays all the characters including herself, Liz. The Narrator also uses the following puppets: a tiger, an elephant, a horse, a male and a female aerialist, and Tom, an actor-friend.

Place: A circus big top. The Narrator uses the facilities of the circus to create other locations across America including an apartment, a dairy barn, a moving car, etc., from New York to West Texas, from Wisconsin to Florida.

Time: The present.

SCENE ONE

The interior of a circus big top. A minimal set suggests the tent and the ring.

The NARRATOR, age 44, plays herself, LIZ, at age 21. LIZ uses the circus facilities to represent her student apartment in Madison, Wisconsin, in March, 1974; a curry brush sitting on a feed pan is a telephone. LIZ picks up the receiver, starts to dial, hangs up.

LIZ: I'd get out of it if I could, but I told this guy I'd do it.

NARRATOR: (*Addressing the audience.*) It's a brand new, one-ring circus! Wayne Franzen, the guy who's starting it, is a schoolteacher. He's 27, and he saved some money and he's gonna do it.

Lots of kids dream about joining the circus—but I never did. My friend Paul did. He got me this job. I ran into him and he said, "I'm gonna be a clown!" I used to play circus with Paul after kindergarten, setting up miniature trucks, corrals—the whole show under his dining room table.

I dream about being an actor. But kids from Northern Wisconsin don't grow up to become actors. It's just not possible. We're teachers and we're good at sewing.

The show opens in three months in Plainfield, a small Wisconsin town. Wayne's brother Neil is the booking agent. Neil made some money working on the Alaskan pipeline, and Wayne convinced him to go into business with him.

They grew up on a farm and Wayne's good with animals so he'll do the animal acts. We're going to have one baby elephant, one horse, three dogs, a mule, seven goats, and a llama.

Neil's wife Suzanne is going to be the cook and she'll do the aerial acts… I'm going to be the ringmistress and the organist at the big show. I also told this guy Wayne I'd play the accordion on the Midway—and do a puppet show at the sideshow.

(*By simply and clearly changing her focus, the NARRATOR plays all the characters.*)

NARRATOR: I told my Mom. She said…

MOTHER: You don't know how to play the organ!

LIZ: I can take lessons.

MOTHER: You don't have any puppets!

LIZ: I can make some!

MOTHER: Oh, honey, you didn't have to go to college to work for a circus!

LIZ: Mom, I'm 21! And the economy is terrible—everyone I know is cleaning houses. And Nixon's in way too much trouble to do anything about it. I might as well work for a circus!

NARRATOR: She started crying and stormed out of the room.

SCENE TWO

Two months later. LIZ is on the phone at her childhood home in Northern Wisconsin. She has a trunk. The NARRATOR also mimes WAYNE on the phone. WAYNE speaks with a Wisconsin accent.

LIZ: Mr. Franzen? This is Liz Bussey. I thought I'd come to your farm a couple weeks early to practice the show. How do I get there?

WAYNE: Take the Polish Memorial Highway east out of town. When you get to the big Catholic Church, turn right on County Road Z. At the end of Z, turn left on County Road ZZ. We're at the end of ZZ.

LIZ: Right.

SCENE THREE

One week later. The dark and dusty interior of a dairy barn outside Amherst Junction, Wisconsin. LIZ has her trunk. WAYNE struggles to control BUCK, an unruly horse.

WAYNE: The organ is out here in the dairy barn, Liz.

(*BUCK whinnies.*)

WAYNE: Whoa, Buck! Easy, boy! Buck just finished practicing his Liberty Act.

LIZ: Liberty Act?

WAYNE: Where a horse performs without a lead.

LIZ: A lead?

WAYNE: A line you lead a horse around with.

(*BUCK whinnies.*)

WAYNE: Settle down, Buck! Mostly you see circus acts where the trainers use leads so they can keep their horses in the ring. I don't like to restrain them like that. That's better, Buck. If you treat them right they'll perform good without a lead.

LIZ: In a "Liberty" Act the horse is "free." What a cool thing—for a horse to dance without a lead. Did you raise Buck?

(*WAYNE brushes BUCK with a curry brush.*)

WAYNE: No. Found him in the want ads for $25. When I went to look at Buck he was standing in a pile of manure that came halfway up his rear end. And would you believe it? The bridle had grown into his skin.

LIZ: His skin?

WAYNE: Wasn't adjusted as he grew.

LIZ: Oh. (*Pointing to a rope hanging from the rafters.*) Is that an aerial act?

WAYNE: Yeah! A Spanish Web! Neil's wife, Miss Suzanne, climbs up the rope and puts her hand through the little loop at the top and then Neil spins her around.

LIZ: Is that it?

WAYNE: Then she hangs upside down. She wears a swimsuit with sequins sewed on it. (*Placing a feed pan in front of BUCK.*) Here's your feed, Buck. Oh-kay. You don't see many of these kinds of acts in Wisconsin!

LIZ: Uh... No. (*LIZ opens the trunk. It contains a red satin costume and a tiger puppet.*) My grandmother made my costume out of some red satin my mom bought to make a Christmas tablecloth. Fully lined!

WAYNE: Good for rainy days. Shoot! I gotta get my band uniform fixed!

LIZ: You're wearing a band uniform?

WAYNE: Yeah, but the hat comes down over my eyes, the sleeves are short, and the pants bunch up around my ankles. I can hardly walk!

LIZ: Right. (*She gets the tiger puppet out of the trunk.*) I made an elephant and a horse puppet and I'm almost finished with this tiger.

WAYNE: A tiger, eh?

LIZ: Yeah. When do you think we'll get to go through the show?

WAYNE: Geez! I gotta pick up that starter for the generator!

(*A cow moos.*)

SCENE FOUR

Two weeks later. The interior of a big top in Plainfield, Wisconsin. It's pouring rain.

NARRATOR: (*Addressing the audience.*) We're in Plainfield! The first performance starts in an hour and we've never had a rehearsal!

(*The NARRATOR takes a marker and prints "Order of Acts" at the top of a piece of poster board.*)

NARRATOR: (*Writing.*) Or-der of Acts. We can't start with that damn horse, Buck; he keeps running out of the ring! (*The NARRATOR prints "Elephant" at the bottom of the poster board.*) If the elephant is last, what's the next best act that could be first? And we should have a good act right before intermission and a good act right after intermission. We don't have that many good acts.

We started to come over here two days ago but Wayne's truck broke down. We finally got here yesterday but no one knew how to put up the tent! We were going to go through the show this afternoon... (*The NARRATOR gets a top hat and whistle out of the trunk. She puts on the top hat.*) But just as I put on my top hat, just as I am about to become "Miss Elizabeth, the ONLY Ringmistress in the History of the Big Top," just as I blow my whistle... (*She blows the whistle.*) And announce, "La-deees and Gentlemen! Wayne and Neil Franzen proudly present..."

(*A strong wind blows through the big top.*)

NARRATOR: A huge gust of wind roars into the tent! The top billows, the sidewall flies straight out, and the quarter poles come loose and fly through the air! AAAAAAHHHHHH!

(*The NARRATOR takes cover from the storm behind a section of ring curb.*)

It's as if the storm started on cue! I blow the whistle and it's one big impossible muddy mess!

(*Loud thunder. The NARRATOR prints "1. Liberty Act" under "Order of Acts." She continues to write the list.*)

NARRATOR: We're gonna have to start with Buck-the-horse and hope he can do his Liberty Act without a lead. We can put that new guy from West Texas right before intermission: Low-wire walker. The clown—my friend Paul—he calls himself "Paulo the Magnificent"—can come after the horse.

Llama! The llama runs around the ring one way, and then the other way. And if he doesn't practice every day, the llama forgets his act!

Wayne's wife JoAnne isn't happy about this circus. She said,

JOANNE: Wayne, I thought we were saving our money for new furniture!

NARRATOR: She thinks someone ought to tell Wayne Franzen, "You can't do this!"

(*Thunder.*)

NARRATOR: All of nature is telling Wayne Franzen, "You can't do this!"

(*Loud thunder.*)

NARRATOR: Miss Suzanne—Spanish Web. Dogs and mule. Low-wire. Intermission. Goats! Paulo the Magnificent. Miss Suzanne—again—Swinging Ladder. Buck's Arithmetic Act! Oh! I almost forgot! The Tumblers! And... Elephant!

(*The NARRATOR tacks the list on a sidewall pole.*)

NARRATOR: I gotta get my costume on!

SCENE FIVE

One month later. A bright summer morning. The NARRATOR stands at the edge of a big open field next to a small town in rural Wisconsin. She carries a small brown cardboard box containing a can of red spray paint, a tape measure, and a rope.

NARRATOR: What a beautiful morning.

The first day in Plainfield—a month ago—we've been in a different town every day since—that first day we drove the tent stakes too far out—so we had to pull all 50 of them and drive them over again! There are two kinds of stakes: wooden ones Wayne made out of trees he chopped down, and old car axles. So the next day we drove the stakes closer in, and it turned out they were in the tent!

Finally, one of the tumblers and I sat down with a pencil and paper and figured it out! The tumblers are really smart. We call them "A Transcendent Tournament of Accomplished Acrobatic Artistry—the High-Flying Toscannis!" Actually, they're Fred and Ralph Hugenon. And they're on the gymnastics team at LaCrosse State University.

So now, I'm the first one to get to the next lot, and I lay it out. Watch!

The crowd's gonna come down that road from town—so the entrance to the tent will be there. That puts the first center pole here.

(*The NARRATOR lays out the lot as she describes it. She marks the location of the center pole with the spray paint. She uses the tape measure to measure the distance to the second center pole, and marks the location of the second center pole.*)

The measurement between the two center poles has to be EXACT! Now! I made this special rope with two knots tied in one end of it. I anchor one end of the rope where one center pole is going to be. Then I use the first knot at the other end to measure the right distance to the stake line and the second knot to measure the right amount of space between each stake. (*The NARRATOR paints the first two points of a semicircle.*) Cool, huh? (*The NARRATOR continues to outline the points of a semicircle.*)

You know, the audience loves this circus! Okha, the baby elephant—she's five years old and an elephant has the life span of a human being—she's the most exciting thing that's ever been in these small towns. The audience even likes Miss Suzanne's "Death-Defying Spin for Life!"

And they love the goat act. It is pretty cool. We call it "The Largest Aggregation of Trained Goats in the World!" I made them costumes. I had to find fabric the goats wouldn't eat! Three of them get on a teeter-totter: Snuff gets at one end, Spike gets at the other end, and then Billy walks back and forth in the middle and makes Spike and Snuff go up and down. After each trick, Wayne says, "Oh-kay!" The goats live to hear that "Oh-kay."

The grand finale of the goat act is a trick called "The Long Mount." Elephants do it at big circuses. All seven goats get in a line and stand up, with their front hooves on the back of the goat in front of them. A little goat named Day is at the back of the line—he's white and his hair is really long. It's shiny—almost silver. He glows in the light at the back of the line.

I'm thinking about applying for drama school. But what's the point? I don't have any money.

(*The NARRATOR looks down the road.*)

They should be pulling onto the lot pretty soon. When we're parked at the edge of town like this, Wayne lets Okha, the little elephant, wander around loose. Last week she disappeared! Wayne hollered, "Where's the elephant?" She was down the street in someone's garden eating vegetables. Wayne hollered, "Okha! Come here!" She looked up, turned around, and trotted across a couple of back yards right up to him.

That breeze feels so good. Can you smell the new-mown hay?

Most of the guys on the canvas crew were students in Wayne's shop classes—Pesheski, Pehoski, Jellinski—they're all sons of Polish potato farmers. When we take the big top down, we all grab hold of the edge of the canvas and then the whole line of us runs across to the other side, folding the big top in half. (*The NARRATOR runs across the stage, miming folding the canvas.*) The wind catches the canvas but it gradually drifts to the ground. Then we all grab hold again and run back to the other side. We do that several times. Then we attach one end to a big spool that Wayne welded on the back of an old potato truck. They start the power take-off!

(*Loud mechanical sound.*)

And we roll up the canvas. (*The NARRATOR mimes rolling up the canvas.*)

There's one thing I don't like. The organ I play is in an old-fashioned circus wagon Wayne built—and it sits off to the side. I can see everything from there—but I don't get to go to the center of the ring to announce the acts! There's no time—as soon as I finish announcing, I have to start the music. I wish I could go to the center of the ring!

(*Music transition: "Polovetzian Dance," upbeat organ.*)

SCENE SIX

Two months later, at dusk. LIZ mimes driving a truck. She reads a sign over the road, pulls onto a small, grassy lot.

LIZ: "Quad Cities, Illinois, Wild Animal Zoo." (*LIZ rolls down the truck window and hollers.*) Wayne!!! Is this where I should park this truck? Thank you. (*LIZ turns off the ignition, opens the door, and struggles to get down out of the cab. She limps across the lot.*) Oh, man!

NARRATOR: (*Addressing the audience.*) Swingin' a 12-pound maul yesterday did me in. Three of us put up the big top—it seats 1,200 people—and I drove a third of the stakes! I'm not makin' this stuff up!

(*LIZ approaches WAYNE. He stands next to a table with a plate of sandwiches on it.*)

LIZ: You gonna replace those guys who went back to school?

WAYNE: We finish in a month. You grow up on a farm?

LIZ: No.

WAYNE: Never seen a city girl work as hard as you. Tell you what. I'll talk to Neil about givin' you a raise—to $120 a week. Hey, why did Paul quit?

LIZ: Said he was "blasted exhausted." Goin' to graduate school. What did Miss Suzanne fix for dinner?

WAYNE: I'd rather eat popcorn.

LIZ: Oh. So why are we parked at a zoo?

WAYNE: They've got a tiger kitten for sale.

LIZ: You gonna get it?

WAYNE: Neil doesn't want to spend the money—only $250. But it'll eat 10 pounds of meat a day. Shoot! I gotta call that man about buyin' some hay! (*WAYNE searches his pants pockets for a scrap of paper with a phone number on it.*) Where'd I put his number?

LIZ: Why don't you just say, "Neil, I'm gonna get that tiger."

WAYNE: Oh no! I'm afraid he'd quit and make me buy him out. Neil thinks the circus did pretty good this year so why don't we keep it the same next year. (*Still searching his pants pockets.*) I don't have enough hay to feed tonight!

LIZ: Is that the number in your shirt pocket?

(*WAYNE finds a scrap of paper in his shirt pocket.*)

WAYNE: Yeah! Oh-kay!

LIZ: (*Beaming.*) So, Wayne, how did you get the idea of starting a circus?

WAYNE: Been in my head since I was five—when I started milking cows. My dad would take me and Neil and our sister Kathy out to the barn before dawn. Dad would tell a story. He had seen the Ringling Circus—they're from Wisconsin, ya know—and he told about somersaulting dogs and Royal Bengal Tigers. I'd forget all about milking and say, "Tell some more." He'd say, "Get back to work, Wayne." It was so cold and dark out there. The idea of circus! It just got to me.

I want the show to be better next year, and better the year after that.

Gotta find a phone. See ya later.

(*WAYNE leaves. LIZ picks up the plate of sandwiches.*)

NARRATOR: (*Addressing the audience.*) These are the same baloney sandwiches we ate yesterday!

LIZ: (*Slamming the plate down on the table.*) YUK!

NARRATOR: (*Addressing the audience.*) You probably think I'm nuts to work this hard—but I'm not quittin'!

LIZ: (*Hollering to Wayne.*) Wayne!

WAYNE: (*Voice-over.*) Yeah?

LIZ: Get the tiger!

SCENE SEVEN

October, 1974. The NARRATOR is in the kitchen of Wayne's farmhouse outside Amherst Junction, Wisconsin.

NARRATOR: (*Addressing the audience.*) Neil quit at the end of the first season. Wayne had to mortgage the farm to buy him out. Neil and Miss Suzanne took off for Mexico this morning where Neil's gonna invest in concrete lawn statues.

Wayne wants to open the show early next year. The low wire walker—his name is Strut—said the spring weather is good in West Texas so he went down there to book. I asked Wayne if he could keep me on to do odd jobs but he can't afford it. I need money. Maybe I could replace Neil as the booking agent for the summer dates up here.

Wayne's out in the barn.

(*Lights change to indicate the interior of the barn.*) He's with his sister, Kathy; she's deaf but she can lip-read. Wayne wants her to do Miss Suzanne's aerial acts for the second season.

(*KATHY's voice is monotone. She has learned to speak by watching other people's mouths. She over-articulates, sounding out every vowel and consonant clearly.*)

KATHY: No way, Wayne. I can't do all those tricks.

(*WAYNE faces KATHY and speaks very clearly. He also mimes what he wants her to do.*)

WAYNE: Climbing up is the hardest part.

KATHY: (*Giggling.*) It will be scary up in the air!

WAYNE: You won't have time to think about that! You'll be thinking about where you're hanging on, and where you're going to hang on next!

KATHY: I'm cold. I want to go in.

WAYNE: Grab the rope—I'll get you started.

KATHY: No! No! I have to finish sewing those flags!

WAYNE: Kathy, stop stalling. It's just like climbing the rope up into the hay mow. Here. Just put one hand on the rope.

(*KATHY reaches for the rope and stops.*)

KATHY: I don't have time to sew a costume!

WAYNE: I'll get you a store-bought one!

KATHY: Wayne...

LIZ: Hi, Wayne. (*LIZ signs an "h" and an "i."*) Hi, Kathy. Wayne, maybe I could get some dates in Minnesota for the second season.

WAYNE: Can't afford another booking agent. Besides, every town we played this year asked us back.

LIZ: But we started late and we had open dates—that we could play in Minnesota.

WAYNE: Do you know how to book a circus?

LIZ: We could do two loops—one in the south—around the Twin Cities—where most of the population is—and then another one up around Duluth and the Iron Range—say in August. There're lots of tourists there at the end of summer. How much would you pay for a contract?

WAYNE: Seventy-five dollars.

LIZ: I'll have a big phone bill. And I'll have to rent a car and stay in motels—and eat.

KATHY: He's cheap!

WAYNE: S'pose I can go a hundred.

LIZ: How about if I try to get seven weeks?

WAYNE: Yeah! Great! Now... (*WAYNE holds out his clasped hands to hoist up KATHY.*) Kathy!

(*Two weeks later. An apartment in Minneapolis. The NARRATOR has a map of Minnesota.*)

NARRATOR: (*Addressing the audience.*) We do one-night stands. Seven weeks means I have to get... 49 contracts! I don't know how to book a circus! ...But I learned how to play the organ!

I take my circus savings and send out 700 letters to every civic organization in Minnesota with a post card they can send back. I get seven back. I get on the phone. I contact the Downtown Business Association, the Band Boosters, the Kiwanis. I schedule a meeting.

(*The NARRATOR consults the map.*) I spend the night with a friend way up in Northeastern Minnesota. I have my first meeting with the Downtown Business Association in Red Lake Falls—250 miles away in Northwestern Minnesota! At ten o'clock tomorrow morning! It snows all night long. You can see your breath in the cabin and it's impossible to sleep. In the morning the pipes are frozen—and I can't get cleaned up! The lane is snowed in and it takes an hour to get my car on the road! I can't keep my eyes open... I pull over for a nap. I call to say...

(*LIZ mimes talking on the phone.*)

LIZ: I can't... I won't... I can't... I'll be late.

(*The NARRATOR mimes driving a car.*)

NARRATOR: The two-lane highway is icy! The wind whips across it. (*The car accelerates.*) I drive 75! 80! 85 miles an hour! (*The car screeches to a halt.*)

I find the clothing store on Main Street where I meet a nice man in a brown plaid wool shirt.

LIZ: Nice shirt!

NARRATOR: We walk down the street—pick up a guy from the furniture store and one from the hardware store. We head for the café. They don't care that I'm late. They don't care that I smell like wood smoke and have coffee breath. I keep thinking they'll say they'll keep the contract and look it over. That they want to check our references. One of them says the date is okay. One of them signs the contract. They all get up and go back to their stores. I have my first signed contract! Whoo-hoo!

I get back on the phone.

(*LIZ mimes talking on a phone.*)

LIZ: No, no, no! The Band Boosters don't give the circus money. You sell advance tickets—and get 40 percent of everything you sell. You can't lose! (*LIZ hangs up the phone and looks at the map.*) Damn!

NARRATOR: (*To audience.*) I've just committed to driving to the Canadian border. (*The NARRATOR mimes driving a car.*) Halfway to Canada I have a conversation with my grandfather. He's been dead for ten years—but I imagine he travels with me—in the passenger's seat.

LIZ: I'm bored, Grandpa Bussey! I can't even find a radio station up here!

GRANDPA BUSSEY: Why don't you memorize a poem?

LIZ: What?

GRANDPA BUSSEY: Didn't your mother give you a book of poetry? You could memorize a poem about snow on these long drives.

(*The NARRATOR gets a scrapbook out of the trunk. She turns the pages and shows the pictures to the audience as she describes them.*)

NARRATOR: I have a scrapbook of circus pictures to show the Band Boosters. It shows the farm at the end of County Road ZZ. It shows all of us sitting on the barnyard fence the week before the show opened. It shows Wayne with his seven goats. It shows children laughing.

A month later I head west to Watertown where I'm scheduled to be the guest speaker at a Kiwanis meeting. I've just had a wisdom tooth pulled. Big flakes of soft snow pour out of the sky. I'll memorize that poem! (*The NARRATOR gets a poetry book out of the trunk and reads from it.*) "Velvet Shoes" by Elinor Wylie: "Silence will fall like dews / On white silence below." Silence will fall like dews... Silence will fall...

The men eat, while I tell them Wayne Franzen's story:

LIZ: His folks were poor Russian dairy farmers. Wayne can remember the day his dad made him clean the barnyard in his bare feet because he didn't want Wayne to get his new shoes dirty.

Farmers are close to their animals. Wayne told me, "On our small farm, we watered each individual calf with a pail." Wayne trained a cow to jump a bale of hay and take a bow. He taught a goat to roll a barrel. His dad exploded: "Forget about circus! It is thing of the past!"

So Wayne went to college and majored in industrial arts education. But he had to write a paper for an English class on "What I Want to Do with My Life." Wayne wrote he always wanted to have a circus. His teacher called him in and said, "You should do this."

After college, Wayne got married and he and his wife bought a farm. But they never put the thermostat above 50 degrees because Wayne hadn't had heat in the house growing up—and he was saving money for his circus. They ate pancakes for breakfast and mashed potato sandwiches for lunch and dinner.

Wayne taught industrial arts and auto mechanics—the perfect background for someone starting a circus. After school in the shop, Wayne built the ring curb, painted it bright blue, and wired it with red and yellow lights. And last summer, when one of our trucks broke down, he just crawled under and fixed it.

Wayne saved $25,000 teaching high school. When he saw a baby elephant advertised for sale in "Amusement Business," he called the number in Pakistan and spoke to a Rajah. He took $8,000 from his savings to buy Okha, the elephant, and spent $1,200 on her airfare. He and his brother met her at the Milwaukee airport and took her home in their pickup truck.

Wayne spent $12,000 on a big top; he bought it used from the Voorhies Brothers—a new circus that had gone broke after only two weeks the previous summer. And he bought an old Allied Van Lines truck to haul his animals around in.

And I am pleased to announce the Franzen Bros. Circus will present a brand new animal act for the 1975 Minnesota tour: "Wayne Franzen and his Jungle Companion, Sophie the Tiger!" Wayne welded Sophie's cage out of a stainless steel vent he bought from a McDonald's. And he bought a corn crib to make into a steel arena for the tiger to perform in.

Gentlemen, we proved Wayne's dad wrong! The circus is not a thing of the past! In fact, every town we played last year has asked us back! And I am confident YOU will ask us back if you book the Franzen Bros. Circus! Thank you. I have never before spoken to a group of men who were all wearing orange sports coats!

NARRATOR: I head back to Minneapolis. The snow is still pouring out of the sky. My jaw hurts! My head is full of Wayne's story; I've told it hundreds of times! I keep hearing Wayne's teacher: "You should do this."

When I was in the fourth grade my parents drove me from the north woods down to Minneapolis to see Jessica Tandy and Hume Cronyn as Sir Politic and Lady Would-Be in <u>Volpone</u>, directed by Sir Tyrone Guthrie. On that day I knew, "That's what I want to do with my life!"

(*The NARRATOR picks up a stack of 49 contracts.*) I've got 49 contracts! I go out to the barn to find Wayne.

(*The NARRATOR puts on the TIGER puppet. She plays WAYNE and the TIGER.*) He's working with the new tiger, Sophie. "Seat," Wayne says. "Hhhh!" Sophie growls at him. "Get up there!" Wayne growls back! Sophie pads to her stool and leaps up on to it. "Wayne..." I say.

WAYNE: Just a sec.

(*The NARRATOR, as WAYNE, takes something representing a small piece of meat out of her pocket and feeds it to the TIGER.*)

NARRATOR: He takes a small piece of meat and gives it to Sophie.

WAYNE: Oh-kay!

(*The NARRATOR takes off the TIGER puppet.*)

NARRATOR: "How can you do that?" I ask.

WAYNE: It's like being an actor. Isn't that what you want to do? When Sophie growls at me, I growl back. If a 650-pound tiger ever attacks you, the tiger's going to win. But, as long as I'm an actor, as long as I growl back louder and fiercer than the tiger, I'm in charge. What d'you got there?

LIZ: The contracts! You owe me $4,900!

(*LIZ hands the 49 contracts to WAYNE. WAYNE thumbs through them.*)

WAYNE: Liz, I'll have to pay you when we play these towns.

LIZ: Oh.

NARRATOR: I go sit in my rented car and cry.

SCENE EIGHT

March, 1975. A dark, windy day in Seagraves, Texas. Howling wind. The NARRATOR is inside a trailer. She mimes trying to shut the door.

NARRATOR: (*Shouting over the wind to the audience.*) I wanna take a nap before the show but I can't get this door shut! If you open your mouth outside, you get a mouthful of sand! The circus lots here in West Texas are either sand or limestone. The sand won't hold the stakes, and you sure can't drive them into the limestone!

(*The NARRATOR manages to shut the door.*)

NARRATOR: This morning we tied the canvas off to the trucks. The wind blew harder than ever and ripped the ropes right out of the tent! We're playing the dates the low-wire walker, Strut, booked because the spring weather is supposed to be good in West Texas. The wind NEVER stops blowing. Business is terrible.

This rickety old wooden trailer is where I live now. I've got the bottom bunk in the back end. (*The NARRATOR mimes lying down and sliding into her bunk.*) To get into my bunk, I lie down, flat on the floor, like this, and, without bending my knees, I slide over and in. I sleep on my back because the bunk is too shallow for me to lie on my side.

When I opened my eyes this morning, the first thing I saw, on the floor next to my bunk, was a snow drift! It's too cold to sleep.

(*The NARRATOR sits up. She mimes hitting her head on the imaginary bunk above her.*)

AAAHHHH! You know, Wayne's wife JoAnne tried to be a good sport when Wayne took her to the Circus World Museum for their honeymoon. But she didn't like it when he bought a Welsh terrier and started teaching it tricks—before they got home. When Wayne trained their collie to walk on his hind legs and push the terrier in a baby carriage, she said...

JOANNE: Wayne, I thought that baby carriage was for a baby!

NARRATOR: JoAnne finally got what she wants. This afternoon she called the local sheriff here in Seagraves, Texas, and asked him to find Wayne on the circus lot and deliver a message. Wayne and JoAnne have a new baby boy—Brian.

(*The trailer door flies open with a loud, violent crash. Loud howling wind. The NARRATOR races to the door and struggles to shut it.*)

NARRATOR: The wind! I hear voices in the wind! The wind asks, "Do you want to have a baby?" I shout back, "NO!" The wind howls, "Do you want to be an actor?" I shout back, "Yes!" The wind howls, "You should do this." I howl back, "It's not possible!" The wind howls, "You should!" "I can't!" "Wayne can!"

(*The NARRATOR slams the door closed.*)

NARRATOR: I can!

SCENE NINE

Two months later. A very bright, sunny day on the back lot of the circus somewhere in Missouri. A loud generator roars offstage.

LIZ: (*Yelling over the sound of the generator to someone offstage.*) Turn off the generator!

NARRATOR: (*Addressing the audience.*) The old generator that came back from Viet Nam died last night. Wayne left right after the show for St. Louis to find a new one. He got back this afternoon with a used one from a hospital.

LIZ: (*Yelling offstage.*) Turn it off! Turn off the generator!

(*The generator noise stops. LIZ approaches WAYNE.*)

LIZ: You all right?

WAYNE: They hooked up the ground wrong! The whole semi was hot—all along there where I tie the goats. One of them wandered into it. See if you can find the shovel.

(*LIZ indicates an equipment box. WAYNE opens it.*)

LIZ: It's in there.

WAYNE: The electricity was running right through me. Didn't think I could pull myself away. Better get your costume on.

LIZ: The bleachers aren't up! Pesheski's arm's messed up from when he got it caught in the spool on the spool truck. The rest of the guys went into Kansas City for a drink last night—and didn't come back! Wayne, there's supposed to be 22 people working for the circus—and there's only eight of us!

WAYNE: Liz! I spent every cent I had to get that generator! We gotta sell some tickets!

LIZ: We don't have any aerial acts! Kathy's out because she fell last week. And Strut has syphilis! That's why he's always scratching his crotch! There's only you, me, and the new clown!

WAYNE: I don't care if everybody quits! Okha and I are doing the show!

(*WAYNE leaves. LIZ "sees" the dead goat offstage.*)

LIZ: Day! The goat with long, shiny, almost silver hair—Day is dead! (*LIZ picks up the shovel and mimes digging a hole.*) I'm gonna bury the little white goat who glowed in the light at the back of the line.

(*Music transition: "Polovetzian Dance," plaintive violin.*)

SCENE TEN

A warm August evening eight years later, 1983, in Northern Michigan. LIZ circles the stage, running, and stops at the entrance to the big top. Out of breath, she looks up and reads the marquis.

LIZ: (*Reading.*) "Franzen Bros. Circus! America's Favorite Show!"

(*LIZ tries to enter the big top.*)

KILLER: Ticket!

LIZ: I drove all the way from New York. I don't want to miss the first act. I'll pay later.

KILLER: Go to the ticket booth, lady; it only costs two dollars.

LIZ: I used to work here—eight years ago. I want to see the tiger act!

NARRATOR: My friend Paul runs up. He's back; he's the ringmaster now.

PAUL: Killer, what's goin' on? This is Liz! She booked the best seven weeks the circus ever had. Liz-the-tiger is named after her! Miss Elizabeth?

(*LIZ takes PAUL's arm. They run into the big top.*)

LIZ: Thanks. That guy's name is "Killer"?

PAUL: He's new—a lost soul. Gotta start the blasted show. Hope you can find a seat!

(*LIZ looks around in wonder. She searches for a seat.*)

LIZ: A straw house!

NARRATOR: (*Addressing the audience.*) That means to squeeze everyone in—more than 1,200 people—there's straw on the ground for the kids to sit on.

I saved $10,000 working for the Franzen Bros. Circus—including the $4,900 Wayne paid me for the Minnesota dates!—and went to drama school in London. Then, for four years, I stage managed theatre tours through North and South Dakota in the dead of winter. I had plenty of experience driving over icy highways—and I loved it! I worked my way up to understudy. One of the actors I toured with had a vacancy in her New York apartment and convinced me to take it.

(*Circus music: "Meadowlands March." The NARRATOR puts on the TIGER puppet. The puppet performs the tricks in the tiger act as the NARRATOR describes them.*)

NARRATOR: Wayne enters the steel arena and works with 10 Royal Bengal tigers! Five of the tigers do a roll-over! That's the hardest trick there is to teach a tiger, because when a tiger rolls over, it exposes its chest, making it vulnerable. But Wayne gets five tigers to lie down on the ground, and all five roll over in unison! Sophie leaps through a hoop of flames! Liz walks on her hind legs! Now Wayne wants Tony to balance on a fiberglass ball! "Hhhhhhhh!" Tony growls at him.

WAYNE: Get up there!!!

NARRATOR: Wayne growls back!!!

(*The NARRATOR balances the TIGER puppet on a big red ball and rolls the ball across the ring.*)

NARRATOR: Tony hops onto the ball and rolls it all the way across the ring! The act is over and Wayne rides Tony out of the steel arena! It's Paulo the Magnificent!

PAUL: Ladies and Gentlemen, the Circus welcomes the newest member of its menagerie, a Royal Bengal tiger, Loo-kah, born on the show earlier this year. Loo-kah is the offspring of two tigers you saw perform this evening. Congratulations Tony, Sophie and Loo-kah!

(*Circus music: "Valse Bleue." The NARRATOR gets the ELEPHANT puppet. The puppet performs the elephant act as the NARRATOR describes it.*)

NARRATOR: Okha knows every trick in the book; she does a fifteen-minute act! She walks a balance beam! Lies down! Sits up! Waltzes! Spins! And salutes! The most famous elephant in the circus world today is Anna Mae in the Big Apple Circus. Everyone is saying Okha is the next Anna Mae!

(*Circus music: "Over the Waves." The NARRATOR gets a MALE AERIALIST puppet and a FEMALE AERIALIST puppet out of the trunk. The puppets perform the act as the NARRATOR describes it.*)

NARRATOR: The aerialists are beautiful: Miss Marlene and Mr. Bob! Hep! (*The AERIALISTS ascend to the high wire.*) Their bodies are slim, well-formed, muscled. They're all blonde! Hep! (*The AERIALISTS ascend to the trapeze.*) They're all husbands and wives and they love each other and hold each other and catch each other and... Hep! ...spot each other. Hep! Hep! The women have long, thick hair and it trails behind them as they fly through the air from one side of the big top to the other. The men are handsome and strong. (*The AERIALISTS bow.*) Tah-dah!

Wayne's son Brian is eight years old and he does the goat act! The farmers in the audience laugh at the goats and ogle the beautiful women. The women in the audience hug their little boys and buy more cotton candy! (*The NARRATOR buys cotton candy.*) The new guy, Killer, hawks cotton candy wearing a clean red and white striped vest. Even the organ sounds good!

(*Circus music: "Polovetzian Dance," upbeat.*)

NARRATOR: Wayne cracks his whip! Twelve Ponies of America thunder into the tent! White horses with black dots all over! The show ends with their Liberty Act... And they stay in the ring!

I make my way through the crowd.

LIZ: Paulo the Magnificent! Look at that tailcoat!

(*PAUL mimes taking off his tailcoat and showing it to LIZ.*)

PAUL: I sewed 2,000 Austrian rhinestones on it! Weighs a ton. We're short-handed so I'm doin' tear-down.

LIZ: I can help.

PAUL: How's the Big Apple?

LIZ: Paul, when I moved there, I made it my full-time job to get acting work. I was rejected—five times a day, five days a week, for five months. I finally got five weeks of work.

So some friends and I started our own theatre company. (*LIZ runs across the stage, miming folding the canvas.*) To get into the rehearsal hall, you have to step over someone passed out on the steps—and the lobby smells like vomit. We rented a small theatre for the performances: there's one bathroom and it's on the stage. (*LIZ runs back across the stage, miming folding the canvas again.*) If we're lucky, we'll get 20 of our friends to come and see it. And we're gonna charge 'em $25 apiece. (*LIZ crosses back, miming folding the canvas again.*)

Yesterday I borrowed an actor-friend's car so I could make this trip. To get my driver's license renewed... (*Loud mechanical sound. LIZ mimes hoisting the huge roll of canvas onto the spool truck as it is rolled up.*) ...I had to stand in line at City Hall for three hours—and the air conditioning was broken. Afterwards I went to the parking lot. A woman stopped me and asked, "Do you know where Chambers Street is?" I said, "God damn it, lady, how should I know?"

Paul, what kind of a person am I becoming?

(*The horses thunder by. Whinnying.*)

LIZ: What's up with the horses?

PAUL: You know Franzen; when we're at a fairgrounds with a big corral like this, he lets all the animals run around loose after the show.

LIZ: That big Belgian horse must be lonely down at the far end—all by himself.

PAUL: There he goes! He likes to charge from one end of the corral to the other!

LIZ: He scattered the 12 Ponies of America! They're gonna run to the end he just left. What the...? The mule is following them!

PAUL: The mule wants to be a Pony of America—white with black dots all over. The little animal following the mule is a Sicilian donkey. The Sicilian donkey thinks the mule is her mother.

LIZ: You're kidding! Ponies, mule, little donkey...!

(*Okha trumpets.*)

LIZ: Here comes Okha!

PAUL: Look out! Okha likes the little Sicilian donkey, and when the little Sicilian donkey takes off, Okha takes off!

LIZ: Ponies, mule, little donkey, elephant. It's a parade! It's like the <u>Bremen Town Musicians</u>! Paul... I wish... I could dance with the horses!

(*Music transition: "Polovetzian Dance," upbeat organ.*)

SCENE ELEVEN

October, 1983. An apartment in Hell's Kitchen, New York.

NARRATOR: (*Addressing the audience.*) Following my 24 hours with the circus, I drive back to New York. My friends and I put on our play and it gets good reviews—but my heart isn't in it.

(*A phone rings.*)

LIZ: A couple weeks later, I don't get out of bed.

(*A phone rings.*)

LIZ: It's easier to lie here—un-groomed.

(*There is a knock on the door.*)

NARRATOR: In the middle of the afternoon my roommate taps on the door.

(*LIZ lies in bed; she doesn't answer.*)

NARRATOR: She says, "There's a phone call for you, Liz."

LIZ: There's no Liz here! Liz has disappeared! She doesn't know who she is anymore! Go away!

NARRATOR: She says, "Lizzie, it's Wayne Franzen." Wayne is calling from Iowa.

(*The NARRATOR uses a hairbrush to represent a telephone. She mimes WAYNE, and LIZ, talking on the phone.*)

WAYNE: This 1983 drought is the worst they've had in Africa, Liz. The elephants are dying. But they're trying to save the baby elephants. A planeload landed in Manhattan this morning. They're being trucked to a game farm in the Catskills. Is that far from where you live?

LIZ: Not too far.

WAYNE: They cost $8,000 a piece. Could you drive up and look them over? I need you to pick out the best two.

LIZ: Wayne, how do you pick out a baby elephant?

WAYNE: They're one year old. An elephant won't wean itself naturally until it's three—so make sure they're eating okay. Don't get them if they're being bottle-fed. I want females. And get two about the same size so they'll look good together in the ring. It's just like buying a horse, Liz. There's something about the look of it—something in the eye.

LIZ: I never bought a horse!

WAYNE: There're three kinds of elephants: the crazies, the stupids, and the normals. Just be sure you get two normals.

(*LIZ brushes her hair.*)

NARRATOR: I call my actor-friend, Tom—the guy with the car.

(*LIZ mimes talking on the phone.*)

LIZ: This could be an interesting experience... If you're willing to drive, we can go shopping for baby elephants!

(*Lights change to indicate the interior of an animal barn. The NARRATOR carries a shoulder-bag.*)

NARRATOR: (*Addressing the audience.*) Have you ever seen a one-year-old elephant? They're... thigh high. They get into everything with their trunks. They throw hay on their backs. I think, "I could take one back to my apartment with me." There are four females. One big one, one little one, and two in the middle. I pick out the two in the middle.

SCENE TWELVE

A rainy day, one year later, September, 1984. The NARRATOR stands across the street from a circus lot in southern Michigan.

NARRATOR: (*Addressing the audience.*) That was a year ago. It has been a struggle—sometimes impossible—for me to get out of bed every day since.

(*Pouring rain. The NARRATOR gets an umbrella out of her shoulder-bag and opens it.*)

NARRATOR: I suppose you're wondering why I'm standing here in the pouring rain—across the street from the circus lot. Wayne's been calling again. He says he's going broke this year because nobody's doing the advance work. I keep telling him the circus is behind me, I'm the hardest working actor in New York... I clean houses. He keeps calling.

There's nothing left in me to say, "No." I'm gonna work for him for three months—just until December—to get the show in off the road. Then I'm going back to New York.

My actor-friend Tom was leaving for the Midwest yesterday and dropped me at a Greyhound bus depot within range of the circus. I spent last night playing video games—Donkey-Kong. I cried all night. I kept going up to the ticket window to get, "Five dollars worth of quarters." I know that woman thought, "She's a crazy."

I memorized a poem about this, "Renascence" by Edna St. Vincent Millay: "Rain it hath a friendly sound to one who's six feet underground."

SCENE THIRTEEN

A warm autumn day one month later. The NARRATOR stands by a corral on a circus lot in northeastern Arkansas.

NARRATOR: (*Addressing the audience.*) Doing the advance work, promotion, I travel 10 days in front of the show. But we're making a loop here in Arkansas: they're coming in and I'm headed out, so I was able to catch them. The local sheriff is here too. He's got divorce papers for Wayne. JoAnne is terminating her career with the Franzen Bros. Circus.

(*The NARRATOR sorts through a stack of mail.*) There's supposed to be a contract in the mail from the Knights of Columbus in Red Bay, Alabama. Here it is. Good. (*The NARRATOR reads another envelope.*) Who's "Fred Zimmer"? From Illinois... Oh, that's Killer!

(*The NARRATOR walks over to two sections of corral tied together with binder twine bows; the bows have very large loops.*)

NARRATOR: He's still here: just look at these bows. Tying bows is a big deal in the circus. When the U.S. got involved in World War II, the Army went to Ringling Bros. to learn how to move out quickly. Everything, EVERYTHING is tied with BOWS: bleacher boards, sidewall poles, sections of the corral—so it can be untied with one little tug. About the time Killer joined the show, someone started tying things together with knots...

(*The NARRATOR sets up Buck's Arithmetic Act. It is a railing holding ten small pieces of wood with the* numbers from one to ten painted on them. Each piece of wood has a loop of rope tacked to the top so Buck can pick it up in his mouth.)

NARRATOR: Killer, Fred, I think, is officially "slow"; he can't have a driver's license. But he goes to work on his bows. And he gets a position: prop guy.

(*The NARRATOR puts on the HORSE puppet and uses it to portray BUCK. BUCK performs the Arithmetic Act as the NARRATOR describes it. The NARRATOR also plays WAYNE and KILLER.*)

NARRATOR: Killer's favorite props job is Buck's Arithmetic Act. He sets it up and then Buck…

BUCK: (*Whinnying.*) E-E-E-E-E-E!

NARRATOR: Takes arithmetic problems from the audience, say, "How much is two plus two?"

(*BUCK trots to the railing, picks out the "four" and trots back to WAYNE.*)

NARRATOR: Buck picks out the right answer! Wayne says, "Oh-kay!" Takes the "four" out of Buck's mouth, and gives him a lump of sugar.

BUCK: (*Whinnying.*) E-E-E-E-E-E!

NARRATOR: Wayne tosses the "four" back to Killer and Killer replaces it on the railing. Sometimes Buck gets in a hurry and gets the wrong answer.

(*BUCK takes the "five" out of the railing.*)

NARRATOR: Then Killer shakes his head and scowls at Buck! You can see him mouthing, "You dummie!"

This spring when the circus came north through Illinois, Killer asked Wayne…

KILLER: Can you give me a lift to see my dad?

NARRATOR: It's a modest home at the end of a long drive. Wayne goes up to the door with Killer. Killer's dad appears.

KILLER'S DAD: What the hell you doin' here? Your sister's graduatin' high school tonight—and we're leavin' right now.

KILLER: Dad, this is my boss, Wayne Franzen. He owns a circus and I'm in charge of the props.

KILLER'S DAD: Huh?

WAYNE: Fred does a good job: gets the right prop in the right place at the right time.

KILLER'S DAD: You made somethin' of yourself? Well… Come on in.

NARRATOR: A lot of these guys are lost souls. But they find a purpose working for the circus. Maybe there's hope for all of us: just look at these bows! He might need extra rope because they have large loops, but Killer learned to tie them.

(*LIZ "sees" KILLER offstage.*)

LIZ: Killer! There's a letter for you! From your Dad!

(*Music transition: "Polovetzian Dance," upbeat oboe.*)

SCENE FOURTEEN

(*One month later. LIZ mimes driving a big car down a road in rural Alabama.*)

LIZ: I feel like I've met every person east of the Mississippi.

NARRATOR: I say to my grandfather.

GRANDPA BUSSEY: Where did you get this car?

LIZ: It belongs to the guy from the Knights of Columbus, the butcher. The van needed to be serviced. I feel like I'm driving a boat. Look! It's got push-button gears. We met in the butcher's freezer! He cut sides of beef with a cleaver while I asked about ticket sales.

NARRATOR: Grandpa Bussey's been dead for 20 years now. I imagine he looks out for me. That he waits in the van while I put up a billboard in rural Mississippi in the middle of the night with a city council man who wants to drink vodka later. That he somehow prevents a truck that comes out of nowhere! From hitting me broadside. That he watches the motel rooms where I stay... Hoping the bugs in the shower won't get me in the night.

GRANDPA BUSSEY: Where are we going?

NARRATOR: In my family, my grandfather is the only person who had a passion; he knew what he wanted to do, did it, and loved it. He taught mathematics. He could impart his love for mathematics to his students, and they loved him for it.

LIZ: There's supposed to be a radio station along here. The butcher wants me to set up an interview with the elephant.

GRANDPA BUSSEY: What?

LIZ: Okha can speak on command! Wayne says, "Okha, speak!" and Okha goes, "EEEMMMRRRR!" The butcher wants the radio station to interview her over the phone.

GRANDPA BUSSEY: Do you like New York?

LIZ: No. I have to run a mile to see a tree. I go to Central Park where the horse drawn carriages are parked so I can smell the manure; it's the only honest smell in Manhattan and it reminds me of the circus. But if I want to work in the theatre, why am I driving across rural Alabama trying to sell circus tickets?

NARRATOR: Having been a college professor, my grandfather is somewhat formal. He's the only person who calls me by my real name, Elizabeth. And I've never-ever seen him wear anything but a suit—even on camping trips.

GRANDPA BUSSEY: Give yourself permission to be yourself, Elizabeth. It's a wonderful thing that you love the goat act and that you believe Wayne Franzen's picture will be on the cover of <u>Time</u> magazine some day.

LIZ: I don't see a radio station. Shoot. I'm gonna turn around in that driveway. Where's the blinker on this thing?

GRANDPA BUSSEY: What is it about Wayne Franzen you respect so much?

LIZ: Well... He works hard. But guess what? I work hard, and look at me! I'm trying to turn around this boat of a car with huge fins in... What the...? What's that white stuff? Shoot. How do you put this thing in reverse?

GRANDPA BUSSEY: So... You need to work hard. What else?

LIZ: Whoa! We're not in any gear at all.

GRANDPA BUSSEY: WHAT DO YOU NEED BESIDES HARD WORK?

(*Beat.*)

LIZ: It's Wayne's belief. He believes in himself. He believes he can do it. He grew up in a dairy barn but he believes he can train an elephant. It never occurs to him his circus won't make it. You know, Grandpa Bussey, I worked hard... but... it never occurred to me I'd make it in New York.

A-ha! This button with the "R" on it must be reverse!

How do you learn to believe in yourself?

NARRATOR: My grandfather is warm. He takes off his hat and passes his hand through a few remaining strands of white hair.

GRANDPA BUSSEY: It comes from deep down in. And it grows. You'll know when it's there. And then when you get an opportunity, you have to jump in.

LIZ: There's the radio station! We've been here the whole time! That butcher didn't tell me it was in the middle of a cotton field!

(*Music transition: "Polovetzian Dance," upbeat strings.*)

SCENE FIFTEEN

January, 1985. The NARRATOR sits at a table in an Airstream trailer parked at a county fairgrounds in central Florida.

NARRATOR: (*Addressing the audience.*) The show is parked at this county fairgrounds in Central Florida for the winter. It's Wayne and his new wife and me and the ex-cons. I'm dating a human blockhead.

I'm booking circus dates in Kentucky by phone. I have a friend who's the director of a community theatre there.

(*LIZ mimes talking on the phone with HAL. HAL has a Southern accent.*)

LIZ: We have an incredible advance operation! Your community theatre can make $5,000 in one day!

HAL: I'm leavin' this job, Liz. Why don't you come and take it?

LIZ: Yeah... I'm... Yeah... I'm jumpin' in.

SCENE SIXTEEN

Ten years later, September, 1995. An early morning at the county fairgrounds in Dixon, Tennessee. The NARRATOR carries the actor-friend TOM puppet in her right hand and plays the scene with it.

NARRATOR: It's ten years later. I'm trying to explain my career to my actor-friend Tom.

LIZ: The community theatre job meant starting at the bottom again—but at least I was back climbing my own shaky, swinging ladder. Now I'm at a professional theatre. We have a thrust stage—just like the Guthrie! And we do great plays.

NARRATOR: Tom's acting career in New York has been dodgy.

(*TOM looks at LIZ.*)

LIZ: One beer commercial since the last time I saw you?

(*TOM looks away.*)

NARRATOR: Now Tom's moving to California to make it. It's seven a.m. Tom and I are walking across the circus lot.

(*A car drives up.*)

NARRATOR: A woman in a big car drives up. "I'm the new promotion director," she says. "Did you hear? Wayne's second wife left him."

(*An air horn sounds.*)

LIZ: The circus is here!

(*The NARRATOR places the TOM puppet on the ring curb. LIZ and TOM "see" the circus activity offstage.*)

LIZ: Tom! Have you ever seen a big top go up? Watch! Those guys are gonna drive the stakes... with a pneumatic stake driver! Wayne's son Brian is the boss canvas man. See! He's putting a harness on Okha so she can pull up the tent! Okay... Now they're unrolling the canvas from the spool truck... Whoa! Something's wrong... Oh man... That's a huge tear! They're gonna have to fix that.

Liz's Circus Story

(*The NARRATOR picks up the ELEPHANT puppet and uses it to portray OKHA. She crosses to the ring curb, sits next to the TOM puppet, and holds OKHA over her head.*)

NARRATOR: Okha wanders. She comes over to Tom and me.

LIZ: Hello, Okha! (*LIZ address TOM.*) I've known this elephant since she was five years old. She's 26 now.

NARRATOR: Okha's standing right over us. She rocks back and forth.

OKHA: MMMMMMMHHHH!

LIZ: Don't be afraid. I've seen her pick a bouquet of dandelions!

NARRATOR: Okha's even closer to us. She's rocking back and forth.

OKHA: MMMHHH!

NARRATOR: I'm trying to be cool in front of Tom. My knuckles are white. Okha's trunk is huge. I know in a heartbeat she can fling either Tom or me across the fairgrounds.

OKHA: MMMHHH!

LIZ: (*To Brian, offstage.*) Brian! The elephant's a little close!

NARRATOR: Brian looks up.

BRIAN: (*With a Wisconsin accent.*) Okha, come here!

(*The NARRATOR rises and trots the OKHA puppet toward BRIAN.*)

NARRATOR: Okha turns around and trots over to him. They take a break and Brian comes over.

LIZ: What was going on with the elephant?

BRIAN: Wha'd'ya mean?

LIZ: She was standin' right over us. She kept goin', "MMMMMHHHH."

BRIAN: Oh. She was glad to see you, Liz. She was purring!

LIZ: Oh.

NARRATOR: Wayne bursts out of his trailer.

(*Twenty years have passed since we've heard WAYNE speak; his voice is scratchy, and cracks.*)

WAYNE: It's Liz Bussey!

LIZ: (*To Tom.*) His voice is shot from years of hollering at lost souls.

WAYNE: Gotta set up the tiger act. Hey, do you know why Paul has gone into the seminary?

LIZ: Guess he's still searching.

WAYNE: Okha killed one of the Ponies of America. That horse used to pick on the little Sicilian donkey Okha liked. One of the dummies let them loose in the same corral. Okha tusked the horse to death. Buck's out to pasture on a farm in Florida. Hey, Liz, why don't you come back to work for the circus? I could use your help.

(*Beat.*)

LIZ: No, Wayne. I'm an actor at a real theatre now.

WAYNE: Oh-kay!

(*The tigers growl. The NARRATOR picks up the TOM puppet and crosses to an imaginary tiger cage.*)

LIZ: Tom, let's look at the tigers. They travel right in their cages on this truck. Which one was born on the show?

WAYNE: (*Pointing out a tiger.*) Loo-kah.

(*LOO-KAH growls.*)

WAYNE: Don't get too close.

(*TOM looks at WAYNE.*)

WAYNE: Last week someone popped a balloon by her cage and since then she's been a little crazy... skittish.

(*TOM walks away from the tiger cage.*)

NARRATOR: Tom wants to get back on the road.

LIZ: (*To Tom.*) I feel bad about turning down Wayne for that job.

TOM: (*In a deep, resonant voice, enunciating each syllable clearly.*) What's the big deal about Wayne Franzen, Liz? Isn't he just an old man with a whip?

LIZ: You don't get it! Why don't you take off your damn sunglasses? You won't... You'll never get acting work in California! You only got that beer commercial because the casting agent liked your clothes! Wayne Franzen designed and built that tiger truck! He... He created something from nothing! I mean, he started a circus—an impossible...! It's dark! TAKE OFF YOUR DAMN SUNGLASSES! You won't take them off because there's nothing there! I'd hide behind sunglasses, too!

(*LIZ throws TOM into the equipment box and closes it.*)

SCENE SEVENTEEN

April, 1996. The interior of Liz's house in Horse Cave, Kentucky. A doorbell rings. LIZ runs offstage.

LIZ: (*Off.*) Thank you!

(*LIZ enters carrying a large, brown paper package. She unwraps it.*)

NARRATOR: (*Addressing the audience.*) My mom is cleaning out the attic. I asked her to send me this stuff.

(*LIZ takes out her red satin ringmistress costume.*)

LIZ: Wow! My rainy day costume!

NARRATOR: If it weren't for Wayne Franzen, this red satin would have ended up on a dining room table. (*The NARRATOR puts on the costume.*) Red satin! It's no coincidence that red is the color of the circus, that in the circus' hey day, every show had its own shade of red. You cut your leg shaving in the bathtub and you see beautiful red blood! It's the color of life!

(*The NARRATOR finishes putting on the costume.*) It fits!

SCENE EIGHTEEN

May 7, 1997. The interior of a circus big top during a show in Carrollton, Pennsylvania.

NARRATOR: It's Wednesday night, May 7th, 1997. In Carrollton, Pennsylvania, Wayne Franzen enters the steel arena. He wears a new costume—with large, puffy, shiny, metallic sleeves. Balloon-like.

(*Circus music under: "The Meadowlands March."*)

NARRATOR: The tigers are let into the steel arena one at a time. (*The NARRATOR mimes opening a huge steel gate on the back of a truck.*) KRRRR! One at a time they are taken under control, and seated. (*The NARRATOR mimes closing the gate.*) KRRRR! "Seat!" Wayne says. There are ten tigers in all. Loo-kah is the fourth tiger in. (*The NARRATOR mimes opening the gate.*) KRRRR! Three of them are on their seats and under control when Loo-kah comes in.

(*The NARRATOR mimes closing the gate.*) KRRRR! Loo-kah likes the new costume. Loo-kah bats at the puffy, shiny sleeve. The audience loves it. Wayne offers his arm and 650-pound Loo-kah bats at it harder, and knocks Wayne down. Wayne is on the ground, on his back, between two growling, 650-pound tigers already seated on stools. Loo-kah is stalking him! AAAAAAAAAHHHHHHHH!!!!

(*Black-out. A phone rings. Lights change to indicate the interior of Liz's house in Horse Cave, Kentucky. LIZ uses a curry brush sitting on top of a feed pan to represent a telephone. She answers the phone.*)

LIZ: Hello, Paulo the Magnificent! Oops—sorry—I know, you're a monk now. Hello, Brother Paul Vincent... No, I haven't heard.

(*Lights change.*)

NARRATOR: I hear the story from my friend Paul, and I read it in USA Today, and in the paper my mother sends from Northern Wisconsin. But all the versions are different! So I find Wayne's son Brian and I make him tell me.

(*The NARRATOR carries OKHA, the ELEPHANT puppet. She plays BRIAN walking alongside OKHA.*)

NARRATOR: Brian is giving elephant rides. We walk alongside Okha, loaded with five laughing children.

BRIAN: Yeah, Liz, I was letting the tigers out of their cages. I saw it happen. Easy, Okha. He was in a awkward position. And he tried to growl at the tiger, to scare it away. But there was nothin' he could do. Gee, Okha. Come on, gee! Get around! Loo-kah went for his jugular. She tore out his jaw. I went in there with a steel pipe but it was too late. There was blood everywhere. I beat Loo-kah off with the pipe but there was nothing I could do. My dad died right away. I don't know how I did it but I got the tigers back in the truck. Easy, Okha. Didn't go to the funeral. We drove to the next town in the morning and put up the big top. Had to get money to feed the tigers. That's good, Okha. Oh-kay.

(*The NARRATOR puts down the ELEPHANT puppet.*)

BRIAN: My dad had a good life, Liz. He did what he wanted to do.

(*The lights change. LIZ brings her hand up to her jaw.*)

LIZ: "Silence will fall...." I drive down the road. And sometimes, I think I still see a circus truck coming toward me on the freeway. Wayne Franzen is driving the truck! He doesn't have a jaw!

(*LIZ roars back at the image.*) GGGRRRRAAAAAAAAAHHHHHHHHH!!!!!!! I GROWL BACK! I... I am trained by Wayne Franzen! Wayne Franzen trained all of us.

And 12 dancing horses! The best horse act in the country! All white with black dots. Like Dalmatian horses. And they dance through the big top. They turn in circles to the music, make figure-eights in the ring, and waltz in pairs. And then Wayne twirls the whip above their heads and he cries, "HIGHEEE!" and all 12 rise up on their hind legs and walk across the ring, all 12 in a line on their hind legs!

And you put your hands up to your head! You've never seen anything like it!

And that horse act was in the imagination of a boy who grew up in a dairy barn in Northern Wisconsin!

What's in my imagination? I will create something from nothing! I will perform without a lead! I WILL BE POSSIBILITY! I will dance with the horses! (*LIZ sings the first few notes of "The Polovetzian Dance."*) Dee dee dee, de de dee, de dee, de de dee...

(*Circus music: "The Polovetzian Dance." LIZ dances. The dance is abstract. As LIZ dances, her movements are more and more free, transcendent. She dances with the horses. The dance ends with a horse bow center stage. LIZ stands tall.*)

LIZ: Oh-kay!

THE END

Liz Bussey Fentress with Tom, an actor friend, in *Liz's Circus Story* by Liz Bussey Fentress, Horse Cave Theatre, 2001

LIZ BUSSEY FENTRESS

Born and raised in Northern Wisconsin, Liz Bussey Fentress is a graduate of the University of Wisconsin–Madison, and the Webber-Douglas Academy of Dramatic Art in London. A playwright, director and actor, Liz now makes her home with her husband, Larry, in Louisville, where her hobbies include knitting, gardening and beekeeping. During thirteen seasons at Horse Cave Theatre, Liz served on both the artistic and management teams, coordinating the Kentucky Voices program for the development of new plays by or about Kentuckians for many years. Liz's plays have been produced across the U.S. and staged in London's West End, and she has received playwriting awards from the North American Actors Association, the National Educational Television Association, the Kentucky Arts Council, and the Kentucky Foundation for Women.

Afterword

Although I didn't work at Horse Cave Theatre during every season in which one of these fourteen world premieres was produced, circumstances allowed me to see them all. Revisiting the plays, by serving as one of the editors of this anthology, has been a joy. Stationed at my desk during "The Great Kentucky Ice Storm of 2009," I loved meeting the characters again, journeying with them, in my mind's eye, to their Kentucky homes, workplaces, hang-outs, hide-outs—and the sheriff's office. While tree limbs cracked and fell to the frozen ground outside my window, I was miles away, witness to heroes and heroines in struggles with spouses, lovers, children, bosses, enemies, themselves and God.

I count myself lucky to have worked at Horse Cave Theatre during nine of the seventeen seasons in which world premieres were produced. The plays were presented in rotating repertory—meaning the theatre had several plays running at the same time, usually three, and they were performed in rotation. The world premiere of a Kentucky Voices production was likely to be "in rep" with a recent Broadway hit, an American classic, a French farce, or a Shakespeare play. For instance, Jim Peyton's *East of Nineveh* ran with Eugene O'Neill's *Desire Under the Elms*, and Nancy Gall-Clayton's *Just Taking Up Space* played with Thornton Wilder's *The Matchmaker*. Ron Mielech was presented alongside both Richard Brinsley Sheridan and Arthur Miller, and John Howell with Samuel Beckett. Kentucky playwrights stood shoulder to shoulder, deservedly, with the greatest names in dramatic literature.

According to Warren Hammack, Horse Cave Theatre's founding producing artistic director, doing shows in rotating repertory is what made the production of the world premieres possible. A new play by a Kentucky writer had no track record of success—in fact, it could have bombed. While this never happened, in the event of a slow start the repertory system meant that box office income could be maintained through ticket sales to plays by the likes of Moss Hart or Neil Simon. Furthermore, a count of the number of performances of most shows reveals they only ran for about three weeks. However, because the shows were "in rep," the three weeks of dates were stretched out over an entire summer—allowing for positive word-of-mouth to develop, and for previously unknown Kentucky plays to find their audiences.

Performing different characters in different plays back to back was a great challenge—and the actors loved it. Tess Campbell appeared in Billy Edd Wheeler's *Mossie and the Strippers,* and was back on stage within hours in A.R. Gurney's *The Dining Room*. Pamela White played lead roles in both Betty Peterson's *Desert Flower* and Georges Feydeau's *A Flea in her Ear* the same summer. Robert Brock, in his first season as an actor in Horse Cave, appeared as an over-worked public defender in *Just Taking Up Space*, while also performing as the lovable Cornelius Hackle in *The Matchmaker* and as the odious media professor, Bernard Nightingale, in Tom Stoppard's *Arcadia*.

Later, Robert would lead Horse Cave Theatre (now Kentucky Repertory Theatre), taking over at the end of Warren's 25th season.

The technical challenges presented by the repertory system could be counted on for lively discussions with designers and technicians who did most of the heavy lifting that made the rotating productions possible. In the early days, sets from the two shows not on stage were stored in a semi-trailer parked outside a backstage door. Following a $1.3 million addition and renovation project in 1993, the sets were rolled offstage through huge, steel-framed openings into an all-new backstage area. A quick glance at this anthology reveals the names of dozens of designers and "techies" who worked on the productions of new plays by or about Kentuckians.

Others who made a special commitment to Horse Cave Theatre's mission include numerous board members, innumerable funders, and the theatre's long-time office manager/bookkeeper Susan Dyche; in 19 years she never missed a payroll.

Pamela White, associate director and a company member for 25 years, made invaluable contributions to Horse Cave Theatre and to the Kentucky Voices program; simply put, neither would have happened without her. She brought vision, tenacity, artistry and beauty to her work—both in the administrative offices and, at the other end of the street, on stage.

Pamela is my connection to Horse Cave. We met many years ago at drama school in London, where we shared a flat. My first visit to Horse Cave was in 1977, during the theatre's first season, to see Pamela in *Candida*. I rode a Greyhound Bus from my hometown in Northern Wisconsin to Louisville, where Pamela met me. We drove the rest of the way together, through the magnificent countryside, to Horse Cave, population 2,300, in Southern Kentucky. Pamela introduced me to Warren and, later, got me a job. I am profoundly grateful to Pamela for sharing Horse Cave Theatre with me.

Producing the plays in repertory allowed audiences to see three plays in two days—and theatre-goers from across Kentucky and the entire Midwest benefited. Large groups from Louisville, including the Louisville Women's Club and the Cherokee Roundtable, regularly came for a theatre weekend. Similarly, friends and families from Nashville gathered in Horse Cave to see two plays on Saturday, and a third on Sunday. Groups and parties also came from Lexington, Cincinnati, Indianapolis and Chicago, among many other places. I remember talking with a couple from Gary, Indiana, who had come to the area as tourists to visit Mammoth Cave; upon discovering Horse Cave Theatre, their trip to Southern Kentucky became an annual event. Audiences were further boosted by a 1997 article in *The New York Times* characterizing Horse Cave Theatre as "a sophisticated theatre with a history of producing challenging dramatic works." Whether they were coming for the weekend or were devoted subscribers to Horse Cave Theatre's regular season, all audience members came to look forward to the Kentucky Voices productions.

The world premieres found even wider audiences through productions at other theatres: Ron Mielech's *The Dancers of Cannan* was produced at Ohio Dominican College in Columbus, Ohio; *East of Nineveh* was produced in Louisville; and my play, *Liz's Circus Story*, toured in Kentucky and Wisconsin, and was later produced at Long Lake Theatre in Hubbard, Minnesota.

Some of the world premieres, *East of Nineveh* and *Liz's Circus Story,* found audiences through award-winning productions on Kentucky Educational Television; in 1985, *East of Nineveh* won the Ohio State award from the Ohio Institute for Educational Broadcasting, the nation's oldest award for excellence in educational TV, and *Liz's Circus Story* won the National Educational Television Award for Best Dramatic Narrative in 2005.

The playwrights themselves have continued to find audiences for their work near and far. Recently, Sallie Bingham's plays *A Dangerous Personality* and *Treason* were both produced at The Perry Street Theatre in New York. Sallie's work has also been produced in Maryland, Texas and Virginia. Following her early experience in Horse Cave, Nancy Gall-Clayton has now seen her work in 16 states, as well as in Australia and Canada. Betty Peterson's plays *The Dollmaker, The Good Daughter* and *River Dreams* have been produced across Kentucky, and Billy Edd Wheeler's *Johnny Appleseed, Voices in the Wind* and *Young Abe Lincoln* have been produced in Ohio, North Carolina and Indiana. The playwrights are also well-known novelists and poets, with many publications and awards to their names.

Several of the writers whose plays are in this anthology still meet, continuing to use the play-development process they learned from Warren. Plays from this workshop have been produced or staged in London, England; Boothbay Harbor, Maine; Cincinnati and Columbus, Ohio; Minneapolis; New York; and in Covington, Elkhorn City, Frankfort, Horse Cave, Lexington, Louisville, Murray, Scottsville and Somerset, Kentucky. Other Kentucky writers have joined the group including Temple Dickinson from Glasgow, Bill Forsyth from Pikeville, and Walter May from Lexington.

One of the more recent members of the workshop has been Kate Larken, a talented playwright, actor and musician, and, coincidentally, the founding owner of MotesBooks, publisher of this anthology. Driving down I-65 to the playwriting workshop one evening a couple of years ago, Kate asked if I thought she should consider publishing some of the new work coming out of Horse Cave. I wasn't clear if she meant work from the current workshop or the plays Warren had produced when he was artistic director. A native Kentuckian who grew up in a family who published weekly newspapers in small towns in the Jackson Purchase area, Kate exclaimed, "Warren Hammack produced world premieres by Kentucky writers? I've got to publish those!" Upon hearing that Kate was going to do a book of the plays, Betty Peterson e-mailed me, "God bless Kate Larken!" Amen.

The playwrights whose work is in this anthology have generously agreed to donate their royalties to a fund at The Community Foundation of Louisville. Called the MotesBooks Kentucky Voices Fund, any Kentucky 501(c)3 organization working on a project involving the development or production of a new play by or about Kentuckians can apply for support. More information about the MotesBooks Kentucky Voices Fund can be found at www.cflouisville.net

As I sit at my desk finishing up this Afterword, I notice the seasons have changed. The trees outside my window are leafed out in green and "The Great Kentucky Ice Storm of 2009" is long gone. Several questions, however, linger in my mind: Will there be other productions of these plays? Will these playwrights write more plays? Will there be more world premieres of plays by or about Kentuckians? I sincerely hope the answer to these questions is yes. I see the clover is in bloom—and imagine the honeybees will find it soon.

– Liz Bussey Fentress

www.ingramcontent.com/pod-product-compliance
Lightning Source LLC
Chambersburg PA
CBHW080918180426
43192CB00040B/2444